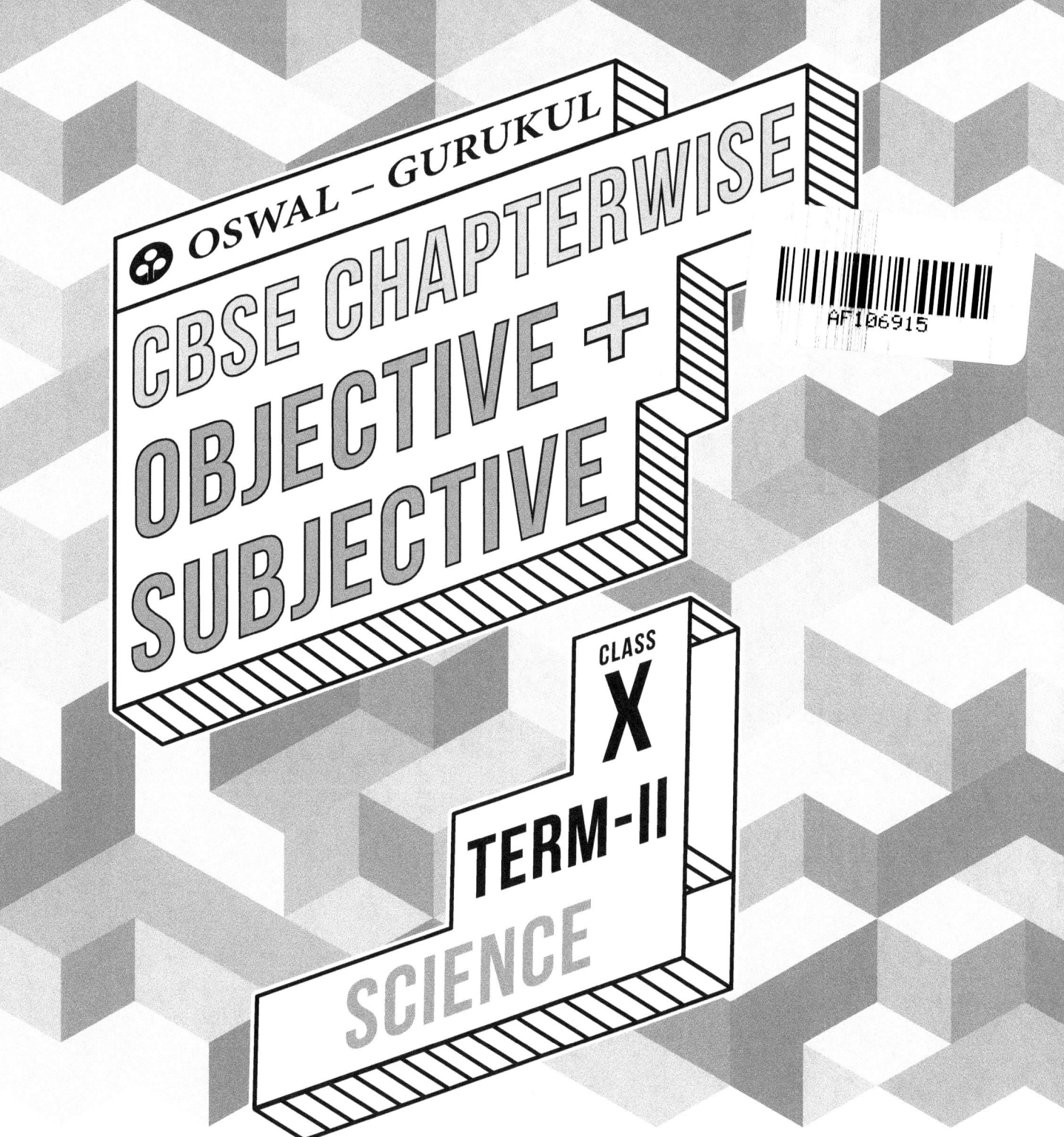

By
PANEL OF AUTHORS

© **COPYRIGHT RESERVED BY THE PUBLISHERS**

All rights reserved. No part of this publication may be reproduced in any form without the prior permission of the Oswal Publishers.

DISCLAIMER
With the ambition of providing standard academic resources, we have exercised extreme care in publishing the content. In case of any discrepancies in the matter, we request readers to excuse the unintentional lapse and not hold us liable for the same. Suggestions are always welcome.

EDITION : 2022

ISBN : 978-93-92563-07-2

PRICE : ₹ 299.00

PUBLISHED BY
OSWAL PUBLISHERS

Head Office : 1/12, Sahitya Kunj, M.G. Road, Agra - 282 002
Phone : (0562) 2527771-4
Whatsapp : +91 74550 77222
E-mail : info@oswalpublishers.in
Website : www.oswalpublishers.com

The cover of this book has been designed using resources from Freepik.com

PREFACE

Board exams are a crucial milestone for every student. For students to perform well in this exam, we have introduced CBSE Chapterwise Objective and Subjective book for the TERM II Examinations for class X. We have designed this book, keeping in mind all the changing scenarios and exam patterns. The content of the book is strictly based on the latest circular (Acad- 51 and 53) issued by the board in July, 2021 for TERM II examinations. This book will help the learners achieve the learning objectives in an easy to grasp manner.

This book contains matter compiled by highly proficient teachers and subject matter experts from across the country. Questions are segregated as per their respective chapters to facilitate easy navigation between them. Every attempt has been made to keep the language of the book crisp and accessible.

We hope you will find this book helpful in your preparations for Std. X board examinations. We would advise you to stay calm and manage your time wisely. Don't be overwhelmed with the amount of resources and study guides available; be selective and efficient in your preparation.

—Publisher

Note : Questions marked with :
* are board exam questions from previous years.
** are frequently asked board exam questions.

oswal.io

create your own exam sample papers in 2 mins

Prepare a chapter, take practice test & get evaluated to perform better

Create unlimited tests based on the latest board paper pattern once you are done practicing the book questions

Scan the **QR code** and get instant access to **oswal.io** for **free**. Just register & get started!

A winning effort begins with daily practice of tests

Easy steps to follow :

Step 1 - In a few clicks, you can completely customize your test

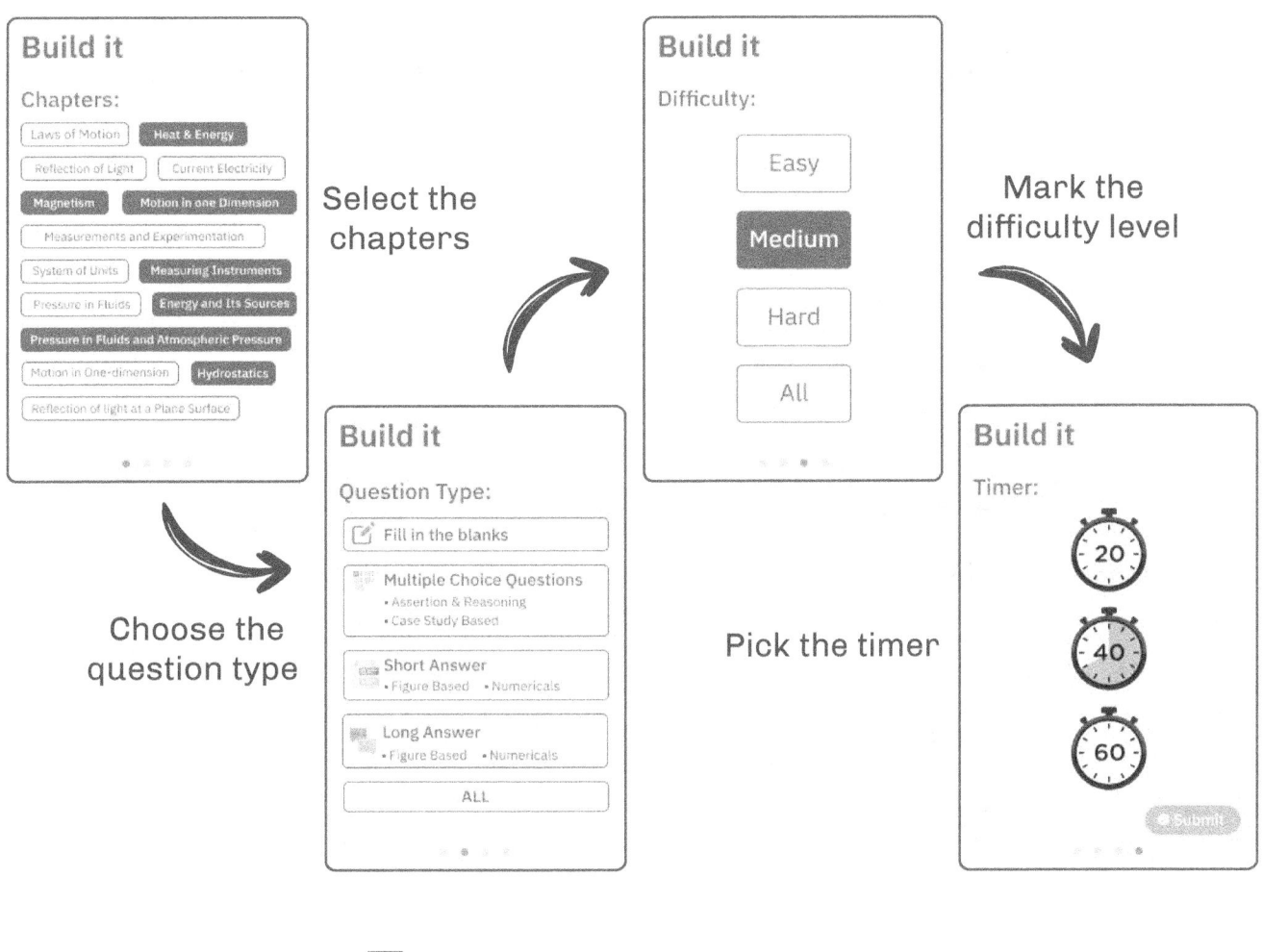

Step 2 - Test is based on the selected question type, chapters, difficulty, time

Step 3 - Click on start and type your answers in the given space

Step 4 - Use insert TeX equation editor to quickly & accurately insert the difficult math/physics/chem formulas

Step 5 - Skip any question if not sure, proceed to next & submit

Step 6 - You will get your result emailed right away

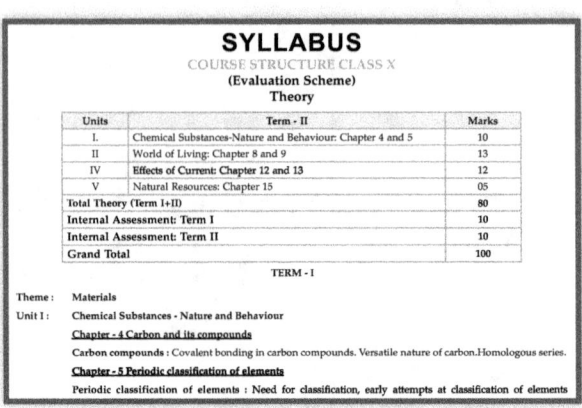

Questions focused on the New Paper Pattern, according to the latest circular issued by the Board (Acad-51 and 53) in July 2021.

Study material strictly based on the reduced syllabus issued by the Board in July 2021 for TERM-II examination.

Based on the board's most recent typologies of Objective Type Questions:

Stand-Alone MCQs
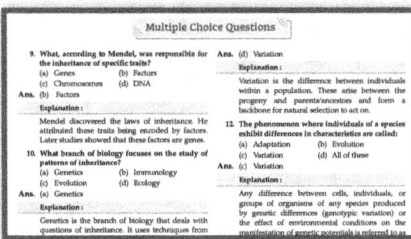

Assertion-Reason Questions
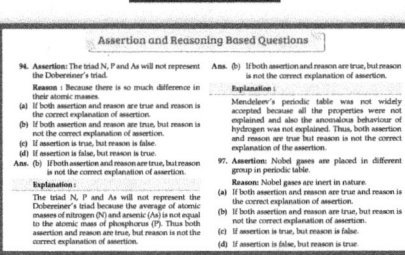

MCQs with Case Study
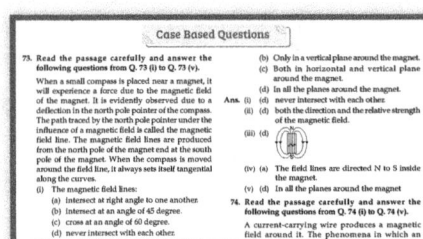

1500+ New Chapter-wise Questions Included

It consists of questions from the official CBSE Question Bank

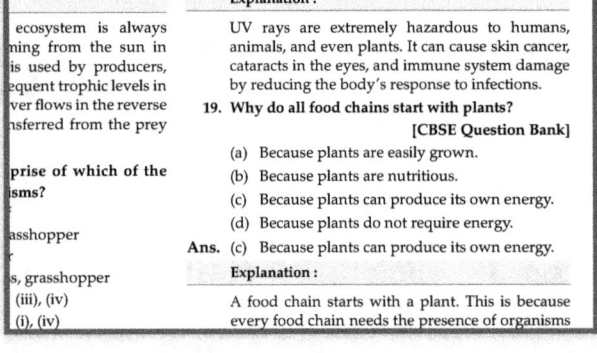

NCERT & NCERT Exemplar Questions Included

Detailed Explanations for MCQs

15. Floods can be prevented by:
 (a) Afforestation (b) Removing top soil
 (c) Deforestation (d) Agriculture
Ans. (a) Afforestation

Explanation :
Afforestation also prevents mass wasting which reduces the amount of soil entering the river and keeps the rivers capacity high. When combined with floodplain zoning, afforestation can be very effective at reducing the risk of flooding. Planting trees help prevent erosion because the roots bind the soil.

natural resource.

19. _____ is a not a greenh...
 (a) Nitrous oxide (b)
 (c) Carbon dioxide (d)
Ans. (d) Nitrogen

Explanation :
Carbon dioxide, methan ozone, nitrous oxide, examples of greenhouse g

20. Which of the following is...

Recent Years Board Questions Included

thus leading to depletion of ozone layer. Hence harmful UV rays can easily pass through ozone layer and cause various types of disorders in humans, plants and animals.

163. Show the reactions of formation of ozone from oxygen in the atmosphere? Name the pollutant and its role in depletion of ozone layer.
Ans. Ozone is formed by absorption of UV rays coming from sun.
$$O_2 \leftrightarrow O + O$$
$$O + O_2 \rightarrow O_3$$
UV radiations splits oxygen molecules to oxygen atoms and the oxygen atoms combine with oxygen molecule to form ozone.

* are board exam questions from previous years

(a) Replacement of Chlorofluorocarbons with hydrochlorofluorocarbons because it breaks down more quickly.
(b) Safe disposal of old appliances such as refrigerators and freezers.

166. Define a food chain. Design a terrestrial food chain of four trophic levels. If a pollutant enters at the producer level, the organisms of which trophic level will have the maximum concentration of the pollutant in their bodies? What is this phenomenon called?*
Ans. It is the sequence of arrangement of living organism in a community in which one organism consumes another organism to transfer food energy.

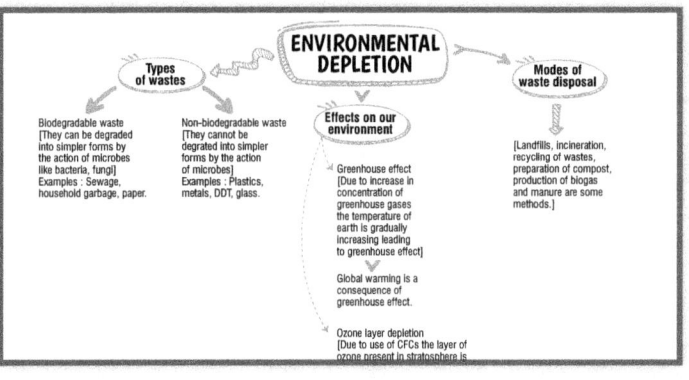

New Illustrated Chapter Summary for easy & quick revision

Very Short Questions

Very Short Answer Type Questions

130. What is the role of decomposers in the ecosystem? [NCERT]
Ans. Decomposers act upon dead and decay organisms and convert them into simpler forms. These simple substances get mixed up in the soil and are used as nutrients by the producers. From producers it goes to consumers and so on. They maintain the balance in the ecosystem and provide space for new life in ecosystem.

131. What will happen if we kill all the organisms in one trophic level? [NCERT]
Ans. If we kill all the organisms of one trophic level, it will lead to an increase in the number of organisms at the lower trophic level and decrease in the number of organisms at the higher trophic level. This will result in disruption in the food web and hence the ecosystem.

132. In following food chain, grass provides 4000 J of energy to the grasshopper.

133. Consider a food chain of the following: Fish, crab, plankton, shark.
Arrange the above chain in proper order of trophic level. Assign trophic level to shark.
Ans. Plankton → Crab → Fish → Shark.
Shark occupies fourth tropic level (Tertiary consumer).

134. What limits the number of trophic levels in a food chain?
Ans. The flow of energy in each trophic level follows 10% law i.e., only 10% of the energy is available to the next higher trophic level hence the amount of energy goes on decreasing at each trophic level which limits the number of trophic levels in a food chain.

135. Write the full name of the group of compounds mainly responsible for the depletion of ozone layer?

Short Questions

Short Answer Type Questions

112. Answer the following questions:
(a) What do you mean by 'magnetic field' of a magnet?
(b) What are magnetic field lines? List two characteristic properties of these lines.*
Ans. (a) The space or region around a magnet in which the force of attraction or repulsion due to the magnet can be detected is called the magnetic field.
(b) The lines drawn in a magnetic field along which north magnetic pole moves, are called magnetic field lines.
The characteristic properties of magnetic field lines are :
(i) The magnetic lines originate from north pole and ends at south pole.
(ii) The magnetic lines do not intersect each other.

113. Answer the following questions:
(a) State Ampere's swimming rule.

when you hold a current carrying conductor in your right hand in such a way that your thumb points in the direction of the current then the direction in which your fingers encircle the conductor will give the direction of magnetic field around it.

114. Answer the following questions:
(a) Name and state the rule to determine the polarity of the two faces of a current carrying circular loop.
(b) State Fleming's Left Hand Rule. [NCERT]
Ans. (a) Clock face rule is used to determine the polarity of the two faces of a current carrying circular loop.
According to this rule, "If the current around the face of circular wire flows in the clockwise direction, then that face of the circular wire will be south pole (S-Pole) and if the current around the face of circular wire flows in the

Long Questions

Long Answer Type Questions

185. Answer the following questions:
(i) Name the different types of asexual reproduction seen in living organisms. Give examples for each.
(ii)

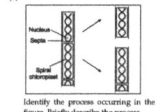

Identify the process occurring in the above figure. Briefly describe the process.
Ans. (i) The different types of asexual reproduction seen in living organisms are:

(ii) The figure depicts fragmentation process in Spirogyra. In the process of fragmentation organism after maturation breaks into smaller fragments and each fragment grows into a new individual. This process is called fragmentation.

186. With the help of suitable diagrams explain the various steps of budding in Hydra.
Ans. Budding is a form of asexual reproduction and is the process of production of new individual from an outgrowth called bud formed on the parent body. Regenerative cells present in Hydra are used for budding. Due to repeated mitotic divisions an outgrowth called bud develops from the parent body which enlarges in size and finally develops into a small hydra. After attaining suitable maturity the offspring gets detached from the parent body and becomes an independent individual.

Syllabus	9
Summary	11–17
4. Carbon and its Compounds	18–36
5. Periodic Classification of Elements	37–65
Summary	66–69
8. How Do Organisms Reproduce ?	70–107
9. Heredity and Evolution	108–135
Summary	136–138
12. Electricity	139–170
13. Magnetic Effects of Electric Current	171–199
Summary	200–204
15. Our Environment	205–237
16. Sustainable Management of Natural Resources	238–264

SYLLABUS
COURSE STRUCTURE CLASS X
(Evaluation Scheme)
Theory

Units	Term - I	Marks
I	Chemical Substances–Nature and Behaviour : Chapter 1, 2 and 3	16
II	World of Living : Chapter 6	10
III	Natural Phenomena : Chapter 10 and 11	14
Units	Term - II	Marks
I.	Chemical Substances-Nature and Behaviour: Chapter 4 and 5	10
II	World of Living: Chapter 8 and 9	13
IV	Effects of Current: Chapter 12 and 13	12
V	Natural Resources: Chapter 15	05
Total Theory (Term I+II)		80
Internal Assessment: Term I		10
Internal Assessment: Term II		10
Grand Total		100

TERM - I

Theme : Materials

Unit I : Chemical Substances - Nature and Behaviour

Chapter - 4 Carbon and its compounds

Carbon compounds : Covalent bonding in carbon compounds. Versatile nature of carbon. Homologous series.

Chapter - 5 Periodic classification of elements

Periodic classification of elements : Need for classification, early attempts at classification of elements (Dobereiner's Triads, Newland's Law of Octaves, Mendeleev's Periodic Table), Modern periodic table, gradation in properties, valency, atomic number, metallic and non-metallic properties.

Theme : The World of the Living

Unit II : World of Living

Chapter - 8 How do organisms reproduce?

Reproduction : Reproduction in animals and plants (asexual and sexual) reproductive health-need and methods of family planning. Safe sex vs HIV/AIDS. Child bearing and women's health.

Chapter - 9 Heredity and Evolution

Heredity: Heredity; Mendel's contribution- Laws for inheritance of traits: Sex determination: brief introduction;

Theme : Natural Phenomena

Unit IV : Effects of Current

Chapter - 12 Electricity

Ohm's law; Resistance, Resistivity, Factors on which the resistance of a conductor depends. Series combination of resistors, parallel combination of resistors and its applications in daily life. Heating effect of electric current and its applications in daily life. Electric power, Interrelation between P, V, I and R.

Chapter - 13 Magnetic effects of current

Magnetic effects of current : Magnetic field, field lines, field due to a current carrying conductor, field due to current carrying coil or solenoid; Force on current carrying conductor, Fleming's Left Hand Rule, Electric Motor, Electromagnetic induction. Induced potential difference, Induced current. Fleming's Right Hand Rule.

Theme : **Natural Resources**

Unit V : **Natural Resources**

Chapter - 15 Our Environment

Our environment : Eco-system, Environmental problems, Ozone depletion, waste production and their solutions. Biodegradable and non-biodegradable substances.

ONLY FOR INTERNAL ASSESSMENT

Note: Learners are assigned to read the below listed part of Unit V. They can be encouraged to prepare a brief write up on any one concept of this Unit in their Portfolio. This may be an assessment for Internal Assessment and credit may be given (Periodic assessment/Portfolio). This portion of the Unit is not to be assessed in the year-end examination.

Chapter–16 Management of natural resources: Conservation and judicious use of natural resources. Forest and wild life; Coal and Petroleum conservation. Examples of people's participation for conservation of natural resources. Big dams: advantages and limitations; alternatives, if any. Water harvesting. Sustainability of natural resources.

ASSESSMENT AREA (THEORY)
CLASS X
Subject : Science (086)

Theory Total Maximum Marks : 80

Competencies	Marks
Demonstrate Knowledge and Understanding	46%
Application of Knowledge/Concepts	22%
Analyze, Evaluate and Create	32%

Note :
- Internal choice would be provided.

Internal Assessment – Term I and II (10 Marks each)
- **Periodic Assessment -** 03 marks
- **Multiple Assessment -** 02 marks
- **Subject Enrichment** (Practical Work) - 03 marks
- **Portfolio -** 02 marks

CHAPTER - 4 : CARBON AND ITS COMPOUND

- The study of carbon compounds is called organic chemistry.
- Carbon is a non-metal having atomic number 6.
- Bonding in carbon : Covalent bonding is present in carbon.

COVALENT BONDING

Formation
Covalent bond is formed by sharing of electrons.

Examples
H_2, O_2, N_2, HCl, CCl_4

Properties
- Generally soft.
- Low melting and boiling point.
- Bad conductors of electricity.
- Insoluble in polar solvents.
- Shows molecular reactions.

ALLOTROPES OF CARBON

Diamond
Structure
Each carbon is bonded to four other carbon atoms.

Properties
Bad conductor of electricity. Hardest substance known.

Uses
Used in jewellery, cutting glasses and as an abrasive.

Graphite
Structure
Each carbon is joined to three carbon atoms.

Properties
Soft and slippery to touch, good conductor of electricity.

Uses
Used in pencil and electrodes.

Fullerene
Structure
60 carbon atoms are linked to form a stable structure.

Properties
Atoms are arranged in shape of football.

CHEMICAL PROPERTIES OF CARBON COMPOUNDS

Oxidation Reaction
Heating in the presence of oxygen.
$C + O_2 \rightarrow CO_2$

Addition Reaction
Reaction which involves addition of two reactants to form a single product.
$CH_2 = CH_2 + H_2 \rightarrow CH_3—CH_3$

Substitution Reaction
The reaction in which a reagent substitutes an atom or a group of atoms.
$CH_4 + Cl_2 \rightarrow CH_3Cl + HCl$

IMPORTANT CARBON COMPOUNDS

Ethanoic acid or Acetic acid [CH_3COOH]

Properties

- Colourless pungent odour liquid

- Reacts with ethanol to give ester
  $CH_3COOH + C_2H_5OH \rightarrow CH_3COOC_2H_5 + H_2O$

- React with base to give salt.
  $CH_3COOH + NaOH \rightarrow CH_3COONa$

- React with carbonates to give CO_2 gas
  $2CH_3COOH + Na_2CO_3 \rightarrow 2CH_3COONa + H_2O + CO_2$

Uses

- For making vinegar
- Making pickles
- Ester preparation

Ethanol [C_2H_5OH]

Properties

- Liquid, colourless and have distinct smell.

- Soluble in water.

- Reacts with sodium to form sodium ethoxide and H_2 gas.
  $C_2H_5OH + Na \rightarrow C_2H_5ONa + H_2$

- It reacts with conc. H_2SO_4 to give ethene.
  $C_2H_5OH \xrightarrow{Conc. H_2SO_4} CH_2 = CH_2$

Uses

- Used in all alcoholic drinks
- As an antiseptic.
- In medicines like tincture of iodine, cough syrup, tonic etc.
- As hypnotic.

Number of carbon atoms in one molecule	Greek name (Alk)
One carbon atom	Meth
Two carbon atoms	Eth
Three carbon atoms	Prop
Four carbon atoms	But
Five carbon atoms	Pent
Six carbon atoms	Hex
Seven carbon atoms	Hept
Eight carbon atoms	Oct

FORMULAE OF THE FIRST FIVE MEMBERS OF ALKANES

Number Of Carbon Atoms: One

- **IUPAC Name** » Meth-ane
- **Molecular formula** » CH_4
- **Condensed formula** » CH_4
- **Structural formula** »

$$\begin{array}{c} H \\ | \\ H-C-H \\ | \\ H \end{array}$$

Number Of Carbon Atoms: Two

- **IUPAC Name** » Eth-ane
- **Molecular formula** » C_2H_6
- **Condensed formula** » CH_3-CH_3
- **Structural formula** »

$$\begin{array}{c} H \quad H \\ | \quad | \\ H-C-C-H \\ | \quad | \\ H \quad H \end{array}$$

Number Of Carbon Atoms: Three

- **IUPAC Name** » Prop-ane
- **Molecular formula** » C_3H_8
- **Condensed formula** » $CH_3-CH_2-CH_3$
- **Structural formula** »

$$\begin{array}{c} H \quad H \quad H \\ | \quad | \quad | \\ H-C-C-C-H \\ | \quad | \quad | \\ H \quad H \quad H \end{array}$$

Number Of Carbon Atoms: Four

- **IUPAC Name** » n-But-ane
- **Molecular formula** » C_4H_{10}
- **Condensed formula** » $CH_3-CH_2-CH_2-CH_3$
- **Structural formula** »

$$\begin{array}{c} H \quad H \quad H \quad H \\ | \quad | \quad | \quad | \\ H-C-C-C-C-H \\ | \quad | \quad | \quad | \\ H \quad H \quad H \quad H \end{array}$$

Number Of Carbon Atoms: Five

- **IUPAC Name** » n-Pent-ane
- **Molecular formula** » C_5H_{12}
- **Condensed formula** » $CH_3-CH_2-CH_2-CH_2-CH_3$
- **Structural formula** »

$$\begin{array}{c} H \quad H \quad H \quad H \quad H \\ | \quad | \quad | \quad | \quad | \\ H-C-C-C-C-C-H \\ | \quad | \quad | \quad | \quad | \\ H \quad H \quad H \quad H \quad H \end{array}$$

FORMULAE OF THE FIRST FIVE MEMBERS OF ALKENES

Number Of Carbon Atoms: One

- **IUPAC Name** » **Meth**-ene (Methylene)
- **Molecular formula** » CH_2
- **Condensed formula** » Not possible, as there must be a double bond ($-C=C-$) between two carbon atoms.
- **Structural formula** »

Number Of Carbon Atoms: Two

- **IUPAC Name** » **Eth**-ene (Ethylene)
- **Molecular formula** » C_2H_4
- **Condensed formula** » $CH_2 = CH_2$
- **Structural formula** » H—C=C—H
                          H   H

Number Of Carbon Atoms: Three

- **IUPAC Name** » **Prop**-ene (Propylene)
- **Molecular formula** » C_3H_6
- **Condensed formula** » $CH_3-CH = CH_2$
- **Structural formula** »

Number Of Carbon Atoms: Four

- **IUPAC Name** » **But**-ene (Butylene)
- **Molecular formula** » C_8H_8
- **Condensed formula** » $CH_3-CH = CH-CH_3$
- **Structural formula** »

Number Of Carbon Atoms: Five

- **IUPAC Name** » **Pent**-ene (Pentylene)
- **Molecular formula** » C_5H_{10}
- **Condensed formula** » $CH_3-CH = CH-CH_2-CH_3$
- **Structural formula** »

FORMULAE OF THE FIRST FIVE MEMBERS OF ALKYNES

Number Of Carbon Atoms: One

- **IUPAC Name** » Meth-yne (—)
- **Molecular formula** » C
- **Condensed formula** » Not possible, as there must be a triple bond (—C≡C—) between two carbon atoms.
- **Structural formula** »

Number Of Carbon Atoms: Two

- **IUPAC Name** » Eth-yne (Acetylene)
- **Molecular formula** » C_2H_2
- **Condensed formula** » CH≡CH
- **Structural formula** » H—C≡C—H

Number Of Carbon Atoms: Three

- **IUPAC Name** » Prop-yne (Mehtyl acetylene)
- **Molecular formula** » C_3H_4
- **Condensed formula** » CH≡CH—CH₃
- **Structural formula** »
$$H-C\equiv C-\overset{\overset{H}{|}}{\underset{\underset{H}{|}}{C}}-H$$

Number Of Carbon Atoms: Four

- **IUPAC Name** » But-yne (Dimethyl acetylene)
- **Molecular formula** » C_4H_6
- **Condensed formula** » $CH_3-CH\equiv C-CH_3$
- **Structural formula** »
$$H-\overset{\overset{H}{|}}{\underset{\underset{H}{|}}{C}}-C\equiv C-\overset{\overset{H}{|}}{\underset{\underset{H}{|}}{C}}-H$$

Number Of Carbon Atoms: Five

- **IUPAC Name** » Pent-yne (Ethylmethyl acetylene)
- **Molecular formula** » C_5H_8
- **Condensed formula** » $CH_3-CH_2-C\equiv C-CH_3$
- **Structural formula** »
$$H-\overset{\overset{H}{|}}{\underset{\underset{H}{|}}{C}}-\overset{\overset{H}{|}}{\underset{\underset{H}{|}}{C}}-C\equiv C-\overset{\overset{H}{|}}{\underset{\underset{H}{|}}{C}}-H$$

CHAPTER - 5: PERIODIC CLASSIFICATION OF ELEMENTS

CLASSIFICATION OF ELEMENTS

- Dobereiner's Triad
- Newland's Law of Octaves
- Mendeleev's Periodic Table
- Modern Periodic Table

DOBEREINER'S TRAID

Law
When elements are arranged in order of increasing atomic mass, mass of middle element is arithmetic mean of other two.

Example
Li(7), Na(23), K39)
$= \frac{7+39}{2}$
$= \frac{46}{2}$
$= 23$ (Na)

Limitations
All known elements could not be arranged in Dobereiner's triad.

NEWLAND OF OCTAVES

The property of eight element was repetition of first element.

Example
H and F
F and Cl

Limitations
Applicable to elements upto calcium only.

EFFECT OF OXIDATION IN EVERYDAY

Characteristics
- Horizontal Columns-Periods.
- Vertical Columns-groups.
- 7 periods and nine groups.

Merits
- Systematic study of elements.
- Correction of atomic masses of elements.
- Prediction of new elements.

Demerits
- Position of hydrogen.
- Anomalous pair.
- Position of isotopes.
- Uncertainty in prediction of new elements.

MODERN PERIODIC TABLE

Law
"Physical and chemical properties of elements are periodic function of atomic number."

Characteristics
- Vertical columns are called groups. There are 18 groups.
- Horizontal columns are called periods. There are 7 periods.

Merits
- Position of isotopes.
- Anomalous position of some elements.
- Easy to remember and reproduce.

Demerits
Position of hydrogen is not certain.

TRENDS IN MODERN PERIODIC TABLE

Valency
Combining capacity of an element.

Valency is same in a group.

Atomic Size
Distance between nucleus and outermost shell.

Increases down the group and decreases in a period.

Ionisation Enthalpy
Energy required to remove loosely bonded electron.

Increases in a period, decreases down a group.

Electron Affinity
Energy released when an electron is added to an isolated atom.

Increases in a period and decreases in a group.

Electronegativity
Tendency to accept electron pair.

Increases in a period and decreases down the group.

Carbon and its Compounds

Chapter 4

Definitions

1. **Bond angle:** The angle that is formed between two adjacent bonds on the same atom.
2. **Bond length:** The equilibrium distance between the nuclei of two groups or atoms that are bonded to each other.
3. **Hydrocarbons:** An organic compound containing only carbon and hydrogen atoms.
4. **Saturated hydrocarbons:** A substance in which the atoms are linked by single bonds.
5. **Unsaturated hydrocarbons:** A substance in which atoms are linked by double or triple bond.
6. **Allotropy:** The phenomenon of existence of two or more different physical forms of a chemical element.
7. **Catenation:** The property of self linking of elements to form a long chain.
8. **Homologous series:** A homologous series is a group of organic chemical compounds, usually listed in order of increasing size, that have a similar structure (and hence also have similar properties) and whose structures differ only by the number of CH_2 units in the main carbon chain.
9. **Tetravalency:** Tetravalency is the state of an atom in which there are four electrons available with the atom for covalent chemical bonding.
10. **Isomers:** Compounds having similar molecular formula but different chemical structure.
11. **Isomerism:** The phenomenon in which the compounds have the same molecular formula and different structural formula.

Multiple Choice Questions

12. **Carbon exists in the atmosphere in the form of:**

    [NCERT Exemplar]
    (a) Carbon monoxide only
    (b) Carbon monoxide in traces and carbon dioxide
    (c) Carbon dioxide only
    (d) Coal

    Ans. (c) Carbon dioxide only

    Explanation :

    Carbon exists in the atmosphere in the form of carbon dioxide gas (CO_2) in air (Only 0.03%) and in the earth crust it exists in the form of the minerals like carbonates. It also occurs in the form of fossil fuels, organic compounds, wood, cotton and wool, etc.

13. **What is true about covalent compounds? They:**
    (a) have high melting and boiling point
    (b) are mostly soluble in water
    (c) are formed between atoms of metals and non-metals
    (d) are formed by the sharing of electrons in the bonding atoms

    Ans. (d) Are formed by the sharing of electrons in the bonding atoms.

    Explanation :

    Covalent compounds are held together by weak intermolecular forces which fail to hold the compound bonded tightly. Thus, a small amount of heat energy is capable of breaking these weak intermolecular forces, therefore, the melting and boiling points of covalent compounds are low. Covalent compounds are non-polar in nature which means they do not dissolve in water, instead make a separate layer on the surface of water. Hence, Compounds having covalent bonds are insoluble in water. Covalent compounds are formed by the sharing of electrons in the bonding atoms between two non-metals.

14. **Covalent compounds are _____ conductors of electricity.**
    (a) Good   (b) Bad
    (c) Moderate   (d) None of them

    Ans. (b) Bad.

    Explanation :

    Covalent compounds are bad conductors of electricity because they do not produce ions in solution.

15. **Buckminster fullerene is an allotropic form of :**

    [NCERT Exemplar]

    (a) Phosphorus (b) Sulphur
    (c) Carbon (d) Tin

    Ans. (c) Carbon.

    Explanation :

    Buckminsterfullerene (C_{60}) is an allotropic form of carbon. It has carbon atoms arranged in the form of football and due to their resemblance with football they are also known as Bucky balls.

16. **Which of the following statements are correct for carbon compounds?**

    (i) Most carbon compounds are good conductors of electricity.
    (ii) Most carbon compounds are poor conductors of electricity.
    (iii) Force of attraction between molecules of carbon compounds is not very strong.
    (iv) Force of attraction between molecules of carbon compounds is very strong.

    (a) (ii) and (iv) (b) (ii) and (iii)
    (c) (i) and (iv) (d) (i) and (iii)

    Ans. (b) (ii) and (iii)

    Explanation :

    Most carbon compounds are poor conductors of electricity because they are formed by the sharing of electrons and therefore they do not have free electrons. Current results from motion of electrons or ions. On dissolving them in water they do not form ions. So, they are generally poor conductors of electricity. Force of attraction between molecules of carbon compounds is not very strong because they form covalent bond by sharing their valence electron in order to attain stable electronic gas configuration.

17. **Which of the following statements are usually correct for carbon compounds ? These :**

    [NCERT Exemplar]

    (i) Are good conductors of electricity.
    (ii) Are poor conductors of electricity.
    (iii) Have strong forces of attraction between their molecules.
    (iv) Do not have strong forces of attraction between their molecules.

    (a) (i) and (iii) (b) (ii) and (iii)
    (c) (i) and (iv) (d) (ii) and (iv)

    Ans. (d) (ii) and (iv)

    Explanation :

    Carbon compounds do not have strong forces of attraction between their molecules because they are bonded to each other through covalent bonds which is weaker than ionic bond. They are poor conductors of electricity because of the absence of free ions.

18. **How many number of carbon atoms are joined in a spherical molecule of Buckminsterfullerene?**

    (a) 30 (b) 60
    (c) 90 (d) 120

    Ans. (b) 60

    Explanation :

    Buckminsterfullerene is the first discovered fullerene. It is a molecule of carbon in the form of a soccer ball consisting of 60 C-atoms and is having the formula C-60. These 60 carbon atoms are joined together by strong covalent bonds and are arranged in interlocking hexagonal and pentagonal rings of carbon atom.

19. **The allotrope of carbon which is a good conductor of heat and electricity is**

    (a) Diamond (b) Graphite
    (c) Charcoal (d) None of these

    Ans. (b) Graphite

    Explanation :

    The allotrope of carbon which is a good conductor of heat and electricity is graphite. This is because, in its planar structure it has three electrons which are covalently bonded and fourth electron is free to move along the layers from one carbon atom to the next when connected to an external battery.

20. **In diamond, each carbon atom is bonded to four other carbon atoms to form:**

    (a) A hexagonal array
    (b) A rigid three-dimensional structure
    (c) A structure in the shape of a football
    (d) A structure of a ring

    Ans. (b) A rigid three-dimensional structure

    Explanation :

    In diamond, each carbon atom is bonded to four other carbon atoms tetrahedrally to form a rigid three-dimensional structure. This rigid three dimensional structure of carbon is responsible for the hardness and rigidity of diamond.

21. **How many electrons are there in the outermost shell of carbon?**

    (a) 1 (b) 2
    (c) 3 (d) 4

    Ans. (d) 4

    Explanation :

    Carbon is a member of group 14 elements and has four electrons in its outer shell. Carbon typically shares electrons to achieve a complete valence shell, forming bonds with multiple other atoms.

22. **Hydrocarbons are mainly composed of:**

    (a) Hydrogen, carbon and nitrogen
    (b) Hydrogen and carbon

(c) Hydrogen
(d) Hydrogen, oxygen and carbon

Ans. (b) Hydrogen and carbon

Explanation :

A hydrocarbon is an organic chemical compound composed exclusively of hydrogen and carbon atoms. For example, the simplest hydrocarbon is Methane molecule with the molecular formula of CH_4.

23. **Complete combustion of hydrocarbons gives:**
    (a) Carbon dioxide and water
    (b) Carbon monoxide and water
    (c) Carbon monoxide and hydrogen
    (d) Carbon dioxide and hydrogen

Ans. (a) Carbon dioxide and water

Explanation :

The simple word equation for the stoichiometric combustion of a hydrocarbon in air is:
Fuel + Oxygen = Water + Nitrogen + Carbon dioxide
$$CH_4 + 2O_2 = 2H_2O + CO_2$$

24. **Carbon forms four covalent bonds by sharing its four valence electrons with four univalent atoms, *e.g.*, hydrogen. After the formation of four bonds, carbon attains the electronic configuration of:**

    [NCERT Exemplar]
    (a) Helium   (b) Neon
    (c) Argon   (d) Krypton

Ans. (b) Neon

Explanation :

The electronic configuration of carbon (C) is 2, 4. To complete its octet, it will share its 4 valence electrons with hydrogen atom and forms CH_4 molecule. As carbon is sharing its 4 valence electrons, it will form four covalent bonds.
Now, the electronic configuration of C in CH_4 is 2, 8
Electronic configuration of Ne (atomic number = 10) is 2, 8. Hence, after the formation of four covalent bonds, carbon attains the electronic configuration of Neon.

25. **Which of the following is not a straight chain hydrocarbon ?**
    (a) $H_3C-CH_2-CH_2-CH_2-CH_2$
                              |
                              CH_3
    (b) $H_3C-CH_2-CH_2-CH_2-CH_2-CH_3$
    (c) $\overset{CH_3}{\underset{|}{H_2C}}-H_2C-H_2C-CH_2$
                                       |
                                       CH_3
    (d) $\begin{matrix}H_3C\\H_3C\end{matrix}\!\!>\!\!CH-CH_2-CH_2-CH_3$

Ans. (d) $\begin{matrix}H_3C\\H_3C\end{matrix}\!\!>\!\!CH-CH_2-CH_2-CH_3$

Explanation :

In straight chain hydrocarbons, carbon atoms are connected through covalent bond in one continuous chain with no branches. In the structure (a), (b) and (c), all the carbon atoms are connected to each other in a continuous straight chain:
(a) $H_3\overset{1}{C}-\overset{2}{C}H_2-\overset{3}{C}H_2-\overset{4}{C}H_2-\overset{5}{C}H_2$
                                                          |
                                                          $\overset{6}{C}H_3$
(b) $H_3\overset{1}{C}-\overset{2}{C}H_2-\overset{3}{C}H_2-\overset{4}{C}H_2-\overset{5}{C}H_2-\overset{6}{C}H_3$
(c) $\overset{1}{C}H_3$
    $\underset{|}{\overset{2}{H_2C}}-\overset{3}{H_2C}-\overset{4}{H_2C}-\overset{5}{C}H_2$
                                                    |
                                                    $\overset{6}{C}H_3$

In structure (d), $-CH_3$ group is attached to the second carbon atom of the chain forming a branch. Hence, compound in structure (d) is a branched chain hydrocarbon.

$\begin{matrix}\overset{1}{H_3C}\\H_3C\end{matrix}\!\!>\!\!\overset{2}{C}H-\overset{3}{C}H_2-\overset{4}{C}H_2-\overset{5}{C}H_3$

26. **In double covalent bond there is sharing of:**
    (a) 2 electrons   (b) 4 electrons
    (c) 6 electrons   (d) 3 electrons

Ans. (b) 4 electrons

Explanation :

A double covalent bond is formed when two pairs of electrons are shared between them. For example, in an oxygen molecule, there is a double bond between two oxygen atoms as they share two pairs of electrons *i.e.* 4 electrons.

27. **The bond between two identical non-metallic atoms has a pair of electron :**
    (a) unequally shared between two atoms.
    (b) transferred completely from one atom to another.
    (c) with identical spins.
    (d) equally shared between them.

Ans. (d) equally shared between them.

Explanation :

The bond between two identical non-metallic atoms has a pair of electron equally shared between them. This is due to the equal sharing of electrons between the bonded atoms. Hence, the bonded atoms will hold on the shared pair of electrons.

28. **Which of the following properties is not true regarding organic compounds ?**
    (a) They are generally covalent compounds.
    (b) Show isomerism.
    (c) Compounds have high melting and boiling points.

(d) Generally insoluble in water.

Ans. (c) Compounds have high melting and boiling points.

Explanation:

Organic compounds have low melting and boiling point because they are made of weak covalent bonds. Thus, the property which is not true regarding organic compounds is that they have high melting and boiling points.

29. **Which of the following is not an allotropic form of carbon ?**
    (a) Fluorine   (b) Fullerene
    (c) Diamond   (d) Graphite

Ans. (a) Fluorine

Explanation:

Carbon is found in many forms in nature which differ from each other in various physical properties but they exist in same state. These forms of carbon are known as allotropes of carbon. From the given options, fullerene, diamond, graphite are all different types of allotropes. Whereas, fluorine is a non-metal which belongs to halogen family. Hence, fluorine is not an allotrope of carbon.

30. **The term 'Isomerism' applies to organic compounds with same :**
    (a) Molecular formula but different structural formulae.
    (b) Molecular formula but different empirical formula.
    (c) Empirical formula but different molecular formula.
    (d) Structural formula but different molecular formula.

Ans. (a) Molecular formula but different structural formulae.

Explanation:

The term isomerism refers to the organic compounds with same molecular formula but different structural formulae. An example is the compound with the molecular formula C_5H_{12}. It has three isomers: n-pentane, Isopentane and neopentane which differ from each other in their structure but they have same molecular formula.

```
      H  H  H  H  H
      |  |  |  |  |
   H—C—C—C—C—C—H
      |  |  |  |  |
      H  H  H  H  H
         n-Pentane
```

```
      H  H  H  H
      |  |  |  |
   H—C—C—C—C—H
      |  |  |  |
      H  H  |  H
           H—C—H
              |
              H
       2-Methyl butane
```

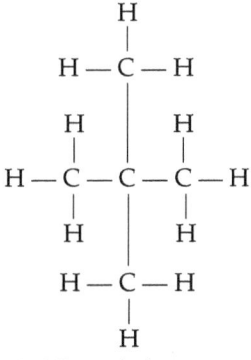

2, 2-Dimethyl propane

31. **Which of the following is not a characteristic of Diamond ?**
    (a) Hardest substance
    (b) High thermal conductivity
    (c) High refractive index
    (d) Good conductor of electricity

Ans. (d) Good conductor of electricity

Explanation:

Diamond is the hardest substance known, this is due to its structure in which carbon atoms are arranged in a lattice giving it a giant covalent structure with great forces of attraction.
Diamond has high thermal conductivity, this is due to the stiff chemical bonds between the carbon atoms. It has high refractive index which gives it the transparency and brilliance and it is a bad conductor of electricity because of the absence of free mobile electrons.

32. **A hydrocarbon should have minimum how many carbon atoms to show isomerism?**
    (a) Three   (b) Four
    (c) Five   (d) Six

Ans. (b) Four

Explanation:

Since branching is not possible with carbon 1, 2, 3 so the minimum number of the carbons required by the hydrocarbon to show isomerism is Four.

33. **The amount of carbon present in the earth crust as minerals is:**
    (a) 0.03%   (b) 0.02%
    (c) 0.05%   (d) 0.08%

Ans. (a) 0.02%

Explanation:

The amount of carbon present in the earth crust as minerals is 0.02%. In the earth's crust only 0.02% carbon is found in the form of minerals like carbonates, hydrogen carbonates, coal and petroleum. and the atmosphere has 0.03% of carbon dioxide. In spite of this small amount of carbon available in nature, the importance of carbon is immense.

34. Carbon compounds are ……….. conductors of electricity"
    (a) Poor (b) Good
    (c) Semi (d) None of the above
Ans. (a) Poor

Explanation :

Current results from motion of electrons or ions. Carbon compounds are covalent in nature as they are formed by the sharing of electrons. They do not dissociate into ions in aqueous solution and also it does not have free electrons. Since, there is no flow of charge (i.e., electrons or ions), it is a poor conductor of electricity.

35. Carbon compounds have ………….. melting point and ……………. boiling point:
    (a) Low, high (b) Low, Low
    (c) High, low (d) High, high
Ans. (b) Low, Low

Explanation :

Carbon compounds generally have low melting points and boiling points because the force of attraction between the molecules of carbon compounds is not very strong. These weak intermolecular forces make them very easy to pull apart from each other. Since carbon compounds are easy to separate, they have low melting and boiling point.

36. Which among the following properties does not comply with graphite?
    (a) Presence of hexagonal rings of carbon
    (b) Layer tightly held by strong forces of attraction
    (c) High melting point close to that of diamond
    (d) Electrical conductivity comparable to metals
Ans. (b) Layer tightly held by strong forces of attraction

Explanation :

Graphite has layer lattice structure in which layer of hexagonal rings are held by weak forces of attraction

37. Which of the statement is correct
    (a) Reactivity of element is explained on the tendency to attain completely filled outer shell
    (b) Ionic compound attain stability via gaining and losing electron from the outermost shell
    (c) Carbon can gain or lose electron four electron to attain noble gas configuration
    (d) All of the above
Ans. (d) All of the above

Explanation :

All the above given statements are correct.

38. Carbon attain stability by ……………. its valence electron
    (a) Donating (b) Gaining
    (c) Sharing   (d) Transferring
Ans. (c) Sharing

Explanation :

Carbon has four electrons in its valence shell. It can either gain electron forming an anion (C^{4-}) or it can lose its valence electrons and form cation(C^{4+}) but in former case it is difficult for nucleus to hold 10 electrons with number of protons to be 6 and in the latter case, it requires large amount of energy for the release of valence electrons. Hence, it can attain stability by sharing of its valence electron

39. Carbon is …………. compound:
    (a) Tetravalent (b) Pentavalent
    (c) Hexavalent   (d) Octavalent
Ans. (a) Tetravalent

Explanation :

The electronic configuration of carbon is 2,4 which means it has four electrons in its outermost shell. Carbon atoms can achieve the inert gas electronic configuration only by sharing of electrons, so carbon always forms covalent bonds. As the valency of carbon is four because one carbon atom requires 4 electrons to achieve the nearest inert gas configuration. Thus, we can say that carbon is a tetravalent compound.

40. Bonds which are formed by sharing of an electron pair between two atom is known as
    (b) Ionic (b) Covalent
    (c) Coordinate (d) electrovalent
Ans. (b) Covalent

Explanation :

The wide variation of properties in different forms of elementary carbon and existence of innumerable compounds of carbon are due to unique nature of bonding between carbon atoms. Carbon atom generally participates in bond formation by sharing electron. Hence termed as covalent bonding

41. Graphite structure is formed by …………array:
    (a) Tetragonal (b) Hexagonal
    (c) Pentagonal (d) None of the above
Ans. (b) Hexagonal

Explanation :

In graphite, each atom of carbon is surrounded by three other carbon atoms by single bonds, thereby forming a layer of hexagonal structures. The fourth valence electron of each carbon atom forms a weak bond between the layers of hexagonal structure.

42. ……………… is the hardest substance:
    (a) Carbon (b) Diamond
    (c) Graphite (d) C-60
Ans. (b) Diamond

Explanation :

In diamond, carbon atoms are compactly arranged by very strong covalent bonds, diamond is very hard. Due to the compact arrangement of carbon atom, diamond has very high density and tends to be hardest substance.

43. **Graphite is .... and.......... in nature.**
    (a) Smooth, slippery
    (b) Hard, slippery
    (c) Smooth, non-slippery
    (d) None of these

Ans. (a) Smooth, slippery

Explanation :

In graphite, each atom of carbon is surrounded by three other carbon atom by single bonds, thereby forming a layer of hexagonal structures. The fourth valence electron of each carbon atom forms a weak bond between the layers of hexagonal structure Graphite can be used as a dry lubricant in machine where large amount of heat is produced due to friction between different parts of machine. Ordinary lubricating oil gets charred due to generation of heat. The soft slippery nature and high resistance to heat makes graphite useful.

44. **............. is an allotrope of carbon:**
    (a) Fullerenes
    (b) Diamond
    (c) Graphite
    (d) All of them

Ans. (d) All of them

Explanation :

All of them are formed through carbon linkages and possess different physical property and same chemical property.

45. **Which of the following characteristics does not comply with all non-polar covalent substance?**
    (a) Do not undergo ionization
    (b) Soluble only in organic solvent
    (c) Exist only in gaseous state
    (d) They do not conduct electricity

Ans. (c) Exist only in gaseous state

Explanation :

Non polar covalent compound can exist either in gaseous state or in liquid state. This statement does not hold good as a feature of all non–polar covalent substance.

46. **Compound formed from carbon are:**
    (a) Methane
    (b) Bio gas
    (c) CNG
    (d) All of these

Ans. (d) All of these

Explanation :

Methane is CH_4, Biogas is mixture of gases primarily consisting of methane and CO_2. CNG is composed methane (CH_4). They all have carbon as the element

47. **Chlorine forms................ Molecule:**
    (a) Diatomic
    (b) Monoatomic
    (c) Triatomic
    (d) Tetraatomic

Ans. (a) Diatomic

Explanation :

Chlorine atom has 7 electrons and need one electron to attain stability hence sharing of electron between two chlorine atom leads to chlorine molecule

48. **Identify the correct statement among the following:**
    (i) Three bond pair and one lone pair of electron are present in a molecule of ammonia.
    (ii) Two bond pair and two lone pairs of electrons are present in molecule of water
    (iii) Only one bond pair of electron is present in molecule of chlorine
    (iv) One bond pair and three lone pairs of electron are present in molecule of HF
    (a) (i) and (ii)
    (b) (i), (ii), (iii)
    (c) (ii) and (iv)
    (d) (i), (ii), (iii), (iv)

Ans. (c) (ii) and (iv)

Explanation :

Chlorine molecule has one bond pair and six lone pair of electron. Each chlorine atom has electron 2,7 and requires one electron for its octet to get complete therefore single bond between the atoms led to formation of chlorine molecules leaving six lone pair of electrons in chlorine

49. **From which of the following substance pencil lead is formed?**
    (a) Charcoal
    (b) Wood
    (c) Lead
    (d) Graphite

Ans. (d) Graphite

Explanation :

Reason: Pencil lead is formed of graphite. Graphite is an allotropic form of carbon in which each carbon atom is joined to three others, forming layers:

These layers are put together by weak van der Waals forces which enable the layers to slide over each other, making graphite soft and slippery. So graphite is used as pencil 'lead'. As the pencil moves across the paper, layers of graphite rub off leaving the dark marks on paper.

50. **How many number of carbon atoms are joined in a spherical molecule of buckminsterfullerene?**
    (a) 30
    (b) 60
    (c) 90
    (d) 120

Ans. (b) 60

Explanation :

Buckminsterfullerene is a molecule of carbon in the form of a hollow sphere consisting of 60 C-atoms and is having the formula C_{60}.

51. **Which of the following statements about graphite and diamond is true?**
    (a) They have the same crystal structure
    (b) They have the same degree of hardness
    (c) They have the same electrical conductivity
    (d) They can undergo the same chemical reactions

Ans. (d) They can undergo the same chemical reactions

Explanation :

Both Graphite and diamond being the allotropes of the same element, carbon, have similar chemical properties. So they undergo the same chemical reactions.

52. **Identify the carbon compound in which carbon not exhibit the property of catenation as well multiple bond formation**
    (a) Propene   (b) Benzene
    (c) Acetone   (d) Methane

Ans. (d) Methane

Explanation :

In methane there is only one carbon atom and no double or triple bond. So in methane there is no catenation of carbon and multiple bond.

53. **Self-linking property of carbon is called............**
    (a) Catenation   (b) Versatile
    (c) Homologus   (d) None of these

Ans. (a) Catenation

Explanation :

The ability of an atom to combine with other atom of the same element and form long chain –like structure is called catenation property. The maximum catenation is observed in the compounds of carbon. The chain of carbon compound can be straight, branched or closed like a ring. The formation of different kind of chain of different length by carbon atom is possible because of its four valence electron.

54. **The property of self-linkage among identical atoms to form long chain compounds is known as:**
    (a) Catenation   (b) Isomerisation
    (c) Superposition   (d) Halogenation

Ans. (a) Catenation

Explanation :

Catenation is the property of self-linking of an element by which an atom combines with the other atoms of the same element to form long chains. This property is exhibited by carbon as it forms covalent bonds with other carbon atoms to form longer chains and structures. This is the reason for the presence of the vast number of organic compounds in nature.

55. **Which of the following belongs to homologous series of alkynes? C_6H_6, C_2H_6, C_2H_4, C_3H_4.**
    (a) C_6H_6 (b) C_2H_4
    (c) C_2H_6 (d) C_3H_4

Ans. (d) C_3H_4

Explanation :

Homologous series is the series comprising of compounds that share same chemical properties and functional groups. Alkynes have general formula, C_nH_{2n-2}, where n is number of carbon atoms. Thus, from given options, C_3H_4 belongs to the homologous series of alkynes.

56. **The number of isomers of pentane is:**
    (a) 2   (b) 3
    (c) 4   (d) 5

Ans. (b) 3

Explanation :

Isomerism is a phenomenon in which two or more compounds have the same chemical formula but possesses different structural formulas. Pentane is an organic compound and an alkane with molecular formula C_5H_{12}. There are five carbons in its structure which can be arranged in three different ways to form 3 different structural isomers of pentane. These are n-pentane, iso-pentane and neo-pentane.

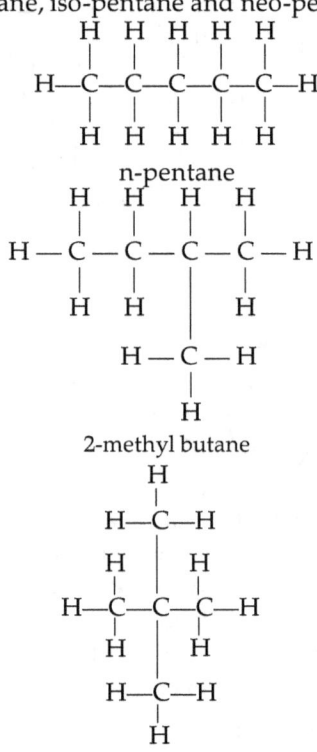

57. **C_3H_8 belongs to the homologous series of:**
    (a) Alkynes   (b) Alkenes
    (c) Alkanes   (d) Cyclo alkanes

Ans. (c) Alkanes

Explanation :

A homologous series is a family of compounds with the same general formula, same functional group and similar chemical properties. Each family of organic compound is called a homologous series for example,

Homologous series of Alkanes has the general formula C_nH_{2n+2}

Homologous series of Alkene has the general formula C_nH_{2n}

Homologous series of Alkyne has the general formula C_nH_{2n-2}

Hence, from the general formula of the homologous series of alkanes, this can be confirmed that C_3H_8 belongs to the homologous series of alkanes.

58. Pentane has the molecular formula C_5H_{12}. It has :
[NCERT Exemplar]
(a) 5 covalent bonds (b) 12 covalent bonds
(c) 16 covalent bonds (d) 17 covalent bonds

Ans. (c) 16 covalent bonds

Explanation :

Structural formula of pentane is:

$$H-\underset{\underset{H}{|}}{\overset{\overset{H}{|}}{C}}-\underset{\underset{H}{|}}{\overset{\overset{H}{|}}{C}}-\underset{\underset{H}{|}}{\overset{\overset{H}{|}}{C}}-\underset{\underset{H}{|}}{\overset{\overset{H}{|}}{C}}-\underset{\underset{H}{|}}{\overset{\overset{H}{|}}{C}}-H$$

Pentane

Number of C–C covalent bonds = 4
Number of C–H covalent bonds = 12
Hence, the total number of covalent bonds in the structure of pentane is 16.

59. The first member of the alkyne homologous series is:
[NCERT Exemplar]
(a) ethyne (b) ethene
(c) propyne (d) methane

Ans. (a) Ethyne

Explanation :

The first member of the alkyne family is Ethyne (C_2H_2), with two carbon atoms bonded by a triple bond. It is a hydrocarbon and the simplest alkyne. Its molecular weight is 26.04g/mol.

60. Which of the following does not belong to the same homologous series ?
[NCERT Exemplar]
(a) CH_4 (b) C_2H_6
(c) C_3H_8 (d) C_4H_8

Ans. (d) C_4H_8

Explanation :

CH_2, C_2H_6, C_3H_8 are all saturated carbon compounds with general formula C_nH_{2n+2} whereas C_4H_8 is an alkene with general formula C_nH_{2n}. Thus, C_4H_8 does not belong to the same homologous series as it is an alkene.

61. By how much atomic mass unit successive members of a homologous series vary ?
(a) One (b) Sixteen
(c) Fourteen (d) Twelve

Ans. (c) Fourteen

Explanation :

In homologous series, the two consecutive members will differ by CH_2 unit or 14 amu.
The molecular masses of first three members of alkanes with general formula C_nH_{2n+2} are shown below:
Methane (CH_4) = 16 amu
Ethane (C_2H_6) = 30 amu
Propane (C_3H_8) = 44 amu
From the above examples, it is clear that atomic mass unit of successive members of a homologous series vary by 14 amu.

Assertion and Reasoning Based Questions

62. Assertion: Carbon and its compounds used as fuels for most applications.

Reason: When carbon is heated in presence of excess of air or oxygen, it forms carbon dioxide. During its formation, a large amount of heat and light are released. Further, once ignited, carbon and its compounds keep on burning without needing additional heat energy.

(a) If both assertion and reason are true and reason is the correct explanation of assertion.
(b) If both assertion and reason are true, but reason is not the correct explanation of assertion.
(c) If assertion is true, but reason is false.
(d) If assertion is false, but reason is true.

Ans. (a) If both assertion and reason are true and reason is the correct explanation of assertion.

Explanation :

Carbon and its compounds have maximum number of carbon and hydrogen, which makes them of high calorific value. Thus, most of the carbon compounds release high amount of energy. This is the cause that carbon and its compounds are used as fuels for most applications.

63. Assertion: Graphite and diamond have same chemical properties

Reason: Graphite and diamond are allotropes of carbon

(a) If both assertion and reason are true and reason is the correct explanation of assertion.
(b) If both assertion and reason are true, but reason is not the correct explanation of assertion.
(c) If assertion is true, but reason is false.
(d) If assertion is false, but reason is true.

Ans. (a) If both assertion and reason are true and reason is the correct explanation of assertion.

Explanation :

Allotropes of an element exhibit same chemical properties. Graphite and diamond are allotropes of carbon. Thus both assertion and reason are correct and reason is the correct explanation for assertion.

64. Assertion: Coal generally burns red hot without flame

Reason: Coal contains sulphur and nitrogen which produce volatile oxides on burning

(a) If both assertion and reason are true and reason is the correct explanation of assertion.
(b) If both assertion and reason are true, but reason is not the correct explanation of assertion.
(c) If assertion is true, but reason is false.
(d) If assertion is false, but reason is true.

Ans. (a) If both assertion and reason are true, but reason is not the correct explanation of assertion.

Explanation :

Coal and charcoal are solid fuels. So, they generally burn red hot without flame. Coal contains sulphur and oxygen to form volatile oxides. Thus both assertion and reason are correct but reason is not the correct explanation for assertion.

65. **Assertion:** Carbon and its compounds are used as fuels.
    Reason: They give lot of heat and light when burnt in air.
    (a) If both assertion and reason are true and reason is the correct explanation of assertion.
    (b) If both assertion and reason are true, but reason is not the correct explanation of assertion.
    (c) If assertion is true, but reason is false.
    (d) If assertion is false, but reason is true.

Ans. (a) If both assertion and reason are true and reason is the correct explanation of assertion.

Explanation :

Carbon and its compounds are used as fuels for most applications because most of the carbon compounds give a lot of heat and light when burnt in air. Saturated hydrocarbons burn with a clean flame and no smoke is produced. The carbon compounds, used as a fuel, have high calorific values. Thus, both assertion and reason are true and reason is the correct explanation of the assertion.

66. **Assertion:** Covalent compounds are poor conductors of electricity.
    Reason: It is because they do not form the ions.
    (a) If both assertion and reason are true and reason is the correct explanation of assertion.
    (b) If both assertion and reason are true, but reason is not the correct explanation of assertion.
    (c) If assertion is true, but reason is false.
    (d) If assertion is false, but reason is true.

Ans. (a) If both assertion and reason are true and reason is the correct explanation of assertion.

Explanation :

Covalent compounds are poor conductors of electricity because they do not form the ions. Thus both assertion and reason are true and reason is the correct explanation of the assertion.

67. **Assertion:** Graphite and diamond are the allotropes of carbon.
    Reason: It is because they have large network like structure.
    (a) If both assertion and reason are true and reason is the correct explanation of assertion.
    (b) If both assertion and reason are true, but reason is not the correct explanation of assertion.
    (c) If assertion is true, but reason is false.
    (d) If assertion is false, but reason is true.

Ans. (c) If assertion is true, but reason is false.

Explanation :

Graphite and diamond are the allotropes of carbon because they have network like structure. Thus, assertion is true but reason is false.

68. **Assertion:** Covalent compounds have high melting and boiling points.
    Reason: It is because the forces present in covalent bonds are held together by weak Van der Waals forces.
    (a) If both assertion and reason are true and reason is the correct explanation of assertion.
    (b) If both assertion and reason are true, but reason is not the correct explanation of assertion.
    (c) If assertion is true, but reason is false.
    (d) If assertion is false, but reason is true.

Ans. (d) If assertion is false, but reason is true.

Explanation :

The forces present in covalent bonds are held together by weak Vander Waals forces and the force of attraction between these molecules are not very strong. A supply of a small amount of energy can weaken this force to a great extent that is why carbon compounds have low melting and boiling point. Thus, assertion is false but reason is true.

69. **Assertion:** Carbon forms ionic compounds.
    Reason: It is because of its valency of 4.
    (a) If both assertion and reason are true and reason is the correct explanation of assertion.
    (b) If both assertion and reason are true, but reason is not the correct explanation of assertion.
    (c) If assertion is true, but reason is false.
    (d) If assertion is false, but reason is true.

Ans. (d) If assertion is false, but reason is true.

Explanation :

Carbon forms covalent compounds because of its valency of 4 due to which it can share its 4 electrons easily. Thus, assertion is false but reason is true.

70. **Assertion:** Mass number of a carbon is 12.
    Reason: Carbon possesses equal number of all three fundamental particles.
    (a) If both assertion and reason are true and reason is the correct explanation of assertion.

(b) If both assertion and reason are true, but reason is not the correct explanation of assertion.
(c) If assertion is true, but reason is false.
(d) If assertion is false, but reason is true.

Ans. (a) If both assertion and reason are true and reason is the correct explanation of assertion.

Explanation :

Number of electrons, protons and neutrons in carbon are equal, that is 6. The mass number of carbon is 12. Thus, both assertion and reason are true and reason is the correct explanation of the assertion.

71. **Assertion:** Carbon forms large number of compounds

    Reason: Carbon has small size and is tetravalent
    (a) If both assertion and reason are true and reason is the correct explanation of assertion.
    (b) If both assertion and reason are true, but reason is not the correct explanation of assertion.
    (c) If assertion is true, but reason is false.
    (d) If assertion is false, but reason is true.

    Ans. (b) If both assertion and reason are true, but reason is not the correct explanation of assertion.

    Explanation :

    Carbon has the property of self-linkage among identical atoms to form large number of compound. This is because it is smaller in size and is tetravalent which means it has a valency of four and is capable of bonding with four other atoms. These bonds that carbon forms with other elements are very strong making these compounds exceptionally stable. Thus, both assertion and reason are true and reason is the correct explanation of assertion.

72. **Assertion:** Catenation is shown by carbon.

    Reason: Catenation is shown by carbon because it has valency of 5.
    (a) If both assertion and reason are true and reason is the correct explanation of assertion.
    (b) If both assertion and reason are true, but reason is not the correct explanation of assertion.
    (c) If assertion is true, but reason is false.
    (d) If assertion is false, but reason is true.

    Ans. (c) If assertion is true, but reason is false.

    Explanation :

    Catenation is shown by carbon because it has valency of 4 and it can form large number of compounds with other compounds. Thus, assertion is true but reason is false.

73. **Assertion:** In a homologous series of alcohols, the formula for the second member is C_2H_5OH and the third member is C_3H_7OH.*

    Reason: The difference between the molecular masses of the two consecutive members of a homologous series is 144.
    (a) If both assertion and reason are true and reason is the correct explanation of assertion.
    (b) If both assertion and reason are true, but reason is not the correct explanation of assertion.
    (c) If assertion is true, but reason is false.
    (d) If assertion is false, but reason is true.

    Ans. (c) If assertion is true, but reason is false.

    Explanation :

    In homologous series two consecutive members differ by $-CH_2$ and differ in molecular masses by 14. Thus, assertion is true but reason is false.

74. **Assertion:** General formula of alkanes is C_nH_{2n+2}.

    Reason: It is because they are saturated compounds.
    (a) If both assertion and reason are true and reason is the correct explanation of assertion.
    (b) If both assertion and reason are true, but reason is not the correct explanation of assertion.
    (c) If assertion is true, but reason is false.
    (d) If assertion is false, but reason is true.

    Ans. (b) If both assertion and reason are true, but reason is not the correct explanation of assertion.

    Explanation :

    Alkanes are saturated compounds because they are very unstable. Thus, both assertion and reason are true but reason is not the correct explanation of the assertion.

75. **Assertion:** Following are the members of a homologous series :

    $CH_3OH, CH_3CH_2OH, CH_3CH_2CH_2OH$

    Reason: A series of compounds with same functional group but differing by —CH_2— unit is called a homologous series.
    (a) If both assertion and reason are true and reason is the correct explanation of assertion.
    (b) If both assertion and reason are true, but reason is not the correct explanation of assertion.
    (c) If assertion is true, but reason is false.
    (d) If assertion is false, but reason is true.

    Ans. (a) If both assertion and reason are true and reason is the correct explanation of assertion.

    Explanation :

    The Homologous series of the compounds differ by $-CH_2$ units and molecular mass of each member differs by 14 amu. Thus, both assertion and reason are true and reason is the correct explanation of the assertion.

* are board exam questions from previous years

Case Based Questions

76. Read the following passage carefully and answer the following questions from 76 (i) to 76 (v):

The phenomenon of the existence of an element in two or more physical forms within the same physical state is known as allotropy. Allotropes have similar chemical properties but they differ in chemical properties. In crystalline form, Carbon occurs as graphite, diamond, and fullerenes. Diamond is the hardest natural substance known and is used in cutting marbles, granite, and glass. Graphite is a greyish black and opaque substance, lighter than a diamond with comparative low density. Graphite has a sheet-like structure having hexagonal layers. One layer slides over the other layer due to weak forces and hence it is soft to touch and breaks easily. Graphite is also used as a lubricant.

(i) Substance A is a moderate conductor of electricity. Observe the structure of substance A given below.

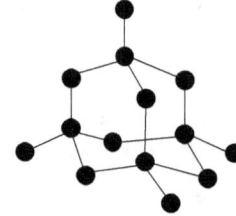

Choose the correct statements regrading substance A.
Statement I - It is a covalent compound.
Statement II - It has a giant molecular structure.
Statement III - It has the same structure as graphite.
Statement IV - It has the same structure as diamond.
(a) I and III (b) II and III
(c) II and IV (d) I, II and IV

(ii) Which of the following is correct about the structure of diamond?
(a) Carbon atoms are held together by single covalent bonds.
(b) Electrons move freely through the structure.
(c) Layers of atoms slide easily over each other.
(d) Carbon atoms conduct electricity in the molten state.

(iii) Which three allotropes of carbon do the given figures represent?

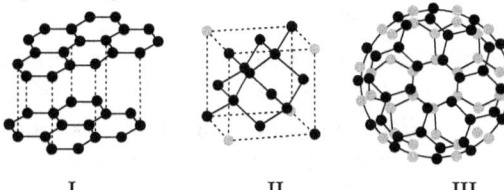

I II III

(a) I-Graphite II-Diamond III-Fullerene
(b) I-Diamond II-Fullerene III-Graphite
(c) I-Graphite II-Fullerene III-Diamond
(d) I-Fullerene II-Graphite III-Diamond

(iv) Identify the incorrect statement(s):
I. Diamond is the hardest substance known while graphite breaks easily.
II. Each carbon atom in diamond is bonded to 4 other carbon atoms in a tetrahaderal manner to form a giant lattice. All carbon atoms are bonded by strong covalent bonds.
III. Graphite is poor conductor of electricity unlike other non metals.
IV. In each layer of graphite, each carbon atom is bonded to three other carbon atoms foming hexagonal rings of carbon atoms.
(a) I and III (b) Only III
(c) II and IV (d) I, II and IV

(v) The number of carbon atoms surrounding each carbon atom in a diamond are:
(a) 3 (b) 4
(c) 2 (d) 5

Ans. (i) (c) II and IV
(ii) (a) Carbon atoms are held together by single covalent bonds
(iii) (a) I-Graphite II-Diamond III-Fullerene
(iv) (b) Only III
(v) (b) 4

77. Read the following passage carefully and answer the following questions from 77(i) to 77(iv):

As a versatile element, carbon can form large compounds because of its tetravalency and the property of catenation that it exhibits. Here, catenation refers to the combination of carbon atoms with itself to form large molecules. Carbon forms stronger covalent bonds with itself and other elements such as hydrogen, oxygen, sulphur, nitrogen and chlorine. This is because its nucleus has a strong force of attraction and holds these bonds tightly together.

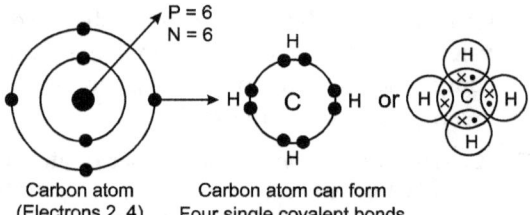

Carbon atom (Electrons 2, 4)   Carbon atom can form Four single covalent bonds e.g. CH_4 (Methane)

(i) Match the columns:

Column A	Column B
(1) Methane	(p) C_8H_{18}
(2) Propane	(q) C_4H_{10}
(3) Butane	(r) C_5H_{12}
(4) Pentane	(s) C_3H_8
(5) Octane	(t) CH_4

(a) (1)-(q), (2)-(s), (3)-(t), (4)-(p), (5)-(r)
(b) (1)-(p), (2)-(r), (3)-(s), (4)-(q), (5)-(t)
(c) (1)-(t), (2)-(s), (3)-(q), (4)-(r), (5)-(p)
(d) (1)-(t), (2)-(q), (3)-(s), (4)-(r), (5)-(p)

(ii) Which of the following statements regarding carbon is incorrect?
(a) A single atom of carbon can participate in two double bonds
(b) A single atom of carbon can participate in three single bonds and one double bond
(c) A single atom of carbon can participate in four single bonds
(d) A single atom of carbon can participate in two single bonds and one double bond

(iii) Put the elements in the right order in terms of their valency, starting with the element of lowest valency?
(a) O, C, N, H   (b) C, O, N, H
(c) H, C, O, N   (d) H, O, N, C

(iv) Which of the following does not represent the molecular formula C_6H_{14}?

(a) H—C—C—C—C—C—C—H (chain of 6 C with H's)

(b) 5-carbon chain with one branch

(c) central C with 4 CH3 groups (neopentane-like)

(d) 4-carbon chain with one branch

Ans. (i) (c) (1)-(t), (2)-(s), (3)-(q), (4)-(r), (5)-(p)
(ii) (b) A single atom of carbon can participate in three single bonds and one double bond
(iii) (d) H, O, N, C
(iv) (c)

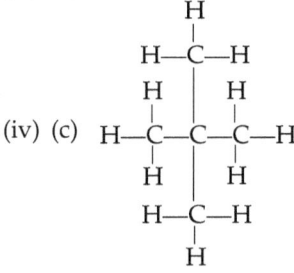

78. Read the following passage carefully and answer the following questions from Q 78 (i) to 78 (v):

The compounds which have the same molecular formula but differ from each other in physical or chemical properties are called isomers and this phenomenon is known as isomerism. Structural isomerism is when isomers have difference in the arrangement of atoms within the molecule, without any reference to space. We can say that compounds which have the same molecular formula but different structural formula show structural isomerism. Compounds of carbon show this phenomenon as the atoms can be linked together in the form of straight chains, banched chains or even rings.

(i) Among the following sets of compounds, choose the set having the same molecular formulae:
(a) Butane and iso-butane
(b) Cyclohexane and hexene
(c) Propanal and propanone
(d) All

(ii) The minimum number of carbon atoms required in an organic compound, in order to form branching:
(a) 3   (b) 4
(c) 5   (d) 2

(iii) Which of the following pairs show isomerism?
(a) Ethane and ethene
(b) Propane and butane
(c) Ethane and propane
(d) Butane and 2-methyl propane

(iv) Which among the following has the longest chain?
(a) Iso-pentane
(b) 2-methylpentane
(c) 2,2-dimethylbutane
(d) neopentane

(v) The number of isomers of pentane is:
(a) 4   (b) 3
(c) 2   (d) 5

Ans. (i) (d) All

(ii) (b) 4
(iii) (d) Butane and 2-methyl propane
(iv) (b) 2-methylpentane
(v) (b) 3

Reasoning Based Questions

79. Why are carbon and its compounds used as fuels for most applications?* **[NCERT]**

Ans. Carbon and its compounds are used as fuels for most applications because most of the carbon compounds give a lot of heat and light when burnt in air. Saturated hydrocarbons burn with a clean flame and no smoke is produced. The carbon compounds, used as a fuel, have high calorific values.

80. Why is fullerene so called?

Ans. Fullerene is so called because it resembles the framework of dome shaped halls designed by American architect Buckminster fuller.

81. Catenation is the ability of an atom to form bonds with other atoms of the same element. It is exhibited by both carbon and silicon. Compare the ability of catenation of the two elements. Give reasons.

Ans. Carbon has the maximum capacity of catenation. The reason for this is the smaller size of of carbon which makes the C–C bonds strong. The size of sulphur is greater than Carbon. This makes Si—Si bonds comparatively weaker than C-C bond.

Very Short Answer Type Questions

82. Answer the following questions:
  (i) What are the two properties of carbon which lead to the huge number of carbon compounds we see around us? **[NCERT]**
  (ii) Which element exhibit the property of catenation to maximum extent and why*?

Ans. (i) The two features of carbon that give rise to a large number of compounds are as follows:
  (a) **Catenation:** The ability to form bonds with other atoms of carbon to form a long chain
  (b) **Tetravalency:** With the valency of four, carbon is capable of bonding with four other atoms.
  (ii) Carbon exhibits the property of catenation to maximum extent. It is due to strong tetra valency of carbon.

83. Answer the following questions:
  (i) What is homologous series of carbon compounds?*
  (ii) Write the name and formula of the 2nd member of homologous series having general formula (C_nH_{2n+2}).*
  (iii) Write the molecular formula of the 2nd and 3rd member of the homologous series where the first member is ethyne.*
  (iv) What is the difference in molecular formula of any two consecutive members of a homologous series?

Ans. (i) The series of organic compounds having same functional group and similar chemical properties is called homologous series. Each member differs from successive member by – CH_2 group. The difference in molecular weight between two successive members is $14u$.

(ii) The name of 2nd member of alkanes: Ethane. The formula of 2nd member of alkanes: C_2H_6 or $CH_3 – CH_3$.
(iii) 2nd member of alkyne series is propyne (C_3H_4),
3rd member of alkyne series is butyne (C_4H_6).
(iv) The molecular formula of two consecutive members of a homologous series differ by – CH_2.

84. State the following:
  (i) Two properties of carbon which lead to the formation of a large number of carbon compounds.
  (ii) Write the next homologue of C_2H_4 and C_4H_6.
  (iii) Write the name and molecular formula of the first member of the homologous series of alkyne.
  (iv) Write the next two members of homologous series for C_2H_6 and C_3H_8?
  (v) Write the name and formula of second member of homologous series having general formula (C_nH_{2n}).
  (vi) Write the name and formula of second member of homologous series having general formula ($C_nH_{2n–2}$).
  (vii) Write the names of any two isomers represented by the molecular formula C_5H_{12}.

Ans. (i) Catenation and tetravalency.
(ii) C_3H_6 and C_5H_8
(iii) Ethyne (C_2H_2)
(iv) C_4H_{10} and C_5H_{12}
(v) Propene (C_3H_6)
(vi) Propyne (C_3H_4)
(vii) Isopentane and neopentane.

---
* are board exam questions from previous years

Carbon and its Compounds | 31

Short Answer Type Questions

85. What are covalent compounds ? Why are they different from ionic compounds? List their three characteristics properties.*

Ans. The compounds which are formed by sharing of electrons between two or more same atoms or between two or more non-metals are called covalent compounds. They are different from ionic compounds as:
(a) Covalent compounds are bad conductors of electricity whereas ionic compounds are good conductors of electricity in molten state.
(b) Covalent compounds are directional and ionic compounds are non-directional.

Characteristics of Covalent compounds:
(a) They have low melting and boiling point.
(b) These compounds are generally insoluble in water.
(c) These compounds are bad conductors of electricity.

86. Explain the nature of the covalent bond using the bond formation in CH_3Cl. [NCERT]

Ans. Carbon has 4 valence electrons. It completes its octet by sharing its four electrons with other carbon atoms or with atoms of other elements as it can neither lose four of its electrons nor gain four electrons since both the processes require extra amount of energy and would make the system unstable. Such bonds that are formed by sharing of electrons and are known as covalent bonds. In covalent bonding, both the atoms share the valence electrons, i.e., the shared electrons belong to the valence shells of both the atoms.

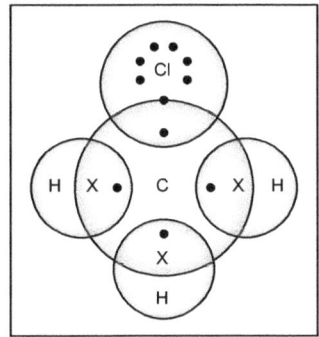

In the formation of CH_3Cl, carbon requires 4 electrons to complete its octet, while each hydrogen atom requires one electron to complete its duplet. Also, chlorine requires an electron to complete the octet. Therefore, all of these share the electrons and as a result, carbon forms 3 bonds with hydrogen atom and one with chlorin atom.

87. Carbon has the unique property to form bonds with other carbon atoms:*
(i) Name the unique property of carbon.
(ii) Give reason for unique property of carbon atom.
(iii) Draw the structure of cyclohexane.

Ans. (i) Catenation.
(ii) It is due to tetra valency of carbon atom.
(iii) Cyclohexane.

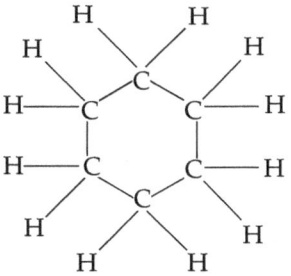

88. What is a homologous series? Explain with an example. [NCERT]

Ans. A homologous series is a series of carbon compounds that have different numbers of carbon atoms but contain the same functional group. There is a difference of —CH_2 unit between each successive member and mass differ by $14u$.

For example, methane, ethane, propane, butane, etc., are all part of the alkane homologous series. The general formula of this series is C_nH_{2n+2}.

Long Answer Type Questions

89. Explain why carbon forms compounds mainly by covalent bond. Explain in brief two main reasons for carbon forming a large number of compounds. Why does carbon forms strong bonds with most other elements?*

Ans. Carbon is tetravalent. Carbon has 4 electrons in its outer most shell. To complete the octet it needs 4 electrons. Thus, it can either gain or lose 4 electrons. But loosing or gaining 4 electrons is not possible due to energy consideration. Hence, in place of gaining or losing 4 electrons, carbon does sharing of these 4 electrons and covalent bonds.

Reason for carbon forming a large number of compounds:
(a) **Catenation:** The tendency of carbon to form chains of identical atoms is known as catenation. Carbon forms long chains by combining with other carbon atoms through covalent bonds.
(b) **Tetravalency:** It has 4 valence electrons, so it can form 4 covalent bonds with four different atoms, or two double bonds or a single and a triple bond with other atoms. This tendency helps carbon to form a large range of compounds.

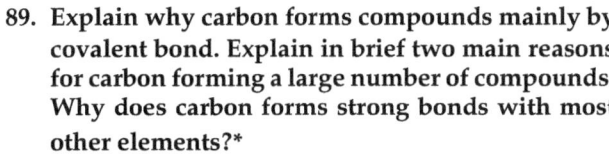

* are board exam questions from previous years

Carbon forms strong bonds with most of other elements like H, O, S, N, Cl. Br, I etc. due to its small size which helps it to attract more number of electrons.

90. **Answer the following questions:**
    (i) **State any three physical property of carbon compounds.**
    (ii) **Carbon is a versatile element. Justify this statement.***

Ans. (i) The properties of carbon compounds are:
   (a) Carbon possesses property of catenation:
   (b) Poor conductor of electricity.
   (c) Low melting and boiling point as compared to ionic compounds.
   (ii) Carbon is a versatile element because of its properties. It shows the property of catenation due to which it forms a large number of compounds. Carbon is tetravalent. Due to this, it forms covalent compounds only.

91. **State the reason why carbon can neither form C^{4+} cations nor C^{4-} anions, but forms covalent compounds. Also state reasons to explain why covalent compounds:***
    (i) **Are bad conductors of electricity?**
    (ii) **Have low melting and boiling point?**

Ans. Carbon needs 4 electrons to complete its octet. It has 4 electrons in its valence shell. Thus, carbon can either gain or lose 4 electrons. But due to energy consideration, it is not possible. Therefore, in place of gaining or losing 4 electrons, carbon does sharing of these 4 electrons to form covalent bonds. Therefore, can neither form C^{4+} cations nor C^{4-} anions but forms covalent compounds only by sharing of electrons.
   (i) Covalent compounds are bad conductors of electricity because they do not contain ions.
   (ii) Covalent compounds have usually low melting and boiling point because the force of attraction between the molecules of covalent bond is very weak.

92. **Elements forming ionic compounds attain noble gas configuration by either gaining or losing electrons from their valence shells. Explain giving reason why carbon cannot attain such a configuration in this manner to form its compounds. Name the type of bonds formed in ionic compounds and in the compounds formed by carbon. Also explain with reason why carbon compounds are generally poor conductors of electricity.***

Ans. Carbon needs 4 electrons to complete its octet. It has 4 electrons in its valence shell. Thus, carbon can either gain or lose 4 electrons. But due to energy consideration, it is not possible. Therefore, in place of gaining or losing 4 electrons, carbon does sharing of these 4 electrons to form 4 covalent bonds.
Electrovalent or ionic bond is present in ionic compounds whereas covalent bond is present in Carbon compounds. Carbon compounds are poor conductors of electricity because of absence of ions.

93. **Why certain compounds are called hydrocarbons? Write the general formula for homologous series of alkanes, alkenes and alkynes and also draw the structure of the first member of each series. Write the name of the reaction that converts alkenes into alkanes and also write a chemicals equation to show the necessary conditions for the reaction to occur.***

Ans. Compounds containing only carbon and hydrogen are called hydrocarbons.
General formula for the homologous series of alkanes is C_nH_{2n+2} First member of the alkane family is methane.

$$\begin{array}{c} H \\ | \\ H-C-H \\ | \\ H \end{array}$$

General formula for the homologous series of alkenes is C_nH_{2n}. First member of the alkene family is ethene.

$$\begin{array}{c} H \quad\quad H \\ \diagdown \quad \diagup \\ C = C \\ \diagup \quad \diagdown \\ H \quad\quad H \end{array}$$

General formula for the homologous series of alkynes = C_nH_{2n-2}. First member of the alkyne family is ethyne.

$$H — C \equiv C—H$$

Catalytic hydrogenation is the reaction used to convert alkenes to alkanes.

$$CH_2 = CH_2 + H_2 \xrightarrow[300°C]{Nickel} C_2H_6$$

Differentiate Between

94. **Differentiate between diamond and graphite.**

Ans.

	Diamond	Graphite
(a)	Diamond has 3-dimensional network structure.	Graphite has hexagonal sheet layer structure.
(b)	Each carbon in diamond is bonded to four other carbon atoms.	Each carbon has one free electron with it.

* are board exam questions from previous years

| (c) | No free electron is left. | It is a good conductor of electricity. |
| (d) | It is a bad conductor of electricity. | It is soft and slippery. |

Analysis and Evaluation Based Questions

95. Carbon is so versatile in nature that organic chemistry forms a separate branch of chemistry which deals mainly with carbon and its compounds. Carbon is an element with symbol "C", atomic number 6. Carbon element has a property of catenation. Carbon has a valency of four. So, it is capable of bonding with four other atoms of carbon or atoms of some other monovalent element. Compounds of carbon are formed with oxygen, nitrogen, hydrogen, sulphur, chlorine and many other elements, giving rise to compounds with specific properties which depend on the elements other than the carbon present in the molecule.

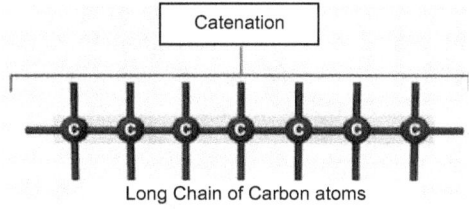

(i) Name the term used to define property of carbon to form bond with another carbon atom.

(ii) Name the group and period to which carbon belong.

(iii) Name the term used for four valency of carbon.

(iv) Which of these statements is incorrect?

(a) Valence electrons of carbon are 4.

(b) Carbon has a valency of four.

(c) Organic chemistry forms a separate branch of chemistry which deals mainly with carbon and its compounds.

(d) Electronic configuration of carbon is 2,6.

Ans. (i) Catenation is the term used to define property of carbon to form bond with another carbon atom.

(ii) Carbon belongs to second period and fourteenth group of periodic table.

(iii) The term used for four valency of carbon is tetravalency.

(iv) Total electrons present in carbon are 6. Out of these 6 electrons, 2 are present in first shell and other four in next shell. This gives electronic configuration of carbon to be 2,4. Hence, the incorrect option is (d).

96. The solid element A exhibits the property of catenation. It is also present in the form of a gas B in the air which is utilised by plants in photosynthesis. An allotrope C of this element is used in glass cutters.

(i) What is element A?

(ii) What is the gas B?

(iii) Name the allotrope C.

(iv) State another use of allotrope C (other than in glass cutters).

(v) Name another allotrope of element A which exists as spherical molecules.

(vi) Name yet another allotrope of element A which conducts electricity.

Ans. (i) Element A: Carbon

(ii) Gas B: Carbon dioxide

(iii) Allotrope C: Diamond

(iv) Used for making jewellery

(v) Buckminsterfullerene

(vi) Graphite

97. A colourless organic liquid X of molecular formula $C_2H_4O_2$ turns blue litmus to red. Another colourless organic liquid Y of molecular formula C_2H_6O has no action on any litmus but it is used as a nail polish remover. A yet another colourless organic liquid Z of molecular formula C_2H_6O has also no action on litmus but it is used in tincture of iodine.

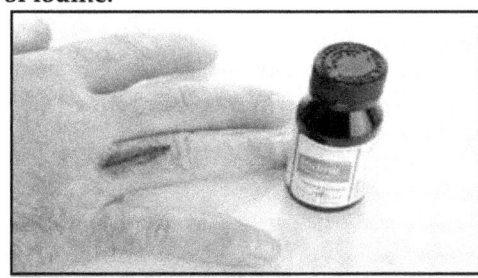

(i) Name the liquid X. To which homologous series does it belong ? Give the name of another member of this homologous series.

(ii) Name the liquid Y. To which homologous series does it belong ? Write the name of another member of this homologous series.

(iii) Can you name an organic compound having the same molecular formula as liquid Y but which belongs to a different homologous series? What is this homologous series?

(iv) Name the liquid Z. To which homologous series does it belong ? Write the name of another member of this homologous series.

Ans. (i) Liquid X is ethanoic acid; it belongs to homologous series of carboxylic acids.

Methanoic acid is another member of this homologous series.

(ii) Liquid Y is Propanone; it belongs to homologous series of ketones. Butanone is another member of this homologous series.

(iii) Propanal; it belongs to homologous series of aldehydes.

(iv) Liquid Z is ethanol; it belongs to homologous series of alcohols. Methanol is another member of this homologous series.

Creating Based Questions

98. The solid element A exhibits the property of catenation. It is also present in the form of a gas B in the air which is utilised by plants in photosynthesis. An allotrope C of this element is used in glass cutters.

(i) What is element A ?

(ii) What is the gas B ?

(iii) Name the allotrope C.

(iv) State another use of allotrope C (other than in glass cutters).

(v) Name another allotrope of element A which exists as spherical molecules.

(vi) Name a yet another allotrope of element A which conducts electricity.

Ans. (i) Element A : Carbon

(ii) Gas B : Carbon dioxide

(iii) Allotrope C : Diamond

(iv) Used for making jewellery

(v) Buckminsterfullerene

(vi) Graphite

99. From the given table, answer the following questions :

	Column I	Column II
1.	[structure image]	• Used as gems and for making jewellery. • They can be synthesized by subjecting pure carbon to very high pressure and temparature.
2.	[structure image]	• Used in several lubricant products, such as grease and forging lubricants, in blast furnace linings. • Its amorphous form is used in the manufacturing of lead used in pencils.
3.	[structure image]	• Used as an anti-aging and anti-damage agent in the cosmetic sector, used as antiviral agents. • Poor conductor of electricity.

(i) Identify all three structures mentioned in the table.

(ii) What type of property bound these following structures?

(iii) Which one is the good conductor of electricity?

(iv) What is difference between the first two structures?

Ans. (i) (a) Dimond

(b) Graphite

(c) Buckminsterfullerene

(ii) Catenation property

(iii) Graphite.

(iv) Diamond is the hardest substance while graphite is smooth and slippery and also graphite is good conductor of electricity.

100. Based on the information given below answer the following questions:

Carbon has the versatile nature it shows the property of catenation and has the tetravalency. Catenation is the ability of an atom to form bonds with other atoms of the same element. Carbon has the valency of 4 due to which it can form the covalent compounds with the other elements as well and thus it forms hydrocarbons as well which exist in the nature in a form of a series known as the Homologous series.

(i) List the three characteristics of the Homologous series.

(ii) Why carbon forms the covalent compounds?

(iii) Which element other than carbon exhibits the property of catenation?

Ans. (i) **Characteristics of homologous series of carbon compound:**

(a) All the members of a homologous series can be represented by the same general formula and they have same functional group.

(b) Any two adjacent homologues differ by 1 carbon atom and 2 hydrogen atoms in their molecular formulae.

(c) The difference in the molecular masses of any two adjacent homologues is 14 u.
(ii) Electricity is conducted by moving electrons. But carbon forms covalent bonds by sharing of electrons. It does not have free electrons.
(iii) Silicon.

101. Give two possibilities through which carbon can attain the inert gas configuration.

Ans. Carbon has two possibilities to attain noble gas configuration.
(a) One of the possibilities is to attain four electrons and form C^{4-} anion. But it will be difficult for the nucleus to hold four more electrons firmly.
(b) Another possibility is to lose four electrons forming C^{4+} cation. But this will also be difficult due to the requirement of large energy to lose four electrons from the outermost shell. As a result the atom will contain six protons and two electrons.

102. Study the table related to three hydrocarbons X, Y and Z carefully and answer the following questions from Q 102 (i) to 102 (iii):

Hydrocarbon	Molecular Formula
X	C_3H_8
Y	C_5H_{10}
Z	C_4H_6

(i) X, Y and Z are classified as hydrocarbons because these contain:
(a) Hydrogen
(b) Oxygen
(c) Carbon
(d) Both carbon and hydrogen

(ii) To which series C_5H_{10} belongs?
(a) C_nH_{2n+2} (b) C_nH_{2n}
(c) C_nH_{2n-2} (d) C_nH_{n+2}

(iii) Choose the incorrect statement regarding above three hydrocarbons
(a) All have different general formula
(b) X and Y differ by –CH_2 unit
(c) Z is an alkyne
(d) Y is an alkene

Ans. (i) (d) Both carbon and hydrogen
(ii) (b) C_nH_{2n}
(iii) (b) X and Y differ by –CH_2 unit

103. Study the table given below carefully and answer any four questions from Q 103 (i) to 103 (iv):

Hydrocarbon	Property
H	has the molecular formula $C_{10}H_{22}$
J	has two carbon atoms less than (H) and belongs to the same homologous series.
K	has two carbon atoms more than (H) and belongs to the same homologous series.

(i) What is the molecular formula of J?
(a) $C_{12}H_{26}$ (b) C_8H_{16}
(c) C_8H_{18} (d) C_8H_{14}

(ii) Compounds H, J, K belong to which homologous series?
(a) C_nH_{2n} (b) C_nH_{2n-2}
(c) C_nH_{2n+2} (d) C_nH_{2n+1}

(iii) What is the molecular formula of K?
(a) $C_{12}H_{26}$ (b) $C_{12}H_{24}$
(c) $C_{12}H_{22}$ (d) $C_{12}H_{28}$

(iv) Choose the correct statements regarding compounds H, J and K
(a) All have the same chemical properties
(b) All have different general formula
(c) All differ by –CH_2 unit
(d) All have same melting and boiling points

Ans. (i) (c) C_8H_{18}
(ii) (c) C_nH_{2n+2}
(iii) (a) $C_{12}H_{26}$
(iv) (a) All have the same chemical properties

104. Question number 104(i)-104(iv) are based on the table given below. Study the table and answer the following questions.

Homologous Series	General Formula	Functional Group	Example
Alkanes	C_nH_{2n+2}	C – C	Methane, CH_4 Ethane, C_2H_6 Propane, C_3H_8 Butane, C_4H_{10}
Alkenes	C_nH_{2n}	C = C	Ethene, C_2H_4 Propene, C_3H_6 Butene, C_4H_8

(i) Give the name of the fifth member of the homologous series of Alkanes.
(ii) What type of bond is present in Alkanes?
(iii) Which hydrocarbon is also known as marsh gas?
(iv) Give one use of the ethene.

Ans. (i) Pentane (C_5H_{12}).
(ii) Single bond is present in alkanes.
(iii) Methane.
(iv) In the manufacture of many important polymers like polyethene and polyvinyl chloride (PVC).

105. Based on the structures given below answer the following questions:

$$H-\underset{\underset{H}{|}}{\overset{\overset{H}{|}}{C}}-\underset{\underset{H}{|}}{\overset{\overset{H}{|}}{C}}-H$$

Ethane

H H
| |
H — C = C — H
Ethene

H H
| |
C = C
Ethyne

(i) Give the name of the third member of the homologous series of alkene.

(ii) Write the number of covalent bonds in the molecule of butane.

(iii) Write the number of covalent bonds in the molecule of propane.

(iv) Draw the structure of butane.

Ans. (i) Butene (C_4H_8).

(ii) Thirteen

(iii) 10 bonds

(iv)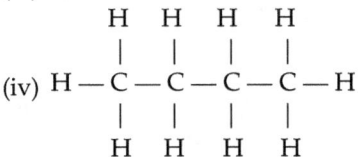

Self-Assessment

106. Define bond length.
107. Define allotropy.
108. Which of the following is used in pencil lead?
    (a) Diamond   (b) Graphite
    (c) Coke   (d) All the above
109. Which of the following is not a characteristic of graphite?
    (a) Soft and slippery
    (b) Good conductor of electricity
    (c) Heavier than diamond
    (d) Contains free electrons
110. Which one is called buckminsterfullerene?
    (a) C_{60} (b) C_{70}
    (c) C_{80} (d) C_{90}
111. **Assertion:** Carbon and its compounds are used as fuels.
    Reason: They give lot of heat and light when burnt in air.
112. What its catenation?
113. What do you mean by isomers?
114. What is general formula of alkanes?
115. Which of the following is an example of triple bond?
    C_2H_6, C_2H_2, C_2H_4, C_3H_4
116. What are non–crystalline allotropes of carbon?
117. Classify the following compounds as alkanes, alkenes and alkynes: C_2H_4, C_3H_4, C_4H_8, C_5H_{12}, C_5H_8, C_3H_8, C_6H_6.

Periodic Classification of Elements

Chapter 5

Definitions

1. **Element:** A substance that cannot be separated into simpler substances and that singly or in combination constitute all matter.
2. **Periods:** It is a horizontal row of periodic table.
3. **Groups:** It is a vertical column of the periodic table.
4. **Atomic mass:** Atomic mass of an element is the sum of protons and neutrons.
5. **Atomic radius:** It is defined as the distance from the centre of nucleus to the outermost shell of the atom. It is generally expressed in Picometer (pm).
6. **Periodicity:** The recurrence of similar physical and chemical properties of elements when arranged in a particular order.
7. **Valency:** It is defined as the combining capacity of an atom of an element to acquire the next inert gas configuration.
8. **Electronegativity:** The relative tendency of an atom to attract shared pair of electrons towards itself.
9. **Electron affinity:** The amount of energy released when an electron is added to an isolated gaseous atom.
10. **Ionisation energy:** The amount of energy required to remove most loosely bonded electron from an isolated gaseous atom.
11. **Isotopes:** Atoms of same element having similar atomic number but different atomic mass.
12. **Isobars:** Atoms of different elements having different atomic number but same atomic mass.

Multiple Choice Questions

13. **The Law of Octaves was applicable upto which element in the Periodic table:**
    (a) Oxygen (b) Calcium
    (c) Cobalt (d) Potassium

    Ans. (b) Calcium.

    Explanation :
    Newland's law of octaves was applicable only to lighter elements having atomic masses up to 40 u i.e., up to calcium. After calcium, every eighth element did not possess properties similar to that of the first element.

14. **According to Mendeleev's Periodic Law, the elements were arranged in the periodic table in the order of:** [NCERT, Exemplar]
    (a) Increasing atomic number
    (b) Decreasing atomic number
    (c) Increasing atomic masses
    (d) Decreasing atomic masses

    Ans. (c) Increasing atomic masses.

    Explanation :
    According to Mendeleev's periodic law, the elements were arranged in the periodic table in the order of increasing atomic masses.

15. **In Mendeleev's periodic table, gaps were left for the elements to be discovered later. Which of the following elements found a place in the perioidc table later.** [NCERT, Exemplar]
    (a) Germanium (b) Chlorine
    (c) Oxygen (d) Silicon

    Ans. (a) Germanium.

    Explanation :
    Chlorine, oxygen and silicon were included in Mendeleev's periodic table. Germanium was discovered later which fit into the empty spaces left by Mendeleev and matched to the expected properties.

16. **How many elements were arranged by Mendeleev in his periodic table ?**
    (a) 98 (b) 63
    (c) 42 (d) 21

    Ans. (b) 63.

    Explanation :
    Mendeleev included 63 known elements arranged it according to increasing atomic weight;

Mendeleev also left spaces for as yet undiscovered elements for which he predicted according to the atomic weights.

17. What type of oxide would Eka– aluminium form ? [NCERT, Exemplar]
(a) EO_3
(b) E_3O_2
(c) E_2O_3
(d) EO

Ans. (c) E_2O_3

Explanation :
Aluminium is Al having the oxidation state: +3, it can form Al^{3+} and it has valency = +3. So it will form Al_2O_3. Gallium and aluminium belong to the identical group and hence their valency is also going to the same which is 3. Eka Aluminium comes after Aluminium, and it is called Gallium. E_2O_3 is the type of oxide Eka – aluminium would form.

18. Which element was not known when Mendeleev proposed his classification ?
(a) Hydrogen
(b) Sodium
(c) Calcium
(d) Germanium

Ans. (c) Germanium

Explanation :
The elements which were unknown when Mendeleev gave his classification were geranium, gallium and scandium. He left gaps for the unknown elements and predicted correctly the properties of some of the unknown elements.

19. According to Mendeleev's Periodic Law, the elements were arranged in the periodic table in order of their:
(a) increasing atomic number
(b) decreasing atomic number
(c) increasing atomic mass
(d) decreasing atomic mass

Ans. (c) increasing atomic mass

Explanation :
Mendeleev realized that the chemical and physical properties of elements were related to their atomic mass in a 'periodic' way, and arranged them so that groups of elements with similar properties fell into vertical columns in his table. So, according to Mendeleev's periodic table elements were arranged according to their atomic mass.

20. Which of the following statements about Newland' slaw of octaves is correct?
(a) It was applicable to all elements.
(b) It was applicable to elements up to calcium only.
(c) Every first and seventh element had similar properties.
(d) Noble gases werediscovered that time

Ans. (b) It was applicable to elements up to calcium only.

Explanation :
Out of the total 56 known elements, Newland could arrange elements only up to calcium. Every eighth element did not show properties similar to that of the first after calcium.

21. In Mendeleev's periodic table, gaps were left for the elements to be discovered later. Which of the following elements found a place in the periodic table later?
(a) Chlorine
(b) Silicon
(c) Oxygen
(d) Germanium

Ans. (d) Germanium

Explanation :
Chlorine, oxygen and silicon were included in Mendeleev's periodic table. Germanium was discovered later which fit into the empty spaces left by Mendeleev and matched to the expected properties.

22. The law of octaves was given by ___.
(a) Mendeleev
(b) Newlands
(c) Bohr
(d) Moseley

Ans. (b) Newlands

Explanation :
The law of octaves was given by Newlands.

23. The position of element in the periodic table is generally determined by its:
(a) no of valence electrons
(b) no of shells
(c) both (a) and (b)
(d) none of the above

Ans. (c) both (a) and (b)

Explanation :
Electronic configuration is the arrangement of electrons in the shells. Outer electrons tells us about thegroup number and the number of shells tells us about period number.

24. Vertical columns in a periodic table are called:
(a) rows
(b) periods
(c) groups
(d) patters

Ans. (c) groups

Explanation :
Horizontal rows in the periodic table are called periods and vertical columns are called groups.

25. The elements having seven valence electrons in their outermost shell are known as:
(a) alkalis
(b) halogens
(c) alkaline earth metals
(d) noble gases

Ans. (b) halogens

Periodic Classification of Elements | 39

Explanation :

The family of elements having seven electrons in the valence shell is halogens, i.e., chlorine, fluorine, bromine, iodine, astatine. Halogens are the most electronegative elements in the periodic table.

26. **Non metals usually forms :**
    (a) acidic oxides   (b) basic oxides
    (c) neutral oxides   (d) amphoteric oxides

Ans. (a) acidic oxides

Explanation :

Non-metals react with oxygen to form acidic compounds of oxides which are held together by covalent bonds. These compounds can also be called as acid anhydrides.

27. **The number of shells in elements of the third period is:**
    (a) three   (b) two
    (c) four   (d) one

Ans. (a) three

Explanation :

Number of shells = Period number

28. **Which of the following group has the maximum radii in a group when considered in the same period?**
    (a) Halogens   (b) Alkaline earth metals
    (c) Alkali metals   (d) Noble gases

Ans. (c) Alkali metals

Explanation :

Atomic radii decreases on moving across a period from left to right, so moving from group 1 to 18 atomic radii decreases and group 1 has the largest atomic radii as compared to the other groups of the same period.

29. **An element X has 4 shells and 3 valence electrons. What is its period number?**
    (a) 3   (b) 5
    (c) 6   (d) 4

Ans. (d) 4

Explanation :

Number of shells = Period number

30. **The electronic configuration of an element M is 2, 8, 4. In modern periodic table, the element M must be placed in:**
    (a) 4th group   (b) 2nd group
    (c) 14th group   (d) 18th group

Ans. (c) 14th group

Explanation :

In the periodic table, elements having 4 valence electrons are placed in group 14.

31. **Which group elements are called transition metals?**
    (a) Group number 1 to 2
    (b) Group number 13 to 18
    (c) Group number 3 to 12
    (d) Group number 1 to 8

Ans. (c) Group number 3 to 12

Explanation :

The elements occurring in group 3 to 12 are named as transition metals because they are metallic elements that form a transition between the main group elements, which occur in groups 1 and 2 on the left side, and groups 13–18 on the right side of the periodic table.

Transition elements have following properties:
(a) They are good conductors of heat and electricity.
(b) They can be hammered or bent into shape easily.
(c) They have high melting points (but mercury is liquid at room temperature).
(d) They are usually hard and tough.
(e) They have high densities.

32. **Elements of which group has only 2 shells and both are completely filled?**
    (a) Helium   (b) Neon
    (c) Calcium   (d) Boron

Ans. (b) Neon

Explanation :

Neon with the atomic number 10, has the electronic configuration as 2,8. Hence, both its K and L shells are completely filled.

33. **The elements A, B and C belong to group 2, 14 and 16 respectively, of the periodic table. Which two elements of these will form covalent bonds?**
    (a) A and B   (b) B and C
    (c) C and A   (d) None of these

Ans. (b) B and C

Explanation :

The covalent bond is formed by the sharing of electrons between two atoms. As the element B (which belongs to group 14) has 4 valence electrons which it can share with two atoms of the elements of C (from group 16 each having 6 valence shell electrons) to complete the octet of each included atom, B and C will form covalent bond with each other.

34. **An element M is in group 13th of the periodic table. The formula for its oxide is:**
    (a) MO   (b) M_2O_3
    (c) M_3O_2 (d) None of these

Ans. (b) M_2O_3

Explanation :

As the element M belongs to group 13th of the periodic table so it has 3 valence electrons, i.e., it can have +3 oxidation state while oxygen atom (with 2 valency) has −2 oxidation state. So the formula for the corresponding oxide is M_2O_3.

35. Which of these belong to the same period?

Element	A	B	C
Atomic number	2	10	5

   (a) A, B (b) B, C
   (c) C, A (d) A, B and C

Ans. (b) B, C

Explanation :
B = 10 (2, 8), C = 5 (2, 3) Both have 2 shell, so they both belong to same period.

36. Carbon belongs to the second period and group 14 while silicon belongs to the third period and group 14 of the periodic table. If atomic number of carbon is 6, the atomic number of silicon should be:
   (a) 7   (b) 14
   (c) 24 (d) 16

Ans. (b) 14

Explanation :
Silicon and carbon belong to the same group. They have same number of valence electron in their outermost shell i.e. 4. Hence, they will differ in atomic numbers by 8. So, 6 + 8 = 14.

37. Consider the following elements
   20Ca, 8O 18Ar, 16S, 4Be, 2He
   Which of the above elements would you expect to be in group 16 of the Periodic Table?
   (a) 20Ca and 16S (b) 20Ca and 8O
   (c) 18Ar and 16S (d) 8O and 16S

Ans. (d) 8O and 16S

Explanation :
The electronic configuration of oxygen and sulphur is 2,6 and 2,8,6 respectively. Both of them have 6 electrons in their outermost shell. To know the group number 10 is added. The output is 16. Therefore both of them belong to group 16.

38. The atom of an element has electronic configuration 2, 8, 7. To which of the following elements would it be chemically similar?
   (a) N(7)   (b) P(15)
   (c) Na(11) (d) F (9)

Ans. (d) F (9)

Explanation :
Electronic configuration of chlorine and the given element is 2,7, and 2,8,7. Both are having same number of valence electron. Hence they would be similar in their chemical property.

39. How many groups are there in the periodic table?
   (a) 18 (b) 8
   (c) 28 (d) 17

Ans. (a) 18

Explanation :
Vertical columns of the periodic table are known as groups. There are 18 groups in the periodic table.

40. Atomic mass number is equal to the:-
   (a) total number of p and n
   (b) total number of p and e
   (c) number of Protons
   (d) number of neutrons

Ans. (a) total number of p and n

Explanation :
Mass number is the sum of the number of protons and the number of neutrons in an atom.

41. Five elements A, B, C, D and E have atomic numbers 2, 3, 7, 10 and 18 respectively. The elements which belong to the same period of the periodic table are:
   (a) A,B,C (b) B, C,D
   (c) A,D, E (d) B,D,E

Ans. (b) B, C,D

Explanation :
B,C and D, with atomic number 3,7,10 respectively, belong to the same period of periodic table. This is because the elements B,C and D have the same valence shell (L).

42. The alkaline earth metal present in group 2 and period 3 of the periodic table is:
   (a) sodium   (b) magnesium
   (c) calcium (d) potassium

Ans. (b) magnesium

Explanation :
The alkaline earth metal present in group 2 and period 3 of the periodic table is magnesium.

43. The position of three elements A, B and C in the Periodic Table are shown below:

Group 16	Group 17
–	–
–	A
–	–
B	C

Which type of ion, cation or anion, will be formed by element A?
   (a) cation   (b) anion
   (c) both (a) and (b) (d) none of these

Ans. (b) anion

Explanation :
A will form an anion as it accepts an electron to complete its octet, and achieve the nearest gas configuration.

44. Given below is the electronic configuration of two elements. Which of these will be more electronegative?

A = 2,3
B = 2,3,5
(a) A
(b) B
(c) Both (a) and (b)
(d) None of these

Ans. (a) A

Explanation :

Nitrogen is more electronegative than phosphorus, because on moving down a group, the number of shell increases and electronegativity also decreases.

45. Where would you locate the element with electronic configuration 2,7 in the Modern Periodic Table?
(a) Group 8
(b) Group 9
(c) Group 18
(d) Group 10

Ans. (b) Group 9

Explanation :

It is the electronic configuration of Fluorine with atomic number 9. It is the hologen and is most electronegative elements.

46. The atomic number of element of second period and sixth group is ?
(a) 20
(b) 56
(c) 38
(d) 55

Ans. (b) 56

Explanation :

The element of second period and sixth group is Barium.

47. Which of the following elements do not belong to same group?
(a) P, As
(b) Tc, Re
(c) Ag, Hg
(d) Ne, Xe

Ans. (c) Ag, Hg

Explanation :

Ag and Hg do not belong to same group. Ag belongs to group 11 and Hg belongs to group 12 of the periodic table.

48. Given below is the elements of group 14 of periodic table,

6 C Carbon 12.0
14 Si Silicon 28.1
32 Ge Germanium 73.6
50 Sn Tin 118.7
82 Pb Lead 207.2
114 Fl Flerovium (289)

(i) How many metals are there in the group?
(a) 1
(b) 2
(c) 3
(d) 0

Ans. (c) 3

Explanation :

Sn, Pb and Fl are metals.

(ii) Which type of bond is formed by elements if this group?
(a) Ionic
(b) Covalent
(c) Coordinate
(d) Metallic bond

Ans. (b) Covalent

Explanation :

The group is having valence of 4. So, covalent bond is formed.

49. In the following set of elements, which one of the following element does not belong to the set.

Calcium, Magnesium, Sodium, Beryllium
(a) Calcium
(b) Magnesium
(c) sodium
(d) Beryllium

Ans. (c) Sodium

Explanation :

Sodium does not belong to the set. This is because all other elements belong to group 2 but sodium belongs to group 1 of the periodic table.

50. Which of the period in periodic table has only gaseous elements?
(a) 1
(b) 2
(c) 3
(d) 4

Ans. (a) 1

Explanation :

It contains two elements H and He, both are gases.

51. Which amongst the given below elements does not belong to the same period.
$_6P_{12}$, $_7Q_{14}$, $_8R_{16}$, $_{11}S_{23}$,
(a) P, Q and R
(b) P and R
(c) P, Q, R and S
(d) Q and R

Ans. (a) P, Q and R

Explanation :

The electronic configuration of the elements is given as:

Element	Atomic number	Electronic configuration
P	6	2, 4
Q	7	2, 5
R	8	2, 6
S	11	2, 8, 1

Element P, Q and R have only two electrons shells and hence, they belong to the same period i.e, 2nd period.

52. **Identify the nature of the element:**
    Period = 3
    Valency = 4
    Physical property = hard
    Nature of compounds : Oxide- acidic halide - covalent.
    (a) Metal
    (b) Non-metal
    (c) Metalloid
    (d) Inner Transition elements

Ans. (c) Metalloid

Explanation :

The element is silicon with atomic number 14. It belongs to 3rd period and its valency is 4. It is a metalloid and exhibit properties of both metals and non-metals. It forms covalent halides as its outermost shell has 4 electrons.

53. **Where would you locate the element with electronic configuration 2, 8 in the Modern Periodic Table?** [NCERT, Exemplar]
    (a) Group 8 (b) Group 2
    (c) Group 18 (d) Group 10

Ans. (c) Group 18.

Explanation :

Element with the electronic configuration of 2, 8 is Neon having the atomic number 10. In the modern periodic table, noble gas elements are present in the group 18. Hence, the element with electronic configuration 2, 8 will be in the 18th group of the Modern Periodic Table.

54. **The outermost shell for elements of period 2 will be:**
    (a) K shell (b) L shell
    (c) M shell (d) N shell

Ans. (b) L shell.

Explanation :

The elements having two valence shells are placed in the second period. Thus, the outermost shell of these elements is L-shell.

55. **An element 'X' is forming an acidic oxide. Its position in modern periodic table will be:***

(a) Group 1 and Period 3
(b) Group 2 and Period 3
(c) Group 13 and Period 3
(d) Group 16 and Period 3

Ans. (d) Group 16 and Period 3

Explanation :

An element 'X' is forming an acidic oxide. Its position in modern periodic table will be placed in the group 16 and 3rd period of the periodic table since the elements of the group 16 forms the acidic oxides.

56. **The number of electrons in the valence shell is equal to its ....**
    (a) atomic mass (b) group number
    (c) period number (d) atomic volume

Ans. (b) group number.

Explanation :

The number of electrons in the valence shell is equal to its group number. For example: Valence electrons in P is 5 and its group number is also 5.

57. **Consider the following statements about an element 'X' with number of protons 13.***
    (A) It forms amphoteric oxide.
    (B) Its valency is three.
    (C) The formula of its chloride is XC_3.
    The correct statements (s) is/are.
    (a) only (A) (b) only (B)
    (c) (A) and (C) (d) (A), (B) and (C)

Ans. (d) (A), (B) and (C)

Explanation :

An element having the protons 13 has the atomic number 13 and the element having the atomic number 13 is Aluminium, it forms the amphoteric oxide which are both acidic and basic in nature and it has the valency 3 and its oxide is of the formula XC_3 such as Al_2O_3.

58. **The element with atomic number 14 is hard and forms acidic oxide and a covalent halide. To which of the following categories does the element belong ?** [NCERT, Exemplar]
    (a) Metal
    (b) Metalloid
    (c) Non-metal
    (d) Left-hand side element

Ans. (b) Metalloid

Explanation :

The element will be a metalloid since the elements present in the group 14 have the characteristics of both metals and the non-metals also they have the valence shell electrons as 4 thus, they form the covalent molecules with the other atoms.

59. **The modern periodic law is given by............**
    (a) Mendeleev (b) Einstein
    (c) Bohr (d) Mosley

Ans. (d) Mosley

---
* are board exam questions from previous years

Explanation :

The modern periodic law was given by Henry Mosley and his periodic table was based on the fact that "The physical and chemical properties of the elements are periodic functions of their atomic numbers". The atomic number is equal to the number of electrons or protons in a neutral atom."

60. Which one of the following property does not increase while moving down the group in the periodic table ?
(a) Atomic radius
(b) Metallic character
(c) Valence electrons
(d) Number of shells in an element

Ans. (c) Valence electrons

Explanation :

The number of valence electrons does not increase while moving down the group in the periodic table.

61. On moving from left to right in a period in the periodic table, the size of the atom:
[NCERT, Exemplar]
(a) increases
(b) decreases
(c) does not change appreciably
(d) first decreases and then increases

Ans. (b) decreases

Explanation :

On moving from left to right in a period, the atomic size decreases as the atomic number (i.e., the number of protons and electrons) increases but the number of shells remain the same. Therefore, the force of attraction between the nucleus and the outermost shell of electrons (effective nuclear charge) increases, thus leading to a decrease in the size.

62. A liquid non-metal is ....
(a) phosphorous (b) mercury
(c) bromine (d) nitrogen

Ans. (c) bromine

Explanation :

Bromine is the liquid non-metal present in the group 17 of the Periodic table.

63. The period that contains only gaseous elements are:
(a) 1 (b) 2
(c) 3 (d) 4

Ans. (a) 1

Explanation :

Period 1 has only gaseous elements namely hydrogen and helium.

64. The pairs of elements with the following atomic numbers have the same chemical properties:

(a) 13 and 12 (b) 3 and 11
(c) 4 and 24 (d) 2 and 1

Ans. (b) 3 and 11

Explanation :

The elements with the atomic number 3 and 11 have the same properties because both elements have same valence shell electronic configuration, *i.e.*, ns^1.

65. The positions of four elements A, B, C and D in the Modern Periodic Table are shown below. Which element is most likely to form an acidic oxide ?

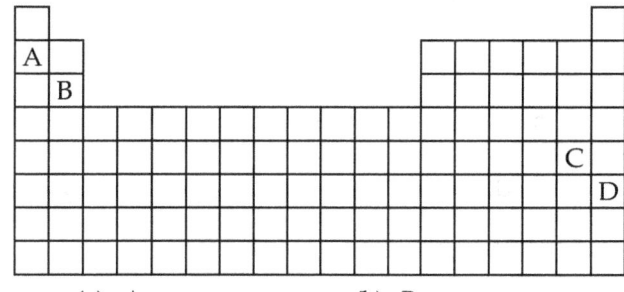

(a) A (b) B
(c) C (d) D

Ans. (c) C

Explanation :

From the position of element C in the periodic table, it is clear that it is a non-metal. Therefore C will form the acidic oxide since oxides of non-metals are acidic in nature.

66. Elements P, Q, R and S have atomic numbers 11, 15, 17 and 18 respectively. Which of them are reactive non-metals ?
(a) P and Q (b) P and R
(c) Q and R (d) R and S

Ans. (c) Q and R.

Explanation :

We are given that elements P, Q, R and S have atomic numbers 11, 15, 17, and 18.

We have to find reactive non metals in given elements.

We know that atomic number of sodium = 11
Therefore, P is sodium.
Sodium is metal not non metal.
We know that atomic number of phosphorus, P = 15
Therefore, Q is phosphorus.
It is not a metal because it requires 3 electrons to complete its octet.
Atomic number of chlorine = 17
Therefore, element R is chlorine.
It is a non metal since it requires an electron to complete its octet.
Atomic number of argon = 18
Therefore, element S is argon.

It is noble gas because it has completely filled shells. It is non reactive because it does not require any electron to complete its octet.

Hence, Q and R are reactive non metals.

67. Which of the given elements A, B, C, D and E with atomic number 2, 3, 7, 10 and 30 respectively belong to the same period ? [NCERT, Exemplar]
(a) A, B, C
(b) B, C, D
(c) A, D, E
(d) B, D, E

Ans. (b) B, C, D.

Explanation :

The first period contains 2 elements. Whereas, both second and third period contains 8 elements. Therefore, the first period contains 1 to 2 atomic number. The second period contains 3 to 10 atomic number. The third contains 11 to 18 atomic number. The fourth period contains 19 to 36 atomic number. Therefore, B, C and D belong to the same period.

68. Which pair of elements belong to the same group if elements A, B, C, D and E have atomic number 9, 11, 17, 12 and 13 respectively.
(a) A and B
(b) B and D
(c) A and C
(d) D and E

Ans. (c) A and C.

Explanation :

Since both A and C elements have the same number of valence electrons which is 7, hence they belong to the same group, i.e. 17th group of the periodic table.

69. _____ element would lose an electron easily ?
(a) Mg
(b) Na
(c) K
(d) Ca

Ans. (d) Ca.

Explanation :

The electronic configuration of calcium is 2, 8, 8, 2. It will lose two electron from its outermost shell because on losing two electrons it will acquire the nearest Nobel gas configuration and will become more stable.

70. Which among the following elements has the largest atomic radii ? [NCERT, Exemplar]
(a) Na
(b) Mg
(c) K
(d) Ca

Ans. (d) Ca.

Explanation :

Calcium will have the highest atomic radii since with the increase in the atomic number atomic radii also increases due to the increase in the number of the electronic shells.

71. The correct increasing order of the atomic radii of O, F and N will be:
(a) O, F, N
(b) N, F, O
(c) O, N, F
(d) F, O, N

Ans. (c) O, N, F.

Explanation :

The increasing order of atomic radii is F, O, N as atomic number of F, O and N are 9, 8 and 7 respectively and as the atomic number increases the atomic radii also increases due to the increase in the number of the electronic shells.

72. Which one of the following elements exhibits maximum number of valence electrons ? [NCERT, Exemplar]
(a) Na
(b) Al
(c) Si
(d) P

Ans. (d) P

Explanation :

Valence electrons in Na, Al, Si and P are 1, 3, 4 and 5. Hence, phosphorus has maximum number of valence electrons.

73. The least reactive element in group 17 is............
(a) Fluorine
(b) Chlorine
(c) Bromine
(d) Iodine

Ans. (d) Iodine.

Explanation :

Iodine is the least reactive element in the group 17 of the periodic table since with the increase in the number of the shells the hold of the nucleus on the electron becomes weak and thus, it is less reactive in nature.

74. Three elements B, Si and Ge are: [NCERT, Exemplar]
(a) metals
(b) non-metals
(c) metalloids
(d) metal, non-metal and metalloid respectively

Ans. (c) metalloids

Explanation :

The elements B, Si and Ge are metalloids since they have the characteristics of both metals and the non-metals also they have the valence shell electrons as 4 and they form the covalent bonds with the other elements.

75. In periodic table, helium is placed at:
(a) top left corner
(b) bottom right corner
(c) bottom left corner
(d) top right corner

Ans. (d) top right corner

Explanation :

Helium is the second element on the periodic table. It is located in period 1 and group 18 or 8A on the right-hand side of the table. This group contains the noble gases, which are the most chemically inert elements on the periodic table. Thus it is placed on the top right corner in the periodic table.

Periodic Classification of Elements | 45

76. A factor that affects the ionisation potential of an element is ....
(a) atomic size (b) electron affinity
(c) electro-negativity (d) neutrons

Ans. (a) atomic size

Explanation :
Larger the atomic size, smaller is the ionisation potential. It is due to that the size of atom increases the outermost electrons farther away from the nucleus and nucleus loses the attraction on that electrons and hence can be easily removed and thus it affects the ionisation potential of the atom.

77. Which of the following element forms basic oxide?
(a) Phosphorous (b) Argon
(c) Chlorine (d) Potassium

Ans. (d) Potassium

Explanation :
The elements which can donate their valence electrons to other atoms are the metallic elements which form basic oxides as they give hydroxides in their aqueous solutions.

78. Which of the two elements will form covalent bonds?
X = Group 2
Y = Group 14
Z = Group 16
(a) X and Y (b) Y and Z
(c) Z and A (d) None of the above

Ans. (b) Y and Z

Explanation :
Covalent bond is formed by elements having less difference in their electronegativity. Since the covalent bond is formed between two non-metal elements. Now, out of X, Y and Z the element Y (of group 14) and element Z of group (16) are non-metals. Thus the elements Y and Z will form covalent bonds.

79. The correct order of decreasing metallic character of elements Na, Si, Cl, Mg, Al
(a) Cl > Si > Al > Mg > Na.
(b) Na > Mg > Al > Si > Cl
(c) Na > Si > Mg > Al > Cl
(d) Al > Na > Si > Cl > Mg

Ans. (b) Na > Mg > Al > Si > Cl

Explanation :
Sodium has 1, Mg has 2 and Al and 3, Si has 4 electrons in outermost orbits. But Cl has 7 electrons in its outermost orbit. Hence, sodium shows the maximum character of metallic elements, and chlorine shows the character of a non-metallic elements. Electropositive elements are metallic in character.

80. The positions of four elements A, B, C and D in the modern periodic table are shown below.

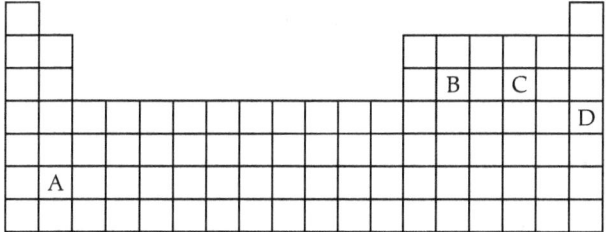

The correct order of increasing order of atomic size is:
(a) C < B < D < A (b) A < B < C < D
(c) B < C < A < D (d) D < C < B < A

Ans. (a) C < B < D < A

Explanation :
Atomic size decreases along a period and increases down the group.

81. As we move down the group, the number of shells:
(a) increases (b) decreases
(c) remain Same (d) none of the above

Ans. (a) increases

Explanation :
As we move down in the group ,number of shells increases .Hence,size of the atom also increases.

82. The commonly used unit of atomic radii is:
(a) angstrom (b) meters
(c) millimetres (d) centimetres

Ans. (a) angstrom

Explanation :
Atomic radius is usually expressed in Angstrom units. It is because the size of atom is very small. It is equivalent to $1\times 10-10$ metres.

83. Nuclear charge is directly proportional to the:
(a) number of electrons
(b) number of neutrons
(c) number of protons
(d) number of nucleons

Ans. (c) number of protons

Explanation :
Protons and neutrons are present in the nucleus and both are collectively called nucleons. Protons are charged particles and neutrons are neutral or do not have any charge on them. So ,thetotal charge on the nucleus is due to the number of protons present in the nucleus.

84. What happens to the nuclear charge as we move down the group in a periodic table?
(a) Increases (b) Decreases
(c) Remains the same (d) None of the above

Ans. (a) Increases

Explanation :

Nuclear charge is a function of the number of protons present in an atom. If we move from right to left or from top to bottom in a periodic table we can always observe an increase in the number of protons as there is an increase in the number of electrons.

85. **The maximum amount of energy required to remove the most loosely bounded electron from an isolated, neutral, gaseous atom is known as:**
    (a) electron Affinity (b) ionisation energy
    (c) electro negativity (d) none of the above

Ans. (b) ionisation energy

Explanation :

Ionization Energy is the amount of energy required to remove an electron from an isolated atom or molecule.

86. **Which of the following elements has the highest electro negativity?**
    (a) Fluorine (b) Oxygen
    (c) Boron (d) Beryllium

Ans. (a) Fluorine

Explanation :

The electro negativity values for the VIIA group or Halogen value are the highest in their period or row, and decreases as the atomic number of the Halogen increases. The group VIIA/17 or Halogens have a valance electron configuration of 2, 8, 7. This gives the Halogens 7 valance electrons.

The electron configuration causes the Halogens to have a strong pull for one more electron. The definition of electronegativity is the pull of the element for more electrons. Thus the VIIA or Halogens will have the highest electronegativity of any element in their row, or period.

87. **Which of the following has the highest atomic size?**
    (a) Magnesium (b) Sodium
    (c) Sulphur (d) Chlorine

Ans. (b) Sodium

Explanation :

Sodium, Magnesium, Sulphur and Chlorine belongs to the third period. For elements of same period, size decreases while going from left to right across a period

88. **Which of the following alkali metals is radioactive in nature?**
    (a) Potassium (b) Rubidium
    (c) Caesium (d) Francium

Ans. (d) Francium

Explanation :

Francium is the second rarest element on the earth. It has a half-life of about 22 minutes only. It is used in cancer diagnostics, spectroscopic experiments, etc.

89. **Which of the following has zero electron affinity?**
    (a) Halogens
    (b) Alkali metals
    (c) Alkaline earth metals
    (d) Noble gases

Ans. (d) Noble gases

Explanation :

Noble gases have zero electron affinity due to stable electronic configuration.

90. **Which of the following is the correct order of the atomic radii of the elements oxygen, fluorine and nitrogen?**
    (a) $O < F < N$ (b) $N < F < O$
    (c) $O < N < F$ (d) $F < O < N$

Ans. (d) $F < O < N$

Explanation :

Oxygen (8), fluorine (9) and nitrogen (7) belong to the same period of the periodic table, in the order nitrogen, oxygen and fluorine. Now in a period, on moving from left to right the atomic radius of the elements decreases. Therefore, the atomic radius of nitrogen is the largest.

91. **Element X forms a chloride with the formula XCl_2, which is a solid with a high melting point. X would most likely be in the same group of the Periodic Table as**
    (a) Na (b) Mg
    (c) Al (d) Si

Ans. (b) Mg

Explanation :

Group 2 alkaline earth metal atoms have two valence electrons each. They can donate their two valence electrons to two other chlorine atoms to form the solid compounds of the form XCl_2. This XCl_2 compound being ionic in nature, has a very strong electrostatic force of attraction between 2 chloride ions and 1 metal ion. Thus, a large amount of heat is required to break these strong bonds, causing the compounds to have very high melting and boiling points.

92. **Out of Li and Be which has higher ionisation energy?**
    (a) Li (b) Be
    (c) Both have same (d) None

Ans. (a) Li

Explanation :

Ionization Potential is the amount of energy required to remove the electron from an atom. It is also known as Ionization energy. Ionization energy increases across the period with increase in atomic number. Li and Be belongs to the same period having electronic configuration 2,1 and 2,2 respectively. Hence Be will have more ionization energy tan Li.

93. Observe the following table:

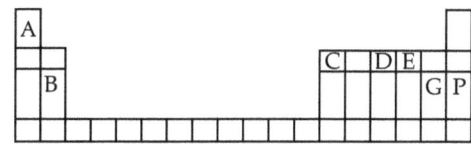

(i) Which element will form an ionic compound with G?

(a) A (b) B
(c) C (d) D

Ans. (i) (b)

Explanation :

B belongs to group 2 alkaline earth metal and G belongs to group 17 halogens which are non-metals. Ionic compound is formed between metal and a non-metal.

Assertion and Reasoning Based Questions

94. **Assertion:** The triad N, P and As will not represent the Dobereiner's triad.

    Reason : Because there is so much difference in their atomic masses.

    (a) If both assertion and reason are true and reason is the correct explanation of assertion.
    (b) If both assertion and reason are true, but reason is not the correct explanation of assertion.
    (c) If assertion is true, but reason is false.
    (d) If assertion is false, but reason is true.

    Ans. (b) If both assertion and reason are true, but reason is not the correct explanation of assertion.

    Explanation :

    The triad N, P and As will not represent the Dobereiner's triad because the average of atomic masses of nitrogen (N) and arsenic (As) is not equal to the atomic mass of phosphorus (P). Thus both assertion and reason are true, but reason is not the correct explanation of assertion.

95. **Assertion:** The elements of the same group have similar chemical properties.

    Reason: The elements of the same group have the different number of valence electrons.

    (a) If both assertion and reason are true and reason is the correct explanation of assertion.
    (b) If both assertion and reason are true, but reason is not the correct explanation of assertion.
    (c) If assertion is true, but reason is false.
    (d) If assertion is false, but reason is true.

    Ans. (c) If assertion is true, but reason is false.

    Explanation :

    The elements of same group have similar chemical properties due to the same number of valence electrons. Thus assertion is true but reason is False.

96. **Assertion:** Mendeleev's periodic table was not widely accepted.

    Reason: It is because hydrogen was not placed properly.

    (a) If both assertion and reason are true and reason is the correct explanation of assertion.
    (b) If both assertion and reason are true, but reason is not the correct explanation of assertion.
    (c) If assertion is true, but reason is false.
    (d) If assertion is false, but reason is true.

    Ans. (b) If both assertion and reason are true, but reason is not the correct explanation of assertion.

    Explanation :

    Mendeleev's periodic table was not widely accepted because all the properties were not explained and also the anomalous behaviour of hydrogen was not explained. Thus, both assertion and reason are true but reason is not the correct explanation of the assertion.

97. **Assertion:** Nobel gases are placed in different group in periodic table.

    Reason: Nobel gases are inert in nature.

    (a) If both assertion and reason are true and reason is the correct explanation of assertion.
    (b) If both assertion and reason are true, but reason is not the correct explanation of assertion.
    (c) If assertion is true, but reason is false.
    (d) If assertion is false, but reason is true.

    Ans. (a) If both assertion and reason are true and reason is the correct explanation of assertion.

    Explanation :

    Noble gases are placed in a separate group because these are inert elements. They have properties which are different from all other elements. Thus both assertion and reason are true and reason is the correct explanation of the assertion.

98. **Assertion:** The elements of the different group have similar chemical properties.

    Reason: It is because they have same number of valence electrons.

    (a) If both assertion and reason are true and reason is the correct explanation of assertion.
    (b) If both assertion and reason are true, but reason is not the correct explanation of assertion.
    (c) If assertion is true, but reason is false.
    (d) If assertion is false, but reason is true.

    Ans. (d) If assertion is false, but reason is true.

    Explanation :

    The elements of the same group have similar chemical properties because of the presence of same number of valence electrons. Thus, assertion is false but reason is true.

99. **Assertion:** Metalloids are present in zig-zag rows in periodic table.
    Reason: Metalloids have same properties.
    (a) If both assertion and reason are true and reason is the correct explanation of assertion.
    (b) If both assertion and reason are true, but reason is not the correct explanation of assertion.
    (c) If assertion is true, but reason is false.
    (d) If assertion is false, but reason is true.
Ans. (b) If both assertion and reason are true, but reason is not the correct explanation of assertion.

   Explanation :
   It is because they have some properties of metals and some properties of non-metals. Thus, both assertion and reason are true but reason is not the correct explanation of the assertion.

100. **Assertion:** Chlorine is called halogen.
    Reason: It is because chlorine reacts with metals to form salts.
    (a) If both assertion and reason are true and reason is the correct explanation of assertion.
    (b) If both assertion and reason are true, but reason is not the correct explanation of assertion.
    (c) If assertion is true, but reason is false.
    (d) If assertion is false, but reason is true.
Ans. (d) If assertion is false, but reason is true.

   Explanation :
   Elements such as chlorine, bromine and iodine are called halogens because they react with metals to form salts. Thus, assertion is false but reason is true.

101. **Assertion:** Across a period atomic radius decreases.
    Reason: It is because electron is added to the same shell.
    (a) If both assertion and reason are true and reason is the correct explanation of assertion.
    (b) If both assertion and reason are true, but reason is not the correct explanation of assertion.
    (c) If assertion is true, but reason is false.
    (d) If assertion is false, but reason is true.
Ans. (a) If both assertion and reason are true and reason is the correct explanation of assertion.

   Explanation :
   Atomic radius decreases across a period because electron is added in the same shell. Thus attraction between nucleus and valence shell increases due to which outermost shell is pulled closer to the nucleus. Nuclear charge is also increasing. Thus, effective nuclear charge increases and atomic size decreases. Thus, both assertion and reason are true and reason is the correct explanation of the assertion.

102. **Assertion:** Sodium is a metal whereas sulphur is a non-metal.
    Reason: From left to right metallic character decreases.
    (a) If both assertion and reason are true and reason is the correct explanation of assertion.
    (b) If both assertion and reason are true, but reason is not the correct explanation of assertion.
    (c) If assertion is true, but reason is false.
    (d) If assertion is false, but reason is true.
Ans. (a) If both assertion and reason are true and reason is the correct explanation of assertion.

   Explanation :
   Metallic character of elements decreases in a period from left to right. Hence, sodium which is at left is metal and sulphur is a non-metal. Thus, both assertion and reason are true and reason is the correct explanation of the assertion.

103. **Assertion:** Non-metals are placed on the right-hand side in the periodic table.
    Reason: Metalloids shows properties of both metals and non-metals.
    (a) If both assertion and reason are true and reason is the correct explanation of assertion.
    (b) If both assertion and reason are true, but reason is not the correct explanation of assertion.
    (c) If assertion is true, but reason is false.
    (d) If assertion is false, but reason is true.
Ans. (b) If both assertion and reason are true, but reason is not the correct explanation of assertion.

   Explanation :
   Non-metals are placed on the right-hand side in the periodic table and metalloids in the middle. Thus both assertion and reason are true, but reason is not the correct explanation of assertion.

104. **Assertion:** The atomic radius decreases in moving from left to right along a period.
    Reason: This is due to an increase in nuclear charge.
    (a) If both assertion and reason are true and reason is the correct explanation of assertion.
    (b) If both assertion and reason are true, but reason is not the correct explanation of assertion.
    (c) If assertion is true, but reason is false.
    (d) If assertion is false, but reason is true.
Ans. (a) If both assertion and reason are true and reason is the correct explanation of assertion.

   Explanation :
   Increased nuclear change is due to increase in nuclear charge which tends to pull the electrons closer to the nucleus and reduces the size of the atom. Thus both assertion and reason are correct and reason is the correct explanation of the assertion.

105. **Assertion :** Out of the Na, Mg and Ar, Ar has the highest ionisation enthalpy.
    Reason: Ar has stable inert gas configuration.

(a) If both assertion and reason are true and reason is the correct explanation of assertion.
(b) If both assertion and reason are true, but reason is not the correct explanation of assertion.
(c) If assertion is true, but reason is false.
(d) If assertion is false, but reason is true.

Ans. (a) If both assertion and reason are true and reason is the correct explanation of assertion.

Explanation :

The elements having inert gas configuration has highest ionisation enthalpy. Thus both assertion and reason are correct and reason is the correct explanation of the assertion.

106. **Assertion:** Metallic character decreases across a period.
    Reason: Non metals are electropositive in nature.
    (a) If both assertion and reason are true and reason is the correct explanation of assertion.
    (b) If both assertion and reason are true, but reason is not the correct explanation of assertion.
    (c) If assertion is true, but reason is false.
    (d) If assertion is false, but reason is true.

Ans. (c) If assertion is true, but reason is false.

Explanation :

Non metals are electronegative in nature and metallic character decreases across a period. Thus assertion is true but reason if False.

107. **Assertion:** The ionisation energy of Mg is more than sodium.
    Reason: The ionisation energy decreases in a period from left to right.
    (a) If both assertion and reason are true and reason is the correct explanation of assertion.
    (b) If both assertion and reason are true, but reason is not the correct explanation of assertion.
    (c) If assertion is true, but reason is false.
    (d) If assertion is false, but reason is true.

Ans. (b) If both assertion and reason are true, but reason is not the correct explanation of assertion.

Explanation :

The ionisation energy increases in a period from left to right. Therefore, ionisation energy of Mg is more than sodium. Thus, both assertion and reason are true but reason is not the correct explanation of the assertion.

108. **Assertion:** Periodicity in elements is the basis for the periodic table.
    Reason: Henry Mosley gave the modern periodic law.
    (a) If both assertion and reason are true and reason is the correct explanation of assertion.
    (b) If both assertion and reason are true, but reason is not the correct explanation of assertion.
    (c) If assertion is true, but reason is false.
    (d) If assertion is false, but reason is true.

Ans. (b) If both assertion and reason are true, but reason is not the correct explanation of assertion.

Explanation :

Repetition of properties after regular intervals is the main cause of periodicity of elements. Thus, both assertion and reason are true but reason is not the correct explanation of the assertion.

109. **Assertion:** Chlorine is less electronegative than fluorine.
    Reason: It is because of its small size.
    (a) If both assertion and reason are true and reason is the correct explanation of assertion.
    (b) If both assertion and reason are true, but reason is not the correct explanation of assertion.
    (c) If assertion is true, but reason is false.
    (d) If assertion is false, but reason is true.

Ans. (b) If both assertion and reason are true, but reason is not the correct explanation of assertion.

Explanation :

Electronegativity decreases in a group from top to bottom. Therefore, chlorine is less electronegative than fluorine. Thus, both assertion and reason are true but reason is not the correct explanation of the assertion.

Case Based Questions

110. **Read the following passage carefully and answer the following questions from Q 110 (i) to 110 (v).**

    With the constant discovery of a large number of elements, it became necessary to classify them and arrange them according to their periodic properties. Dobereiner arranged the elements with similar properties into groups. He classified some groups of three elements having similar physical and chemical properties, called Dobereiner's triads. John Newland's later arranged all elements in order of increasing atomic masses and found that every eighth element has similar properties as the first one in the chart.

    (i) {Cl, Br, I} is a Dobereiner's triad. In this triad, if the atomic masses of Cl and I are 35.5 and 127 respectively, what is the atomic mass of Br?
       (a) 162.5   (b) 91.5
       (c) 45.625 (d) 81.25

    (ii) Which is a Dobereiner's triad:
       (a) K, Al, Ca   (b) Li, Al, Ca
       (c) Li, Na, K   (d) Li, K, Na

    (iii) Newland's law of Octaves is obeyed by two elements A and B showing similar properties. The number of elements between A and B is:
       (a) 8   (b) 6
       (c) 7   (d) 5

(iv) Properties of Magnesium are similar to those of which element according to Newland's law of octaves?
(a) Beryllium (b) Lithium
(c) Potassium (d) Sodium

(v) Elements are arranged in Dobereiner's triad on the basis of:
(a) Atomic mass
(b) Atomic Number
(c) Number of Electrons
(d) Number of Neutrons

Ans. (i) (d) 81.25
(ii) (c) Li, Na, K
(iii) (b) 6
(iv) (a) Beryllium
(v) (a) Atomic mass

111. **Read the following passage carefully and answer the following questions from Q 111 (i) to 111 (v).**
When elements are arranged in the increasing order of their atomic numbers, we observe the recurrence of properties of the elements after certain regular intervals. This recurrence is known as periodicity. A number of physical properties such as atomic size, metallic and non-metallic character, etc. show periodic variation. Properties vary differently moving from left to right in a period and top to down in a group. Moving in a period from left to right, the number of shells remain the same but valence electron increase by one number. This results in an increase in nuclear charge. Going down in a group, the number of valence shells increases while the valence electrons remain the same. Observe some periodic table trends in the given figure.

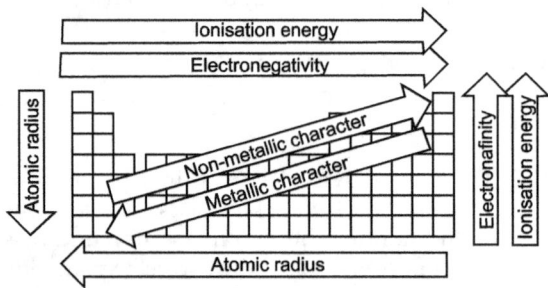

(i) As we go down in a group in the periodic table, the electropositive character of the element
(a) Decreases
(b) Increases
(c) Changes but irregularly
(d) Remains constant

(ii) In the second period in the table, which element has the largest size
(a) N (b) F
(c) Li (d) Be

(iii) Which of the following elements has three valence electrons?
(a) Al (b) S
(c) Cs (d) Ca

(iv) In the periodic table, the metallic character of the elements:
(a) Increases from left to right and decreases down the group
(b) Decreases from left to right and increases down the group
(c) Increases from left to right and increases down the group
(d) Deceases from left to right and decreases down the group

(v) Moving along a period results in an increase of
(a) Atomic size
(b) Number of valence electrons
(c) Electropositive character
(d) All of the above

Ans. (i) (b) Increases
(ii) (c) Li
(iii) (a) Al
(iv) (b) Decreases from left to right and increases down the group
(v) (b) Number of valence electrons

112. **Read the following and answer the following questions from Q 112 (i) to 112 (v).**

Metallic character: The ability of an atom to donate electrons and form positive ion (cation) is known as electropositivity or metallic character. Down the group, metallic character increases due to increase in atomic size and across the period, from left to right electro-positivity decreases due to decrease in atomic size.

Non-metallic character: The ability of an atom to accept electrons to form a negative ion (anion) is called non-metallic character or electronegativity. The elements having high electronegativity have a higher tendency to gain electrons and form anion. Down the group, electronegativity decreases due to increase in atomic size and across the period, from left to right electronegativity increases due to decrease in atomic size.

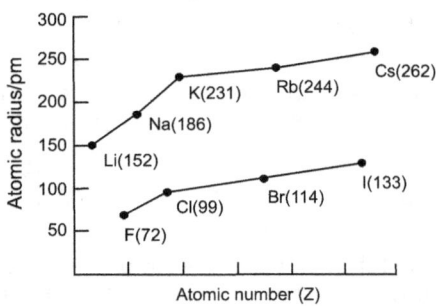

(i) Which of the following correctly represents the decreasing order of metallic character of Alkali metals plotted in the graph?
(a) Cs > Rb > Li > Na > K
(b) K > Rb > Li > Na > Cs
(c) Cs > Rb > K > Na > Li
(d) Cs > K > Rb > Na > Li

(ii) Hydrogen is placed along with Alkali metals in the modern periodic table though it shows non-metallic character:

(a) as Hydrogen has one electron and readily loses electron to form negative ion
(b) as Hydrogen can easily lose one electron like alkali metals to form positive ion
(c) as Hydrogen can gain one electron easily like halogens to form negative ion
(d) as Hydrogen shows the properties of non-metals

(iii) Which of the following has highest electronegativity?
(a) F (b) Cl
(c) Br (d) I

(iv) Identify the reason for the gradual change in electronegativity in halogens down the group.
(a) Electronegativity increases down the group due to decrease in atomic size
(b) Electronegativity decreases down the group due to decrease in tendency to lose electrons
(c) Electronegativity decreases down the group due to increase in atomic radius/tendency to gain electron decreases
(d) Electronegativity increases down the group due to increase in forces of attractions between nucleus and valence electrons

(v) Which of the following reason correctly justifies that, "Fluorine (72pm) has smaller atomic radius than Lithium (152pm)"?
(a) F and Li are in the same group. Atomic size increases down the group.
(b) F and Li are in the same period. Atomic size increases across the period due to increase in number of shells.
(c) F and Li are in the same group. Atomic size decreases down the group.
(d) F and Li are in the same period and across the period atomic size/radius decreases from left to right.

Ans. (i) (c) Cs > Rb > K > Na > Li
(ii) (b) As Hydrogen can easily lose one electron like alkali metals to form positive ion
(iii) (a) F
(iv) (c) Electronegativity decreases down the group due to increase in atomic radius/tendency to gain electron decreases.
(v) (d) F and Li are in the same period and across the period atomic size/radius decreases from left to right.

113. **Read the following passage carefully and answer the following questions from Q 113 (i) to 113 (v).**
Atomic radius is defined as the distance between the center of the nucleus and the outermost shell of electrons. As the effective nuclear charge increases as we move left to right along a period, hence the atomic radii decreases. There is a decrease in atomic size from Li to F in the second period and from Na to Cl in the third period. In any period the noble size has the largest radius.

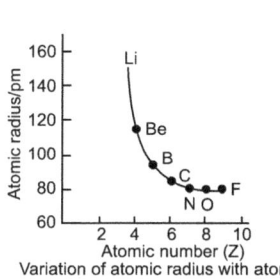
Variation of atomic radius with atomic number across the second period

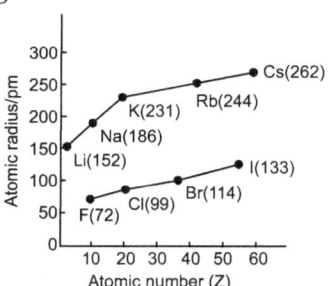
Variation of atomic radius with atomic number for alkali metals with halogens

(i) Which among the following has the maximum atomic radius?
(a) Si (b) P
(c) Mg (d) Al

(ii) The element which has the smallest size in group 13 is:
(a) Aluminum (b) Gallium
(c) Boron (d) Thallium

(iii) The reason due to which atomic radius decreases as we move across a period is:
(a) atomic number decreases
(b) electrons are removed from the atom
(c) atomic mass increases
(d) effective nuclear charge increases

(iv) The element having the smallest size in the third period of the periodic table is:
(a) Argon (b) Chlorine
(c) Silicon (d) Sodium

(v) The correct order of increasing atomic radii for the element set [O, C, F, Cl, Br] is:
(a) F, O, C, Cl, Br (b) F, C, O, Cl, Br
(c) F, Cl, Br, O, C (d) C, O, F, Cl, Br

Ans. (i) (c) Mg
(ii) (c) Boron
(iii) (d) effective nuclear charge increases
(iv) (b) Chlorine
(v) (a) F, O, C, Cl, Br

Reasoning Based Questions

114. **How does the tendency of the elements to lose electrons change in the Modern Periodic Table in (i) a group, (ii) a period and why?***

Ans. (i) Increase down a group.

*are board exam questions from previous years

Reason: At each succeeding element down a group the number of shells from the nucleus increases, and the effective nuclear force of attraction decreases on the last shell, so it becomes easy for the atom to lose electrons.

(ii) Decreases in a period from left to right.

Reason: As the effective nuclear charge on the valence shell electron increases, the attraction between the valence electron and nucleus increases, so it becomes difficult to lose electrons.

115. **Write the name given to the vertical columns and horizontal rows in the Modern Periodic Table. How does the metallic character of elements vary on moving down a vertical column? How does the size of atomic radius vary on moving left to right in a horizontal row? Give reason in support of your answer in the above two cases.***

Ans. Vertical columns are called groups and horizontal rows are called periods. Metallic character increases down the group. As the size increases, the distance between electron and nucleus increases and attraction between nucleus and valence electrons decreases.

Atomic size decreases on moving left to right in a period because electron is added in the same shell. So attraction between nucleus and valence shell increases due to which the outermost shell is pulled in closer to the nucleus. Nuclear charge is also increasing. Thus, effective nuclear charge increases and atomic size decreases.

116. **The elements Li, Na and K each having one valence electron are in the period 2, 3 and 4 respectively of Modern Periodic Table.***
    (i) In which group of the periodic table should they be?
    (ii) Which one of them is least reactive?
    (iii) Which one of them has the largest atomic radius? Give reason to justify your answer.

Ans. (i) They belong to group 1 because they have one valence electrons.
(ii) Lithium is least reactive.
(iii) Potassium has largest size because atomic size increases down the group.

117. **In the modern periodic table a zig-zag line separates metals from non-metals. What are these elements called and why?**

Ans. A zig-zag line of elements that separates metal from non-metals are known as metalloids because they have some properties of metals and some properties of non-metals.

118. **Why are elements chlorine, bromine and iodine called halogens?**

Ans. Element chlorine, bromine and iodine are called halogens because these elements reacts readily with alkali metal and alkaline earth metals to form halide salts. (halo - salt, gene - producer.).

119. **Why do you think the noble gases are placed in a separate group?**

Ans. Noble gases are placed in a separate group because these are inert elements. They have properties which are different from all other elements.

120. **What is meant by atomic radius? Explain why it the decreases across a period?***

Ans. The distance from centre of nucleus to outermost shell of an atom is atomic radius.

Atomic radius decrease across a period because electron is added in the same shell. So attraction between nucleus and valence shell increases due to which outermost shell is pulled in closer to the nucleus. Nuclear charge is also increasing. Thus, effective nuclear charge increases and atomic size decreases.

121. **Na, Mg and Al are the element of the same period of modern periodic table having one, two and three valence electrons respectively, which of these elements (i) has the largest atomic radius, (ii) is least reactive? Justify your answer starting reason for each case.***

Ans. (i) Atomic radius decreases along the period with increase in atomic number. Therefore, the element with largest atomic radius is Na.
Na > Mg > Al
(ii) All these elements are metals. Reactivity of metals decreases with decrease in atomic radius along the period. Hence, Na is most reactive among the three. So, the order of reactivity is Na > Mg > Al.

122. **How does the metallic character of elements change along a period of the periodic table from the left to the right and why?***

Ans. The metallic character goes on decreasing along a period from left to right because atomic size goes on decreasing therefore, tendency to lose electrons decreases.

123. **Nitrogen (Atomic number 7) and phosphorous (atomic number 15) belong to group 15 of the periodic table. Write the electronic configuration of these two electrons. Which of these will be more electronegative and why?***

Ans. Nitrogen = 2, 5
Phosphorous = 2, 8, 5
N is more electronegative than P as from top to bottom down a group, electronegativity decreases. This is because number of shell increases down a group, and thus there is an increased distance between the valence electrons and nucleus, or a greater atomic radius.

124. **Explain why:**
(i) The elements of the same group have similar chemical properties.
(ii) The elements of the same period have different properties.

Ans. (i) The elements of the same group have similar chemical properties because of the presence of same number of valence electrons.
(ii) The elements of the same period have different properties because number of valence electrons are different.

---
* are board exam questions from previous years

Very Short Answer Type Questions

125. What were the criteria used by Mendeleev in creating his periodic table? [NCERT]

Ans. Mendeleev's periodic table was based on atomic masses and similarity in formula of hydrides and oxides of elements. According to him, the properties of elements are a periodic function of their atomic masses.

126. Besides gallium, which other elements have since been discovered that were left by Mendeleev in his Periodic Table? (any two) [NCERT]

Ans. Scandium and Germanium.

127. Did Dobereiner's triads also exist in the columns of Newlands' Octaves? Compare and find out. [NCERT]

Ans. Yes, Dobereiner's triads also exist in the columns of Newlands' Octaves.
For example, the triad formed by the elements Li, Na, and K of Dobereiner's triads also occurred in the columns of Newlands' octaves.

128. What were the limitations of Dobereiner's classification? [NCERT]

Ans. The limitation of Dobereiner's classification is that the elements known at that time could not be classified into groups of triads on the basis of their properties.

129. In the Modern Periodic Table, which are the metals among the first ten elements? [NCERT]

Ans. Among the first ten elements H, He, Li, Be, B, C, N, O, F, Ne; Lithium (Li) and Beryllium (Be) are metals.

130. Write two reasons responsible for late discovery of noble gases.*

Ans. (a) They are inert gases.
(b) Their valency is zero.

131. State one reason for placing Mg and Ca in the same group of the periodic table.*

Ans. They have same number of valence electrons and show similar chemical properties.

132. By considering their position in the periodic table, which one of the following elements would you expect to have maximum metallic characteristic? [NCERT]

Ga, Ge, As, Se, Be

Ans. Metallic character of an element is defined as the easiness of its atom in losing electrons. According to the modern periodic table, the metallic character of an element decreases while moving from left to right across a period and increases down the group. Among the elements Ga, Ge, As, Se Be, Be and Ga are expected to be most metallic and out of Be and Ga, Ga is bigger in size and hence has a greater tendency to lose electrons than Be. Thus, Ga is more metallic than Be.

133. Compare the radii of two species X and Y. Give reasons for your answer. [NCERT]

(i) X has 12 protons and 12 electrons, (ii) Y has 12 protons and 10 electrons.

Ans. Y has less electrons than X. This means that Y is cation of X. Therefore, radii of Y is less than X.

134. If an element X is placed in group 14, what will be the formula and the nature of bonding of its chloride? [NCERT]

Ans. If an element X is placed in group 14, its chemical formula is XCl_4. The nature of bonding of its chloride is covalent bonding.

135. The electronic configuration of two elements X and Y are 2, 8, 8, 3 respectively. Write atomic numbers of X and Y.*

Ans. Atomic number of X = 2, 8, 7 = 17
Atomic number of Y = 2, 8, 8, 3 = 21

136. Write the atomic numbers of two elements 'X' and 'Y' having electronic configuration 2, 8, 2 and 2, 8, 6 respectively.*

Ans. Atomic number of X = 2 + 8 + 2 = 12
Atomic number of Y = 2 + 8 + 6 = 16

137. The atomic numbers of three elements A, B and C are 12, 18, and 20 respectively. State giving reason, which two elements will show similar properties.

Ans. A and C will show similar properties due to same number of valence electrons i.e., 2.

138. Write any one difference between the electronic configuration of group-1 and group -2 elements.*

Ans. Group 1 elements have 1 valence electron while group 2 elements have 2 valence electrons.

139. The atomic numbers of three elements X, Y and Z are 3, 11 and 17, respectively. State giving reason which two elements will show similar chemical properties.*

Ans. The two elements X and Y will show same chemical properties because they have same number of valence electron in group. They form positively charged ions by losing one electron.

140. Write the name, symbol and electronic configuration of an element X whose atomic number is 11.*

Ans. The element whose atomic number is 11 is sodium. Its symbol is Na.
Electronic configuration—2, 8, 1
Valency 1

141. Answer the following questions:
(i) How would the tendency to lose electrons change as we go from left to right across a period of the periodic table?
(ii) How do the atomic radii of elements change as we go from left to right in a period of the periodic table?

Ans. (i) On moving from left to right in a period, the tendency of atoms to lose electrons decreases.
(ii) On moving from left to right in a period, the atomic size decreases.

* are board exam questions from previous years

142. Elements have been arrangement in the following sequence on the basis of their increasing atomic masses.

F, Na, Mg, Al, Si, P, S, Cl, Ar, K

(i) Pick two sets of elements which have similar properties.
(ii) The given sequence represents which law of classification of elements?

Ans. (i) (a) F and Cl (b) Na and K.
(ii) Newland's law of octaves.

143. State the following:
(i) Write the formulae of chlorides of Eka-silicon and Eka-aluminium. **[NCERT]**
(ii) Write the number of elements in 2nd and 5th period in Modern Periodic Table?
(iii) Write the number of a group in which metallic, metalloid and non-metallic, all three types of elements, are present.
(iv) Write the number of horizontal rows in the modern periodic table. What are these rows called?
(v) Write the number of vertical columns in the modern periodic table. What are these columns called?
(vi) Write the formula used to determine the maximum numbers of electrons which a shell in an atom can accommodate?

Ans. (i) $GeCl_4$, $GaCl_3$
(ii) 2nd period has 8 elements, 5th period has 18 elements.
(iii) Group 14.
(iv) There are seven horizontal rows in the modern periodic table. These rows are called periods.
(v) There are 18 vertical columns in the modern periodic table. These are known as groups.
(vi) $2n^2$, where n is the number of shell.

Short Answer Type Questions

144. State the main aim of classifying elements. Which is the more fundamental property of elements that is used in the development of modern periodic table? Name and state the law based on this fundamental property. On which side of the periodic table one can find metals, non- metals and metalloids?*

Ans. The main aim of classification is to make study of elements systematic and easy. The fundamental property of elements that is used in the development of modern periodic table is Atomic number. According to Modern Periodic law, "Physical and Chemical Properties of the elements are a periodic function of their atomic numbers". In a periodic table, metals are on the left and non-metals are on the right. Metalloids at the border of metals and beginning of non- metals.

145. What is Newlands' law of octaves? Explain with an example.

Ans. According to this law, when elements are arranged in the order of increasing atomic masses, the properties of the eighth element (starting from a given element) are a repetition of the properties of the first element.
For example: Lithium shows similarity with sodium.

146. State Mendeleev's periodic law. Write two achievements of Mendeleev's periodic table.

Ans. Mendeleev's Periodic Law states that 'Properties of elements are the periodic function of their atomic masses.
Achievements :
(a) It could classify all the elements discovered at that time and helped in the discovery of new elements
(b) It helped in correction of atomic mass of some of the elements.

147. Answer the following questions:
(i) In Mendeleev's periodic table the elements were arranged in the increasing order of their atomic masses. However, cobalt with atomic mass of 58.93 amu was placed before nickel having an atomic mass of 58.71 amu. Give reason for the same.
(ii) In the classification of the then known elements, Mendeleev was guided by two factors. What are those two factors?

Ans. (i) This is done so that the elements with similar properties could be grouped together. Therefore, to arrange elements with similar properties together, cobalt is placed before Nickel neglecting its atomic mass.
(ii) The two factors are as follows:
(a) Increasing atomic masses.
(b) Grouping together of elements having similar properties.

148. Which group of elements could be placed in Mendeleev's periodic table without disturbing the original order? Give reason.

Ans. Noble gases could be placed in Mendeleev's periodic table without disturbing the original order. According to Mendeleev's classification, the properties of elements are the periodic function of their atomic masses and there is a periodic recurrence of elements with similar physical and chemical properties. Noble gas being inert, could be placed in a separate group without disturbing the original order.

149. How it can be proved that the basic structure of the Modern Periodic Table is based on the electronic configuration of atoms of different elements?*

Ans. Modern periodic law states that the physical and chemical properties of an element are the periodic function of the atomic number of that element.

---
* are board exam questions from previous years

Electronic configuration of the elements plays an important role in the placement of element in the modern periodic table. The valence shell electron on an element decides its position in a particular group or period for example, if the configuration of an element is 2, 1 it means that the element is lithium (Li = 2, 1) and it belongs to the 2nd period and 1st group of the modern periodic table.

150. Use Mendeleev's periodic table to predict the formulae for the oxides of the following elements: K, C, Al, Si, Ba. [NCERT]

Ans. K belongs to group 1. Therefore, the oxide will be K_2O.

C belongs to group 4. Therefore, the oxide will be CO_2.

Al belongs to group 3. Therefore, the oxide will be Al_2O_3.

Si belongs to group 4. Therefore, the oxide will be SiO_2.

Ba belongs to group 2. Therefore, the oxide will be BaO.

151. Can the following groups of elements be classified as Dobreiner's triad?
(a) Na, Si, Cl, (b) Be, Mg, Ca.
Atomic mass of Be 9; Na 23; Mg 24; Si 28; Cl 35; Ca 40
Explain by giving reason.

Ans. (a) Na, Si, Cl cannot be classified as Dobereiner's triad because here the elements do not belong to the same group and have different electronic configuration.
Na–2, 8, 1; Si–2, 8, 4 and Cl–2, 8, 7

(b) Be, Mg, Ca are the elements of Dobereiner's triad because the mass of Mg is the arithmetic mean of the other two elements.

i.e., Be and Ca = $\frac{9+40}{2}$ = 24.

152. How could the Modern periodic table remove various anomalies of Mendeleev's periodic table? [NCERT]

Ans. Modern periodic table removes various anomalies of Mendeleev's periodic table on the following points :

(a) Position of isotopes : As Modern periodic table is based on atomic number, isotopes can be placed at one place in same group in modern periodic table.

(b) Anomalous position of some pair of elements: In Mendeleev periodic table, some of the elements having higher atomic mass are placed before the elements having lower atomic mass. This defect of Mendeleev periodic table was overcome in Modern periodic table since it is based on atomic numbers.

(c) Prediction of new elements : In long form of periodic table, the position and properties of new elements can be predicted easily on the basis of their atomic numbers or electronic configuration.

153. Answer the following questions:
(i) What is the basic difference in approach between Mendeleev's periodic law and the Modern periodic law?
(ii) In between nitrogen and oxygen; whose ionisation energy is high and why?

Ans. (i) The basic difference in approach between Mendeleev's periodic law and Modern periodic law is the change in basis of classification of elements from atomic weight to atomic number.

(ii) The electronegativity of N is greater than O because Nitrogen has stable and exactly half-filled p-orbitals.

154. Answer the following questions:*
(i) How many groups and periods are there in the modern periodic table? How do the atomic size and metallic character of elements vary as we move:
(a) down a group and
(b) from left to right in a period
(ii) State the changes in valency and metallic character of elements as well as we move from left to right in a period. Also state the changes, if any, in the valency and atomic size of elements as we move down a group.

Ans. (i) There are a total of 18 groups and 7 periods in a periodic table.
(a) As we move down the group the atomic size as well as metallic character of elements increases.
(b) Both metallic character and atomic size decreases as we move from left to right in a period.

(ii) Valency increases and the metallic character decreases as we move from left to right. Valency remains same and the size increases as we move down the group in periodic table.

155. The position of three elements A, B and C in the Periodic Table are shown below: [NCERT]

Group 16	Group 17
—	—
—	A
—	—
B	C

(i) State whether A is a metal or non-metal.
(ii) State whether C is more reactive or less reactive than A.
(iii) Will C be larger or smaller in size than B?
(iv) Which type of ion, cation or anion, will be formed by element A?

Ans. (i) A is a non-metal.
(ii) C is less reactive than A, as reactivity decreases down the group in halogens.
(iii) C will be smaller in size than B as moving across a period, the nuclear charge increases

and therefore, electrons come closer to the nucleus.
(iv) A will form an anion as it accepts an electron to complete its octet.

156. An element belongs to third period and group 16 of modern periodic table.*
(i) Determine the number of valence electrons and valency of T.
(ii) Molecular formula of the compound when X reacts with hydrogen and write its electron dot structure.
(iii) Name the element X and state whether it is metallic or non-metallic.

Ans. (i) Valency electron = 6
Valency = 2
(ii) H_2S
(iii) Sulphur, Non-metal.

157. The elements of the second period of the Periodic Table are given below: Li, Be, B, C, N, O, F.
(i) Give reason to explain why atomic radii decrease from Li to F.
(ii) Identify the most (a) metallic and (b) non-metallic element.

Ans. (i) On moving from left to right in a period force of attraction between nucleus and electrons increases which results in decrease in size.
(ii) (a) Most metallic element is 'Li'.
(b) Most non-metallic element is 'F'.

158. Answer the following questions:
(i) What property do all elements in the same column of the periodic table as boron have in common?
[NCERT]
(ii) What property do all elements in the same column of the periodic table as fluorine have in common?

Ans. (i) All the elements in the same column as boron have the same number of valence electrons i.e., 3. Hence, they all have valency equal to 3.
(ii) All the elements in the same column as fluorine have the same number of valence electrons i.e., 7. Hence, they all have valency equal to 1.

159. An element X of group 15 exists as diatomic molecule and combines with hydrogen at 773 K in presence of the catalyst to form a compound, ammonia which has a characteristic pungent smell.
(i) Identify the element X. How many valence electrons does it have?
(ii) Draw the electron dot structure of the diatomic molecule of X. What type of bond is formed in it?
(iii) Draw the electron dot structure for ammonia and what type of bond is formed in it?

Ans. (i) Nitrogen (atomic no. 7). Its electronic configuration is 2, 5; it has 5 valence electrons.

(b) 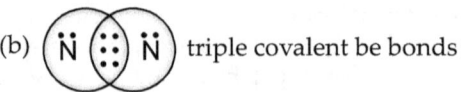 triple covalent be bonds

(c) 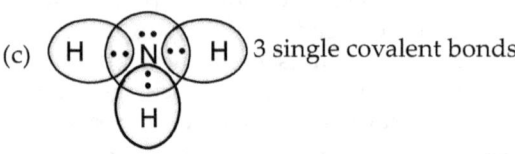 3 single covalent bonds

160. Which element has: [NCERT]
(i) two shells, both of which are completely filled with electrons?
(ii) the electronic configuration 2, 8, 2?
(iii) a total of three shells, with four electrons in its valence shell?
(iv) a total of two shells, with three electrons in its valence shell?
(v) twice as many electrons in its second shell as in its first shell?

Ans. (i) Neon has two shells, both of which are completely filled with electrons (2 electrons in K shell and 8 electrons in L shell).
(ii) Magnesium has the electronic configuration 2, 8, 2.
(iii) Silicon has a total of three shells, with 4 electrons in its valence shell (2 electrons in K shell, 8 electrons in L shell and 4 electrons in M shell).
(iv) Boron has a total of two shells, with three electrons in its valence shell (2 electrons in K shell and 3 electrons in L shell).
(v) Carbon has twice as many electrons in its second shell as in its first shell (2 electrons in K shell and 4 electrons in L shell).

161. An element X (atomic number 17) reacts with an element Y (atomic number 20) to form a divalent halide.
(i) Where in the periodic table are elements X and Y placed?
(ii) Classify X and Y as metal (s), non-metal (s) or metalloid (s).
(iii) What will be the nature of oxide of element Y? Identify the nature of bonding in the compound formed.
(iv) Draw the electron dot structure of the divalent halide.

Ans. (i) X belongs to Group 17 and 3rd period Y belongs to Group 2 and 4th period.
(ii) X — Non-metal and Y — Metal.
(iii) Basic oxide; Ionic bonding.
(iv) $Y\overset{..}{\underset{..}{X}} + \overset{..}{\underset{..}{X}} \longrightarrow [Y^{2+}(\overset{..}{\underset{..}{X}})_2]$

162. From the following elements:*
4Be ; 9F ; 19K ; 20Ca
(a) Select the elements having one electron in the outermost shell.
(b) Two elements of the same group.

*are board exam questions from previous years

Write the formula of the compound and mention the nature of the compound formed by the union of 19 K and element X(2, 8, 7).

Ans. (a) 'K' has only one electron in the outermost shell

19K: 2, 8, 8, 1

(b) Be and Ca both are the members of 2nd group. K has only one electron in its outermost shell while the element X is only one electron short from its octet. So there would be transfer of one electron from K to X. Formula of compound: KX Nature of compound: Ionic or Electrovalent.

163. Answer the following questions:*
(i) What are metalloids?
(ii) Name any four metalloids?
(iii) Predict which of the following elements will form cation and will form anions?
  (a) Na,
  (b) Al,
  (c) Cl,
  (d) O.
(iv) Name two elements that are inert in nature.*

Ans. (i) Borderline elements which are intermediate in properties between metals and non-metals are called metalloids.
(ii) Boron, silicon, germanium and arsenic.
(iii) Na and Al are metals. They form cations.
(iv) Cl and O are non-metals. They form anions.

164. Name the following elements: **[NCERT]**
(i) Three elements that have a single electron in their outermost shells.
(ii) Two elements that have two electrons in their outermost shells.
(iii) Three elements with filled outermost shells.
(iv) Name two elements you would expect to show chemical reactions similar to magnesium. What is the basis for your choice? **[NCERT]**

Ans. (i) Lithium (Li), Sodium (Na), and Potassium (K) have a single electron in their outermost shells.
(ii) Magnesium (Mg) and Calcium (Ca) have two electrons in their outermost shells.
(iii) Neon (Ne), Argon (Ar) and Xenon (Xe) have filled outermost shells.
(iv) Calcium (Ca) and strontium (Sr) are expected to show chemical reactions similar to magnesium (Mg). This is because the number of valence electrons (2) is same in all these three elements and they belong to same group.

165. Answer the following questions:
(i) Lithium, sodium, potassium are all metals that react with water to liberate hydrogen gas. Is there any similarity in the atoms of these elements? **[NCERT]**
(ii) Helium is an unreactive gas and neon is a gas of extremely low reactivity. What, if anything, do their atoms have in common?

Ans. (i) Yes, they all belong to group 1 i.e, their atoms have one electron in their outermost shell.
(ii) Both Helium (He) and Neon (Ne) have filled outermost shells. Helium has a duplet i.e., two electrons in its K shell, while neon has an octet i.e, 8 electrons in its L shell.

166. An atom has electronic configuration 2, 8, 7.
[NCERT]
(i) What is the atomic number of this element?
(ii) To which of the following elements would it be chemically similar ? (Atomic numbers are given in parentheses.) N(7), F(9), P(15), Ar(18).

Ans. (i) The atomic number of this element is 17.
(ii) It would be chemically similar to F(9) with configuration as 2, 7.

167. Nitrogen (atomic number 7) and phosphorus (atomic number 15) belong to group 15 of the Periodic Table. Write the electronic configuration of these two elements. Which of these will be more electronegative? Why? **[NCERT]**

Ans.

Element	K	L	M
Nitrogen	2	5	
Phosphorus	2	8	5

Nitrogen is more electronegative than phosphorus, because on moving down a group, the number of shell increases and electronegativity decreases.

168. Answer the following questions:*
(i) Three elements X, Y and Z belong to 17th group but 2nd, 3rd and 4th period respectively. Number of valence electrons in Y is 7. Find the number of valence electrons in X and Z.
(ii) Na, Mg, Al and P belong to third period but are placed in first, second, thirteen and fifteenth group. Number of shells occupied in Mg is three. What is the number of occupied shells in Na, Al and P. Give reasons for your answer.
(iii) The atomic radius of three elements A, B and C of a periodic table are 186 pm, 104 pm and 143 pm respectively. Giving a reason, arrange these elements in the increasing order of atomic numbers in a period.

Ans. (i) Number of valence electrons in X and Z will be 7 because the number of electrons in the outermost shell in the elements in same group is same.
(ii) In Na, Al and P number of occupied shells are three. The reason for this is that elements with same number of occupied shells are placed in same period.
(iii) Order of atomic number of elements will be : A < C < B. Out of three, A has largest atomic radius, then C and finally B and atomic radius decreases along a period.

169. Name any two elements of group one and write their electronic configuration. What similarity do

---
* are board exam questions from previous years

you observe in their electronic configuration? Write the formula of oxide of any of the above said elements.*

Ans. Two elements of group 1 are Sodium (11) and Potassium (19).
Electronic configuration,
Na = 2, 8, 1.; K = 2,8,8,1.
Both have one electrons in their valence shell. The formula of their oxide is: Na$_2$O and K$_2$O.

170. Na, Mg and Al are the elements of the same period of modern periodic table having one, two and three valence electrons respectively. Which of these element (i) has the largest atomic radius, (ii) is least reactive ? Justify your answer stating reason for each case.*

Ans. (i) Na or Sodium. The atomic size decreases from left to right due to the increase in nuclear charge.
(ii) Al is least reactive because the tendency to lose electron decreases from, left to right.

171. Give an example of:*
(i) A metal that is liquid at room temperature.
(ii) A non-metal that is liquid at room temperature.
(iii) An inert gas (At. No. < 20)

Ans. (i) Mercury
(ii) Bromine
(iii) Helium or Neon or Argon.

172. The electronic configuration of an element is 2, 8, 4. State its:*
(i) Group and period in the Modern Periodic Table.
(ii) Name and write its one physical property.

Ans. (i) Si = 2, 8, 4
(a) It means that it belongs to 3rd period and 14th group.
(b) The name of element is silicon.
(ii) It is a metalloid. (i.e., element that has properties of both metals and non-metals).

173. Based on the group valency of elements write the molecular formula of the following compounds giving justification for each :*
(i) Oxide of first group elements.
(ii) Halide of the elements of group thirteen, and
(iii) Compound formed when an element, A of group 2 combines with an element, B of group seventeen.

Ans. (i) Sodium is a group one element (Na) so its configuration is 2, 8, 1 and its valency is 1.
Oxide has a valency of 2.
So, their formula would be

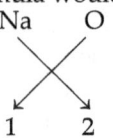

Formula for sodium oxide is Na$_2$O.

(ii) Halide is any Halogen. Group 13 means for example, we take Aluminium (Al), its configuration is 2, 8, 3, valency of Al is 3, valency of Cl is 1.
So

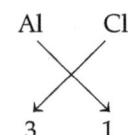

Formula would be AlCl$_3$ (Aluminium chloride).

(iii) Element of group 2 for example Mg 2, 8, 2, its valency would be 2.
Element of group 17 would be Cl 2, 8, 7, valency would be 1.

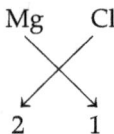

Formula would be MgCl$_2$ (Magnesium chloride).

Long Answer Type Questions

174. List the merits and demerits of Mendeleev periodic table.

Ans. Merits of Mendeleev periodic table:
(a) At some places the order of atomic weight was changed in order to justify the chemical and physical nature.
(b) Mendeleev left some gap for new elements which were not discovered at that time.
(c) One of the strengths of Mendeleev's periodic table was that, when inert gases were discovered they could be placed in a new group without disturbing the existing order.

Demerits of Mendeleev periodic table:
(a) **Position of hydrogen:** Hydrogen resembles alkali metals (forms H$^+$ ion just like Na$^+$ ions) as well as halogens (forms H$^-$ ion similar to Cl$^-$ ion).Therefore, it could neither be placed with alkali metals (group I) nor with halogens (group VII).

(b) **Position of isotopes:** Different isotopes of same elements have different atomic masses, therefore, each one of them should be given a different position in the periodic table. On the other hand, because they are chemically similar, they had to be given same position.

(c) **Anomalous pairs of elements:** At certain places, an element of higher atomic mass has been placed before an element of lower atomic mass. For example, Argon (39.91) is placed before potassium (39.1).

175. Answer the following questions:
(i) The modern periodic table has been evolved through the early attempts of Dobereiner,

---
* are board exam questions from previous years

Newland and Mendeleev. List one advantage and one limitation of all three attempts.*
(ii) Name the scientist who first of all showed that atomic number of an element is a more fundamental property than its atomic mass.
(iii) State Modern Periodic law.

Ans. (i) **(a) Dobereiner:**
Advantage: Group three elements having similar properties they were called as the Dobereiner triads. He arranged them in order of increasing atomic mass and the mass of middle element was equal to the average of the other two elements.
Limitation: He was able to identify only 4 traids but he failed in his attempt to group nitrogen, phosphorus and arsenic because atomic mass of phosphorus is not the average of other two.
(b) Newland:
Advantages: He arranged the elements in horizontal rows in order of increasing in atomic mass. The property of every 8th element was similar to the 1st element.
Limitation: His arrangement was only applicable to lighter elements.
(c) Mendeleev:
Advantage: He arranged the elements in order of there increasing atomic mass and he corrected the mass of beryllium from 4.5 to 13.5 u.
Limitation: Position of hydrogen and isotopes were not justified in his periodic table.
(ii) Henry Moseley showed that atomic number of an element is a more fundamental property than its atomic mass.
(iii) Modern periodic law states that "the properties of elements are the periodic function of their atomic number. Repetition of properties is due to the same outer electronic configuration."

176. Answer the following questions:
(i) List any three observations which posed a challenge to Mendeleev's Periodic law.*
(ii) How does the metallic character of elements vary on moving from
(a) left to right in a period,
(b) from top to bottom in a group of the Modern Periodic Table?
Give reason for your answer.

Ans. (i) Three observations which posed a challenge to Mendeleev's Periodic law are:
(a) The position of isotopes could not be explained.
(b) Wrong order of atomic masses of some elements could not be explained.
(c) A correct position could not be assigned to hydrogen in the periodic table.

(ii) (a) On moving from left to right in a period, the metallic character of elements increases because electropositive character decreases.
(b) On going down in a group of the periodic table, the metallic character of elements increases because electropositive character of elements increases.

177. Answer the following questions:
(i) What is a group in the periodic table? In which part of a group would you separately expect the elements to have : (a) the greatest metallic character, (b) the largest atomic size?
(ii) In what respects do the properties of group 1 elements differ from those of group 17 elements?
(iii) From the stand point of atomic structure, what determines which element will be the first and which is the last in a period of the periodic table?
(iv) Explain why, the properties of elements are repeated after 2, 8, 18 and 32 elements in the periodic table.
(v) What are the advantages of the periodic table?

Ans. (i) The vertical columns in a periodic table are called groups.
(a) The greatest metallic character is found in the elements in the lowest part of the group.
(b) The largest atomic size is found in the lowest part of the group.
(ii) Group 1 elements have 1 valence electron and are ionic in chemical reactions, whereas, the elements of group 17 have 7 valence electrons. They all are non-metals.
(iii) The number of valence electrons in the atoms of elements decides which element will be the 1st element in a period and which will be the last in a period.
(iv) The properties of elements are repeated after 2, 8, 18 and 32 elements in the periodic table because the electronic configurations of the elements are repeated in this manner.
(v) Advantages of the periodic table:
(a) It is easier to remember the properties of an element if its position in the periodic table is known.
(b) The type of compounds formed by an element can be predicted by knowing its position in the periodic table.

178. The electronic configuration of three elements A, B and C is given below:
A = 2. B = 2, 6 C = 2, 8, 2
(i) Which element belongs to the second period?
(ii) Which one of them is a noble gas?
(iii) What is the valency of B?
(iv) Name the element C.
(v) Which is a metal?

---
* are board exam questions from previous years

Ans. (i) B belongs to second period as its valency is two.
(ii) A(2 = helium) is a noble gas.
(iii) 2 (8-6).
(iv) Magnesium (At. No. 12)
(v) C is a metal.

179. **The electrons in the atoms of four elements A, B, C and D are distributed in three shells having 1, 3, 5 and 7, electrons respectively in their outermost shells. Write the group numbers in which these elements are placed in the Modern Periodic Table. Write the electronic configuration of the atoms of B and D, and the molecular formula of the compound formed when B and D combine.***

Ans. A—1st group.
B—13th group.
C—15th group.
D—17th group.
Electronic configuration
B ⟶ Atomic number = 13
  K L M
  2 8 3
D ⟶ Atomic number = 17
  K L M
  2 9 7

The molecular formula of the compound when B and D combine is BD_3.

180. **Atoms of eight elements A, B, C, D, E, F, G and H have the same number of electronic shells but different number of electrons in their outermost shell. It was found that elements A and G combine to form an ionic compound. This compound is added in a small amount to almost all vegetable dishes during cooking. Oxides of elements A and B are basic in nature while those of E and F are acidic. The oxide of D is almost neutral. Based on the above information answer the following questions:***
   (i) To which group or period of the Periodic Table do the listed elements belong?
   (ii) What would be the nature of compound formed by a combination of elements B and F?
   (iii) Which two of these elements could definitely be metals?
   (iv) Which one of the eight elements is most likely to be found in gaseous state at room temperature?
   (v) If the number of electrons in the outermost shell of elements C and G be 3 and 7 respectively, write the formula of the compound formed by the combination of C and G.

Ans. (i) A and B belong to group 1 and 2 because they form basic oxides. C belongs to group 13 as it has 3 valence electrons. D belongs to group 14 as it forms almost neutral oxide. E and F belong to group 15 and 16 as they form acidic oxides, G belongs to group 17 as it has 7 valence electrons and H belongs to group 18. They belong to 3rd period of the periodic table because AG is NaCl, added in a small amount to almost all vegetable dishes during cooking and Na and Cl belong to 3rd period.
(ii) Ionic compounds will be formed because 'B' is metal and 'F' is non-metal. 'B' can lose two electrons and 'F' can gain two electrons.
(iii) A and B are definitely metals as they form basic oxides.
(iv) G and H are in gaseous state at room temperature.
(v) CG_3 is the formula of the compound formed by combination of C and G.

181. **Explain the periodicity of following properties of elements:**
   (i) Atomic radius
   (ii) Ionisation enthalpy
   (iii) Electronegativity

Ans. (i) **Atomic radius:** In a period, atomic radius generally decreases from left to right. In a period there is a gradual increase in the nuclear charge. Since valence electrons are added in the same shell, they are more and more strongly attracted towards nucleus. This gradually decreases atomic radii.

Atomic radii increase in a group from top to bottom. As we go down a group the number of shells increases and valence electrons are present in higher shell and the distance of valence electrons from nucleus increases. Both the factors decrease the force of attraction between nucleus and valence electron. Therefore, atomic size increases on moving down a group.

(ii) **Ionisation enthalpy:** Ionisation energy decreases in a group from top to bottom. This is due to the fact that the force of attraction between valence electrons and nucleus decreases in a group from top to bottom. Thus, less energy is required to remove electron from atom.

On the either hand, the force of attraction between valence electron and nucleus increases in a period from left to right. As a consequence of this, the ionisation energy increases in a period from left to right.

(iii) **Electronegativity:** Electronegativity is relative tendency of a bonded atom to attract the bond-electrons towards itself. Electronegativity decreases in group from top to bottom. In a period, electronegativity increases from left to right because atomic size decreases.

---
* are board exam questions from previous years

Differentiate Between

182. Compare and contrast the arrangement of elements in Mendeleev's periodic Table and the Modern Periodic Table.

Ans.

	Mendeleev's periodic table	Modern periodic table
(a)	Elements are arranged in the increasing order of their atomic masses.	Elements are arranged in the increasing order of their atomic numbers.
(b)	There are a total of 7 groups and 6 periods.	There are a total of 18 groups and 7 periods.
(c)	Elements having similar properties were placed directly under one another.	Elements having the same valence shell are present in the same period while elements having the same number of valence electrons are present in the same group.
(d)	Position of isotopes is not clear.	Position of isotopes is clear.
(e)	Electronic configuration cannot be predicted from the position of element.	Electronic configuration can be predicted from the position of element.

Analysis and Evaluation Based Questions

183. Mendeleev arranged 63 elements known at that time in the periodic table. According to Mendeleev "the properties of the elements are a periodic function of their atomic masses." The table consists of eight vertical columns called 'groups' and horizontal rows called 'periods'. Merits of Mendeleev's Periodic Table: At some places the order of atomic weight was changed in order to justify the chemical and physical nature. Mendeleev left some gap for new elements which were not discovered at that time. One of the strengths of Mendeleev's periodic table was that, when inert gases were discovered they could be placed in a new group without disturbing the existing order. Its main characteristics are that the elements are arranged in vertical rows called groups and horizontal rows called periods.

(i) What is the basis of arrangement of elements in Mendeleev's periodic table?

(ii) Why were there some gaps in Mendeleev's periodic table?

(iii) State whether the statement is true or false. Mendeleev's periodic table consists of eight vertical columns called 'groups' and horizontal rows called 'periods'.

(iv) X, Y and Z are the elements of a Dobereiner's triad. If the atomic mass of X is 7. and that of Z is 39. What should be the atomic mass of Y?

Ans. (i) In Mendeleev's periodic table, elements are arranged according to atomic masses.

(ii) There were some gaps in Mendeleev's periodic table for unknown elements.

(iii) Mendeleev's periodic table was divided into groups and columns. Therefore, the given statement is true.
(iv) According to Dobereiner's triad, the atomic mass of middle element is the average of other two elements. Therefore, (7 + 39) = 46/2 Y = 23.

184. An element belongs to group 2 and element Q belongs to group 17 of long form of periodic table.
(i) How many valence electrons are there in P?
(ii) What is the valency of P?
(iii) How many valence electrons are there in Q?
(iv) What is the valency of Q?
(v) Write the chemical formula of P and Q.

Ans. (i) P has 2 valency electrons as valence electrons are equal to group number.
(ii) Valency of P is +2.
(iii) Q has 7 valence electrons.
(iv) Valency of Q is – 1. (valency = group number – 18 i.e., 17 -18)
(v) The formula of the compound is PQ_2.

185. By giving reasons state which amongst the given below elements does not belong to the same period.

$_6P12, \ _7Q14, \ _8R16, \ _{11}S23$

Ans. The electronic configuration of the elements is given as:

Element	Atomic No.	Electronic configuration
P	6	2, 4
Q	7	2, 5
R	8	2, 6
S	11	2, 8, 1

Element P, Q and R have only two electron shells and hence, they belong to the same period i.e., 2nd period.

186. An element X has both K and L shell completely filled with electrons. The element has atomic number 10.
(i) Identify the element.
(ii) To which group does it belong?
(iii) Write its electronic configuration.

Ans. (i) The element is Neon.
(ii) It belongs to group 18 of periodic table.
(iii) Electronic configuration: 2,8.

187. In each of the following pairs, choose the atom having the bigger size:
(i) Mg (At. No.12) or Cl (At. No. 17)
(ii) Na (At. No. 11) or K (At. No. 19)

Ans. (i) Mg since atomic size decreases from left to right in a period.
(ii) K since atomic size increases on going down a group.

188. Answer the following questions:
(i) An element X has mass number 40 and contains 21 neutrons in its atom. To which group of the periodic table does it belong?
(ii) The element X forms a compound X_2Y. Suggest an element that Y might be and give reasons for your choice.

Ans. (i) Group 1 (2, 8, 8, 1).
(ii) Oxygen (X is monovalent so Y has to be divalent to form the compound X_2Y)

189. The elements A, B and C belong to groups 1, 14 and 17 respectively of the periodic table.
(i) Which two elements will form a covalent compound?
(ii) Which two elements will form an ionic compound?
(iii) Noble gases do not react with other elements. Why?
(iv) Atom is electrically neutral but still it has a tendency to form an ion. Why?

Ans. (i) B and C, will form covalent compounds since both are non-metals.
(ii) A and C will form on ionic compound since A is an alkali metal and C is non-metal.
(iii) Elements react in order to complete its octet. Noble gases have complete octet. Therefore, they do not react with other elements.
(iv) The elements have valence electrons. Metals have less valence electrons and give out the valence electrons to form cations to complete the outermost shell and attain nearest noble gas configuration. Likewise, non metals attain electrons to form anions to complete the outermost shell and attain nearest noble gas configuration.

190. The atomic numbers of the three elements X, Y and Z are 2, 6 and 10 respectively. Which two elements belong to the same group ? Which two elements belong to the same period ? Give reasons for your choice.

Ans. X (2) and Z (2, 8). Both X and Z have zero valency hence they belong to same group: noble gases.
Y and Z. Y: 2, 4 and Z: 2, 8 so, both of them belong to second period with two shells filled.

Creating Based Questions

191. Write the contrasting points present in modern periodic table, against the following given points of Mendeleev's table :
(i) Elements arranged according to atomic mass.
(ii) It has 8 groups and 6 periods.

Ans. The contrast points can be written as :

(i) In modern periodic table the elements are arranged according to atomic number.
(ii) Modern periodic table has 18 groups and 7 periods.

192. Study the chart carefully and answer the following questions from Q 192 (i) to 192 (v).

GROUP → PERIOD ↓	1	2	3-12	13	14	15	16	17	18
2	A				B				C
3				D	E				F

(i) Which element present in the chart has the same number of electrons as K^+ and Cl^-?
   (a) C   (b) D
   (c) E   (d) F

(ii) Which formula is correct for oxide of D?
   (a) DO   (b) D_2O
   (c) D_2O_3 (d) D_2O_5

(iii) Most metallic character is shown by which of the following:
   (a) D   (b) E
   (c) F   (d) B

(iv) Chloride of element E has the formula
   (a) ECl_5 (b) ECl_4
   (c) ECl_2 (d) ECl_3

(v) Character of metalloid is shown by which of the following?
   (a) E   (b) A
   (c) B   (d) C

Ans. (i) (d) F
(ii) (c) D_2O_3
(iii) (a) D
(iv) (b) ECl_4
(v) (a) E

193. Read the following information the and answer the following questions from Q 193 (i) to 193 (v).

The following table shows the position of the elements A, B, C, D, E, F, G, H, I, J, K, L, M, N in the period table.

Groups→ Periods ↓	1	2	3-12	13	14	15	16	17	18
2		A		B		C		D	E
3	F			G	H			I	
4	J	K				L	M		N

With reference to the table, answer the following:

(i) Which elements have complete outer electronic configuration?
   (a) F and J   (b) D and E
   (c) E and N   (d) M and N

(ii) Atomic size refers to the radius of an atom. The atomic size may be visualised as the distance between the centre of the nucleus and the outermost shell of an isolated atom.
Study the given graph which represents the trend of atomic size with respect to the periodic table.

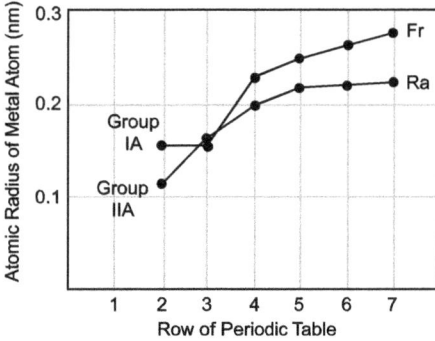

Which of the following is the correct order for atomic size?
   (a) A > B > C > D > E
   (b) F < G < H < I
   (c) J > K > L < M > N
   (d) E < F < G < H < I

(iii) Which of the following states Modern Periodic Law?
   (a) Properties of elements are the periodic function of their atomic number
   (b) Properties of elements are the periodic function of their atomic size
   (c) Properties of elements are the group function of their atomic number
   (d) Properties of elements are the periodic function of their valency

(iv) Which of the following reason correctly justifies that "bromine has smaller atomic radius than potassium"?
   (a) Br and K are in the same group. Atomic size increases down the group.
   (b) Br and K are in the same period. Atomic size increases across the period due to increase in number of shells.
   (c) Br and K are in the same group. Atomic size decreases down the group.
   (d) Br and K are in the same period. Atomic size decreases across the period from left to right.

(v) Identify the correct elements from the table.
   (a) B- boron, C- Neon, M- oxygen
   (b) G-aluminium, I- Chlorine, K-calcium
   (c) F- sodium, K- caesium, L- Lithium
   (d) B- boron, H- carbon, L- Nitrogen

Ans. (i) (c) E and N
(ii) (a) A > B > C > D > E
(iii) (a) Properties of elements are the periodic function of their atomic number.
(iv) (d) Br and K are in the same period. Atomic size decreases across the period from left to right.
(v) (b) G-aluminium, I- Chlorine, K-calcium

194. Consider the following elements, A, B, C and D in the given periodic table:

Group 16	Group 1	Group 2
----	----	----
----	B	D
A	----	----
----	C	----

(i) Which element is the most electronegative element?
(ii) Which element is the most unreactive?
(iii) Which element forms acidic oxides?
(iv) Which element has 6 electrons in outer orbital?

Ans. (i) Element B would be the most electronegative element.
(ii) Element D would be the most unreactive element.
(iii) Element B and C forms acidic oxides.
(iv) Element A has 6 electrons in outer orbital.

195. Question number 194(i)-194(iv) are based on table given below. Study the table and answer the following questions.

Atomic number	Element	Electronic configuration
1	Hydrogen	1
8	Oxygen	2, 6
6	Carbon	2, 4
9	Flourine	2, 7

(i) What is valency of oxygen?
(ii) Give the chemical formula formed by hydrogen and oxygen.
(iii) What is the electron dot structure of above formed compound in (ii) part?
(iv) What is the chemical formula for element H, F used for bond formation?
    (a) H_2F (b) HF
    (c) HF_2 (d) HF_3

Ans. (i) Valency of oxygen is 2.
(ii) $2H + O \rightarrow H_2O$
     1   2, 6
The chemical formula formed is H_2O.
(iii)

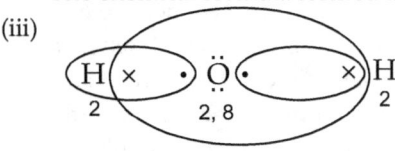

(iv) (b) HF.

196. The position of eight elements in the modern periodic table is given below with atomic numbers.

Period Number	Elements	
2	Li (3)	Be (4)
3	Na (11)	Mg (12)
4	K (19)	Ca (20)
5	Rb (37)	Sr (38)

Answer the following question with reference to the above table.
(i) Write the electron configuration of Calcium (Ca).
(ii) Predict the number of valence electrons in Strontium (Sr).
(iii) What is the number of shells in Rubidium (Rb)?
(iv) Predict whether K is a metal or a non-metal?

Ans. (i) Electronic configuration of Calcium is 2, 8, 8, 2.
(ii) The number of valence electrons in Strontium (Sr) is 2.
(iii) The number of shells in Rubidium (Rb) is 5.
(iv) Potassium (K) is a metal, which has one valence electron.

197. Based on the table given below answer the following questions:

Period	Group 1	Group 2
1.	A (3)	E (4)
2.	B (11)	F (12)
3.	C (19)	G (20)
4.	D (37)	H (38)

(i) What is the electronic configuration of F?
(ii) What is the number of valence electrons in the atom of F?
(iii) Write the size of the atoms of E, F, G and H in decreasing order.
(iv) Out of B, E and F which one has the biggest atomic size?

Ans. (i) 'F' has electronic configuration 2, 8, 2.
(ii) 'F' has two valence electrons.
(iii) H > G > F > E is decreasing order of size of atoms.
(iv) 'B' is having biggest atomic size among B, E and F.

198.

Period	Group 1	Group 2
1.	A (3)	E (4)
2.	B (11)	F (12)
3.	C (19)	G (20)
4.	D (37)	H (38)

(i) What is the electronic configuration of F?
(ii) What is the number of valence electrons in the atom of F?
(iii) Write the size of the atoms of E, F, G and H in decreasing order.
(iv) Out of B, E and F which one has the biggest atomic size?

Ans. (i) 'F' has electronic configuration 2, 8, 2.
(ii) 'F' has two valence electrons.
(iii) H > G > F > E is decreasing order of size of atoms.
(iv) 'B' is having biggest atomic size among B, E and F.

Periodic Classification of Elements | 65

199. An element X forms a chloride with the formula XCl_2, which is a solid with a high melting point. Predict the most likely outer orbital electronic configuration of X and also name two more elements from same group of the Periodic Table to which elements X belongs.

Ans. The element X has 2 electrons in outer orbital as it forms a dichloride (XCl_2). So, this element belongs to group 2 of periodic table. Other elements of group 2 are magnesium (Mg) and beryllium (Be).

200. Oxygen (atomic number 8) and sulphur (atomic number 16) belong to group 16 of the periodic table. Write the electronic configuration of the two elements. Which of them will be more electronegative ? Why ?

Ans. Oxygen has atomic number 8, electronic configuration will be ⎯⎯→ 2, 6
Sulphur has atomic number 16, electronic configuration will be ⎯⎯→ 2, 8, 6
Oxygen with two shells will be more electronegative because it can easily gain electron due to its smaller size of atom, the nuclear charge attracts the electron easily to become negative ion.

201. Consider the following elements, A, B, C and D in the given periodic table :

Group 16	Group 17	Group 18
……	……	……
……	B	D
A	……	……
……	C	……

(i) Which element is the most electronegative element ?
(ii) Which element is the most unreactive ?
(iii) Which element forms acidic oxides ?
(iv) Which element has 6 electrons in outer orbital ?

Ans. (i) Element B would be the most electronegative element.
(ii) Element D would be the most unreactive element.
(iii) Element B and C forms acidic oxides.
(iv) Element A has 6 electrons in outer orbital.

Self- Assessment

202. What is Newland's Law of octaves?

203. How isotopes of all the elements posed a challenge to Mendleev's periodic table?

204. What is Newland's law of Octaves? Explain with an example.

205. What name is given to the horizontal rows in a periodic table?

206. Why does silicon is classified as metalloid?

207. What are isotopes?

208. What is Modern periodic Law?

209. The valency of group 13 elements is:
(a) 1 (b) 2
(c) 3 (d) 4

210. Which of the following is a metalloid?
(a) Carbon (b) Silicon
(c) Tin (d) Lead

211. Which of the following statements is not correct about the trends when going from left to right across the long form of periodic table?
(i) Elements become less metallic in nature.
(ii) Number of valence electrons increases.
(iii) Elements lose their electrons more easily.
(iv) The oxides become more acidic.

212. An element with atomic number 14 is hard and forms an acidic oxide and a covalent halide. To which of the following categories does the element belong?
(i) Metal
(ii) Metalloid
(iii) Non-metal
(iv) Left hand side element

213. Define the following terms:
(i) Periodicity
(ii) Electrongain enthalpy
(iii) Electronegativity
(iv) Ionisation energy

214. A set of alkaline earth metals are:
(a) Ca, Sr, Ba (b) Na, K, Ca
(c) Na, Li, K (d) Na, K, Rb

215. The element which is essentially an essential constituent of all organic compounds belong to:
(a) Group 1 (b) Group 14
(c) Group 15 (d) Group 16

216. In the following set of elements, one element does not belong to the set. Select this element and state why it does not belong:
Oxygen, Nitrogen, Carbon, Chlorine, Fluorine

217. Consider the following elements:
Na, Ca, Al, K, Mg, Li
(i) Which of these elements belong to the same period of the periodic table?
(ii) Which of these elements belong to the same group of the periodic table?

218. An element belongs to the first group and third period of the periodic table. What conclusion can you draw from its position?

219. How does electronic configuration of atoms change in a period with increase in atomic number?

220. **Assertion:** The ionization energy of Mg is more than that of sodium.
Reason: The ionization energy decreases in a period from left to right.

CHAPTER-8: HOW DO ORGANISMS REPRODUCE

- Reproduction is the biological process by which new individual organisms (offspring) are produced from their parents. Reproduction is a fundamental feature of all known life. Each individual organism exists as the result of reproduction.
- The inheritance of features from parents can be transferred to their offsprings through chromosomes present in the nucleus of the cell.
- Basic event in reproduction is the creation of a DNA copy.
- Some changes in DNA copying produces variations in organisms known as mutations.

TYPES OF REPRODUCTION

Asexual Reproduction
[It involves single parent and there is no gametes formation]

- Spore formation
  [Reproduction occurs by formation of spores. Examples - Mucor, Rhizopus]
- Fission
  [When an organism splits into two or more individuals by mitotic divisions]
  - **Binary**
    [Division of a parent cell into two identical daughter cells] Examples - Binary fission in amoeba, paramecium
  - **Multiple**
    [Division of a parent cell into several small daughter cells] Examples - Fission in plasmodium malarial parasite
- Fragmentation
  [The body of the organism divides into smaller fragments and each fragment grow into new individuals. Example - Spirogyra]
- Regeneration
  [The ability of an organism to regenerate its lost or injured part of the body. Example - Regeneration in Planaria]
- Budding
  [Production of new individuals from outgrowth of the parent. Example - Budding in Hydra]

Sexual Reproduction
[It involves mixing of genetic material through fusion of gametes and two parents are involved]

- Vegetative propagation in plants is also an example of asexual reproduction. New plants can be grown from different vegetative parts of the plants like roots, stems, leaves etc.
- Some plants like Bryophyllum develops adventitious buds on their leaves which develops into new plants.
- Modified tuberous roots like sweet potato can be propagated vegetatively when planted in soil.
- Artificial methods of vegetative propagation includes cutting, layering, grafting etc.

SEXUAL REPRODUCTION

In Plants

Flower is the main reproductive organ

- Pollination
  [Transfer of pollen grains from anther of the stamen to the stigma of carpel]
- Fertilisation
  [Fusion of male and female gametes to form zygote]

Self pollination
Transfer of pollen grains from anther of a flower to the stigma of the same flower or flower borne on the same plant

Cross pollination
Transfer of pollen grains from anther of one flower to stigma of another flower of different plant but of same species

In Human Beings

Male Reproductive System
- Testes
- Vas deferens
- Urethra
- Penis

Female Reproductive System
- Ovaries
- Oviducts
- Vagina
- Vulva

- The parts of a flower are calyx, corolla, androecium and gynoecium.
- Calyx is the outermost whorl of a flower which is a collection of sepals mostly green in colour and they are protective in function.
- Corolla is the collection of petals, they are brightly coloured and helps in attraction of insects for pollination.
- Androecium is a collection of stamens which are the male reproductive organs of a flower. A stamen consists of anther and filament. Anther contains pollen sacs in which pollen grains are produced. Pollen grains contain male gametes.
- Gynoecium is a collection of carpels which are the female reproductive organs of a flower.
- A carpel consists of stigma, style and ovary.
- The ovary contains ovules which contains the female gametes.
- Double fertilisation is a complex fertilisation mechanism in flowering plants. This process involves the fusion of a female gametophyte (megagametophyte, also called the embryo sac) with two male gametes (sperm).
- Ovules grow into seeds and ovaries grow into fruits after fertilisation.

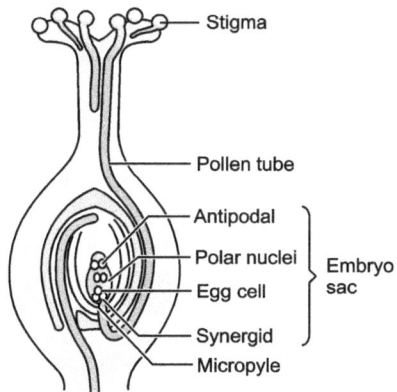

- Gonads are primary sex organs in humans. Testes are male gonads which produces sperms whereas ovaries are female gonads which produce eggs.
- Testes are found within sac like structures called scrotum. Vas deferens or sperm ducts carry sperms from testis.
- Ovaries produce eggs. The fertilisation of egg with sperms occurs at oviduct. After fertilisation zygote is formed which develops into embryo that grows in uterus to a full term baby in about 280 days which is called gestation period.
- If fertilisation does not occur the egg disintegrates and along with blood and mucus it comes out through the vagina. This cycle occurs every month in females known as menstrual cycle.

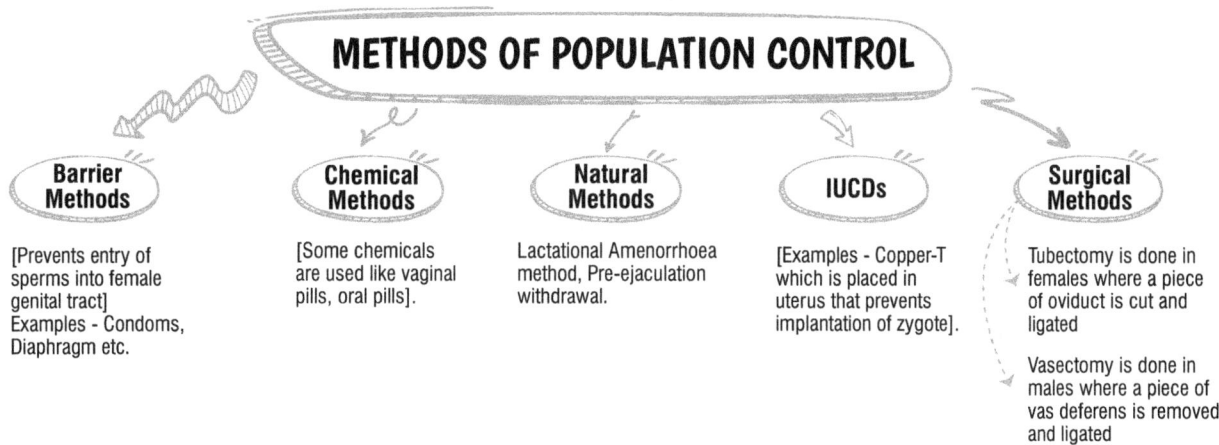

- To avoid rapid growth of population some preventive measures are taken which is called birth control.
- The infectious diseases which spread from an infected person to a healthy ones through sexual contact are called Sexually Transmitted Diseases or STDs. Examples are AIDS, syphilis, gonorrhea.

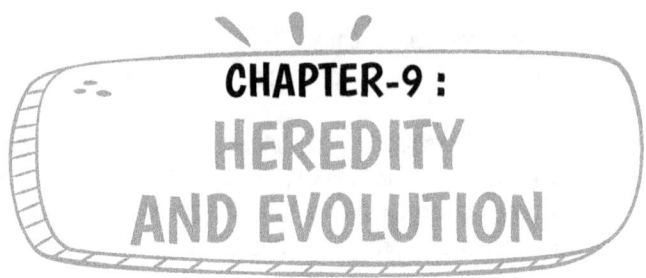

CHAPTER-9 : HEREDITY AND EVOLUTION

- Genetics is the process of transmission of body features from parents to offsprings and the laws related to transmission. In other words we can say Genetics deals with study of both heredity and variations.
- The word " Genetics " was coined by **William Bateson in 1906**.

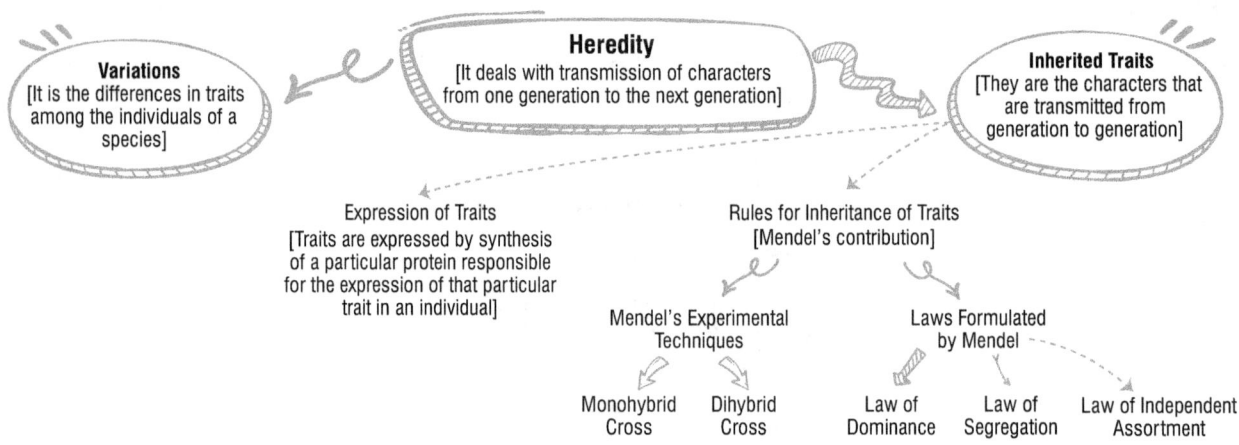

- Variations are mainly seen during sexual reproduction due to the following reasons :
(i) Crossing over during meiosis process.
(ii) Alterations in genetic material due to mutations.
(iii) Mixing of female and male gametes that come from two different individuals i.e., father and mother.
- **Gregor Johann Mendel** is considered as **"Father of Genetics."** He had formulated the Laws of Inheritance by performing hybridisation experiments on Pisum sativum – Garden pea plant.
- He had studied seven contrasting pairs of characters in pea plants.
(i) Height of the plant – Tall or short
(ii) Colour of flower – Purple or white
(iii) Shape of seed – Round or wrinkled
(iv) Colour of seed – Yellow or green
(v) Colour of pod – Green or yellow
(vi) Shape of pod – Inflated or constricted
(vii) Position of flower –Axial or terminal
- The cross between the two pure breeding varieties of an organism taking into account only a single character at a time is called monohybrid cross.
- Example of monohybrid cross : A pure tall pea plant is crossed with pure dwarf pea plant. In F_1 generation tall pea plants are produced with heterozygous condition i.e., they carry both dominant and recessive alleles. When these plants are crossed they give tall and dwarf plants in the ratio 3 : 1 which is also called phenotypic ratio and their genotypic ratio is 1 : 2 : 1.

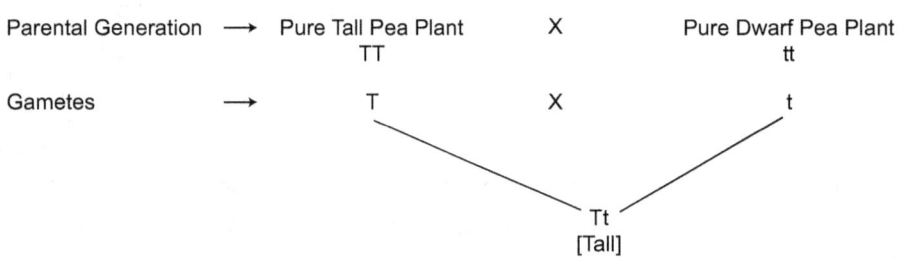

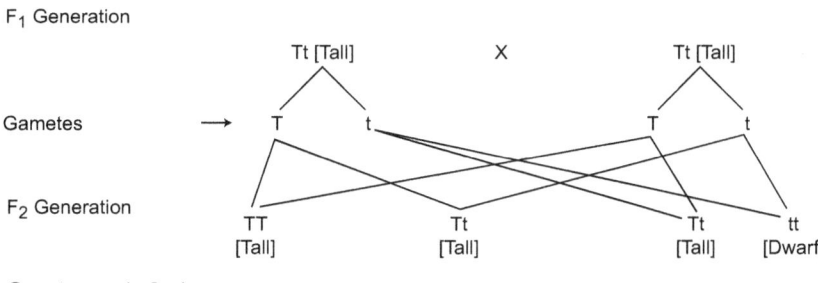

Genotype : 1 : 2 : 1
Phenotype : 3 : 1

- The cross between the two pure breeding varieties of an organism taking into account two characters at a time is called dihybrid cross.
- When a pure pea plant with round yellow seeds is crossed with pure pea plant having green wrinkled seeds, in F1 generation hybrid plants with round yellow seeds are produced. But again when these plants are crossed they produce round-yellow, round-green, wrinkled-yellow, wrinkled-green in the ratio 9 : 3 : 3 : 1, which is the phenotypic ratio.

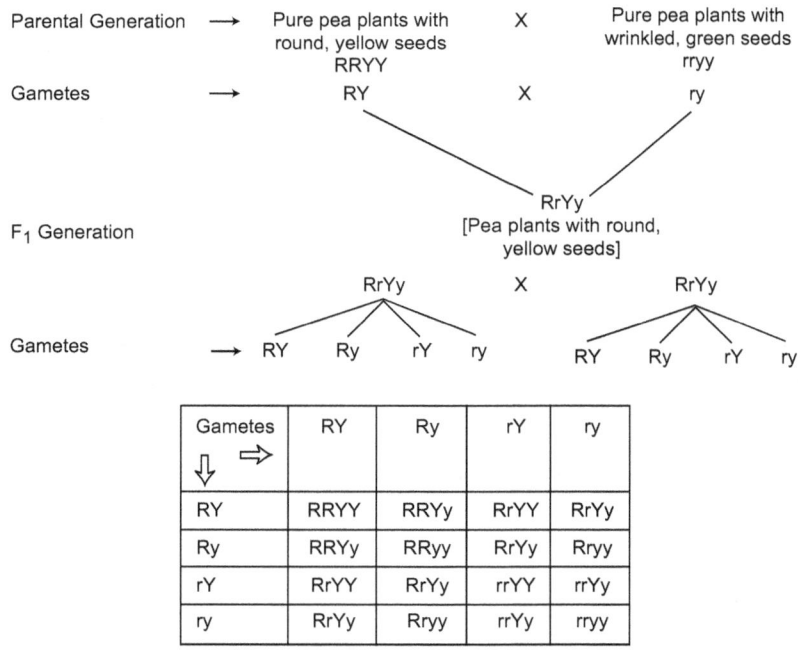

Phenotype : 9 : 3 : 3 : 1

- Based on Mendel's breeding experiments three Laws were deduced.
- **Law of Dominance :** The phenomenon of appearance of only one of the two contrasting traits in F1 generation is called dominance. The other character remains suppressed which is known as recessive character.
- **Law of Segregation :** At the time of reproduction when gametes are formed the factors segregate so that each gamete receives only factor of each character. This is called Law of purity of gametes.
- **Law of independent assortment :** At the time of reproduction, two pairs of factors of each of the two traits in a dihybrid cross segregated independently during gamete formation and randomly formed combinations in F2 generation. Inheritance of factors controlling a particular trait in an organism is independent of the other.
- The mechanism by which sex of an individual is determined when it begins its life is called sex determination.
- In human beings, sex is determined by XX-XY mechanism. Males have XY sex chromosomes whereas females have XX sex chromosomes.
- In some reptiles sex is determined by environmental factors.
- Gene is a fragment of DNA molecule that has a particular nucleotide sequence which encodes for a particular protein.
- Evolution is the constant process of gradual change occurring in an organism since the origin of life which gives rise to variety of complex organisms on the surface of earth.

How Do Organisms Reproduce ?

Chapter 8

Definitions

1. **Asexual reproduction:** The process of producing offsprings which involves a single parent without the formation of gametes is called asexual reproduction.
2. **Spore:** A spore is a single-celled or multi-celled reproductive structure which gets separated from its parent and under favourable conditions gives rise to new individual.
3. **Seed:** A seed is the reproductive unit of a plant from which a new plant grows.
4. **Vegetative propagation:** It is mainly seen in plants and is an asexual mode of reproduction where a new plant grows from different parts of plant like roots, stem, leaves etc., rather than from a seed.
5. **Tissue culture:** The production of new plants from a small piece of plant tissues or cells removed from the growing tips of a plant in a suitable growth medium is called tissue culture.
6. **Pollination:** The process of transfer of pollen grains from anthers of stamens to the stigma of carpel within the same flower or different flower of same plant or to any other flowers of different plants but of same species is called pollination.
7. **Double fertilisation:** The process by which a male gamete fuses with an egg to form zygote and the second male gamete unites with two polar nuclei to form endosperm is called double fertilisation.
8. **Primary sex organs:** They are the gonads i.e., testes and ovaries which produce gametes and secrete sex hormones.
9. **Gametes:** The special cells involved in sexual reproduction to produce the offsprings are called gametes or sex cells.
10. **Puberty:** The age at which sex hormones are produced, reproductive organs become matured and have the capacity to give rise to new individual and there is development of secondary sexual characters in both males and females.
11. **Fertilisation:** The process of fusion of male and female gametes to produce the zygote is called fertilisation.
12. **Gestation period:** It is the time from fertilisation till the birth of the new born.
13. **Parturition:** The delivery of full term baby from the uterus of mother after the end of gestation period is called parturition.

Multiple Choice Questions

14. A _____ fuses with a _____ in generative fertilisation.
    (a) Secondary nucleus, polar nucleus
    (b) Polar nucleus, female gamete
    (c) Male gamete, female gamete
    (d) All of the above

    Ans. (c) Male gamete, female gamete

    Explanation :
    In double fertilisation, triple fusion (vegetative fertilisation) and syngamy (generative fertilisation) occur. In generative fertilisation, a male gamete fuses with a female gamete and forms diploid zygote.

15. Which of the statements is incorrect?
    (a) The filiform apparatus blocks the entry of pollen and sperm cells
    (b) The secondary nuclei form a polar nucleus prior to fertilisation
    (c) Androecium is a part of the carpel
    (d) All of the above

    Ans. (d) All of the above

    Explanation :
    Filiform apparatus are the finger-like projections that direct the entry of pollen tube and aid in sperm discharge. The definitive nucleus is a secondary nucleus generated by the fusion of two polar nuclei. Stamens are the male parts of a flower; together, they make up the androecium.

16. **Which of the following is a product of meiosis?**
    (a) Microspore mother cell
    (b) Endosperm nucleus (primary)
    (c) Megaspore mother cell
    (d) Megaspore

Ans. (d) Megaspore

Explanation :

Megaspore is a haploid cell that is formed forms when the megaspore mother cell undergoes meiosis. It is the initial cell female gametophyte.

17. **To perform an experiment to identify the different parts of an embryo of a dicot seed, first of all you require a dicot seed. Select dicot seeds from the following group*.**

    Wheat, Gram, Maize, Pea, Barley, Ground-nut
    (a) Wheat, Gram and Pea
    (b) Gram, Pea and Ground-nut
    (c) Maize, Pea and Barley
    (d) Gram, Maize and Ground-nut

Ans. (b) Gram, Pea and Ground-nut.

Explanation :

Monocot and dicot plants are the two types of angiosperm plants. The seeds of dicot plants have two cotyledons. Ground-nut, gram, and pea are examples of dicot plants.

18. **On observing an embryo of a pea seed, a student listed its various parts as given below :**

    Micropyle, Cotyledon, Plumule, Testa, Radicle, Tegmen

    On examining the list the teacher remarked that out of these only three parts belong to embryo. Select these three parts* :
    (a) Testa, Radicle, Cotyledon
    (b) Tegmen, Radicle, Micropyle
    (c) Cotyledon, Plumule, Radicle
    (d) Cotyledon, Plumule, Testa

Ans. (c) Cotyledon, Plumule, Radicle

Explanation :

Pea is a dicot plant with testa, cotyledons, and embryonic axis in its seed. The cotyledon, plumule, and radicle make up the embryo. Cotyledons are fleshy spherical structures on the embryonic axis that carry reserve feeding resources. The radicle is found on the micropylar end of embryonic axis, while the plumule is found on the other end.

19. **In the following figure different stages of binary fission in Amoeba are depicted, which are not in proper sequence:***

  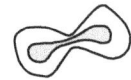

   I   II   III   IV

* are board exam questions from previous years

The correct sequence is :
(a) II, III, IV, I   (b) I, II, IV, III
(c) III, IV, II, I   (d) I, III, IV, II

Ans. (a) II, III, IV, I

Explanation :

In Amoeba, binary fission is an asexual method of reproduction. (II) represents the parent cell, which replicates the genetic material as shown in (III). The cytoplasm divides after karyokinesis, resulting in two cells (IV). The two cells illustrated in (I) are the daughter cells that result from binary fission.

20. **The correct sequence of reproductive stages seen in flowering plants is :** [NCERT Exemplar]
    (a) gametes, zygote, embryo, seedling
    (b) zygote, gametes, embryo, seedling
    (c) seedling, embryo, zygote, gametes
    (d) gametes, embryo, zygote, seedling

Ans. (a) gametes, zygote, embryo, seedling

Explanation :

The male gamete present in the pollen grain and the female gamete egg in the embryo sac are formed by meiosis. The zygote is formed when the male and female gametes unite. The embryo is formed by multiple divisions of the zygote. In the seed, the embryo develops and matures. The seed germinates by absorbing water and growing into a new seedling.

21. **In Rhizopus tubular thread like structures bearing sporangia at their tips are called :**
    [NCERT Exemplar]
    (a) Filaments   (b) Rhizoids
    (c) Roots   (d) Hyphae

Ans. (d) Hyphae

Explanation :

In fungi, hyphae are filamentous structures that branch out and spread beneath a substratum's surface. Hyphae may rise upright above the surface during its life cycle, with its contents forming a bulge at the tip. The sporangium is formed by this bulge. Spores are generated in the sporangium.

22. **Factors responsible for the rapid spread of bread mould on slices of bread are:** [NCERT Exemplar]
    (i) large number of spores.
    (ii) availability of moisture and nutrients in bread.
    (iii) presence of tubular branched hyphae.
    (iv) formation of round shaped sporangia.
    (a) (i) and (iii)   (b) (ii) and (iv)
    (c) (i) and (ii)   (d) (iii) and (iv)

Ans. (c) (i) and (ii)

Explanation :

The sporangium of the bread mould releases huge number of spores, which germinate on a suitable substratum and form hyphae. Fungi are saprophytes so profuse growth is only possible in the presence of an appropriate substratum, such as bread, that provides a considerable amount of moisture and nutrients.

23. From the figure identify parts labeled a, b and c.

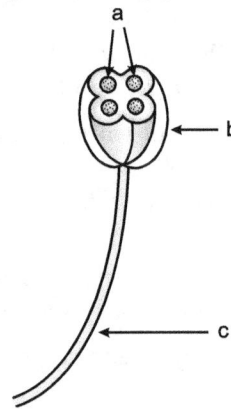

(a) Pollen grains, anther, filament
(b) Anther, pollen grains, filament
(c) Filament, anther, pollen grains
(d) Filament, pollen grains, anther

Ans. (a) Pollen grains, anther, filament

Explanation :

Anther is the part of the stamen where pollen is produced. Pollen forms in the anther, which is supported by the filament. Each pollen grain is made up of two male gametes in a single cell.

24. Length of pollen tube depends on the distance between : [NCERT Exemplar]
    (a) pollen grain and upper surface of stigma.
    (b) pollen grain on upper surface of stigma and ovule.
    (c) pollen grain in anther and upper surface of stigma.
    (d) upper surface of stigma and lower part of style.

Ans. (b) pollen grain on upper surface of stigma and ovule.

Explanation :

The length of pollen tube is determined by the distance between pollen grain on the upper surface of stigma and ovule. This is because pollen germinates and forms pollen tube that reaches up to ovule in ovary and releases male gamete to combine with female gamete.

25. Asexual reproduction takes place through budding in: [NCERT]
    (a) Amoeba   (b) Yeast
    (c) Plasmodium   (d) Leishmania

Ans. (b) Yeast

Explanation :

Both asexual and sexual reproduction are possible for yeast. Budding is the process through which yeast multiply asexually.

26. Which structure in the plant carries the male organ?
    (a) Sperm   (b) Ovule
    (c) Pollen grain   (d) Spores

Ans. (c) Pollen grain

Explanation :

The pollen grains carry the male organ. Mostly the male organs are the motile gamete while the female organ is stationary. It is necessary for the male organs to be small and light for easy propagation by the environmental agents.

27. The ability of a cell to divide into several cells during reproduction in Plasmodium is called :
    (a) Budding   (b) Reduction division
    (c) Multiple fission (d) Binary fission

Ans. (c) Multiple fission

Explanation :

Plasmodium reproduces asexually after feeding on red blood cells, a process known as schizogony or multiple fission. Plasmodium divides into numerous cells during multiple fission.

28. What is the disadvantage of parthenogenesis?
    (a) Wastage of germplasm
    (b) Retention of genotype
    (c) Lack of adaptability
    (d) Variety in population

Ans. (c) Lack of adaptability

Explanation :

Since there is no fertilisation of gametes in parthenogeneis, there will be no crossing over of genes. This hence causes no variations in the generations. Which makes it difficult for the offspring to adapt to the changing environmental conditions.

29. The anther contains :
    (a) Sepals   (b) Ovules
    (c) Carpel   (d) Pollen grains

Ans. (d) Pollen grains

Explanation :

Pollen grains are microscopic structures produced by an anther. When anther opens, pollen is released, which is subsequently transferred by the wind, insects, or birds to different plants for pollination.

30. What is the event after zygote formation called?
    (a) Pre-fertilisation   (b) Post-fertilisation
    (c) Fertilisation   (d) Gametogenesis

Ans. (b) Post-fertilisation

Explanation :

Sexual reproduction is divided into 3 events: Pre-fertilisation, fertilisation and post-fertilisation events. Pre-fertilisation events occur before fusion of gametes (gametogenesis), fertilisation is the fusion of gametes to form zygote and post-fertilisation events occur after zygote formation.

31. Anthers and filaments form the _____ .
(a) gynoecium (b) calyx
(c) androecium (d) corolla

Ans. (c) androecium

Explanation :

Androecium consists of the anthers and filaments. They are the male reproductive structures. Male gametes that are in pollen grains are on the anthers. Depending on the species, the stamens (anthers and filaments) may or may not protrude out of the flower.

32. Variation pattern are studied in the offspring of sexually and asexually reproducing organisms. State your observation:
(a) More variations are observed in the offspring of sexually reproducing organisms.
(b) More variations are observed in the offsprings of asexually reproducing organisms.
(c) No difference in variation is observed in offspring of sexually and asexually reproducing organisms.
(d) Cannot be determined.

Ans. (a) More variations are observed in the offspring of sexually reproducing organisms.

Explanation :

There is always a possibility of diversity of characters in the offsprings of sexually reproducing organism because the offspring is formed as a result of fusion of two gametes produced by two different individuals the male and the female parents. So, there is an opportunity for new combinations of characters.

33. Name the process shown in the above diagram of getting back a full organism from its body parts:

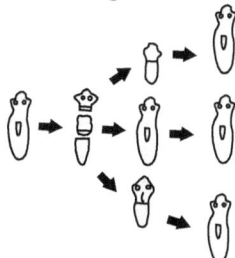

(a) Regeneration (b) Budding
(c) Fragmentation (d) Fission

Ans. (a) Regeneration

Explanation :

The process of getting back a full organism from its body parts is called regeneration. The simple animals like hydra and planaria show regeneration. If the body of planaria gets cut into a number of pieces, then each body piece can regenerate into a complete planaria by growing all the missing parts. The regeneration of an organism from its cut body part occurs by the process of growth and development. The cells of cut body part divide rapidly to make a ball of cells. The cells then become specialised to form different types of tissues which again form various organs and body parts.

34.

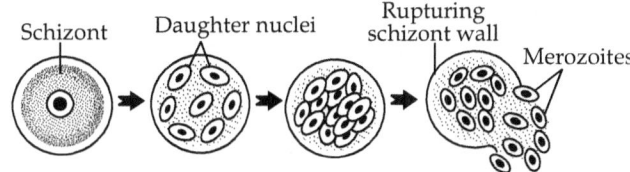

Which of the following two combinations are correct?

	Multiple Fission	Binary fission
(a)	2 daughter cells are formed.	Many daughter cells are formed.
(b)	Both the Nucleus and cytoplasm divide simultaneously.	First, the nucleus divides and is surrounded by cytoplasm.
(c)	Divides repeatedly.	Divides only once.
(d)	Includes a definite pattern of division.	Has no definite pattern of division.

Ans. (c) Divides repeatedly—Divides only once.

Explanation :

Both binary fission and multiple fission are asexual reproduction and occur with the presence of only one parent. In binary fission, the parent cell divides itself into two equal and identical daughter cells. It is the most common form of reproduction in prokaryotes such as bacteria. In multiple fission, a single parent cell is divided into many daughter cells. It is the most common form of reproduction in protists and in some parasitic species.

35. The Correct Sequence of Reproductive Stages Occurring in Flowering Plants is
(a) Gametes, Zygote, Embryo, Seed
(b) Zygote, Gametes, Embryo, Seed
(c) Seed, Embryo, Zygote, Gametes
(d) Gametes, Embryo, Zygote, Seed

Ans. (a) Gametes, Zygote, Embryo, Seed

Explanation :

Gametes of flowers fuse to form a zygote. This zygote develops into an embryo that later forms the seed.

74 | CBSE Chapterwise Objective + Subjective – X

36. In which of the given figures, budding is not shown?

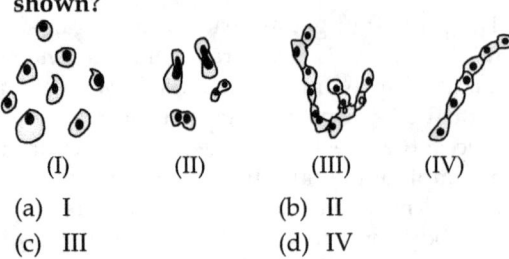

(I) (II) (III) (IV)

(a) I (b) II
(c) III (d) IV

Ans. (a) I

Explanation :

Budding is a asexual reproduction process that involves the formation of a bud that is an outgrowth in the parent body and later breaks down to form a new organisms. Due to repeated cell division the hydra forms an outgrowth in a particular site. This bud develops into a new individual and when it matures it detaches from the parent body and becomes a new independent individual. In the given image, the diagram I do not show any bud formation.

37. Slides A and B were examined and interpreted by four students as a, b, c and d. Identify the correct option:

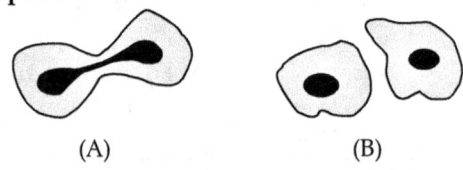

(A) (B)

	Slide A	Slide B
(a)	Binary fission in Amoeba	Daughter cells of Amoeba
(b)	Budding in yeast	Buds of Yeast
(c)	Binary fission in Amoeba	Buds of Yeast
(d)	Budding in yeast	Daughter cells of Amoeba

Ans. (a) Slide A—Binary fission in *Amoeba*.
Slide B—Daughter cells of *Amoeba*.

Explanation :

The binary fission is an asexual reproduction observed in amoeba. After the replication process through mitotic division, the amoeba cell divides into two equal halves and is considered as the daughter cells. In this process, the daughters cells thus produce through cell division are identical to each other as shown in the diagram.

Budding is also a asexual reproduction process that involves the formation of a bud that is an outgrowth in the parent body that later breaks down to form a new organisms and the diagram do not show the bud formation.

38. In the sunflower, the anther matures before the stigma, which ensures that its pollen cannot fertilise the same flower. Such adaptations favour cross-pollination over self-pollination.

Which of the given options correctly represents self-pollination or cross-pollination.

	Self-pollination	Cross-pollination
(a)	Flowers of different plants (of same species) are involved	Flowers of the same plant are involved
(b)	Pollinating agent is not necessary	Pollinating agent is necessary
(c)	the stamen and carpel mature at the different time.	the stamen and carpel mature at the same time.
(d)	leads to greater genetic diversity	leads to the production of plants with less genetic diversity

Ans. (b) Pollinating agent is not necessary— Pollinating agent is necessary

Explanation :

Self-pollination occurs when the pollen from the anther is deposited on the stigma of the same flower, or another flower on the same plant. Cross-pollination is the transfer of pollen from the anther of one flower to the stigma of another flower on a different individual of the same species. Self-pollination occurs in flowers where the stamen and carpel mature at the same time, and are positioned so that the pollen can land on the flower's stigma. This method of pollination does not require an investment from the plant to provide nectar and pollen as food for pollinators. Self-pollination leads to the production of plants with less genetic diversity, since genetic material from the same plant is used to form gametes, and eventually, the zygote. In contrast, cross-pollination or out-crossing leads to greater genetic diversity because the microgametophyte and megagametophyte are derived from different plants.

39. In which of the following aspects does multiple fission differs from binary fission?

(i) Number of offsprings produced.
(ii) Level of genetic variation in offsprings.
(iii) Number of parents involved.
(iv) Multiple fission happens in Plasmodium whereas binary fission happens in Leishmania.

(a) Only (i) is correct
(b) Both (i) and (iv) are correct
(c) (iii) is correct
(d) (ii) is correct

Ans. (b) Both (i) and (iv) are correct

Explanation :

Multiple fission produces many off springs whereas binary fission produces only two. Off springs produced through multiple fission as well as binary fission are genetically identical to each other and to their parents. Both multiple fission and binary fission require only one parent. Plasmodium, the protozoan that causes malaria reproduces through multiple fission. Leishmania causes Kala-azar and it reproduces through binary fission.

40. **What happens when a Planarian (plural-Planaria) is cut into many fragments?**
    (a) All fragments regenerate into new organisms.
    (b) Only the head containing fragment regenerates into a new organism.
    (c) Nearly half of the fragments regenerate into new organisms.
    (d) No changes are seen in fragments. Planaria reproduce by budding.

Ans. (a) All fragments regenerate into new organisms.

Explanation :

Cells that cause regeneration in a Planarian are present all over the body. Cells that cause regeneration are present all over the body of a Planarian. So, when a Planarian is cut into many fragments, all fragments regenerate into new organisms. Cells that cause regeneration in Planarian are present all over the body including the head.

41. **Study the following diagram showing various stages of binary fission in Amoeba: the correct sequence of these diagrams should be**

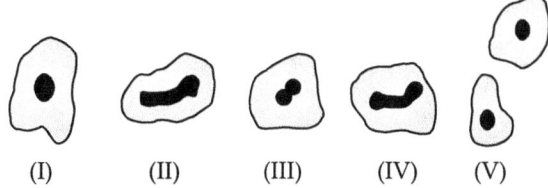

    (I)   (II)   (III)   (IV)   (V)
    (a) I, IV, III, II, V   (b) III, I, IV, II, V
    (c) I, II, IV, III, V   (d) I, III, IV, II, V

Ans. (d) I, III, IV, II, V

Explanation :

Asexual reproduction is a process of reproducing the offspring through simple division of cells, this type of reproduction is observed in single cell organisms, it does not undergo fusion of gametes therefore, and the offspring produced by asexual reproduction are genetically identical. The asexual reproduction is further divided into; binary fission, budding, fragmentation, and sporogenesis.

The binary fission is an asexual reproduction observed in amoeba. After the replication process through mitotic division, the amoeba cell divides into two equal halves and is considered as the daughter cells. In this process, the daughters cells thus produce through cell division are identical to each other.

The amoebas that are about to divide grow eventually larger the nucleus gets extended and divided into two. The nuclear division is followed by the cytoplasmic division. Therefore, two amoebas are produced from a single amoeba.

42. **Which of the following statements about binary fission is true?**
    (a) Some multicellular organisms also reproduce through binary fission.
    (b) Binary fission produces two new organisms.
    (c) Binary fission in amoeba happens only in the vertical plane.
    (d) Binary fission in Leishmania can happen in any plane.

Ans. (b) Binary fission produces two new organisms.

Explanation :

Only unicellular organisms reproduce through binary fission. In binary fission, a unicellular organism (a cell) divides to form two unicellular organisms (two cells). Binary fission in Amoeba can happen in any plane. Binary fission in Leishmania happens in a definite orientation (plane) to the body because Leishmania has somewhat organised structure.

43. **Identify A, B and C in the given diagram and match the labelling referred in column I and correlate with the function in column II.**

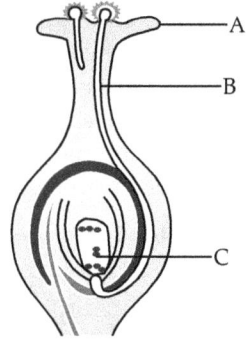

Column I	Column II
A.	(i) special reproductive female sex cell which combines with male gamete to form zygote.
B.	(ii) A male gamete moves down though it towards the female gamete in the ovary
C.	(iii) receiving the pollen grains from the anther of stamen during pollination.

(a) A-(iii), B-(ii), C-(i)   (b) A-(ii), B-(i), C-(iii)
(c) A-(i), B-(ii), C-(iii)   (d) A-(iii), B-(i), C-(ii)

Ans. (a) A-(iii), B-(ii), C-(i)

Explanation :

A – Stigma. The top part of carpel is called stigma. Stigma is for receiving the pollen grains from the anther of stamen during pollination.

B – Pollen tube. When a pollen grain falls on the stigma, it bursts open and grows a pollen tube downward through the style towards the female gamete in the ovary. A male gamete moves down the pollen tube.

C–Female gamete (ovum). It is a special reproductive female sex cell which combines with male gamete to form zygote.

44. **Which of the following statements is NOT true regarding asexual reproduction in plants?**
    (a) Plants that reproduce asexually reach maturity faster than those who reproduce sexually.
    (b) Plants that reproduce asexually have greater genetic diversity than those who reproduce sexually.
    (c) Plants that reproduce asexually are more stable than those who reproduce sexually.
    (d) Plants that reproduce asexually create offspring that are identical to the parent plant.

Ans. (b) Plants that reproduce asexually have greater genetic diversity than those who reproduce sexually.

Explanation :

Sexual reproduction provides genetic diversity because the sperm and egg that are produced contain different combinations of genes than the parent organisms. Asexual reproduction, on the other hand, does not need sperm and eggs since one organism splits into two organisms that have the same combination of genes.

45. **Which of the following options shows correct sequence of asexual reproduction in hydra?**

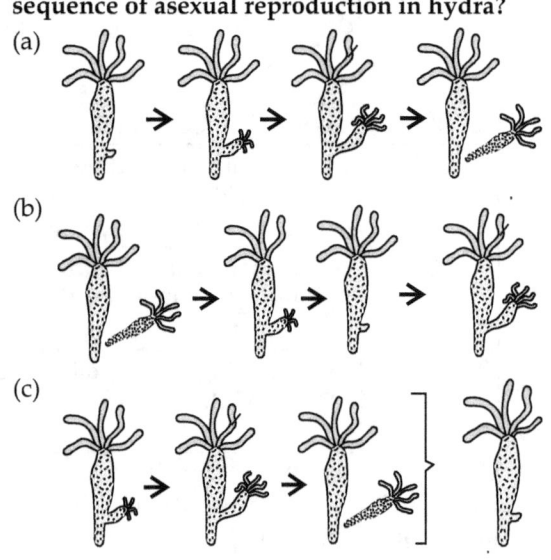
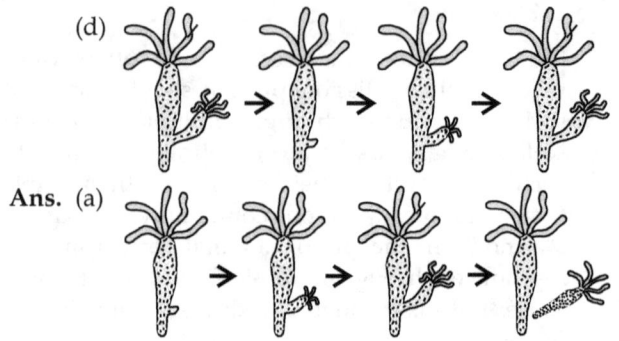

Ans. (a)

Explanation :

In Hydra, a bud develops as an outgrowth due to repeated cell division at one specific site. These buds develop into tiny individuals and when fully mature, detach from the parent body and become new independent individuals.

46. **A Feature of Reproduction that is Common to Amoeba, Yeast and Bacterium is that :**
    (a) They Are All Multicellular
    (b) They Are All Unicellular
    (c) They Reproduce Only Sexually
    (d) They Reproduce Asexually

Ans. (d) They Reproduce Asexually

Explanation :

Amoeba, Yeast and Bacterium are unicellular organism and reproduce asexually.

47. **In the list of organisms given below, those that reproduce by the asexual method are**

[NCERT Exemplar]

    (i) banana   (ii) dog
    (iii) yeast   (iv) *Amoeba*
    (a) (ii) and (iv)   (b) (i), (iii) and (iv)
    (c) (i) and (iv)   (d) (ii), (iii) and (iv)

Ans. (b) (i), (iii) and (iv)

Explanation :

Asexual reproduction takes place without the process of gamete formation and only one parent is needed. Examples include *Amoeba* which reproduces by binary fission (divison of cell into two similar cells).

Yeast, reproduces by budding (small buds develop from body wall of parent that separate and grow further).

Banana, reproduces by vegetative propogation (Vegetative parts of a plant such as root, stem, etc., can produce new plants).

In dog, sexual reproduction takes place, (i.e., it involves two sexes-male and female whose gametes fuse constituting sexual reproduction).

48. **In a flower, the parts that produce male and female gametes (germ cells) are**

[NCERT Exemplar]

(a) stamen and anther
(b) filament and stigma
(c) anther and ovary
(d) stamen and style

Ans. (c) anther and ovary

Explanation :

In a flower, the parts that produce male and female gametes are anther and ovary respectively. Stamen is the male reproductive unit of the flower. It contains a bilobed anther at the top which produces male gametes. Filament is the stalk of the stamen that supports anther.

Pistil (carpel) is the female reproductive part of the flower. It consists of ovary (forms ovules-female gametes), stigma (receives pollen) and style (elongated tube).

49. **Which of the following is the correct sequence of events of sexual reproduction in a flower?**
    [NCERT Exemplar]
    (a) Pollination, fertilisation, seedling, embroy
    (b) Seedling, embryo, fertilisation, pollination
    (c) Pollination, fertilisation, embryo, seedling
    (d) Embryo, seedling, pollination, fertilisation

Ans. (c) Pollination, fertilisation, embryo, seedling

Explanation :

The correct sequence of events are
↓
Pollination (transfer of pollen from stamen to stigma)
↓
Fertilisation (fusion of germ cells to form zygote)
↓
Embryo formation (zygote divides several times to form an embryo within the ovule)
↓
Seedling (ovule develops a tough coat and converts into a seed).

50. **Offspring formed by asexual method of reproduction have greater similarity among themselves because** [NCERT Exemplar]
    (i) Asexual reproduction involves only one parent.
    (ii) Asexual reproduction does not involve gametes.
    (iii) Asexual reproduction occurs before sexual reproduction.
    (iv) Asexual reproduction occurs after sexual reproduction.
    (a) (i) and (ii)   (b) (i) and (iii)
    (c) (ii) and (iv)   (d) (iii) and (iv)

Ans. (a) (i) and (ii)

Explanation :

Offspring have greater similarity as only one parent is involved in asexual reproduction thus no gametes are formed. The basis of asexual reproduction is mitosis (division of a nucleus into two identical daughter nuclei). Each daughter nucleus has same genetic make up because of replication of parental DNA. The new offspring produced are called clones.

51. **Characters transmitted from parents to offspring are present in** [NCERT Exemplar]
    (a) cytoplasm   (b) ribosome
    (c) golgi bodies (d) genes

Ans. (d) genes

Explanation :

Characters are transmitted from parents to offspring through genes. Genes are the heriditary units of the body in living organisms. Chromosomes in the nucleus of a cell contain information for the inheritance of features from parents in the form of DNA (Deoxyribonucleic acid). This DNA contains genes.

52. **Characters that are transmitted from parents to offspring during reproduction show**
    [NCERT Exemplar]
    (a) only similarities with parents.
    (b) only variations with parents.
    (c) both similarities and variations with parents.
    (d) neither similarities nor variations.

Ans. (c) both similarities and variations with parents.

Explanation :

In sexual reproduction, the offspring are not identical to the parents or to one another. This is because the offspring receive some genes from mother and some from father.

Because of mixing of genes on re-establishment of number of chromosome in various differents combinations, the offspring show both similarities and variations with characters of parents.

53. **A feature of reproduction that is common to *Amoeba, Spirogyra* and yeast is that**
    [NCERT Exemplar]
    (a) they reproduce asexually.
    (b) they are all unicellular.
    (c) they reproduce only sexually.
    (d) they are all multicellular.

Ans. (a) they reproduce asexually.

Explanation :

Amoeba and yeast are unicellular while *Spirogyra* is multicellular. But all the three reproduce asexually.

54. **In *Spirogyra*, asexual reproduction takes place by**
    [NCERT Exemplar]
    (a) breaking up of filaments into smaller bits.
    (b) division of a cell into two cells.

(c) division of a cell into many cells.
(d) formation of young cells from older cells.

Ans. (a) breaking up of filaments into smaller bits.

Explanation:
In *Spirogyra*, asexual reproduction takes place by fragmentation, i.e., organism simply breaks up into smaller pieces upon maturation. Each piece grows into new individual without forming any gametes.

55. **The number of chromosomes in parents and offspring of a particular species remains constant due to** [NCERT Exemplar]
   (a) doubling of chromosomes after zygote formation.
   (b) halving of chromosomes during gamete formation.
   (c) doubling of chromosomes after gamete formation.
   (d) halving of chromosomes after gamete formation.

Ans. (b) halving of chromosomes during gamete formation.

Explanation:
The number of chromosomes in parents and offspring of a particular species remains constant due to halving of chromosomes during gamete formation.

The gametes are special type of cells which contain only half the amount of DNA as compared to normal cells of an organism. So, when a male gamete combines with a female gamete during sexual reproduction, then the new cell 'zygote' will have normal amount of DNA.

56. **Vegetative propagation refers to formation of new plants from** [NCERT Exemplar]
   (a) stem, roots and flowers
   (b) stem, roots and leaves
   (c) stem, flowers and fruits
   (d) stem, leaves and flowers

Ans. (b) stem, roots and leaves

Explanation:
In vegetative propagation, vegetative parts of a plant such as root, stem, leaf, etc., can produce new plants. Vegetative reproduction is seen in plants like orchids, ornamental plants, grasses, banana, rose, jasmine, etc.

57. **Which of the following statements are true for flowers?** [NCERT Exemplar]
   (i) Flowers are always bisexual.
   (ii) They are the sexual reproductive organs.
   (iii) They are produced in all groups of plants.
   (iv) After fertilisation they give rise to fruits.
   (a) (i) and (iv)   (b) (ii) and (iii)
   (c) (i) and (iii) (d) (ii) and (iv)

Ans. (d) (ii) and (iv)

Explanation:
Flowers are the sexual reproductive organs of a plant. They are produced in angiosperms. Majority of flowers are bisexual. After fertilisation, they give rise to fruits.

58. **Which among the following statements are true for unisexual flowers?** [NCERT Exemplar]
   (i) They possess both stamen and pistil.
   (ii) They possess either stamen or pistil.
   (iii) They exhibit cross pollination.
   (iv) Unisexual flowers possessing only stamens cannot produce fruits.
   (a) (i) and (iv)   (b) (ii), (iii) and (iv)
   (c) (iii) and (iv)   (d) (i), (iii) and (iv)

Ans. (b) (ii), (iii) and (iv)

Explanation:
The flowers which are unisexual (papaya, watermelon) contain either stamens or carpels. Since only one reproductive organ is present in them, they depend on cross pollination to form zygote after fertilisation. Both stamen and carpels are required for fertilisation, so only one of them cannot produce fruits.

59. **Which among the following statements are true for sexual reproduction in flowering plants?** [NCERT Exemplar]
   (i) It requires two types of gametes.
   (ii) Fertilisation is a compulsory event.
   (iii) It always results in formation event.
   (iv) Offspring formed are clones.
   (a) (i) and (iv)   (b) (i), (ii) and (iv)
   (c) (i), (ii) and (iii) (d) (i), (ii) and (iv)

Ans. (c) (i), (ii) and (iii)

Explanation:
Sexual reproduction creates variation in organisms. So clones cannot be produced through it. Clones are identical copies of parent organism. Sexual reproduction needs two type of gametes, i.e., male and female to form zygote after fertilisation.

60. **In figure, the parts A, B and C are sequentially** [NCERT Exemplar]

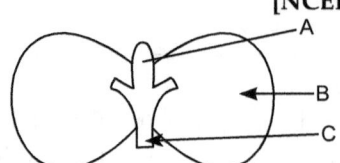

   (a) cotyledon, plumule and radicle
   (b) plumule, radicle and cotyledon
   (c) plumule, cotyledon and radicle
   (d) radicle, cotyledon and plumule

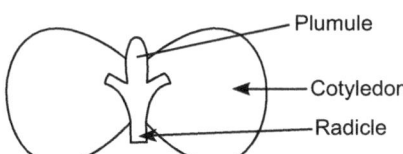

Ans. (c) plumule, cotyledon and radicle

Explanation :

Plumule 'A' grows into shoots, cotyledon 'B' stores food and radicle 'C' grows into roots.

61. Reproduction is essential for living organisms to order to
(a) keep the individual organism alive.
(b) fulfill their energy requirement.
(c) maintain growth.
(d) continue the species generation after generation.

Ans. (d) continue the species generation after generation.

Explanation :

Reproduction is not essential for the survival of an individual, but it is an important function of a living being as it helps an organism to perpetuate its own kind.

Through this process, new individuals are produced, that grow and reproduce again, so as to continue the species generation after generation. Reproduction is a process to maintain the progeny of an organism.

62. The Ratio of Number of Chromosomes in a Human Zygote and a Human Sperm is:
(a) 2 : 1   (b) 3 : 1
(c) 1 : 2   (d) 1 : 3

Ans. (a) 2 : 1

Explanation :

The number of chromosomes in a human sperm is half the number of chromosomes in a zygote i.e their ratio is 2 : 1.

63. The diagram shows the female reproductive system during the fertile period of the menstrual cycle. Select what happens in the ovary during this time?

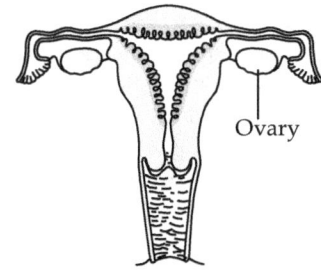

(a) Implantation occurs.
(b) Fertilisation takes place.
(c) A sperm fuses (joins) with an egg.
(d) An egg is released.

Ans. (d) An egg is released.

Explanation :

Ovulation is the process in which a mature egg is released from the ovary.

64. Name the part labelled X in the diagram that produces fluids which help the sperm to swim.

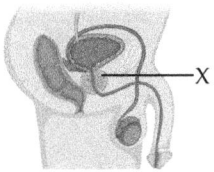

(a) Prostate gland   (b) Scrotum
(c) Urethra   (d) Ureter

Ans. (a) Prostate Gland

Explanation :

The structures of the male reproductive system include the testes, the Epididymis, the penis, and the ducts and glands that produce and carry semen. The seminal vesicles and prostate gland add fluids to the sperm to create semen. Prostate gland is a doughnut-shaped gland that secretes a milky fluid that helps to activate the swimming movements of sperm.

65. The figure is given alongside shows the human male reproductive organs. Which structures make sperms and seminal fluid?
(a) V makes sperms and X makes seminal fluid
(b) W makes sperms and Y makes seminal fluid
(c) X makes sperms and W makes seminal fluid
(d) Y makes sperms and V makes seminal fluid

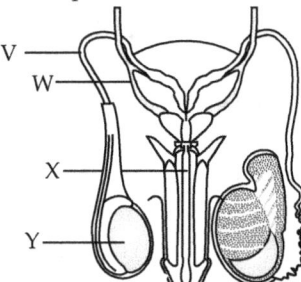

Ans. (d) Y makes sperms and V makes seminal fluid

Explanation :

Explanation: Y represents the testes that produce sperms and V represents the prostate gland that produces seminal fluid.

66. The male human reproductive system consists of the testes and the male accessory glands.
Which of the following statements about male accessory glands is false?
(a) The prostate gland also synthesises sperm.
(b) The prostate gland and seminal vesicles are found outside the testes.

(c) The secretions of prostate gland and seminal vesicles make semen fluid and provide nutrition.
(d) Male accessory glands contribute to semen.

Ans. (a) The prostate gland also synthesises sperm.

Explanation :

Sperm is synthesized only by the testes. The prostate gland and seminal vesicles are found outside the testes along the path of vas deferens. Secretions from the prostate gland and seminal vesicle glands contribute to the composition of semen. The seminal vesicles secretions include fructose and nourishment for sperm cells. Secretions from the prostate gland contribute to the fluid in semen.

67. **In human males, the testes lie in the scrotum, because it helps in the** [NCERT Exemplar]
    (a) process of mating
    (b) formation of sperm
    (c) easy transfer of gametes
    (d) all of the above

Ans. (b) formation of sperm

Explanation :

Formation of germ cells or sperms takes place in the testes and it lies in the scrotum. In the scrotum (outside the abdominal cavity), the temperature is about 3°C lower than the temperature of the body. Testes lie in scrotum because the sperm formation requires a lower temperature than the normal body temperature.

68. **Which among the following is not function of tests at puberty?** [NCERT Exemplar]
    (i) Formation of germ cells
    (ii) Secretion of testosterone
    (iii) Development of placenta
    (iv) Secretion of estrogen
    (a) (i) and (ii)   (b) (ii) and (iii)
    (c) (iii) and (iv)   (d) (i) and (iv)

Ans. (c) (iii) and (iv)

Explanation :

Development of placenta and secretion of estrogen are related to female reproductive system, hence are not the function of testes at puberty.

69. **The correct sequence of organs in the male reproductive system for transport of sperms is** [NCERT Exemplar]
    (a) testis → vas deferens → urethra
    (b) testis → ureter → urethra
    (c) testis → urethra → ureter
    (d) testis → vas deferens → ureter

Ans. (a) testis → vas deferens → urethra

Explanation :

Sperms formed in testis are delivered through the vas deferens which joins with another tube called urethra coming from the urinary bladder.

70. **What do seminal vesicles add into the semen?**
    (a) Proteins   (b) Sugar Fructose
    (c) Sperm   (d) Both (a) and (b)

Ans. (d) Both (a) and (b)

Explanation :

The fluid from the seminal vesicles is viscous and contains fructose, which provides energy to the sperm; prostaglandins, which aids in sperm movement and viability; and proteins, which produce minor coagulation reactions in the semen following ejaculation.

71. **Which of the functions are performed by the ovaries?**
    (a) Formation of ovum
    (b) Secretion of Progesterone
    (c) Secretion of Estrogen
    (d) All of the above

Ans. (d) All of the above

Explanation :

In the female body, the ovaries perform two main reproductive functions. They produce the reproductive hormones estrogen and progesterone. They also produce ovum (eggs) for fertilisation.

72. **Which of the following statements are incorrect?**
    (a) The umbilical cord is the conduit between the foetus and the placenta.
    (b) The placenta can exchange materials between the foetus and the mother.
    (c) Antibodies cannot reach the foetus through the mother's placenta.
    (d) All of the above.

Ans. (c) Antibodies cannot reach the foetus through the mother's placenta

Explanation :

The transfer of maternal IgG antibodies to the foetus through the placenta is an important method that protects the infant when his or her humoral reaction is ineffective. The only antibody class that crosses the human placenta in a considerable amount is IgG.

73. **Which of the following is not a part of the female reproductive system in human beings?** [NCERT]
    (a) Ovary   (b) Uterus
    (c) Vas deferens   (d) Fallopian tube

Ans. (c) Vas deferens

Explanation :

The ovaries, fallopian tubes, uterus, vagina, and external genitals make up the female reproductive system. Vas deferens is a male reproductive organ that connects the epididymis to the urethra and transports sperm from the testis to the urethra.

74. **Offspring formed as a result of sexual reproduction exhibit more variations because:**
    [NCERT Exemplar]
    (a) sexual reproduction is a lengthy process.
    (b) genetic material comes from two parents of the same species.
    (c) genetic material comes from two parents of different species.
    (d) genetic material comes from many parents.

Ans. (b) genetic material comes from two parents of the same species.

Explanation :

Sexual reproduction is a process in which two individuals of the same species collaborate to produce two distinct gametes, one male and one female. The fusion of gametes results in the mixing of genetic material, resulting in the formation of a diploid cell with new combinations.

75. **In human females an event that reflects onset of reproductive phase is :**
    (a) growth of body
    (b) change in voice
    (c) changes in hair pattern
    (d) menstruation

Ans. (d) menstruation

Explanation :

Menstruation is an event that occurs in human females and signals the start of the reproductive phase. The endometrial lining and the unfertilised egg are discharged through the vaginal canal during this phase, which lasts about 5-7 days.

76. **Which of the following is considered a barrier form of contraception?**
    (a) Vasectomy   (b) Femidom
    (c) Copper T   (d) Silver T

Ans. (b) Femidom

Explanation :

Femidom, often known as a female condom, is a device that inhibits pregnancy by forming a barrier between sperm and ovum during sexual intercourse.

77. **Which of the following sexually transmitted diseases is caused by a virus?**
    (a) Syphilis   (b) Chlamydia
    (c) Hepatitis B   (d) Cholera

Ans. (c) Hepatitis B

Explanation :

Infected blood, semen, and vaginal secretions contain the hepatitis B virus. It is a sexually transmitted infection (STI) that spreads through unprotected sexual contact and also by contaminated needles and syringes.

78. **Which of the following is another barrier method of contraception?**
    (a) Diaphragm   (b) Withdrawal
    (c) Sterilisation (d) All of these

Ans. (a) Diaphragm

Explanation :

Barrier methods of birth control prevent sperm to reach the egg to prevent pregnancy. Condoms, diaphragms, cervical caps, and the contraceptive sponge are examples of barrier techniques.

79. **Which of the following sterilisation methods is permanent?**
    (a) Vasectomy   (b) Tubal Sterilisation
    (c) IUD   (d) Both (a) and (b)

Ans. (d) Both (a) and (b)

Explanation :

Female sterilisation via tubal ligation, commonly known as "tied tubes," transcervical sterilisation, and male sterilisation or vasectomy are the three types of permanent birth control.

80. **Which among the following diseases is not sexually transmitted ?**   [NCERT Exemplar]
    (a) HIV-AIDS   (b) Hepatitis
    (c) Syphilis   (d) Gonorrhoea

Ans. (b) Hepatitis

Explanation :

Hepatitis is a virus-induced inflammation of the liver that spreads through the person's body fluids, blood, and other bodily fluids. Syphilis and Gonorrhea are sexually transmitted bacterial diseases. AIDS is a sexually transmitted viral disease caused by HIV.

81. **During adolescence several changes occur in the human body. Mark one change associated with sexual maturity in boys.**
    [NCERT & NCERT Exemplar]
    (a) Loss of milk teeth (b) Increase in height
    (c) Weight gain   (d) Cracking of voice

Ans. (d) Cracking of voice

Explanation :

Cracking of voice is associated with sexual maturity in boys which occurs during adolescence. Loss of milk teeth, height gain, and weight gain are all part of the natural growing process for both boys and girls as they become older.

Assertion and Reasoning Based Questions

82. **Assertion:** Non flowering plants cannot reproduce sexually.

    Reason: Flower is only reproductive part of the plant that can produce gametes.

    (a) If both assertion and reason are true and reason is the correct explanation of assertion.
    (b) If both assertion and reason are true, but reason is not the correct explanation of assertion.
    (c) If assertion is true, but reason is false.
    (d) If assertion is false, but reason is true.

    Ans. (a) If both assertion and reason are true and reason is the correct explanation of assertion.

    Explanation :

    Gametes are mandatory for sexual reproduction. Though plants can reproduce through other parts like stem and roots (vegetative reproduction), but they cannot reproduce sexually in absence of flowers. Thus, both assertion and reason are true and reason is the correct explanation of the assertion.

83. **Assertion:** Meiosis takes place only in gametes.

    Reason: To restore the total number of chromosomes in offspring.

    (a) If both assertion and reason are true and reason is the correct explanation of assertion.
    (b) If both assertion and reason are true, but reason is not the correct explanation of assertion.
    (c) If assertion is true, but reason is false.
    (d) If assertion is false, but reason is true.

    Ans. (a) If both assertion and reason are true and reason is the correct explanation of assertion.

    Explanation :

    Both the sperm and ovum have 23 pairs of chromosomes, so when the zygote is formed after their fusion it forms 46 chromosomes in the zygote, and hence the number of chromosome is restored in the offspring. Thus, both assertion and reason are true and reason is the correct explanation of the assertion.

84. **Assertion:** The flower of papaya is called unisexual flower.

    Reason: The flower contains stamens only as a sex organ.

    (a) If both assertion and reason are true and reason is the correct explanation of assertion.
    (b) If both assertion and reason are true, but reason is not the correct explanation of assertion.
    (c) If assertion is true, but reason is false.
    (d) If assertion is false, but reason is true.

    Ans. (c) If assertion is true, but reason is false.

    Explanation :

    Unisexual flowers are those which can have either stamen or carpels as sex organ. It is not true that it has only stamen in it. It can have only carpel also, so either of these will describe a unisexual flower. Thus, assertion is true but reason is false.

85. **Assertion:** Plants raised by vegetative propagation can bear flower and seed earlier than those produced from seeds.

    Reason: Plants which have lost the capacity to bear viable seeds, can propagate through vegetative propagation.

    Ans. (b) If both assertion and reason are true, but reason is not the correct explanation of assertion.

    Explanation :

    The plant which are unable to produce seed reproduce by the means of vegetative propagation. This process is a type of asexual reproduction which is much faster than sexual reproduction. Thus both assertion and reason are true, but reason is not the correct explanation of assertion.

86. **Assertion:** XX chromosome give rise to female child whereas XY give rise to male child.

    Reason: The Y chromosome in males is smaller than X chromosome.

    (a) If both assertion and reason are true and reason is the correct explanation of assertion.
    (b) If both assertion and reason are true, but reason is not the correct explanation of assertion.
    (c) If assertion is true, but reason is false.
    (d) If assertion is false, but reason is true.

    Ans. (b) If both assertion and reason are true, but reason is not the correct explanation of assertion.

    Explanation :

    Smaller Y chromosome, does not decide the gender of the child. Its presence is important not the size. Thus, both assertion and reason are true but reason is not the correct explanation of the assertion.

87. **Assertion:** Lumen of fallopian tube is lined by ciliated epithelium.

    Reason: Ciliated epithelium helps in moving the zygote towards the uterus for implantation.

    (a) If both assertion and reason are true and reason is the correct explanation of assertion.
    (b) If both assertion and reason are true, but reason is not the correct explanation of assertion.
    (c) If assertion is true, but reason is false.
    (d) If assertion is false, but reason is true.

Ans. (a) If both assertion and reason are true and reason is the correct explanation of assertion.

Explanation :

Lumen of Fallopian tube is lined by ciliated epithelium as
Cilia have a rhythmic waving and beating motion that helps substances to travel from one place to another. Thus, both assertion and reason are true and reason is the correct explanation of the assertion.

88. **Assertion:** Placenta is connected to the embryo through an umbilical cord which helps in the transport of substances to and from the embryo.

    Reason: Placenta acts as an endocrine tissue.
    (a) If both assertion and reason are true and reason is the correct explanation of assertion.
    (b) If both assertion and reason are true, but reason is not the correct explanation of assertion.
    (c) If assertion is true, but reason is false.
    (d) If assertion is false, but reason is true.

Ans. (b) If both assertion and reason are true, but reason is not the correct explanation of assertion.

Explanation :

Placenta performs both the given functions. But they are not related to each other. Being an endocrine tissue it releases hormones like progesterone, estrogen and others, but does not help in transport of materials to and from the embryo. Thus, both assertion and reason are true but reason is not the correct explanation of the assertion.

89. **Assertion:** High chances of fertilisation is during the mid of the menstrual cycle.

    Reason: Sperms are very active during that time.
    (a) If both assertion and reason are true and reason is the correct explanation of assertion.
    (b) If both assertion and reason are true, but reason is not the correct explanation of assertion.
    (c) If assertion is true, but reason is false.
    (d) If assertion is false, but reason is true.

Ans. (c) If assertion is true, but reason is false.

Explanation :

Ovulation takes place on the 14th day of the menstrual cycle, so if the sperm happens to meet the ovum during that phase fertilisation will take place. Thus, assertion is true but reason is false.

90. **Assertion:** The testes descend into the scrotum just before birth.

    Reason: Human males have 2 testes in the body.
    (a) If both assertion and reason are true and reason is the correct explanation of assertion.
    (b) If both assertion and reason are true, but reason is not the correct explanation of assertion.
    (c) If assertion is true, but reason is false.
    (d) If assertion is false, but reason is true.

Ans. (b) If both assertion and reason are true, but reason is not the correct explanation of assertion.

Explanation :

Human males have 2 testes and the testes descend into the scrotum just before the birth for the movement of the foetus in the canal. Thus, both assertion and reason are true but reason is not the correct explanation of the assertion.

91. **Assertion:** Copper-T can be used as a contraceptive method.

    Reason: It prevents from sexually transmitted disease.
    (a) If both assertion and reason are true and reason is the correct explanation of assertion.
    (b) If both assertion and reason are true, but reason is not the correct explanation of assertion.
    (c) If assertion is true, but reason is false.
    (d) If assertion is false, but reason is true.

Ans. (c) If assertion is true, but reason is false.

Explanation :

Copper-T is a contraceptive method, which is inserted inside the uterus, it prevents implantation. It does not prevent sexually transmitted disease. Thus, assertion is true but reason is false.

92. **Assertion:** Male is responsible for the sex determination in humans.

    Reason: It has similar kind of chromosomes XX.
    (a) If both assertion and reason are true and reason is the correct explanation of assertion.
    (b) If both assertion and reason are true, but reason is not the correct explanation of assertion.
    (c) If assertion is true, but reason is false.
    (d) If assertion is false, but reason is true.

Ans. (c) If assertion is true, but reason is false.

Explanation :

Male is responsible for the sex determination in humans because it has different kinds of chromosomes namely XY. A child which inherits X chromosome from his father will be a girl and the one who inherits Y chromosome will be a boy. Thus, assertion is true but reason is false.

93. **Assertion:** Ovary releases one egg every month.

    Reason: The lining of uterus is always thick and spongy.

Ans. (c) If assertion is true, but reason is false.

Explanation :

The thick and spongy lining of the uterus, the endometrium, is developed during each menstrual cycle after ovulation. The endometrium serves as an anchorage for the developing foetus. Thus assertion is true, but reason is False.

94. **Assertion:** HIV/AIDS is a viral disease.

    Reason: HIV infection is spread by sexual contact with an infected person.

Ans. (b) If both assertion and reason are true, but reason is not the correct explanation of assertion.

Explanation :

HIV infection is caused by the human immunodeficiency virus. One can get HIV from contact with infected blood, semen, or vaginal fluids. Most people get the virus by having unprotected sex with someone who has HIV. Another common way of getting it is by sharing drug needles with someone who is infected with HIV. Thus both assertion and reason are true, but reason is not the correct explanation of assertion.

95. **Assertion:** Pollen grains reaches directly to the egg, which is seated deep in the ovarian cavity.

    Reason: To effect fertilization, the pollen grains germinate on the stigma.

Ans. (d) If assertion is false, but reason is true.

Explanation :

In angiosperms the female gametophyte is seated deep in the ovarian cavity, quite away from the stigma. The stigma. In seed plants the male gametes are brought to the egg containing female gametophyte by a pollen tube. A pollen grain does not pass down the stigma. Only its pollen tube does so. Thus assertion is false, but reason is true.

96. **Assertion:** In male reproductive system, transport of sperm takes place in a fluid which also provide nutrition.

    Reason: Prostate glands and seminal vesicles secrete their secretions

Ans. (a) If both assertion and reason are true and reason is the correct explanation of assertion.

Explanation :

Semen (seminal fluid) contains the sperm cells as well as the seminal plasma. The seminal plasma is the secretion from the tubules of the seminal tract (seminal vesicles, etc) and from the seminiferous tubules in the testicles. It nourishes the sperm cells from ejaculation up to fertilization. The vas deferens joins the ends of the seminal vesicles to form the ejaculatory ducts. Thus both assertion and reason are true and reason is the correct explanation of assertion.

Case Based Questions

97. **Read the passage carefully and answer the following questions from Q. 97 (i) to 97 (v).**

    Reproduction is a biological process by which new individual organisms are produced. Reproduction is a fundamental feature of all life forms; each individual exists due to the process of reproduction. Reproduction is the mechanism of species continuation. Mechanism and process of reproduction varies for different species in this world.

    (i) Which of the following statement is not true about reproduction?
    - (a) Organisms create exact copies of themselves.
    - (b) Creation of a DNA copy is a basic event in reproduction.
    - (c) Simply breaking up into smaller pieces upon maturation is also a method of reproduction.
    - (d) Cell division in unicellular organisms is the method of reproduction.

    (ii) The ability of cell to divide into several cells during reproduction in plasmodium is called _____.
    - (a) budding
    - (b) reproductive division
    - (c) multiple fission
    - (d) binary fission

    (iii) Vegetative propagation is a type of:
    - (a) farming
    - (b) reproduction
    - (c) cooking
    - (d) movement control

    (iv) Organisms in which reproduction is a function of a specific cell type are:
    - (a) multicellular organisms
    - (b) amoeba
    - (c) unicellular organisms
    - (d) bacteria

    (v) Which one of the following is not a method of reproduction?
    - (a) Regeneration
    - (b) Budding
    - (c) Spore formation
    - (d) Vegetation

Ans. (i) (a) Organisms create exact copies of themselves.
(ii) (c) multiple fission
(iii) (b) reproduction
(iv) (a) multicellular organisms
(v) (d) Vegetation

98. **Read the passage carefully and answer the following questions from Q 98 (i) to 98 (v).**

    Asexual reproduction, in which offspring arise from a single organism, occurs in a variety of prokaryotes and eukaryotes including plants, fungi, and animals. It may have some advantages over the sexual reproduction, in which individuals of two genders, females and males, must be involved but only females can give birth to new individuals. There are several different methods of asexual reproduction. Asexual reproduction can be very rapid. This is an advantage for many organisms. It allows them to crowd out other organisms that reproduce more slowly.

(i) Budding is a mode of asexual reproduction in:
  (a) amoeba (b) plasmodium
  (c) yeast (d) leishmania

(ii) The specific reproductive part in Rhizopus responsible for reproduction is:
  (a) sporadic (b) stick
  (c) hyphae (d) sporangia

(iii) Buds produced in the notches along the leaf margin of Bryophyllum fall on the soil and develop into new plants. This is an example of:
  (a) vegetation
  (b) vegetative propagation
  (c) sexual reproduction
  (d) clone formation

(iv) *Hydra* and *Planaria* can be cut into any number of pieces and each piece grows into a complete organism. This is known as:
  (a) regeneration (b) budding
  (c) fragmentation (d) speciation

(v) In amoeba the splitting of the two cells during division can take place in _____ plane.
  (a) single (b) perpendicular
  (c) directional (d) any

Ans. (i) (c) yeast
(ii) (d) sporangia
(iii) (b) vegetative propagation
(iv) (a) regeneration
(v) (d) any

99. Read the passage carefully and answer the following questions from Q 99 (i) to 99 (v).

Sexual reproduction is the most common method of reproduction in animals and plants. One male and one female parent are involved in the process of sexual reproduction. Sexual reproduction involves fusion of two types of reproductive cells known as gametes to form a single cell called zygote. The zygote multiplies repeatedly and undergoes specific changes to form a new individual.

(i) What is the source of variations in populations of organisms?
  (a) DNA copying is error free
  (b) DNA copying is not error free
  (c) Protein formation
  (d) Involvement of only one parent

(ii) The reproductive parts of angiosperms are located in the:
  (a) fruit (b) flower
  (c) pistil (d) stigma

(iii) _____ is the male reproductive part in a plant and it produces pollen grains that are yellowish in colour.
  (a) Stamen (b) Pistil
  (c) Carpel (d) Petal

(iv) In plants, after fertilisation, the zygote divides several times to form an embryo within the ovule. The ovule develops a tough coat and is converted gradually into a:
  (a) bud (b) seed
  (c) fruit (d) plant

(v) As the rate of general body growth begins to slow down, reproductive tissues begin to mature. This period during adolescence is known as:
  (a) puberty (b) adulthood
  (c) germination (d) reproduction

Ans. (i) (b) DNA copying is not error free.
(ii) (b) flower
(iii) (a) Stamen
(iv) (b) seed
(v) (a) puberty

100. Read the passage carefully and answer the following questions from Q 100 (i) to 100 (v).

Sexual reproduction is a method to give rise to one's progeny. In higher animals, male and female gametes are produced by different individuals to carry out sexual reproduction. Such individuals are said to be unisexual. However, in some animals like flatworm, earthworm, leech, and hydra both male and female gametes are produced by the same individual. Such organisms are said to be hermaphrodites or bisexual. Male and female gametes fertilise to form a zygote that has trail of characters from both the parents.

(i) Where does fertilisation occur in human females?
  (a) Cervix (b) Vagina
  (c) Uterus (d) Oviduct

(ii) The offspring formed by sexual reproduction exhibit more variations because _____.
  (a) sexual reproduction is a lengthy process
  (b) genetic material comes from two parents of same species
  (c) genetic material comes from two parents of different species
  (d) genetic material comes only from one parent

(iii) Why are pollens spiny?
  (a) Help in Fertilisation
  (b) For easy pollination

(c) To attach to bodies of insects
(d) Appearance
(iv) What is the principle of natural contraceptive methods?
(a) Avoiding sperm and ovum to meet
(b) Avoiding release of egg
(c) Avoiding release of sperm
(d) Abortion when pregnant
(v) The number of chromosomes present in parents and offspring of a particular species remains constant due to _____.
(a) doubling of chromosomes during zygote formation
(b) halving of chromosomes during gamete formation
(c) doubling of chromosomes after gamete formation
(d) halving of chromosomes after gamete formation

Ans. (i) (d) Oviduct
(ii) (b) genetic material comes from two parents of same species.
(iii) (c) To attach to bodies of insects
(iv) (a) Avoiding sperm and ovum to meet
(v) (b) halving of chromosomes during gamete formation

101. The below given picture shows a few methods of contraception and avoiding sexually transmitted diseases in humans. See the picture carefully and answer the following questions from Q 101 (i) to 101 (v).

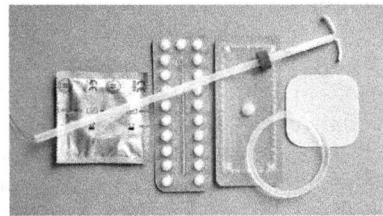

(i) Which one out of the below given terms is STD?
(a) Kala azar (b) Jaundice
(c) Pyorrhea (d) Syphilis
(ii) IUCD is used for:
(a) Vegetative propagation
(b) Prevent miscarriage
(c) Contraception
(d) In vitro fertilisation
(iii) Use of condom for contraception is a:
(a) mechanical method
(b) surgical method
(c) hormonal method
(d) chemical method
(iv) The best way to avoid sexually transmitted diseases is by use of:
(a) a condom (b) medicine
(c) chemical (d) IV injection
(v) Which one of the following statements is not true?
(a) Prenatal sex determination has been prohibited by law in India.
(b) Illegal sex-selective abortion of female foetus in India is the prime reason for unbalanced male to female sex ratio.
(c) Contraceptive pills change hormonal balance in a female body.
(d) Mechanical barriers for contraception is available only for males.

Ans. (i) (d) syphilis
(ii) (c) contraception
(iii) (a) mechanical method
(iv) (a) a condom
(v) (d) Mechanical barriers for contraception is available only for males.

Reasoning Based Questions

102. Why is vegetative propagation practiced for growing some types of plants? **[NCERT]**

Ans. Vegetative propagation is practiced for growing some types of plants because:
(a) The plants which cannot produce seeds or produce non-viable seeds also can be easily propagated by this method.
(b) It is a very easy, quick and cheapest method of propagation.
(c) Seedless plants can be produced by vegetative propagation.
(d) Flowers and fruits are produced in very short time.
(e) Parental features are preserved.

103. Explain why fertilisation is possible if mating takes place during the middle of menstrual cycle?

Ans. Mostly in an healthy woman ovulation occurs on 14th day of 28 days menstrual cycle which is the middle day of the cycle hence if mating occurs in the middle of cycle there is maximum chance of fertilisation.

104. Why does menstruation occur in human females? **[NCERT]**

Ans. Menstruation occurs in human females when egg is not fertilised. Every month the ovary releases an egg and uterus prepares itself to receive the embryo. The wall of uterus gets thickened and they are richly supplied with blood which provides nutrition to the growing embryo from mother. If egg is not fertilised then there is no need of rich supply of blood and thick lining of uterine wall and egg also disintegrates thus egg along with blood andmucus comes out through vagina in the form of menstrual flow.

Very Short Answer Type Questions

105. Name the life process of an organism that helps in the growth of its population.*

Ans. Reproduction.

106. Where is DNA found in cell?

Ans. DNA is found inside the nucleus in a cell.

107. What is termed as the blue print of life and why?

Ans. DNA is termed as the blue print of life because it carries all the information for the organisms to grow, survive and reproduce. Proteins which are the structural and functional unit of cells are synthesized according to the information stored in DNA.

108. Can you consider cell division as a type of reproduction in unicellular organisms? Justify.

Ans. Yes, cell division can be considered as a type of reproduction in unicellular organisms because through cell division two or more daughter cells are produced from a parent cell.

109. What is the end product of double fertilisation?

Ans. In double fertilisation one of the male gametes fuse with egg cell to form a zygote whereas the other male gamete fuses with two polar nuclei to form primary endosperm that provides nourishment to the growing embryo.

110. Name the plant that reproduces vegetatively by leaf?

Ans. Bryophyllum reproduces vegetatively by leaf.

111. Name the method by which Hydra reproduces? Is this method sexual or asexual?

Ans. Hydra can reproduce by budding and regeneration. Both are asexual method, of reproduction.

112. In a bisexual flower inspite of the young stamens being removed artificially the flower produces fruit. Provide a suitable explanation for the above situation.

Ans. Though the stamens are removed but pistils are present so cross pollination might have taken place which leads to fertilisation and finally to the formation of fruits.

113. Is the chromosome number of zygote, embryonal cells and adult of a particular organism always constant? How is the constancy maintained in these three stages?

Ans. Yes, the chromosome number of zygote, embryonal cells and adult of a particular organism is always constant. This is because zygote is diploid and it undergoes mitotic divisions to form embryonal cells and finally adult and during mitosis the chromosome number remains constant.

114. Where is the zygote located in the flower after fertilisation?

Ans. Zygote is located inside the ovule which is present in the ovary part of the pistil.

115. What is a clone? Why do offsprings formed by asexual reproduction exhibit remarkable similarity?

Ans. Clone is an exact replica of an organism produced as a result of asexual reproduction. Since all the offsprings formed by asexual reproduction have exact copies of DNA of their parent so they exhibit remarkable similarity.

116. Name the method by which spirogyra reproduces under favourable conditions. Is this method sexual or asexual?

Ans. Spirogyra reproduces under favourable conditions by fragmentation which is an asexual mode of reproduction.

117. Name the types of asexual reproduction in which two individuals are formed from a single parent and the parental identity is lost. Write the first step from where such a type of reproduction begins.*

Ans. Binary fission is a type of asexual reproduction in which two individuals are formed from a single parent and the parental identity is lost. The reproduction starts from Karyokinesis i.e., division of nucleus.

118. How does Planaria reproduce? Is this method sexual or asexual?*

Ans. Planaria reproduces by regeneration process. This method is an asexual mode of reproduction. In this process, if Planaria is cut into many pieces each piece grows into a new Planaria.

119. State the method of growing rose plant and jasmine plant ?

Ans. Vegetative propagation like cutting is used to grow rose plant and layering method is used to grow jasmine plant.

120. Name a tiny fresh water animal which reproduces by the same method as that of yeast ? What is this method known as ?

Ans. Hydra is a tiny fresh water animal which reproduces by the same method as that of yeast and this method is known as budding.

* are board exam questions from previous years

121. Name the causative agent of the disease kala-azar and its mode of asexual reproduction.

Ans. Leishmania causes kala-azar and its mode of asexual reproduction is binary fission.

122. Name a unisexual and a bisexual flower.

Ans. Watermelon is an unisexual flower whereas Hibiscus is a bisexual flower.

123. What are those organisms called which bear both the sex organs in the same individual? Give one example of such organism.

Ans. Organisms having both the sex organs in the same individual are called Hermaphrodite. E.g., Earthworm.

124. Explain the vegetative reproduction in Bryophyllum.

Ans. Bryophyllum has a special case of vegetative propagation. The buds are generated from the margins of the leaves. These buds grow up to be new saplings on the leaf itself and fall off to the ground to be rooted and matured. These buds are formed from mitosis of meristematic type tissues in the phylloclade of the plant. They are called epiphyllous buds since they are present on top of the leaves. Buds in Bryophyllum are known as epiphyllous buds.

125. Name the agents which bring about cross pollination.

Ans. Insects, wind, water, animals etc., are the agents which bring about cross pollination.

126. Name the method by which Hydra reproduces? Is this method sexual or asexual?

Ans. Hydra can reproduce by budding and regeneration. Both are asexual method.

127. How many gametes are produced after germination of angiosphermous pollen grains over the stigma of carpel?

Ans. Two male gametes are produced after germination of angiosphermous pollen grains over the stigma of carpel.

128. An organism which is a worm has very simple eyes, that are really eye spots which detect light. Name the organism.

Ans. Planaria.

129. List two functions performed by testes in human beings.

Ans. In human testes, sperms are produced by the process of spermatogenesis and interstitial cells present in testes produce the male hormone testosterone.

130. Explain the roles of gamete and zygote in sexual reproduction?

Ans. Gametes play an important role in sexual reproduction because fusion of male and female gametes lead to formation of a zygote. Zygote formed as a result of fertilisation develops into embryo and finally into a new individual.

131. List two functions of ovary of human female reproductive system?

Ans. Ovaries produces the ova or eggs and they produce hormones like oestrogen and progesterone. Oestrogen helps in development of secondary sexual characters in females at the time of puberty whereas progesterone prepares the uterus for receiving the fertilised egg.

132. Name the largest cell present in the human body.

Ans. Ovum is the largest cell present in the, human body.

133. What is the significance of testes being located in scrotal sacs outside abdomen?

Ans. The formation of sperms requires a temperature of 2°C–3°C lower than body temperature. So testes are located in a sac like structures called scrotum outside the abdomen.

134. What is the effect of DNA copying which is not perfectly accurate in the reproduction process?

Ans. If DNA copying is not perfectly accurate in the reproduction process it would lead to variations in the populations which may prove a better survival option to the species.

135. If a woman is using copper-T, will it help her in protecting from sexually transmitted diseases?

Ans. No, copper-T will not help her in protecting from sexually transmitted diseases. It only prevents the implantation of embryo inside uterus.

136. What would be the ratio of chromosome number between an egg and its zygote? How is the sperm genetically different from the egg?

Ans. The ratio of chromosome number between an egg and its zygote is 1 : 2. Sperms are of two types 50% of sperms have X chromosome and rest 50% Y chromosomes. But eggs have only one type of chromosome i.e., X chromosome.

137. How does the chemical method help in preventing pregnancy?

Ans. Chemical methods prevent the ovaries from releasing the egg hence no fertilisation can occur thus preventing pregnancy.

138. Expand: (a) IUCD (b) STDs.

Ans. (a) **IUCD:** Intra Uterine Contraceptive Devices.

(b) **STDs:** Sexually Transmitted Diseases.

139. What are the benefits of using mechanical barriers during sexual act?

Ans. Mechanical barriers like condoms prevent unwanted pregnancies and transmission of sexually transmitted diseases like AIDS, syphilis etc.

Short Answer Type Questions

140. Why is variation beneficial to the species but not necessary for the individual? [NCERT]

Ans. Due to recombination and crossing over in meiosis process during formation of gametes as well as during sexual reproduction the mixing up of male with female gametes produce some variations in the offsprings. These variations are necessary for survival of a particular species to the changing environment. If there would be no variations then there will be less chance of a particular species to get adapted to the changed environment and with course of time that particular species may extinct. Variations also lead to evolution of the species. Thus it is said that variation is beneficial to the species but not necessary for the individual.

141. How will an organism be benefited if it reproduces through spores? [NCERT]

Ans. An organism can be benefited if it reproduces through spores by following ways:
 (a) Spores are covered with thick walls which protect them from adverse environmental conditions like drought, high temperature etc. So, they can survive even in these conditions.
 (b) They are very light, small and can be easily dispersed through wind, water, animals and on getting favourable conditions they germinate and give rise to new individuals.
 (c) This mode of reproduction is simple and faster.
 (d) Large numbers of spores are produced at one time within a sporangium.

142. What is the importance of DNA copying in reproduction? [NCERT]

Ans. DNA copying is necessary as parents transmit their characters to offsprings through DNA. Due to this, the offsprings resemble in some of the features with their parents. But DNA copying also produces some variations in the offsprings that helps them to adapt to the changing environment.

143. Can you think of reasons why more complex organisms cannot give rise to new individuals through regeneration? [NCERT]

Ans. Complex organisms have highly and well developed tissue and organ system to perform a particular function. There is division of labour in the body of complex organisms. Their body is highly complicated and the tissue and organ system are highly differentiated and are made up of different kinds of cells. So, it is very difficult for complex organisms to give rise to new individuals through regeneration, which is seen in simple organisms like Hydra, Planaria etc.

144. Distinguish between pollination and fertilisation. Mention the site and the product of fertilisation in a flower.

Ans. (a) The transfer of pollen grains from anther of a stamen to the stigma of a carpel is called pollination whereas fertilisation is the process when the male gamete present in pollen grain joins the female gamete present in ovule.
 (b) Pollination is an external mechanism whereas fertilisation is an internal mechanism which takes place inside the flower.
 (c) Site of fertilization in flower is ovary. Product of fertilization in flower is Zygote.

145. How are the methods of reproduction different in unicellular and multicellular organisms? [NCERT]

Ans. An unicellular organism has a single cell so there is no specific organ system for reproduction. They divide by the process of cell division. The different modes of reproduction in unicellular organism are binary fission, multiple fission, budding etc. But in multicellular organism there are specific tissues and organ system to carry out this process. There is formation of male and female gametes. It is a very complex process and normally takes more time as compared in unicellular organisms.

146. How does reproduction help in providing stability to population of species? [NCERT]

Ans. There is a natural cycle of born and death, through reproduction the lost species can be replenished. Stability of a particular species is maintained by equalizing birth and death ratios which is possible through reproduction. It ensures the survival of a particular species which might extinct if there is no reproduction process.

147. How is the process of binary fission different in Amoeba and Leishmania?

Ans. In amoeba, the process of binary fission occurs in any plane but in Leishmania binary fission occurs in a definite orientation. Leishmania has a whip like structure at one end of the cell. The division occurs longitudinally in relation to this whip like structure.

148. Fallen leaves of Bryophyllum on the ground produce new plants whereas the leaves of rose do not. Explain this difference between the two plants?

Ans. In Bryophyllum new plants develop from the adventitious buds on their leaves through vegetative propagation but buds do not develop from the leaves of rose plants hence new plants cannot grow from the fallen leaves of rose plant.

149. Answer the following:
 (i) With the help of a diagram demonstrate the process of regeneration as seen in Planaria?

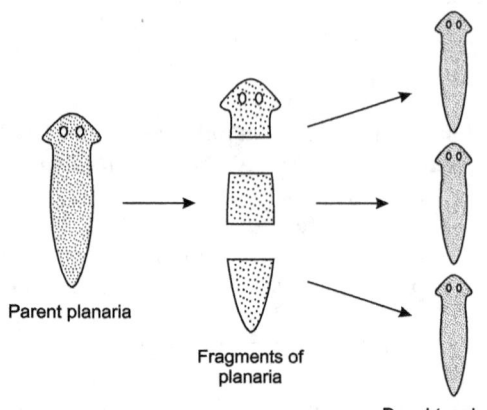

Parent planaria

Fragments of planaria

Daughter planaria

(ii) Which type of cells are used by such multicellular organisms to regenerate?

Ans. (i) Regeneration is the process by which an organism has an ability to regenerate its lost parts of the body which might have been removed by injury or by some other methods. When Planaria is cut into many pieces, each piece grows into a complete organism. Regeneration is carried out by specialised cells which have the capacity to develop, proliferate and differentiate into various cell types and tissues.

(ii) A single pluripotent adult stem cell type (neoblasts) is used by such multicellular organisms to regenerate.

150. **What are the advantages of vegetative propagation?**

Ans. Some advantages of vegetative propagation are:
(a) It is cheaper, easier and rapid method.
(b) The plants which cannot produce seeds also can be easily propagated by this method.
(c) The plants produced by this method bear fruits and flowers earlier.
(d) It produces new individuals with exactly identical qualities as the parent, which preserves the parental characteristics.

151. **Answer the following:**
(i) Name the structures where spores are formed? Give the terms used for non-flagellated, non-motile spores and flagellated, motile spores?
(ii) Give one example of plant where modified tuberous roots can be propagated vegetatively when planted in soil?

Ans. (i) Spores are formed in sporangia. Non-flagellated, non-motile spores are called aplanospores and flagellated, motile spores are called zoospores.
(ii) Sweet potato is an example of plant where modified tuberous roots can be propagated vegetatively when planted in soil.

152. **When a cell reproduces what happens to its DNA?***

Ans. During the process of reproduction DNA is transmitted from parents to offspring. But DNA is replicated before reproduction i.e., two copies of DNA are produced. During the time of cell division the two copies of DNA are equally distributed between the two daughter cells. Each daughter cell receives same type and amount of DNA from parent cell. Thus, the consistency in type and amount of DNA is maintained in the particular species of a living organism.

153. **Newly formed DNA copies may not be identical at times. Give one reason.***

Ans. During the time of DNA replication most of the base sequence in daughter cells is identical to the parent DNA but sometimes due to mutations or some errors during replication some changes in the newly formed DNA copies may occur. So, it is said that newly formed DNA copies may not be identical at times.

154. **List the two types of reproduction. Which one of the two is responsible for bringing in more variations in its progeny and how?***

Ans. There are two types of reproduction- sexual and asexual. Sexual reproduction is responsible for bringing in more variations in its progeny as it involves fusion of male and female gametes from two different organisms which leads to more diversity of characters in offsprings. Gametes are formed by meiosis process which brings new combinations of genes due to crossing over and homologous recombination. Due to all these factors sexual reproduction is responsible for bringing in more variations in its progeny.

155. **Students were asked to observe the permanent slides showing different stages of budding in yeast under high power of a microscope.***
(i) Which adjustment screw were you asked to move to focus the slides?
(ii) Draw diagrams in correct sequence to show budding in yeast.

Ans. (i) Fine adjustment screws were moved to focus the slides.
(ii)

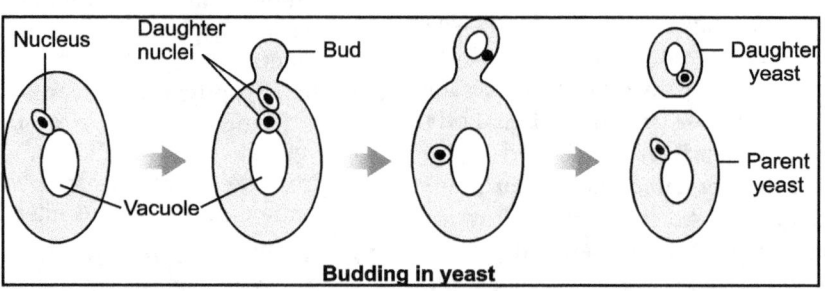

Budding in yeast

---
* are board exam questions from previous years

156. **Write one main difference between asexual and sexual mode of reproduction. Which species is likely to have comparatively better chances of survival–the one reproducing asexually or the one reproducing sexually? Give reasons to justify your answer.**

Ans. Asexual reproduction involves only one parent and the offsprings produced are clone and similar copies of their parents where as sexual reproduction involves two parents and the offsprings produced are different from their parents. Offsprings produced by sexual reproduction have better chances of survival.

Sexual reproduction leads to variation because it leads to the formation of offspring by the combination of DNA from both the parents, so the species will have better adaptability and better survival rate.

157. **What is carpel? Write the function of its various parts.***

Ans. The flask-shaped organ in the centre of a flower is called carpel. It is also called as female reproductive organ of the plant.

It is made up of three parts:
1. Stigma
2. Style
3. Ovary

(a) Stigma is the top part of carpel and is sticky. So, it receives the pollen from the anther of stamen.
(b) Style connects stigma to ovary.
(c) Ovary contains female gametes of the plant and helps in reproduction.

158. **Answer the following questions:**
   (i) Budding, fragmentation and regeneration, all are considered as asexual mode of reproduction. Why?
   (ii) With the help of neat diagrams, explain the process of regeneration in Planaria.

Ans. (i) Budding, fragmentation and regeneration are considered as asexual mode of reproduction because only one parent is involved no sex cells are involved.
   (ii) Regeneration in planaria.

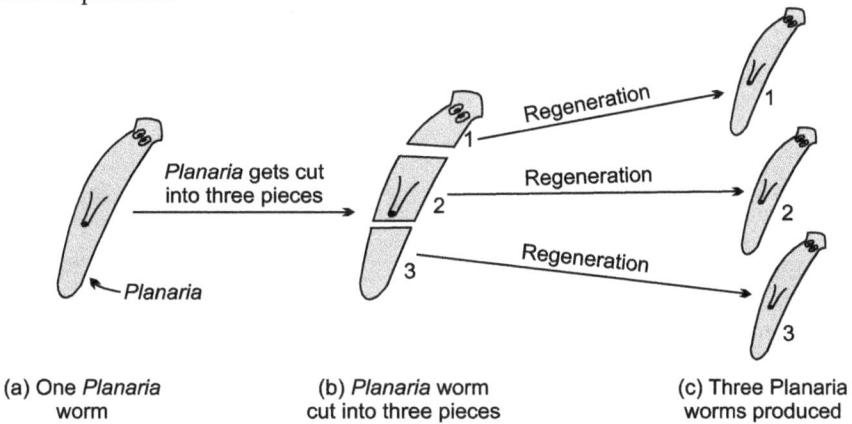

(a) One *Planaria* worm   (b) *Planaria* worm cut into three pieces   (c) Three Planaria worms produced

Fig. Regeneration in Planaria

The process of getting back a full organism from its body parts is called regeneration. Planaria reproduces by this method in which if the body of Planaria somehow gets cut into a number of pieces, then each body piece can regenerate into a complete Planaria by growing all the missing parts.

159. **How is the process of pollination different from fertilisation?** [NCERT]

Ans. Pollination is the process of transfer of pollen grains from anther to the stigma of pistil. It is carried out by various pollinating agents like water, wind, insects, animals etc., whereas fertilisation is the process of fusion of male gamete with a female gamete to produce a zygote. It occurs in the embryo sac present inside ovule.

160. **What are the advantages of sexual reproduction over asexual reproduction?**

Ans. The advantages of sexual reproduction over asexual reproduction are :
   (a) Variations are produced due to sexual reproduction which helps in better survival of offsprings to the changing environment.
   (b) More diversity is seen in case of sexual reproduction as compared to asexual reproduction.
   (c) Due to recombination and crossing over in meiosis process during formation of gametes and as there is mixing of male and female gametes, genetic variations are seen which is the main cause of evolution.

161. **What are stamen and carpel in a flower? What is the name of yellow powdery substance present in the anther of a flower?**

Ans. Stamen is the male reproductive part of a flower whereas carpel is a female reproductive part of a flower. The yellow powdery substance present in the anther of a flower is pollen grains.

162. **What happens when:**
   (i) Planaria gets cut into two pieces.

*are board exam questions from previous years

(ii) A mature Spirogyra filament attains considerable length.
(iii) On maturation sporangia burst.

Ans. (i) Each piece regenerates into a new Planaria.
(ii) When a mature Spirogyra filament attains considerable length it breaks into two or more fragments and each fragments grow into a new individual.
(iii) On maturation when sporangia burst, spores are liberated and they are dispersed.
On getting a suitable substratum and under favourable conditions each spore germinates into new mycelium.

163. Name the two reproductive parts of a bisexual flower which contain the germ cells. State the location and function of its female reproductive part.

Ans. Stamen and carpel are the two reproductive parts of a bisexual flower which contain the germ cells. Carpel- the female reproductive part is located at the centre of a flower. Carpel has three parts, the tip part is stigma which is sticky and receives the pollen grains, style is long and middle part through which pollen tube from pollen grains travel to reach ovary. Ovary is the swollen, bottom part of carpel which contains the female gametes where fertilisation occurs.

164. Write one difference between sexual and asexual mode of reproduction. Which species is likely to have better chances of survival the one reproducing asexually or the one reproducing sexually? Justify your answer?

Ans. In sexual reproduction male and female gametes from two different individuals unite leading to variations in offsprings due to mixing up of genetic material whereas in case of asexual reproduction only single parent is involved and there is no formation of gametes. The ones that are produced sexually have better chances of survival as due to mixing up of genetic material between two different individuals there is increase in genetic variations in the offsprings which provides maximum chances for the survival of species in the changing environment as well as under unfavourable conditions. This variation in species is also essential for evolution.

165. Name the following parts:
(i) The organ where foetus develop during gestation period.
(ii) A funnel like structure near the posterior end of ovary.
(iii) Technical term given to the stalk of the flower.
(iv) Three parts of carpel.

Ans. (i) Uterus
(ii) Fallopian tube
(iii) Pedicel
(iv) Stigma, style, ovary

166. Answer the following questions:
(i) What happens to the ovule and ovary after fertilisation?
(ii) Which group of plants show double fertilisation?

Ans. (i) After fertilisation ovule develops into seeds and ovary into fruit.
(ii) Mostly angiosperms show double fertilisation.

167. Answer the following questions:
(i) Write the names of those parts of a flower which serve the same functions as the following do in the animals.
(a) Testis, (b) Sperm, (c) Ovary, (d) Egg
(ii) State the function of flowers in the flowering plants?

Ans. (i) (a) Testis – Anther; (b) Sperm – Pollen grains; (c) Ovary – Ovary; (d) Egg – Ovum
(ii) Flowers are the main organs of sexual reproduction. They contain the reproductive organs.

168. State the basic requirements for sexual reproduction? Write the importance of such reproduction in nature?*

Ans. The basic requirements for sexual reproduction are involvement of a father and mother, parents which will contribute the male and female gametes respectively. The gametes are haploid which are produced through meiosis which on fusion produce a zygote and normal diploid number of chromosome is restored in offsprings.

Importance of sexual reproduction:
(a) It involves variations in species.
(b) Two individuals are required one male and another female.
(c) Specialized cells called sex cells are involved in this type of reproduction.
(d) It promotes diversity of characters in offsprings.
(e) It results in recombination of genes thus increase chances of genetic variations.
(vi) It plays an important role in origin of new species.

169. What are the changes seen in girls at the time of puberty? [NCERT]

Ans. Changes seen in girls during puberty are:
(a) Appearance of thick hair in genital parts and under arm pits.
(b) Enlargement of breasts.
(c) Darkening of skin surrounding the nipples.
(d) Start of menstrual cycle.
(e) Oily skin and pimples.

170. What is the role of seminal vesicles and prostate glands? [NCERT]

Ans. Seminal vesicles and prostate glands are accessory reproductive organs. The secretion from seminal vesicles provides nourishment and motility to the

---
* are board exam questions from previous years

sperms. Prostate glands secretion neutralizes the acidic pH of vagina so that sperms can easily pass through vagina.

171. How does the embryo gets nourishment inside the mother's body? [NCERT]

Ans. The embryo gets nourishment inside the mother's body through a disc shaped structure called placenta. It connects embryo with mother's blood. It supplies nutrients, oxygen to the growing embryo and removes carbon dioxide, wastes from embryo. Through this structure the blood of embryo comes in close contact with mother's blood and by diffusion process exchange of nutrients occurs. The placenta is formed by interlocking of two sets of villi, which provides maximum surface area for absorption of nutrients and oxygen gas.

172. List six specific characteristics of sexual reproduction.

Ans. Characteristics of sexual reproduction are:
  (a) In sexual reproduction, two parents are involved (male and female).
  (b) The new organism produced is genetically different from both parents.
  (c) During gamete formation meiosis occurs. After fertilization all divisions are mitotic.
  (d) Sexual reproduction helps in evolution.
  (e) Fertilization of gametes leads to zygote formation. This zygote grows and develops to form a new organism.
  (f) Humans, fish, dogs, hens, cats, cows, horses, deer, rabbit; lions and tigers all reproduce by the method of sexual reproduction. Most of the flowering plants also reproduce by sexual reproduction.

173. The embryo gets its nutrition from the mother's blood with the help of special tissue.
  (i) What is this special tissue called?
  (ii) Give any other function of this tissue apart from one mentioned above.
  (iii) Explain the structure of this special tissue.

Ans. (i) This special tissue is called placenta.
  (ii) Besides providing nutrition to the embryo, placenta helps in removing waste products from embryo, it also helps in providing oxygen to the embryo and eliminating carbon dioxide from embryo.
  (iii) Placenta is a disc like structure which is attached to the wall of the uterus. It is formed by two sets of minute finger like process called villi. One set from uterine wall and other set from the embryo. The blood flows through fine capillaries of the placenta.

174. Answer the following questions:
  (i) Trace the path of the sperms from where they are produced in the human body to the exterior?

  (ii) Write the functions of seminal vesicles and prostate glands in human male reproductive system?

Ans. (i) Seminiferous tubules → Epididymis → Sperm duct → Urethra
  (ii) Seminal vesicles secretion serves as a medium for transportation of sperms and also they activate and nourish the sperms. The secretion of prostate gland makes the medium alkaline and neutralises the acidic medium of female vagina.

175. Reproduction is essentially a phenomenon that is not for survival of an individual but for the stability of a species. Justify?

Ans. For an organism to survive it has to perform various life processes like nutrition, respiration, circulation, excretion etc. Reproduction is not required for survival of an organism. During reproduction there is replication of DNA and only genetic material is transferred from one generation to the next producing certain variations in the offsprings. This process helps in maintaining the continuity of a species.

176. Write the functions of each of the following parts in a human female reproductive system.
  (i) Ovary
  (ii) Uterus
  (iii) Fallopian tube

Write the structure and functions of placenta in a human female.

Ans. (i) **Ovary:** It produces female gametes and female sex hormones like estrogen, progesterone.
  (ii) **Uterus:** It supports and nourishes the developing foetus. It expands according to the growth of the baby.
  (iii) **Fallopian tube:** They are the site of fertilisation and carry eggs from ovary to uterus.

Placenta connects baby with mother's body. It is a disc like structure embedded in uterine wall. It is a special tissue formed by the interlocking of two sets of villi, one set given by wall of uterus and other set from embryo. It is the site of exchange of materials between the blood of mother and baby. It provides nutrients, oxygen from mother to foetus and removes excretory substances, carbon dioxide from foetus.

177. Answer the following questions:
  (i) Name the organ that produces sperms as well as secretes a hormone in human males. Name the hormone it secretes and write its functions.
  (ii) Name the parts of the human female reproductive system where fertilisation occurs.
  (iii) Explain how the developing embryo gets nourishment inside the mother's body?*

Ans. (i) Testes produces sperms as well as secretes a hormone in human males. The hormone secreted by testes is testosterone and its functions are:
  (a) It stimulates sperm production.

(b) It stimulates development of secondary sexual characters in males.

(c) It involves the development, maturation and functioning of male accessory sex organs.

(ii) Fallopian tubes are the site of fertilisation in the human female reproductive system.

(iii) A specialised tissue called placenta connects developing foetus with uterine wall of mother that provides nutrients from mother to child. Placenta is formed by interlocking of finger like projections called villi which provides a large surface area for diffusion of nutrients like glucose and respiratory gases like oxygen from mother. Carbon dioxide gas and metabolic wastes released by foetus are removed by placenta.

178. What are different methods of contraception? [NCERT]

Ans. The methods or devices used to prevent fertilisation and implantation are referred to as contraceptive methods. Some of the methods are:

(a) **Barrier methods:** Use of condoms in male and diaphragms in female prevents the entry of sperms into uterus.

(b) **Chemical methods:** Use of various hormonal pills prevents the release of egg from ovary. They cause a change in menstrual cycle thus delaying ovulation.

(c) **IUCDs:** Use of IUCDs devices like copper-T which is fitted inside uterus that prevents implantation of embryo into the wall of uterus.

(d) **Surgical methods:** Tubectomy is done in female where a small portion of oviducts are removed and ligated to prevent the entry of egg from ovaries. Vasectomy is done in males where a small portion of vas deferens is cut and ligated preventing passage of sperms.

(e) **Natural methods:** To avoid copulation around the time of ovulation.

179. What could be the reasons for adopting contraceptive method? [NCERT]

Ans. The reasons for adopting contraceptive method are:

(a) Preventing unwanted pregnancies to control population growth.

(b) It protects from sexually transmitted diseases like AIDS, Syphillis etc.

(c) Proper health of mother and child can be maintained by preventing frequent pregnancies.

(d) Sufficient gap between the offsprings, which ensures the proper health of the mother and child.

180. List four points of significance of reproductive health in a society. Name any two areas related to reproductive health which have improved over the past 50 years in our country.

Ans. Significance of reproductive health in a society are:

(a) It helps in controlling population growth.

(b) It helps in preventing the transmission of sexually transmitted diseases like syphilis, AIDS etc.

(c) It helps in family planning.

(d) It helps in knowing the suitable age for marriage and giving birth to child so that the mortality rates of mother and new born child can be reduced.

The two areas related to reproductive health which have improved over the past 50 years in our country are less mortality rate in new borns and mother.

181. Answer the following questions:

(i) List two sexually transmitted diseases in each of the following cases:

(a) Bacterial infections (b) Viral infections

(ii) How may the spread of such diseases be prevented?

Ans. (i) (a) Gonorrhoea and syphilis are bacterial infections.

(b) AIDS, warts are viral infections.

(ii) They can be prevented by avoiding sexual contact with the infected persons, using barriers like condoms, maintaining personal hygiene.

182. List four points of significance of reproductive health in a society. Name any two areas related to reproductive health which have improved over the past 50 years in our country.

Ans. Significance of reproductive health in a society are:

(a) It helps in controlling population growth.

(b) It helps in preventing the transmission of sexually transmitted diseases like syphilis, AIDS etc.

(c) It helps in family planning.

(d) It helps in knowing the suitable age for marriage and giving birth to child so that the mortality rates of mother and new born child can be reduced.

The two areas related to reproductive health which have improved over the past 50 years in our country are less mortality rate in new born and mother.

183. Rajeev, a sales executive in a MNC was not keeping well for a long time. He underwent a complete medical check-up and was diagnosed as HIV+. He was terminated on account of this condition.

(i) To which category of disease does AIDS belong to? Give its causative organism.

(ii) Do you think it was a right decision by the head of the company? Justify?

(iii) What concern should the society show towards HIV+ individuals?

Ans. (i) AIDS is a sexually transmitted disease. Its causative organism is HIV.

(ii) No it was not a right decision by the head of the company because HIV is not spread by shaking hands, mixing with HIV infected individuals. Instead he should be given equal rights, justice and freedom so that he should feel happy and should not get depressed.

(iii) The society should show positive attitude towards HIV positive persons. They should be given proper care and treatment. Everybody should support them so that they can lead a healthy life without getting mental depression. We should not isolate them but we should provide proper education and create awareness among people about HIV and AIDS.

184. Mohan was watching his mother cutting some potatoes into small pieces, each with one or two buds. These buds have started sprouting. She planted them in kitchen garden and started watering them daily. Mohan asked his mother why she planted them as they have no seeds.
(i) What is this method of propagation called?
(ii) Which part of plant is used in this case?
(iii) Is it sexual or asexual mode of reproduction?

Ans. (i) It is called vegetative propagation.
(ii) The stem tuber is used.
(iii) It is asexual mode of reproduction as there is no involvement of gametes and it involves single parent.

Long Answer Type Questions

185. Answer the following questions:
(i) Name the different types of asexual reproduction seen in living organisms. Give examples for each.
(ii)

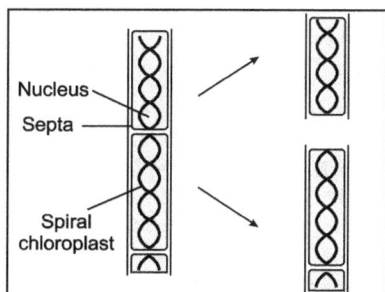

Identify the process occurring in the above figure. Briefly describe the process.

Ans. (i) The different types of asexual reproduction seen in living organisms are:
(a) **Fission:** It is the process in which a unicellular organism splits into two or more daughter cells. They are mainly of two types- Binary fission which is seen in Amoeba, Leshmania, Paramecium and Multiple fission seen in Plasmodium.
(b) **Fragmentation:** It is seen in Spirogyra.
(c) **Regeneration:** It is seen in Hydra, Planaria.
(d) **Budding:** It is seen in Yeast, Hydra.
(e) **Spore formation:** Here reproduction occurs through formation of spores. Spores under favourable conditions give rise to new individuals. It is seen in Rhizopus, Mucor etc.
(f) **Vegetative propagation:** It is mainly seen in plants.

(ii) The figure depicts fragmentation process in Spirogyra. In the process of fragmentation organism after maturation breaks into smaller fragments and each fragment grows into a new individual. This process is called fragmentation.

186. With the help of suitable diagrams explain the various steps of budding in Hydra.

Ans. Budding is a form of asexual reproduction and is the process of production of new individual from an outgrowth called bud formed on the parent body. Regenerative cells present in Hydra are used for budding. Due to repeated mitotic divisions an outgrowth called bud develops from the parent body which enlarges in size and finally develops into a small hydra. After attaining suitable maturity the offspring gets detached from the parent body and becomes an independent individual.

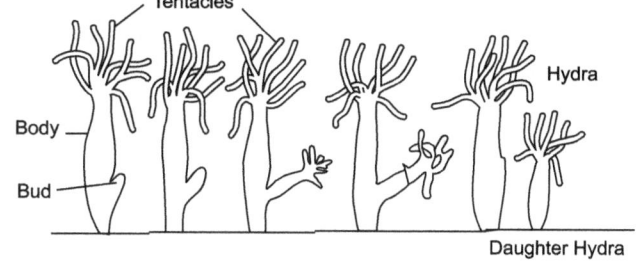

Fig. Budding in Hydra

187. Answer the following questions:
(i) Draw the female reproductive part of a flower and label:
(a) The part which is sticky and receptors of pollen grains.
(b) The part that transfers male gametes.
(c) The part that contains the female gametes.

(ii) How do the pollen grains reach to the female reproductive part in a flower?
(iii) Describe how male and female gametes unite in a flowering plant with suitable diagrams.

Ans.

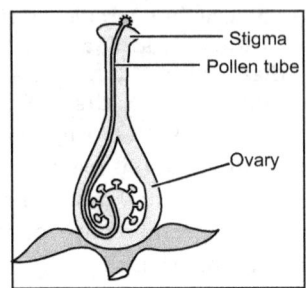

(i) (a) Stigma is sticky in nature and receptors of pollen grains.
(b) Pollen tube which arises from pollen grains transfers male gametes by passing through style into ovary.
(c) Ovary contains ovules that carry an embryo sac which contains the female gametes.

(ii) Pollen grains reach the stigma of carpel through pollination process by various pollinating agents like wind, insects, water etc.

(iii)

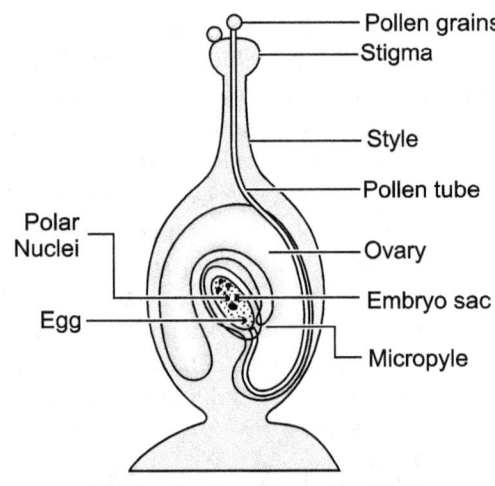

Fertilisation in a Flowering Plant

The process of mixing of male and female gametes to form a zygote is called fertilisation. By pollination process pollen grains gets deposited on stigma of carpel. Under suitable conditions they germinate. A long pollen tube containing two male gametes arises and it passes through style to reach the ovary. The ovary contains ovule which has a embryo sac. Female gamete is present inside embryo sac. The pollen tube enters the ovule through micropyle and penetrates through the embryo sac. One male gamete fuses with female gamete to produce zygote whereas the second male gamete fuses with polar nuclei to form endosperm. This process is called double fertilisation.

188. Define pollination. Explain the different types of pollination. List two agents of pollination. How does suitable pollination lead to fertilisation?*

Ans. Pollination is the transfer of pollen from the anther of the stamen to the stigma of the pistil with the help of air, water and insects.

Types of pollination:
(a) **Self pollination:** Transfer of pollen grain from the anther to the stigma of the same flower.
(b) **Cross pollination:** Transfer of pollen grain from the anther of one flower to the stigma of other flower of the same species.

Two agents of pollination are air, water, insects, etc. When correct species of pollen grain lands on the stigma it results in some chemical response from the ovary that causes the growth of pollen tube from pollen grain. The pollen grain slides down the pollen tube and enters the ovary where it meets the egg. This process is called as fertilisation and leads to the formation of zygote.

189. What is vegetative propagation? Describe various methods of vegetative propagation?

Ans. The growth of new plants from vegetative parts of the plant like roots, stem, leaves other than the seeds is called vegetative propagation. Various methods of vegetative propagation are:
(a) **Cutting:** Small piece of plant part like roots, stem or leaves is cut and is used for propagation. Examples: Rose, china-rose, sugarcane etc.
(b) **Layering:** It is the process where roots are induced when a stem comes in contact with the ground. Examples: Grapevine, jasmine, litchi, mango etc.
(c) **Grafting:** It is a process of joining a part of a living plant like stem or bud to another plant and they grow as one plant. Examples: Lime, lemon etc.
(d) **Propagation by plant tissue culture:** In this method plant cells are cultured in an artificial culture media, where a cell divides into undifferentiated mass of cells called callus which is transferred to different nutrient medium to grow into plantlets.

All the above methods are artificial method of vegetative propagation.
In natural methods of vegetative propagation underground roots [Root tubers of Dahlia] or underground stems [bulbs of onions, rhizomes of ginger] or adventitious buds on leaves [Bryophyllum] grow into new plants.

190. Study the below diagram and answer the following:
(i) Label the parts A, B, C and D.

---
* are board exam questions from previous years

(ii) Which parts represent the male and female reproductive part respectively.
(iii) What is the function of the parts labeled A and D ?
(iv) What do you mean by pollination and explain the different types of pollination?

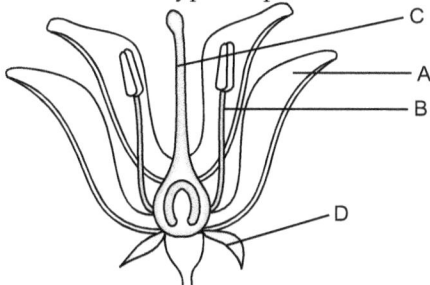

Ans. (i) A – Petals; B – Stamens; C – Pistil; D – Sepals
(ii) Part B [Stamens] represent male reproductive part and part C [Pistil] represent female reproductive part of a flower.
(iii) The main function of petal is to attract insects for pollination so they are large, showy and brightly coloured. The main function of sepal is to protect the stamens and pistils.
(iv) Pollination is the process of transfer of pollen grains from anther to the stigma of the carpel by various pollinating agents like wind, insects etc. There are two types of pollination :
(a) **Self-pollination** : The transfer of pollen grains from anther of a flower to stigma of the same flower or different flower but in same plant is called self pollination.
(b) **Cross pollination** : The transfer of pollen grains from anther of flower of one plant to stigma of another flower of different plant but of same species is called cross pollination.

191. Describe the role of the following in a male reproductive system and label them in a figure:
(i) Testis
(ii) Vas deferens
(iii) Epididymis
(iv) Scrotum
(v) Seminal vesicle

Ans. (i) Testes are the primary sex organs in a human male which produce sperms by the process of spermatogenesis. They also produce male sex hormone testosterone which helps in the development of secondary male characteristics at the time of puberty.
(ii) Vas deferens also called sperm ducts carries the sperms from testes to urethra.
(iii) Epididymis stores the sperms for some days where they get mature and become motile in nature.
(iv) Scrotum or scrotal sacs are pouch like structures located outside the abdomen in which testes are placed. It provides an optimum temperature for sperm formation.
(v) The secretion of seminal vesicles helps in transportation of sperms and provides nourishment to the sperms.

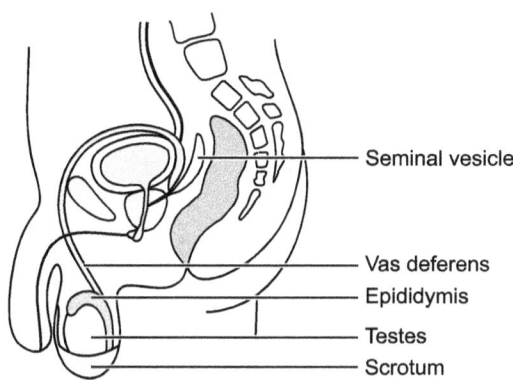

192. Answer the following questions:
(i) Write the function of following parts in human female reproductive system:
(a) Ovary
(b) Oviduct
(c) Uterus
(ii) Describe in brief the structure and function of placenta.

Ans. (i) (a) **Ovary:** It produces egg for fertilisation. It secretes estrogen and progesterone. Estrogen regulates secondary sexual characters and progesterone controls the thickness of the lining of uterus.
(b) **Oviduct:** It is the site of fertilisation and carries egg or fertilised ovum (zygote) to the uterus.
(c) **Uterus:** It helps to nourish the fertilised ovum that will develop into foetus. It holds the baby till it is ready for birth.
(ii) Placenta is a disc shaped structure on uterine wall before implantation of embyro. It provides oxygen and nutrients to the foetus. It helps to remove waste also. The placenta is composed of both material tissues and tissue derived from the embryo. The chorion is the embryonic derived portion of the placenta. It is composed of foetal blood vessels and trophoblasts which are organised into finger-like structures called chorionic villi.

193. Answer the following questions:
(i) Identify the given diagram. Name the parts 1 to 5.

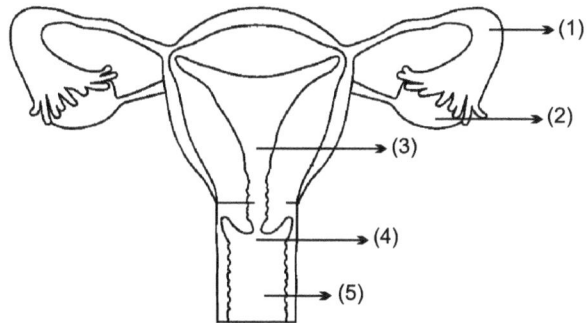

(ii) What is contraception? List three advantages of adopting contraceptive measures.

Ans. (i) The parts of the female reproductive system are as follows:
(1) Fallopian tube or Oviduct
(2) Ovary
(3) Uterus
(4) Cervix
(5) Vagina

(ii) Contraception is the method by which a female inhibits fertilisation and hence prevents pregnancy.

The three advantages of contraception are:
(a) It makes the people more aware about the concept of family planning.
(b) It educates the people about sexually transmitted diseases and ways to avoid it.
(c) It helps the female to space children.
(d) It reduces the risk of unwanted pregnancies.

194. Answer the following related to AIDS.
(i) Expand AIDS, HIV.
(ii) Is AIDS an infectious disease?
(iii) State few methods of transmission of this disease.
(iv) Give some preventive measures for control of AIDS.
(v) When is World AIDS day celebrated?

Ans. (i) AIDS – Acquired Immuno Deficiency Syndrome
HIV – Human Immuno deficiency Virus
(ii) Yes, AIDS is an infectious disease.
(iii) Few methods of transmission of this disease are:
(a) Sexual contact with an infected person.
(b) Transfusion of blood from an infected person.
(c) From mother to child through placenta during pregnancy.
(d) Sharing of infected needles for injection of drugs or vaccines.

(iv) Some preventive measures for control of AIDS are:
(a) Using disposable syringes.
(b) Using condoms for sex.
(c) Before blood transfusion, blood should be tested for AIDS.
(d) Educating people about transmission and prevention of AIDS.

(v) World AIDS day is celebrated on December 1 every year.

195. Given below are few questions based on analogy. Fill in the blanks with appropriate answer in each.
(i) Diaphragm: Barrier methods: : Copper-T : _____.
(ii) Removal of vas deferens surgically: Vasectomy: : _____ : Tubectomy
(iii) HIV : AIDS : : _____ : Gonorrhoea
(iv) Ovary: Oestrogen: : Testis : _____
(v) Propagation by tissue culture: _____ : : Development of new plants from adventitious buds in Bryophyllum : Natural Methods of vegetative propagation.

Ans. (i) Intrauterine Contraceptive Device (IUCD)
(ii) Removal of oviduct surgically
(iii) Nisseria gonorrhoeae
(iv) Testosterone
(v) Artificial Methods of vegetative propagation

Diagram Based Questions

196. Draw in sequence (showing the four stages), the process of binary fission in amoeba.

Ans. Binary fission is an asexual mode of reproduction in amoeba where a single parent cell divides into two daughter cells and each daughter cell receives a copy of genetic material.

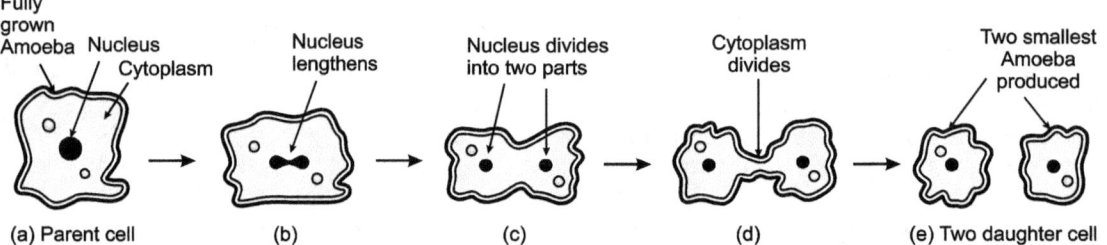

Binary Fission in Amoeba

197. A student is observing a permanent slide showing sequentially the different stages of asexual reproduction taking place in yeast. Name this process and draw diagrams of what he observes in a proper sequence.

Ans. This process is called budding.

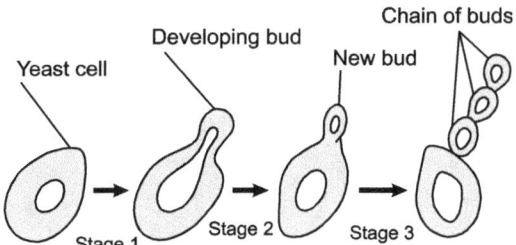

198. Study the diagram and answer the following:

(i) What does the figure represents?

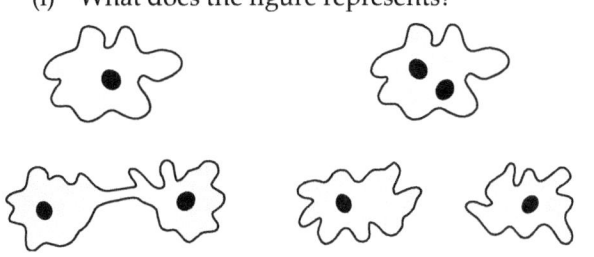

(ii) Give an example of organism which shows this process.
(iii) Describe the process shown in the picture.

Ans. (i) The figure represents binary fission which is an asexual mode of reproduction.
(ii) Amoeba and Paramecium show this mode of reproduction.
(iii) The genetic material first duplicates through mitosis leading to duplication of nucleus through karyokinesis and a constriction appears in the cell membrane which deepens and finally a single parent cell divides into two daughter cells. The division of cytoplasm is called cytokinesis. This mode of asexual reproduction is called binary fission.

199. Draw a diagram of Rhizopus labelling the reproductive and non-reproductive parts. Explain the process of reproduction in Rhizopus.

Ans. Spores are reproductive parts and Hyphae are non-reproductive parts of Rhizopus.

Rhizopus reproduces through asexual method by spore formation. During spore formation a structure called sporangium develops from the fungal hypha. The nucleus divides several times within the sporangium and each nucleus with small amount of cytoplasm develops into a spore. The spores are liberated and develop into new hypha on the substratum when conditions become favourable.

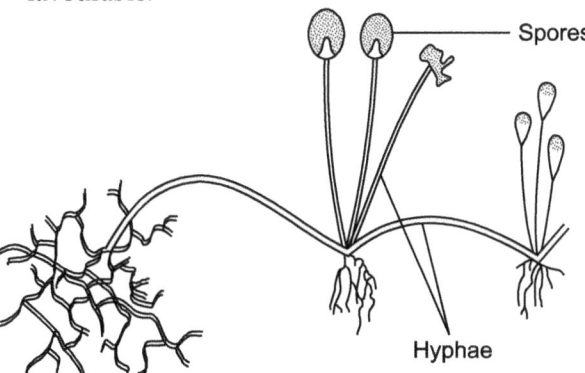

200. The picture given below depicts the process of reproduction in a single cell organism. Answer the following questions based on it:

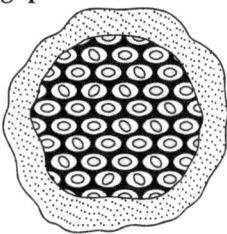

(i) Name the process depicted above and define it?
(ii) What is meant by asexual reproduction?

Ans. (i) The diagram given above represents multiple fission. The process by which there is division of a parent cell into several daughter cells is called multiple fission. During this process the nucleus of parent cell divides into many daughter nuclei along with the division of cytoplasm.
(ii) The reproduction which involves only one parent and occurs without the formation and fusion of gametes and there is no mixing of genetic material is called asexual reproduction.

201. Answer the following questions:

(i) Identify the process depicted in the diagram given below:
(ii) The spores have a covering of thick walls around it. What is its advantage?
(iii) What are hyphae?

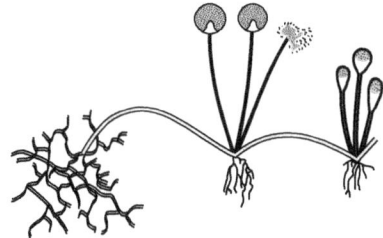

Ans. (i) The process is known as spore formation in rhizopus.
(ii) Spores are covered by a thick structure to withstand unfavourable conditions like drought, high temperature etc., so that they can survive for a long time.
(iii) Hyphae are long, thread, branched filaments of fungus which release enzymes to absorb nutrients from food sources.

202. Draw the diagram of a flower and label the four whorls. Write the names of gametes producing organs in the flower.

Ans. Anther of stamen produce male gametes and ovary pistil produce female gametes.

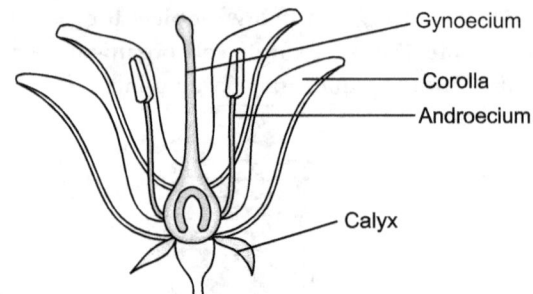

203. Draw a labelled diagram of the longitudinal section of a flower. **[NCERT]**

Ans.

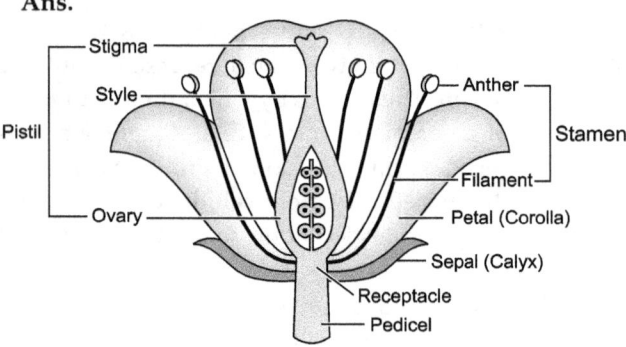

L.S. of a Flower

204. Study the diagram and answer the following questions.

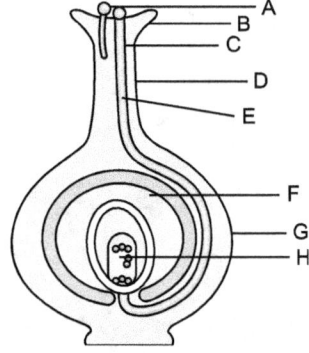

(i) What does the figure indicate?
(ii) Label the parts A, B, C, D, E, F, G, H.
(iii) Mention the role of parts B, E?

Ans. (i) The figure indicates fertilisation process in flowering plant.
(ii) A – Pollen grains, B – Stigma, C – Male gametes, D – Style, E – Pollen tube, F – Ovule, G – Ovary, H – Embryo sac
(iii) Stigma is the part of carpel which receives pollen grains during pollination.
Pollen tube contains the male gamete which passes through the style and finally reaches the ovary. It carries the male gametes towards female gametes for fertilisation.

205. Draw and label the diagram of embryo of a gram seed. Give the functions of each parts labeled by you ?

Ans. Cotyledons store food for the growth of embryo.
Radicle becomes root in future plant.
Plumule becomes shoot in future plant.

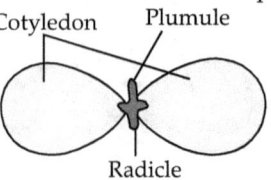

206. Answer the following by carefully studying the figure:
(i) Identify the image shown below.
(ii) Label in the figure the ovary, oviduct, uterus, vagina.
(iii) State the functions of the labeled parts in part b.

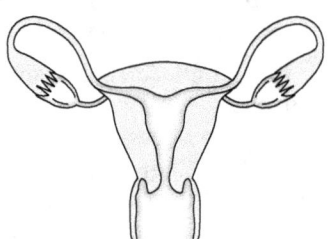

Ans. (a) The figure represents female reproductive system.
(b) The figure is as shown.

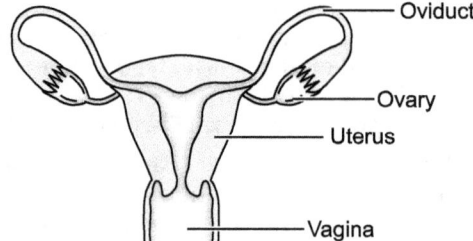

207. Study the diagram and answer the following:
(i) What does the figure represent and label the parts A and B.
(ii) Name a hormone produced by X and what is its function?
(iii) Mention the substances carried by ducts C and D.

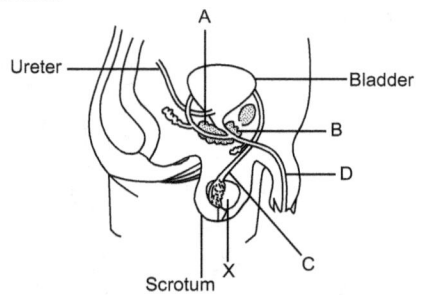

Ans. (i) The figure represents human male reproductive system. Part A is seminal vesicle and B is prostate gland.

(ii) The organ represented by X is testes and Hormone produced by it is testosterone which helps in developing secondary sexual characters in males at the time of puberty.

(iii) Duct C is vas deferens which carries sperms and Duct D is urethra which carries both sperms and urine.

Differentiate Between

208. What is the difference between albuminous seed and ex-albuminous seed?

Ans.

Albuminous seeds	Ex-albuminous seeds
Endosperm is present and cotyledons are thin and surrounded by membrane. Examples: Cereals, custard apple.	They lack endosperm and cotyledons are thick and fleshy because they store food. Examples: Gram, peas.

209. How does binary fission differ from multiple fission? [NCERT]

Ans.

	Binary fission	Multiple fission
(a)	A single parent cell divides into two daughter cells.	It results in production of many daughter cells.
(b)	Nucleus divides once and then each nucleus gets surrounded by cytoplasm to form two individuals.	Nucleus divides repeatedly to form many nuclei and each gets surrounded by cytoplasm to form many daughter cells.
(c)	It occurs under favourable conditions. Example: Binary fission in Amoeba, Paramecium.	It occurs under unfavourable conditions. Example: Plasmodium.

210. Distinguish between a gamete and zygote?

Ans.

Gamete	Zygote
The germ cells that are mixed during sexual reproduction are called gametes, e.g. sperm (male) and ova (female).	It is the product of the fusion of male gametes and female gametes during sexual reproduction.
Gametes are unfertilised reproductive cells.	Zygote is a fertilised egg or a fertilised egg.
As a product of meiosis, gametes are always haploid cells.	Since zygote is the product of the fusion of the male and female gamete haploid, it is a diploid structure.
Haploid	Diploid
Meiosis and cytokinesis occur.	Compaction and formation of blastula occur.
Found in gonads	Found in fallopian tube
No new individuals are formed.	New individuals are formed.
Has one copy of all autosomes and one sex chromosome, either X or Y.	Have two copies of all of the autosomes. Sex chromosomes may be either XX or XY.
Giving rise to the zygote.	Giving rise to the foetus.
Sperm: very motile. Oocyte: no-motile	Non-motile

Analysis and Evaluation Based Questions

211. What is the advantage of reproduction through spores in the case of Rhizopus?

Ans. Spores are highly resistant to adverse environmental conditions like drought, heat etc. They have a thick wall which protects them and on exposure to suitable conditions they germinate and give rise to new individuals.

212. A potato is cut into a number of small pieces, these potato pieces are placed on wet cotton kept in a tray. After a few days, green shoots and roots appear only from some potato pieces and not from all potato pieces, why?

Ans. In those potato pieces which possess the buds on getting moisture, light, oxygen new plants develop from them which is an example of natural methods of vegetative propagation and those potato pieces which do not have buds, from them new plants do not grow.

213. Hormones are powerful. It takes only a tiny amount to cause big changes in cells or even your whole body. That is why too much or too little of a certain hormone can be serious. Laboratory tests can measure the hormone levels in your blood, urine, or saliva.

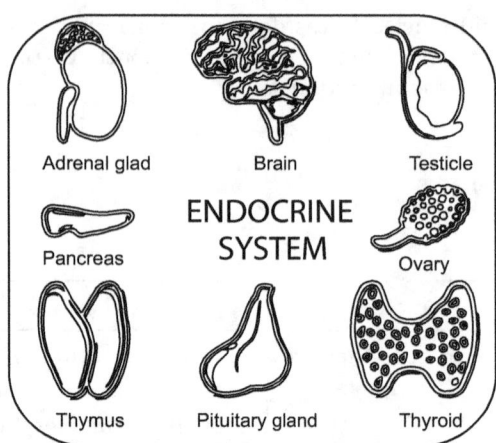

(i) Name the part of the brain that regulates the release of hormones.
(ii) Name any two endocrine glands that are common in both males and females.
(iii) Name the endocrine gland which is present only in the males. Also, name the hormone that is produced by this gland.
(iv) Name the endocrine gland which is present only in the females and the hormone that is produced by this gland.

Ans. (i) The part of the brain that controls and regulates the release of hormones is the hypothalamus.
(ii) Pituitary gland and thyroid gland.
(iii) Testis which produces a hormone named testosterone is present only in males.
(iv) Ovary which produces the hormones progesterone and estrogen is the endocrine gland which is present only in the females.

214. Colonies of yeast fail to multiply in water but multiply in sugar solution. Give one reason for this.

Ans. Sugar solution provides energy which cannot be provided by water for the growth of yeast colonies.

215. Why is the number of sperms produced always more than the number of eggs Produced?

Ans. A single ejaculation produces about 400 million sperms. Sperms are motile in nature and they have to travel long distance to reach the egg for fertilisation. They also compete with each other to reach the egg, very few are able to climb through uterus to reach oviduct whereas rest die and are absorbed on the way. Only one sperm in the end fuses with egg so to fertilise a single egg million number of sperms are produced.

216. Answer the following:
(i) Complete the sentence by filling in X and Y. The ovary contains the X and the X contains the Y.
(ii) If a farmer wishes to develop a mango with characters of two related species, what method of vegetative propagation should he use?

Ans. (i) X is Ovule, Y is embryo sac which contain egg cell and two polar nuclei.
(ii) Grafting method is used.

217. The sexual act always has the potential to lead to pregnancy. Pregnancy will make major demands on the body and the mind of the woman, and if she is not ready for it, her health will be adversely affected. Therefore, many ways have been devised to avoid pregnancy.

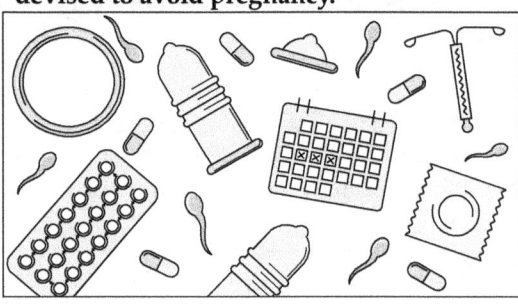

(i) Name any two bacterial diseases that are caused due to unprotected sex.
(ii) How a pill helps in preventing pregnancy?
(iii) What is vasectomy?
(iv) What are the common side-effects of using contraceptive pills?

Ans. (i) The two bacterial diseases that are caused due to unprotected sex are gonorrhea and syphilis.
(ii) The pill helps in preventing pregnancy as it prevents the release of the ovum, by changing the hormonal balance.
(iii) Vasectomy is the surgical process by which the vas deferens is cut. This prevents the sperms from reaching the ejaculatory duct.
(iv) The common side-effects of using contraceptive pills are irritation, nausea, and mood swings.

Practical Based Questions

218. To perform an experiment to identify the different parts of an embryo of a dicot seed, first of all you require a dicot seed. Select dicot seeds from the following group.*
Wheat, gram, maize, pea, barley, ground-nut.
(i) Wheat, gram and pea
(ii) Gram, pea and ground-nut
(iii) Maize, pea and barley
(i) Gram, maize and ground-nut

Ans. (ii) Gram, pea and ground-nut.

219. Which among the following organism is capable of reproducing through spores?

---
* are board exam questions from previous years

(i) Amoeba
(ii) Plasmodium
(iii) Hydra
(iv) Rhizopus

Ans. (iv) Rhizopus

Explanation: Asexual reproduction by spore formation is the common method of reproduction in fungi and bacteria. Example: Rhizopus During spore formation a structure called sporangium develops from the fungal hypha. The nucleus divides several times within the sporangium and each nucleus with small amount of cytoplasm develops into a spore. The spores are liberated and develop into new hypha on the substratum when conditions become favourable.

220. Write any two precautions while studying different parts of an embryo of a dicot seed?

Ans. Two precautions are:
(a) The slide should first be observed under low power magnification compound microscope and then under high power magnification compound microscope.
(b) The slides should be focused properly.

221. Name three dicot seeds. Seeds on germination give rise to _____ and _____.

Ans. The three dicot seeds are gram, peas and beans. Seeds on germination give rise to plumule and radicle.

222. Are binary fission and budding faster processes of reproduction when compared to sexual reproduction? Justify.

Ans. Yes, binary fission and budding are faster processes of reproduction when compared to sexual reproduction because in sexual reproduction there are lot of events like formation of gametes, fusion of gametes, development of a zygote to a young one etc.

223. Name the type of asexual reproduction in which two individuals are formed from a single parent and the parental identity is lost. Draw the initial and the final stages of this type of reproduction. State the event with which this reproduction starts.

Ans. Binary fission is the type of asexual reproduction in which two individuals are formed from a single parent and the parental identity is lost.

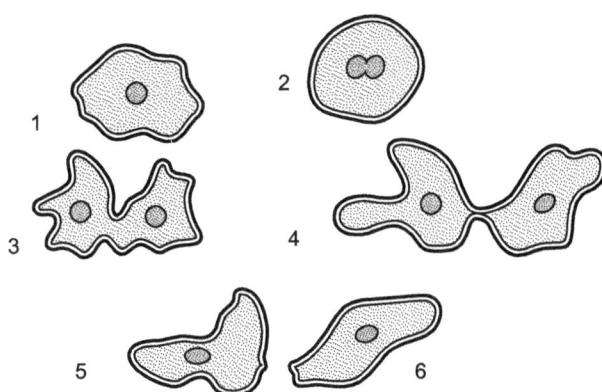

This reproduction starts with elongation of Nucleus.

224. Answer the following questions:
(i) A slide showing several amoeba was given to a student and was asked to focus the Amoeba undergoing binary fission. What will the student look for to correctly focus on a dividing Amoeba?
(ii) How can you identify the daughter cells which are formed due to binary fission in amoeba?

Ans. (i) Student should observe the Amoeba which will have a elongated nucleus along with a constriction in the middle of cytoplasm.
(ii) The daughter cells would be smaller in size than their respective parent cells.

225. Answer the following questions:
(i) Name the remaining structure after removing the testa from water soaked gram seed.
(ii) How many cotyledons are present in the embryo of gram?

Ans. (i) Full mature embryo
(ii) Two cotyledons

226. A student is made to observe two permanent slides. He was asked to identify the mode of reproduction in the respective organism. The student observed the following slides:

 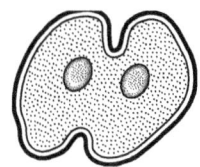

Slide I   Slide II

Ans. Slide I is showing budding in yeast and slide II is showing the process of binary fission in Amoeba.

Application Based Questions

227. Ravi took three bread slices and kept the three pieces of the slices in the following conditions.

(i) Slice 1 in a dried and dark place.
(ii) Slice 2 in a moist and dark place.

(iii) Slice 3 in moist and in refrigerator.

What would he observe in each of the above conditions? Give reasons for your answer.

Ans. In slice 1, no spores will develop as there is lack of moisture. In slice 2, white spongy mass like structures with black spots will be seen as both moisture and darkness favours the growth of bread moulds. In slice 3, there will be no formation of spores even though moisture is present because the low temperature in refrigerator does not favour the growth of spores.

228. A student noticed that an organism by mistake was cut in two parts. After sometime both the parts developed into new individuals.
(i) Name the mode of reproduction used by the organism.
(ii) State the type of cells which carry this process.
(iii) Write examples of two organisms which multiply by this process.

Ans. (i) Regeneration method of asexual mode of reproduction.
(ii) Specialised regenerative cells.
(iii) Planaria and Hydra multiply by this process.

229. Ram and Shyam went for a trip to Botanical garden. They saw some plants with beautifully coloured and scented flowers. They wondered why some flowers were beautifully coloured and scented. Then they saw in a flower bed, rose plants with same coloured flowers and of same size. Next day when they went to school they asked teacher about that.
(a) Why flowers are beautifully coloured and scented?
(b) Why all the flowers in the flower bed were of same size and colour?

Ans. (a) Flowers are beautifully coloured and scented to attract insects for pollination. Pollination would lead to fertilization and finally formation of fruits and seeds.
(b) Rose plants might have propagated by vegetative propagation so they resemble their parents i.e., all the rose plants are of same size and of same colour.

230. (i) Dissolve about 10 gm of sugar in 100 mL of water.
(ii) Take 20 mL of this solution in a test tube and add a pinch of yeast granules to it.
(iii) Put a cotton plug on the mouth of the test tube and keep it in a warm place.
(iv) After 1 or 2 hours, put a small drop of yeast culture from the test tube on a slide and cover it with a cover slip.

Observe the slide under a microscope.

Ans. Formation of yeast cells by budding process could be seen. Some may show a chain of yeast cells attached to each other.

231. (i) Wet a slice of bread, and keep it in a cool, moist and dark place.
(ii) Observe the surface of the slice with a magnifying glass.

Record your observations for a week.

Ans. A white cottony mass appears on the moist bread which later becomes black to produce sporangiosphores which contain spores in them. This is called Rhizopus or bread mould.

232. (i) Observe a permanent slide of Amoeba under a microscope.
(ii) Similarly observe another permanent slide of Amoeba showing binary fission.

Now, compare the observations of both the slides.

Ans. One slide shows an amoeba containing a nucleus and cytoplasm whereas the second slide shows amoeba undergoing binary fission i.e., nucleus to be dividing, constriction appearing on the cytoplasm, a single amoeba divides to produce two daughter amoeba.

233. (i) Collect water from a lake or pond that appears dark green and contains filamentous structures.
(ii) Put one or two filaments on a slide.
(iii) Put a drop of glycerine on these filaments and cover it with a coverslip.
(iv) Observe the slide under a microscope.

Can you identify different tissues in the Spirogyra filaments ?

Ans. Spirogyra is a multicellular, filamentous, green algae where cells are alike and there is no differentiation of tissues.

234. (i) Take a potato and observe its surface. Can notches be seen ?
(ii) Cut the potato into small pieces such that some pieces contain a notch or bud and some do not.
(iii) Spread some cotton on a tray and wet it. Place the potato pieces on this cotton. Note where the pieces with the buds are placed.
(iv) Observe changes taking place in these potato pieces over the next few days. Make sure that the cotton is kept moistened.

Which are the potato pieces that give rise to fresh green shoots and roots ?

Ans. Potatoes having buds show the growth of fresh green shoots and roots and those who do not have buds does not show any growth of new plants.

235. (i) Select a money-plant.
(ii) Cut some pieces such that they contain at least one leaf.
(iii) Cut out some other portions between two leaves.
(iv) Dip one end of all the pieces in water and observe over the next few days.

Which ones grow and give rise to fresh leaves ?

Ans. The portion of money plant having at least one leaf develops fresh leaves and branch as they have axillary bud present in exile of leaf. Other parts did not show any growth.

236. (i) Soak a few seeds of Bengal gram (chana) and keep them overnight.
   (ii) Drain the excess water and cover the seeds with a wet cloth and leave them for a day. Make sure that the seeds do not become dry.
   (iii) Cut open the seeds carefully and observe the different parts.
   Compare your observations with the below Fig. and see if you can identify all the parts.

Ans. The seed contains two cotyledons which store food, when seed germinates plumule and radicle are seen which grows into shoot and root respectively. Yes we can see all the parts as shown in figure above.

237. **It is a well known fact that pregnant woman's health is a backbone of every family, society and thus nation.**
   (i) Which tissue is responsible for providing nutrition from mother to growing embryo?
   (ii) According to you, what can likely be the measures to maintain woman health during pregnancy.

Ans. (i) Placenta is responsible for providing nutrition from mother to growing embryo.
   (ii) Following measures should be maintain for the proper health of woman during pregnancy:
     (a) Well balanced and proper nutritious diet.
     (b) She should not take alcohol, smoke cigarette.
     (c) She must be kept stress free away from family problems.
     (d) Regular check-ups and visits to doctor.
     (e) Avoid use of excess medicines and do light exercises.

238. **We hear and read about female foeticide, which is really a wrong practice. In some families, be it rural or urban, females are tortured for giving birth to a girl child. They do not seem to understand the scientific reason behind the birth of a boy or a girl.**
   In your opinion, the approach of the society towards mother in this regard is correct or not? Explain the scientific reason.

Ans. No, it is not correct. Mother should not be blamed for this. There is no difference between a male and female child, both are equal. A female is born if it receives the X bearing sperms from father as father carries both X and Y chromosomes and mother carries only X chromosomes.

239. **Study the table given below and answer the questions.**

Contraceptive method	Duration of efficiency	Hormonal exposure
Copper IUD	10 years	No
Pills	Use days	Yes
Diaphragm	Reusable	No

   (i) What are STDs?
   (ii) Which of the bacteria is responsible for causing syphilis?
   (iii) Name the contraceptive device that is commonly used by the males?
   (iv) What is the part of the male reproductive organ that is cut in the process of vasectomy?

Ans. (i) There are a number of diseases that are caused by sexual intercourses. These diseases are called STDs "Sexually transmitted disease".
   (ii) *Treponema pallidum* is the bacterium that causes a disease called syphilis in humans.
   (iii) The contraceptive device that is commonly used by the males is the condom.
   (iv) The vas deferens is cut in the process of vasectomy. This prevents the sperms from reaching the ejaculatory duct.

Creating Based Questions

240. **Elaborate the statement 'DNA contains the blueprint of the next generation'.**

Ans. DNA is the hereditary material. It stores the blueprint in the genes which are the sequence of nucleotides. Genes control synthesis of proteins. These proteins act as enzymes which control biochemical reactions of the body. Genes are responsible for transmitting characters from parents to offspring. Before transmitting characters from parents to offspring prior to cell division DNA makes its copies by replication. Hence, DNA contains the blueprint of the next generation.

241. **Due to his recent travel and the location of sores, Dr. Gonzala suspects that Mike may have contracted Leishmaniasis.**
   (i) Name the parasite that causes Leishmaniasis.
   (ii) The parasite that causes Leishmaniasis reproduce through which mode?
   (iii) How it is transmitted?

Ans. (i) Leishmaniasis infection caused by the parasite Leishmania.
   (ii) Leishmania reproduce through binary fission.
   (iii) Leishmania is transmitted through the bite of an infected sand-fly. Leishmania (which cause

kala-azar), have a whip-like structure at one end of the cell.

242. **Study the table given below and answer the questions.**

Disease	Causative agent
Syphilis	*Treponema pallidum*
Genital herpes	HSV-2
AIDS	HIV
Trichomoniasis	*Trichomoniasis vaginalis*

(i) What are STDs?
(ii) What is the full form of HIV and AIDS?
(iii) Is syphilis a bacterial infection or a viral infection?
(iv) Is trichomoniasis a bacterial infection?

Ans. (i) There are a number of diseases that are caused by sexual intercourses. These diseases are called STDs "Sexually transmitted disease".
(ii) The full form of HIV is the Human Immunodeficiency Virus, and the full form of AIDS is Acquired Immunodeficiency Syndrome.
(iii) The syphilis is a bacterial infection as it is caused by a bacteria named *Treponema pallidum*.
(iv) No, trichomoniasis is not a bacterial infection as it caused by a protozoan named *Trichomoniasis vaginalis*.

143. **The diagram represents gametes P and Q fusing to give cell R. This cell then produces gametes S.T.U and V.**

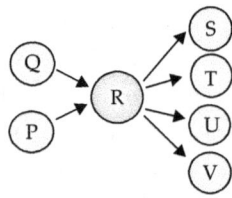

(i) State whether P, Q and R are Haploid or diploid.
(ii) What is the Ratio of Number of Chromosomes in a Human Zygote and a Human Sperm?
(iii) The parental cell divides and gives rise to two daughter cells. Each division doubles the number of cells. How many numbers of cells will be there in third generation? If starting cells is considered as 0 generation.

Ans. (i) P and Q are haploid gametes while R is zygote and diploid.
(ii) The number of chromosomes in a human sperm is half the number of chromosomes in a zygote i.e their ratio is 2:1
(iii) The number of cells increases exponentially and can be expressed as 2n, where n is the number of generations. If we apply the formula 2n, where n is equal to 3, the single cell would give rise to 23 i.e 8 cells.

244. **Mrs. Alka, 37 years old, was diagnosed with secondary infertility. The experts diagnosed her for tubal factor infertility that was obstructing her second pregnancy. Later, she was suggested to go for In-Vitro Fertilisation (IVF). She conceived in the first attempt of the treatment and delivered a healthy baby. Why it is difficult to conceive if fallopian tube is blocked?**

Ans. In case the fallopian tube is blocked, the passage for sperm to get to the eggs, as well as the path back to the uterus for the fertilised egg, is blocked. To prevent pregnancy in females quite often the fallopian tube is blocked by surgery due to which the egg released by the ovary is not able to reach the uterus and hence fertilisation does not occur. If the fallopian tube is blocked then the female cannot conceive. The process of fertilisation starts in the fallopian tube hence if it is blocked then it is difficult for the female to get pregnant.

245. **A 25-year-old young man with his partner of 3 years decides not to have babies and undergoes a surgical procedure to prevent pregnancy. This led to permanent sterilisation of young mam.**
(i) Name the surgery performed.
(ii) Which part is cut during this process?
(iii) How does this process prevent pregnancy?

Ans. (i) Vasectomy is a surgical procedure for male sterilisation or permanent contraception.
(ii) During the procedure, the male vasa deferentia are cut and tied or sealed.
(iii) Cutting and sealing of vasa deferentia prevents sperm from entering into the urethra and thereby prevent fertilisation of a female through sexual intercourse.

Self-Assessment

246. Which parts of plants can grow vegetatively?
247. What is syngamy?
248. Answer the following related to diagrams given below:

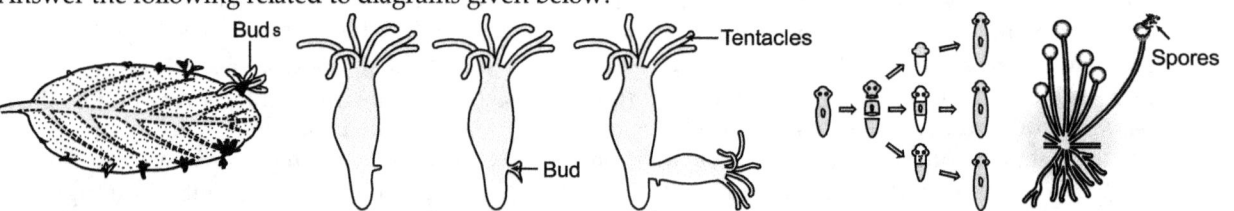

Figure (A) Figure (B) Figure (C) Figure (D)

(i) Identify the organisms in figure A, B, C and D.
(ii) Identify the life process shown in all the figures.
(iii) How is the life process advantageous to the organisms?

249. From the internet, gather information about the chromosome numbers of five animals and five plants. Correlate the number with the size of the organism and answer the following questions:
   (i) Do larger organisms have more number of chromosomes or cells?
   (ii) Can organism with fewer chromosomes reproduce more easily than organisms with more number of chromosomes?
   (iii) More the number of chromosomes or cells greater is the DNA content. Justify.

250. (i) Draw a longitudinal section of flower exhibiting germination of pollen on stigma and label ovary, male-germ cell, female-germ cell, ovule on it.
   (ii) After fertilisation in a flower, mention the structures that develop into the embryo and seed.

251. What are the different methods of asexual reproduction? Explain budding and regeneration with diagrams?

252. List two differences between self-pollination and cross-pollination?

253. Give one difference between binary fission and budding.

254. Explain budding in yeast with proper diagram?

255. What are the various parts of an embryo of a dicot seed?

256. What is the role of Seminal Fliud ?

257. Which hormone stimulates the release of egg from ovary almost every month after puberty in woman?

258. Discuss what will be the effect of DNA copying which is not perfectly accurate in the reproduction process?

259. Mention secondary sexual characters in human male and female.

260. Give reason for the statement— "Since the ovary releases one egg every month, the uterus also prepares itself every month by making its lining thick and spongy."

261. List distinguishing features between sexual and asexual types of reproduction in tabular form.

262. Answer the following:
   (i) List two advantages of sexual reproduction over asexual reproduction?
   (ii) How will an organism be benefitted if it reproduces through spores.
   (iii) Name a sexually transmitted disease and a method to avoid it.
   (iv) Illustrate the following with the help of suitable diagrams:
      (a) Spore formation in Rhizopus
      (b) Multiple fission in Plasmodium

263. **Assertion:** XX chromosome give rise to female child whereas XY give rise to male child.

   Reason: The Y chromosome in males is smaller than X chromosome.

Chapter 9

Heredity and Evolution

Definitions

1. **Heredity:** Transmission of genetically based characters from one generation to the next generation is called heredity.
2. **Gene:** It is a specific segment of DNA on a chromosome occupying specific position and determines the hereditary characters.
3. **Traits:** The alternative forms of a character are called traits.
4. **Genetics:** It is the branch of biology that deals with the study of heredity and variations.
5. **Monohybrid cross:** A breeding experiment which involves the alternative traits of one single character is called monohybrid cross.
6. **Dihybrid cross:** A cross between two pure breeding individuals taking into consideration alternative traits of two different characters is called a dihybrid cross.
7. **Variation:** It is the differences in the traits shown by the individuals of a species and also by the offsprings of the same parents are called variations.
8. **Sex determination:** The mechanism by which sex of an individual is determined when it begins its life.

Multiple Choice Questions

9. What, according to Mendel, was responsible for the inheritance of specific traits?
   (a) Genes (b) Factors
   (c) Chromosomes (d) DNA

   Ans. (b) Factors

   Explanation:
   Mendel discovered the laws of inheritance. He attributed these traits being encoded by factors. Later studies showed that these factors are genes.

10. What branch of biology focuses on the study of patterns of inheritance?
    (a) Genetics (b) Immunology
    (c) Evolution (d) Ecology

    Ans. (a) Genetics

    Explanation:
    Genetics is the branch of biology that deals with questions of inheritance. It uses techniques from various disciplines like Molecular biology, Cell biology, and many more to understand the basis of inheritance.

11. What determines the differences between the progeny and parents?
    (a) Inheritance (b) Heritage
    (c) Genetics (d) Variation

    Ans. (d) Variation

    Explanation:
    Variation is the difference between individuals within a population. These arise between the progeny and parents/ancestors and form a backbone for natural selection to act on.

12. The phenomenon where individuals of a species exhibit differences in characteristics are called:
    (a) Adaptation (b) Evolution
    (c) Variation (d) All of these

    Ans. (c) Variation

    Explanation:
    Any difference between cells, individuals, or groups of organisms of any species produced by genetic differences (genotypic variation) or the effect of environmental conditions on the manifestation of genetic potentials is referred to as variation (phenotypic variation).

13. Which of the following statements is incorrect?
    (a) Gene is a sequence of nucleotides.
    (b) During the process of gene expression, DNA is first copied into RNA.
    (c) Genes can acquire mutations in their sequence.

(d) Genes cannot acquire mutations in their sequence.

Ans. (c) Genes can acquire mutations in their sequence.

Explanation :

Genes can acquire mutations. A gene mutation is a change in the DNA sequence that makes up a gene that is permanent and differs from the sequence found in most people.

14. **Which part of the DNA provides information for a protein?**
    (a) Chromosome (b) Mitochondria
    (c) RNA (d) Gene

Ans. (d) Gene

Explanation :

The information needed to build proteins is stored in the DNA of an organism. A unique portion of DNA is called a gene code for each protein. A gene is a piece of DNA that is required to make a single protein.

15. **Which of the following is controlled by genes?**
    (a) Eye colour (b) Height
    (c) Hair colour (d) All of these

Ans. (d) All of these

Explanation :

Characters or traits are the characteristics that a person expresses and can be seen in their phenotype. Height, eye colour, and body colour are all controlled by genes and can be inherited.

16. **The discipline of Biology that deals with the study of inheritance is**
    (a) Cytology (b) Evolution
    (c) Genetics (d) Morphology

Ans. (c) Genetics

Explanation :

Genetics is the branch of biology concerned with the study of the DNA and its inheritance in the organisms.

17. **Germinal variations are those variations which**
    (a) are inheritable
    (b) affect only somatic cells
    (c) are not inheritable
    (d) None of the above

Ans. (a) are inheritable

Explanation :

Germinal variations occur in germ cells that get passed to the next generation through gametes produced by the germ cells.

18. **When a gene exists in more than one form, the different forms are terms as**
    (a) alleles (b) heterozygotes
    (c) genotypes (d) homozygotes

Ans. (a) alleles

Explanation :

An allele is a variant form of a gene.

19. **The terms 'genotype' and 'phenotype' were coined by**
    (a) Darwin (b) Bateson
    (c) Johannsen (d) Mendel

Ans. (c) Johannsen

Explanation :

Danish botanist Wilhelm Johannsen coined the word gene to describe the Mendelian units of heredity. He also made the distinction between the outer appearance of an individual (phenotype) and its genetic traits (genotype).

20. **Two pink coloured flowers on crossing resulted in 1 red, 2 pink and 1 white flower progeny. The nature of the cross will be:** [NCERT Exemplar]
    (a) double fertilisation
    (b) self pollination
    (c) cross fertilisation
    (d) no fertilisation

Ans. (c) cross fertilisation

Explanation :

In incomplete dominance, the cross between plants with pure red and white flowers results in F1 generation plants with all pink flowers. The self-pollination or fertilisation of these plants results in progenies (F2 generation) with red, pink and white flowers in a ratio of 1 : 2 : 1 respectively.

21. **Which of the following statement is true?**
    (a) The characteristics or traits of parents are transmitted to their progeny (offspring) through genes present on their chromosomes during the process of sexual reproduction.
    (b) The genes which dominate other genes are called dominant genes and the genes which get dominated are called recessive genes.
    (c) The progeny inherits two genes for each trait from its parent but the traits shown by the progeny depends on which inherited gene is dominant of the two.
    (d) All of the above

Ans. (d) All of the above

Explanation :

Here, all the statements are correct. Hence, the answer will be option [d].

22. **Dominant alleles are expressed exclusively in a heterozygote, while recessive traits are expressed only if the organism is ....for the recessive allele.**
    (a) homozygous (b) heterozygous
    (c) normal (d) none of these

Ans. (a) homozygous

Explanation :

Mendel's law of dominance states that in a heterozygote, one trait will conceal the presence of another trait for the same characteristic. Rather than both alleles contributing to a phenotype, the dominant allele will be expressed exclusively. The recessive allele will remain "latent," but will be transmitted to offspring by the same manner in which the dominant allele is transmitted. The recessive trait will only be expressed by offspring that have two copies of this allele.

23. **From the list given below select the character which can be acquired but not inherited.**

    [NCERT Exemplar]
    - (a) Colour of eye
    - (b) Colour of skin
    - (c) Size of body
    - (d) Nature of hair

    Ans. (c) Size of body

Explanation :

Environmental factors influence the development of acquired traits. It is because the availability of less or more food can modify the size of the body, it is an acquired feature. The other three- eye and skin colour, and nature of hair, are inherited characteristics from the parents.

24. **Select the group which shares maximum number of common characters.**
    - (a) Two individuals of a species
    - (b) Two species of a genus
    - (c) Two genera of a family
    - (d) Two genera of two families

    Ans. (a) Two individual of a species

Explanation :

As we move from higher taxonomic rank to lower one, common characters increase. Among species, genus, family and families; species is the lowest taxonomic rank. Hence, two individuals of the same species will share maximum number of common characters.

25. **A Mendelian experiment consisted of breeding tall pea plants bearing violet flowers with short pea plants bearing white flowers. The progeny all bore violet flowers but almost half of them were short. This suggests that the genetic make-up of the tall parent can be depicted as:** [NCERT]
    - (a) TTWW
    - (b) TTww
    - (c) TtWW
    - (d) TtWw

    Ans. (c) TtWW

Explanation :

According to the law of dominance, hybridisation between two pure-breeding varieties yields uniforms F_1 generation of all dominant offspring. Since here F_1 generation consists of short plants with violet flowers and tall plants with violet flowers in an exceedingly 1:1 ratio, the dominant parent is not pure-bred. The absence of a dominant allele for flower colour (violet) would make the phenotype of the dominant parent tall with white flowers.

26. **A cross between a tall plant (TT) and short pea plant (tt) resulted in progeny that were all tall plants because:** [NCERT Exemplar]
    - (a) tallness is the dominant trait.
    - (b) shortness is the dominant trait.
    - (c) tallness is the recessive trait.
    - (d) height of pea plant is not governed by gene 'T' or 't'.

    Ans. (a) tallness is the dominant trait.

Explanation :

A cross between a tall plant (TT) and short pea plant (tt) resulted in progeny that were all tall plants because tallness is the dominant trait. In F1 generation, the cross between TT and tt will result in all tall plants. Thus, tallness is the dominant trait.

27. **The process where characteristics are transmitted from parent to offsprings is called:**
    - (a) Variation
    - (b) Heredity
    - (c) Gene
    - (d) Allele

    Ans. (b) Heredity

Explanation :

The process where characteristics are transmitted from parent to offsprings is called as heredity. During the process of sexual reproduction, characteristics from parents are passed down to offspring which are the combinations of female and male parent. This is known as heredity.

28. **_____ is the observable set of characteristics of an organism.**
    - (a) Phenotype
    - (b) Genes
    - (c) DNA
    - (d) All of these

    Ans. (a) Phenotype

Explanation :

The term "phenotype" refers to an organism's observable physical properties, such as its appearance, development, and behaviour.

29. **When a new plant is formed as a result of cross-pollination from different varieties of a plant, the newly formed plant is called:**
    - (a) Dominant plant
    - (b) Mutant plant
    - (c) Hybrid plant
    - (d) All of these

    Ans. (a) Dominant plant

Explanation :

The process of crossing pollen from one flower to the pistils of another flower is known as cross-pollination. When a new plant is formed as a result of cross-pollination from different varieties of a plant, the newly formed plant is called hybrid plant.

30. **Which of the following is a recessive trait in pea plants?**
    (a) Dwarf stem height (b) Violet flowers
    (c) Axial flowers (d) Inflated pods

Ans. (a) Dwarf stem height

Explanation :

Recessive traits are the ones that require both alleles to be present to result in the expression of the gene product. Of the mentioned traits, only dwarf stem height is a recessive trait, in pea plants.

31. **If you were to sample garden pea plants in Mendel's garden, which of the following statements would hold?**
    (a) Round seeds were more abundant than wrinkled seeds.
    (b) Wrinkled seeds were more abundant than round seeds.
    (c) Both round and wrinkled seeds were equally abundant.
    (d) Answer depends on the time of day when sampling is done.

Ans. (a) Round seeds were more abundant than wrinkled seeds.

Explanation :

Dominant allele can express even in the presence of a recessive allele. Hence, dominant phenotype is more common. Round seeds are dominant over wrinkled seeds; hence would be more abundant.

32. **Which of the following can be inherited from parents to offspring?**
    (a) Swimming technique
    (b) Big nose
    (c) Sculpted body
    (d) All of the above

Ans. (b) Big nose

Explanation :

Big nose is an inherited trait which can be passed from parents to offspring.

33. **Which of the following is an example of genetic variation?**
    (a) One person has a scar but his friend does not.
    (b) One person is older than the other.
    (c) Reeta eats meat but her sister Geeta is a vegetarian.
    (d) Two children have different eye colour.

Ans. (d) Two children have different eye colour.

Explanation :

Variation in gene frequencies is referred to as genetic variation. Eye colour is determined by variations in genes of a person. Two children having different eye colour is an example of genetic variation.

34. **In peas, a pure tall (TT) is crossed with a pure short plant(tt). The ratio of pure tall plants to pure short plants in F_2 generation is:**
    (a) 1:3 (b) 3:1
    (c) 1:1 (d) 2:1

Ans. (c) 1:1

Explanation :

In the F_2 generation, the ratio of pure tall plants to pure short plants will be 1:1. The other two plants that are produced will be tall as well, but will not be pure.

35. **Humans have two different sex chromosomes, X and Y. Based on Mendel's laws, a male offspring will inherit which combination of chromosomes?**
    (a) Both the X chromosomes from one of its parents.
    (b) Both the Y chromosomes from one of its parents.
    (c) Combination of X chromosomes from either of its parents.
    (d) Combination of X and Y chromosome from either of its parents.

Ans. (d) Combination of X and Y chromosome from either of its parents.

Explanation :

The X and Y chromosomes are found in humans and most other mammals. Males have both X and Y chromosomes in their cells, whereas females have two X chromosomes. X chromosomes are found in all egg cells, while X or Y chromosomes are found in sperm cells.

36. **Two pea plants one with round green seeds (RR yy) and another with wrinkled yellow (rrYY) seeds produce F_1 progeny that have round yellow (RrYy) seeds. When F_1 plants are self pollinated, the F_2 progeny will have a new combination of characters. Choose the new combinations from the following.**
    [NCERT Exemplar]
    (i) Round, yellow (ii) Round, green
    (iii) Wrinkled, yellow (iv) Wrinkled, green
    (a) (i) and (ii) (b) (i) and (iv)
    (c) (ii) and (iii) (d) (i) and (iii)

Ans. (b) (i) and (iv)

Explanation :

The new combination in F_2 progeny will be round yellow and wrinkled green. The phenotypic ratio obtained in a dihybrid cross is 9 : 3 : 3 : 1. The phenotypic ratio will be - Round Yellow: Round green: Wrinkled yellow: Wrinkled green = 9 : 3 : 3 : 1.

37. If Mendel would have carried out cross pollination of a pea plant having tt trait with pea plant having Tt trait then the F1 Progeny plants would have been?
    (a) Two dwarf and Two tall plant
    (b) One dwarf and three tall plant
    (c) All Tall
    (d) All dwarf

Ans. (a) Two dwarf and Two tall plant

Explanation :

The cross will be as shown in the table:

	T	t
t	Tt	tt
t	Tt	tt

So, there will be two tall and two dwarf plants.

38. Mendel conducted his experiments with
    (a) chick pea   (b) garden pea
    (c) wild pea   (d) pigeon pea

Ans. (b) garden pea

Explanation :

Garden pea or Pisum sativum was used by Mendel to study inheritance. He used this particular plant because it has easily identifiable traits.

39. A pea plant with round and green seeds (RRyy) is crossed with another pea plant with wrinkled and yellow seeds (rrYY). What would be the nature of seeds in the first generation (F1 generation).
    (a) Round green   (b) Wrinkled green
    (c) Wrinkled yellow (d) Round yellow

Ans. (d) Round yellow

Explanation :

The characters that appear in the first generation are dominant. In this case, round seeds and yellow colour is dominant.

40. A group of laboratory mice having tails are bred together and their progeny is studied. The progeny had tails. However, the scientist removed the tails surgically and again bred them for four successive generations. In your opinion, what would be the nature of the new progeny?
    (a) All mice born will have tails.
    (b) All mice born will have no tails.
    (c) The ratio of tailless to the tailed mice will be 1 : 3.
    (d) The ratio of tailless to the tailed mice will be 1 : 4.

Ans. (a) All mice born will have tails.

Explanation :

By surgical removal of the tails the scientist is not able to produce any change in the germ cells. Basically, he is not able to influence the cause of germinal variations, which is DNA (genes). Thus, this change of tail removal does not get inherited by the progeny.

41. When a cross is made between two parents with respect to a single character, it is called a
    (a) dihybrid cross   (b) monohybrid cross
    (c) trihybrid cross   (d) None of these

Ans. (b) monohybrid cross

Explanation :

A monohybrid cross is a cross between two organisms with different variations at one genetic locus of interest. For example, a cross between a tall pea plant and a dwarf pea plant that is considering only the height of the parents is a monohybrid cross.

42. The genotype of the offspring formed from the cross depicted as Tt × tt will be
    (a) TT and tt   (b) Tt and tt
    (c) Only tt   (d) Only TT

Ans. (b) Tt and tt

Explanation :

This is a test cross. A test cross is a cross of any genotype showing dominant phenotype with a recessive homozygote to determine the genotype of a dominant parent, i.e., whether it is a heterozygous or a homozygous dominant. In the above case, the parent is heterozygous dominant because offspring contains dwarf plants as well.

43. Which of the following statements is not true with respect to variations?
    (a) All variations in a species have equal chances of survival.
    (b) Change in genetic composition results in variation.
    (c) Selection of variants by environmental factors forms the basis of evolutionary processes.
    (d) Variation is minimum in asexual reproduction.

Ans. (a) All variations in a species have equal chances of survival.

Explanation :

All variations in a species do not have equal chances of survival. Some of the variations may be so drastic that the new DNA copy cannot sustain in the cellular environment in which it is inherited.

44. According to Mendel, the genotypic ratio of F2 generation in a monohybrid cross is
    (a) 3 : 1   (b) 9 : 3 : 3 : 1
    (c) 1 : 1   (d) 1 : 2 : 1

Ans. (d) 1 : 2 : 1

Explanation :

A monohybrid cross is mating between individuals who have different alleles at one genetic locus of interest. In a monohybrid cross, the pure breed tall and dwarf homozygous plants are crossed.

Genotype:	TT	X	tt
Gametes:	T		t
Offspring:	Tt		
Selfing of F1:	Tt	X	Tt
Gametes:	T, t		T, t
F2 generation:	TT, Tt, Tt and tt		
Genotypic ratio:	1 : 2 : 1		

45. Recessive genes can be expressed only in
(a) homozygous condition
(b) heterozygous condition
(c) Both of the above conditions
(d) None of the above conditions

Ans. (a) homozygous condition

Explanation :

In a homozygous condition, recessive allele can express itself as there is no dominant allele to mask its effect.

46. A plant (homozygous for flower colour) with red coloured flowers is crossed with a plant having white flowers. The red and white colour of the flowers is controlled by a single gene. Red is dominant over white. The F1 progeny is self-pollinated and the flower colour in F2 generation is observed.

Given the above information, what is the expected phenotypic ratio of plants with different flower colours in F2?
(a) All plants will be with red flowers.
(b) Red : White flowers will be in the ratio of 3 : 1.
(c) Pink : White flowers will be in the ratio of 3 : 1.
(d) Red : Pink : White flowers will be in the ratio of 1 : 2 : 1.

Ans. (b) Red : White flowers will be in the ratio of 3 : 1.

Explanation :

Red is dominant. When the F1 progeny is self-crossed (Rr X Rr), the cross will yield the following genotypes in the F2 generation:

F2 generation—RR, Rr and rr in the ratio of 1 : 2 : 1, but the phenotypic ratio will be Red : White in the ratio of 3 : 1.

47. The sex of the child depends on the chromosomes present in the
(a) egg of the female   (b) sperm of the male
(c) Both (a) and (b)   (d) None of these

Ans. (b) sperm of the male

Explanation :

The sex of the child depends on the male chromosome which is transferred to the offspring. This happens because males have a mismatched pair of sex chromosome (XY) which is responsible for deciding the sex of the child.

48. Which of the following conditions of the zygote would lead to the birth of the normal human female child?
(a) Two X chromosomes
(b) Only one Y chromosome
(c) Only one X chromosome
(d) One X and one Y chromosome

Ans. (a) Two X chromosomes

Explanation :

Human beings contain 44 autosomes and one pair of allosome. In females, the allosome composition is XX and in males it is XY. The other combinations such as XO, XXY, etc., will lead to different genetic disorders.

49. In humans, sex determination is controlled by
(a) allosomes   (b) autosomes
(c) temperature   (d) All of the above

Ans. (a) allosomes

Explanation :

In humans, sex is determined by the sex chromosomes or a pair of allosomes (XX in females, XY in males).

50. In humans, the sex Chromosomes comprises one pair of the total of 23 pairs of chromosomes. The other 22 pairs of chromosome are called:
(a) autosomes   (b) chromosomes
(c) meiosis   (d) all of these

Ans. (a) autosomes

Explanation :

In humans, each cell normally contains 23 pairs of chromosomes, for a total of 46. Twenty-two of these pairs, called autosomes, look the same in both males and females. The 23rd pair, the sex chromosomes, differ between males and females. Females have two copies of the X chromosome, while males have one X and one Y chromosome.

51. The number of pairs of sex chromosomes in the zygote of humans is:
(a) 1   (b) 2
(c) 3   (d) 4

Ans. (a) 1

Explanation :

In the human zygote, the number of pairs of autosomes and sex chromosomes is the same as in an adult human. A human adult possesses 23 pairs of chromosomes, 22 of which are autosomes and 1 of which is a sex chromosome.

52. In human males all the chromosomes are paired perfectly except one. These unpaired chromosomes are:
(i) Large chromosome (ii) Small chromosome
(iii) Y-chromosome   (iv) X-chromosome

(a) (i), (ii) (b) (iii) only
(c) (iii), (iv) (d) (ii), (iv)
Ans. (c) (iii), (iv)

Explanation :

In human males, one pair called as the sex chromosomes are unpaired. Here, one is a normal sized X chromosome while other is a short Y chromosome. Women have a perfect pair of sex chromosomes, both called as X. Whereas the X and Y chromosomes are paired well.

53. **Which chromosomes do not play any role in the determination of the sex of an individual?**
    (a) Autosomes
    (b) Metacentric chromosomes
    (c) Acrocentric chromosomes
    (d) None of the above

Ans. (a) Autosomes

Explanation :

Autosomes do not play any role in the determination of the sex of an individual since they are alike in both the males and the females and are 22 in pairs.

54. **The two versions of a trait which are brought in by the male and female gametes are situated on:** [NCERT Exemplar]
    (a) copies of the same chromosome
    (b) two different chromosomes
    (c) sex chromosomes
    (d) any chromosomes

Ans. (a) copies of the same chromosome

Explanation :

The two versions of a trait which are brought in by the male and female gametes are situated on different copies of the same chromosome, different alleles are present. One chromosome is inherited from the father via the male gamete, while the other chromosome is inherited from the mother via the female gamete. After fertilisation, a zygote with 23 pairs of chromosomes is created, with alleles for a trait present on the homologous pair.

55. **In human males, all the chromosomes are paired perfectly except one. This/these unpaired chromosome is/are** [NCERT Exemplar]
    (i) large chromosome
    (ii) small chromosome
    (iii) Y-chromosome
    (iv) X-chromosome
    (a) (i) and (ii) (b) (iii) only
    (c) (iii) and (iv) (d) (ii) and (iv)

Ans. (c) (iii) and (iv)

Explanation :

In human males, one pair called the **sex chromosomes** are unpaired. Here, one is a normal-sized X-chromosome while other is a short Y-chromosome. Women have a perfect pair of sex chromosomes, both called X.

56. **The maleness of a child is determined by** [NCERT Exemplar]
    (a) the X-chromosome in the zygote.
    (b) the Y-chromosome in zygote.
    (c) the cytoplasm of germ cell which determines the sex.
    (d) sex is determined by chance.

Ans. (b) the Y-chromosome in zygote.

Explanation :

The maleness of a child is determined by the Y-chromosome in zygote inherited from the father. If X-chromosome is inherited from the father, the zygote will develop into girl.

57. **A zygote which has an X-chromosome inherited from the father will develop into a** [NCERT Exemplar]
    (a) boy
    (b) girl
    (c) X-chromosome does not determine the sex of child
    (d) either boy or girl

Ans. (b) girl

Explanation :

A zygote that has an X-chromosome inherited from father will develop into a girl. All children whether boys or girls inherit an X-chromosome from their mother. Thus, sex is determined by what they inherit from their father. A child who inherits X-chromosome from her father will be a girl, and one who inherits a Y-chromosome from him will be a boy.

Assertion and Reasoning Based Questions

58. **Assertion:** Changes in non-reproductive tissues can be passed on the DNA of the germ cells.

    Reason: Inherited traits include the traits developed during the lifetime of an individual that cannot be passed on the its progeny.

    (a) If both assertion and reason are true and reason is the correct explanation of assertion.
    (b) If both assertion and reason are true, but reason is not the correct explanation of assertion.
    (c) If assertion is true, but reason is false.
    (d) If assertion is false, but reason is true.

Ans. (d) If assertion is false, but reason is true.

Explanation :

Changes in non-reproductive tissues cannot be passed on the DNA of the germ cells. The traits developed during the lifetime of an individual that cannot be passed on to its progenies are acquired traits. Thus assertion is false, but reason is true.

Reason: It is represented by capital letter, *e.g.,* T.

59. **Assertion:** Variations are seen in offspring produced by asexual reproduction.

    Reason: DNA molecule generated by replication is not exactly identical to original DNA.
    (a) If both assertion and reason are true and reason is the correct explanation of assertion.
    (b) If both assertion and reason are true, but reason is not the correct explanation of assertion.
    (c) If assertion is true, but reason is false.
    (d) If assertion is false, but reason is true.

Ans. (d) If assertion is false, but reason is true.

Explanation :

Variations are not seen in the offspring produced by the asexual reproduction since only a single parent is involved the variations are not there and thus assertion is false, but reason is true.

60. **Assertion:** The genetic complement of an organism is called genotype.

    Reason: Genotype is the type of hereditary properties of an organism.
    (a) If both assertion and reason are true and reason is the correct explanation of assertion.
    (b) If both assertion and reason are true, but reason is not the correct explanation of assertion.
    (c) If assertion is true, but reason is false.
    (d) If assertion is false, but reason is true.

Ans. (b) If both assertion and reason are true, but reason is not the correct explanation of assertion.

Explanation :

The genetic constitution of a cell or an organism is referred to as a genotype. It consists of the total of all recessive and dominant genes and the various genes are the heredity material that serves to transfer the genetic information from one generation to the next. This makes genotype an inherited property of organisms. Hence, the reason is correct. However, it is not a correct explanation for the assertion. Thus, both assertion and reason are true but reason is not the correct explanation of assertion.

61. **Assertion:** If the weight of the beetle is reduced because of starvation, that will not change the DNA of the germ cells.

    Reason: Acquired traits are not inherited.
    (a) If both assertion and reason are true and reason is the correct explanation of assertion.

    (b) If both assertion and reason are true, but reason is not the correct explanation of assertion.
    (c) If assertion is true, but reason is false.
    (d) If assertion is false, but reason is true.

Ans. (a) If both assertion and reason are true and reason is the correct explanation of assertion.

Explanation :

Acquired traits are not inherited because they do not cause any change in the DNA of the organism. Therefore, low weight is not a trait that can be inherited by the progeny of a starving beetle. Therefore, even if some generations of beetles are low in weight because of starvation, that is not an example of evolution, since the change is not inherited over generations. Thus, both assertion and reason are true and reason is the correct explanation of the assertion.

62. **Assertion:** Dominant allele is an allele whose phenotype expresses even in the presence of another allele of that gene.

    Reason: It is represented by a capital letter, *e.g.* T.
    (a) If both assertion and reason are true and reason is the correct explanation of assertion.
    (b) If both assertion and reason are true, but reason is not the correct explanation of assertion.
    (c) If assertion is true, but reason is false.
    (d) If assertion is false, but reason is true.

Ans. (b) If both assertion and reason are true, but reason is not the correct explanation of assertion.

Explanation :

Dominant allele is an allele whose phenotype expresses even in the presence of another allele of that gene and is generally represented by the capital letters. Thus both assertion and reason are true but reason is not the correct explanation of the assertion.

63. **Assertion:** Mendel was successful in his hybridisation experiments.

    Reason: Garden pea proved as an ideal experimental material.
    (a) If both assertion and reason are true and reason is the correct explanation of assertion.
    (b) If both assertion and reason are true, but reason is not the correct explanation of assertion.
    (c) If assertion is true, but reason is false.
    (d) If assertion is false, but reason is true.

Ans. (a) If both assertion and reason are true and reason is the correct explanation of assertion.

Explanation :

The pea plant which Mendel choose for conducting experiments, is most ideal for controlled breeding, since it can easily be subjected to cross pollination.

He identified very clear contrasting characters in the pea plants. Thus, both assertion and reason are true and reason is the correct explanation of the assertion.

64. **Assertion:** Dominant allele is an allele whose phenotype expresses even in the presence of another allele of that gene.
    (a) If both assertion and reason are true and reason is the correct explanation of assertion.
    (b) If both assertion and reason are true, but reason is not the correct explanation of assertion.
    (c) If assertion is true, but reason is false.
    (d) If assertion is false, but reason is true.

Ans. (b) If both assertion and reason are true, but reason is not the correct explanation of assertion.

Explanation :

Dominant allele is an allele whose phenotype will be expressed even in the presence of another allele of that gene. It is represented by a capital Letter, e.g., T. Both assertion and reason are true but reason is not the correct explanation of assertion.

65. **Assertion:** Chromosomes are capable of self-reproduction and maintaining morphological and physiological properties through successive generations.

    Reason: Chromosomes are capable of self-reproduction and maintaining morphological and physiological properties through successive generations.
    (a) If both assertion and reason are true and reason is the correct explanation of assertion.
    (b) If both assertion and reason are true, but reason is not the correct explanation of assertion.
    (c) If assertion is true, but reason is false.
    (d) If assertion is false, but reason is true.

Ans. (a) If both assertion and reason are true and reason is the correct explanation of assertion.

Explanation :

Chromosomes are known as heredity vehicles because they are capable of self-reproduction and maintains the characteristics in an individual generation after generation. Thus both assertion and reason are true and reason is the correct explanation of the assertion.

66. **Assertion:** Mendel selected the pea plant for his experiments.

    Reason: Pea plant is cross-pollinating and has unisexual flowers.
    (a) If both assertion and reason are true and reason is the correct explanation of assertion.
    (b) If both assertion and reason are true, but reason is not the correct explanation of assertion.
    (c) If assertion is true, but reason is false.
    (d) If assertion is false, but reason is true.

Ans. (a) If both assertion and reason are true and reason is the correct explanation of assertion.

Explanation :

The flowers of pea plant are bisexual and they are self-pollinating, and thus, self and cross-pollination can easily be performed. They have a shorter life span and are the plants that are easier to maintain. Therefore Mendel choose the pea plant. Thus both assertion and reason are true and reason is the correct explanation of the assertion.

67. **Assertion:** Mendel self-crossed F_1 yellow with round seeds to obtain F_2 generation.

    Reason: F_1 progeny of a yellow with round seeds and a green with wrinkled seeds are all green and wrinkled seeds.
    (a) If both assertion and reason are true and reason is the correct explanation of assertion.
    (b) If both assertion and reason are true, but reason is not the correct explanation of assertion.
    (c) If assertion is true, but reason is false.
    (d) If assertion is false, but reason is true.

Ans. (c) If assertion is true, but reason is false.

Explanation :

Mendel took two contradicting traits together for crossing i.e., colour and shape of seeds. He chose a round yellow seed and a wrinkled green seed and crossed them. He obtained only round yellow seeds in the F_1 generation. Then, F_1 progeny ws self-pollinated, which gave four different combinations of seeds i.e., round-yellow, wrinkled-yellow, round green and wrinkled green seeds in the F_2 generation. So, assertion is true but reason is false.

68. **Assertion:** A geneticist crossed two pea plants got 50% tall and 50% dwarf in the progeny.

    Reason: One plants was heterozygous tall and the other was dwarf.
    (a) If both assertion and reason are true and reason is the correct explanation of assertion.
    (b) If both assertion and reason are true, but reason is not the correct explanation of assertion.
    (c) If assertion is true, but reason is false.
    (d) If assertion is false, but reason is true.

Ans. (a) If both assertion and reason are true and reason is the correct explanation of assertion.

Explanation :

The given cross can be illustrated as follows:
or 50% tall, 50% dwarf progeny.

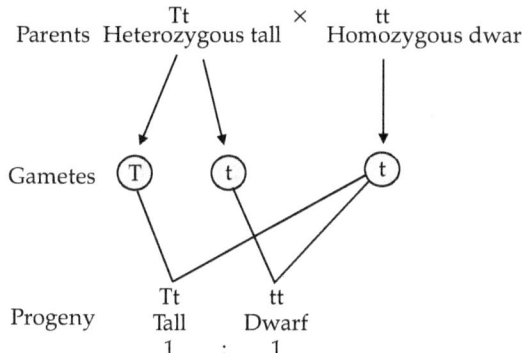

Thus both assertion and reason are true and reason is the correct explanation of assertion.

69. **Assertion:** The low of independent assortment can be studies by maeas of dihybrid cross.

    Reason: The law of independent assortment is applicable only to linked genes.
    (a) If both assertion and reason are true and reason is the correct explanation of assertion.
    (b) If both assertion and reason are true, but reason is not the correct explanation of assertion.
    (c) If assertion is true, but reason is false.
    (d) If assertion is false, but reason is true.

Ans. (c) If assertion is true, but reason is false.

Explanation:

The law of independent assortment states that two factors of each character assort or separate independent of the factors of other characters at the times of gemete formation and get randomly rearranged in the offspring producing both parental and new combinations of traits. The principle of law of independent assortment is applicable to only those factors or genes which are either located distantly on the same chromosome or occur on different chromosomes. Actually, a chromosome bears hundreds of genes. All the genes of factors present on a chromosome are inherited together except when crossing over takes place. Thus assertion is true but reason is false.

70. **Assertion:** The sex of the children will be determined by chromosome received from the father.

    Reason: A human male has one X and one Y chromosome.
    (a) If both assertion and reason are true and reason is the correct explanation of assertion.
    (b) If both assertion and reason are true, but reason is not the correct explanation of assertion.
    (c) If assertion is true, but reason is false.
    (d) If assertion is false, but reason is true.

Ans. (a) If both assertion and reason are true and reason is the correct explanation of assertion.

Explanation:

If a child inherits X-chromosome from the father will be a girl and one who inherits a Y-chromosome will be a boy. Thus, both assertion and reason are true and reason is the correct explanation of assertion.

Case Based Questions

71. **Read the passage carefully and answer the following questions from Q 71 (i) to 71 (v).**

    Heredity is the passing on of some specific characteristics from one generation to the next, from parent to offspring. The study of heredity is called genetics. The traits are passed on by genes in our DNA. A gene gives instructions about making a certain protein to determine a trait for the person like the colour of eyes or hair. The genes are located inside a DNA molecule which is a material found in chromosomes. Genes may be dominant or recessive.

    (i) What was the model organism used by Mendel to give the laws of inheritance?
      (a) Garden peas (b) Wild peas
      (c) Basket peas (d) Bottle gourd
    (ii) A zygote which has an X-chromosome inherited from the father will develop into a:
      (a) girl.
      (b) boy.
      (c) either boy or girl.
      (d) X-chromosome does not influence the sex of a child.
    (iii) The factor which expresses in homozygous and heterozygous states is called _____.
      (a) dominant (b) recessive
      (c) gene (d) allele
    (iv) The study of the pattern of chromosomes from parents to the offspring is called:
      (a) Genetics
      (b) Evolution
      (c) Offspring analysis
      (d) Genetical analysis
    (v) In Mendel's experiment, the trait which did not appear in the F1 generation was:
      (a) dominant (b) recessive
      (c) recession (d) allele

Ans. (i) (a) Garden peas
    (ii) (a) girl
    (iii) (a) dominant
    (iv) (a) Genetics
    (v) (b) recessive

72. **Read the passage carefully and answer the following questions from Q 72 (i) to 72 (v).**

The study of heredity is called genetics. Traits are characteristics such as hair colour, eye colour, artistic or athletic ability, height, and more. Every living organism, plant, or animal, receives its characteristics or traits from its parents. In plants these traits may include seed colour, flower position, length of stem, and much more. The first person to discover this passing of traits was a scientist named Gregor Mendel. He is considered as the father of genetics. He studied pea plants and discovered that certain traits were passed on, or inherited from parent to offspring.

(i) Pure-breed pea plant A is crossed with pure-breed pea plant B. It is found that the plants which look like A do not appear in F_1 generation but re-emerge in F_2 generation. Which of the plants A and B are tall and dwarf?
   (a) A are tall and B are dwarf.
   (b) A are tall and B are also tall.
   (c) A are dwarf and B are also dwarf.
   (d) A are dwarf and B are tall.

(ii) In humans if gene B gives brown eyes and gene b gives blue eyes, what will be the colour of eyes of the persons having combinations?
   (i) Bb and (ii) BB
   (a) (i) Blue and (ii) Brown
   (b) (i) Brown and (ii) Blue
   (c) (i) Brown and (ii) Brown
   (d) (i) Blue and (ii) Blue

(iii) If a round, green seeded pea plant (RRyy) is crossed with a wrinkled yellow seeded pea plant (rrYY), the seeds produced in F_1 generation are:
   (a) round and green
   (b) round and yellow
   (c) wrinkled and green
   (d) wrinkled and yellow

(iv) A cross between two individuals results in a ratio of 9: 3: 3:1 for four possible phenotypes of progeny. This is an example of a:
   (a) Monohybrid cross
   (b) Dihybrid cross
   (c) Test cross
   (d) F_1 generation

(v) A man with blood group A marries a woman having blood group O. What will be the blood group of the child?
   (a) O only
   (b) A only
   (c) AB
   (d) Equal chance of acquiring blood group A or blood group O

Ans. (i) (d) A are dwarf and B are tall
(ii) (c) (i) Brown and (ii) Brown
(iii) (b) round and yellow

(iv) (b) Dihybrid cross
(v) (d) Equal chance of acquiring blood group A or blood group O.

73. Read the following and answer the following questions from Q. 73 (i) to 73 (v):

Gregor Johann Mendel is known as a "Father of modern genetics" for his work in the field of genetics. He gave three laws of inheritance followed as Law of dominance, Law of segregation and Law of independent assortment. He conducted his experiment on garden pea plants having contrasting characteristics. He performed self-pollination and cross-pollination to understand the inheritance patterns of traits.

(i) After cross-fertilisation of true-breeding tall and dwarf plants, the F1 generation was self-fertilised. The resultant plants have genotype in the ratio:
   (a) 1:2:1 (homozygous tall: heterozygous tall: dwarf).
   (b) 1:2:1 (heterozygous tall: homozygous tall: dwarf).
   (c) 3:1 (tall: dwarf).
   (d) 3:1 (dwarf: tall).

(ii) Which of the following characteristics of pea plants was not used by Mendel in his experiments?
   (a) Seed colour   (b) Seed shape
   (c) Pod length   (d) Flower position

(iii) Mendel took _____ contrasting characteristics of pea plants.
   (a) eight   (b) seven
   (c) six   (d) five

(iv) The maleness of a child is determined by:
   (a) the X-chromosome in the zygote.
   (b) the Y-chromosome in zygote.
   (c) the cytoplasm of germ cell which determines the sex.
   (d) sex is determined by chance.

(v) Test cross determines:
   (a) whether two traits are linked or not.
   (b) the genotype of F_2 plant.
   (c) whether the two species will breed successfully or not.
   (d) number of alleles in a gene.

Ans. (i) (a) 1:2:1 (homozygous tall: heterozygous tall: dwarf).
(ii) (c) Pod length
(iii) (b) Seven
(iv) (b) the Y-choromosome in zygote
(v) (b) the genotype of F_2 plant.

74. Read the passage carefully and answer the following questions from Q 74 (i) to 74 (v).

Gregor Mendel, in 1865, paved the way for the analysis of the underlying genetic basis of traits by setting out to understand the principles of heredity. As per Darwin's observations, in nearly all populations individuals tend to produce far more offspring than are needed to replace the parents. He also observed that it is very rare for any two individuals to be exactly alike. All the natural variations among individuals lead to natural selection. Individuals born with variations that present an advantage in obtaining resources or mates have greater chances of living and reproducing offspring who would inherit and carry forward the favourable variations. At the same time, individuals with different variations might be less likely to reproduce.

(i) VV, Vv and vv are _____, while violet and white are _____.
    (a) genotypes, phenotypes
    (b) phenotypes, genotypes
    (c) genotypes, genotypes
    (d) phenotypes, phenotypes

(ii) Which one of the following traits is most likely to pass from one generation to other?
    (a) Artificial hair coloured by a mother during pregnancy.
    (b) Acquired skills by a father.
    (c) Brown eye colour.
    (d) Six fingers in right hand of a person.

(iii) _____ is simply the generation of diversity and the shaping of the diversity by environmental selection.
    (a) Evolution   (b) Speciation
    (c) Heredity   (d) Natural selection

(iv) Which one of the following statements is not true?
    (a) Excavating, time-dating, studying fossils, and determining DNA sequences are tools to study evolution.
    (b) Variations arising during the process of reproduction cannot be inherited.
    (c) Variations in the species may confer survival advantages or merely contribute to the genetic drift.
    (d) Classification of organisms is based on tracing evolutionary relationships.

(v) Frequency of certain _____ in a population changes over generations to bring about evolution.
    (a) members   (b) progenies
    (c) genes   (d) ideas

Ans. (i) (a) genotypes, phenotypes
(ii) (c) Brown eye colour
(iii) (a) Evolution
(iv) (b) Variations arising during the process of reproduction cannot be inherited
(v) (c) genes

75. **Read the passage carefully and answer the following questions from Q 75 (i) to 75 (v).**

Inheritance is the acquiring of genetic characteristics or traits from parents by their offspring. In humans, both parents equally contribute to the inheritance of traits. In 1860, Gregor Mendel studied the rules of inheritance of traits. He conducted an experiment on pea plants for the same. He cultivated pea plants and observed their pattern of inheritance from one generation to the next generation. This observation resulted in the discovery of three laws of inheritance, famously known as Mendel's laws of Inheritance.

(i) _____ is the observable set of characteristics of an organism.
    (a) Phenotype   (b) Genes
    (c) DNA   (d) All of these

(ii) Select the statements that describe characteristics of genes:
    (A) Genes are specific sequence of bases in a DNA molecule.
    (B) A gene does not code for proteins.
    (C) In individuals of a given species, a specific gene is located on a particular chromosome.
    (D) Each chromosome has only one gene.
    (a) (A), (B)   (b) (A), (C)
    (c) (A), (D)   (d) (B), (D)

(iii) A group of moths some brown and some green lived in a grassland having dry bushes and dry grass. This phenomenon is called:
    (a) Variation   (b) Natural selection
    (c) Mutations   (d) None of them

(iv) The two versions of a trait which are brought in by the male and female gametes are situated on :
    (a) copies of the same chromosome.
    (b) two different chromosomes.
    (c) sex chromosomes.
    (d) any chromosomes.

(v) If a round, green seeded pea plant (RRyy) is crossed with wrinkled, yellow seeded pea plant (rrYY), the seeds produced in F1 generation are :
    (a) round and yellow
    (b) round and green
    (c) wrinkled and green
    (d) wrinkled and yellow

Ans. (i) (a) Phenotype
(ii) (b) (A), (C)
(iii) (b) Natural selection
(iv) (a) copies of the same chromosome
(v) (a) Round and yellow

76. **Read the passage carefully and answer the following questions from Q 76 (i) to 76 (v).**

A genetic disorder is an inherited medical condition. It can be passed from parents to their children.

Examples include cystic fibrosis, sickle cell disease and haemophilia.

Parents who are heterozygous for these conditions are called carriers. They do not usually have the disorder themselves. This is shown in this Punnett square for cystic fibrosis.

An individual who is homozygous (cc) with the recessive allele will develop cystic fibrosis.

	C	c
C	CC	Cc
c	Cc	cc

(i) State the probability percentage of children Without cystic fibrosis
  (a) 75%   (b) 25%
  (c) 10%   (d) 5%

(ii) State the probability percentage of children with cystic fibrosis.
  (a) 75%   (b) 25%
  (c) 10%   (d) 5%

(iii) Genetic disorders are:
  (a) Inherited
  (b) Acquired
  (c) Cannot be determined
  (d) None of the above

(iv) Which of the following statement is correct in reference to cystic fibrosis?
  (a) Two heterozygous parents (carriers) have a two in four chance of passing it to their children.
  (b) Two heterozygous parents (carriers) have a one in four chance of passing it to their children.
  (c) Two heterozygous parents (carriers) have a three in four chance of passing it to their children.
  (d) Two heterozygous parents (carriers) will surely pass it to their children.

(v) State the probability of percentage of children with cystic fibrosis, if the parents are homozygous (cc) with the recessive allele.
  (a) 75%   (b) 25%
  (c) 100%   (d) 5%

Ans. (i) (a) 75%. Since, An individual who is homozygous (cc) with the recessive allele will develop cystic fibrosis. Without cystic fibrosis – three from four so 75%
(ii) (b) With cystic fibrosis – one from four so 25%
(iii) (a) Inherited
(iv) (b) one
(v) (c) 100%

Very Short Answer Type Questions

77. What is the functional unit of heredity?
Ans. Genes.

78. How many laws were given by Mendel?
Ans. Three laws.

79. What is Law of Dominance?
Ans. Law of Dominance says that a gene has two contrasting alleles and one always expresses itself in the organism.

80. What are homologous chromosome?
Ans. A pair of similar chromosomes (one received from the father and one from the mother) containing the same genes are termed homologous chromosomes.

81. Where are genes located?
Ans. Genes are found on tiny spaghetti-like structures called chromosomes

82. What will be the blood group of an individual with genetic combination IA IB?
Ans. An individual with genetic combination IA IB, will have blood group AB.

83. Which is the safest blood group for donation if an accident victim of an unknown blood group has to be given immediate blood transfusion?
Ans. Sometimes there may not be time or facility available for prior ascertaining of the blood group. Immediate blood transfusion is possible if the blood group is known. If unknown, the safest blood group for transfusion is O negative (O group and Rh-).

84. How can a person be normal for a trait even when carrying one defective gene for that trait?
Ans. The other member of the pair is dominant and masks the effect of the recessive gene.

85. How does the creation of variations in species promote survival? [NCERT]
Ans. The changes in the environment brings out Variations in the species. Such variations enable stability to the population of various species by preventing them from getting wiped out during adverse conditions. Thus, variations help a species in survival.

86. What are the different ways in which individuals with particular trait may increase in a population? [NCERT]
Ans. The different ways in which individuals with particular trait may increase in a population are natural selection, genetic drift and availability of food in abundance.

87. Why are traits acquired during the lifetime of an individual not inherited? [NCERT]

Ans. The traits which are acquired during the individual's lifetime do not cause changes in the DNA of germ cells which are transmitted through generations, but they produce changes only in the somatic cells which are not transmitted. Hence traits acquired during the lifetime of an individual are not inherited.

88. **What factors could lead to the rise of a new species?** [NCERT]

Ans. The factors that could lead to the rise of a new species are genetic variations, genetic drift, reproductive isolation and natural selection.

89. **When a black guinea pig is crossed with a white guinea pig, what coloured guinea pigs are obtained in F1 generation if black colour is dominant over white?**

Ans. Guinea pigs of black colour will be obtained in F_1 generation.

90. **In a cross between a tall pea plant (TT) and a short pea plant (tt), what will be the characteristics shown by the F_1 generation?**

Ans. As Tall is a dominant trait and short is recessive so in F_1 generation plants will be tall (Tt).

91. **In a cross between round yellow seeds (RRYY) and wrinkled green seeds (rryy) of pea plant, what is the ratio of plants obtained in F_2 generation?**

Ans. The ratio of plants obtained in F_2 generation is 9: 3: 3: 1.

92. **In turtle, high incubation temperature leads to the development of female offspring. On the other hand in lizards, high incubation temperature leads to the development of male offspring. What determines the sex of the offspring in these examples?**

Ans. In the examples given in the question sex of the offspring is determined by environmental factors.

93. **All the variations in a species do not have equal chances of survival. Why?**

Ans. According to 'Survival of the fittest', only the species which can adapt themselves to the environment can survive. Selection of the variants occurs by the different environmental factors. This forms the basis for evolution. Also, when a new change or variation occurs it means that the DNA constitution and the bodily cell apparatus also undergo genetic changes which result in the formation of a new variant. However, this change in the DNA might not be able to survive in the new environment. So, the DNA may get damaged and may stop functioning regularly which will affect the survival of the variant. The variations or the changes that are helpful and help in the evolution of the species will survive while the others will perish.

94. **How do the variations in a species promote survival?***

Ans. Variations increases the adaptability of an individual to its changing environment thus promotes survival of the species.

95. **A Mendelian experiment consisted of breeding pea plants bearing violet flowers with pea plant bearing white flowers. What will be the result in F_1 progeny?***

Ans. All the progeny of F_1 generation will have violet flowers because violet colour is dominant over the recessive white colour.

96. **Give the respective scientific terms used for studying:**
    (i) The mechanism by which variations are created and inherited.
    (ii) The development of new type of organisms from the existing ones.

97. **What is a recessive trait?**

Ans. A trait which is not expressed in the presence of a dominant allele is known as recessive.

98. **A Mendelian experiment consisted of breeding pea plants bearing violet flowers with pea plant bearing white flowers. What will be the result in F_1 progeny?***

Ans. All the progeny of F_1 generation will have violet flowers because violet colour is dominant over the recessive white colour.

Ans. (i) Genetics
(ii) Evolution

99. **Give any two examples where sex determination is regulated by environmental factors?**

Ans. In turtles and lizards sex determination is regulated by environmental factor temperature. In turtle high incubation temperature leads to development of female offsprings. In lizards high incubation temperature leads to development of male offsprings.

100. **What will be the sex of a child who inherits Y chromosome from his or her father?**

Ans. The child will be a male because the sex chromosome that the child inherits from his or her father will determine the sex as mother has only X chromosome. Here as the child inherits Y chromosome from his father so he will be a male (XY).

101. **Do genetic combinations of mothers play a significant role in determining the sex of a new born?**

Ans. No, because mother has only one type of sex chromosomes *i.e.*, X chromosomes but a father has two types of chromosomes X and Y chromosomes. So all children will inherit X chromosome from mother and whether X or Y bearing sperm from father fertilise the egg will determine the sex of new born.

102. **How many pairs of chromosomes are autosomes?**

Ans. Out of the 23 pairs of chromosomes, 22 pairs are termed autosomes. The 23rd pair (X and X in females and X and Y in males) are called sex chromosomes.

---
* are board exam questions from previous years

103. Why Pre-natal Diagnostic Techniques (Regulation and Prevention of Misuse) Act, 1994, was enacted?

Ans. The Pre-natal Diagnostic Techniques (Regulation and Prevention of Misuse) Act, 1994, was enacted and brought into operation from 1st January, 1996, in order to check female foeticide. The Act prohibits determination and disclosure of the sex of foetus. It also prohibits any advertisements relating to pre-natal determination of sex and prescribes punishment for its contravention. The person who contravenes the provisions of this Act is punishable with imprisonment and fine.

104. Discuss the types of egg and sperm in reference to X and Y chromosome.

Ans. Ova or eggs are of one kind only. These contain 22 autosomes and a single X chromosome. Sperms are of two kinds (i) having 22 autosomes and one X chromosome, or (ii) having 22 autosomes and a Y chromosome

105. If Y bearing sperm fuses with the egg what will be the sex of the child? Also state the chromosomal constitution.

Ans. If Y bearing sperm fuses with the egg then a male child results with chromosomal constitution of 44 autosomes and one X and one Y chromosome.

106. How many X chromosomes can be found in the cells of the body of (i) a boy, and (ii) a girl.

Ans. Females have two X chromosomes, while males have one X and one Y chromosome.

107. If a X bearing sperm fuses with an egg, what will be the sex of the individual developing from the zygote?

Ans. When X bearing sperm fuses with the egg, a female child results with 44 autosomes, and two X chromosomes.

Reasoning Based Questions

108. Give reasons why acquired characters are not inherited?

Ans. The changes in the environment brings out Variations in the species. Such variations enable stability to the population of various species by preventing them from getting wiped out during adverse conditions. Thus, variations help a species in survival.

109. Why do all the gametes formed in human females have an X-chromosome? [NCERT]

Ans. The sex chromosome in human female is homomorphic i.e., they contain same chromosome XX. During meiosis process at the time of gamete formation all egg cells will get one copy of X chromosome, hence all the gametes formed in human females have an X-chromosome.

Short Answer Type Questions

110. How can variation occur in asexually reproducing organisms?

Ans. There would be only very minor differences in asexual reproduction, generated due to small inaccuracies in DNA copying. Unlike sexual reproduction, asexual reproduction only introduces genetic variation into the population if a random mutation in the organism's DNA is passed on to the offspring.

111. What are mutations? Can mutation be inherited?

Ans. A mutation is a random change in DNA which therefore affects a gene and/or chromosome. Most mutations have no effect on the phenotype. Some influence phenotype to some extent. Very few create a new phenotype. Mutations can be inherited and therefore passed on from one individual to another. If a mutation causes a new phenotype that makes an organism better suited to a particular environment, it can lead to rapid change in the characteristics of the individuals in that species.

112. (i) State the observation of Mendel on self-pollination of first generation plants.

(ii) Which is a small section of DNA that is the genetic code for a characteristic?

Ans. (i) Mendel cross-breed peas with 7 pairs of pure-breed traits. First-generation (F1) progeny only showed the dominant traits, but recessive traits reappeared in the self-pollinated second-generation (F2) plants in a 3:1 ratio of dominant to recessive traits.

(ii) A gene is a small section of DNA which is the genetic code for a characteristic.

113. Here are the three possible genotypes for hair length in cats. Complete the table below, Remember short hair is dominant.

Genotype	Phenotype
HH (homozygous dominant)	
Hh (heterozygous)	
hh (homozygous recessive)	

Ans.

Genotype	Phenotype
HH (homozygous dominant)	Short hair
Hh (heterozygous)	Short hair - because H is dominant over h
hh (homozygous recessive)	Long hair

114. **(i)** Will all organisms from a cross between two homozygous dominant organisms would have the same phenotype?
   (ii) What proportion of offspring from BB v Bb would be BB?
   (iii) What proportion of offspring from Cc v Cc would be cc?
   (iv) What proportion of offspring from tt v Tt would be tt?
   (v) What proportion of offspring from two homozygous recessive organisms would be homozygous recessive?

Ans. **(i)** True, all organisms from a cross between two homologous dominant organisms would have the same phenotype which would be homozygous dominant.
   (ii) 50% of offspring would be BB (homozygous dominant) and the other 50% would be Bb (heterozygous).
   (iii) One in four (25%) of offspring would be cc (homozygous recessive). Another 25% would be CC (homozygous dominant) and the final 50% would be Cc (heterozygous).
   (iv) 50% of offspring would be tt (homozygous recessive) and the other 50% would be Tt (heterozygous).
   (v) All offspring (100%) would be homozygous recessive. Without a dominant gene or genes offspring cannot result in heterozygous or homozygous dominant.

115. **Complete the square below for two heterozygous short-haired cats. Work out the probability percentage of genotype and phenotype of the offspring, remember short hair (H) is dominant.**

	H	h
H		
h		

Ans.

	H	h
H	HH	Hh
h	Hh	hh

- HH – one from four so 25%
- Hh – two from four so 50%
- hh – one from four so 25%
- Short hair – three from four so 75%
- Long hair – one from four so 25%

116. **Characteristics in an individual organism are caused by both genetic and environmental variation. Complete the table below stating whether the characteristic is genetic or environmental variation.**

Trait	Genetic only / Environmental only/ can be both
Eye colour	
Tattoos	
Attached earlobes	
Weight	

Ans.

Trait	Genetic only / Environmental only/ can be both
Eye colour	Genetic only
Tattoos	Environmental only
Attached earlobes	Genetic only
Weight	can be both

117. **A study found that children with light coloured eyes are likely to have parents with light-coloured eyes. On this basis can we say anything about whether the light eye colour trait is dominant or recessive? Why or why not?** [NCERT]

Ans. No we cannot say whether the light eye colour trait is dominant or recessive as the child inherits one copy of the trait from father and other from mother and here nature of the trait is not known. The nature can be known from at least three generations but here data is given only for two generations i.e., parents [P] and offsprings [F1].

118. **Only variations that confer an advantage to an individual organism will survive in a Population. Do you agree with this statement? Why or why not?** [NCERT]

Ans. Yes, we agree with this statement that only variations that confer an advantage to an individual organism will survive in a population because those variations which occur in an individual that favours the organism to get adapt to the environment will be able to survive otherwise it may not. The chances of survival depend upon the nature of variations. Different individuals would have different kinds of advantages. For example– A bacteria which can withstand heat will be able to survive in hot springs otherwise it will die. Selection of variants by environmental factors forms the basis for evolutionary process.

119. **Gene controls traits. Explain this with an example?**

Ans. Genes are a specific sequence on nucleotides on chromosome which encodes a particular protein which express in form of a particular trait in the body. Each gene has two alternative forms for a particular character. These alternative forms are called alleles, one is dominant allele and other is recessive allele. For example – Height of a plant, plant height depends on the amount of hormones synthesised. The amount of hormones synthesised depends upon the efficiency of the process for making it. If the protein needed for this process is synthesised and works efficiently plant would be tall. On the other hand if the gene is altered, the protein synthesised will be less efficient and hence hormones produced would be less and plant would be dwarf.

120. How do Mendel's experiments show that traits may be dominant or recessive? [NCERT]

Ans. When Mendel crossed pure tall (TT) pea plants with pure dwarf (tt) pea plants, in F_1 generation he found that all pea plants were tall (Tt). There were no dwarf plants produced in F_1 generation. When he self-pollinated these F_1 plants, in F_2 generation he obtained tall and dwarf plants in the ratio 3: 1. Thus as three-fourths of the plant in F_2 generation are tall and one-fourth is dwarf so tall is a dominant trait whereas dwarf is a recessive trait [which expressed itself only in homozygous condition]. So he concluded that for a particular trait [here in this example height of the plant] it may be dominant or recessive.

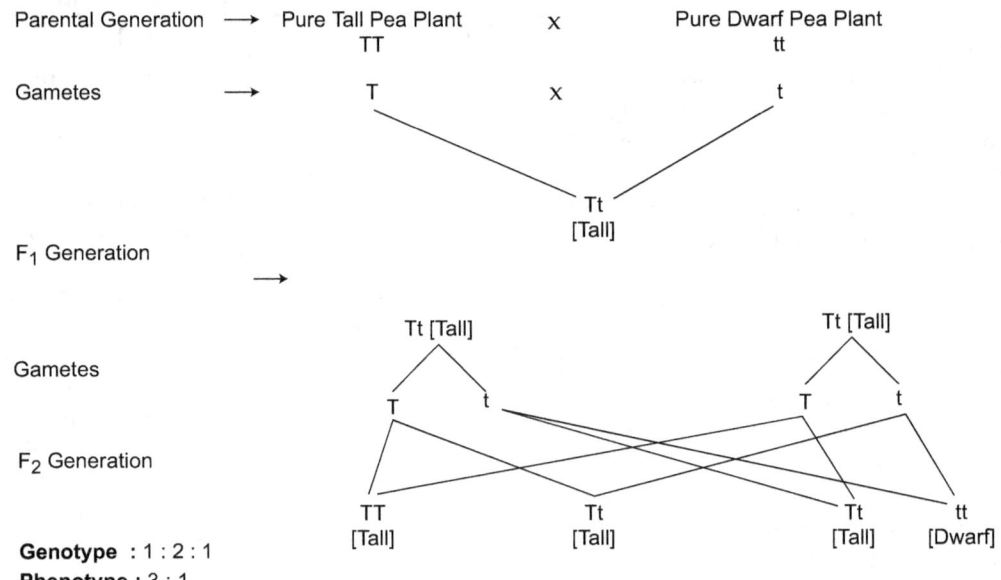

Genotype : 1 : 2 : 1
Phenotype : 3 : 1

121. If a trait A exists in 10% of a population of an asexually reproducing species and trait B exists in 60% of the same population, which trait is likely to have arisen earlier? [NCERT]

Ans. Trait B would have arisen earlier than trait A because as species are asexually reproducing, there would be very minor differences generated due to small inaccuracies in DNA copying which results in variations in trait A. But as trait B occurs in more number in the population as compared to trait A so Trait B would have arisen earlier than trait A.

122. Outline a project which aims to find the dominant coat colour in dogs. [NCERT]

Ans. Consider a homozygous black coat colour male dog (BB) breed with homozygous white coat colour female dog (bb). In F_1 generation all dogs with black coat colour are produced. When these are again bred we get black and white coat colour dogs in F_2 generation in the ratio 3 : 1. Thus we can say black colour is dominant over white.

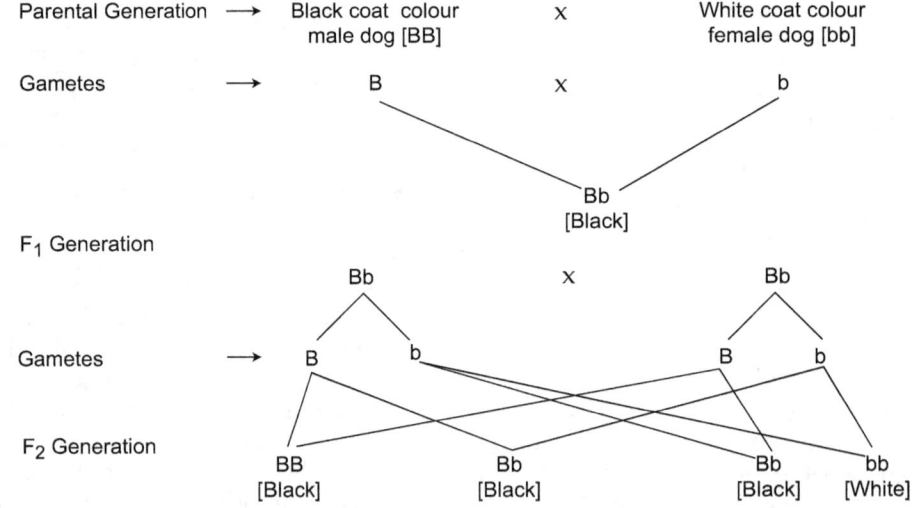

123. A man with blood group A marries a woman with blood group O and their daughter has blood group O. Is this information enough to tell you which of the traits blood group A or O is dominant? Why or why not? **[NCERT]**

Ans. No, this information is not enough to find out which blood group is dominant. Blood group A can be represented as IAIA or IAIO which is the father's blood group. Blood group O is represented as IOIO which is the mother's blood group. The blood group of daughter is also O which might be inherited from her mother or father so it is difficult to assume which blood group is dominant.

124. A study found that children with light coloured eyes are likely to have parents with light-coloured eyes. On this basis can we say anything about whether the light eye colour trait is dominant or recessive? Why or why not? **[NCERT]**

Ans. No, we cannot say whether the light eye colour trait is dominant or recessive as the child inherits one copy of the trait from father and other from mother and here nature of the trait is not known. The nature can be known from at least three generations but here data is given only for two generations *i.e.*, parents [P] and offsprings [F_1].

125. Name the plant Mendel used for his experiment. What type of progeny was obtained by Mendel in F_1 and F_2 generations when he crossed the tall and short plants? Write the ratio he obtained in F_2 generation plants.*

Ans. Mendel used pea plant (*Pisum sativum*) when he crossed tall and short plants the progeny obtained in F_1 generation were tall. When the F_1 plants were selfed the F_2 generations showed three tall and one dwarf plant. The genotypic ratio of F_2 generation is 1: 2: 1.
(TT: Tt: Tt: tt)
The phenotypic ratio 3: 1 (Tall: Dwarf)

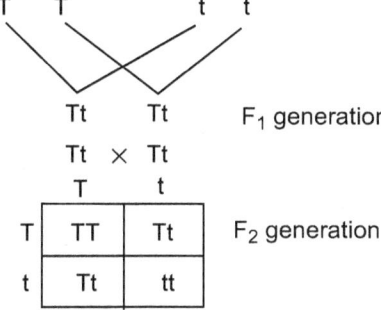

126. How is the sex of the child determined in human beings? **[NCERT]**

Ans. In human beings, there are two types of sex chromosome X and Y; female have XX chromosome whereas male have XY chromosome. Females produce eggs which carry only X chromosomes but males contain half of the sperms with X chromosomes and other half with Y chromosomes. During fertilisation when X carrying sperms fuse with an egg which contains X chromosome the offsprings will be a female (XX). But when Y bearing sperms fuse with an egg (X) the offspring will be male (XY). Thus the sex of a child is determined by the type of sex chromosome X or Y received by the male gamete.

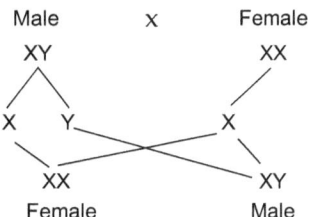

127. Answer the following:
   (i) Who are more closely related— A brother and sister or two cousins? Why?
   (ii) Why do all the gametes formed in human females have an X-chromosome ?

Ans. (i) A brother and sister are more closely related than two cousins as they have a common ancestor.
   (ii) The sex chromosome in human female is homomorphic *i.e.*, they contain same chromosome XX. During meiosis process at the time of gamete formation all egg cell will get one copy of X chromosome, hence all the gametes formed in human females have an X chromosome.

128. How is the equal genetic contribution of male and female parents ensured in the progeny? **[NCERT]**

Ans. Human beings contain 23 pairs of chromosomes-22 pairs are autosomes and one pair sex chromosomes. During meiosis process gametes are formed in sex cells where the chromosome number is halved(n). At the time of fertilisation when male gamete fuses with female gamete the diploid number (2n) is restored back in zygote. Thus half of the chromosomes come from father and other half from mother. In this way meiosis process ensures equal genetic contribution of male and female parents in the progeny.

129. Why are human beings who look so different from each other in terms of size, colour and looks said to belong to the same species? **[NCERT]**

Ans. Human beings belong to a same species called Homo sapiens. Based on the study of fossils, molecular phylogeny involving DNA sequence though human beings, who look so different from each other in terms of size, colour and looks belong to a single species. The study of fossils suggests that they have originated in Africa. Gradually their number increases and they spread throughout the whole continent, some also migrate to other parts of the world. The geographical and climatic variations in different regionslead to variations in their genes as a result their colour, looks, size also varies.

* are board exam questions from previous years

130. How is the equal genetic contribution of male and female parents ensured in the Progeny? [NCERT]

Ans. Human beings contain 23 pairs of chromosomes-22 pairs are autosomes and one pair sex chromosomes. During meiosis process gametes are formed in sex cells where the chromosome number is halved (n). At the time of fertilisation when male gamete fuses with female gamete the diploid number ($2n$) is restored back in zygote. Thus half of the chromosomes come from father and other half from mother. In this way meiosis process ensured equal genetic contribution of male and female parents in the progeny.

131. How many pairs of chromosomes are present in human beings? Out of this how many are sex chromosomes? How many types of sex chromosomes are found in human beings?

Ans. There are 23 pairs of chromosomes present in human beings. One pair is sex chromosome. They are XX and XY. So there are two types of sex chromosomes.

132. How many pairs of chromosomes are present in human beings? Out of this how many are sex chromosomes? How many types of sex chromosomes are found in human beings?*

Ans. There are 23 pairs of chromosomes present in human beings. One pair is sex chromosome. They are XX and XY. So there are two types of sex chromosomes.

Long Answer Type Questions

133. Why did Mendel choose pea plants for his experiments? Give any five reasons.

Ans. Mendel is known as the father of modern genetic because of genetic experiments with Pea or *Pisum Sativum*. The reason for the selection of pea plants for the genetic experiments are:

(a) Easy to grow in the garden.

134. Give the basic features of the mechanism of inheritance?

Ans. The basic features of mechanism of inheritance are:

(a) Traits are controlled by genes.
(b) Genes are present on chromosomes.
(c) Each gene controls one character.
(d) There may be two or more forms of a gene.
(e) One form may be dominant over the other.
(f) An individual possesses two forms of genes which may be similar or dissimilar.
(g) The two forms of gene separate at the time of gamete formation.
(h) The two forms of gene are brought together in a zygote after fertilisation.

135. Give the cross between RRYY × rryy for both F1 and F2 generation? What are the combinations of characters produced in F2 generation and give reasons for appearance of new progeny?

Ans.

Parental Generation → Pure pea plants with round, yellow seeds RRYY × Pure pea plants with wrinkled, green seeds rryy

Gametes → RY × ry

F₁ Generation → RrYy [Pea plants with round, yellow seeds]

RrYy × RrYy

Gametes: RY Ry rY ry   RY Ry rY ry

Gametes ⇓ ⇒	RY	Ry	rY	ry
RY	RRYY	RRYy	RrYY	RrYy
Ry	RRYy	RRyy	RrYy	Rryy
rY	RrYY	RrYy	rrYY	rrYy
ry	RrYy	Rryy	rrYy	rryy

Round-yellow, round-green, wrinkled-yellow, wrinkled-green in the ratio of 9: 3: 3: 1 are produced in F2 generations. New characters round-green and wrinkled-yellow are produced because when pure round-yellow pea plants are crossed with pure wrinkled-green pea plants the inheritance of one pair of character is independent of other pair i.e., the inheritance of character of round seed is not linked with yellow seed or the inheritance of wrinkled seed is not linked with green seed. The contrasting traits segregate and inherits independently and results in the formation of new combination of characters.

(b) The flowers of pea plants are hermaphrodite, *i.e* flowers have bisexual characteristics.

---
* are board exam questions from previous years

(c) Easy to obtain pure breed plant through self-fertilisation
(d) The generation time of pea plants is less.
(e) They have excellent disease resistance and have an optimal rate of survival.

136. A blue flower plant denoted by BB is crossed with that of white coloured flower plant denoted by bb.
(i) State the colour of flower you would expect in their F_1 generation plants.
(ii) What must be the percentage of white flower plants in F_2 generation if flower of F_1 plants are self – pollinated?
(iii) State the expected ratio of the genotypes BB and bb in the F_2 progeny?

Ans. (i) In the first generation *i.e.* in F1, generation, all the flower plants will be of blue colour. It can be shown as follows:

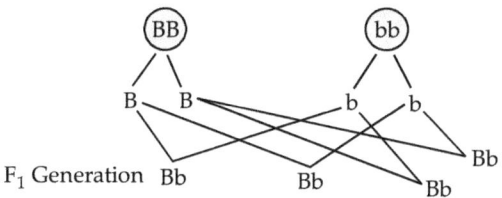

(ii) When flowers of f_1 generation are self-pollinated:

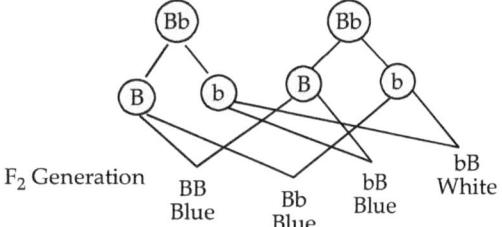

So, in F_2 generation, there will be three blue Flowers and one white flower. So the ratio of blue flower plant to ratio of white flower plant is 3 : 1 but we need to find the ratio percentage of white flower which is calculated as follows:

$$\text{Percentage} = \frac{\text{no. of white flower plant}}{\text{Total plants in F2 generation}} \times 100$$

$$\text{Percentage} = \frac{1}{4} \times 100$$

So, Ratio percentage of white flower plant is 25%

(iii) The expected ratio of the genotypes BB and Bb in the F_2 progeny is as follows:

Genotype in F_2 generation: (BB) (Bb) (Bb) (bb)

Phenotype in F_2 generation: Blue Blue Blue White

137. How do Mendel's experiments show that the:*
(i) Traits may be dominant or recessive
(ii) Traits are inherited independently.

Ans. (i) When Mendel crossed pure tall pea plants with pure dwarf pea plants in F_1 generation only tall plants were produced. When these F_1 plants were self-pollinated in F_2 generation both tall and dwarf plants were produced in the ratio of 3: 1. In F_1 generation only tall plants were found so it showed that tall is a dominant character. In F_2 generation dwarf plants appeared which shows that dwarf is a recessive trait which is expressed only in recessive condition.

Parental Generation →	Pure Tall Plant TT	×	Pure Dwarf Plant tt
Gametes →	T		t
F_1 Generation		Tt [Tall]	
	Tt	×	Tt
Gametes →	Tt Tt		
F_2 Generation →	TT [Tall] Tt [Tall]	Tt [Tall]	tt [Dwarf]

(ii) When Mendel crossed pure pea plants with round, yellow seeds with pure plants with wrinkled, green seeds in F_1 generation all pea plants with round and yellow seeds were produced. This shows that round and yellow are dominant characters whereas green and wrinkled are recessive characters. Again when these F_1 plants were crossed round, yellow pea plants as well as green, wrinkled seeds pea plants were produced. But in addition to these two new characters were produced i.e., round and green, wrinkled and yellow seeds pea plants were produced.

This shows that two pair of characters combine in F_1 generation but they get separated and behave independently in F_2 generation.

---
* are board exam questions from previous years

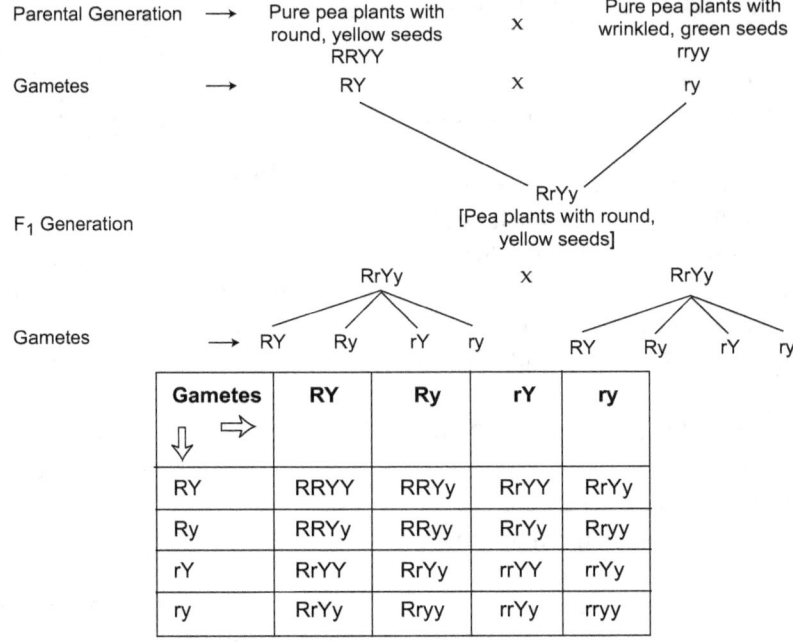

Round-yellow, round-green, wrinkled-yellow, wrinkled-green – 9: 3: 3: 1

138. Answer the following questions:
(i) What are dominant and recessive traits?*
(ii) "Is it possible that a trait is inherited but may not be expressed in the next generation? Give a suitable example to justify this statement.*

Ans. (i) The trait which can express its effect over contrasting trait is called dominant trait whereas the trait which cannot express its effect over contrasting trait or which gets suppressed by the contrasting trait is called recessive trait. The inherited trait which is not expressed will be a recessive trait.

(ii) In Mendel's experiment, when pure tall pea plants were crossed with pure dwarf pea plants, only tall pea plants were obtained in F_1 generation. On selfing the pea plants of F_1 generation both tall and dwarf pea plants were obtained in F_2 generation. Reappearance of the dwarf pea plants in F_2 generation proves that the dwarf trait was inherited but not expressed in F_1 generation. The recessive trait does not express itself in the presence of the dominant trait. So, it is possible that one trait may be inherited but may not be expressed in an organism.

139. The given box diagram represents the ratio of females to males or the sex ratio in our country for 10 decades (1901 to 2001). Answer the following questions in the light of your knowledge of sex determination and the data presented in the box diagram.*

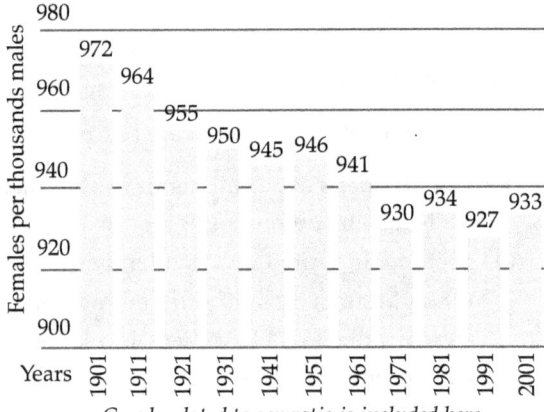

Graph related to sex ratio is included here

(i) What does the bar diagram show?
(ii) As per scientific knowledge regarding sex determination, what should be the sex ratio or the male to female ratio at a given point of time?
(iii) Assign one reason to the trend showing deviation from the expected sex ratio.
(iv) Suggest a way by which such a trend can be stopped.

Ans. (i) Bar diagram shows the proportion of females in the population over a decade.
(ii) 1 : 1
(iii) Female foeticide
(iv) Banning sex tests of unborn baby; increasing awareness and education.

140. The sex of a new born child is a matter of chance and none of the parents may be considered responsible for it. Draw a flowchart showing determination of sex of a newborn to justify this statement.*

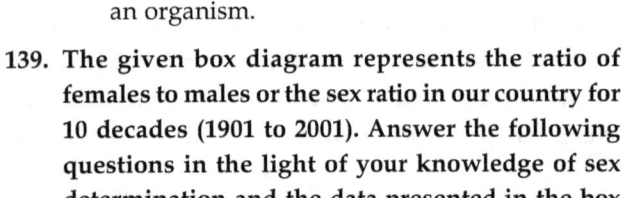

* are board exam questions from previous years

Ans. In human beings, there are two types of sex chromosome X and Y; female have XX chromosome whereas male have XY chromosome. Females produce eggs which carry only X chromosomes but males contain half of the sperms with X chromosomes and other half with Y chromosomes. During fertilisation when X carrying sperms fuse with an egg which contains X chromosome the offsprings will be a female (XX). But when Y bearing sperms fuses with an egg (X) the offspring will be male (XY). Thus the sex of a child is determined by the type of sex chromosome X or Y received by the male gamete.

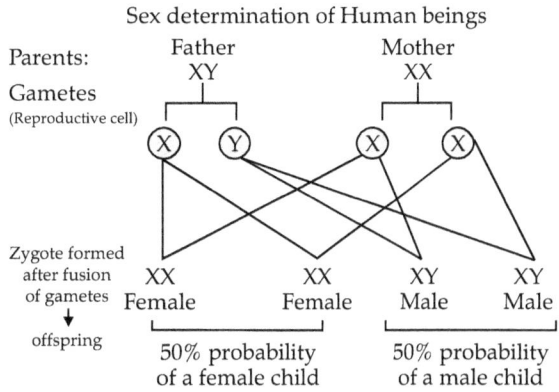

Differentiate Between

141. Difference between Recessive and Dominant Traits

Ans.

	Dominant Trait	Recessive Trait
(a)	Dominant traits are always expressed when the connected allele is dominant, even if only one copy exists.	Recessive traits are expressed only if both the connected alleles are recessive. If one of the alleles is dominant, then the associated characteristic is less likely to manifest.
(b)	Dominant allele is denoted by a capital letter.	Recessive allele is denoted by a small letter.

142. List two differences between acquired traits and inherited traits by giving an example of each.*

Ans.

	Acquired traits	Inherited traits
(a)	These are somatic variations and do not bring any change in DNA.	These are genetic variations and bring about changes in the DNA.
(b)	These traits develop throughout the life time of an individual. Example, learning of dance and music.	These traits are transferred by or (inherited) by the parents to the offsping. Example, Eye colour, hair colour.

Analysis and Evaluation Based Questions

143. Study carefully the given flowchart depicting cross between pea plant with yellow seeds and pea plant with green seeds and answer the following:

(i) What kind of cross it depicts?

(ii) In which proportions the characters will appear in F_1 and F_2 generation?

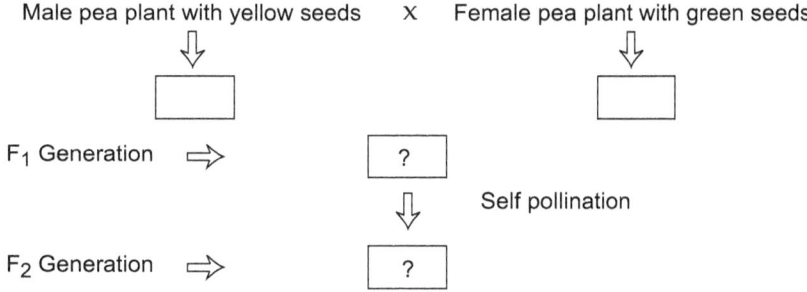

Ans. (i) It depicts monohybrid cross.

(ii) In F_1 generation all pea plants with yellow seeds will be produced whereas in F_2 generation pea plants with yellow and green seeds in the ratio 3:1 will be produced.

---
* are board exam questions from previous years

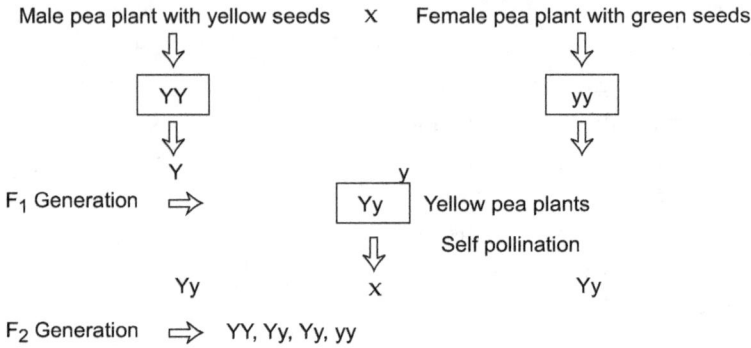

144. Acquiring characteristics or traits from one generation to the other is nothing but inheritance. Here, both the parents contribute equally to the inheritance of traits. It was Gregor Mendel, known as the Father of Genetics, who conducted immense research and studied this inheritance of traits. It was with his research on plant breeding that he came up with the laws of inheritance in living organisms. He conducted his experiments on pea plants to show the inheritance of traits in living organisms. He observed the pattern of inheritance from one generation to the other in these plants.

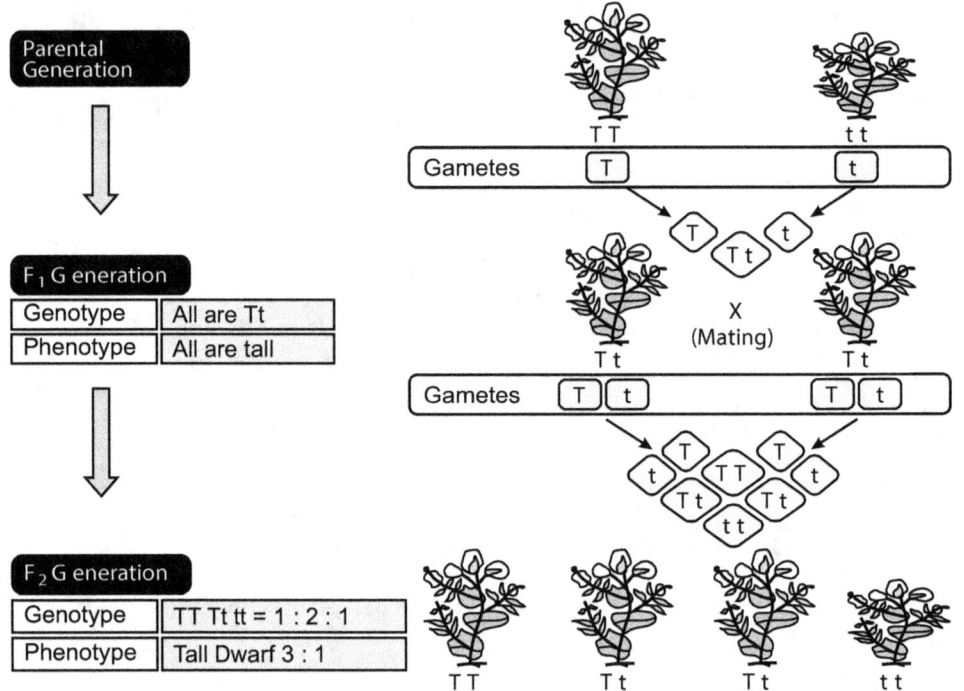

   (i) Name which Mendel's experiments shows that traits are inherited indepedently?
   (ii) What is observed by Mendel in his experiment about the phenotype and genotype?
   (iii) Define the term Genotype.
   (iv) What do you understand by dominant alleles?

Ans. (i) The Dihybrid cross experiment that Mendel performed with the pea plants, shows that traits are inherited independently. In a cross between two plants with two pairs of contrasting characters, the expression of traits occurs independently.

   (ii) In F_2, the phenotype ratio is 9: 3: 3: 1. The genotype ratio is a very complex one.

   (iii) **Genotype:** It is the complete heritable genetic identity of an organism. It is the actual set of alleles that are carried by the organism.

   (iv) When an allele affects the phenotype of an organism, then it is a dominant allele. It is denoted by a capital letter. For example, 'T' to express tallness.

145. Given below is the experiment carried out by Mendel to study inheritance of two traits in garden pea.

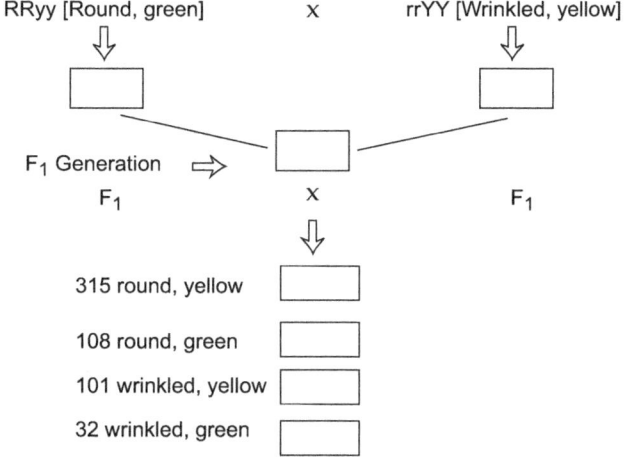

(i) Fill the boxes.
(ii) Why did Mendel carry experiment with two traits?
(iii) What were his findings with respect to inheritance of traits in F_1 and F_2 generations?

Ans. (i)

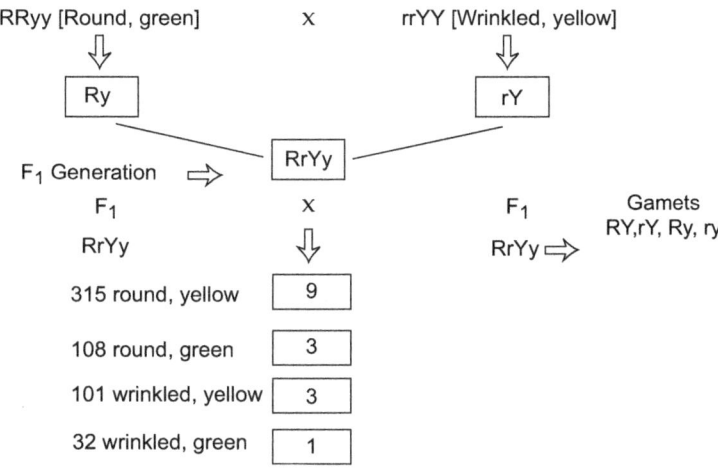

(ii) Mendel carried out experiment with two traits to study the independent assortment of characters during inheritance.

(iii) In F_1 generation though both the traits were inherited but only dominant traits [*i.e.*, round, yellow characters] are expressed, the recessive traits, [wrinkled, green] were not expressed. But in F_2 generation both dominant and recessive traits were expressed in the ratio 9: 3: 3: 1.

146. Observe the ears of all the students in the class. Prepare a list of students having free or attached earlobes and calculate the percentage of students having each (Fig. below). Find out about the earlobes of the parents of each student in the class. Correlate the earlobe type of each student with that of their parents. Based on this evidence, suggest a possible rule for the inheritance of earlobe types.

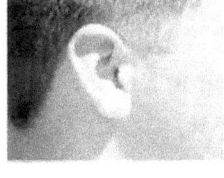
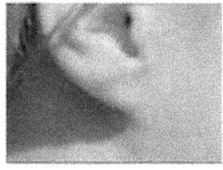

(a)   (b)

Ans. It is observed that earlobe is attached to the side of head in some of students and not in others. Majority of students have free ear lobes. After observing the earlobes of parents it is found that free earlobes always occur in those cases where one or both the parents have free ear lobes. However attached earlobes were observed in atleast one of the two parents of children having attached earlobes.

Earlobe trait is inherited from parents. Suppose earlobe trait is controlled by two alleles L or l. Individuals with free ear lobe have alleles LL or Ll and attached ear lobes have alleles ll. So free ear lobe is dominant trait and attached earlobe is recessive trait.

147. In the given figure below, what experiment would we do to confirm that the F_2 generation did in fact have a 1 : 2 : 1 ratio of TT, Tt and trait combinations?

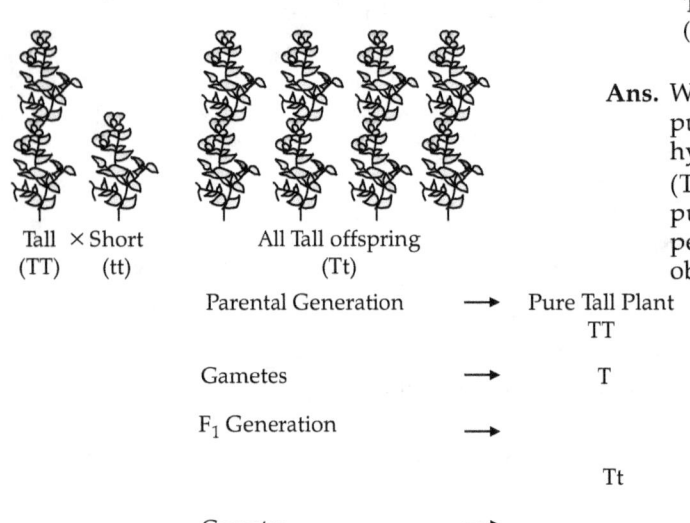

Tall × Short   All Tall offspring
(TT) (tt)   (Tt)

Parental Generation → Pure Tall Plant × Pure Dwarf Plant
                           TT   tt
Gametes → T   t
F_1 Generation → Tt [Tall]

                     Tt × Tt
Gametes → Tt × T tTy
F_2 Generation → TT [Tall], Tt [Tall], Tt [Tall], tt [Dwarf]

Genotypic ratio is 1 : 2 : 1

Inheritance of traits over two generations

Ans. When a pure tall pea plant (TT) was crossed with pure short pea plant (tt) then in F1 generation all hybrid tall pea plants were produced.
(Tt) Again pea plants of F_1 were selfed where pure tall (TT), hybrid tall (Tt) and pure short (tt) pea plants were obtained in the ratio 1 : 2 : 1 were obtained.

Practical Based Questions

148. In a monohybrid cross between tall pea plants (TT) and short pea plants (tt) a scientist obtained only tall pea plants (Tt) in the F_1 generation. However on selfing the F_1 generation pea plants he obtained both tall and short plants in F_2 generation. On the basis of above observations with other angiosperms also can the scientist arrive at a law? If yes, explain the law. If not, give justification for your answer.*

Ans. Yes, the scientist arrives at Law of Dominance according to which the trait that gets expressed in F_1 generation is dominant and the trait which gets expressed along with dominant trait in F_2 generation is recessive trait which expreses itself only in homozygous condition.

Application Based Questions

149. Guinea pig having black colour when crossed with a guinea pig having same colour produced 80 offspring, out of which 60 were black and 20 were white. Now find out:
   (i) What is the possible genotype of the guinea pigs?
   (ii) Which trait is dominant and which trait is recessive?
   (iii) What is this cross called and what is its phenotypic ratio?

Ans. (i) The possible genotype of the guinea pigs is Bb × Bb.
(ii) Black colour is dominant and white colour is recessive.
(iii) This is an example of monohybrid cross and its phenotypic ratio is 3 : 1.

150. A woman with blonde curly hair married a man with black soft hair. All of their children in first generation had black soft hair but in next generation children had different combinations in

* are board exam questions from previous years

the ratio of 9 : 3 : 3 : 1. State the law that governs this expression.

Ans. Law of independent assortment governs this expression which states that inheritance of factors controlling a particular trait in an organism are independent of each other i.e., during the time of reproduction two pairs of factors of each of the two traits in a dihybrid cross segregate independently during gamete formation and randomly formed combinations in F_2 generations.

151. **Mrs. Joshi, an eight months pregnant lady was suggested by her doctor to get an ultrasound done. She went to a radiologist with her husband and got the ultrasound done. When the ultrasound was done, her husband asked doctor about the sex of the baby in the womb.**

(i) Is it ethical to determine the sex of the foetus? Why?

(ii) What is the chance of giving birth to a girl child in human beings?

(iii) What has government done to stop female foeticides?

Ans. (i) No, it is not ethical to determine the sex of the foetus because sex determination may lead to female foeticides which results in death of a girl child and thus the sex ratio become unbalanced in a society.

(ii) The chance of giving birth to a girl child in human beings is 50%.

(iii) Government has imposed a ban on sex determination techniques to stop female foeticides.

Creating Based Questions

152. **Ram met with an accident. John his school mate takes him to the hospital where Ram (AB blood group) needs blood transfusion. John also has AB blood group and is willing to donate his blood but Ram's mother object by saying "John belongs to different community so has different type of blood". Give your opinion about Ram's mother views.**

Ans. Blood group does not depend on community, same blood group is same for all communties. Blood group AB has two alleles A and B in the people of all communities.

153. **Why a mice whose tail has been removed by surgery does not produce tailless mice?**

Ans. A mice whose tail has been removed by surgery does not produce tailless mice because tailless character is not present in germ cells of mice so, it is an acquired character which cannot be passed onto the next generation.

154. **A Blue Colour Flower Plant Denoted by Bb is crossbreed with that of White Colour Flower Plant Denoted by Bb.**

(i) State the Colour of Flower You Would Expect in Their F1 Generation Plants.

(ii) What must be the percentage of white flower plants in F2 generation if flowers of f1 plants are self-pollinated?

(iii) State the expected ratio of the genotypes BB and Bb in the F2 Progeny.

Ans. (i) Blue colour flower plant: BB

(ii) White colour flower plant: bb

(iii) The cross involved is as follows:

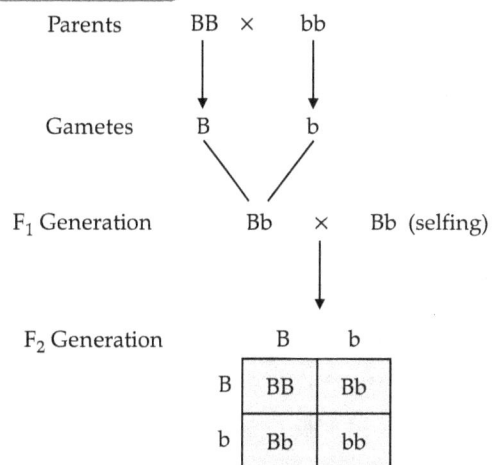

(a) In F1 generation, all plants will have blue flower.

(b) In the F2 generation, 25% of flowers are white in colour.

(c) The ratio of the genotypes BB and Bb in the F2 generation would be 1(BB): 2(Bb).

155. **With the help of two suitable examples, explain why certain experiences and traits earned by people during their lifetime are not passed on to their next generations. When can such traits be passed on?**

Ans. Learning skills like swimming, dancing and low weight of beetle due to starvation earned by people during their lifetime are not passed on to their next generation. If a person knows swimming or dancing, it is not necessary that this trait is seen in the progeny because learning a new skill does not change the genes of the germ cells of humans. Also, low weight in a beetle is not a trait that can be inherited by the progeny of a starving beetle. These traits or experiences occur in the somatic cells which do not involve germ cells and genetic materials. Therefore, these traits are not passed on to their next generation. Traits can be passed only when they have some direct effect on the genes. For example, if a mutation is caused in the germ cells of a person due to exposure to some harmful radiations, it is highly likely that the mutation caused will be passed on to the subsequent generations.

156. **Study the table given below and answer the questions.**

   In a human, how many chromosomes are present in:
   (i) a brain cell?
   (ii) a sperm in the testes?
   (iii) an egg which has just been produced by the ovary?
   (iv) a skin cell?
   (v) a fertilised egg?

   Ans. (i) 46.
   (ii) 23.
   (iii) 23.
   (iv) 46.
   (v) 46.

157. **Study the table given below and answer the following questions.**

Characters	Males	Females
Total number of chromosomes	23 pairs	23 pairs
Number of autosome	22 pairs	22 pairs
Number of sex chromosome	1 pair	1 pair

   (i) What is sex determination?
   (ii) What are the sex chromosomes in the males?
   (iii) What are the sex chromosomes in the females?
   (iv) Is the father responsible for the sex of the child?

   Ans. (i) The process by which the sex of a newborn organism is detected is called sex determination.
   (ii) The males have two sex chromosomes which are X and Y.
   (iii) The sex chromosomes in the females are X and X.
   (iv) Yes, it is the father that gives either the X or Y chromosome to the child. In case, the child receives the X chromosome from the father, then it has XX chromosome, and it develops into a female child. However, if the father gives Y chromosome, then the child develops into a male as it gets XY chromosome.

158. **"A brother and sister are more related to each other in comparison to the case when any one of them is related with his or her cousin". Through this statement what will we get to know about their ancestors?**

   Ans. A brother and sister are more closely related to each other which means that they have common ancestors more recently as compared to the case when any one of them (brother or sister) is related to the cousin. A brother and sister have their "parents" in common while a brother or sister and cousin have "grandparents" in common.

Self-Assessment

159. Write the scientific name of man and garden pea.

160. Which of the following type of reproduction sexual or arexual generates more number of successful variations?

161. Why do mice whose tails were surgically removed just after birth for generations, continue to produce mice with tails?

162. Which of the following represent the round shaped and green coloured seeds of pea plant? [rrYY, RrYy, RRyy, Rryy]

163. A pea plant with blue colour flower denoted by BB is cross bred with a pea plant with white flower denoted by ww.
   (a) What is the expected colour of the flowers in F_1 progeny?
   (b) What will be the % of plants bearing white flower in F_2 generation when the flowers of F_1 plants were selfed?
   (c) State the expected ratio of the genotype BB and Bw in the F_2 progeny.

164. Explain Mendel's experiment with peas on inheritance of characters considering only one visible contrasting characters.

165. Answer the following:
   (a) Define dominant and recessive traits.
   (b) Why are two letters like TT, Tt, tt are used to denote the character of height?
   (c) If a purple pea plant (PP) is crossed with a white coloured pea plant (pp), will we have white flowered pea plant in F_1 generation? Why?

166. The gene for red hair is recessive to the gene for black hair. What will be the hair colour of a person if he inherits a gene for red hair from his mother and a gene for black hair from his father?

167. Explain with an example, how genes control the characteristics (or traits).

168. (i) What is the genotype of dwarf plants which always produced dwarf offspring ?

    (ii) What is the genotype of tall plants which always produced tall offspring ?

169. In human beings, the statistical probability of getting either a male or female child is 50 : 50. Give a suitable explanation.

170. The palisade cells of a species of plant contains 28 chromosomes. How many chromosomes will there be in each gamete produced by the plant?

171. Ram met with an accident. John his schoolmate takes him to the hospital where Ram (AB blood group) needs blood transfusion. John also has AB blood group and is willing to donate his blood but Ram's mother object by saying "John belongs to different community so has different type of blood". Give your opinion about Ram's mother views.

172. A husband has 46 chromosomes and his wife also has 46 chromosomes. Then why do not their offsprings have 46 pairs of chromosomes which is obtained by fusion of male and female gametes?

CHAPTER-12: ELECTRICITY

OHM'S LAW
- According to Ohm's law,
  $V \propto I$ (at constant temperature)
  i.e., $V = IR$

RESISTANCE
- The obstruction offered to the flow of current by a conductor.
- Resistance $(R) = \frac{V}{I}$
- S.I. unit of resistance is ohm.

Factors affecting Resistance

» Length of the conductor $(R \propto l)$
» Area of cross-section of the conductor $(R \propto \frac{1}{A})$
» Nature of the material of the conductor.

Resistivity
- $R \propto l$ and $R \propto \frac{1}{A}$
- $\therefore R \propto \frac{l}{A} \Rightarrow R \propto \frac{\rho l}{A}$
  where ρ is constant known as resistivity or specific resistance.
- S.I. unit is ohm-metre.

Combination of Resistance

Series
- When two (or more) resistances are connected end to end consecutively.

- Current remains constant but voltage varies.
  $V = v_1 + v_2$
- $R_S = R_1 + R_2$

Parallel
- When two (or more) resistances are connected between the same two points.
  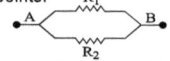
- Voltage remains constant but current varies.
- $I = I_1 + I_2$
- $\frac{1}{R_P} = \frac{1}{R_1} + \frac{1}{R_2}$

Heating Effect of Electric Current
When an electric current is passed through a high resistance wire, like nichrome wire, the resistance wire becomes very hot and produces heat.

Joule's Law of Heating
According to Joule's law of heating,
$H \propto I^2$
$H \propto R$
$H \propto t$
$\therefore$ Heat produced, $H = I^2Rt$

Practical Applications
- In the working of electrical heating appliances such as electric iron, electric kettle, electric toaster etc.
- In electric bulbs for producing light.
- In electric fuse for protecting household wiring and electrical appliances.

ELECTRIC POWER

- The rate at which the electrical energy is dissipated or consumed per unit time in an electric circuit.
- Power $(P) = \frac{\text{Work done (W)}}{\text{Time }(t)}$
  $= VI = \frac{V^2}{R} = I^2R$
- S.I. unit of electric power is watt (W).
- Bigger units of power are:
  1 kilowatt = 1kW
  = 1000 W
  = 10^3 W
  1 megawatt = 1MW
  = 10^6 W

Electrical Energy
- Using Power $(P) = \frac{\text{Electrical energy dissipated (E)}}{\text{Time }(t)}$
  $\Rightarrow E = P \times t$
- The S.I. unit of electrical energy is watt hour.
- The commercial unit of electric energy is kilowatt hour (kWh) commonly known as 'unit'.
- 1 kWh = 1000 watt × 3600 second
  = 3.6×10^6 watt second
  = 3.6×10^6 joule

CHAPTER-13: MAGNETIC EFFECTS OF ELECTRIC CURRENT

Magnetic Effect of Electric Current
An electric current flowing in a wire produces a magnetic field around it".

Magnet
- A substance which attracts small pieces of iron, steel, nickel etc., and points in North-South direction when suspended freely.
- Magnets come in various shapes and sizes depending on their use.
- One of the most common magnets is bar magnet which is a long, rectangular bar of uniform cross-section.

Magnetic Field
- The space surrounding a magnet in which magnetic force is exerted.
- It has both magnitude and direction.
- The direction of magnetic field at a point is the direction of the resultant force acting on a hypothetical north pole placed at that point.

Magnetic Field Lines
- A closed continuous curved path around a magnet such that the tangent at any point on the curve gives the direction of magnetic field at that point.
- **Properties:**
  - Outside the magnet, they are directed from the north pole towards the south pole whereas inside the magnet they are directed from the south pole towards the north pole.
  - They never intersect each other.
  - They are crowded near the poles of magnet where magnetic field is strong and are less crowded (near the centre) where the magnetic field is weak.

MAGNETIC FIELD DUE TO A CURRENT-CARRYING CONDUCTOR

Magnetic field due to Straight Current-carrying Conductor
- The magnetic field lines around a straight conductor carrying current are concentric circles whose centres lie on the wire.
- In this case, the magnitude of magnetic field is :
  - Directly proportional to the current passing in the wire,
  - Inversely proportional to the distance of that point from the wire.

Direction
- **Right Hand Thumb Rule :**

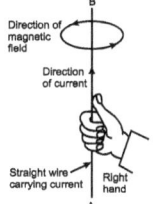

- **Maxwell's Corkscrew Rule :**

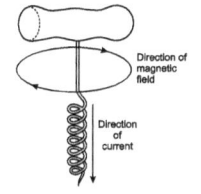

Magnetic field due to a Circular Loop
- The magnetic field lines are represented by concentric circles that appear as straight lines near the centre of loop.
- In this case, the magnitude of magnetic field is :
  - Directly proportional to the current passing through the circular loop,
  - Inversely proportional to the radius of circular loop.

Direction
- **Clock Face Rule**

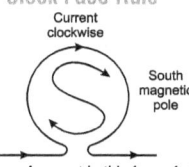

(a) The direction of current in this face of circular wire is clockwise, so this face of circular wire carrying current will act as a South magnetic pole (S-pole)

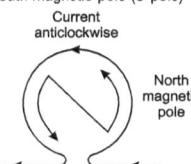

(b) The direction of current in this face of circular wire is anticlockwise, so this face of circular wire carrying current will act as a North magnetic pole (N-pole)

Magnetic field due to a Solenoid
- The solenoid is a long coil containing a large number of close turns of insulated copper wire.
- The magnetic field produced by a current carrying solenoid is similar to the magnetic field produced by a bar magnet.
- In this case, the strength of magnetic field depends on :
  - number of turns in solenoid.
  - strength of current in the solenoid.
  - the nature of 'core material'.

Electromagnet
- A temporary magnet of soft iron which retains magnetism only when current passes through it.
- Used in electric bell, telephone, electric motor etc.
- Factors affecting the strength of an electromagnet :
  - Number of turns.
  - Current flowing in the coil.
  - Length of air gap between its poles.

Force on Current-carrying conductor placed in a magnetic field

- When a current-carrying conductor is placed in a magnetic field, a mechanical force is exerted on the conductor which makes it move.
- The direction of force is:
  (i) perpendicular to the direction of current,
  (ii) perpendicular to the direction of magnetic field.

Direction of Force

- Fleming's left hand Rule:

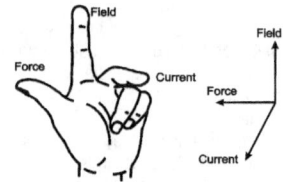

Electric Motor

- A motor is a device which converts electrical energy into mechanical energy.
- It works on the principle that when a rectangular coil is placed in a magnetic field and current is passed through it, a force acts on the coil which rotates it continuously.
- It is mainly used in electric fans, washing machines, refrigerators, electric cars, etc.

Electromagnetic Induction

The production of induced current in a coil placed in a region where the magnetic field changes with time.

Direction of Induced Current

- Fleming's right hand rule:

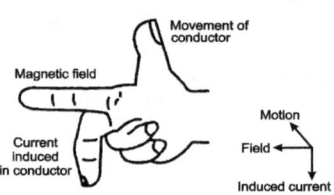

Electricity

Chapter 12

Multiple Choice Questions

1. Two conducting wires of the same material and of equal lengths and equal diameters are first connected in series and then parallel in a circuit across the same potential difference. The ratio of heat produced in series and parallel combinations would be:
(a) 1 : 2 (b) 2 : 1
(c) 1 : 4 (d) 4 : 1

Ans. (c) 1 : 4

Explanation :

As the two conducting wires are of the same material, equal lengths and equal diameters. They will have the same resistance.
Let the resistance of each wire be R and applied potential difference, V.

$$R_{series} = R_1 + R_2$$
$$= R + R = 2R$$
$$P_{series} = \frac{V^2}{R_{series}}$$
$$= \frac{V^2}{(2R)} \quad ...(i)$$

$$\frac{1}{R_{parallel}} = \frac{1}{R_1} + \frac{1}{R_2}$$
$$= \frac{1}{R} + \frac{1}{R}$$
$$R_{parallel} = \frac{R}{2}$$

$$P_{parallel} = \frac{V^2}{R_{parallel}}$$
$$= \frac{2V^2}{R} \quad ...(ii)$$

Dividing equation (i) by equation (ii)
$$\frac{P_{series}}{P_{parallel}} = \frac{1}{4}$$

Hence, the ratio of heat produced is 1/4 or 1 : 4.

2. A student plots V-I graphs for three samples of nichrome wire with resistances R_1, R_2 and R_3. Choose from the following statement that holds true of this graph.

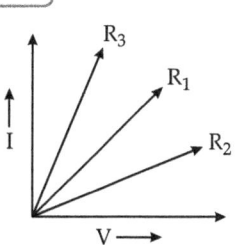

(a) $R_1 = R_2 = R_3$ (b) $R_1 > R_2 > R_3$
(c) $R_3 > R_2 > R_1$ (d) $R_2 > R_1 > R_3$

Ans. (d) $R_2 > R_1 > R_3$

Explanation :

As it is clear from the graph, the current for A_2 conductor is less than A_1 and A_1 is less than A_3 we can say $I_{A2} < I_{A1} < I_{A3}$.
We know
$$R = \frac{V}{I}$$
or
$$R \propto \frac{1}{I}$$

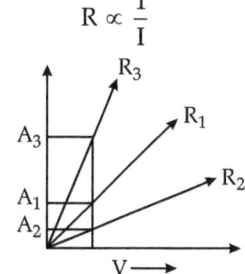

If I is less, then R will be more.
$$I_{A2} < I_{A1} < I_{A3}$$
$$\therefore \quad R_2 > R_1 > R_3.$$

3. The instrument used for measuring electric current is:
(a) galvanometer (b) ammeter
(c) voltmeter (d) potentiometer

Ans. (b) ammeter

Explanation :

Ammeter is a device used for measuring electric current in amperes.

4. Which of the following does not apply to silver ?
(a) The resistance provided is directly proportional to its length.

(b) The resistance provided is inversely proportional to the area of cross section.
(c) Their resistivity is in the range $10^{-8}\,\Omega$ to $10^{-6}\,\Omega$.
(d) The movement of electrons on their outer most orbital is tightly held together.

Ans. (d) The movement of electrons on their outer most orbital is tightly held together.

Explanation:

For a given continuous piece of uniform wire, the resistance is directly proportional to its length. Thus, silver which is a good conductor of electricity and the resistance in it is directly proportional to its length.

Silver is a good conductor of electricity, thus, the resistance provided is inversely proportional to the area of cross section.

Silver has resistivity in the range of $10^{-8}\Omega$ to $10^{-6}\Omega$. Therefore, it is considered as very good conductors.

Hence, the statement that does not apply to silver is the movement of electrons on their outer most orbital is tightly held together.

5. R_1 and R_2 are two resistors and r_1 and r_2 are equivalent resistances in series and parallel respectively, then $\dfrac{R_1}{R_2}$

(a) $\dfrac{r_1 r_2}{r_1 + r_2}$ (b) $\dfrac{r_1 + r_2}{r_1 r_2}$

(c) $\dfrac{r_1 + \sqrt{r_1 - 4r_1 r_2}}{r_1 + \sqrt{r_1 + 4r_1 r_2}}$ (d) $\dfrac{r_1 + \sqrt{r_1^2 - 4r_1 r_2}}{r_1 - \sqrt{r_1^2 - 4r_1 r_2}}$

Ans. (d) $\dfrac{r_1 + \sqrt{r_1^2 - 4r_1 r_2}}{r_1 - \sqrt{r_1^2 - 4r_1 r_2}}$

Explanation:

Here, $r_1 = R_1 + R_2$ ...(i)

and $r_2 = \dfrac{R_1 R_2}{R_1 + R_2}$

$\Rightarrow R_1 R_2 = r_2 r_1$ ...(ii)

Now $(R_1 - R_2)^2 = (R_1 + R_2)^2 - 4 R_1 R_2$
$= r_1^2 - 4 r_2 r_1$

$R_1 - R_2 = \sqrt{r_1^2 - 4r_2 r_1}$

and $R_1 + R_2 = r_1$

$\therefore R_1 = \dfrac{r_1 + \sqrt{r_1^2 - 4 r_1 r_2}}{2}$

and $R_2 = \dfrac{r_1 - \sqrt{r_1^2 - 4 r_1 r_2}}{2}$

$\therefore \dfrac{R_1}{R_2} = \dfrac{r_1 + \sqrt{r_1^2 - 4 r_1 r_2}}{r_1 - \sqrt{r_1^2 - 4 r_1 r_2}}$

6. There are three resistors connected in parallel, the resistance of each resistor is 3 ohm. What is the total resistance of all the three resistors?

(a) $1\,\Omega$ (b) $6\,\Omega$
(c) $15\,\Omega$ (d) $3\,\Omega$

Ans. (a) $1\,\Omega$

Explanation:

It is given that the three resistors are connected in parallel and the resistance of each resistor is $3\,\Omega$. Therefore,

$R_1 = R_2 = R_3 = 3\,\Omega$

From the formula given below, we can calculate the total resistance of all the three resistors:

$$\dfrac{1}{R_p} = \dfrac{1}{R_1} + \dfrac{1}{R_2} + \dfrac{1}{R_3}$$

$$= \dfrac{1}{3} + \dfrac{1}{3} + \dfrac{1}{3} = \dfrac{3}{3}$$

$\therefore R_p = 1\,\Omega$

Hence, the total resistance is $1\,\Omega$.

7. The accumulator which is used for the domestic purpose has the electromotive force of 10 V and with an internal resistance of 0.8 Ω is externally charged by 150 V of the direct current power supply using a series resistor 18 Ω. Calculate the terminal voltage of the accumulator during using.

(a) 16.8 V (b) 17.1 V
(c) 11.3 V (d) 15.9 V

Ans. (d) 15.9 V

Explanation:

$E = V - Ir$
$V = E + Ir$
$= 10 + \left(\dfrac{150 - 10}{18 + 0.8}\right) \times 0.8$
$= 15.9\,V$

8. If a person has five resistors each of value $\dfrac{1}{5}\Omega$, then the maximum resistance he can obtain by connecting them is:

(a) $1\,\Omega$ (b) $5\,\Omega$
(c) $10\,\Omega$ (d) $25\,\Omega$

Ans. (a) $1\,\Omega$

Explanation:

Resistance of one resistor $= \dfrac{1}{5}\,\Omega$

Number of resistors = 5

Maximum resistances can be obtained by combining the resistors in series:

$R_s = R_1 + R_2 + R_3 + R_4 + R_5$
$= \dfrac{1}{5} + \dfrac{1}{5} + \dfrac{1}{5} + \dfrac{1}{5} + \dfrac{1}{5}$
$= \dfrac{1+1+1+1+1}{5} = \dfrac{5}{5} = 1\,\Omega$

Hence, a person on combining five resistors in series gets resistance $1\,\Omega$.

9. Match the components in column A with the symbols in column B.

Column A		Column B
(A) —⊣⊢—		(1) Wire joint
(B) o—▷—o		(2) Capacitor
(C) ⏚		(3) Diode
(D) ⏚		(4) Earth

(a) A-3; B-4; C-3; D-2 (b) A-1; B-2; C-1; D-4
(c) A-4; B-1; C-2; D-3 (d) A-2; B-3; C-4; D-1

Ans. (d) A-2; B-3; C-4; D-1

Explanation:

The correct options are:
A-2; B-3; C-4; D-1

Column A		Column B
(A) —⊣⊢—		(2) Capacitor
(B) o—▷—o		(3) Diode
(C) ⏚		(4) Earth
(D) ⏚		(1) Wire joint

10. The resistance of the wire when the length of the wire increases two times:
(a) becomes 2 times (b) becomes 3 times
(c) becomes 6 times (d) becomes 4 times

Ans. (a) becomes 2 times

Explanation:

The electrical resistance of a wire can be expressed as:

$$R = \frac{\rho L}{A}$$

Where, A = Area of cross section of the conductor
L = Length of the conductor
ρ = Resistivity

From this relation, it is clear that the resistance is directly proportional to the length and inversely proportional to area of cross-section.
If length becomes 2L, then

$$R' = \frac{\rho(2L)}{A} = 2\frac{\rho L}{A}$$

So, $R' = 2R$

Thus, the resistance becomes 2 times if the length of the wire is doubled.

11. Which among the following is the correct way of connecting ammeter and voltmeter in the circuit to determine the equivalent resistance of two resistors in series?
(a) Both ammeter and voltmeter in series
(b) Both ammeter and voltmeter in parallel
(c) Ammeter in parallel and voltmeter in series
(d) Ammeter in series and voltmeter in parallel

Ans. (d) Ammeter in series and voltmeter in parallel

Explanation:

The correct way of connecting ammeter and voltmeter in the circuit to determine the equivalent resistance of two resistors is connecting ammeter in series and voltmeter in parallel. Ammeter is connecting in series, so that whole current passes through it and voltmeter in parallel to it could measure the complete voltage of the circuit.

12. The proper representation of series combination of cells obtaining maximum potential is:

(a) ⊣⊢⊣⊢⊣⊢⊣⊢ (b) ⊣⊢ ⊣⊢ ⊣⊢ ⊣⊢
(c) ⊣⊢⊣⊢⊣⊢⊣⊢ (d) ⊣⊢ ⊣⊢ ⊣⊢ ⊣⊢

Ans. (a) ⊣⊢⊣⊢⊣⊢⊣⊢

Explanation:

The maximum potential is obtained when cells are connected in series such that the negative terminal of the cell is connected to the positive terminal of the second cell and so on.
E.g.,

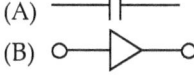

13. The equivalent resistance of a series combination of two resistances is X ohm. It the resistance are of 10 Ω and 40 Ω respectively, the value of X will be:
(a) 10 Ω (b) 20 Ω
(c) 50 Ω (d) 40 Ω

Ans. (c) 50 Ω

Explanation:

We know that
Total Resistance
$R = R_1 + R_2$
$= 10 + 40$
$= 50\ \Omega$

Hence, the value of X is 50 Ω.

14. A cylindrical conductor of length 'l' and uniform area of cross-section 'A' has resistance 'R'. The area of cross-section of another conductor of same material and same resistance but of length '2l' is:

[NCERT Exemplar]

(a) $\frac{A}{2}$ (b) $\frac{3A}{2}$
(c) 2 A (d) 3 A

Ans. (c) 2 A

Explanation:

A cylindrical conductor of length 'l' and uniform area of cross-section 'A' has resistance 'R'. The area of cross-section of another conductor of same material and same resistance but of length '2l' is 2 A. This can be explained as:

$$R = \frac{\rho l}{A}$$

$$\frac{R_1}{R_2} = \left(\frac{L_1}{L_2}\right) \times \left(\frac{A_2}{A_1}\right)$$

$$A_2 = \left(\frac{R_1}{R_2}\right) \times \left(\frac{L_2}{L_1}\right) \times A_1$$

$$A_2 = \left(\frac{R}{R}\right) \times \left(\frac{2l}{l}\right) \times A$$

$$A_2 = 2A$$

15. The maximum resistance which can be made using four resistors each of resistance $\frac{1}{2}\,\Omega$ is :

(a) $2\,\Omega$ (b) $1\,\Omega$
(c) $2.5\,\Omega$ (d) $8\,\Omega$

Ans. (a) $2\,\Omega$

Explanation :

The maximum resistance which can be made using four resistors each of resistance $1/2\,\Omega$ is $2\,\Omega$. This can be explained as:

In series combination, the current in each resistance remains constant and the voltage gets added up. As a result, the individual resistances also get added up.

So, Equivalent Resistance $= R_1 + R_2 + R_3 + R_4$

$$= \frac{1}{2} + \frac{1}{2} + \frac{1}{2} + \frac{1}{2}$$

$$= \frac{4}{2}$$

$$= 2\,\Omega$$

16. A piece of wire of resistance R is cut into five equal parts. These parts are then connected in parallel. If the equivalent resistance of this combination is R', then the ratio R/R' is :

(a) $\frac{1}{25}$ (b) $\frac{1}{5}$

(c) 5 (d) 25

Ans. (d) 25

Explanation :

Given,

A piece of wire with resistance (R) is cut into 5 equal parts

$$R = \frac{R}{5} + \frac{R}{5} + \frac{R}{5} + \frac{R}{5} + \frac{R}{5}$$

$$R = \frac{5R}{5} = R \qquad \text{...(i)}$$

Now, these pieces of wire are connected in parallel then the resistance is (R')

$$\frac{1}{R'} = \frac{5}{R} + \frac{5}{R} + \frac{5}{R} + \frac{5}{R} + \frac{5}{R}$$

So, $\quad \dfrac{1}{R'} = \dfrac{25}{R}$

$$R' = \frac{R}{25} \qquad \text{...(ii)}$$

Now,

$$\frac{R}{R'} = \frac{R}{\frac{R}{25}} \quad \text{[Using (i) and (ii)]}$$

$$\frac{R}{R'} = \frac{25R}{R}$$

$$\frac{R}{R'} = 25$$

17. On which of the given factor, resistance does not depend:
(a) length of conductor
(b) area of cross-section
(c) temperature
(d) density

Ans. (d) density

Explanation :

The resistance of wire can be expressed as:

$$R = \frac{\rho L}{A}$$

Where, A = Area of cross section of the conductor
L = Length of the conductor
ρ = Resistivity

From the above relation, we can see that resistance of a wire is directly proportional to its length and inversely proportional to the area of cross-section. Hence, resistance does not depend on the density.

18. Which of the following obeys Ohm's law ?
(a) Filament of a bulb (b) LED
(c) Nichrome (d) Transistor

Ans. (c) Nichrome

Explanation :

In conductors, resistance remains constant when the current passing through them is increased, they are known as Ohmic conductors. Nichrome which is an alloy is made in such a way that its resistance remains constant for a wide range of temperature. Hence, nichrome obeys Ohm's Law. Whereas, transistor, LED, bulb filament do not obey Ohm's law because with the varied change in temperature their resistance changes.

19. Electrical resistivity of an alloy of copper and nickel is _____ when compared with the electrical resistivity of an alloy of copper, manganese and nickel.
(a) same (b) double
(c) more (d) less

Ans. (c) more

Explanation :

Electrical resistivity of an alloy of copper and nickel is more when compared with the electrical resistivity of an alloy of copper, manganese and nickel. The electrical resistivity of Cu-Ni resistance alloys at different temperatures rises steeply. At 200°C, the electrical resistivity of Cu-Ni alloy is $49 \times 10^{-8}\,\Omega$–m whereas of copper, manganese and nickel $44 \times 10^{-8}\,\Omega$–m.

20. There is a dual of 8 ohm resistance on the aerial. Determine the aerial's new resistance.
    (a) 2 Ω   (b) 4 Ω
    (c) 7 Ω   (d) 10 Ω

Ans. (a) 2 Ω

Explanation :

Let L be the length and A be the area of cross section.

$$R = \rho \frac{l}{A} = 8\,\Omega$$

$$l' = \frac{l}{2}$$

$$A' = 2A$$

$$R' = \rho \frac{l'}{A'}$$

$$= \rho \frac{\frac{l}{2}}{2A}$$

$$= \frac{1}{4}\left(\rho \frac{l}{A}\right)$$

$$= \frac{1}{4} \times 8$$

$$= 2\,\Omega$$

Hence, the aerial's new resistance is 2 Ω.

21. Electrical resistivity of a given metallic wire depends upon:
    (a) its length   (b) its thickness
    (c) its shape   (d) nature of the material

Ans. (d) nature of the material

Explanation :

The resistivity of a material is constant for a particular temperature at a constant temperature. Resistivity of material does not depend on length, thickness and shape of the material. It only depends on the temperature.

22. An electric heater is rated at 2 kW. Electrical energy costs ₹ 4 per kWh. What is the cost of using the heater for 3 hours?
    (a) ₹ 12   (b) ₹ 24
    (c) ₹ 36   (d) ₹ 48

Ans. (b) ₹ 24

Explanation :

Consumption of electrical energy in 3 hours can be calculated by using the formula:
$$E = P \times t$$
$$= 2\,kW \times 3\,hour = 6\,kWh$$
Unit cost of electrical energy
$$= ₹\,4\,per\,kWh$$
Therefore, the cost of energy used for three hours will be: $4 \times 6 = ₹\,24$

23. Consider the room temperature is 24°C in summer, the electrical resistance of thermocoil which is used in the AC unit is 150 Ω. Then calculate the temperature of the thermocoil if the electrical resistance is 175 Ω. Given the temperature coefficient of the thermocoil is $2.98 \times 10^{-4}\,°C^{-1}$.
    (a) 597°C   (b) 583°C
    (c) 546°C   (d) 512°C

Ans. (b) 583°C

Explanation :

$$R_t = R_0 (1 + \alpha \Delta T)$$
$$175 = 150 (1 + 2.98 \times 10^{-4} \Delta T)$$
$$\frac{25}{150} = 2.98 \times \Delta T \times 10^{-4}$$
$$\Delta T = 559.28°C$$
$$T - 24 = 559.28°C$$
$$T = 559.28°C + 24$$
$$T = 583.28°C$$

Hence, the temperature of the thermocoil is 583°C.

24. The values of mA and μA are :
    (a) 10^{-6} and 10^{-9} A respectively
    (b) 10^{-3} and 10^{-6} A respectively
    (c) 10^{-3} and 10^{-9} A respectively
    (d) 10^{-6} and 10^{-3} A respectively

Ans. (b) 10^{-3} and 10^{-6} A respectively

Explanation :

An ampere is the SI unit of electric current.

$1A = 1000\,mA$ or $1\,mA = \frac{1}{1000}\,A = 10^{-3}\,A$

∴ $1\mu A = 10^{-3} \times 10^{-3}\,A = 10^{-6}\,A$

25. The resistance of a resistor is reduced to half of its initial value. In doing so, if other parameters of the circuit remain unchanged the heating effects on the resistor will become:
    (a) two times   (b) half
    (c) one - fourth   (d) four times

Ans. (a) two times

Explanation :

Resistance of a resistor R Ω

New resistance of a resistor $\frac{R}{2}$ Ω.

All other parameters of the circuit remain unchanged

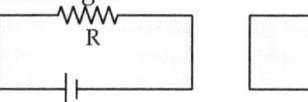 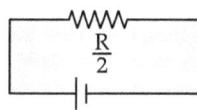

By applying Joule's law of heating
$$H = I^2 Rt$$
As per Ohm's law $V = IR$
or
$$I = \frac{V}{R}$$
∴
$$H = \frac{V}{R} \times \frac{V}{R} \times R \times t$$
or
$$= \frac{V^2}{R} \times t$$

Case-I Case-II
$$H = \frac{V^2}{R} \times t \qquad H' = \frac{V^2}{\frac{R}{2}} \times t$$
$$= \frac{V^2 \times 2}{R} \times t$$
$$H' = H \times 2$$

Hence, the heating effect in the resistor will become two times if all other parameter of the circuit remain same.

26. **An electric fuse is connected with :**
    (a) live wire (b) earthing
    (c) neutral wire (d) parallel to the line wire

Ans. (a) live wire

Explanation :
An electric fuse is connected with live wire because it gets blown up when an excess current tries to pass through in order to save the electrical appliances by restricting the flow of that current.

27. **Which of the following terms does not represent electrical power in a circuit ?**
    (a) I^2R (b) IR^2
    (c) VI (d) V^2/R

Ans. (b) IR^2

Explanation :
We know that,
$$P = VI \qquad \ldots(i)$$
Where, P = Power
V = Potential difference
I = Current
$$V = IR \qquad \ldots(ii)$$
On substituting equation (ii) in equation (i), we get
$$P = I^2R \qquad \ldots(iii)$$
Again, from Ohm's law
$$I = \frac{V}{R} \qquad \ldots(iv)$$
On substituting equation (iv) in equation (i), we get
$$P = \frac{V^2}{R}$$
Hence, option (b) IR^2 does not represent power.

28. **An electric bulb is rated 220 V and 100 W. When it is operated on 110 V, the power consumed will be:**
    (a) 100 W (b) 75 W
    (c) 50 W (d) 25 W

Ans. (d) 25 W

Explanation :
We know that,
$$P = \frac{V^2}{R}$$
Where, P = Electric power
V = Potential difference in a circuit
R = Resistance
Now,
$$R = \frac{V^2}{P}$$
$$R = \frac{220 \times 220}{100} = 484\ \Omega$$
As the voltage drop across the bulb is 110 V. The power consumed by the bulb is:
$$P_b = \frac{V^2}{R}$$
$$= \frac{110 \times 110}{484}$$
$$P_b = 25\ W$$
Hence, the power consumed will be 25 W.

29. **Let us consider that because of the flow of the current flowing through a metallic wire if the temperature of the entire system increases. What will happen from the following options ?**
    (a) Potential difference (V) increases
    (b) Resistance (R) decreases
    (c) Potential difference (V) decreases
    (d) V and R remains the same

Ans. (c) Potential difference (V) decreases

Explanation :
If the temperature of the entire system increases when the current is flowing through a metallic wire, the potential difference (V) decreases.

30. **Which of the following terms does not represent electrical energy in a circuit?**
    (a) I^2Rt (b) IR^2t
    (c) VIt (d) V^2t/R

Ans. (b) IR^2t

Explanation :
Electric power, $P = VI = I^2R = \dfrac{V^2}{R}$

∴ Electrical Energy $= Pt = VIt = I^2Rt = \dfrac{V^2t}{R}$

Assertion and Reasoning Based Questions

(a) If both assertion and reason are true and reason is the correct explanation of assertion.
(b) If both assertion and reason are true, but reason is not the correct explanation of assertion.
(c) If assertion is true, but reason is false.
(d) If assertion is false, but reason is true.

31. **Assertion :** In a series circuit, the current is constant throughout the electric circuit.

    Reason : All electric devices does not need equal currents to operate properly.

Ans. (b) If both assertion and reason are true, but reason is not the correct explanation of assertion.

Explanation :

Current is constant in a series circuit as there is only one path for the flow of current. But different devices connected in a circuit have different power ratings and therefore draw different amount of currents. Thus, both assertion and reason are true and reason is not the correct explanation of the assertion.

32. **Assertion :** When area of the conductor is halved then the resistance of the material gets doubled when length is kept constant.

    Reason : Because resistance is inversely proportional to the area of a cross-section of the material.

    (a) If both assertion and reason are true and reason is the correct explanation of assertion.
    (b) If both assertion and reason are true, but reason is not the correct explanation of assertion.
    (c) If assertion is true, but reason is false.
    (d) If assertion is false, but reason is true.

Ans. (a) If both assertion and reason are true and reason is the correct explanation of assertion.

Explanation :

According to the formula: $R = \rho \dfrac{l}{A}$

Where, R : resistance
ρ : resistivity
l : length of conductor
A : area of cross section of conductor

Here, resistivity of the material never varies. If length is also kept constant and when area is halved then resistance of the material gets doubled as the resistance depends on 3 factors, i.e., length, area and nature of the material.

Thus, both assertion and reason are true and reason is the correct explanation of assertion.

33. **Assertion :** In a circuit which is having 3 series resistors of R Ω each, the total resistance of the circuit will be 3 R.

    Reason : As in parallel circuit the resultant resistance will be $\dfrac{1}{R} = \dfrac{1}{R_1} + \dfrac{1}{R_2} + \dfrac{1}{R_3}$.

    (a) If both assertion and reason are true and reason is the correct explanation of assertion.
    (b) If both assertion and reason are true, but reason is not the correct explanation of assertion.
    (c) If assertion is true, but reason is false.
    (d) If assertion is false, but reason is true.

Ans. (b) If both assertion and reason are true, but reason is not the correct explanation of assertion.

Explanation :

Resultant resistance is the addition of individual resistance present in the series circuit. So, according to the above statement,

Resultant resistance (R) = $R_1 + R_2 + R_3$. So total resistance will be 3 R. In parallel combination, resultant resistance will be $\dfrac{1}{R} = \dfrac{1}{R_1} + \dfrac{1}{R_2} + \dfrac{1}{R_3}$.

Here, both assertion and reason are true, but reason is not the correct explanation of assertion.

34. **Assertion:** The connecting wires are made of copper.

    Reason: The electrical conductivity of copper is high.

    (a) If both assertion and reason are true and reason is the correct explanation of assertion.
    (b) If both assertion and reason are true, but reason is not the correct explanation of assertion.
    (c) If assertion is true, but reason is false.
    (d) If assertion is false, but reason is true.

Ans. (a) If both assertion and reason are true and reason is the correct explanation of assertion.

Explanation :

Due to high electrical conductivity of copper, it conducts the current without offering much resistance. The copper being diamagnetic material does not get magnetised due to current through it and hence does not disturb the current in the circuit. Thus, both assertion and reason are correct and reason is the correct explanation of the assertion.

35. **Assertion :** Voltmeter is always connected in parallel across the circuit while measuring the potential difference.

    Reason : As the voltage in parallel circuits is measured to be the same.

    (a) If both assertion and reason are true and reason is the correct explanation of assertion.
    (b) If both assertion and reason are true, but reason is not the correct explanation of assertion.
    (c) If assertion is true, but reason is false.
    (d) If assertion is false, but reason is true.

Ans. (a) If both assertion and reason are true and reason is the correct explanation of assertion.

Explanation :

Voltage measured in the parallel circuits is always equal. As all the parallel circuits start from one point and end at another point and the potential difference between the two points will always be the same. So, this is the reason why voltmeter is always connected in parallel across the circuit. Thus, both assertion and reason are true and reason is the correct explanation of assertion.

36. **Assertion :** Electric current flowing through a metallic wire is directly proportional to the potential difference across its ends.

    Reason : Ohms law expression V = IR, where R (resistance) of the wire is always varying.

    (a) If both assertion and reason are true and reason is the correct explanation of assertion.

(b) If both assertion and reason are true, but reason is not the correct explanation of assertion.

(c) If assertion is true, but reason is false.

(d) If assertion is false, but reason is true.

Ans. (c) If assertion is true, but reason is false.

Explanation :

Ohm's law states that the electric current flowing through a metallic wire is directly proportional to the potential difference across its two ends. The expression is written as :

$$V = IR$$

Here, R (resistance of the wire) is constant value then only the statement will be valid.

$$V \propto I \text{ only if } \frac{V}{I} = \text{constant}$$

Thus, assertion is true, but reason is false.

37. Assertion : Alloys are commonly used in electrical heating devices like electric iron and heater.*

Reason : Resistivity of an alloy is generally higher than that of its constituent metals but the alloys have low melting points than their constituent metals.

(a) If both assertion and reason are true and reason is the correct explanation of assertion.

(b) If both assertion and reason are true, but reason is not the correct explanation of assertion.

(c) If assertion is true, but reason is false.

(d) If assertion is false, but reason is true.

Ans. (b) If both assertion and reason are true, but reason is not the correct explanation of assertion.

Explanation :

Alloys are the combination of metals and they are used in the heating devices due to their high resistance which produces more heat energy. And alloys are made up of weak bonds, their melting point is lower than their constituents metals. Thus, both assertion and reason are true, but reason is not the correct explanation of assertion.

38. Assertion : An ammeter is always connected in parallel with the circuit for which current has to be measured.

Reason : As the current in a series circuit is same.

(a) If both assertion and reason are true and reason is the correct explanation of assertion.

(b) If both assertion and reason are true, but reason is not the correct explanation of assertion.

(c) If assertion is true, but reason is false.

(d) If assertion is false, but reason is true.

Ans. (d) If assertion is false, but reason is true.

Explanation :

In a series circuit the current measured will be same, this is the reason why ammeter is always connected in series with the circuit for which the measurement has to be done. Thus, assertion is false, but reason is true.

39. Assertion : When more current flows to an electrical equipment it shows more heating of the same.

Reason : Heat flow is directly proportional to the square of current only.

(a) If both assertion and reason are true and reason is the correct explanation of assertion.

(b) If both assertion and reason are true, but reason is not the correct explanation of assertion.

(c) If assertion is true, but reason is false.

(d) If assertion is false, but reason is true.

Ans. (c) If assertion is true, but reason is false.

Explanation :

Heat flow is dependent on three factors :
1. Current flowing through it
2. Time period of flow of current
3. Resistance of the conductor

So, the reason is false that heat flow only depends on square of current. Therefore, assertion is true, but reason is false.

40. Assertion : Bulbs are filled with inactive nitrogen and argon gases.

Reason : As there is a requirement of thermal isolation of the filament.

(a) If both assertion and reason are true and reason is the correct explanation of assertion.

(b) If both assertion and reason are true, but reason is not the correct explanation of assertion.

(c) If assertion is true, but reason is false.

(d) If assertion is false, but reason is true.

Ans. (a) If both assertion and reason are true and reason is the correct explanation of assertion.

Explanation :

Most part of the power consumed by bulb is dissipated as heat but very less part gets converted into light. So, there is a need for thermal isolation in order to reduce heat losses. This is the reason why bulbs are filled with inactive nitrogen and argon. So, both assertion and reason are true and reason is the correct explanation of assertion.

Case Based Questions

41. Read the passage carefully and answer the following questions from Q. 41 (i) to Q. 41 (v).

Ohm's law is the relationship between potential difference and current in a circuit which was first established by George Simon Ohm. The law states that the current passing through a metallic

---
* are board exam questions from previous years

conductor is directly proportional to the potential difference applied between its ends. $V \propto I$ i.e., $V = kI$ where k is the resistance offered by the conductor and is constant for a given conductor. Although a large class of materials is known to follow Ohm's law, there do exist materials used in circuits that do not follow the direct relationship between V & I.

(i) If in a circuit both the potential difference and resistance are doubled, then
   (a) current is doubled.
   (b) current is halved.
   (c) current remains same.
   (d) current is four times.

(ii) When a battery of 9 V is connected across a conductor and the current flowing is 0.1 A, the resistance is:
   (a) 90 Ω   (b) 0.9 Ω
   (c) 9 Ω   (d) 900 Ω

(iii) By increasing voltage across a conductor:
   (a) current will increase.
   (b) current will decrease.
   (c) resistance will decrease.
   (d) resistance will increase.

(iv) The slope of the V-I graph shall give:
   (a) resistance
   (b) reciprocal of resistance
   (c) power
   (d) charge

(v) Four students have plotted the graph between V-I for a conductor. Which one is correct?

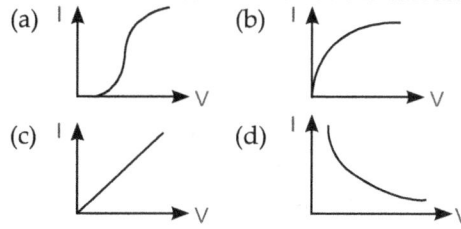

Ans. (i) (c) Current remains same
(ii) (a) 90 Ω
(iii) (d) resistance will increase
(iv) (a) resistance
(v) (c)

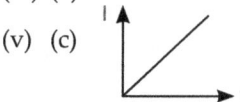

42. Read the passage carefully and answer the following questions from Q. 42 (i) to Q. 42 (v).

In a circuit, several resistors may be combined to form a network. The combination must have two endpoints to connect it with a battery or other elements of the circuit. When the resistors are connected in series then the current flowing in each remains the same but potential differences across each resistor will vary. When the resistances are connected in parallel, the potential difference across each resistor will be the same though a different amount of current will flow in each resistor.

(i) The household circuits are connected in:
   (a) series
   (b) parallel
   (c) both series and parallel
   (d) neither series nor parallel

(ii) The equivalent resistance of two resistors x and y is Z when connected in series and M when connected in parallel. Z:M is:
   (a) xy (b) $x + y \times y$
   (c) $(x + y)^2/xy$ (d) $xy(2x + 2y)$

(iii) Two resistances 10 Ω and 3 Ω are connected in parallel across a battery. If there is a current of 0.2 A in 10 resistors, the voltage supplied by the battery is:
   (a) 2 V   (b) 1 V
   (c) 4 V   (d) 8 V

(iv) Two wires each having a resistance value equal to R are first connected in series and then connected in parallel. The plot shows the graphical representation of resistances in both cases.

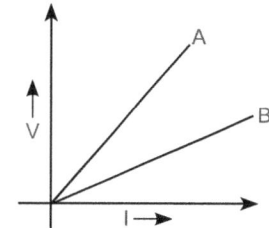

   (a) A denotes parallel combination
   (b) B denotes series combination
   (c) A denotes series combination and B denotes parallel combination
   (d) None of the above

(v) The equivalent resistance (in Ω) of the network across A and B is:

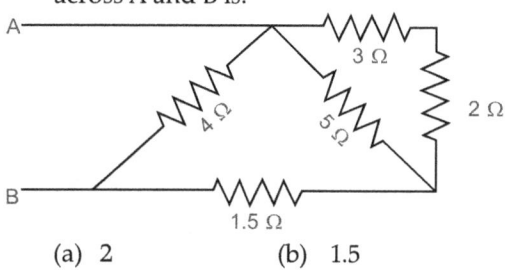

   (a) 2   (b) 1.5
   (c) 2.5   (d) 3

Ans. (i) (b) parallel
(ii) (c) $(x + y)^2/xy$
(iii) (a) 2 V
(iv) (c) A denotes series combination and B denotes parallel combination
(v) (a) 2

43. Read the passage carefully and answer the following questions from Q. 43 (i) to Q. 43 (v).

Resistivity or electric resistivity is the inverse of the electrical conductivity. Resistivity is a fundamental property of a material and it demonstrates how strongly the material resists or conducts electric current. A low resistivity is a clear indication of a material which readily allows electric current. The common representation of resistivity is by the Greek letter ρ. Also, the SI unit of electrical resistivity is ohm-meter (Ω-m). Resistivity refers to the electrical resistance of a conductor of a particular unit cross-sectional area and unit length.

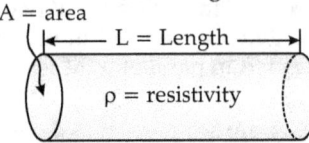

Experts can use resistivity for comparing different materials on the basis of their ability to conduct electric currents. High resistivity is the designation of poor conductors.

(i) The value of resistivity depends upon:
 (a) length of wire
 (b) area of cross section
 (c) nature of conductor
 (d) radius of wire

(ii) A wire has the same resistance as the one given in the figure. Calculate its resistivity if the length of the wire is 10 m and its area of cross section is 2 m.

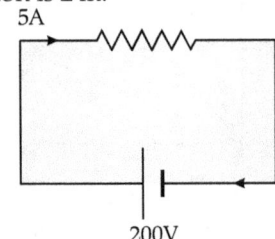

 (a) $16\,\Omega - m$
 (b) $8\,\Omega - m$
 (c) $16\,k\Omega - m$
 (d) $8\,k\Omega - m$

(iii) The resistivity of alloys is:
 (a) very low
 (b) very high
 (c) generally lower than its constituent metals
 (d) more than resistivity of insulators

(iv) A student plotted the graphs as shown below to study the variation of resistances R of a wire with its length l and radius r:

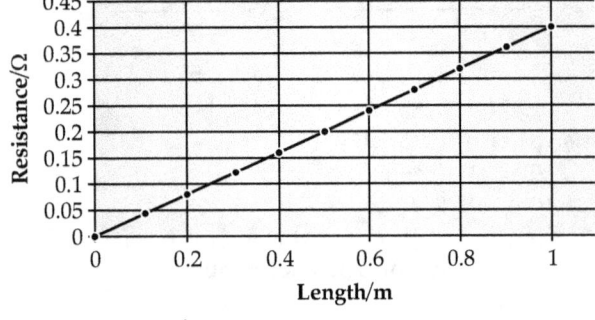

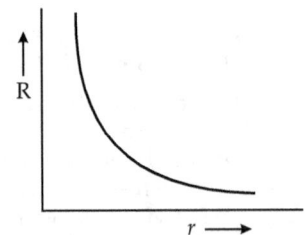

(I) The resistance of a wire is inversely related to the length of the wire, i.e., $R \propto \dfrac{1}{l}$.

(II) The resistance of a wire is directly related to the length of the wire, i.e., $R \propto l$.

(III) The resistance of a wire is inversely related to the radius of the wire, i.e., $R \propto \dfrac{1}{r}$.

(IV) The resistance of a wire is inversely related to the square of the radius of the wire, i.e., $R \propto \dfrac{1}{r^2}$.

 (a) Both (I) and (III)
 (b) Both (II) and (III)
 (c) Both (I) and (IV)
 (d) Both (II) and (IV)

(v) A wire of length l and of radius of cross-section r has a resistance of R Ω. Another wire of same material and of radius of cross-section $2r$ will have the same R if the length is:

 (a) $\dfrac{l}{4}$
 (b) $2l$
 (c) $4l$
 (d) $\dfrac{l}{2}$

Ans. (i) (c) nature of conductor
 (ii) (b) $8\,\Omega - m$
 (iii) (a) very low
 (iv) (d) Both (II) and (IV)
 (v) (c) $4l$

44. Read the passage carefully and answer the following questions from Q. 44 (i) to Q. 44(v).

The electrical energy consumed by an electrical appliance is given by the product of its power rating and the duration for which it is used. SI unit of electrical energy is the joule. Where a large quantity of energy is involved, using a joule is not convenient as a unit. So, for commercial purposes, bigger units of electrical energy are involved. 1 kilowatt-hour is equal to 3.6×10^6 joules of electrical energy.

(i) The value of energy dissipated by a certain heater is E. If the duration of operation of the heater is doubled, the energy dissipated will be:
 (a) halved
 (b) doubled
 (c) four-times
 (d) remains same

(ii) 60 W is the power of a lamp. The energy dissipated in one minute is:
 (a) 360 J
 (b) 36 J
 (c) 3.6 J
 (d) 3600 J

(iii) Calculate the energy transformed by a 5 A current flowing through a resistor of 2 Ω for 30 minutes.
 (a) 90 kJ
 (b) 80 kJ
 (c) 60 kJ
 (d) 40 kJ

(iv) Choose the correct statement:
 (a) 1 watt-hour = 3600 J
 (b) 1 kWh = 36 × 10⁶ J
 (c) Energy in kWh = power in W(watt) × time in hour(h)
 (d) Energy in kWh = V × I × T1000
(v) Choose the incorrect statement.
 (a) Higher the resistance, the lesser the power consumed.
 (b) Lower the resistance, more the voltage drawn.
 (c) Higher the resistance, the higher the current flown.
 (d) Higher the resistance, the lesser the voltage drawn.

Ans. (i) (b) doubled
(ii) (d) 3600 J
(iii) (a) 90 kJ
(iv) (a) 1 watt-hour = 3600 J
(v) (c) Higher the resistance, the higher the current flown.

45. Observe the figure carefully and answer the following questions from Q. 45 (i) to Q. 45 (v).

The following graphs represent the current versus voltage and voltage versus current for six conductors A, B, C, D, E, and F.

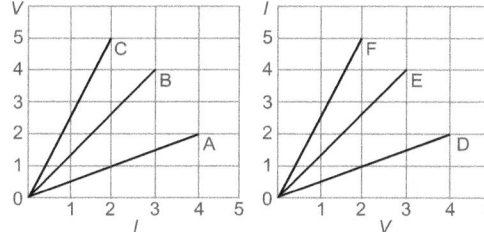

(i) Among conductors A, B, C, D, E, F, the maximum resistance is shown by:
 (a) curve C (b) curve A
 (c) curve F (d) curve D
(ii) Which of the following does not indicate the resistance of curve B?
 (a) The slope of curve B
 (b) The ratio of V-intercept to I-intercept
 (c) The ratio of total grids on the y-axis to total grids on the x-axis
 (d) $\frac{3}{4}$ Ω
(iii) Which indicates the correct sum of least resistances of two graphs?
 (a) Curve C + Curve F
 (b) Curve A + Curve D
 (c) Curve A + Curve F
 (d) Curve C + Curve D
(iv) If resistances shown by curve A and curve E are added, the value will be:
 (a) 1.83 Ω (b) 1.50 Ω
 (c) 1.64 Ω (d) 1.25 Ω

(v) Which is true for these graphs?

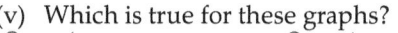
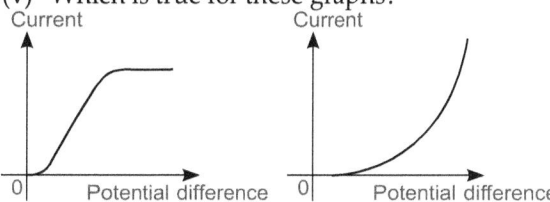

 (a) Both are ohmic conductors
 (b) Curve A is ohmic and B is non-ohmic conductor
 (c) Both are non-ohmic conductors
 (d) Curve B is ohmic and A is non-ohmic conductor

Ans. (i) (a) curve C
(ii) (d) $\frac{3}{4}$ Ω
(iii) (c) Curve A + Curve F
(iv) (d) 1.25 Ω
(v) (c) Both are non-ohmic conductors

46. Read the passage carefully and answer the following questions from Q. 46 (i) to Q. 46 (v).

The graph below is a V-I graph of a metallic circuit drawn at two different temperatures T_1 and T_2.

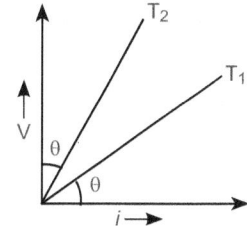

(i) For the above graph choose the correct option depicting which of the two temperatures is higher with justification.
 (a) $T_2 > T_1$; Slope of V-I graph at T_2 is greater than slope at T_1.
 (b) $T_1 > T_2$; resistance increases with increase in temperature.
 (c) $T_2 > T_1$; resistance increases with decrease in temperature.
 (d) $T_1 > T_2$; Slope of V-I graph at T_1 is greater than slope at T_2.
(ii) For the above graph, at which temperature the resistance is higher?
 (a) At T_1
 (b) At T_2
 (c) Resistance does not depend upon temperature
 (d) None of these
(iii) Choose the correct set containing factors on which resistance depends?
 (a) Length, Area of cross section, Temperature, Nature of the material.
 (b) Area of cross section, Temperature, Nature of the material, Colour.

(c) Length, Area of cross section, Temperature, intermolecular attraction.

(d) Temperature, Nature of the material, Length, physical state of material.

(iv) What is likely to happen if current in a wire is passed for a longer time than required?

(a) The wire may get burnt and may melt.

(b) Length of the wire may decrease resulting in lower resistance.

(c) Resistance of wire will drop as it will be very difficult to stop the electrons.

(d) Resistance of the wire will get increased due to joule's heating effect.

(v) If the vertical and horizontal axes of a typical V-I straight line graph are reversed, which graph below is likely to represent the I-V graph? (I on vertical, V on horizontal for I-V graph).

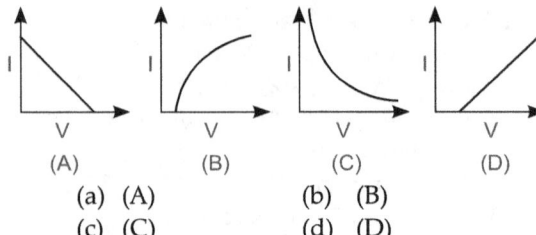

(a) (A) (b) (B)
(c) (C) (d) (D)

Ans. (i) (a) $T_2 > T_1$; Slope of V-I graph at T_2 is greater than slope at T_1.

(ii) (b) At T_2

(iii) (a) Length, Area of cross section, Temperature, Nature of the material.

(iv) (d) Resistance of the wire will get increased due to joule's heating effect.

(v) (d)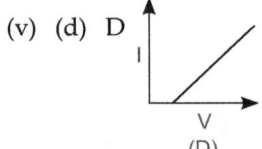

Definitions

47. Define resistance of a conductor.

Ans. The obstruction offered to the flow of current by a conductor is called its resistance.

48. State Ohm's law.

Ans. According to Ohm's law, the current flowing in a conductor is directly proportional to the potential difference applied across its ends, provided the temperature and other physical conditions of the conductor remain constant.

49. Define resistivity.

Ans. The resistivity of a substance is numerically equal to the resistance of a rod of that substance which is 1 metre long and 1 square metre in cross-section.

50. What are ohmic conductors?

Ans. The conductors which obey Ohm's law are called ohmic conductors. The V-I graph for ohmic conductor is a straight line.

51. What are non-ohmic conductors?

Ans. The conductors which does not obey Ohm's law are called non-ohmic conductors. The V-I graph for non-ohmic conductors is not a straight line.

52. State Joule's law of heating.

Ans. Joule's law of heating states that the amount of heat produced in a conductor is directly proportional to:

(a) Square of current (I^2)

(b) Resistance of wire (R)

(c) Time (t), for which current is passed.

53. Define electric power.

Ans. The electrical work done per unit time is called electric power.

54. What does an electric circuit mean? [NCERT]

Ans. A continuous conducting path consisting of wires and other electrical components (like resistance or electric bulb, switch etc.) between the two terminals of a cell or battery, along which an electric current flows, is called an electric circuit.

Formula or S.I. Unit Based Questions

55. Name and define S.I. unit of resistance.*

Ans. The S.I. unit of resistance is ohm (Ω).

The resistance of a conductor is said to be 1 ohm if 1 ampere current flows through it when a potential difference of 1 volt is applied across the ends of the conductor.

$$1 \text{ ohm} = \frac{1 \text{ volt}}{1 \text{ ampere}}$$

56. Write the formula for the equivalent resistance (R) when three resistors R_1, R_2 and R_3 are connected in (a) series, (b) parallel.

Ans. (a) $R = R_1 + R_2 + R_3$

(b) $\dfrac{1}{R} = \dfrac{1}{R_1} + \dfrac{1}{R_2} + \dfrac{1}{R_3}$

57. Write the S.I. unit of resistivity.

Ans. Ohm-metre.

58. What happens to resistance of a conductor when its area of cross-section is increased?*

Ans. Resistance decreases as $R \propto \dfrac{1}{A}$.

---

* are board exam questions from previous years

59. How many joules are equals to 1 kWh ?
Ans. 3.6×10^6 J.

60. A given length of a wire is doubled on itself. By what factor does the resistance of the wire change ?*
Ans. When given length of wire is doubled on itself, its new length $L' = \dfrac{L}{2}$ and new cross-section area $A' = 2A$. Hence, its new resistance

$$R' = \dfrac{\rho L'}{A'} = \dfrac{\rho\left(\dfrac{L}{2}\right)}{(2A)} = \dfrac{1}{4}\dfrac{\rho L}{A} = \dfrac{R}{4}$$

Thus, resistance is reduced to one-fourth of its original value.

61. Derive the relation $R = R_1 + R_2 + R_3$, when resistors are joined in series.*
Ans. In series combination, the same current flows in all the resistances but the potential difference across each of the resistance is different.
According to Ohm's law, we have
$$V_1 = IR_1, V_2 = IR_2, V_3 = IR_3$$
If the total potential difference between A and B is V, then
$$V = V_1 + V_2 + V_3$$
$$= IR_1 + IR_2 + IR_3$$
$$= I(R_1 + R_2 + R_3)$$

Let the equivalent resistance be R, then
$$V = IR$$
and hence $IR = I(R_1 + R_2 + R_3)$
$\Rightarrow$ $R = R_1 + R_2 + R_3$.

62. Derive the relation $\dfrac{1}{R} = \dfrac{1}{R_1} + \dfrac{1}{R_2} + \dfrac{1}{R_3}$ when resistors are joined in parallel.*
Ans. In parallel combination of three resistance R_1, R_2 and R_3, the current in each of the resistance is different. If I is the current drawn from the cell then it is divided into branches as I_1, I_2 and I_3. Thus,
$$I = I_1 + I_2 + I_3$$
The potential difference across each of these resistances is the same.
Thus, from Ohm's law
$$I_1 = \dfrac{V}{R_1}, I_2 = \dfrac{V}{R_2}, I_3 = \dfrac{V}{R_3}$$

If R is the equivalent resistance then,

$$I = \dfrac{V}{R}$$

$$\therefore \quad \dfrac{V}{R} = \dfrac{V}{R_1} + \dfrac{V}{R_2} + \dfrac{V}{R_3}$$

and $\dfrac{1}{R} = \dfrac{1}{R_1} + \dfrac{1}{R_2} + \dfrac{1}{R_3}$.

63. Out of 60 W and 40 W lamps, which one has a higher electrical resistance when in use.
Ans. Power $(P) = \dfrac{V^2}{R}$.

From the above formula, P is inversely proportional to R (resistance) as voltage remaining the same. Hence, 40 We lamp has high resistance.

64. Write the formula for current 'I' flowing through a conductor if 'n' electrons flow through the cross-section of a conductor in time 't'.
Ans. If 'n' electrons pass through the cross-section of a conductor in time 't', the total charge 'Q' passing through the conductor is :
$$Q = ne$$
(e is the charge on an electron = 1.6×10^{-19} C)
The current 'I' in the conductor is :
$$I = \dfrac{Q}{t} = \dfrac{ne}{t}$$

65. What is commercial unit of electrical energy ? Convert it into joules.
Ans. The commercial unit of electrical energy is kWh.
$$1 \text{ kWh} = 1000 \text{ W} \times 1 \text{ hour}$$
$$= 1000 \dfrac{J}{s} \times 60 \times 60 s$$
$$= 3.6 \times 10^6 \text{ J}$$

66. Name the practical unit of power and state its relation with the S.I. unit.
Ans. The practical unit of power is Horse Power (H.P.)
$$1 \text{ H.P.} = 746 \text{ watt.}$$

67. Write the formula of electric power (P) in terms of :
(a) Potential difference (V) and current (I).
(b) Current (I) and resistance (R).
(c) Potential difference (V) and resistance (R).
Ans. (a) $P = VI$
(b) $P = I^2R$
(c) $P = \dfrac{V^2}{R}$

68. Write the formula for the heat produced (H) when a current (I) is passed through a conductor of resistance (R) for second (t).
Ans. Heat produced, $H = I^2Rt$.

69. What is the formula of (a) Resistance (R) of an electric appliance, (b) Safe current (I) in terms of power rating (P) and voltage rating (V).
Ans. (a) Resistance of appliance
$$= \dfrac{\text{(Voltage rating of appliance)}^2}{\text{(Power rating of appliance)}}$$

*are board exam questions from previous years

$$R = \frac{V^2}{P}$$

(b) Safe current = $\frac{\text{Power rating of appliance}}{\text{Voltage rating of appliance}}$

$$I = \frac{P}{V}$$

70. Name the physical quantity that represents the ratio of potential difference and current.
Ans. Resistance.

71. What is commercial units of electrical energy? Convert it into joules.
Ans. The commercial unit of electrical energy is kWh.
$$1 \text{ kWh} = 1000 \text{ W} \times 1 \text{ hour}$$
$$= 1000 \frac{J}{s} \times 60 \times 60 \text{ s}$$
$$= 3.6 \times 10^6 \text{ J}$$

72. Name and define the S.I. unit of electric power.
Ans. The S.I. unit of electric power is watt (W). One watt is the power consumed by an electrical device when it is operated at a potential difference of one volt and carries a current of one ampere.
$$1 \text{ watt} = 1 \text{ volt} \times 1 \text{ ampere.}$$

73. What is meant by saying that the potential difference between two points is 1 V? [NCERT]
Ans. The potential difference between two points is said to be 1 volt if 1 joule of work is done in moving 1 coulomb of electric charge from one point to the other.

74. Define kWh.
Ans. A kilowatt hour (kWh) is the commercial unit of electrical energy. It is the energy consumed when 1 kW (1000 W) power is used for 1 hour.

Very Short Answer Type Questions

75. The radius of conducting wire is doubled. What will be the ratio of its new specific resistance to the old one?
Ans. 1 : 1, specific resistance does not change as it depends on the nature of material only.

76. How are bulbs connected in a fairy light circuit used for decoration of buildings in festivals?
Ans. Series combination.

77. What will happen to the resistivity of a wire of length L if it is cut into three parts?
Ans. Resistivity of the wire will not change even when the wire is cut into three parts as resistivity is a characteristic of the material of the conductor and does not depend on the physical dimensions of the conductor.

78. The following table gives the value of electrical resistivity of some materials :*

Material	Copper	Silver	Constantan
Electrical resistivity (in Ω–m)	1.62×10^{-8}	1.6×10^{-8}	49×10^{-8}

Which one is the best conductor of electricity out of them?
Ans. Silver, because its electrical resistivity is least out of the given materials.

79. What is the resistance of an (a) ideal ammeter and (b) ideal voltmeter?
Ans. (a) Zero
(b) Infinite

80. In series combination which remains constant— current or voltage?
Ans. Current.

81. Name two devices in which electricity is converted into heat.
Ans. Electric heater and electric iron.

82. Name the alloy which is used for making the filament of bulbs.

Ans. Tungsten is used for making the filament of bulbs.

83. Would you connect a fuse in series or in parallel to an electric circuit?
Ans. In series, of the electric circuit before appliances are present in the circuit.

84. Why do electricians wear rubber hand gloves while working?*
Ans. Rubber is an electrical insulator. Hence, electrician can work safely while working on an electric circuit without a risk of getting any electric shock.

85. Electric current flows through a metallic conductor from its one end A to other end B. Which end of the conductor is at higher potential? Why?
Ans. Since, current flows from a region higher potential to a lower potential. So, it flows from A to B where A is the end with higher potential.

86. Write the function of voltmeter in an electric circuit.*
Ans. Voltmeter measures the potential difference across two points in a circuit. It is always connected in parallel in the circuit.

87. Should the resistance of a voltmeter be low or high? Give reason.*
Ans. The resistance of a voltmeter should be high, because voltmeter is connected parallel to the component of a circuit and it also takes negligible current from the circuit in order to measure the potential difference accurately.

88. Which material is the best conductor of electricity?*
Ans. Silver.

89. Which substance is used for making resistance coil of electric heater and why?
Ans. Nichrome, due to its high resistivity.

90. Why is an ammeter connected in series in an electric circuit?
Ans. It is connected in series so that whole of electric current, which it has to measure, passes through it.

* are board exam questions from previous years

Reasoning Based Questions

91. Two wires P and Q are made of copper. The wire P is long and thin, while the wire Q is short and thick. Which will have more specific resistance? Give a reason for your answer.

Ans. Both the wires will have same specific resistance, since they are both made of same material (*i.e.,* copper) and there is no change in temperature.

92. Why should a connection wire be thick?

Ans. Resistance of a wire is inversely proportional to its area of cross-section (or thickness). Hence, a connection wire should be thick to reduce its resistance.

93. Why is a series arrangement not used for domestic circuits?

Ans. Series arrangement is not used for domestic circuits for the following reasons :
1. The voltage of the source gets divided in all the appliances connected in series, in the ratio of their resistances, so each appliance does not operate at its rated voltage.
2. The resistance of the circuit increases and it reduces the current in the circuit, so each appliance gets less power.
3. If any one appliance in series arrangement is switched off (or gets spoilt), no other appliance connected with it in series will then operate.

94. Answer the following questions:
   (a) List the factors on which the resistance of a conductor in the shape of wire depends.
   (b) Why are metals good conductors of electricity whereas glass is a bad conductor of electricity? Give reason.

Ans. (a) Resistance of a conductor depends directly on its length and is inversely proportional to the area of cross-section.
   (b) Metals have free electrons and they move and conduct electricity, whereas glass does not have free electrons and charges to flow as it is an insulator.

95. Name a material which is used for making standard resistors. Give a reason for your answer.

Ans. Standard resistors are made from alloys such as constantan, manganin etc., because they have high specific resistance and the effect of change in temperature on their resistance is negligible.

96. Which of the cables, one rated 5 A and the other 10 A will be of thicker wire? Give a reason for your answer.

Ans. The cable carrying 10 A current will be of thicker wire because to carry a heavy current, the resistance of wire should be low, hence its area of cross-section should be large.

97. Why are copper and aluminium wires used as connecting wires?*

Ans. Copper and aluminium wires are used as connecting wires because they have low resistivity and are good conductors of electricity.

98. Why is tungsten used for filaments of electric lamps?*

Ans. Tungsten has high melting point and great tensile strength that's why it is used as light bulb filament in electric lamps.

99. Why is lead-tin alloy used for fuse wires?*

Ans. Lead-tin alloy is used for fuse wires because it has low melting point. It will melt when high supply come to prevent the electric circuit from fire.

100. Why are the heating elements of electric toasters and electric irons made of an alloy rather than a pure metal?*

Ans. The resistivity of an alloy is generally higher than that of its constituent metals. Alloys do not oxidise (burn) readily at higher temperatures. Therefore, conductors of electric heating devices, such as toasters and electric irons, are made up of an alloy rather than pure metal.

101. Why are coils of electric heaters and electric irons made of an alloy rather than a pure Metal?

Ans. The resistivity of alloys are generally higher than that of its constituent metals and alloys do not oxidize (burn) readily at high temperatures, hence they are commonly used in electrical heating devices, like electric heaters, electric irons etc.

Short Answer Type Questions

102. Answer the following questions:
   (a) Define resistance of a conductor.
   (b) State Ohm's law.
   (c) State Joule's law of heating.

Ans. (a) The obstruction offered to the flow of current by a conductor is called its resistance.
   (b) According to Ohm's law, the current flowing in a conductor is directly proportional to the potential difference applied across its ends, provided the temperature and other physical conditions of the conductor remain constant.
   (c) Joule's law of heating states that the amount of heat produced in a conductor is directly proportional to :
   1. square of current (I^2),
   2. resistance of wire (R), and
   3. time (t), for which current is passed.

103. Answer the following questions:
   (a) What is an ammeter?
   (b) What is a voltmeter?
   (c) Define resistivity.

* are board exam questions from previous years

Ans. (a) Ammeter is an instrument which is used to measure electric current in a circuit. It is always connected in series with the circuit.
(b) A voltmeter is an instrument which is used to measure electric potential in the circuit between two points. It is always connected in parallel with the circuit.
(c) The resistivity of a substance is numerically equal to the resistance of a rod of that substance which is one metre long and one square metre in cross-section.

104. **Answer the following questions:**
(a) Define electric power.
(b) What is a super conductor? Give two examples.
(c) What does an electric circuit mean?
(d) Define conductors and insulators. **[NCERT]**

Ans. (a) The electrical work done per unit time is called electric power.
(b) A superconductor is a substance of zero resistance at very low temperatures.
Example : Mercury below 4.2 K, Lead below 7.25 K.
(c) A continuous conducting path consisting of wires and other electrical components (like resistance or electric bulb, switch etc.) between the two terminals of a cell or battery, along which an electric current flows, is called an electric circuit.
(d) The substances through which electricity can flow are called conductors and the substances through which electricity cannot flow are called insulators.

Differentiate Between

105. **Write three points of difference between Ohmic resistor and non-Ohmic resistor.**
Ans.

S. No.	Ohmic Resistor	Non-Ohmic Resistor
1.	Ohmic resistors obey Ohm's law.	Non-Ohmic resistors do not obey Ohm's law.
2.	The graph for potential difference (V) versus current (I) is a straight line.	The graph for potential difference (V) versus current (I) is not a straight line.
3.	The slope of V-I graph is constant at all values of V or I at a given temperature.	The slope of V-I graph is different at different values of V or I even at a given temperature.

106. **Write two points of difference between resistance and resistivity (or specific resistance).**
Ans.

S. No.	Resistance	Resistivity (or Specific Resistance)
1.	The S.I. unit of resistance is Ohm (Ω).	The S.I. unit of resistivity is ohm-metre (Ω m).
2.	Resistance of a substance depends on its length and thickness.	Resistivity of a substance is independent of its length and thickness.

107. **Write three points of difference between series combination and parallel combination of resistors.**
Ans.

S. No.	Series Combination	Parallel Combination
1.	The current has a single path for its flow, hence, same current flows through each resistor.	The main current from the source divides itself in different arms. The current in each resistors is inversely proportional to its resistance.
2.	The potential difference across the entire circuit is equal to the sum of the potential difference across the individual resistor.	The potential difference across each resistor is same and it is equal to the potential difference across the terminals of the battery (or source).
3.	The equivalent resistance in series combination is greater than the highest resistance in the series combination.	The equivalent resistance in parallel combination is less than the least resistance in the parallel combination.

108. **Distinguish between an open and a closed circuit.**
Ans. An electric circuit is said to be an open circuit when the switch is in 'off' mode (or key is unplugged) and no current flows in the circuit.
The circuit is said to be a closed circuit when the switch is in 'on' mode (or key is plugged) and a current flows in the circuit.

109. **Write two points of difference between electrical energy and electric power.**
Ans.

S. No.	Electrical Energy	Electric Power
1.	Electrical energy consumed by an electrical appliance is given by the product of its power rating and time for which it is used.	It is the rate at which electrical energy is consumed.
2.	It is measured in kWh.	It is measured in watt or kilo-watt.

Diagram Based Questions

110. Identify the components used in circuit diagrams represented by the following symbols :

(a) —+| |−—   (b) —/\/\/\/\—

(c) —/\/\/\/\— (with arrow) (d) —( )—

(e) —(•)—   (f) —+|H H|−—

(g) —+(A)−— (h) —+(V)−—

Ans. (a) An electric cell
(b) A fixed resistance
(c) A variable resistance
(d) Plug key (open)
(e) Plug key (closed)
(f) A battery or combination of cells
(g) Ammeter
(h) Voltmeter

111. What do you mean by an electric circuit ? Carefully study the circuit diagram given below and make the necessary corrections.

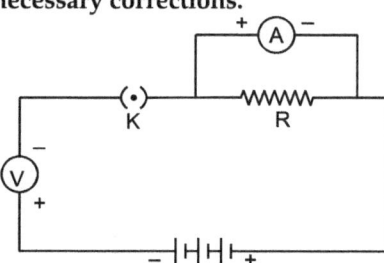

Ans. An electrical circuit is a continuous path comprising conducting wires and other electrical components between the terminals of a battery along which an electric current is set up. It is represented by drawing a circuit diagram.

The corrected circuit diagram given in the question is :

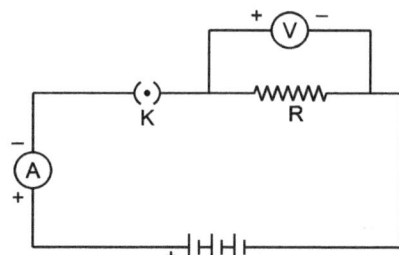

112. The given figure shows the V-I graphs for two resistors. Identify the resistor that obeys Ohm's law. Give a reason for your answer

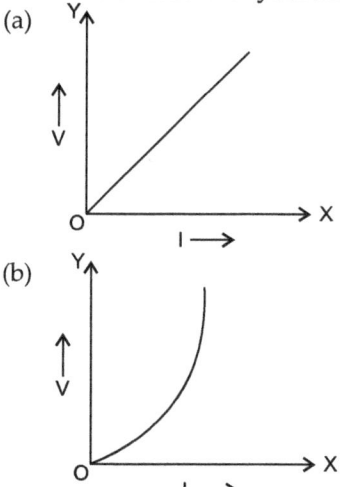

Ans. The figure (a) obeys Ohm's law because the V-I graph is a straight line and its slope (or resistance) is constant.

113. The given figure shows a battery, a switch and two bulbs. Complete the diagram to show the electric connections of the bulbs to the battery. How have you joined the bulbs ? Give a reason.

Ans. The two bulbs are connected in parallel and the complete circuit diagram is drawn below :

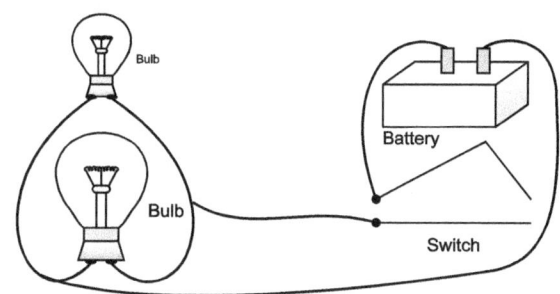

The reason for connecting the two bulbs in parallel is that (i) both the bulbs glow at the same voltage, and (ii) if one bulb stops glowing, the other bulb remains unaffected.

114. The given figures show V-I graphs experimentally obtained for different resistors. Select the graphs for resistors that do not obey Ohm's law.

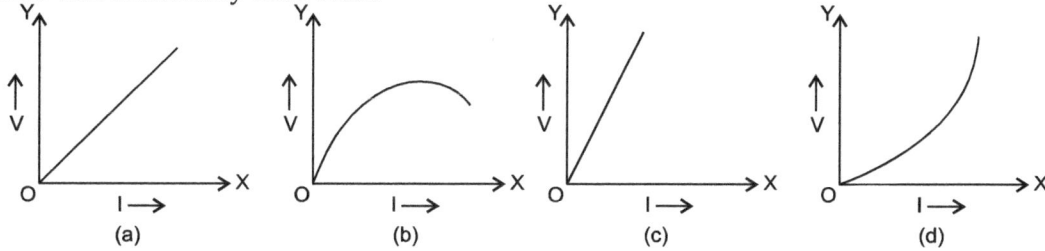

Ans. The figure (b) and (d) do not obey Ohm's law because the V-I graphs are not straight lines.

115. The given figure represents V-I graph for a series combination and for a parallel combination of two resistors. Which of the two, A or B, represents the series combination. Give a reason for your answer.

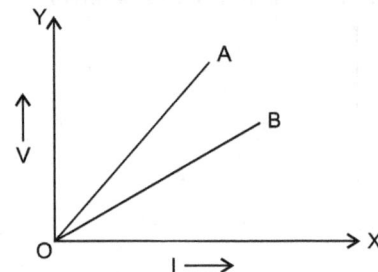

Ans. Since, the straight line A is steeper than B, so the straight line A represents a greater resistance. The equivalent resistance in a series combination is greater than in parallel combination. Hence, A represents series combination.

116. What is the mistake in the circuit given below?

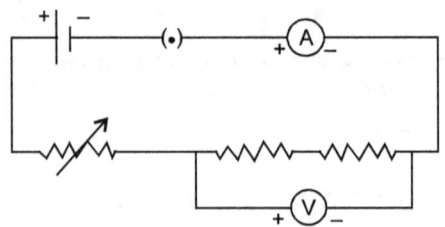

Ans. The terminals of ammeter are wrongly connected.

117. Identify the X, Y and Z in the circuit given below:

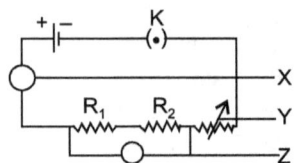

Ans. X = Ammeter, Y = Rheostat, Z = Voltmeter.

Numericals

118. The resistance of a wire of length 150 cm and of uniform area of cross-section 0.015 cm², is found to be 3.0 Ω. Calculate the specific resistance of the wire.

Ans. Here, l = 150 cm; A = 0.015 cm²; R = 3.0 Ω.

Specific resistance, $\rho = \dfrac{RA}{l}$

$= \dfrac{3.0 \times 0.015}{150}$

$= 0\cdot0003$ Ω cm.

119. A wire has a resistance of 5 Ω. Calculate the resistance of a wire of same material, whose length is three times and area of cross-section is four times the first wire.

Ans. **Case I:** R = 5 Ω

Let the area of cross-section be 'A' and length be 'l'.

We know that, $R = \rho \cdot \dfrac{l}{A}$

Where ρ is the specific resistance of the wire.

∴ $5 = \rho \dfrac{l}{A}$ ...(i)

Case II: $R_1 = ?$

Here, length = $3l$, area of cross-section = 4A

∴ $R_1 = \rho \dfrac{3l}{4A}$ ...(ii)

Dividing equation (ii) by (i), we get

$\dfrac{R_1}{5} = \dfrac{\rho \cdot 3l}{4A} \times \dfrac{A}{\rho \cdot l}$

∴ $R_1 = 5 \times \dfrac{3}{4} = 3.75$ Ω.

120. A torch bulb when cold has a resistance of 2·5 Ω. It draws a current 450 mA, when connected to a 6 V battery and glows brightly. Calculate the resistance of the bulb when glowing and explain the reason for the difference in resistance.

Ans. While glowing, I = 450 mA = 0.45 A, V = 6 volt

Using Ohm's law, Resistance of bulb, $R = \dfrac{V}{I} = \dfrac{6}{0.45}$

= 13.33 Ω

The reason for the difference in resistance of bulb when cold (R = 2·5 Ω) and while glowing (R = 13·33 Ω), is that the resistance of filament of bulb increases with the increase in temperature.

121. A uniform wire with a resistance of 32 Ω is divided into four equal parts and they are joined in parallel. Calculate the equivalent resistance of the parallel combination.

Ans. Resistance of each part,

$R_1 = \dfrac{32}{4} Ω = 8 Ω$

When connected in parallel, the equivalent resistance is

$\dfrac{1}{R} = \dfrac{1}{8} + \dfrac{1}{8} + \dfrac{1}{8} + \dfrac{1}{8} = \dfrac{4}{8} = \dfrac{1}{2}$

or $R = 2 Ω.$

122. Calculate the value of x if the equivalent resistance between the points P and Q as shown in figure is 5 Ω.

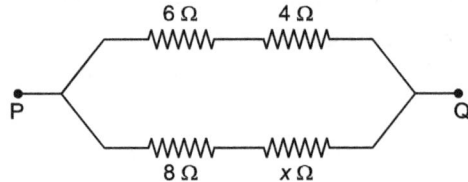

Ans. Equivalent resistance of 6 Ω and 4 Ω in series,

$R_1 = (4 + 6) Ω = 10 Ω$

Equivalent resistance of 8 Ω and x Ω in series,

$R_2 = (8 + x) Ω.$

Now, R_1 and R_2 are in parallel.

Therefore, the equivalent resistance of R_1 and R_2 connected in parallel can be calculated as

$$\frac{1}{R} = \frac{1}{R_1} + \frac{1}{R_2}$$

or $\quad \dfrac{1}{5} = \dfrac{1}{10} + \dfrac{1}{8+x} \quad [\because R = 5\,\Omega]$

or $\quad \dfrac{1}{5} - \dfrac{1}{10} = \dfrac{1}{8+x}$

or $\quad \dfrac{2-1}{10} = \dfrac{1}{8+x}$

or $\quad \dfrac{1}{10} = \dfrac{1}{8+x}$

or $\quad 8 + x = 10$

$\Rightarrow \quad x = 10 - 8 = 2\,\Omega$

$\therefore \quad$ Value of $x = 2\,\Omega$.

123. You have three resistors of r ohm each and a battery of E volts. How would you connect these resistors with the battery to obtain maximum current? Draw a circuit diagram to illustrate your answer and also calculate the current drawn from the battery.*

Ans. Three resistors are connected in parallel. Let its equivalent resistance be R Ω.

$\therefore \quad \dfrac{1}{R} = \dfrac{1}{r} + \dfrac{1}{r} + \dfrac{1}{r}$

$\dfrac{1}{R} = \dfrac{1+1+1}{r} = \dfrac{3}{r}$

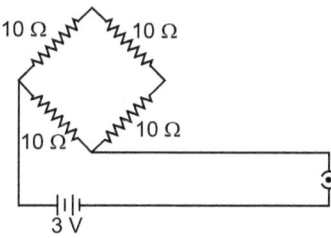

$\Rightarrow \quad R = \dfrac{r}{3}$

By Ohm's law, $\quad E = IR$

$\Rightarrow \quad$ Current $(I) = \dfrac{E \times 3}{r} = \dfrac{3E}{r}$

These resistances should be connected in parallel with the battery to obtain the maximum current.

124. Find the current drawn from the battery by the network of four resistors shown in the figure.*

Ans. The given circuit can be redrawn as shown below :
Resultant resistance of R_1, R_2 and R_3 :

$R' = R_1 + R_2 + R_3$
$\quad = 10 + 10 + 10 = 30\,\Omega$

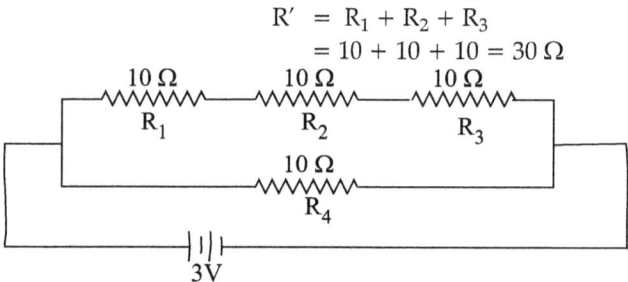

Resultant resistance of the circuit :

$\dfrac{1}{R} = \dfrac{1}{R'} + \dfrac{1}{R_4}$

$= \dfrac{1}{30} + \dfrac{1}{10} = \dfrac{1+3}{30} = \dfrac{4}{30}$

$R = \dfrac{30}{4} = \dfrac{15}{2} = 7.5\,\Omega$

Here, V = 3 volt, I = ?
By Ohm's law, $\quad V = IR$

$\Rightarrow \quad I = \dfrac{V}{R} = \dfrac{3}{7.5} = \dfrac{30}{75} = 0.4\,A$

125. An electric lamp of 100 Ω, a toaster of resistance 50 Ω, and a water filter of resistance 500 Ω are connected in parallel to a 220 V source. What is the resistance of an electric iron connected to the same source that takes as much current as all three appliances and what is the current through it?

[NCERT]

Ans. The combined resistance R of the three electrical devices R_1, R_2 and R_3 connected in parallel is :

$\dfrac{1}{R} = \dfrac{1}{R_1} + \dfrac{1}{R_2} + \dfrac{1}{R_3}$

Here, $R_1 = 100\,\Omega$, $R_2 = 50\,\Omega$ and $R_3 = 500\,\Omega$

$\therefore \quad \dfrac{1}{R} = \dfrac{1}{100} + \dfrac{1}{50} + \dfrac{1}{500}$

$= \dfrac{5+10+1}{500}$

$= \dfrac{16}{500}$

or $\quad R = \dfrac{500}{16}$

$= 31.25\,\Omega$

Now, Potential difference, V
$\quad = 220\,V$
Current, I = ?
Resistance, R = 31.25 Ω

Using Ohm's law : $\dfrac{V}{I} = R$

or $\quad \dfrac{220}{I} = 31.25$

*are board exam questions from previous years

or $\qquad I = \dfrac{220}{7.04}$

$\qquad \qquad = 7.04$ A

Hence, the current passing through the electric iron is 7.04 A.

The resistance of electric iron $R_{iron} = \dfrac{V}{I} = \dfrac{220}{7.04}$

$\qquad \qquad \qquad \qquad = 31.25\ \Omega.$

126. How can three resistors of resistances 2 Ω, 3 Ω and 6 Ω be connected to give a total resistance of (a) 4 Ω and (b) 1 Ω? [NCERT]

Ans. (a) The three resistors of resistances 2 Ω, 3 Ω and 6 Ω have to be combined as shown in the figure to obtain 4 Ω resistance.

Equivalent resistance of 3 Ω and 6 Ω connected in parallel is,

$$\dfrac{1}{R_P} = \dfrac{1}{3} + \dfrac{1}{6}$$

$$= \dfrac{2+1}{6} = \dfrac{3}{6}$$

or $\qquad R_P = \dfrac{6}{3} = 2\ \Omega$

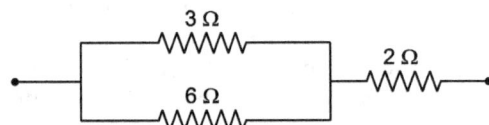

Now, R_P and 2 Ω are joined in series and the equivalent resistance is,

$\qquad R = R_P + 2$

$\qquad \quad = (2 + 2)\ \Omega$

$\qquad \quad = 4\ \Omega$

(b) In order to obtain 1 Ω resistance, the resistors 2 Ω, 3 Ω and 6 Ω have to be combined as shown in figure. 2 Ω, 3 Ω and 6 Ω resistances are connected in parallel,

∴ $\qquad \dfrac{1}{R} = \dfrac{1}{2} + \dfrac{1}{3} + \dfrac{1}{6}$

$\qquad \qquad = \dfrac{3+2+1}{6}$

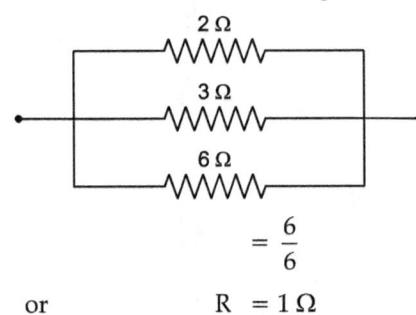

$\qquad \qquad = \dfrac{6}{6}$

or $\qquad R = 1\ \Omega$

127. How many 176 Ω resistors in parallel are required to carry 5 A on a 220 V line? [NCERT]

Ans. Here, Potential difference, V = 220 V, Current, I = 5 A

∴ Resistance, $R = \dfrac{V}{I}$

$\qquad \qquad = \dfrac{220}{5} = 44\ \Omega$

Let the number of 176 Ω resistors to be connected in parallel to give an equivalent resistance of 44 Ω be x. Equivalent resistance of 'x' 176 Ω resistance connected in parallel is $\dfrac{176}{x}\ \Omega$

But, $\qquad \dfrac{176}{x} = 44$

∴ $\qquad x = \dfrac{176}{44} = 4$

Thus, 4 resistors of 176 Ω each should be connected in parallel.

128. In the circuit diagram shown below, calculate : (a) total resistance and (b) current shown by the ammeter A.

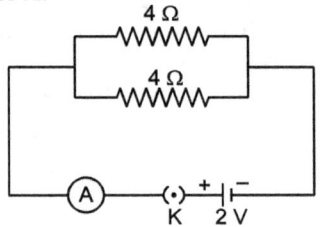

Ans. (a) The two resistors of resistance 4 Ω each are connected in parallel.

∴ $\qquad \dfrac{1}{R} = \dfrac{1}{4} + \dfrac{1}{4}$

$\qquad \qquad = \dfrac{1+1}{4}$

$\qquad \qquad = \dfrac{2}{4} = \dfrac{1}{2}$

∴ $\qquad R = 2\ \Omega$

Now, Potential difference,

$\qquad V = 2$ V

Total resistance, $R = 2\ \Omega$

(b) Using Ohm's law, Current,

$\qquad I = \dfrac{V}{R} = \dfrac{2}{2}$ A = 1 A.

129. In the circuit given below, calculate the value of x, if the equivalent resistance between the points A and B is 6 Ω.

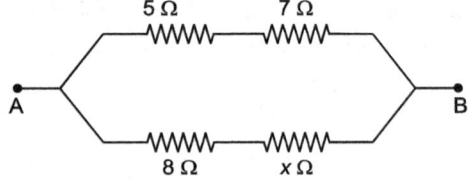

Ans. The network of resistors can be simplified as (∵ 5 Ω and 7 Ω are in series and also 8 Ω and x Ω are in series).

Here, equivalent resistance (R) = 6 Ω, R_1 = 12 Ω, R_2 = (8 + x) Ω

The resistors R_1 and R_2 are connected in parallel.

$$\therefore \quad \frac{1}{R} = \frac{1}{R_1} + \frac{1}{R_2}$$

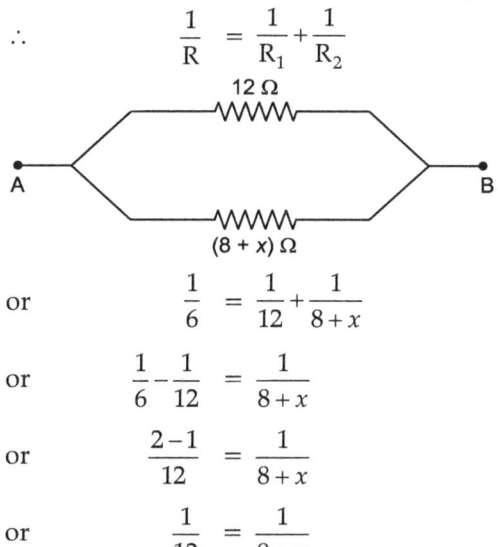

or $\quad \dfrac{1}{6} = \dfrac{1}{12} + \dfrac{1}{8+x}$

or $\quad \dfrac{1}{6} - \dfrac{1}{12} = \dfrac{1}{8+x}$

or $\quad \dfrac{2-1}{12} = \dfrac{1}{8+x}$

or $\quad \dfrac{1}{12} = \dfrac{1}{8+x}$

or $\quad 8 + x = 12$

$\therefore \quad x = 12 - 8 = 4\,\Omega.$

130. Draw a schematic diagram of a circuit consisting of a battery of three cells of 2 V each, a 5 Ω resistor, an 8 Ω resistor, and a 12 Ω resistor and a plug key, all connected in series. Now, connect the ammeter to measure the current through the resistors and a voltmeter to measure the potential difference across the 12 Ω resistors. What would be the readings in the ammeter and the voltmeter?

Ans. The total resistance of the circuit is given by
$$R = 5 + 8 + 12 = 25\,\Omega$$

We know, $\quad R = \dfrac{V}{I}$

Hence, $\quad 25 = \dfrac{6}{I}$

$$I = \dfrac{6}{25} = 0.24\,A$$

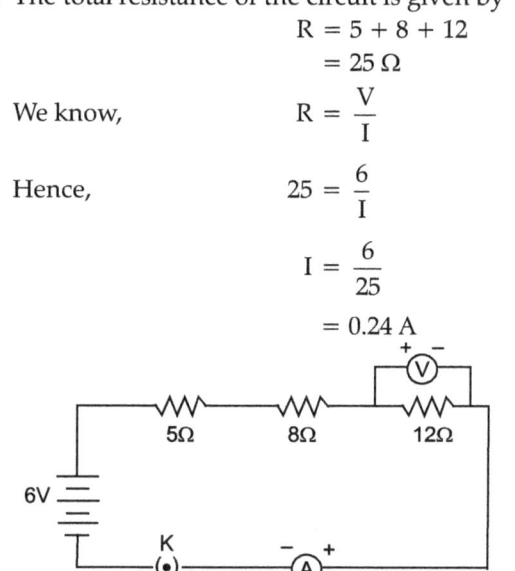

Since, resistances are connected in series, thus electric current remains the same through all resistors.
Here we have,
Electric current, $\quad I = 0.24\,A$
Resistance, $R = 12\,\Omega$
Thus, potential difference (V) through the resistor of 12 Ω is given by
$$V = I \times R = 0.24 \times 12$$
$$= 2.88\,V$$

$\therefore \quad$ Reading of ammeter $= 0.24\,A$
Reading of voltmeter through resistor of 12 Ω $= 2.88\,V$.

131. Calculate the equivalent resistance of the following network:

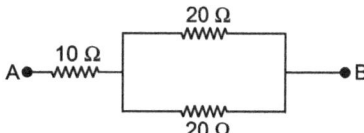

Ans. Let R_p is the equivalent resistance of resistors connected in parallel.
$\therefore$ Equivalent resistance of the circuit
$$\frac{1}{R_p} = \frac{1}{20} + \frac{1}{20}$$
$$\frac{1}{R_p} = \frac{1+1}{20}$$
$$= \frac{2}{20} = \frac{1}{10}$$
$$R_p = 10\,\Omega$$

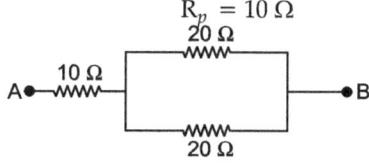

Now, equivalent circuit becomes.
$\because$ 10 Ω and 10 Ω are connected in series.

A●——10 Ω——10 Ω——●B

$\therefore$ Equivalent resistance of the circuit
$$R = 10\,\Omega + 10\,\Omega = 20\,\Omega$$

132. Resistance of a conductor of length 80 cm is 4.0 Ω. Calculate the resistance of a similar conductor of length 400 cm.

Sol. Here, $l_1 = 80$ cm, $R_1 = 4.0\,\Omega$, $l_2 = 400$ cm, $R_2 = ?$

$\therefore \quad \dfrac{R_1}{R_2} = \dfrac{l_1}{l_2}$

or $\quad R_2 = R_1 \cdot \dfrac{l_2}{l_1}$

$$= 4.0 \times \dfrac{400}{80} = 20.0\,\Omega.$$

133. The circuit diagram given below shows the combination of three resistors, $R_1 = 2\,\Omega$, $R_2 = 12\,\Omega$ and $R_3 = 6\,\Omega$:

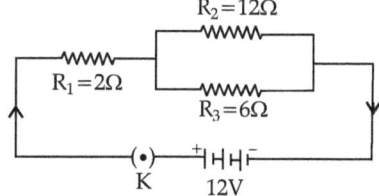

Calculate:

(a) Total resistance of the circuit.
(b) Total current flowing in the circuit.

(c) The potential difference across R_1.
(d) The potential difference across R_2 or R_3.
(e) Current flowing through R_2.

Ans. (a) R_2 and R_3 are in parallel.

∴ Equivalent resistance of R_2 and R_3,

$$R_P = \frac{R_2 \times R_3}{R_2 + R_3}$$

$$= \frac{12 \times 6}{12 + 6} \Omega$$

$$= \frac{72}{18}$$

$$= 4 \Omega.$$

∴ Total resistance of the circuit, $R = R_1 + R_P$

Now, R_1 and R_P are connected in series

$$= (2 + 4) \Omega$$
$$= 6 \Omega$$

(b) Potential difference, $V = 12$ V

Total resistance, $R = 6 \Omega$

Using Ohm's law,

Total current flowing in circuit,

$$I = \frac{V}{R}$$

$$= \frac{12}{6} A = 2 A$$

(c) Potential difference across R_1,

$$V_1 = IR_1$$
$$= 2 \times 2 = 4 V$$

(d) Potential difference across R_2 or R_3,

$$V_2 = IR_P$$
$$= 2 \times 4 = 8 V$$

(e) Let the current flowing through R_2 be I'.

∴ $V_2 = I'R_2$

or $I' = \frac{V_2}{R_2} = \frac{8}{12} A$

$$= 0.67 A.$$

134. In a network of resistors as shown in figure, calculate the equivalent resistance between the points (a) S and R and (b) P and R.

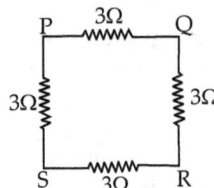

Sol. (a) Between S and R : Between the points S and R the above network of resistors can be represented as :

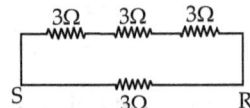

Equivalent resistance of three 3 Ω resistors connected in series,

$$R_1 = (3 + 3 + 3) = 9 \Omega$$

Now, R_1 and 3 Ω are connected in parallel.

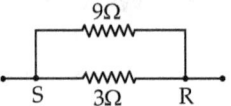

∴ Equivalent resistance R can be calculated as

$$\frac{1}{R} = \frac{1}{9} + \frac{1}{3}$$

$$= \frac{1 + 3}{9}$$

$$= \frac{4}{9}$$

or $R = \frac{4}{9} \Omega = 2.25 \Omega$

(b) **Between P and R :** Between the points P and R the network of resistors can be represented as :

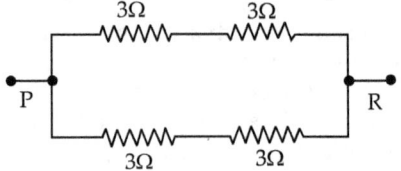

Equivalent resistance of two 3 Ω resistors connected in series is $(3 + 3) = 6 \Omega$

Now, two 6 Ω resistors are connected in parallel.

∴ Equivalent resistance is given by

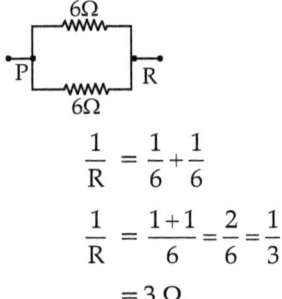

$$\frac{1}{R} = \frac{1}{6} + \frac{1}{6}$$

$$\frac{1}{R} = \frac{1+1}{6} = \frac{2}{6} = \frac{1}{3}$$

$$= 3 \Omega.$$

135. A copper wire has diameter 0.5 mm and resistivity of 1.6×10^{-8} Ω m. What will be the length of this wire to make its resistance 10 Ω ? How much does the resistance change if the diameter is doubled ?

Sol. Here, diameter of wire = 0.5 mm, Resistivity (ρ) = 1.6×10^{-8} Ω M, Resistance (R) = 1 Ω. Let the length of wire l and the resistance when diameter is doubled be R_1.

∴ Radius = $\frac{0.5 \text{mm}}{2}$ = 0.25 mm

$$= \frac{0.25}{1000} = 0.00025 \text{ m}$$

We know that, $R = \rho \frac{1}{A}$

$$\therefore \quad l = \frac{RA}{\rho} = \frac{R\pi r^2}{\rho}$$

$$\Rightarrow \quad l = \frac{10 \times 3.14 \times (0.00025)^2}{1.6 \times 10^{-8}}$$

$$l = \frac{10 \times 3.14 \times 0.00025 \times 0.00025}{1.6 \times 10^{-8}}$$

$$\Rightarrow \quad l = \frac{10 \times 3.14 \times 0.0000000625 \times 10^8}{1.6}$$

$$l = \frac{10 \times 10^8 \times 0.00000196250}{1.6}$$

$$= \frac{196.26}{1.6}$$

$$= 122.65 \text{ m} = 122.7 \text{ m}$$

When diameter wire is doubled then,
Now diameter $= 0.5 \times 2 = 1$ mm

$$\therefore \quad \text{Radius} = \frac{1}{2} \text{mm} = 0.5 \text{ mm}$$

$$= \frac{0.5}{1000} \text{m} = 0.0005 \text{ m}$$

$$\therefore \quad R_1 = \rho \frac{1}{A} = \rho \frac{l}{\pi r^2}$$

$$= 1.6 \times 10^{-8} \times \frac{122.7}{3.14 \times 0.0005 \times 0.0005}$$

$$= \frac{1.6 \times 10^{-8} \times 122.7}{3.14 \times 0.00000025}$$

$$= \frac{1.6 \times 122.7}{3.14 \times 0.00000025 \times 10^8}$$

$$= \frac{196.32}{78.5} = 2.5 \, \Omega$$

136. Show how would you join resistors each resistance 9 Ω so that the equivalent resistance of the combination of combination is (a) 13.5 Ω (b) Ω ?

Sol. (a) To get an equivalent resistance of 13.5 Ω, the resistance should be connected as sown in the figure given below:

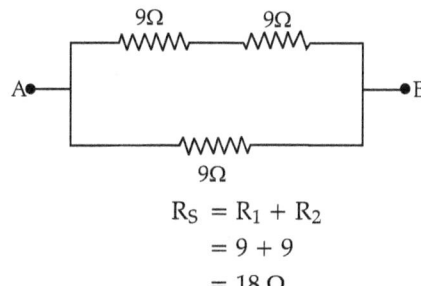

So,
$$\frac{1}{R_p} = \frac{1}{R_1} + \frac{1}{R_2}$$

$$= \frac{1}{9} + \frac{1}{9}$$

$$= \frac{1+1}{9} = \frac{2}{9}$$

$$\frac{1}{R_p} = \frac{2}{9}$$

$$R_P = \frac{9}{2} = 4.5 \, \Omega$$

Now,
$$R_S = R_3 + 4.5 \, \Omega$$
$$= 9 \, \Omega + 4.5 \, \Omega$$
$$= 13.5 \, \Omega$$

(b) To get equivalent resistance of 6 Ω, the resistance should be connected as shown in the given below

$$R_S = R_1 + R_2$$
$$= 9 + 9$$
$$= 18 \, \Omega$$

Now both the resistance are in parallel with each other so,

$$R_P = \frac{1}{18} + \frac{1}{9}$$

$$= \frac{1+2}{18} = \frac{3}{18}$$

$$= \frac{1}{6} \Omega$$

So, $\quad R_P = 6 \, \Omega$

137. An electric bulb of resistance 44 Ω draws a current of 5.0 A. Calculate the line voltage.

Ans. Here, I = 5.0 A, R = 44 Ω, V = ?
Using Ohm's law, $\quad V = IR$
$$= 5.0 \times 44 = 220 \text{ V}$$

138. An electric iron of resistance 20 Ω takes a current of 5 A. Calculate the heat developed in 30 s.
[NCERT]

Ans. Here, Current (I) = 5 A, Resistance (R) = 20 Ω, Time (t) = 30 s

$\therefore$ Heat produced (H) $= I^2 Rt$
$$= (5)^2 \times 20 \times 30$$
$$= 15000 \text{ J}$$

Thus, heat developed is 1.5×10^4 J.

139. Which uses more energy, a 250 W T.V. set in 1 hour or a 1200 W toaster in 10 minutes? [NCERT]

Ans. For T.V. Set : $\quad$ Power, P = 250 W
$\quad$ Time, t = 1 h
Electrical energy consumed $= P \times t$
$$= \frac{250 \times 1}{1000} \text{ kWh}$$
$$= 0.25 \text{ kWh}$$

For toaster : $\quad$ Power, P = 1200 W

Time, $t = 10$ minutes
$$= \frac{10}{60} h = \frac{1}{6} h$$

Electrical energy consumed $= P \times t$
$$= \frac{1200 \times 1}{1000 \times 6} \text{ kWh}$$
$$= 0.20 \text{ kWh}$$

The T.V. set uses more energy (0.25 kWh) whereas the toaster uses less energy (0.20 kWh).

140. When a 12 V battery is connected across an unknown resistor, there is a current of 2.5 mA in the circuit. Find the value of the resistance of the resistor. **[NCERT]**

Ans. Here, Potential difference, $V = 12$ V

Current, $I = 2.5$ mA $= \frac{2.5}{1000}$ A $= 0.0025$ A

Using Ohm's law

Resistance, $R = \frac{V}{I} = \frac{12}{0.0025} = 4800 \; \Omega$

141. The values of current I flowing in a given resistor for the corresponding values of potential difference V across the resistor are given below:

I (ampere)	0.5	1.0	2.0	3.0	4.0
V (volt)	1.6	3.4	6.7	10.2	13.2

Plot a graph between V and I and calculate the resistance of that resistor.

Ans. The graph between V and I is given below:

Let us consider two points A and B on the slope.

Draw two lines, one from point B along X-axis and another from point A along Y-axis, which meet at point C.

The slope of the graph will give the value of resistance, thus

$$\text{Slope} = R = \frac{AC}{BC}$$

Now,
$$BC = 3 - 1 = 2 \text{ A}$$
$$AC = 10.2 - 3.4 = 6.8 \text{ V}$$
$$\text{Slope} = \frac{6.8}{2} = 3.4 \; \Omega$$

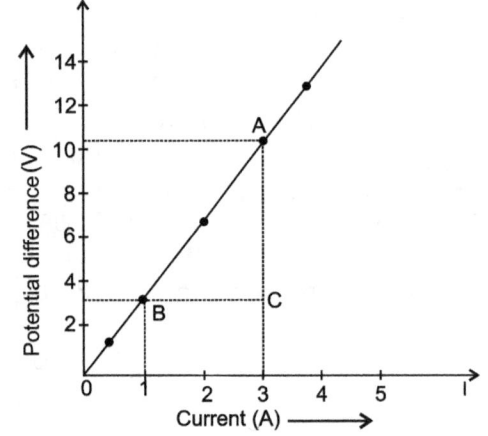

Thus, resistance $(R) = 3.4 \; \Omega$.

142. An electric iron is rated '1 kW – 220 V'. Calculate the following:
(a) The resistance of its heating element.
(b) The amount of current that will flow through the element.
(c) The amount of heat that will be produced in 2 minutes.
(d) The power consumed if the line voltage falls to 200 V.

Ans. Here, $V = 220$ volt, $P = 1$ kW $= 1000$ W, $t = 2$ minute $= 2 \times 60 = 120$ s

(a) Resistance of the heating element,
$$R = \frac{V^2}{P} = \frac{(220)^2}{1000} = 48.4 \; \Omega.$$

(b) Current through the element,
$$I = \frac{P}{V} = \frac{1000}{220} = 4.54 \text{ A}$$

(c) Heat produced in 2 minutes $= P \times t$
$$= 1000 \times 120 = 1.2 \times 10^5 \text{ J}$$

(d) If line voltage falls to 200 V, the power consumed is,
$$P = \frac{V^2}{R} = \frac{(200)^2}{48.4} = 826.44 \text{ W}.$$

143. An electric lamp of resistance 20 Ω and a conductor of resistance 4 Ω are connected to a 6 V battery as shown in the circuit. Calculate:

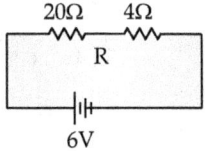

(a) the total resistance of the circuit,
(b) the current through the circuit,
(c) the potential difference across the (i) electric lamp and (ii) conductor,
(d) power of the lamp.

Ans. (a) Given, $R_1 = 20 \; \Omega, R_2 = 4 \; \Omega$
Since, in Series $R = R_1 + R_2$
∴ Total resistance of circuit:
$$R = 20 + 4$$
$$= 24 \; \Omega$$

(b) Current through circuit
$$V = 6 \text{ V}, R = 24 \; \Omega$$
According to Ohm's law
$$V = IR$$
So,
$$I = \frac{V}{R}$$
$$I = \frac{6}{24}$$
$$= \frac{1}{4} = 0.25 \text{ ampere}$$

(c) (i) Potential difference across electric lamp:

$$I = \frac{1}{4} \text{A}, R_1 = 20 \, \Omega$$
$$V_1 = IR_1$$
$$V_1 = \frac{1}{4} \times 20$$
$$= 5 \text{ V}$$

(ii) Potential difference across conductor
$$V_2 = IR_2$$
$$= \frac{1}{4} \times 4$$
$$V_2 = 1 \text{ V}$$

(d) Power of lamp : $P = I^2 R$
$$= \left(\frac{1}{4}\right)^2 \times 20$$
$$= \frac{1}{4} \times \frac{1}{4} \times 20$$
$$= \frac{5}{4} \text{ W}$$
or $P = 1.25$ W.

144. Two bulbs rated (60 W – 220 V) and (60 W – 110 V) respectively. Calculate the ratio of their resistance.

Sol. First bulb:
Power rating $P_1 = 60$ W
Voltage rating $V_1 = 220$ V
$\therefore$ Resistance, $R_1 = \dfrac{V_1^2}{P_1}$
$$= \frac{220 \times 220}{60} \Omega$$

Second bulb:
Power rating $P_2 = 60$ W
Voltage rating, $V_2 = 110$ V
$\therefore$ Resistance, $R_2 = \dfrac{V_2^2}{P_2}$
$$= \frac{110 \times 110}{60} \Omega$$

$$\frac{R_1}{R_2} = \frac{\frac{220 \times 220}{60}}{\frac{110 \times 110}{60}}$$

$$= \frac{220 \times 220}{60} \times \frac{60}{110 \times 110}$$

$$= \frac{4}{1}$$

$$R_1 : R_2 = 4 : 1$$

145. An electric kettle is rated at (100 W – 220 V).
(a) What is the resistance of its element when in use?
(b) What is the safe value of current that can pass through its element?

Sol. Here, Power rating, P = 1000 W
Voltage rating, V = 220 V

(a) Using the relation $P = \dfrac{V^2}{R}$

Resistance of element when in use,
$$R = \frac{V^2}{P} = \frac{220 \times 220}{1000}$$
$$= 48.4 \, \Omega$$

(b) Using the relation $P = VI$
Safe current, $I = \dfrac{P}{V} = \dfrac{1000}{20}$
$$= 4.55 \text{ A}$$

146. Two lamps, one rated 100 W at 220 V, and the other 60 W at 220 V, are connected in parallel to electric mains supply. What current is drawn from the line if the supply voltage is 220 V? **[NCERT]**

Sol. Given: Power of one lamp, $P_1 = 100$ W
Power of second lamp, $P_2 = 60$ W
Since, both the lamps are connected in parallel, thus, potential difference will be equal.
Thus, Potential difference = 220 V
We know, that Power (P) = VI
Thus, the total current through the circuit
$$I = \frac{P_1}{V} + \frac{P_2}{V}$$
$$I = \frac{100}{200} + \frac{60}{200}$$
$$= \frac{100 + 60}{220}$$
$$= \frac{160}{220} = 0.727 \text{ A}$$

Analysis and Evaluation Based Questions

147. If a student wants to connect four cells of 1.5 V each to form a battery of voltage 6 V, then how would he draw the symbol of the battery?

Ans. ─|I|I|I|I─

148. The atoms of copper contain electrons and the atoms of rubber also contain electrons, then, why does copper conduct electricity but rubber does not conduct electricity?

Ans. Copper contains a large number of free electrons, hence is a good conductor of electric current whereas rubber has negligible number of free electrons and is an insulator.

149. You are given three resistors of resistance 2 Ω, 4 Ω and 6 Ω. Show by a diagram, how you can get a 3 Ω resistance with the help of these resistors.

Ans. Connect 2 Ω and 4 Ω in series then this combination is connected with the parallel 6 Ω resistance. By this arrangement we can get resistance 3 Ω as equivalent resistance.

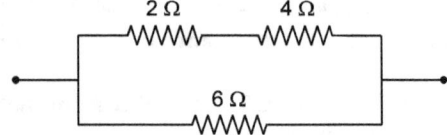

150. How many 10 Ω resistors are required to get a 25 Ω resistor?

Ans. Four 10 Ω resistors are required and they are connected as shown.

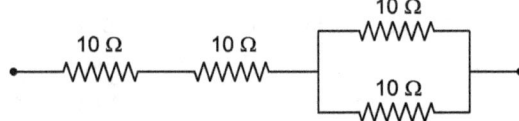

151. You are given fifty 5 Ω resistors. What is (a) smallest and (b) largest resistance can be obtained by using these?

Ans. (a) To get the smallest resistance, all the 5 Ω resistors must be connected in parallel.

Smallest resistance = $\dfrac{5}{50}$ = 0.1 Ω

(b) To get the largest resistance, the 5 Ω resistors must be connected in series.

Largest resistance = 5 × 50 = 250 Ω.

152. Why are fairy decorative lights always connected in parallel?

Ans. When the fairy lights are connected in series the resistance offered will be greater and brightness of the bulbs will be affected. But in parallel connection all the bulbs will glow with same intensity and if any bulb gets fused the other bulbs will continue to glow.

153. What will happen when:
(a) Voltmeter is connected in series?
(b) Ammeter is connected in parallel?

Ans. (a) Negligible current will pass through the circuit because the voltmeter has a very high resistance.
(b) Ammeter will get damaged due to flow of large amount of current through it, because it has low resistance.

154. Arrange 1 Ω, 10 Ω and 100 Ω such that the equivalent resistance is greater than 10 Ω but less than 11 Ω.

Sol. (a) The resistor have to combined as shown in the diagram

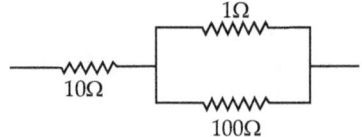

The equivalent resistance of 1 Ω and 100 Ω connected in parallel is:

$\dfrac{1}{R_1} = \dfrac{1}{1} + \dfrac{1}{100}$

$= \dfrac{100+1}{100}$

$= \dfrac{101}{100}$

or $R_1 = \dfrac{100}{101}$ Ω

= 0.99 Ω

Now, 10 Ω and R1 are in series,
Therefore, equivalent resistance R is

R = (10 + 0.99) Ω
= 10.99 Ω

The above value of resistance is greater than 10 Ω but less than 11 Ω.

155. What is (a) the highest, (b) the lowest resistance that can be secured by combination other resistors of 1 Ω, 10 Ω, 100 Ω and 1000 Ω?

Sol. (a) To obtain the highest resistance, the resistors must be connected in series.

∴ Highest resistance, R_S = (1 + 10 + 100 + 1000) Ω
= 1111 Ω

(b) To obtain the lowest resistance, the resistors must be connected in parallel. the lowest resistance is given by

$\dfrac{1}{R_P} = \dfrac{1}{1} + \dfrac{1}{10} + \dfrac{1}{100} + \dfrac{1}{1000}$

$= \dfrac{1000+100+10+1}{1000}$

$= \dfrac{1111}{1000}$

∴ Lowest resistance $R_P = \dfrac{1000}{1111}$ Ω

= 0.9 Ω.

156. If two resistors in series have 'p' number of common points. What will be the value of 'p'?

Ans. One.

157. There are three 2 V cells connected in series. How many joules of energy does 1 C gain on passing through all the three cells?

Ans. Here, the potential difference,
V = 2 + 2 + 2 = 6 V and
charge, Q = 1 C
We know that,
Work done, W = VQ
Substituting the values, we get
W = 6 × 1 = 6 J.

158. The current flowing through a resistor connected in a circuit and the potential difference developed across its ends are as shown in the diagram by milliammeter and voltmeter readings respectively:*

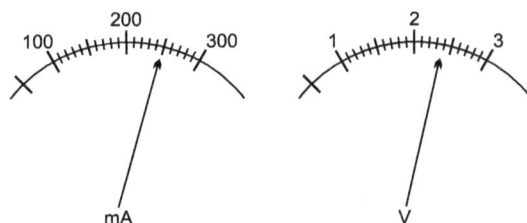

(a) What are the least counts of these meters?
(b) What is the resistance of the resistor?

Ans. (a) 10 mA and 0.1 V
(b) V = 2.4 volt, I = 250 mA = 0.25 A
From Ohm's law. $R = \dfrac{V}{I} = \dfrac{2.4}{0.25} = 9.6 \; \Omega$

159. Why is the tungsten metal more coiled in the bulb and not installed in straight parallel wire form?

Ans. The coiled wire of tungsten increases the surface area of the wire in very less space so as to emit more light and helps in glowing with more intensity.

160. While studying the dependence of potential difference (V) across a resistor on the current (I) passing through it, in order to determine the resistance of the resistor, a student took 5 readings for different values of current and plotted a graph between V and I. He got a straight line graph passing through the origin. What does the straight line signify? Write the method of determining resistance of the resistor using this graph.*

Ans. The straight line in the graph signify that potential difference and current are directly proportional to each other.

The method of determining resistance of resistor using the graph is by Ohm's law, V = IR and by calculating the slope from the points mentioned on the graph.

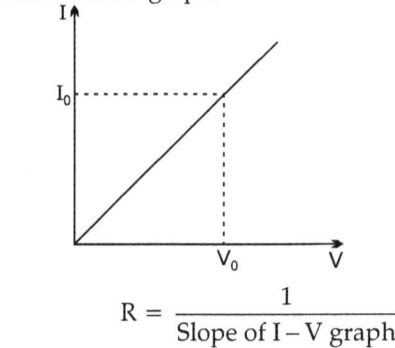

$\therefore \quad R = \dfrac{1}{\text{Slope of I–V graph}}$

161. What would you suggest to a student if while performing an experiment he finds that the pointer/needle of the ammeter and voltmeter do not coincide with the zero marks on the scales when circuit is open? No extra ammeter/voltmeter is available in the laboratory.

Ans. This is called the zero error of the scale of ammeter or voltmeter. If there is a zero error then this error is subtracted from the value that depicts when the circuit is closed otherwise accurate reading will not be recorded.

162. Why we must keep the circuit closed for a relatively shorter time and open for a relatively longer time to ensure minimal changes in the values of resistance?

Ans. Due to heating effect of current, we must keep the circuit closed for a relatively shorter time and open for a relatively longer time to ensure minimal changes in the values of resistance.

Creating Based Questions

163. The following apparatus is available in a laboratory which is summarised in tabular form:

S. No.	Battery	Adjustable from of to 4.5 V
1.	Resistors	3 W and 6 W
2.	Ammeters	A_1 of range 0 to 3 A least count 0.1 A A_2 of range 0 to 1 A least count 0.05 A.
3.	Voltmeters	V_1 of range 0 to 10 V least count 0.5 V V_2 of range of 0 to 5 V least count 0.1 V

(a) For what purpose an ammeter is used ?
(b) If we require the maximum resistance from a number of given resistors we connect :
    (i) all in series
    (ii) all in parallel
    (iii) less resistors in series and more in parallel
(c) The best combination of voltmeter and ammeter for finding the equivalent resistance of the resistors in series would be :
    (i) ammeter A_1 and voltmeter V_1
    (ii) ammeter A_1 and voltmeter V_2
    (iii) ammeter A_2 and voltmeter V_1
    (iv) ammeter A_2 and voltmeter V_2
(d) For the experiment to find the equivalent resistance of the parallel combination of the two given resistors, the best choice would be :
    (i) ammeter A_1 and voltmeter V_1
    (ii) ammeter A_1 and voltmeter V_2
    (iii) ammeter A_2 and voltmeter V_1
    (iv) ammeter A_2 and voltmeter V_2

Ans. (a) To measure current in the circuit.
(b) (i) All in series
(c) (iv) Ammeter A_2 and voltmeter V_2
(d) (iii) Ammeter A_2 and voltmeter V_1

---
* are board exam questions from previous years

164. Shyam designed a burglar alarm circuit in which the resistors are connected in series. The circuit breaks and the current did not flow through the circuit. What is the alternate method he should opt to prevent the circuit break when the resistors are connected in series ?

Ans. There is only a single path which connects from the electric source to the output devices. The electrical appliance damage can be prevented by connecting the **fuse in series** with the mains as well as the electrical appliance. To maintain the current level efficiently series of resistors can be used.

165. Brisilia designed a prototype in which she used a very sensitive electrical device. But she does not know how to protect the sensitive electrical device from high current. Suggest her with one idea to protect the sensitive device from high current.

Ans. The suggestion to protect the sensitive electrical device from high current is by using a **parallel low resistor known as shunt resistor**. The resistance value of shunt resistor is very low. It is made up of the material having low temperature co-efficient of resistance. It measures the electric current, alternating current or direct current.

166. Rita designed a circuit in which resistors are connected in series. Yet she is not satisfied with the series resistors because if there is a fault in some component of the circuit, the whole circuit stops working. What would be your suggestion in alternative to the resistance in series ?

Ans. To overcome the problem faced by Rita, I would suggest to connect the resistors in parallel because if the **resistors are connected parallel**, the whole circuit does not stop working. If the fault is with one component of the circuit, the current continues to flow through the other components of the circuit which makes the device work further.

167. Electrical resistivities of some substance at 20°C are given below.

S. No.	Metal	Resistivity (in Ω·m)
1.	Silver	1.60×10^{-8}
2.	Copper	1.62×10^{-8}
3.	Tungsten	5.20×10^{-8}
4.	Iron	10.0×10^{-8}
5.	Mercury	94.0×10^{-8}
6.	Nichrome	94.0×10^{-8}

Answer the following relations in relation to them.
(a) Among silver and copper, which one is a better conductor ?
(b) Which material would you advise to be used in electrical heating devices ?
(c) Define resistivity.
(d) What is the effect of temperature on resistivity of a substance ?

Ans. (a) Silver
(b) Nichrome
(c) Resistivity of a conductor is defined as the resistance of the conductor of unit length and unit area of cross-section.
(d) Resistivity of a material changes if its temperature changes.

168. Rhea noted the readings of her home's electricity meter on Monday at 9 a.m. and again on Tuesday at 9 a.m. (as shown in figure given below).

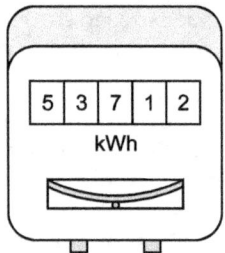 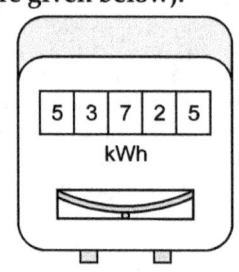

(a) What was the meter reading on Monday ?
(b) What was the meter reading on Tuesday ?
(c) How many units of electrical energy have been used ?
(d) How much time (in hours) have these units been used ?
(e) Calculate the cost of electrical energy used during this time, if the rate is ₹ 8 per unit.

Ans. (a) Meter reading on Monday = 53712
(b) Meter reading on Tuesday = 53725
(c) Number of units of electrical energy used
= 53725 – 53712
= 13 units
(d) Time = 24 hours
(e) Electrical energy consumed = ₹ 8 × 13
= ₹ 104

Miscellaneous Questions

169. What is the limitation of Ohm's law ?

Ans. Ohm's law is obeyed only when the temperature of conductor remains constant.

170. Use the data in table below to answer the following :

	Material	Resistivity (Ω m)
Conductors	Silver	1.60×10^{-8}
	Copper	1.62×10^{-8}
	Aluminium	2.63×10^{-8}
	Tungsten	5.20×10^{-8}
	Nickel	6.84×10^{-8}
	Iron	10.0×10^{-8}
	Chromium	12.9×10^{-8}
	Mercury	94.0×10^{-8}
	Manganese	1.84×10^{-8}
Alloys	Constantan (alloy of Cu and Ni)	49×10^{-8}

	Manganin (alloy of Cu, Mn and Ni)	44×10^{-6}
	Nichrome (alloy of Ni, Cr, Mn and Fe)	100×10^{-6}
Insulators	Glass	$10^{10} - 10^{14}$
	Hard rubber	$10^{13} - 10^{16}$
	Ebonite	$10^{15} - 10^{17}$
	Diamond	$10^{12} - 10^{13}$
	Paper (dry)	10^{12}

(a) Which of these, iron and mercury is a better conductor?
(b) Which material is the best conductor?

Ans. (a) It can be seen from the above table that the resistivity of mercury is more than that of iron. This implies that iron is a better conductor than mercury.
(b) It can be observed from the above table that the resistivity of silver is the lowest among the listed materials. Hence, it is the best conductor.

171. Draw a schematic diagram of a circuit consisting of a battery of three cells of 2 V each, a 5 Ω resistor, an 8 Ω resistor, and a 12 Ω resistor, and a plug key, all connected in series.

Ans.
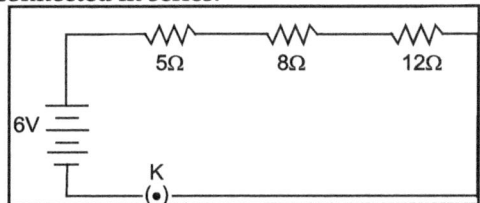

172. How will you infer with the help of an experiment that the same current flows through every part of a circuit containing three resistors in series connected to a battery?

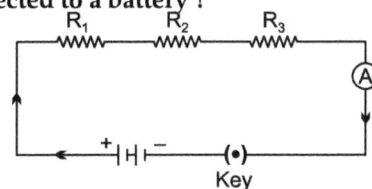

Ans. Let three resistors R_1, R_2 and R_3 are connected in series which are also connected with a battery, an ammeter and a key as shown in figure.
When key is closed, the current starts flowing through the circuit. Take the reading of ammeter. Now change the position of ammeter to anywhere in between the resistors and take its reading. We will observe that in both the cases reading of ammeter will be same showing same current flows through every part of the circuit above.

173. Answer the following question:*
(a) Write Joule's law of heating.
(b) Two lamps, one rated 100 W; 220 V, and the other 60 W; 220 V, are connected in parallel to electric mains supply. Find the current drawn by two bulbs from the line, if the supply voltage is 200 V.

Ans. (a) According to Joule's law of heating, the heat produced in a wire is directly proportional to:
(i) square of current (I^2),
(ii) resistance of wire (R),
(iii) time (t) for which current is passed.
Thus, the heat produced in the wire by current in time 't' is
$$H \propto I^2 Rt$$
or $\quad H = KI^2 Rt$
But K = 1, $\quad H = I^2 Rt$

(b) We know that, P = VI
$$\Rightarrow \quad I = \frac{P}{V}$$

First lamp: $P_1 = 100$ W, V = 220 volt
$$I_1 = \frac{P_1}{V} = \frac{100}{220} = 0.45 \text{ A}$$

Second lamp: $P_2 = 60$ W, V = 220 volt
$$I_2 = \frac{P_2}{V} = \frac{60}{220} = 0.27 \text{ A}$$

So, Total current $= I_1 + I_2$
$= 0.45 + 0.27$
$= 0.72$ A

174. Does Ohm's law hold good for electrolytic solutions and semiconductors?

Ans. No.

175. Define the electric circuit. Draw a labelled, schematic diagram of an electric circuit comprising of a cell, a resistor, an ammeter, a voltmeter and a closed switch

Sol. A continuous conduction path consisting of wires and other resistance (like bulb, fan, etc) and a switch between the two terminals of a cell or a battery along which an electric current flows, is called a circuit.

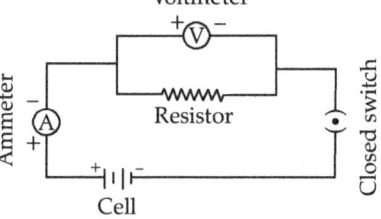

176. For the series combination of three resistors establish the relation:
$$R = R_1 + R_2 + R_3$$
where the symbols have usual meaning. Calculate the equivalent resistance of the combination of three resistor of 6 Ω, 9 Ω and 18 Ω joined in parallel.

Sol. Same current (I) flows through different resistance, when these are joined in series, as shown in the figure.

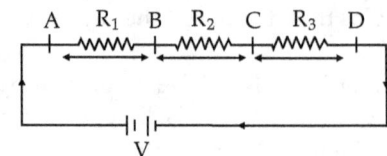

Let R be the combined resistance, then

$$V = IR$$
$$V_1 = IR_1, V_2 = IR_2, V_3 = IR_3$$
$$\because \quad IR = IR_1 + IR_2 + IR_3$$
$$\therefore \quad IR = IR_1 + IR_2 + IR_3$$
$$\Rightarrow \quad IR = I(R_1 + R_2 + R_3)$$
$$\therefore \quad R = R_1 + R_2 + R_3$$

Now, $R_1 = 6\,\Omega, R_2 = 9\,\Omega,$
$R_3 = 18\,\Omega$

In parallel combination

$$\frac{1}{R} = \frac{1}{R_1} + \frac{1}{R_2} + \frac{1}{R_3}$$

$$\Rightarrow \quad \frac{1}{R} = \frac{1}{6} + \frac{1}{9} + \frac{1}{18} = \frac{3+2+1}{18}$$

$$= \frac{6}{18} = \frac{1}{3}$$

$$\Rightarrow \quad \frac{1}{R} = \frac{1}{3}$$

$$\Rightarrow \quad R = 3\,\Omega.$$

177. Let the resistance of an electrical component remains constant while the potential difference across the two ends of the component decreases to half of its former value. What change will occur in the current through it?

Sol. (a) Since Resistance (R) = $\dfrac{\text{Potential difference (V)}}{\text{Electric current (I)}}$

Therefore, if potential between to ends of the component will be halved, and resistance remains constant then electric current would also be halved.

178. What are the advantages of connecting electrical devices in parallel with the battery instead of connecting them in series?

Ans. Advantages of connecting electrical appliances in parallel instead of connecting in series:
(a) Voltage remains same in all the appliances.
(b) The total effective resistance is less.
(c) Switching ON/OFF of one device does not affect others.

179. State the energy conversion taking place in the following electric appliances :
(a) Electric heater, (b) Electric -motor, (c) Loud-speaker, (d) Electrolysis.

Ans. (a) Electrical energy gets converted into heat energy in an electric heater.
(b) Electrical energy changes into mechanical energy in an electric motor.
(c) Electrical energy gets converted into sound energy in a loudspeaker.
(d) Electrical energy changes into chemical energy during electrolysis.

Self-Assessment

180. When a 12 V battery is connected across an unknown resistor, there is a current of 2.5 mA in the circuit. Find the value of the resistance of the resistor. **[NCERT]**

Ans. 4800 Ω

181. A nichrome wire has a resistance of 10 Ω. Find the resistance of another nichrome wire, whose length is three times and area of cross-section is four times the first wire.

Ans. 7.5 Ω

182. The equivalent resistance of the combination of resistors given in figure is 4 Ω. Calculate the value of x.

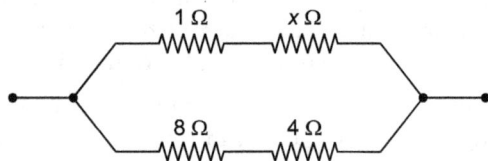

Ans. 5 Ω

183. Explain the difference between resistance and resistivity of a conductor.

184. The given figure shows three lamps and three switches 1, 2 and 3 connected with two cells.

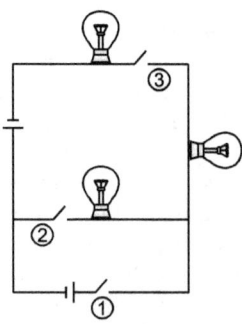

(a) Name the switch/switches to be closed so as to light all the three lamps.
(b) How are the lamps connected : in series or in parallel?

Ans. (a) 2 and 3, (b) in series.

185. Identify the components used in circuit diagram represented by the following symbols :

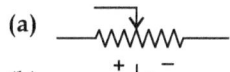

(a) ⎯⎯/\/\/\/⎯⎯
(b) ⎯⎯+| |−⎯⎯
(c) ⎯⎯(•)⎯⎯
(d) ⎯⎯+|H|H|−⎯⎯
(e) ⎯⎯/\/\/\/⎯⎯
(f) ⎯⎯/\/\/\/⎯⎯ (with arrow)

Ans. (a) resistance or rheostat
(b) Electric cell
(c) A closed plug key
(d) Battery
(e) Fixed resistance
(f) Variable resistance

186. Why does the resistance of filament of an electric bulb change when it starts to glow?

187. Why should a voltmeter never be connected in series?

188. Does Ohm's law always hold good? Give examples.

189. What is an electric circuit?

190. What is an electric cell?

191. Define resistance? What are the factors on which it depends?

192. Name (a) S.I. unit, (b) Commercial unit of electrical energy and state the relationship between the two.

193. Define 1 ohm electrical resistance.

194. Name the physical quantity associated with the following units:
(a) ampere, (b) ohm, (c) kilowatt-hour, (d) volt.

195. The given figure shows V-I graph for two conductors A and B.

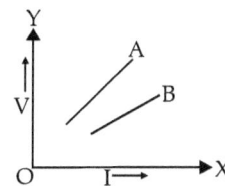

(a) Which conductor obeys Ohm's law?
(b) Which conductor (A or B) has more resistance? Explain your answer.

Ans. (a) Both conductors A and B obey ohm's law.
(b) The slope of V-I graph represents resistance of a conductor. The straight line for conductor A is steeper (or has a greater slope). Hence, conductor A has more resistance.

196. The given figure shows three lamps and three switches 1, 2 and 3 connected with two cells.

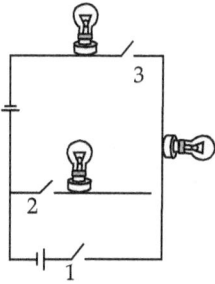

(a) Name the switch/switches to be closed so as to light all the three lamps.
(b) How are the lamps connected: in series or in parallel?

Ans. (a) 2 and 3, (b) in series.

197. Do all conductors obey Ohm's law? State two points of difference between conductors obeying Ohm's law and the ones not obeying Ohm's law.

198. What is the difference between an electric cell and a battery?

199. How many 220 Ω resistors (in parallel) are required to carry 5 A on a 220 V line?

Ans. 5.

200. Several electric bulbs designed to be used on a 220 V electric supply line, are rated 10W. How many lamps can be connected in parallel with each other across the two wires of 220 V line if the maximum allowable current is 5 A? **[NCERT]**

Ans. 110.

201. Which uses more energy:
(a) a 250 W T.V. set in 1 hour
(b) a 1200 W toaster in 10 minutes? **[NCERT]**

Ans. (a) 9×10^5 J, (b) 7.2×10^5 J (T.V. set uses more energy)

202. Study the circuit diagram given in figure carefully and calculate:
(a) Current in main circuit.
(b) Current in each of the resistors in the parallel circuit.

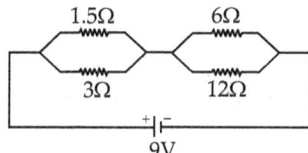

Ans. (a) 1.80 A, (b) 1.2 A and 0.6 A, 1.2 A and 0.6 A.

203. A wire of resistance 1.5 Ω is stretched to double its length. What will be its new resistance?

Ans. 6 Ω.

204. A wire of resistance 36 Ω and length 60 cm is tripled on itself. What is the new resistance?

Ans. 4 Ω.

205. How many electrons are flowing per second past a point in a circuit in which there is a current of 1 A?

Ans. 6.25×10^{18}.

206. The graph between V and I for a conductor is a straight line passing through the origin.
    (a) Name the law illustrated by such a graph ?
    (b) What should remain constant in a statement of this law ?
Ans. (a) Ohm's law, (b) Temperature.
207. Why are alloys such as constantan and manganin used for making standard resistors ?
208. Why are connected wires made of thick copper or aluminium wires ?
209. How is an ammeter connected in an electric circuit and what does it measure ?
210. Name any six components of an electric circuit and draw their symbols.
211. Calculate the least count of voltmeter in which there are 10 divisions between 1.0 V and 1.5 V marks.
Ans. Least count = $\frac{0.5}{10}$ = 0.05.
212. Draw a circuit diagram for the experimental verification of Ohm's law and state the function of each component used.
213. An ammeter has 10 divisions between 0 and 0.5 A marks on its scale. The least count of ammeter is :
    (a) 0.01 A   (b) 0.5 A
    (c) 0.05 A   (d) 0.1 A
Ans. (c)
214. For which of the following substances, resistance decreases with increases in temperature?
    (a) Mercury   (b) Silver
    (c) Copper   (d) Carbon
Ans. (d)
215. Commercial unit of electrical energy is :
    (a) joule   (b) ampere
    (c) volt   (d) kilowatt-hour
Ans. (d)
216. For a parallel combination of three resistors establish the relation :
$$\frac{1}{R} = \frac{1}{R_1} + \frac{1}{R_2} + \frac{1}{R_3}$$
217. Why are coils of electric toasters and electric irons made of an alloy rather than a pure metal ?
218. When a current I flows through a resistance R for time t, the electrical energy spent is given by :
    (a) I^2R/t (b) IRt
    (c) I^2Rt (d) IR^2t
Ans. (c) I^2Rt

219. The electric meter in a house records :
    (a) current   (b) energy
    (c) power   (d) voltage
Ans. (b) energy
220. What is an electric cell ?
221. An electric heater is rated '1500 W, 250 V'. The heater is connected to 250 V mains. Calculate :
    (a) The current drawn.
    (b) The energy consumed in 50 hours.
    (c) The cost of energy consumed at ₹ 6 per kWh.
Ans. (a) 6A, (b) 75 kWh, (c) Rs. 450.
222. Define 1 watt electrical power.
223. A boy noted the readings of his home's electricity meter on 1st June and again on 1st July (as shown in figure given below) :

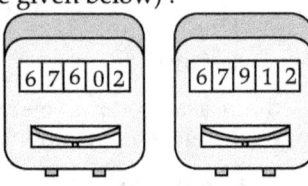

    (a) What was the meter reading on 1st June ?
    (b) What was the meter reading on 1st July ?
    (c) How many units of electrical energy have been used ?
    (d) Calculate the cost of electrical energy used, if the rate is Rs. 5 per unit.
Ans. (a) 67602
    (b) 67912
    (c) 310
    (d) Rs. 1550.
224. In an activity performed by a girl to estimate the monthly bill of her house, she reported that 3 bulbs of 100 W each, 2 fans of 50 W each and 1 T.V. set of 60 W are used daily for an average of 8 hours, 10 hours and 5 hours respectively.
    (a) Calculate the electrical energy (in kWh) consumed in 1 month.
    (b) If the cost of electrical energy is R 6 per unit, what is the monthly bill ?
Ans. (a) 111 kWh
    (b) ₹ 666.
225. Is Joule heating always desirable ?
Ans. No.
226. Name a material whose resistivity becomes zero at a particular temperature.
Ans. Mercury.

Magnetic Effects of Electric Current

Chapter 13

Multiple Choice Questions

1. A toaster of 4 kW is running in an existing circuit 110 volt that has a stream ranking of 4 A. Find the stream of electrons drawn by the toaster.
   (a) 36.36 A
   (b) 23.34 A
   (c) 14.6 A
   (d) 9.06 A

Ans. (a) 36.36 A

Explanation:

The stream of electrons drawn by the toaster is 36.36 A
Given, P = 4 kW, V = 110 V
To find, I = ?
We know that,
$$\text{Power} = VI$$
$$= 110 \times I$$
$$4,000 = 110 \times I$$
$$\therefore \quad I = 36.36 \text{ A}$$

2. The most important safety method used for protecting home appliance from short circuiting on overloading is: [NCERT Exemplar]
   (a) earthing
   (b) use of fuse
   (c) use of stablizers
   (d) use of fuse electric meter

Ans. (b) use of fuse

Explanation:

Use of fuse is most important safety method protecting home appliances from overloading all short circuiting.

3. A finite straight wire carries a current of 3 A, where it is a 2 m long and weighs around 240 g. If it is suspended in the mid-air by a uniform magnetic field then calculate the field B. [Acceleration due to gravity = 9.8 m/s²]
   (a) 0.39 T
   (b) 0.42 T
   (c) 0.61 T
   (d) 0.37 T

Ans. (a) 0.39 T

Explanation:

Given, Mass of the wire = 240 g = 0.24 kg
Length of the wire = 2 m
Current I = 3 A
Magnetic field B = ?
The force acting on the current carrying wire in uniform magnetic field
$$F = BiI \sin \theta$$
$$F = BiI \ (\theta = 90°)$$
Weight of the wire, $w = mg = 0.24 \times 9.8$ N
In the position of suspension
$$BiI = mg$$
$$B = \frac{mg}{iI}$$
$$B = \frac{(0.24 \times 9.8)}{(3 \times 2)}$$
$$B = \frac{(2.352)}{(6)}$$
The magnetic field (B) is 0.39 T

4. If it takes 520 turns to make a solenoid that is 40 cm long with a radius of 1.2 m that carries a current of 6 A, then determine the magnetic field inside the solenoid.
   (a) 7.2×10^{-3} T
   (b) 9.8×10^{-3} T
   (c) 8.4×10^{-4} T
   (d) 10.2×10^{-4} T

Ans. (b) 9.8×10^{-3} T

Explanation:

Given, I = 6 A, L = 40 cm = 0.4 m, r = 1.2 m, N = 520
We know that,
$$B = \frac{\propto_o NI}{L}$$
On substituting the values in above formula
$$= \frac{(4\pi \times 10^{-7} \times 520 \times 6)}{0.4}$$
$$= \frac{(4 \times 3.14 \times 10^{-7} \times 520 \times 6)}{0.4}$$
$$= 97968 \times 10^{-7}$$
$$= 9.8 \times 10^{-3} \text{ T}$$
The magnetic field inside the solenoid is 9.8×10^{-3} T

5. A 3 pin mains plug is fitted to the cable for a 1 kW electric kettle to be used on a 250 V a.c. supply which of the following statements is not correct?

(a) The fuse should be filled in the live wire.
(b) A 13 A fuse is the most appropriate value to use.
(c) The neutral wire is coloured black.
(d) The green wire should be connected to the earth pin.

Ans. (b) A 13 A fuse is the most appropriate value to use

Explanation :

P = 1 kW = 1000 W, V = 250 V

$\therefore$ Current, $I = \dfrac{P}{V}$

$= \dfrac{1000}{250}$

$= 4$ A

Because current drawn is 4 A, a fuse of 13 A cannot be considered the most appropriate.

6. Calculate the magnetic field produced by the solenoid of length 50 cm with no. of turns in the coil 210 when the current passing through it 8 A. (Given permeability, $\mu_0 = 4\pi \times 10^{-7}$ Wb/Am)
   (a) 4.22×10^{-7} T
   (b) 42.24×10^{-7} T
   (c) 422.2×10^{-7} T
   (d) 422.2×10^{-5} T

Ans. (d) 422.2×10^{-5} T

Explanation :

$B = \mu_0 n i$

where, $n = \dfrac{N}{L}$

$= \dfrac{4\pi \times 10^{-7} \times 210 \times 8}{0.50}$

$= 422.2 \times 10^{-5}$ T

7. The strength of an electromagnet after the limit cannot be increased by increasing the current through the solenoid. What is the reason behind this phenomenon?
   (a) Electrons start to corrode the solenoid.
   (b) Voltage through the solenoid gradually starts to decrease.
   (c) Resistance of the solenoid increases.
   (d) Current flowing through the solenoid is saturated.

Ans. (d) Current flowing through the solenoid is saturated.

Explanation :

The strength of an electromagnet after the limit cannot be increased by increasing the current through the solenoid because current flowing through the solenoid is saturated.

8. Two wires are placed in parallel; repulsion force and current in these two wires are "*f*" and "*i*" respectively. What will be a force if the current is doubled in each wire ?

(a) 2*f*
(b) $\dfrac{f}{2}$
(c) $\dfrac{2f}{4}$
(d) 4*f*

Ans. (d) 4*f*

Explanation :

If the current is doubled in each wire the force will be 4*f*. This can be explained as follows:
We know that the force of repulsion per unit length between two wires carrying current in opposite direction is:

$\dfrac{F}{l} = \dfrac{\mu_0 i_1 i_2}{2\pi d}$

Thus when both i_1 and i_2 are doubled, the force between them becomes four times.

9. H_1 and H_2 are heats produced by two copper wires have the same length and different diameters when they are connected in series and parallel respectively. From the above, we infer what of the following ?
   (a) $H_1 > H_2$
   (b) $H_1 < H_2$
   (c) $H_1 = H_2$
   (d) $H_1 \neq H_2$

Ans. (b) $H_1 < H_2$

Explanation :

When wire are connected in series,

$R_s = R_1 + R_2$

in parallel, $R_p = \dfrac{R_1 R_2}{R_1 + R_2}$

$\therefore$ $R_s > R_p$

$\therefore$ $H_1 < H_2$ $\qquad [\because H \propto \dfrac{1}{R}]$

Then $H_1 < H_2$ which implies option (b) is correct.

10. The strength of magnetic field inside a long current carrying straight solenoid is: [NCERT Exemplar]
    (a) more at the ends than at the centre.
    (b) minimum in the middle.
    (c) uniform at all points.
    (d) found to increase from one end to the other.

Ans. (c) uniform at all points.

Explanation :

Inside the solenoid magnetic field lines are straight. This indicates strong magnetic field. Hence, magnetic field is uniform at all points inside the solenoid.

11. Pick out the incorrect statement about magnetic lines of force.
    (a) Magnetic lines of forces start from the North Pole and end on the South Pole.
    (b) No two magnetic lines of force can intersect each other.

(c) Magnetic lines of force are far away from each other at the poles.
(d) Magnetic lines of force are closed continuous curves.

Ans. (c) Magnetic lines of force are far away from each other at the poles.

Explanation :

Magnetic lines of forces are closed continuous curves. They are nearer to each other at the point where magnetic field is strongest and far from each other where magnetic field is weak. At poles magnetic line of forces are nearest to each other because magnetic field is strongest at the pole.

No two magnetic lines of forces intersect with each other at the point of intersection, the compass needle would point towards two directions, which is not possible.

They are continuous, forming closed loops without beginning or end which start from north pole and end at south pole. Hence, statement (c), *i.e.*, Magnetic lines of force are far away from each other at the poles is the incorrect statement.

12. **Strength of the magnetic field at a point in the space surrounding the magnet is measured by:**
    (a) thickness of the magnet.
    (b) number of lines crossing a given point.
    (c) resistance of it.
    (d) length of the magnet.

Ans. (b) number of lines crossing a given point.

Explanation :

The strength of the magnetic field at a point in the space surrounding the magnet is measured by number of lines crossing a given point.

13. **The magnetic field strength of a solenoid can be increased by inserting:**
    (a) a wooden piece into it.
    (b) an iron piece into it.
    (c) a glass piece into it.
    (d) paper roll into it.

Ans. (b) an iron piece into it.

Explanation :

When a piece of soft iron is inserted inside a solenoid then the strength of the magnetic field increases because the iron gets magnetized due to magnetic induction and this combination of the solenoid and the soft iron core so formed is called an electromagnet.

14. **The magnetic field inside the solenoid is:**
    (a) non-uniform   (b) variable
    (c) same at all points (d) zero

Ans. (c) same at all points

Explanation :

The magnetic field inside the solenoid is same at all points. This is because the magnetic field lines inside the solenoid are in the form of parallel straight lines which indicates that the magnetic field is uniform at all points inside the solenoid.

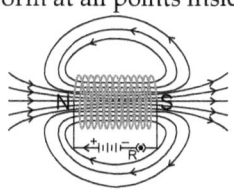

Field lines of the magnetic field through and around a current carrying solenoid.

15. **The magnetic field lines inside a solenoid are in the form of:**
    (a) Curved line   (b) Circular lines
    (c) Zig - zag lines (d) Parallel straight lines

Ans. (d) Parallel straight lines

Explanation :

The field lines inside the solenoid are in the form of parallel straight lines. This indicates that magnetic field is same at all point insides the solenoid.

16. **Which of the following correctly describes the magnetic field near a long straight wire ?**
    (a) The field consists of straight lines perpendicular to the wire.
    (b) The field consists of straight lines parallel to the wire.
    (c) The field consists of radial lines originating from the wire.
    (d) The field consists of concentric circles centred on the wire.

Ans. (d) The field consists of concentric circles centred on the wire.

Explanation :

The magnetic field near a long straight wire are concentric circles and their centres lie on the wire. This can be confirmed by Right-hand Thumb Rule. According to this rule, if we put the thumb of our right hand in the direction of the current flow through the conductor or straight wire and encircle the wire with your fingers, then the direction of those fingers will correspond to the direction of the magnetic field.

Thus, the magnetic field lines will be in concentric circles around the conductor.

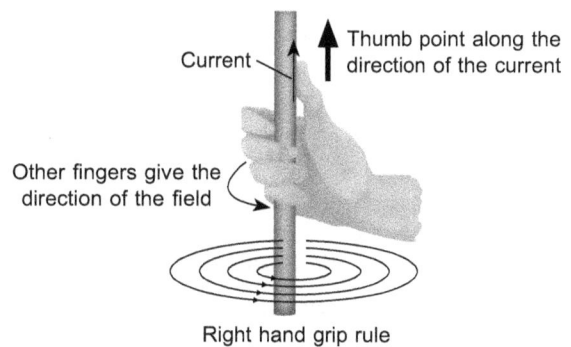

Right hand grip rule

17. **Inside the magnet, the field lines move:**
    (a) from South to North
    (b) from North to South
    (c) away from North pole
    (d) away from South poles

    Ans. (a) from South to North

    Explanation :

    Magnetic field is a vector quantity that has both direction and magnitude. The direction of the magnetic field is taken to be the direction in which a North pole of the compass needle moves inside it. The field lines emerge from North pole and merge in the South pole but inside the magnet the direction of field lines is opposite.

18. **An electron moves with a speed v along positive direction of the x-axis. If a magnetic field B acts along the positive y-direction, then the force on the electron will act along:**
    (a) x-axis (b) y-axis
    (c) $-$ve z-direction (d) $+$ve y-direction

    Ans. (c) $-$ve z-direction

    Explanation :

    As electron is moving in positive x-direction then, according to the Maxwell's right hand thumb rule, the current is moving in negative x-direction and the magnetic field acts on positive y-direction. By applying Fleming's left-hand rule, the thumb will be in negative z-direction which is the direction of force.

19. **The force exerted on a current carrying wire placed in a magnetic field is zero when the angle between wire and the direction of magnetic field is:**
    (a) 45° (b) 60°
    (c) 90° (d) 180°

    Ans. (d) 180°

    Explanation :

    The force exerted on a current carrying wire placed in a magnetic field is zero when the angle between wire and the direction of magnetic field is 180°.
    A force is experienced by the current carrying wire in the presence of an external magnetic field. This can be expressed as:
    $$F = BIL \sin \theta$$
    Where,
    L is the length of the wire.
    I is the current, and
    θ is the angle between the current and the magnetic field.
    We know that sin 180° is 0. Therefore, the force exerted on a current-carrying wire that is placed in a magnetic field is zero when the angle between the wire and the direction of magnetic field is 180°.

20. **In the figure shown below, the point A and B are respectively:**

    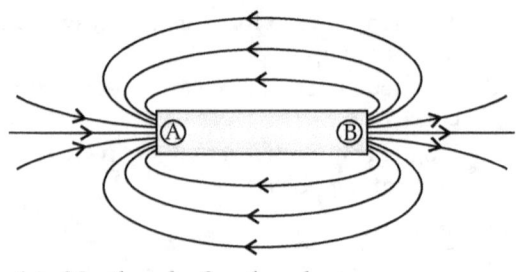

    (a) North pole, South pole
    (b) South pole, North pole
    (c) North pole, North pole
    (d) South pole, South pole

    Ans. (b) South pole, North pole

    Explanation :

    As magnetic lines of forces start from North pole and terminates at S-pole.

21. **The north pole of a long bar magnet was pushed slowly into a short solenoid connected to a galvanometer. The magnet was held stationary for a few seconds with the North pole in the middle of the solenoid and then withdrawn rapidly. The maximum deflection of the galvanometer was observed when the magnet was:**
    (a) Moving towards the solenoid
    (b) Moving into the solenoid
    (c) At rest inside the solenoid
    (d) Moving out of the solenoid

    Ans. (d) Moving out of the solenoid

    Explanation :

    As due to electromagnetic induction.

22. **A rectangular coil of copper wires is rotated in a magnetic field. The direction of the induced current changes once in each:**
    (a) two revolutions (b) one revolution
    (c) half revolution (d) one-fourth revolution

    Ans. (c) half revolution

    Explanation :

    A rectangular coil of copper wires is rotated in a magnetic field. The direction of the induced current changes once in each half revolution. This is because when a rectangular coil is rotated in a magnetic field the direction of the induced current varies once every half revolution. As a result, the current in the coil continues to flow in the same direction.

23. **The magnetic field of the current was discovered by:**
    (a) Maxwell (b) Fleming
    (c) Oersted (d) Faraday

    Ans. (c) Oersted

    Explanation :

    Hans Christian oersted discovered that a compass needle got deflected when electric current passed through a metallic wire placed nearby.

24. Three magnets A, B and C wire dipped one by one in a heap of iron filing. It shows the amount of the iron filling stucking to them:

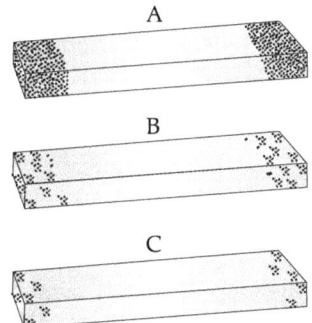

The Strength of these magnets will be:
(a) A > B > C   (b) A < B < C
(c) A = B = C   (d) A < B > C

Ans. (a) A > B > C

Explanation :

As most of the iron fillings got stuck to magnet A. So, it is the most powerful magnet, or it has maximum strength.

25. If we place the magnetic compass near the north pole of the magnet, which pole of the needle will point towards it?

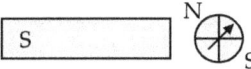

(a) North pole   (b) South pole
(c) Keep deflecting (d) None of these

Ans. (b) South pole

Explanation :

As like poles repel each other and unlike poles attract each other. Therefore when North pole of bar magnet is brought near the compass, it gets defected in south direction.

26. In the circuit shown below, what is direction of the current?

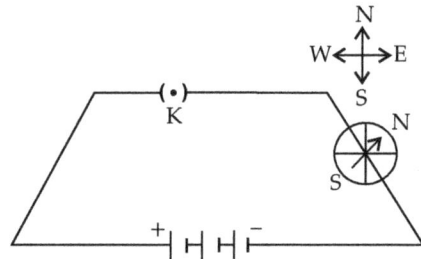

(a) No current flowing (b) Anti-clock wise
(c) Clock wise   (d) Data insufficient

Ans. (c) Clock wise

Explanation :

If the current flows from North to South the compass needle will move towards the last.

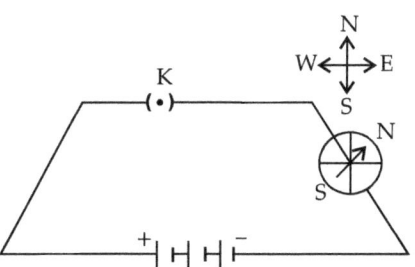

27. A proton enters a magnetic field at right angle to it, as shown below. The direction of force acting on the proton will be:

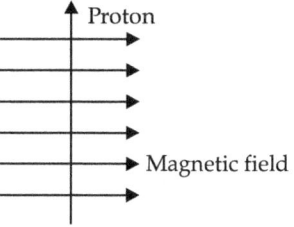

(a) To the right   (b) To the left
(c) Out of the page (d) Into the page

Ans. (d) Into the page

Explanation :

The proton enters a magnetic field at right-angle to it. Therefore, it will experience a force and the direction of force is calculated using Fleming's Left-Hand Rule.

28. A bar magnet is immersed in a heap of iron fillings and pulled out. The amount of iron filling dinging to the:
(a) North pole is almost equal to the South pole
(b) North pole is much more than the South Pole
(c) North pole is almost less equal than the South pole
(d) Magnet will be same all along its length

Ans. (a) North pole is almost equal to the South pole

Explanation :

As the maximum intensity of magnet is on the poles of the magnet.

29. Rashita and her friends were decorating the class bulletin board. She accidently dropped the box of stainless steel pins by mistake. She tried to collect the pins using a magnet. She could not succeed. Why?
(a) They are not using the magnet in right direction
(b) Steel pins are very heavy and cannot be lifted magnet
(c) Steel pins are very long
(d) Steel is not magnetic in nature

Ans. (d) Steel is not magnetic in nature

Explanation :

As steel is not magnetic in nature So it is not attracted by the magnet.

30. If the current is passing through a straight conductor. then, the magnetic field lines around it forms a particular shape. That shape is:
 (a) Straight lines (b) Concentric circles
 (c) Concentric ellipse (d) Concentric parabolas

Ans. (b) Concentric circles

Explanation :

When current passes through a straight conductor, then the magnetic field lines forms concentric circle around it.

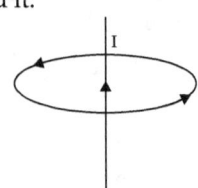

31. The figure given below shows the magnetic field produced by a currents carrying wire. Which of the diagram shows it correctly?

(a) 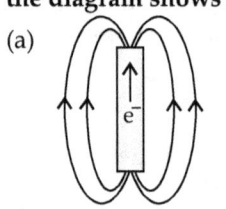 (b)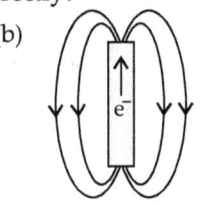

(c) 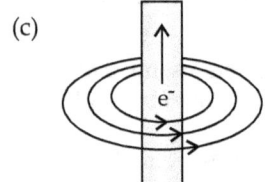 (d)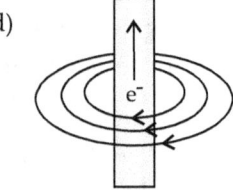

Ans. (d)

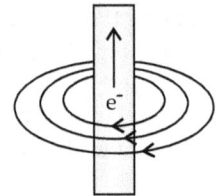

Explanation :

As when current flows through and current-carrying wire, then direction of magnetic field is calculated by right hand thumb rule.

32. Consider the following statements and choose the correct are:
 (a) A magnet is an object which attracts pieces of iron, Nickel and cobalt
 (b) Magnetic effect of electric current means that an electric current flowing in a wire produces a magnetic field around it
 (c) The end of a freely suspended magnet which points towards the north direction is called the north pole of the magnet
 (d) All of the above

Ans. (d) All of the above

Explanation :
 (a) A magnet is an object which attracts pieces of iron, Nickel and cobalt.
 (b) Magnetic effect of electric current means that an electric current flowing in a wire produces a magnetic field around it .
 (c) The end of a freely suspended magnet which points towards the north direction is called the north pole of the magnet.

33. A rectangular loop carrying a current I is situated near a long straight wire such that the wire is parallel to one of the sides of the loop and is in plane of the loop. If steady current I is created in wire as shown in figure below, then the loop:

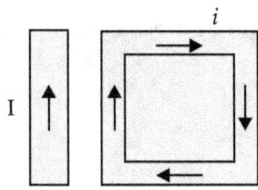

 (a) Rotate about an axis parallel to the wire
 (b) Move towards the wire
 (c) Move away from the wire or towards right
 (d) Remains stationary

Ans. (b) Move towards the wire

Explanation :

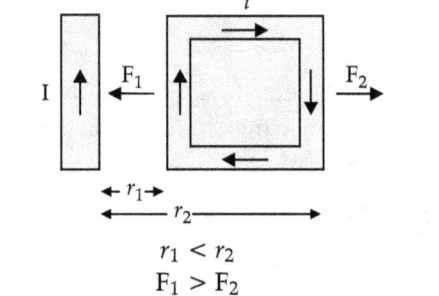

As $\quad r_1 < r_2$
$\therefore \quad F_1 > F_2$
$\therefore \quad F_{net} = F_1 - F_2$
(Directed towards the wire)

34. Which one of the following substances is the magnetic substances?
 (a) Mercury (b) Iron
 (c) Gold (d) Silver

Ans. (b) Iron

Explanation :

Among the given substances, the iron is the only magnetic substances.

35. The magnetic lines of force, inside a current carrying solenoid are:
 (a) Along the axis and are parallel to each other
 (b) Perpendicular to axis and equidistant from each other
 (c) Circular and they do not intersect each other
 (d) Circular at the ends but they are parallel to the axis inside the solenoid

Ans. (a) Along the axis and are parallel to each other

Explanation :

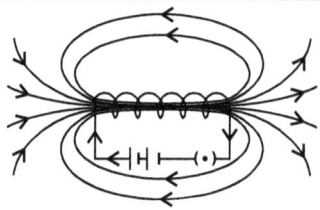

The figure shows the magnetic lines of forces the solenoid.

36. **In the diagram shown below, what is the component A:**

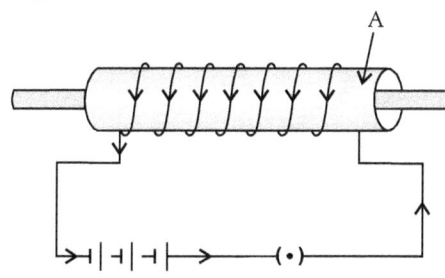

   (a) Solenoid   (b) Glass rod
   (c) Magnetic material (d) None of these

Ans. (c) Magnetic Material

Explanation :

Here, A is a magnetic material on which solenoid as wrapped. As by passing current through it the magnetic material will become an electromagnet.

37. **Which of the following determine the direction of magnetic field due to a current carrying conductor?**
   (a) Faraday's laws of electromagnetic induction
   (b) Fleming's left hand rule
   (c) Lenz's law
   (d) Maxwell's cork screw-rule

Ans. (d) Maxwell's Cork Screw-Rule

Explanation :

According to this rule, if we consider ourselves driving a cork screw in the direction of current, then the direction of the rotation of cork Screw is the direction of the Magnetic field.

38. **Which of the following is not an example of the right hand thumb rule ?**
   (a) D.C. motor
   (b) Solenoid
   (c) A.C. generator
   (d) Cartesian coordinate system

Ans. (c) A.C. generator

Explanation :

Right hand thumb rule is used to find the direction of magnetic field in a coil of wire and the electric current in a straight conductor. A.C. generator is not an example of right hand thumb rule because it works on the principle of electromagnetic induction.

39. **Commercial motors do not use:**

   [NCERT Exemplar]
   (a) an electromagnet to rotate the armature
   (b) effectively large number of turns of conducting wire in the current carrying coil
   (c) a permanent magnet to rotate the armature
   (d) a soft iron core on which the coil is wound

Ans. (c) a permanent magnet to rotate the armature

Explanation :

Commercial motors do not use permanent magnets because they are weak and do not produce strong magnetic field in the region.

40. **The process of inducing a current in a coil of wire by placing it in a region of changing magnetic field is:**
   (a) Electrical effect
   (b) Heating effect of current
   (c) Magnetic effect of current
   (d) Electromagnetic induction

Ans. (d) Electromagnetic induction

Explanation :

The process of inducing a current in a coil of wire by placing it in a region of changing magnetic field is electromagnetic induction.

41. **The core of electromagnet is made of:**
   (a) soft iron   (b) steel
   (c) magnesium   (d) copper

Ans. (a) soft iron

Explanation :

The core of electromagnet is made of soft iron due to following reasons:
- It can be easily magnetised and demagnetised.
- It has low carbon content.
- It has large susceptibility and small retentivity.
- It does not retain its magnetism when the current is switched off.
- It is less corrosive.

42. **Fleming's Right-hand rule gives:**
   (a) Magnitude of the induced current.
   (b) Magnitude of the magnetic field.
   (c) Direction of the induced current.
   (d) Both, direction and magnitude of the induced current.

Ans. (c) Direction of the induced current.

Explanation :

Fleming's Right hand rule gives the direction of the induced current.

Stretch the thumb, forefinger and middle finger of right hand so that they are perpendicular to each other. If forefinger indicates the direction of the magnetic field, thumb shows the direction of motion of conductor, then the middle finger will show the direction of induced current. We can not find out the magnitude of either the induced current or magnetic field by this law.

43. Which of the following property of a proton can change while it moves freely in a magnetic field?
(a) Mass (b) Speed
(c) Velocity (d) Charge

Ans. (c) Velocity

Explanation :

Velocity of a proton can change while it moves freely in a magnetic field because each moving charged particle in a magnetic field experiences a force. The direction of force experienced by a positively charged proton can be studied by Fleming's Left-hand Rule.

The force acting on the proton would change both velocity and momentum when it moves freely in magnetic field. If a charged particle's velocity is completely parallel to the magnetic field, the magnetic field will not exert any force on the particle, and thus the velocity will remain constant. Whereas, if the force is acting perpendicular to the direction of moving charge, work done will be zero. It means kinetic energy does not change. Hence, we can conclude that the force can change the direction of velocity of the proton but not its speed. Thus, momentum and velocity changes.

44. A positively-charged particle (alpha-particle) projected towards west is deflected towards north by a magnetic field. The direction of magnetic field is:
(a) towards south (b) towards east
(c) downward (d) upward

Ans. (d) upward

Explanation :

A positively-charged particle (alpha-particle) projected towards west is deflected towards north by a magnetic field. The direction of magnetic field is upward. This can be explained by Fleming's Left-hand Rule which states that if we stretch our thumb, forefinger and middle figure of our left hand perpendicular to each other in such a way that forefinger points the direction of magnetic field and middle figure points the direction of current then thumb will represent the direction of motion or the force acting on the conductor. Hence, upward is the correct answer.

45. The phenomenon of electromagnetic induction is:
(a) the process of charging a body.
(b) the process of generating magnetic field due to a current passing through a coil.
(c) producing induced current in a coil due to relative motion between a magnet and the coil.
(d) the process of rotating a coil of an electric motor.

Ans. (c) producing induced current in a coil due to relative motion between a magnet and the coil.

Explanation :

The phenomenon of electromagnetic induction is producing induced current in a coil due to relative motion between a magnet and the coil. When a coil is brought near the magnet, and a relative motion is generated between the two by either moving the magnet or the coil, the magnetic flux links through the coil changes. This change in the magnetic flux produces an emf or voltage and hence, subsequent electric current in the coil.

46. The direction of force acting on a current carrying conductor placed in a magnetic field can be obtained by: [NCERT]
(a) Fleming's left hand rule.
(b) Fleming's right hand rule.
(c) Clock face rule.
(d) Ampere's swimming rule.

Ans. (a) Fleming's left hand rule.

Explanation :

The direction of force acting on a current carrying conductor placed in a magnetic field can be obtained by Fleming's left hand rule. According to this rule, when a current-carrying conductor is placed in an external magnetic field, the conductor experiences a force perpendicular to both the field and to the direction of the current flow.

47. The process shown in the diagram below is:

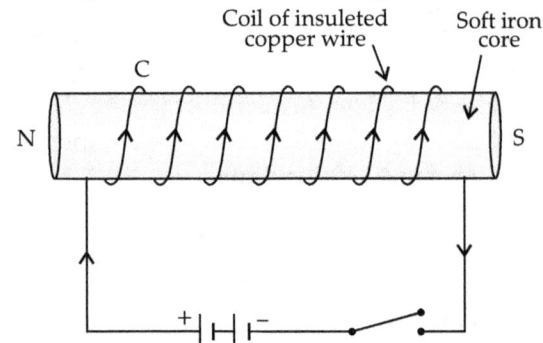

(a) Electriomagnetism (b) Electric generator
(c) Electric Motor (d) Electric fuse

Ans. (a) Electromagnetism

Explanation :

An electromagnet produces a magnetic field so long as current flows in its coil.

48. Which of the given options represents the correct pair?

(a)	Right-hand thumb rule	Direction of force
(b)	Galvanometer	Adjust current in circuit
(c)	Earth wire	Red colour
(d)	MRI	Magnetic Resonance Imaging

Ans. (d) MRI → Magnetic Resonance Imaging

Explanation :

MRI is a technique used to obtain the image of different body parts by using magnetic field.

49. **The phenomenon of electromagnetic induction is:**
    (a) The process of charging a body
    (b) The process of generating magnetic field due to a current passing through a coil
    (c) Producing induced current in a coil to relative motion between a magnet and the coil
    (d) The process of rotating a coil of an electric motor

Ans. (c) Producing induced current in a coil the relative motion between a magnet and the coil

Explanation :

Electromagnetic induction is a process in which current is induced when a current carrying conductor is moved in the magnetic field.

50. **In the given electric circuit, the device X is:**

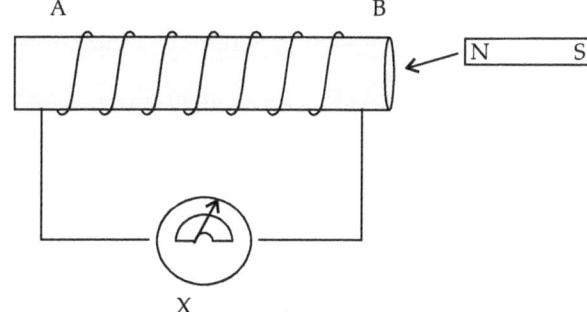

    (a) Ammeter   (b) Resistance
    (c) Galvanometer   (d) Voltmeter

Ans. (c) Galvanometer

Explanation :

Galvanometer is an instrument that is used to detect the presence of the current in the circuit. And when magnet is moved near the coil, the current is included in the coil.

51. **The figure below shows the Fleming's left hand rule. Identify the correct label with the function?**

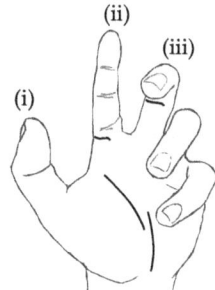

    (a) Thumb force
    (b) Fore finger field
    (c) Middle finger-correct
    (d) All of these

Ans. (d) All of these

Explanation :

According to Fleming's left hand rule stretch the thumb, fore finger and middle finger of your left hand side that they are mutually perpendicular. If the first finger points in the direction of magnetic field and second finger in the direction of current, then thumb will point in the direction of force.

52. **Mutual induction is a process in which current is induced in the neighbouring coil if current flows in a coil. In the figure shown below:**

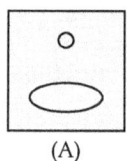 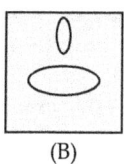 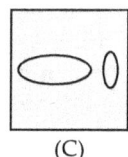
(A)   (B)   (C)

    (a) Maximum in situation (A)
    (b) Maximum in situation (B)
    (c) Maximum in situation (C)
    (d) Same in all situation

Ans. (a) Maximum in situation (A)

Explanation :

As both the coils are in the same plane. And induced current is found to be highest when the direction of the coil is at right angle to the magnetic field.

53. **A charged particle enters at right angle into a uniform field as shown. What should be the nature of charge on the particle if it begins to move in a direction pointing vertically out of the page due to its interaction with the magnetic field?**

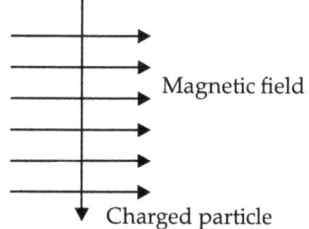

    (a) Positive   (b) Negative
    (c) Natural   (d) Can't decide

Ans. (a) Positive

Explanation :

Using Fleming's left hand rule, the nature of charged particle is positive.

54. **A current flows in a wire, running between the S and N poles of a magnet lying horizontally as shown in the figure below:**

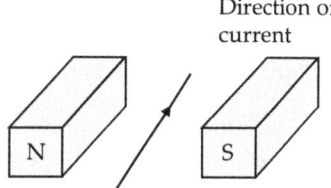

The force on the wire due the magnet is directed.
(a) From N to S
(b) From S to N
(c) Vertically downwards
(d) Vertically upwards

Ans. (c) Vertically downwards

Explanation :

Force on conductor is calculated using Fleming's left hand rule.

55. A student learns that magnetic field strength around a bar magnet is different at every point which diagram shows the correct magnetic field lines around a bar magnet?

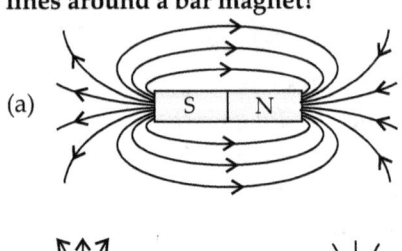
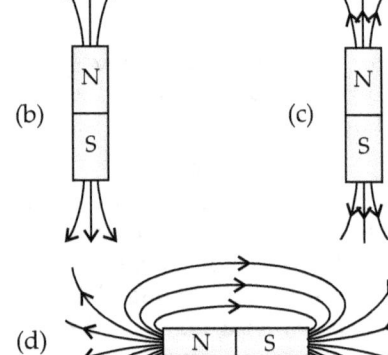
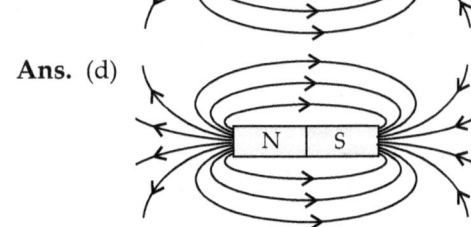

Ans. (d)

Explanation :

As magnetic lines of forces are continuous curves and originate from N-pole and ends at the S-pole

56. Which of the following is not true?
(a) Induction proceeds attractions
(b) We cannot isolate a single pole
(c) We can magnetic an iron ring
(d) A permanent magnet retains its magnetism even when heated on a flame

Ans. (d) A permanent magnet looses its magnetism when heated on the flame

Explanation :

A permanent magnet does not loose its magnetism even when heated on a flame.

57. Which of the following combination is not correct?
(a) Electric Motor—Fleming's right hand rule
(b) Electric generator—Electromagnetic induction
(c) Earth wire—Green colour
(d) Compass Needle—Small Magnet

Ans. (a) Electric Motor—Fleming's right hand rule

Explanation :

A electric motor works on the principle of Fleming's left hand rule.

58. By removing the inducing magnets, the induced magnetism is:
(a) Finished after sometime
(b) Finished just after
(c) Non-finished for a long time
(d) Not Charged

Ans. (b) Finished just after

Explanation :

As induced magnetism takes place, as long as the induced magnet is present.

59. A copper wire is held between the poles of a magnet:

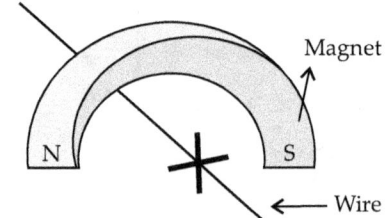

The current in the wire can be reversed. The pole of the magnet can also be changed over. In how many of the four directions shown can the force act on the wire?
(a) 1   (b) 2
(c) 3   (d) 4

Ans. (b) 2

Explanation :

By Fleming's left hand rule, we know that the force on the wire is perpendicular to the current in the wire and the magnetic field.
That it, there are only two possibilities is for the direction of force i.e., upward or downward.

60. Commercial electric motors do not use:
(a) An, electromagnetic to rotate the armature
(b) Effectively large number of conducting wire in the current carrying coil
(c) A permanent magnet to rotate the armature
(d) A soft iron core on which the coil is wound

Ans. (c) A permanent to rotate the armature

Explanation :

Using, electromagnet, the magnetic field strength further increase by, increasing. the current. Hence, it will enhance the power of electric motor.

Assertion and Reasoning Based Questions

61. Assertion: Iron filings are kept near a magnet it gets arranged in a particular fashion.

Reason: Magnetic field is a scalar quantity.

(a) If both assertion and reason are true and reason is the correct explanation of assertion.
(b) If both assertion and reason are true, but reason is not the correct explanation of assertion.
(c) If assertion is true, but reason is false.
(d) If assertion is false, but reason is true.

Ans. (c) If assertion is true, but reason is false.

Explanation:

Magnetic field is not a scalar quantity rather it is a vector quantity which has both magnitude and direction. So, when iron filings are placed around a magnet, they get arranged in a fashion similar to that of magnetic lines. So, assertion is correct, but reason is false.

62. Assertion: A current carrying rod is suspended between U-shaped magnet, the rod deflects.

Reason: A force is exerted on the rod due to magnetic field.

(a) If both assertion and reason are true and reason is the correct explanation of assertion.
(b) If both assertion and reason are true, but reason is not the correct explanation of assertion.
(c) If assertion is true, but reason is false.
(d) If assertion is false, but reason is true.

Ans. (a) If both assertion and reason are true and reason is the correct explanation of assertion.

Explanation:

A force is always exerted due to magnetic field in the same way electric current flowing through any conductor produces magnetic field. And in this case, Fleming's left-hand rule is used to predict directions of the magnetic field, current and displacement.

So, assertion and reason both are true and reason is the correct explanation of assertion.

63. Assertion: The energy of charged particle moving in a uniform magnetic field does not change.

Reason: Work done by magnetic field on the charge is zero.

(a) If both assertion and reason are true and reason is the correct explanation of assertion.
(b) If both assertion and reason are true, but reason is not the correct explanation of assertion.
(c) If assertion is true, but reason is false.
(d) If assertion is false, but reason is true.

Ans. (a) If both assertion and reason are true and reason is the correct explanation of assertion.

Explanation:

The force on a charged particle moving in a uniform magnetic field always acts in direction perpendicular to the direction of motion of the charge. As work done by magnetic field on the charge is zero, so the energy of the charged particle does not change. Thus, both assertion and reason are true and reason is the correct explanation of assertion.

64. Assertion: A current carrying conductor experiences a force in a magnetic field.

Reason: The net charge on a current carrying conductor is zero.

(a) If both assertion and reason are true and reason is the correct explanation of assertion.
(b) If both assertion and reason are true, but reason is not the correct explanation of assertion.
(c) If assertion is true, but reason is false.
(d) If assertion is false, but reason is true.

Ans. (b) If both assertion and reason are true, but reason is not the correct explanation of assertion.

Explanation:

When a current carrying conductor having no net charge is placed in a magnetic field, the free electrons of the conductor move towards the positive end of the conductor with same drift velocity, hence a magnetic force acts on them. The positive ions of the conductor being stationary, do not experience any magnetic field. Thus, both assertion and reason are correct but reason is not the correct explanation of the assertion.

65. Assertion: Magnetic field lines do not intersect each other.

Reason: There are two direction of the magnetic field at a point.

(a) If both assertion and reason are true and reason is the correct explanation of assertion.
(b) If both assertion and reason are true, but reason is not the correct explanation of assertion.
(c) If assertion is true, but reason is false.
(d) If assertion is false, but reason is true.

Ans. (a) Both A & R re true and R is the correct explanation of assertion

Explanation:

Magnetic field lines do not intersect, because it happen so then at that point two direction of magnetic field lines exist, which is not possible.

66. Assertion: The principle of electromagnetic induction was discovered by Micheal Faraday

Reason: The principle is used only in DC generators

(a) If both assertion and reason are true and reason is the correct explanation of assertion.

(b) If both assertion and reason are true, but reason is not the correct explanation of assertion.
(c) If assertion is true, but reason is false.
(d) If assertion is false, but reason is true.

Ans. (c) If assertion is true, but reason is false.

> **Explanation :**
>
> Not only DC generators but AC generators also work on the principle of electromagnetic induction.

67. **Assertion:** Electric Motor converts electric energy into mechanical energy.
    Reason: Electric Motor is based on the principle of Fleming's right hand rule.
    (a) If both assertion and reason are true and reason is the correct explanation of assertion.
    (b) If both assertion and reason are true, but reason is not the correct explanation of assertion.
    (c) If assertion is true, but reason is false.
    (d) If assertion is false, but reason is true.

Ans. (c) If assertion is true, but reason is false.

> **Explanation :**
>
> Electric motor is based on the principle of Fleming's left hand rule.

68. **Assertion:** A compass is kept near a wire carrying current gets deflected.
    Reason: Electric current is capable of producing a magnetic effect.
    (a) If both assertion and reason are true and reason is the correct explanation of assertion.
    (b) If both assertion and reason are true, but reason is not the correct explanation of assertion.
    (c) If assertion is true, but reason is false.
    (d) If assertion is false, but reason is true.

Ans. (a) If both assertion and reason are true and reason is the correct explanation of assertion.

> **Explanation :**
>
> Here while carrying out an experiment if a compass needle is placed near a wire carrying current then due to the effect of magnetism which is produced due to electric current produced in the wire the needle gets deflected. It shows that the magnetism and electricity are interlinked. So, both assertion and reason are true and reason is the correct explanation of assertion.

69. **Assertion:** Deflection of the iron filings changes when current in the conductor varies.
    Reason: Magnitude of the magnetic field does not change with the magnitude of current.
    (a) If both assertion and reason are true and reason is the correct explanation of assertion.
    (b) If both assertion and reason are true, but reason is not the correct explanation of assertion.
    (c) If assertion is true, but reason is false.
    (d) If assertion is false, but reason is true.

Ans. (c) If assertion is true, but reason is false.

> **Explanation :**
>
> Assertion is correct but the reason is wrong. As the current changes in the conductor, magnitude of the magnetic field produced also varies which is the reason for a change in the deflection of the iron filings.

70. **Assertion:** A pump operated by electric motor starts pumping liquid.
    Reason: Motor converts mechanical energy to electrical energy.
    (a) If both assertion and reason are true and reason is the correct explanation of assertion.
    (b) If both assertion and reason are true, but reason is not the correct explanation of assertion.
    (c) If assertion is true, but reason is false.
    (d) If assertion is false, but reason is true.

Ans. (c) If assertion is true, but reason is false.

> **Explanation :**
>
> An electric motor converts electrical energy to mechanical energy which is used for pumping liquids through the pumps. It produces a rotating force when electricity is given to it. So, assertion is true, but reason is false.

71. **Assertion:** Galvanometer is used to measure polarity.
    Reason: Galvanometer is an instrument which is used to detect current in any circuit.
    (a) If both assertion and reason are true and reason is the correct explanation of assertion.
    (b) If both assertion and reason are true, but reason is not the correct explanation of assertion.
    (c) If assertion is true, but reason is false.
    (d) If assertion is false, but reason is true.

Ans. (b) If both assertion and reason are true, but reason is not the correct explanation of assertion.

> **Explanation :**
>
> Both the statements are correct, but reason is not the correct explanation of assertion. In testing purposes galvanometer is used to measure polarity. There is a torque acting on a current carrying coil suspended in a magnetic field which produces deflection.
>
> Deflection is directly proportional to current flowing through the galvanometer coil.

72. **Assertion:** Current can be induced in a coil by changing the magnetic field around it.
    Reason: A Galvanometer connected to a coil can deflect either to the left or right of the zero mark.
    (a) If both assertion and reason are true and reason is the correct explanation of assertion.
    (b) If both assertion and reason are true, but reason is not the correct explanation of assertion.
    (c) If assertion is true, but reason is false.
    (d) If assertion is false, but reason is true.

Ans. (b) If both assertion and reason are true, but reason is not the correct explanation of assertion.

Magnetic Effects of Electric Current | 183

Explanation :

Current is induced in a coil due to a changing magnetic field and this process is known as electromagnetic induction.

Galvanometer is a device that detects the presence of current by deflecting the needle to one side of the zero mark but this does not explain the current induced in the coil.

Case Based Questions

73. **Read the passage carefully and answer the following questions from Q. 73 (i) to Q. 73 (v).**

    When a small compass is placed near a magnet, it will experience a force due to the magnetic field of the magnet. It is evidently observed due to a deflection in the north pole pointer of the compass. The path traced by the north pole pointer under the influence of a magnetic field is called the magnetic field line. The magnetic field lines are produced from the north pole of the magnet end at the south pole of the magnet. When the compass is moved around the field line, it always sets itself tangential along the curves.

    (i) The magnetic field lines:
    (a) intersect at right angle to one another.
    (b) intersect at an angle of 45 degree.
    (c) cross at an angle of 60 degree.
    (d) never intersect with each other.

    (ii) Magnetic field lines can be used to determine:
    (a) the shape of the magnetic field.
    (b) only the direction of the magnetic field.
    (c) only the relative strength of the magnetic field.
    (d) both the direction and the relative strength of the magnetic field.

    (iii) The magnetic field lines due to a bar magnet are correctly shown in:

    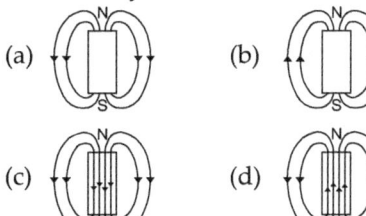

    (iv) Which of the following is incorrect regarding magnetic field lines?
    (a) The field lines are directed N to S inside the magnet.
    (b) The Crowdedness of the field lines shows the strength of the magnet.
    (c) The field is tangent to the magnetic field line.
    (d) Magnetic field lines are closed and continuous curves.

    (v) A strong bar magnet placed vertically above a surface. The magnetic field lines will be:
    (a) Only in a horizontal plane around the magnet.
    (b) Only in a vertical plane around the magnet.
    (c) Both in horizontal and vertical plane around the magnet.
    (d) In all the planes around the magnet.

    Ans. (i) (d) never intersect with each other.
    (ii) (d) both the direction and the relative strength of the magnetic field.
    (iii) (d)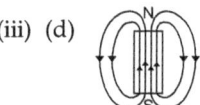
    (iv) (a) The field lines are directed N to S inside the magnet.
    (v) (d) In all the planes around the magnet

74. **Read the passage carefully and answer the following questions from Q. 74 (i) to Q. 74 (v).**

    A current-carrying wire produces a magnetic field around it. The phenomena in which an electromotive force and current are induced by changing magnetic field through it is called induced current. It can be concluded that the induced current flows in a conductor as long as the magnetic force changes within the conductor. For the motion of the coil with respect to the magnet or vice versa, the direction of the current flowing in the conductor is determined by the direction of the relative motion of the conductor with respect to the magnetic field. The induced emf or current is directly proportional to the rate of change in the magnetic field.

    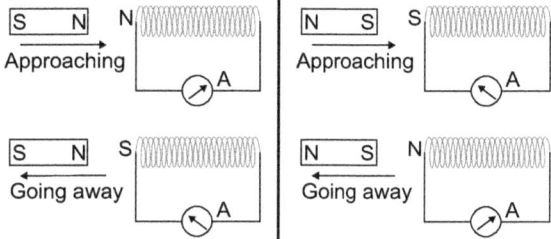

    (i) What is the condition of electromagnetic induction?
    (a) There must be relative motion between galvanometer and coil of wire.
    (b) There must be a relative motion between galvanometer and magnet.
    (c) There must be a relative motion between galvanometer and electric motor.
    (d) There must be a relative motion between the coil of wire and a magnet.

    (ii) An induced emf is produced when a magnet is plugged into a coil. The magnitude of induced emf does not depend upon:

(a) The number of turns in the coil.
(b) The speed with which the magnet is moved.
(c) The resistivity of the material of the coil.
(d) The strength of the magnet.

(iii) A bar magnet is pushed steadily into a long solenoid connected to a meter.

Which of the following would affect the magnitude of the deflection of the meter?
(a) How fast the magnet is pushed into the coil.
(b) Direction in which the coil is wound.
(c) End of the solenoid where the magnet enters.
(d) Pole of the magnet which enters the coil first.

(iv) A conducting rod moves across two magnets as shown in the figure and the needle in the galvanometer deflects momentarily. This physical phenomenon is called:

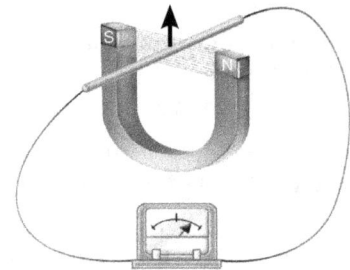

(a) Induced magnetism
(b) Electromagnetism
(c) Static induction
(d) Electromagnetic induction

(v) Magnetic lines of force inside current-carrying solenoid are:
(a) perpendicular to axis.
(b) along the axis and are parallel to each other.
(c) parallel inside the solenoid and circular at the ends.
(d) circular.

Ans. (i) (d) There must be a relative motion between the coil of wire and a magnet.
(ii) (c) The resistivity of the material of the coil
(iii) (a) How fast the magnet is pushed into the coil
(iv) (d) Electromagnetic induction
(v) (b) along the axis and are parallel to each other

75. Read the passage carefully and answer any four questions from Q. 75 (i) to Q. 75 (v).

Hans christian Oersted, one of the leading scientists of the 19th century, play a crucial role in understanding electromagnetism. In 1820, he accidentally discovered that a compass needle got defected when an electric current passed through a metallic wire placed nearby. Through this observation Oersted showed that electricity and magnetic were related phenomenon. This research later created technologies such as radio, television and fibre optics. The unit of magnetic field was named as Oersted in his honour. Electromagnetism is the study of electromagnetic force. It is a type of interface that happens between electrically charged particles. The electromagnetic force generally exhibits electromagnetic fields like magnetic fields, electric fields and light, and is one of the four essential interactions commonly known as forces in nature. The other 3 important interactions are the strong interaction, gravitation and the weak.

(i) Oersted experiment is used to explain which effect of current?
(a) Electric field   (b) Magnetic field
(c) Both (a) and (b)   (d) None of these

(ii) Which instrument helps to detect the presence of magnetic field at a point?
(a) Strong magnet
(b) Solenoid
(c) Compass needle
(d) Current carrying line

(iii) In the diagram below, the direction of magnetic field is:

(a) Clockwise
(b) Anti clockwise
(c) Not any fixed direction
(d) None of these

(iv) On reversing the direction of the current in a wire, the magnetic fixed produced by it:
(a) Gets reversed in direction
(b) Increase in strength
(c) Decreases in strength
(d) Remains unchanged in strength and direction

Ans. (i) (b) Magnetic field

Explanation:

He make to understand that current carrying wire has magnetic field around it.

(ii) (c) Compass needle

Explanation:

Compass needle is a small bar magnet, whose ends are approximately towards the north and south direction.

(iii) (a) Clockwise

Explanation:

It is evaluated by using Right Hand Thum Rule.

(iv) (a) Gets reversed in direction

Explanation:

When direction of current change, then direction of magnetic field produced changes accordingly.

76. Read the passage carefully and answer the following questions from Q. 76 (i) to Q. 76 (v).

A magnet must exert an equal and opposite force on a current-carrying conductor. We know that current is due to the charge in motion. Thus, it is evident that a charge moving in a magnetic field experiences a force. If the direction of motion is perpendicular to the direction of the magnetic field, the magnitude of force experienced depends upon the charge, velocity, and strength of the magnetic field. Fleming's left-hand rule gives the direction of the magnetic force.

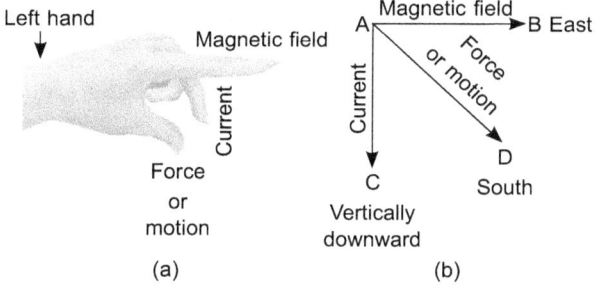

(i) If a charged particle is moving along a magnetic field line, the magnetic force on the particle is:
 (a) along with its velocity.
 (b) opposite to its velocity.
 (c) perpendicular to its velocity.
 (d) zero.

(ii) An electron is travelling horizontally towards the east. A magnetic field in the vertically downward direction will exert a force in:
 (a) East (b) West
 (c) North (d) South

(iii) A uniform magnetic field exists from left to right on a surface. An electron and proton moving in the directions as shown in the figure will experience:

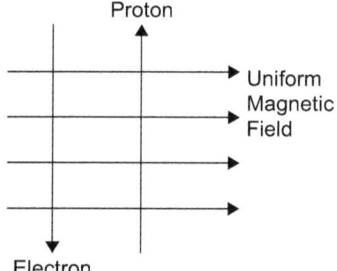

 (a) Forces both pointing into the plane of the surface.
 (b) Forces both pointing out of the plane of the surface.
 (c) The electron will experience into the plane and proton out of the plane.
 (d) The electron will experience opposite to and proton along the direction of the uniform magnetic field.

(iv) Magnetic field exerts no force on:
 (a) a stationary electric charge.
 (b) a magnet.
 (c) an electric charge moving perpendicular to its direction.
 (d) an unmagnetized iron bar.

(v) In Fleming's left-hand rule, the thumb's direction shows the:
 (a) current (b) field
 (c) motion (d) charge

Ans. (i) (d) zero
 (ii) (d) South
 (iii) (a) Forces both pointing into the plane of the surface
 (iv) (a) a stationary electric charge
 (v) (c) motion

77. Read the passage carefully and answer the following questions from Q. 77 (i) to Q. 77 (v).

The space surrounding a magnet in which magnetic force is exerted, is called a magnetic field. The direction of magnetic field lines at a place can be determined by using a compass needle. A compass needle placed near a magnet gets deflected due to the magnetic force exerted by the magnet.

The north end of the needle of the compass indicates the direction of magnetic field at the point where it is placed. When the magnet shown in the diagram below is moving towards the coil, the galvanometer gives a reading to the right.

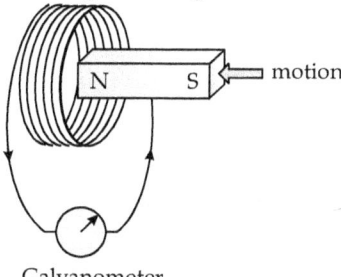

Galvanometer

(i) The direction of induced current is given by:
 (a) Right hand thumb rule
 (b) Fleming's right hand rule
 (c) Fleming's left hand rule
 (d) Maxwell's rule

(ii) What is the condition of electromagnetic induction?
 (a) There must be a relative motion between the coil of wire and galvanometer.
 (b) There must be a relative motion between the galvanometer and a magnet.
 (c) There must be a relative motion between galvanometer and generator.
 (d) There must be a relative motion between the coil of wire and a magnet.

(iii) A student writes a few statements after studying the principles of electromagnetism and working of electric motor:
 (I) Fleming's left hand rule is used to make electromagnet.
 (II) Fleming's left hand rule is used in electric motor.

(III) Fleming's right hand rule is used in electric motor.
(IV) Right hand thumb rule is used in electric motor.

Choose the correct statement(s) from the following:
(a) Only (I) (b) Only (II)
(c) (I) and (III) (d) (II), (III) and (IV)

(iv) When the magnet is moved away from the coil, it is observed that:
(a) the galvanometer needle deflects to the left
(b) the galvanometer needle deflects to the right
(c) the galvanometer needle first deflects to the left and then to the right
(d) the galvanometer needle first deflects to the right and then to the left.

(v) The induced current is highest when:
(a) direction of magnetic field is parallel to the direction of motion of coil.
(b) direction of magnetic field is opposite to the direction of motion of coil.
(c) direction of magnetic field is perpendicular to the direction of motion of coil.
(d) direction of magnetic field is in straight line to the direction of motion of coil.

Ans. (i) (b) Fleming's right hand rule
(ii) (d) There must be a relative motion between the coil of wire and a magnet.
(iii) (b) Only (II)
(iv) (a) the galvanometer needle deflects to the left.
(v) (c) direction of magnetic field is perpendicular to the direction of motion of coil.

Definitions

78. Define magnetism.

Ans. The property by virtue of which a magnet attracts certain metals such as iron, cobalt, nickel etc., is termed as magnetism.

79. What do you mean by 'magnetic field' of a magnet?

Ans. The space or region around a magnet in which the force of attraction or repulsion due to the magnet can be detected is called the magnetic field.

80. State Ampere's swimming rule.

Ans. If a swimmer swims in the direction of current, facing the magnetic needle, then the north pole of the magnetic needle deflects towards his left hand i.e., west and the south pole towards his right hand i.e., east.

81. State Fleming's Left Hand Rule. [NCERT]

Ans. According to this rule, stretch the thumb, forefinger and middle finger of your left hand such that they are mutually perpendicular to each other. If the first finger points in the direction of magnetic field and the second finger in the direction of current, then the thumb will point in the direction of motion or the force acting on the conductor.

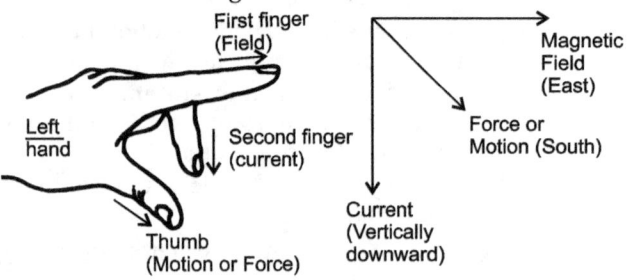

82. What is an electric motor?

Ans. An electric motor is a device which converts the electrical energy into mechanical energy.

83. What is the principle of an electric motor? [NCERT]

Ans. Electric motor works on the principle that 'when a rectangular coil is placed in a magnetic field and current is passed through it, a force acts on the coil which rotates it continuously. Thus, when the coil rotates, the shaft attached to it also rotates converting the electrical energy supplied to the motor to the mechanical energy of rotation.

84. What is a galvanometer?

Ans. A galvanometer is an instrument which can detect the presence of electric current in a circuit.

85. Define electromagnetic induction.

Ans. The production of electricity from magnetism is called electromagnetic induction.

86. What is a permanent magnet? Give one use of it.

Ans. A permanent magnet is a magnet made from steel such that once magnetized, it does not lose it magnetism easily.

87. Define a compass.

Ans. A compass is a device used to show magnetic field direction at a point. It consists of a tiny pivoted magnet usually in the form of a pointer which can turn freely in the horizontal plane.

Very Short Answer Type Questions

88. How is the strength of the magnetic field at a point near a wire related to the strength of the electric current flowing in the wire?

Ans. Strength of magnetic field is directly proportional to the strength of current flowing in the wire.

89. State the conclusion that can be drawn from the observation that a current-carrying wire deflects a magnetic needle placed near it.

Ans. A magnetic field is produced around a current-carrying conductor.

90. Why does a current-carrying conductor experience a force when it is placed in a magnetic field?

Ans. A current-carrying conductor produces a magnetic field around it. This magnetic field interacts with the externally applied magnetic field and as a result the conductor experiences a force.

91. What is the function of a galvanometer in a circuit?

Ans. Galvanometer is a device that detects the presence of current in a circuit. It is also used for measuring the amount of current in the circuit.

92. Why does a current carrying freely suspended solenoid rest along a particular direction? State the direction in which it rests.

Ans. A current carrying solenoid behaves like a bar magnet. It rest in geographic north-south direction.

93. At what place of the magnet are the magnetic field lines closer?*

Ans. Near the poles of the magnet.

94. How is the strength of the magnetic field at a point near a wire related to the strength of the electric current flowing in the wire?*

Ans. Strength of magnetic field is directly proportional to the strength of current flowing in the wire.

95. State the observation made by Oersted on the basis of his experiment with current-carrying conductors?*

Ans. Every current-carrying conductor has a magnetic field around it.

96. What is the shape of a current-carrying conductor whose magnetic field pattern resembles that of a bar magnet?*

Ans. A solenoid

97. Name the two factors that completely define a magnetic field at a point.*

Ans. The strength and the direction of magnetic field at the given point.

98. A stationary charge is placed in a magnetic field. Will it experience a force? Give reason to justify your answer.

Ans. No, a magnetic field exerts a force only on a moving charge.

99. Where will be the value of magnetic field maximum due to current-carrying circular conductor?*

Ans. At the centre of current-carrying circular loop.

100. State the conclusion that can be drawn from the observation that a current-carrying wire deflects a magnetic needle placed near it.*

Ans. A magnetic field is produced around a current-carrying conductor.

101. Why does a current-carrying conductor experience a force when it is placed in a magnetic field?*

Ans. A current-carrying conductor produces a magnetic field around it. This magnetic field interacts with the externally applied magnetic field and as a result the conductor experiences a force.

102. Why steel is not used for making electromagnets?

Ans. The steel does not lose all its magnetism when the current is stopped and becomes a permanent magnet. That's why it is not used for making electromagnets.

103. What happens to the magnetic field lines due to a current-carrying conductor when the current is reversed?*

Ans. The direction of magnetic field (and magnetic field lines) gets reversed on changing the direction of flow of current in a straight conductor.

104. Name five main parts of a D.C. motor.

Ans. An electric motor is a device which converts the electrical energy into mechanical energy.
The five main parts of a D.C. motor are:
(a) Strong field magnet,
(b) Armature coil,
(c) Split ring or commutator,
(d) Carbon brushes, and
(e) Battery.

105. What is the role of a split ring in an electric motor? **[NCERT]**

Ans. In an electric motor, after every half rotation the direction of coil gets reversed due to change in orientation of the magnetic field. To ensure a continuous rotation; a split ring is attached to the coil so that the polarity of the coil changes after every half rotation. This changes the direction of current and thus the armature keeps on rotating continuously.

---
* are board exam questions from previous years

Reasoning Based Questions

106. Why does a compass needle get deflected when brought near a bar magnet? [NCERT]

Ans. When a compass needle is brought near a bar magnet, the compass needle experiences a deflection due to the interaction of magnetic fields of the compass needle and the bar magnet.

107. Why don't two magnetic lines of force intersect each other?

Ans. The tangent drawn at any point on the magnetic field line gives the direction of magnetic field at that point. Hence, if two magnetic field lines would intersect each other, it would result in two tangents at one point which in turn would result in two directions at one point which is impossible. That is why two magnetic field lines never intersect each other.

108. Why does a magnetic needle show a deflection when brought close to a current carrying conductor?

Ans. A current carrying conductor produces a magnetic field around it and the magnetic needle in this magnetic field experiences a torque due to which it deflects to align itself in the direction of magnetic field.

109. Why steel is not used for making electromagnets?

Ans. The steel does not lose all its magnetism when the current is stopped and becomes a permanent magnet. That's why it is not used for making electromagnets

110. Why is soft iron generally used as the core of the electromagnet?

Ans. Soft iron is generally used for making electromagnets because it can easily gain magnetic properties when current is passed around the core and quickly loses when current is stopped.

111. Explain why, an electromagnet is called a temporary magnet?

Ans. An electromagnet is called a temporary magnet because as we keep on passing electric current it will work as magnet, if we stop passing electric current, it will no longer work as magnet.

Short Answer Type Questions

112. Answer the following questions:
(a) What do you mean by 'magnetic field' of a magnet?
(b) What are magnetic field lines? List two characteristic properties of these lines.*

Ans. (a) The space or region around a magnet in which the force of attraction or repulsion due to the magnet can be detected is called the magnetic field.
(b) The lines drawn in a magnetic field along which north magnetic pole moves, are called magnetic field lines.
The characteristic properties of magnetic field lines are :
(i) The magnetic lines originate from north pole and ends at south pole.
(ii) The magnetic lines do not intersect each other.

113. Answer the following questions:
(a) State Ampere's swimming rule.
(b) Name and state the rule to determine the direction of magnetic field produced by a straight wire carrying current.

Ans. (a) If a swimmer swims in the direction of current, facing the magnetic needle, then the north pole of the magnetic needle deflects towards his left hand i.e., west and the south pole towards his right hand i.e., east.
(b) Maxwell's right hand thumb rule is used to determine the direction. According to this rule, when you hold a current carrying conductor in your right hand in such a way that your thumb points in the direction of the current then the direction in which your fingers encircle the conductor will give the direction of magnetic field around it.

114. Answer the following questions:
(a) Name and state the rule to determine the polarity of the two faces of a current carrying circular loop.
(b) State Fleming's Left Hand Rule. [NCERT]

Ans. (a) Clock face rule is used to determine the polarity of the two faces of a current carrying circular loop.
According to this rule, "If the current around the face of circular wire flows in the clockwise direction, then that face of the circular wire will be south pole (S-Pole) and if the current around the face of circular wire flows in the anticlockwise direction, then that face of the circular wire will be north pole (N-Pole)."
(b) According to this rule, stretch the thumb, forefinger and middle finger of your left hand such that they are mutually perpendicular to each other. If the first finger points in the direction of magnetic field and the second finger in the direction of current, then the thumb will point in the direction of motion or the force acting on the conductor.

---
* are board exam questions from previous years

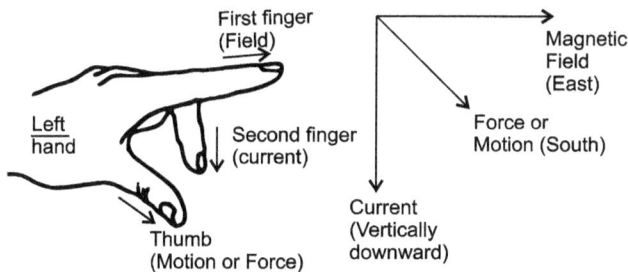

Fig. Fleming's left hand rule

115. Answer the following questions:
(a) What is the principle of an electric motor? **[NCERT]**
(b) What is the role of a split ring in an electric motor? **[NCERT]**
(c) Define magnetism.

Ans. (a) Electric motor works on the principle that 'when a rectangular coil is placed in a magnetic field and current is passed through it, a force acts on the coil which rotates it continuously. Thus, when the coil rotates, the shaft attached to it also rotates converting the electrical energy supplied to the motor to the mechanical energy of rotation.

(b) In an electric motor, after every half rotation the direction of coil gets reversed due to change in orientation of the magnetic field. To ensure a continuous rotation; a split ring is attached to the coil so that the polarity of the coil changes after every half rotation. This changes the direction of current and thus the armature keeps on rotating continuously.

(c) The property by virtue of which a magnet attracts certain metals such as iron, cobalt, nickel etc., is termed as magnetism.

116. State the rule to determine the direction of a :
(a) Magnetic field produced around a straight current carrying conductor.
(b) Force experienced by a current-carrying straight conductor placed in a magnetic field which is perpendicular to it.
(c) Current induced in a coil due to its rotation in a magnetic field.

Ans. (a) Right hand thumb rule or Maxwell's Corkscrew rule.
(b) Fleming's left hand rule.
(c) Fleming's right hand rule.

117. Answer the following questions:
(a) What do you mean by Overloading?
(b) Define an electromagnet.
(c) What is a galvanometer?

Ans. (a) Overloading is the process of overheating of a wire due to excess current drawn by all the appliances than the permitted limit for that wire.

(b) An electromagnet is a magnet consisting of a long coil of insulated copper wire wrapped around a soft iron core that is magnetized only when electric current is passed through the coil.

(c) A galvanometer is an instrument which can detect the presence of electric current in a circuit.

118. Answer the following questions:
(a) Define electromagnetic induction.
(b) What is a permanent magnet? Give one use of it.
(c) Define a compass.

Ans. (a) The production of electricity from magnetism is called electromagnetic induction.

(b) A permanent magnet is a magnet made from steel such that once magnetized, it does not lose its magnetism easily.

(c) A compass is a device used to show magnetic field direction at a point. It consists of a tiny pivoted magnet usually in the form of a pointer which can turn freely in the horizontal plane.

119. State Fleming's right hand rule.

Ans. It states that, "Stretch your right hand in such a way that the first finger, the central finger and the thumb are mutually perpendicular to each other. If the first finger points along the direction of magnetic field and the thumb points along the direction of motion of the conductor, then the direction of induced current is given by the direction of the central finger."

This rule is also called dynamo rule.

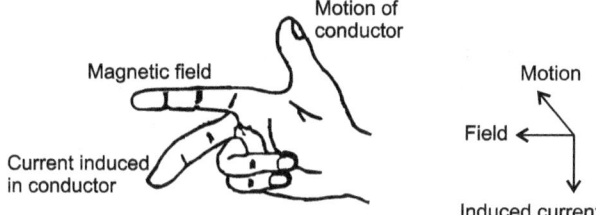

Fig. Fleming's right hand rule.

Differentiate Between

120. State five differences between an electromagnet and a permanent magnet.

Ans.

S. No.	Electromagnet	Permanent Magnet
1.	It is made up of soft iron.	It is made up of steel.
2.	The magnetic field strength can be changed.	The magnetic field strength can not be changed.
3.	The magnetic field can be very strong.	The magnetic field is not so strong.

4.	The polarity of an electromagnet can be reversed.	The polarity of a permanent magnet cannot be reversed.
5.	It can be easily demagnetized by switching off the current.	It cannot be easily demagnetized.

Diagram Based Questions

121. What is a solenoid ? Draw the pattern of magnetic field lines of (i) a current carrying solenoid and (ii) a bar magnet. List two distinguishing features between the two fields.*

Ans. Solenoid is a long cylindrical coil of wire consisting of a large number of turns bound together very tightly.

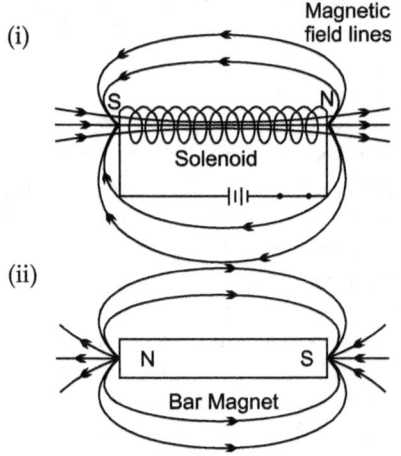

Distinguishing features are as follows :
1. Magnetic field outside the solenoid is negligible as compared to the bar magnet.
2. Magnetic field of solenoid can be varied as per our requirement just by changing current or core of solenoid but in bar magnet it is fixed.

122. In the diagram XY is a straight conductor carrying current in the direction marked by the arrow. The conductor is held vertically by passing it through a horizontal cardboard sheet. Draw three magnetic lines of force on the board and mark the direction of magnetic field in your diagram. State two factors on which magnitude of magnetic field at a point, depends.

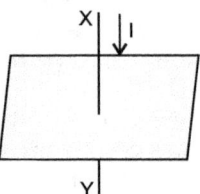

Ans. The magnetic lines of force due to current in the straight conductor XY are shown in figure given alongside. The arrows on the magnetic lines of force show the direction of magnetic field.

The magnitude of magnetic field at a point depends on :
(i) The strength of current in the conductor, and
(ii) The distance of point from the conductor.

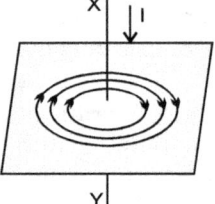

123. Given below are three diagrams showing entry of an electron in a magnetic field. Identify the case in which the force on electron will be maximum and minimum respectively. Give reason for your answer. Find the direction of maximum force acting on electron.*

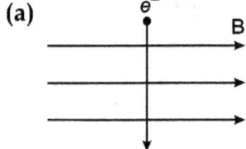 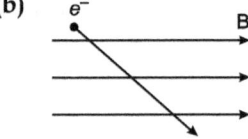 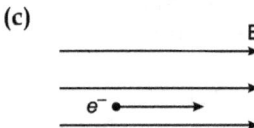

Ans. Force on electron is maximum in fig. (a) because here direction of motion of electron is at right angles to that of magnetic field 'B'. The force is minimum (or zero) in fig. (c) because here electron is moving along the direction of magnetic field B.

The direction of maximum force acting on electron is perpendicular to the plane of paper and directed into it.

124. Sketch the lines of force of the magnetic field of a solenoid. How does its field compare with that of a bar magnet ?

Ans. The magnetic field of a solenoid is very similar to that of a bar magnet. this is shown in figure (a) and (b) respectively, which shows the lines of force of the magnetic field of a current carrying solenoid and a bar magnet.

---
* are board exam questions from previous years

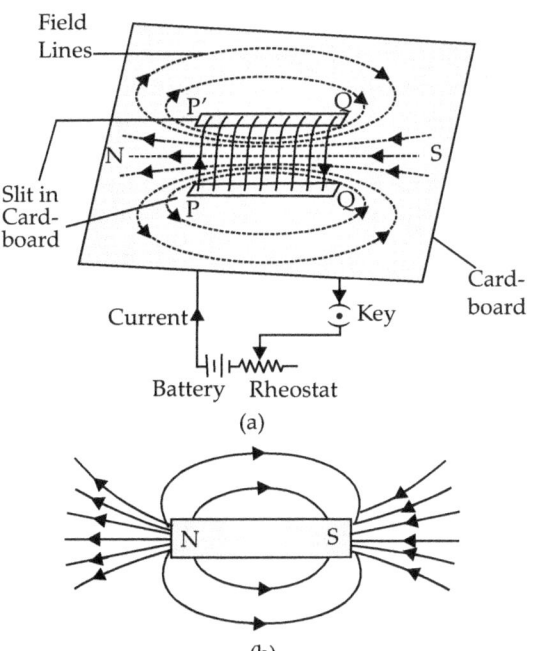

(a)

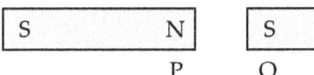

(b)

125. Two magnets are lying side by side as shown below. Draw magnetic field lines between poles P and Q.

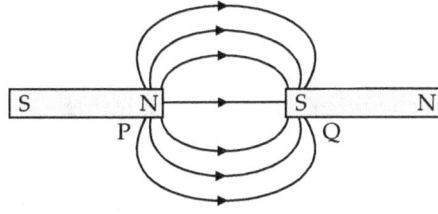

Ans. Magnetic field lines are shown below:

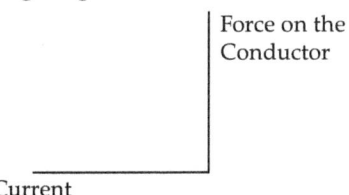

126. State the direction of magnetic field in the following diagram.

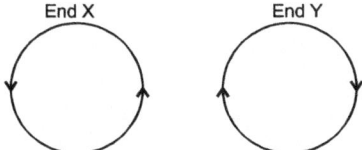

Ans. As per Fleming's left hand rule, the magnetic field is directed out of the paper.

127. The directions of current flowing in the coil of an electromagnet at its two ends X and Y are as shown in given figure.
(a) What is the polarity of end X?
(b) What is the polarity of end Y?
(c) Name the rule which you have used to determine the polarities.

Ans. (a) Since current at end X is anticlockwise, the polarity at that end is North pole.
(b) Current at end Y is clockwise, hence polarity at that end is South pole.
(c) Clock-face rule is used to determine the polarities of the two faces of a current carrying circular loop.

128. AB is a current carrying conductor in the plane of the paper as shown in figure. What are the directions of magnetic fields produced by it at points P and Q? Given $r_1 > r_2$, where will the strength of the magnetic field be larger?

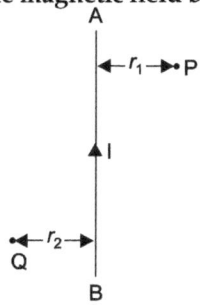

Ans. Since the direction of the current in the current carrying conductor AB is upwards, the direction of the magnetic field would be anti-clockwise as deduced by applying right hand thumb rule. Consequently, the magnetic field at point P would be towards the plane and, at point Q, the direction of the magnetic field would be away from the plane. Since the strength of the magnetic field is inversely proportional to the distance (r), the field at P would be weaker as compared to Q [$\because r_1 > r_2$].

129. Two coils A and B are placed close to each other. If the current in coil A is changed, will some current be induced in the coil B? Given reason. [NCERT]

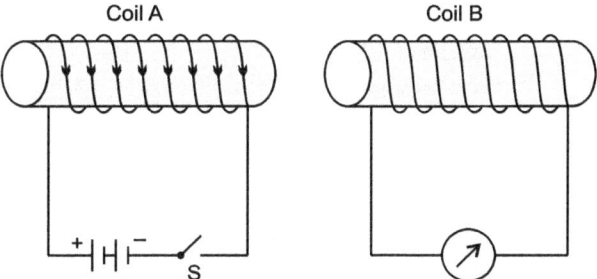

Ans. When we switch on current in coil A, it becomes an electromagnet and produces a magnetic field around coil B. So, an induced current flows in coil B for a moment. When the current in coil A becomes steady, its magnetic field also becomes steady and the current in coil B stops.

When we switch off the current in coil A, then the magnetic field in coil B stops quickly and in this case an induced current flows in coil B in the opposite direction.

130. The diagram shows a current carrying coil passing through a cardboard sheet. Draw three magnetic lines of force on the board. State two factors on which magnitude of magnetic field at the centre depends.

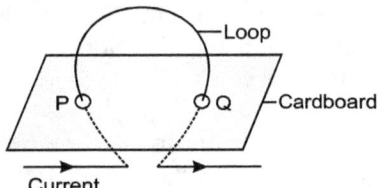

Ans. Figure shows the magnetic lines of force due to current carrying coil.

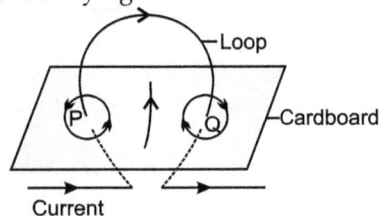

The magnitude of magnetic field at the centre of coil depends on : (a) the strength of current in the coil, and (b) the number of turns in the coil.

131. **Answer the following question:**
   (a) A straight wire conductor passes vertically through a piece of cardboard sprinkled with iron filings. Copy the diagram and show the setting of iron filings when a current is passed through the wire in the upward direction and the cardboard is tapped gently. Draw arrows to represent the direction of the magnetic field lines.
   (b) Name the law which helped you to find the direction of the magnetic field lines.

Ans. (a)

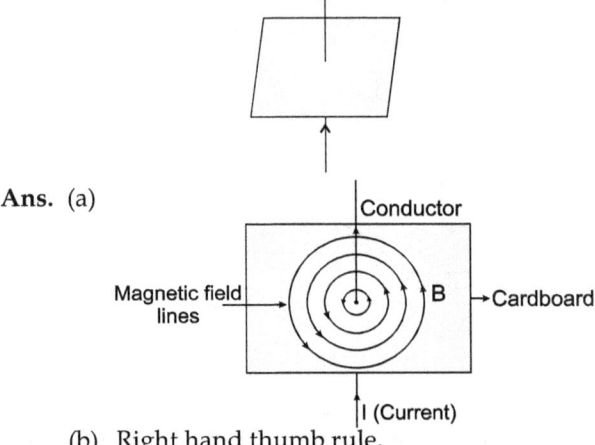

   (b) Right hand thumb rule.

Analysis and Evaluation Based Questions

132. **Answer the following question:**
   (a) What type of magnetic field is produced due to a straight current carrying conductor?
   (b) The magnetic field lines produced by a straight solenoid resemble the magnetic field lines produced by another object. Identify that object.

Ans. (a) Magnetic field lines are concentric circular loops in a plane perpendicular to the straight conductor. The centres of the circular lines lie on the conductor.
   (b) The magnetic field produced due to a straight solenoid is similar to that produced by a bar magnet.

133. **Why does it become more difficult to move a magnet towards a coil when the number of turns in a coil have been increased?**

Ans. It becomes more difficult to move a magnet towards a coil when the number of turns in the coil is increased because the induced current in the coil due to electromagnetic induction increases and the induced current opposes the motion of the magnet towards the coil.

134. **When is the force experienced by a current-carrying conductor placed in a magnetic field largest?**

[NCERT]

Ans. The force experienced by a current-carrying conductor placed in a magnetic field is largest when the current-carrying conductor is placed perpendicular to the direction of magnetic field.

135. **State the condition in each case of the magnitude of force on a current carrying conductor placed in a magnetic field to be (a) zero and (b) maximum.**

Ans. (a) The magnitude of force acting on a current carrying conductor placed in a magnetic field will be zero, when the current carrying conductor is in the direction of magnetic field.
   (b) The magnitude of force acting on a current carrying conductor placed in a magnetic field will be maximum, when the current carrying conductor is normal (perpendicular) to the magnetic field.

136. **When an iron bar is placed inside a solenoid carrying current, it becomes a magnet as long as current flows through the solenoid. Such a magnet is known as electromagnet. In fact, the magnetic field inside the solenoid magnetises the soft iron bar placed in it, which acts as an electromagnet.**
   (a) What type of core is used to make an electromagnet?
   (b) State two ways by which the strength of an electromagnet can be increased.
   (c) State one use of electromagnet.
   (d) Basically electromagnet is a :
      (i) Magnet   (ii) Solenoid
      (iii) Wire   (iv) Coil

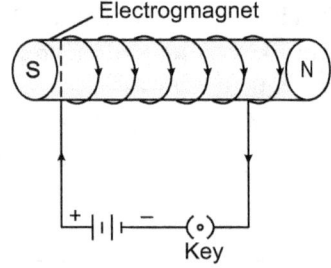

Ans. (a) Soft iron core.
   (b) 1. By increasing the number of turns in the winding on the soft iron core.
       2. By increasing the strength of the current through the winding.
   (c) Electromagnet are used to lift heavy iron pieces.
   (d) (ii) Solenoid

137. How will you decide whether the magnetic field at a point is due to some current carrying conductor or due to earth?

Ans. Place a compass needle at the given point. If it stays in the north-south direction, then the magnetic field is due to earth. If the needle points along any direction other than north-south direction, then the field is due to some current carrying conductor.

138. A metallic wire loop is suspended freely and a bar magnet is brought near it as shown in the diagram. What will be the direction of induced current in the wire loop when the magnet is moved towards it?

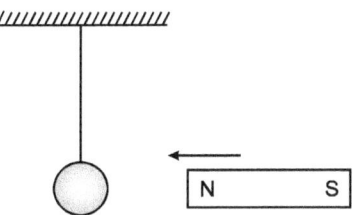

Ans. Anticlockwise from the side of a magnet. As when magnet is brought near it the magnetic flux increases so the induced current will flow in the direction so as to oppose the current. So, current will be anticlockwise.

139. The wire in the figure below is being moved downwards through the magnetic field, so as to produce induced current.
What would be the effect of:
(a) moving the wire at a higher speed?
(b) moving the wire upwards rather than downwards?
(c) using a stronger magnet?
(d) holding the wire still in the magnetic field?

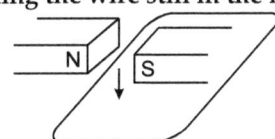

Ans. (a) The induced current increases at a higher speed.
   (b) The induced current is reversed.
   (c) The induced current increases.
   (d) The induced current is zero.

140. Draw the pattern of magnetic field lines produced around a current carrying straight conductor passing perpendicularly through a horizontal cardboard. State and apply right-hand thumb rule to mark the direction of the field lines. How will the strength of the magnetic field change when the point where magnetic field is to be determined is moved away from the straight conductor? Give reason to justify your answer.*

* are board exam questions from previous years

Ans. Maxwell's Right Hand Thumb rule states that if current carrying wire is imagined to be held in the right hand so that thumb points in the direction of current, then the direction in which fingers encircle the wire will give the direction of magnetic field lines around the wire. If we hold the current carrying straight wire so that thumbs in upward direction points the direction of current, the direction of magnetic field lines will be anticlockwise. The strength of magnetic field is inversely proportional to the distance of the point of observation from the wire. So, as we move away from the wire the strength of magnet decreases.

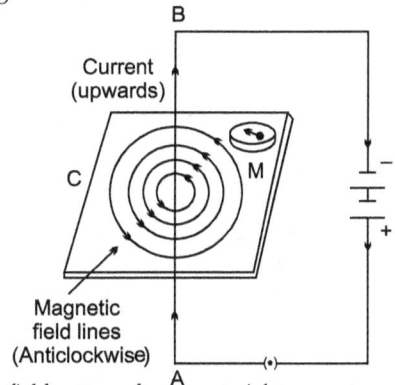

Magnetic field pattern due to a straight current-carrying wire

141. Imagine that you are setting in a chamber with your back to one wall. An electron beam, moving horizontally from back wall towards the front wall, is deflected by a strong magnetic field to your right side. What is the direction of magnetic field?

Ans. As the electron beam moves from back wall towards the front wall, it implies that the current is travelling from front to back wall. Deflection towards right side indicate the direction of the force. Thus by using Fleming's left hand rule, the direction of the magnetic field would be from of the room towards the floor, *i.e.*, from top to bottom or downwards.

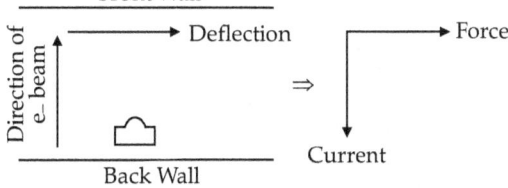

142. Which way does the wire carrying current in the given figure tend to move?

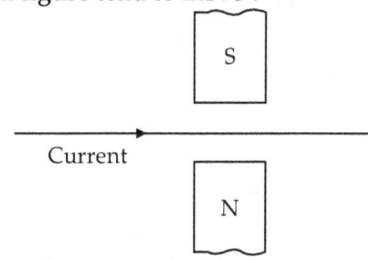

Ans. Applying Fleming's left hand rule, the wire carrying current tends to move upwards (out of the page).

143. A wire is placed between N and S poles of a magnet as shown in figure. If current flows in the wire as

194 | CBSE Chapterwise Objective + Subjective – X

shown, in which direction does the wire tend to move?

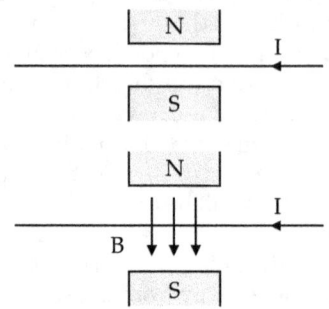

Ans. The direction of magnetic field is from N-pole to S-pole; on applying Fleming's left-hand rule, the wire tends to move perpendicular to plane of paper upward.

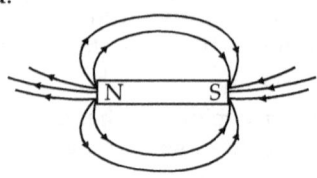

Practical Based Questions

144. A student wound an insulated copper wire around a soft iron rod. He then connected one end to the rheostat and the other free end to the battery via a key. He closed the key and observes the deflection in the magnetic needle placed nearby. Now he altered the current using by reversing the connections of the battery and again noted the change in the deflection of the needle.
(a) Why do the student perform this activity?
(b) What did the student observe?
(c) Comment on the statement "a material in the middle of a current carrying coil gets magnetised".

Ans. (a) The student conducted this activity to make an electromagnet.
(b) The electrical current flowing through a coil will create a uniform magnetic field. This magnetic field causes the needle to turn. Reversing, the connections to the battery, reverses the direction of the current flow and the needle will point in the opposite direction.
(c) When an iron rod is placed along the axis of a current carrying coil, it gets magnetised under the influence of the magnetic field produced by the coil through induction. But this magnetism lasts as long as the current supply is not withdrawn.

145. Answer the following question:
(a) A coil of insulated wire is connected to a galvanometer. What would be seen if a bar magnet with its south pole towards one face of the coil is :*
(i) moved quickly towards it
(ii) moved quickly away from it
(iii) placed near its one face?
These activities are then repeated with north pole of the magnet. What will be the observations?
(b) Name and define the phenomenon involved in above activities.
(c) Name the rule which can determine the direction of current in each case.

Ans. (a) A coil of insulated wire is connected to a galvanometer and if a bar magnet with its south pole towards one face of the coil is

(i) Moved quickly towards it, the galvanometer is deflected towards the left.
(ii) Moved quickly away from it, the galvanometer is deflected towards the right.
(iii) If the magnet is held stationary inside the coil, the deflection of the galvanometer is zero as no change in flux.

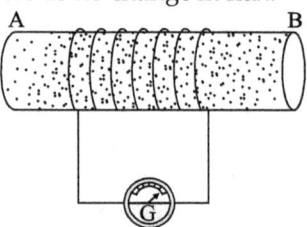

If this activity is repeated with north pole of the magnet :
(i) If the magnet is pushed into the coil, the galvanometer is deflected towards the right.
(ii) If the magnet is withdrawn from the coil, the galvanometer is deflected towards the left.
(iii) If the magnet is held stationary inside the coil, the deflection of the galvanometer is zero.

(b) The phenomenon involved in this activity is electromagnetic induction. The production of electric current by moving a magnet inside a fixed coil of wire is called electromagnetic induction.

(c) The direction of induced current is determined by 'Fleming's right hand rule'.

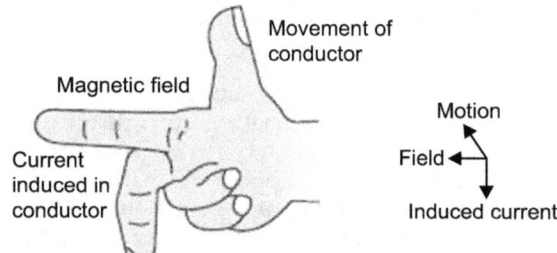

146. Consider a circular loop of wire lying in the plane of the table. Let the current pass through the loop clock-wise. Apply the right hand rule to find out

*are board exam questions from previous years

the direction of the magnetic field inside and outside the loop. **[NCERT]**

Ans. Since, the current is flowing clockwise through a circular loop. The direction of magnetic field around the conductor can be found by using the right hand thumb rule. As the figure shows, the magnetic field would be towards the plane of the paper when it is inside the loop. On the other hand, the magnetic field would be away from the paper when it is outside the loop.

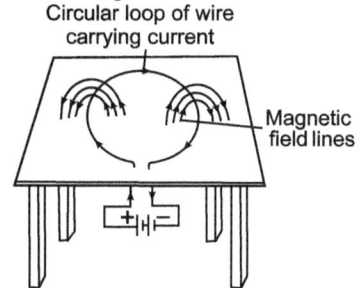

147. A coil of insulated copper wire is connected to a galvanometer. What will happen if a bar magnet is :
    (a) pushed into the coil ?
    (b) held stationary inside the coil ?
    (c) withdrawn from the coil ? **[NCERT]**

Ans. (a) When a bar magnet is pushed into the coil, a momentary deflection is observed in the galvanometer.
(b) When the bar magnet is held stationary inside the coil, there is no deflection in the galvanometer.
(c) When the bar magnet is withdrawn from the coil, the deflection in the galvanometer is in the opposite direction.

Creating Based Questions

148. **Using the following informations form a pathway that defines the working of the electric motor. And also include informations that are not mentioned below to complete it.**
    Battery, Horse-shoe magnet, vertical position, Commutator, rectangle coil, Magnetic force, horizontal position.

Ans. Rectangle coil is placed between horse-shoe magnet ⟶ **Coil is connected to the battery** through brush and commutator ⟶ The **current flow through the coil which is placed between magnetic field** ⟶ **Rectangle coil rotates** from the horizontal position ⟶ The **current stops flowing when the coil attains vertical position** because the brush and the commutator ring will not be in connection ⟶ Though the coil keeps **rotating because of the momentum** from the earlier rotation ⟶ Now the coil attains horizontal position ⟶ Coil again starts to rotate ⟶ With the help of **Fleming's left-hand rule**, the direction of the rotation of the coil is determined.

149. **Using the following informations form an instruction to draw magnetic lines. And also include informations that are not mentioned below to complete it.**
    Magnetic compass, repel, board, Bar magnet, Needle, attract, Merge, Emerge.

Ans. Place a board ⟶ Place a bar magnet in the **middle** ⟶ Mark the boundary of the bar magnet ⟶ Place the magnetic compass near the **North Pole of the bar magnet** ⟶ **North side of the needle points away from the north side of the magnet** ⟶ Same poles repel each other ⟶ different poles attract each other ⟶ Now place the **pin in the direction the needle points** ⟶ Move the compass to **new position where south pole points** the previous position of the north pole ⟶ Repeat the procedure ⟶ Magnetic lines emerge at north pole ⟶ Magnetic lines merge at south pole ⟶ This forms **concentric magnetic lines around bar magnet.**

150. **What would be the inference made by Prashant about the magnetic strength when current passed through a circular coil produces a magnetic field ?**

Ans. Magnetic field lines form in concentric circles around a cylindrical current-carrying conductor, such as a length of wire. The strength of the magnetic field at the centre of a circular coil carrying current is inversely proportional to the radius of the circular coil *i.e.*, the field strength reduces as the radius of the coil increases.

151. **Selena measures the magnetic field produced by an infinitely long wire, a rectangular loop, a solenoid of finite length, a circular loop where all the four carries the same amount of current. After her experiment, she tends to notice that the magnetic field produced by certain cases is similar to the magnetic field produced by the bar magnet. Find out the cases in which both the magnetic fields are equal ?**

Ans. Solenoid is the only thing which is tightly-packed and wound in terms of close loops. If current is passed inside a solenoid which is of finite length, the closely packed loops inside it produce a magnetic field which resembles the magnetic field of a bar magnet. Other than this, the circular or rectangular loop doesn't produce much magnetic field as that of a bar magnet.

152. **Blair wants to measure magnetic field. Suggest her a better instrument which would measure magnetic field approximately.**

Ans. Blair can use Flux meter to measure the magnetic field since it can be used to predict the flux amount produced in the permanent magnet due to its low controlling torque and its heavy electromagnetic damping. It is better than a ballistic galvanometer since it has high torque and its accuracy is less.

153. Using the following informations form an instruction to draw magnetic lines. And also include informations that are not mentioned below to complete it.

Magnetic compass, repel, board, Bar magnet, Needle, attract, Merge, Emerge.

Ans. Place a board ⟶ Place a bar magnet in the **middle** ⟶ Mark the boundary of the bar magnet ⟶ Place the magnetic compass near the **North Pole of the bar magnet** ⟶ **North side of the needle points away from the north side of the magnet** ⟶ Same poles repel each other ⟶ different poles attract each other ⟶ Now place the **pin in the direction the needle points** ⟶ Move the compass to **new position where south pole points the previous position of the north pole** ⟶ Repeat the procedure ⟶ Magnetic lines emerge at north pole ⟶ Magnetic lines merge at south pole ⟶ This forms **concentric magnetic lines around bar magnet**.

154. What would be the inference made by Prashant about the magnetic strength when current passed through a circular coil produces a magnetic field?

Ans. Magnetic field lines form in concentric circles around a cylindrical current-carrying conductor, such as a length of wire. The strength of the magnetic field at the centre of a circular coil carrying current is inversely proportional to the radius of the circular coil i.e., the field strength reduces as the radius of the coil increases.

155. Read the passage carefully and answer any four questions from Q.155(i) to Q.155(v).

The magnetic field lines of an infinite wire are circular and centered at the wire and they are identical in every plane perpendicular to the wire as shown in the figure.

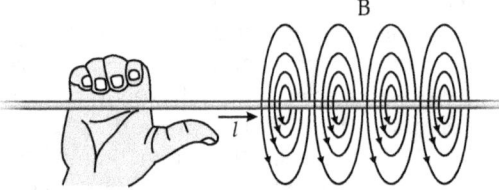

Since the field decreases with distance from the wire, the spacing of the field lines must increase correspondingly with distance. The direction of this magnetic field may be found with a second form of the right-hand rule. If you hold the wire with your right hand so that your thumb points along the current, then your fingers wrap around the wire in the same sense as $\vec{B}$.

(i) A vertical wire carries an electric current out of the page. What is the direction of the magnetic field at point P located to the west from the wire?

N

W •P ⊙I E

S

(a) North (b) South
(c) East   (d) Down

(ii) A student writes the following statements on the characteristics of magnetic field lines:
(I) The magnetic field lines are imaginary lines.
(II) The magnetic field lines has only magnitude.
(III) The magnetic field lines are closed curves.
(IV) The magnetic field lines emerge from the south pole of a magnet.

Choose the correct statement(s) from the following:
(a) Only (I)
(b) Both (I) and (II)
(c) Both (I) and (III)
(d) Both (II) and (IV)

(iii) A current carrying conductor is held in exactly vertical direction. In order to produce a clockwise magnetic field around the conductor, the current should be passed in the conductor:
(a) from top to bottom
(b) from left to right
(c) from bottom to top
(d) from right to left

(iv) A student plotted the variation of magnetic field around a straight current carrying wire and the distance from the wire where the magnetic field is measured. Study the graph below and answer the question that follows:

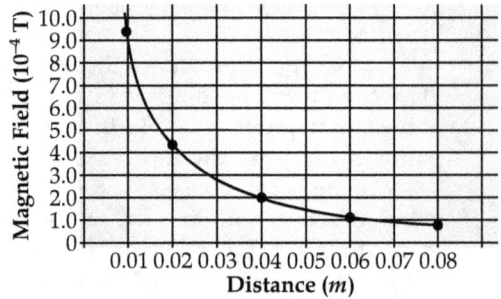

The magnetic field around a current carrying straight wire:

(a) increases linearly with increase in distance.

(b) decreases with increase in distance.

(c) remains constant.

(d) magnetic field at a point does not depend on distance.

(v) A positive charge is moving towards a person. The direction of magnetic field lines will be in:

(a) clockwise direction

(b) anticlockwise direction

(c) vertically upward direction

(d) vertically downward direction

Ans. (i) (b) South

(ii) (c) Both (I) and (III)

(iii) (a) from top to bottom

(iv) (b) decreases with increase in distance

(v) (b) anticlockwise direction

156. Using the following informations form a pathway to determine the direction of the motor in an electric motor. And also include informations that are not mentioned below to complete it.

Motion of the conductor, Direction of current, three fingers, Magnetic field, Index finger, motion of the conductor.

Ans. Three fingers ⟶ **In left-hand** ⟶ Index finger ⟶ Middle finger ⟶ Thumb ⟶ **At right angle** ⟶ **Middle finger represents** the direction of the current ⟶ **Index finger represents** the direction of the magnetic field ⟶ **Thumb represents** the direction of the motion of the conductor ⟶ Used to define the direction of the motion of the conductor in electric motor ⟶ Also known as motor rule.

157. Using the following informations form a pathway that defines the working of the electric motor. And also include informations that are not mentioned below to complete it.

Battery, Horse-shoe magnet, vertical position, Commutator, rectangle coil, Magnetic force, horizontal position.

Ans. Rectangle coil is placed between horse-shoe magnet ⟶ **Coil is connected to the battery** through brush and commutator ⟶ **The current flows through the coil which is placed between magnetic field** ⟶ **Rectangle coil rotates** from the horizontal position ⟶ **The current stops flowing when the coil attains vertical position** because the brush and the commutator ring will not be in connection ⟶ Though the coil keeps **rotating because of the momentum** from the earlier rotation ⟶ Now the coil attains horizontal position ⟶ Coil again starts to rotate ⟶ With the help of **Fleming's left-hand rule**, the direction of the rotation of the coil is determined.

158. Using the following informations form a pathway to determine the direction of the motor in an electric motor. And also include informations that are not mentioned below to complete it.

Motion of the conductor, Direction of current, Three fingers, Magnetic field, Index finger, motion of the conductor.

Ans. Three fingers ⟶ **In left-hand** ⟶ Index finger ⟶ Middle finger ⟶ Thumb ⟶ **At right angle** ⟶ **Middle finger represents** the direction of the current ⟶ **Index finger represents** the direction of the magnetic field ⟶ **Thumb represents** the direction of the motion of the conductor ⟶ Used to define the direction of the motion of the conductor in electric motor ⟶ Also known as **motor rule**.

159. For experimenting purpose, Ram made two electromagnets by wrapping a few turns of wire on one nail and doubled the number of turns of wire for the other nail and let the same amount of electric current passed through it. From his inference, which one tends to have larger magnetic strength ?

Ans. The number of turns of the wire wrapped over the two iron nails is in the ratio of 2 : 1. Electromagnetic strength has a direct relationship with the number of turns wrapped over it. The strength of electromagnet increases with increase in a number of turns of the wire wrapped over the nail and the current passing through them. Hence, the one with more number of turns tends to have more magnetic strength.

160. Suggest a method by which Simran could determine the direction of the magnetic field in a generator.

Ans. Fleming's right-hand rule is generally used for determining the direction of the current, magnetic field and the motion of the conductor in a generator. Here, one can determine the directions by placing the thumb, forefinger and the middle finger of the right-hand perpendicular to each other. The thumb represents the motion of the conductor, the forefinger and the middle finger represent the direction of the magnetic field and the induced current respectively.

Miscellaneous Questions

161. Draw the pattern of magnetic field lines around a current carrying straight conductor. How does the strength of the magnetic field produce change :*
(a) with the distance from the conductor?
(b) with an increase in current in a conductor?

Ans. (a) The strength of a magnetic field is inversely proportional to the square of the distance from the conductor i.e., strength of an electric field decreases with increase in distance.
(b) The strength of the magnetic field is directly proportional to the current passing in the wire i.e., strength of the magnetic field increases with the increase in current.

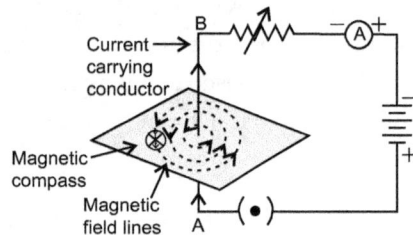

162. The magnetic field in a given region is uniform. Draw a diagram to represent it.

Ans.

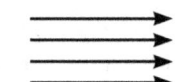

163. How will the direction of force be changed, if the current is reversed in the conductor placed in a magnetic field?

Ans. The direction of the force will be reversed.

164. Write the factors on which the strength of magnetic field produced by a current carrying solenoid depends?

Ans. The strength of magnetic field produced by a current carrying solenoid depends on:
1. The number of turns in the solenoid: Larger the number of turns in the solenoid, greater will be the magnetism produced.
2. The strength of current in the solenoid: Larger the current passed through solenoid, stronger will be the magnetism produced.
3. The nature of core material used in making solenoid: The use of soft iron rod as core in a solenoid produces the stronger magnetism.

165. Draw magnetic field lines around a bar magnet.

Ans.

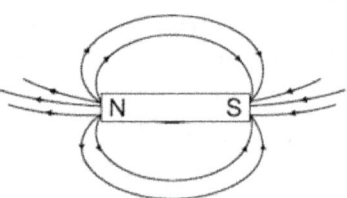

166. List the properties of magnetic lines of force.

Ans. Properties of magnetic field lines:
(a) Magnetic field lines follow the direction from the North Pole to the South Pole.
(b) Magnetic field lines always form closed circular loops.
(c) Magnetic field lines do not cross one another.
(d) Closer the field lines; stronger is the magnetic field and vice-versa.
(e) Magnetic field lines are closer near the poles; which shows greater strength of magnetic field near the poles.

167. Name some devices in which electric motors are used. [NCERT]

Ans. Electric fan, mixer grinder, tape recorder, CD player, hard disk drive, washing machine, cooler, toy car, vacuum cleaner, etc., are some devices in which electric motor is used.

168. List three sources of magnetic fields.

Ans. Three methods of producing magnetic fields are as follows:
(a) By permanent magnet.
(b) By electromagnet
(c) By current carrying conductors.

169. (a) State Fleming's left hand rule.*
(b) Write the principle of working of an electric motor.
(c) Explain the function of following parts of an electric motor:
(a) Armature (ii) Brushes (iii) Split ring.

Ans. (a) According to this rule, stretch the thumb, forefinger and middle finger of your left hand such that they are mutually perpendicular. If the first finger points in the direction of magnetic field and the second finger in the direction of current, then the thumb will point in the direction of motion or the force acting on the conductor.

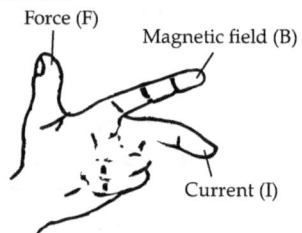

(b) **Principle of electric motor:** When a coil carrying current is placed in a magnetic field, it will experience a force. As a result of this force, the coil begins to rotate.

(c) (i) **Armature:** It creates a magnetic field and the second role is to generate electromotive force.

---
* are board exam questions from previous years

(ii) **Brushes:** Carbon brushes are used to make contract with the rotating rings of the commutator and through them to supply current to the coil.

(iii) **Split ring:** Split rings are used to reverse the direction of current flowing through the coil every time the coil just passes the vertical position during a revolution.

170. **Explain different ways to induce current in a coil.** [NCERT]

Ans. The different ways to induce current in a coil are :
1. By moving the coil in a magnetic field.
2. By changing the magnetic field around the coil.

171. **Complete the following sentences :**
(a) A current carrying solenoid behaves like a ....
(b) A current or a moving charge produces a .... around it.

Ans. (a) bar magnet   (b) magnetic field.

172. **What are the factors affecting the strength of an electromagnet ?**

Ans. Factors affecting the strength of an electromagnet : The strength of an electromagnet depends on :
1. The number of turns in the coil : If we increase the number of turns in the coil, the strength of electromagnet increases.
2. The current flowing in the coil : If the current in the coil is increased, the strength of electromagnet increases.
3. The length of air gap between its poles : If we reduce the length of air gap between the pole of an electromagnet, then its strength increases.

Self-Assessment

173. Answer the following questions:
(a) What are magnetic field lines?
(b) List any two properties of magnetic field lines.
174. Consider a straight conductor passing vertically through a card-board having some iron filings sprinkled on it. A current is passed in the conductor in downward direction and the card-board is gently tapped. Show the setting of iron filings on the card-board and draw arrows to represent the direction of magnetic field lines.
175. A coil of insulated copper wire is connected to a galvanometer. What will happen if the coil is :
(a) pushed towards a bar magnet.
(b) taken away from a bar magnet.
(c) held stationary near a bar magnet.
176. How can you demonstrate that a momentary current?
177. The presence of magnetic field at a point can be detected by means of :
(a) a solenoid
(b) a compass needle
(c) a bar magnet
(d) a current carrying wire

Ans. (b) a compass needle

178. Name and state the rule through which the polarity at the ends of a current carrying solenoid is determined.
179. Which way does the wire carrying current in given figure tend to move ?

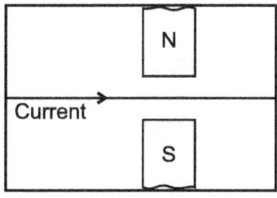

Ans. Downward (into the page)

180. The direction of induced current is obtained by :
(a) Right hand thumb rule
(b) Fleming's left hand rule
(c) Fleming's right hand rule
(d) Clock face rule.

Ans. (c) Fleming's right hand rule

181. State the rule which gives the direction of a magnetic field produced by a straight current carrying conductor.
182. State the rule which determines the direction of induced current in electromagnetic induction.
183. Why is soft iron generally used as the core of an electromagnet ?
184. If you hold a coil of wire next to a magnet, no current, flows in the coil. What else is needed to induce a current ? Explain your answer.
185. **Assertion :** The force experienced by a current carrying conductor placed in a magnetic field is largest when they both are perpendicular to each other.

Reason : According to Fleming's Right Hand Rule, the magnetic field is largest when both forces are perpendicular to each other.
186. State Fleming's left hand rule.
187. Give the principle of electric motor?
188. What is electromagnetic induction?
189. What is induced potential difference and induced current?
190. State Fleming's Right hand rule.
191. Give the difference between Fleming's left and right hand rule.

CHAPTER-15 : OUR ENVIRONMENT

- Environment is everything that is around us which includes both biotic and abiotic components.
- Abiotic components are the non-living components i.e., the physical factors like temperature, light, wind, water, humidity, soil, minerals, etc.
- The biotic components are the living organisms like plants, animals, human beings etc. Both biotic and abiotic components interact with each other to form an environment as a whole.
- An ecosystem includes all living organisms along with the abiotic components which interact with each other to maintain a balance in the nature.
- The term ecosystem was introduced by Tansley in 1935.

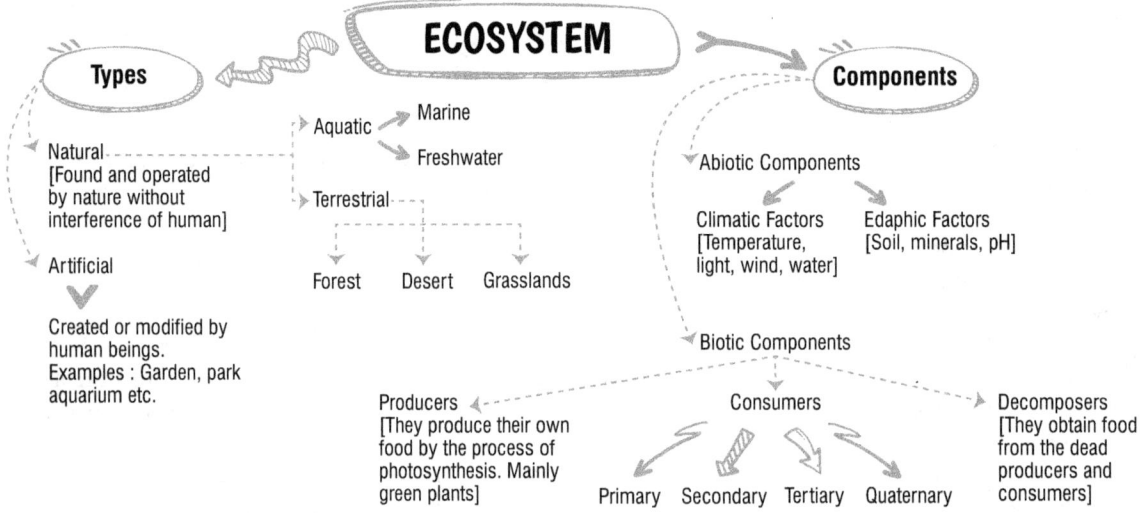

- Producers are mainly autotrophs.
- Consumers cannot prepare their own food. They depend on autotrophs directly or indirectly for food. They are primary consumers [which eat plants or plants products], secondary consumers. [Feed upon primary consumers], tertiary consumers [feed upon secondary consumers], quaternary consumers [feed upon tertiary consumers and are at the top most level of food chain].
- Decomposers like bacteria, fungi etc., feed upon the decay of dead producers and consumers.
- The transfer of food energy from plant sources through a series of organisms in an ecosystem is known as food chain.
- The interlinking sequence starting from an autotroph to herbivores, carnivores and top most level consumers is called a food chain.

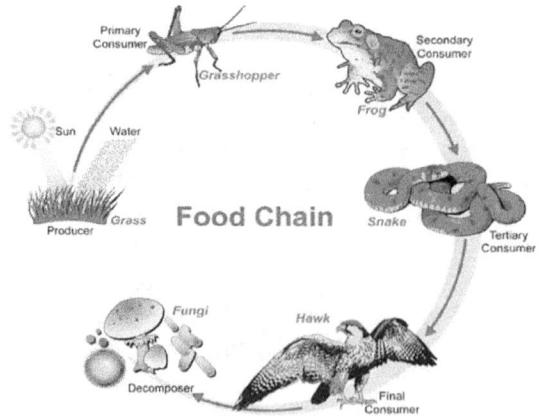

- A food chain shows one path how energy in form of food flows from producers to consumers.
- A food web shows many paths i.e., it is a network of food chains where an organism eat several types of organisms or eaten by many different organisms.

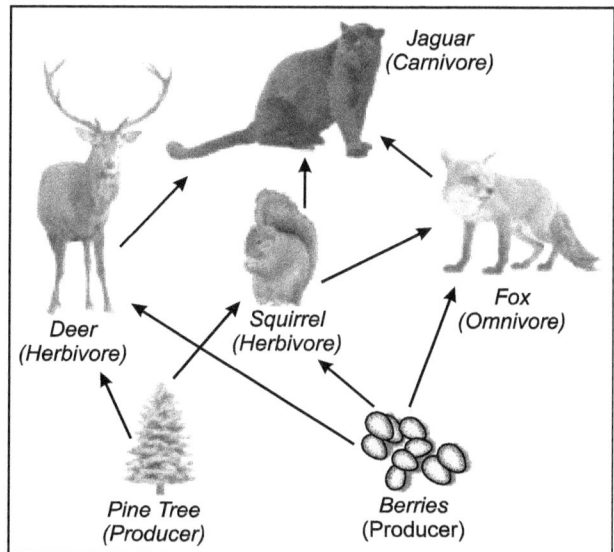

- The distinct sequential steps in the food chain where transfer of energy occurs are referred to as different trophic level, which is represented as under.

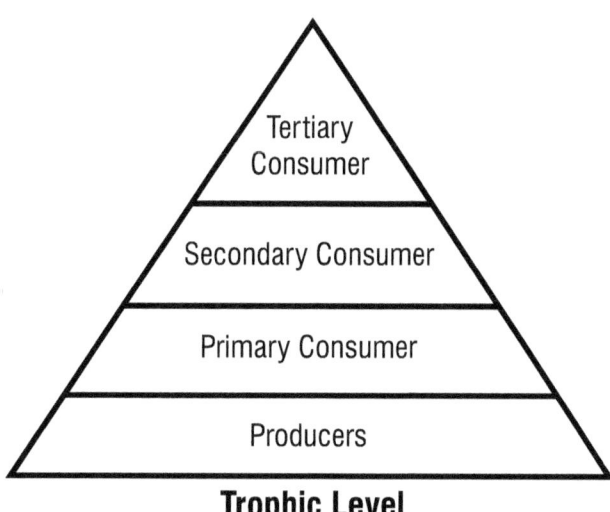

Trophic Level

- Energy flow in an ecosystem is unidirectional i.e., it flows from autotrophs to herbivores to secondary consumers, tertiary consumers in one direction.
- At each trophic level some amount of energy is lost. Lindeman suggested a Ten percent rule which states that the rate of transfer of energy from one trophic level to the next trophic level is of the order of 10%.
- For example if energy produced by a green plant is 100 calories only 10 calories is available to herbivores then 1 calorie to secondary consumers and very less energy i.e., 0.1 calorie to tertiary consumers. So at each trophic level the energy goes on decreasing hence a food chain or food web consists of 3-4 levels or maximum 5.
- Biomagnification is the process which involves the progressive increase in the concentration of toxic or harmful substances at different trophic levels. So the organisms that are at the top of food chain have accumulated a maximum concentration of harmful chemicals in their body. Example : Accumulation of pesticides like DDT.

ENVIRONMENTAL DEPLETION

Types of wastes

Biodegradable waste
[They can be degraded into simpler forms by the action of microbes like bacteria, fungi]
Examples : Sewage, household garbage, paper.

Non-biodegradable waste
[They cannot be degrated into simpler forms by the action of microbes]
Examples : Plastics, metals, DDT, glass.

Effects on our environment

Greenhouse effect
[Due to increase in concentration of greenhouse gases the temperature of earth is gradually increasing leading to greenhouse effect]

Global warming is a consequence of greenhouse effect.

Ozone layer depletion
[Due to use of CFCs the layer of ozone present in stratosphere is gradually depleting leading to serious consequences]

Modes of waste disposal

[Landfills, incineration, recycling of wastes, preparation of compost, production of biogas and manure are some methods.]

- Ozone layer prevents the harmful UV rays of sun from entering to the earth's surface.
- CFCs which is the main cause of depletion of ozone layer is found mainly in aerosol sprayers, refrigerators, air-conditioners etc.
- The depleting ozone layer has many harmful consequences like it causes cancer, causes genetic variations due to mutation, damages our eyes, decline of photosynthesis rate in plants.
- The first ozone hole was discovered over Antarctica.

CHAPTER-16 : SUSTAINABLE MANAGEMENT OF NATURAL RESOURCES

- Natural resources comprises of those substances or materials that exist in nature which are being exploited for supporting life and meeting the needs of human beings.

NATURAL RESOURCES

Classification

- Renewable resources [They can be used repeatedly and can be replenished naturally. Examples : Wind energy, solar energy, tidal energy etc.]

- Non-renewable resources [These resources once exhausted cannot be replenished. Examples : Fossil fuels like coal, petroleum etc.]

Need to Manage Natural Resources

- Natural resources are limited and increased rate of population demands more exploitation of these resources.

- For the use of our future generations.

- Over exploitation of natural resources leads to damage of the environment.

- Everyone should get equal benefits by using these resources.

Conservation of Natural Resources

Natural resources to be conserved for sustainable development

5 R's to save our environment

- Reduce [Less use]
  Examples : (i) Switching off lights, fans, computers, TV, when not in use.
  (ii) Closing water taps when not in use while brushing or shaving.
  (iii) Using public transport rather than personal ones to save fuels.

- Reuse [Use things again and again]
  Examples : (i) We can give our old clothes, toys, books, etc., to poor and needy people.
  (ii) We can repair our mobiles, music players, TV, etc., instead of throwing and buying new ones.

- Recycle [Some wastes can be recycled to produce new ones.]
  Examples : (i) Old newspaper can be recycled.
  (ii) Plastics, metals, etc., can be recycled to make new things.

- Refuse [Say no to the things of no need]
  Examples : (i) Refuse single use plastics, like disposable coffee cups, utensils and straws.
  (ii) Looking into reusable alternatives.

- Repurpose [To recover]
  Examples : (i) Waste plastic bottle can be used to make boat.
  (ii) Waste oils that cannot be refined or in vehicles can be burnt for energy recovery.
  (iii) Recovering the energy from waste oil reduces our dependence on coal and imported oil.

- In 1731, **Amrita Devi Bishnoi** sacrificed her life for protection of "**Khejri trees**" in *Khejrali village* near Jodhpur in Rajasthan.
- Recovery of sal forests of Arabari by the involvement of local people by West Bengal Forest Department.

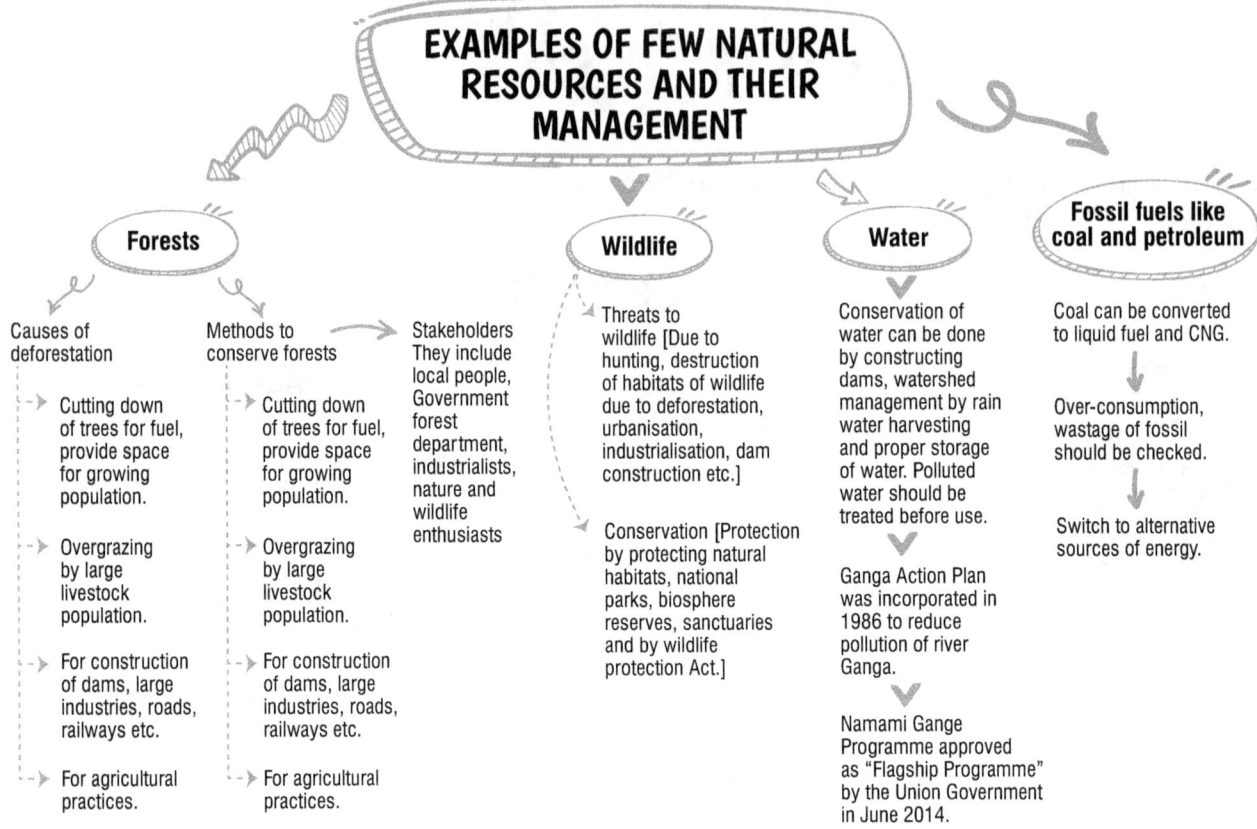

- Various traditional techniques of rain water harvesting like Kuls, Khadins etc., were practiced in different parts of our country.
- Watershed management is concerned with scientific soil and water conservation to increase production of biomass.
- Watershed management increases crop production, reduces the chance of droughts and floods, enhances the life of downstream dam and reservoirs.
- Some aspects of Ganga Action Plan are treatment of effluents before letting them into water bodies, setting of effluent treatment plants by industries, non-disposal of dead bodies into water, construction of community toilets, checking quality of river water from time to time in terms of BOD, coliform count, TDS and pH.
- 'Namami Gange Programme', is an Integrated Conservation Mission, approved as "Flagship Programme" by the Union Government in June 2014 with budget outlay of 20,000 Crore to accomplish the twin objectives of effective abatement of pollution, conservation and rejuvenation of the National River Ganga. Namami Gange is being implemented by the National Mission for Clean Ganga (NMCG), and its state counterparts—State Programme Management Groups. NMCG would establish field offices wherever necessary. The National Mission for Clean Ganga is the implementation wing set up in October, 2016.

Our Environment

Chapter 15

Definitions

1. **Ecosystem:** It is the structural and functional unit of biosphere which comprises of both biotic and abiotic components that interact with each other to form a stable and self-supporting system.
2. **Natural ecosystem:** The ecosystems which operate themselves in nature without any interference of human beings are called natural ecosystems.
3. **Artificial ecosystem:** The ecosystem which is maintained by human beings like croplands, aquarium etc. is called artificial ecosystem.
4. **Abiotic components:** The non-living physio-chemical factors like soil, humidity, sunlight, rainfall, temperature etc. are the abiotic components.
5. **Biotic components:** The living organisms like autotrophs, heterotrophs forms the biotic components.
6. **Food chain:** The sequential interlinking of organisms involving transfer of food energy starting with a producer through a series of organisms where one is eaten by the other is called a food chain.
7. **Trophic levels:** The distinct sequential steps in the food chain where transfer of energy occurs are referred to as trophic levels.
8. **Food web:** A network of food chains which are interconnected at various trophic levels to form a number of feeding connections among different organisms is called a food web.
9. **Biodegradable wastes:** The wastes which get degraded in a natural process by the action of microbes into simpler forms are called biodegradable wastes. Example, food waste, human waste, paper waste, manure, sewage etc.
10. **Non-biodegradable wastes:** The wastes which cannot be degraded by the action of microbes in a natural way and they persist in environment for a longer period of time are called non-biodegradable wastes. Examples, Glass, metal, batteries, plastic bottles, tetra packs.

Multiple Choice Questions

11. **The % of solar radiation absorbed by all the green plants for the process of photosynthesis is about:** [NCERT Exemplar]
    (a) 1%   (b) 5%
    (c) 8%   (d) 10%

    Ans. (a) 1%
    Explanation:
    For the process of photosynthesis, green plants capture roughly 1% of the energy of sunlight that falls on their leaves. This energy is converted into chemical energy, which is then used to make food.

12. **Which of the following statements is incorrect?**
    (a) All green plants and blue green algae are producers.
    (b) Green plants get their food from organic compounds.
    (c) Producers prepare their own food from inorganic compounds.
    (d) Plants convert solar energy into chemical energy.

    Ans. (b) Green plants get their food from organic compounds.
    Explanation:
    Green plants and algae are both producers which means that they can make their own food with the help of inorganic substances and sun energy, through the process of photosynthesis.

13. **At which trophic level is maximum energy available in the figure given below for the various tropic levels in a food chain?**

    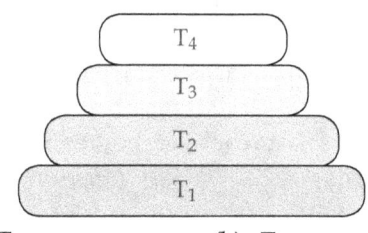

    (a) T_4 (b) T_2
    (c) T_1 (d) T_3

Ans. (c) T_1

Explanation :

All ecosystems are characterised by a unidirectional flow of energy. At each trophic level, most of the energy available is utilised for respiration and excretion and only ten percent of the available energy is passed on to the next level because only ten percent of the available energy can be passed on to the next trophic level, higher trophic levels have substantially less energy content and the number of trophic levels in a food chain is limited. The lower the trophic level higher will be energy content. Hence, the greatest amount of energy is expected to be in trophic level T1.

14. **What will happen if deer is missing in the food chain given below ?** [NCERT Exemplar]
    Grass → Deer → Tiger
    (a) The population of tiger increases.
    (b) Tiger will start eating grass.
    (c) The population of grass decreases.
    (d) The population of tiger decreases and the population of grass increases.

Ans. (d) The population of tiger decreases and the population of grass increases.

Explanation :

The tiger is a secondary consumer which eats deer. If the deer is missing, there will be no food for the tiger. So if deer are missing, the population of grass will increase.

15. **Flow of energy in an ecosystem is always:** [NCERT Exemplar]
    (a) unidirectional (b) bidirectional
    (c) multidirectional (d) no specific direction

Ans. (a) unidirectional

Explanation :

The energy flow in an ecosystem is always unidirectional. Energy coming from the sun in most natural ecosystems, is used by producers, and then passed on to subsequent trophic levels in the form of food. Energy never flows in the reverse direction, it always get transferred from the prey to the predator.

16. **Food chain does not comprise of which of the following groups of organisms?**
    (i) Grass, lion, rabbit, wolf
    (ii) Plankton, man, fish, grasshopper
    (iii) Wolf, grass, snake, tiger
    (iv) Frog, snake, eagle, grass, grasshopper
    (a) (i), (iii) (b) (iii), (iv)
    (c) (ii), (iii) (d) (i), (iv)

Ans. (c) (ii), (iii)

Explanation :

The flow of energy from one organism to another taking part at various biotic levels forms a food chain. A food chain describes the feeding relationships between the organisms within that ecosystem. Food chain (ii) is an aquatic food chain so grasshopper cannot be a part of it. In food chain (iii), wolf, snake and tiger all are carnivores. There is no herbivore to eat grass or herbivore is missing from the chain.

17. **In an ecosystem, the 10% of energy available for transfer from one trophic level to the next is in the form of :*** [NCERT Exemplar]
    (a) heat energy (b) light energy
    (c) mechanical energy (d) chemical energy

Ans. (d) chemical energy

Explanation :

The sun is the ultimate source of energy in an ecosystem, and green plants capture it and convert it to chemical energy, which is then stored in the form of carbohydrates. This chemical energy, in the form of food, is transmitted down the food chain in the ecosystem from one trophic level to the next following 10 per cent law according to which only 10% of the chemical energy is transferred from one trophic level to subsequent higher trophic level.

18. **Excessive exposure of humans to UV rays results in :** [NCERT Exemplar]
    (i) damage to immune system
    (ii) damage to lungs
    (iii) skin cancer
    (iv) peptic ulcers
    (a) (i), (ii) (b) (ii), (iv)
    (c) (i), (iii) (d) (iii), (iv)

Ans. (c) (i), (iii)

Explanation :

UV rays are extremely hazardous to humans, animals, and even plants. It can cause skin cancer, cataracts in the eyes, and immune system damage by reducing the body's response to infections.

19. **Why do all food chains start with plants?** [CBSE Question Bank]
    (a) Because plants are easily grown.
    (b) Because plants are nutritious.
    (c) Because plants can produce its own energy.
    (d) Because plants do not require energy.

Ans. (c) Because plants can produce its own energy.

Explanation :

A food chain starts with a plant. This is because every food chain needs the presence of organisms that can manufacture their own food. Green plants are called as producers as they can synthesis their

---
* are board exam questions from previous years

own food in the presence of sunlight and therefore, most of the food chains start with plants.

20. **Which of the following limits the number of trophic levels in a food chain?**
   [NCERT Exemplar]
   (a) Decrease in energy at higher trophic levels
   (b) Deficient food supply
   (c) Polluted air
   (d) Water

Ans. (a) Decrease in energy at higher trophic levels

Explanation:

A considerable amount of energy is used to keep organisms alive at each trophic level. As an organism progresses through the trophic levels, it receives less and less energy. The number of trophic levels is restricted to 3-4 since the energy available for the next level is insufficient to keep the organisms alive after that.

21. **Which of the following constitute a food chain?**
   (a) Grass, wheat and mango
   (b) Grass, goat and human
   (c) Goat, cow and elephant
   (d) Grass, fish and goat

Ans. (b) Grass, goat and human

Explanation:

A food chain is a group of creatures that are all dependent on one another for food. Grass is the food chain's primary producer, goats eat grass (herbivores), and humans eat goat (carnivore).

22. **If a grasshopper is eaten by a frog, then the energy transfer will be from:**
   (a) producer to decomposer
   (b) producer to primary consumer
   (c) primary consumer to secondary consumer
   (d) pecondary consumer to primary consumer

Ans. (c) primary consumer to secondary consumer.

Explanation:

If a frog eats a grasshopper, energy is transferred from primary consumer to secondary consumer in a food chain. Grasshoppers eat producers, such as grass and plants. So, it is classified as a primary consumer. As a result, frogs, which eat grasshoppers, become the secondary consumer.

23. **Organisms of a higher trophic level which feed on several types of organisms belonging to a lower tropic level constitute the:** [NCERT Exemplar]
   (a) food web
   (b) ecological pyramid
   (c) ecosystem
   (d) food chain

Ans. (a) food web

Explanation:

A food web is a network of interrelated food chains. In a food chain, a creature can occupy more than one trophic level. It eats a variety of organisms of lower trophic level and may be devoured by organisms of higher trophic level.

24. **In the given food chain, suppose the amount of energy at fourth trophic level is 5 kJ, what will be the energy available at the producer level?**

   Grass → Grasshopper → Frog → Snake → Hawk
   (a) 5 kJ   (b) 50 kJ
   (c) 500 kJ   (d) 5000 kJ

Ans. (d) 5000 kJ

Explanation:

According to the 10 per cent law only 10% of the energy available in a trophic level is passed on to the next trophic level. As a result, if the energy available at the fourth trophic level is 5 kJ, then the energy available at the producer level is 5,000 kJ: 5 → 50 → 500 → 5,000.

25. **The decomposers in an ecosystem:**
   [NCERT Exemplar]
   (a) convert inorganic material to simpler forms.
   (b) convert organic material to inorganic forms.
   (c) convert inorganic materials into organic compounds.
   (d) do not break down organic compounds.

Ans. (b) convert organic material to inorganic forms.

Explanation:

Decomposers in an ecosystem transform organic material into inorganic forms, which are then re-used by plants in the soil. Decomposers eat dead bodies, waste products, and organisms.

26. **In the food web, which two organisms are competing for food?** [CBSE Question Bank]

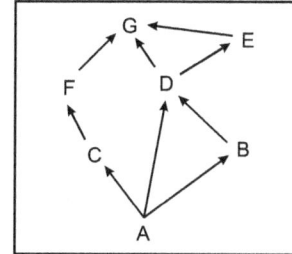

   (a) A and B   (b) A and C
   (c) D and F   (d) B and D

Ans. (d) B and D

Explanation:

When members of various species compete for the same resource in an environment, competition develops. Here, B and D are competing for the same resources or food in this food web.

27. **The _____ is the functional unit of environment.**
   (a) genus   (b) ecosystem
   (c) class   (d) biome

Ans. (b) ecosystem

Explanation :

The ecosystem is the structural and functional unit of the environment through which various biotic and abiotic components interact with one another in relation to their surroundings.

28. _____ are producers.
    (a) Amoeba   (b) Mushrooms
    (c) Sunlight   (d) Green plants

Ans. (d) Green plants

Explanation :

Green plants are producers. They produce their own food, which provides them with the energy they require to grow, reproduce, and survive. They are the only living beings on earth capable of producing their own supply of food energy, which makes them unique.

29. _____ is not an abiotic factor.
    (a) Humidity   (b) Animals
    (c) Temperature   (d) Altitude

Ans. (b) Animals

Explanation :

Both plants and animals are the biotic components of a habitat as they are the species that live there. The abiotic components of the ecosystem are non-living materials like rocks, soil, air, and water.

30. _____ is a herbivore.
    (a) Whales   (b) Eagle
    (c) Bear   (d) Cow

Ans. (d) Cow

Explanation :

An herbivore is a creature that receives its energy only from eating plants or grass. Cows, elk, buffalo are examples of herbivores.

31. _____ are biotic factors.
    (a) Mountains   (b) Rocks
    (c) Grass   (d) All of these

Ans. (c) Grass

Explanation :

Any living component that impacts another organism or shapes the environment is referred to as a biotic component, or biotic factor. Animals, plants, grass, fungus, bacteria, and protists are examples of biotic factors.

32. A _____ is considered a terrestrial ecosystem.
    (a) ocean
    (b) pond
    (c) underground caves
    (d) forest

Ans. (d) forest

Explanation :

A terrestrial ecosystem is a land-based population of species that includes biotic and abiotic interactions in a specific area. Therefore a forest is considered a terrestrial ecosystem.

33. _____ is an omnivore.
    (a) Panther   (b) Bear
    (c) Wolf   (d) Lion

Ans. (b) Bear

Explanation :

An omnivore is an organism that feeds on both plants and animals. Examples of omnivores are dogs, bears, pigs, etc.

34. Ozone has the chemical formula _____.
    (a) O_5 (b) O_4
    (c) O_3 (d) O_2

Ans. (c) O_3

Explanation :

The inorganic molecule ozone, often known as trioxygen, has the chemical formula O_3. It is a pale blue gas with a distinctively pungent odour.

35. Which of the following is an abiotic component of the ecosystem?
    (a) Lichens on a bare rock
    (b) Weathered rock
    (c) Planktons in a pond
    (d) Sea-weed

Ans. (b) Weathered rock

Explanation :

Weathered rock is an abiotic or non-living component of the ecosystem.

36. The depletion of ozone layer is caused by
    (a) carbon dioxide and methane
    (b) burning of fossil fuels
    (c) sulphur dioxide and cabon monoxide
    (d) chlorofluorocarbons and other halons

Ans. (d) chlorofluorocarbons and other halons

Explanation :

Use of chlorofluorocarbons and other halons causes ozone depletion.

37. Which of the following occupies the first trophic level in the food chain they form together?
    (a) Apple tree   (b) Honey bee
    (c) Grasshopper   (d) Mouse

Ans. (a) Apple tree

Explanation :

Producers occupy the first trophic level in a food chain, which in this case is the apple tree.

38. Cutting of forests for growing crops would
(a) reduce the stability of the ecosystem
(b) enhance the stability of the ecosystem
(c) not affect the stability of the ecosystem
(d) first increase and then decrease the stability of the ecosystem

Ans. (a) reduce the stability of the ecosystem

Explanation :
Cutting a large number of trees would affect all the other organisms dependent on those plants. Many organisms would even die. Some would migrate to other places. All such events would disturb the ecological balance and thus would decrease the stability of the ecosystem.

39. The amount of energy that is passed from one trophic level to the next is _____.
(a) 1%   (b) 10%
(c) 11%   (d) 1.1 %

Ans. (b) 10%

Explanation :
Only 10% of the energy is passed from one trophic level to the next.

40. Ozone prevents the entry of
(a) UV radiations from the sun
(b) IR radiations
(c) all solar radiations
(d) all radiations with the large wavelength

Ans. (a) UV radiations from the sun

Explanation :
Ozone prevents the UV radiations from reaching the earth.

41. Which of the following is NOT a type of natural ecosystem?
(a) Sea   (b) Crop field
(c) Lakes and ponds   (d) Estuaries

Ans. (b) Crop field

Explanation :
A crop field is made by humans. Hence, it is not a type of natural ecosystem.

42. In an area, the frog population decreased due to the spread of some diseases. Frogs are prey for snakes, but no major effect was seen in the population of snakes. Instead, there was a decline in the pesticide sale. What could be the possible reason?
(a) Frogs stopped eating grains due to their infection.
(b) There is no relation between the decrease in frog population and pesticide sales.
(c) Both frog and snake migrated to some other are.
(d) Snakes now depended on other organisms that must be the pests for the crops grown.

Ans. (d) Snakes now depended on other organisms that must be the pests for the crops grown.

Explanation :
Given scenario is an example of a food we(b) Infection in frogs could have possibly made snakes shift towards another prey such as rats. Rats destroy the stocked grains. When snakes started eating rats, the sale of pesticides against rats decrease(d)

43. Supriya listed some important points for energy transfer in a food chain. She made an error. Point out that error.
(i) Primary consumers transfer 10% of energy to the next trophic level in the food chain.
(ii) The population at a lower trophic level is greater than the population at a higher trophic level.
(iii) Producers depend entirely on sunlight to make food
(iv) Decomposers work at a double pace to convert complex molecules into simpler forms in case of an epidemi(c)
(a) Only (ii)   (b) Only (iv)
(c) (i) and (iii) (d) All of the above

Ans. (b) Only (iv)

Explanation :
The populations at a lower trophic are greater in number than the populations at higher trophic level to fulfil the energy demand of the latter. The population of decomposers might vary but not the pace.

44. Which of the following gets the minimum amount of energy through the food chain in an ecosystem?
(a) Herbivore   (b) Carnivore
(c) Producer   (d) Large carnivore

Ans. (d) Large carnivore

Explanation :
When the energy is transferred in an ecosystem, only 10% of the energy is passed to the next trophic level. Therefore, the large carnivore, being at the highest level, receives the minimum energy.

45. The population at each trophic level is less than the previous one. How does this phenomenon help?
(i) It maintains a balance in the energy demand and supply.
(ii) Organisms at lower trophic levels are more complex and organise(d)
(iii) Organisms at higher trophic levels are less complex, and hence, this decreases the population of lower trophic levels.
(iv) Organisms at higher trophic levels have lesser energy demands than the ones at lower levels.

(a) Only (i) (b) Only (ii)
(c) Only (iv) (d) (i), (ii) and (iii)

Ans. (a) Only (i)

Explanation :
A higher population at lower trophic levels and lower populations at higher trophic levels maintains a balance in demand and supply of energy and organic matter in the ecosystem.

46. **UV rays are harmful to the life on earth. However, they play an important role in the upper atmosphere. Which of the following statements holds for this fact?**
    (i) UV rays are needed for the formation of the ozone layer in the upper atmosphere.
    (ii) UV rays are less active and inside the atmosphere, they become activated due to the other atmospheric contents.
    (iii) In the upper atmosphere, UV rays have less energy and are not harmful and form the part of the atmosphere.
    (a) Only (i) (b) Only (ii)
    (c) Only (iii) (d) Both (i) and (iii)

Ans. (a) Only (i)

Explanation :
In the upper atmosphere, high energy UV rays are required for the formation of the ozone layer. Ozone prevents the entry of UV rays into the earth's atmosphere.

47. **Which of the statements given below is correct?**
    (a) Omnivores are in the middle of the food chain.
    (b) Omnivores are either in the middle or at the top of the food chain.
    (c) Omnivores are at the top of the food chain.
    (d) Omnivores are capable of modifying the natural food chain.

Ans. (b) Omnivores are either in the middle or at the top of the food chain.

Explanation :
Omnivores can consume plants (producers) as well as animals (consumers). They can be at the middle just after plants or at the top of the food chain.

48. **In an ecosystem, if a species of secondary consumers is affected by a deadly disease, this will affect the ecosystem by _____.**
    (a) giving more opportunity of survival to the prey of the secondary consumer
    (b) giving more opportunity of survival to the predators of the secondary consumer
    (c) disturbing the food chain of which the secondary consumer is a part
    (d) decreasing the population of the producers

Ans. (c) disturbing the food chain of which the secondary consumer is a part

Explanation :
Change in the population of the organism at any trophic level can distress the whole food chain in the ecosystem. This can be detrimental to the balance of energy transfer in the ecosystem.

49. **In an ecosystem, the matter is recyclable because of**
    (a) decomposition activity of decomposers
    (b) the sun, which is an ultimate source of energy
    (c) the fact that matter is made up of atoms
    (d) None of these

Ans. (a) decomposition activity of decomposers

Explanation :
Decomposers convert the complex organic molecules into simpler ones and make them available for other organisms.

50. **All the organisms are not capable of utilising the sun's energy directly for meeting their energy requirements. This gap is filled by**
    (i) all green plants
    (ii) some species of bacteria
    (iii) algae
    (iv) all bacterial species and plant species
    (a) (ii) and (iv) (b) (i) and (iii)
    (c) (i), (ii) and (iii) (d) Only (i)

Ans. (b) (i) and (iii)

Explanation :
All green plants, some species of bacteria and green algae are capable of converting sunlight into a useful form by the process of photosynthesis.

51. **Despite the presence of an adequate amount of decomposers, a lot of waste is accumulating in the ecosystem because**
    (a) decomposers keep mutating
    (b) there is a high amount of non-biodegradable wastes being generated in that ecosystem
    (c) decomposers are unable to survive in this ecosystem
    (d) the rate at which waste is generated is higher than the rate of decomposition

Ans. (b) there is a high amount of non-biodegradable wastes being generated in that ecosystem

Explanation :
Generation of a large amount of non-biodegradable wastes can lead to their accumulation in the ecosystem.

52. **Identify A, B and C in the given food chain.**
    Sunlight → A → B → C → Large fish
    (a) A: Phytoplanktons; B: Zooplanktons; C: Small fish
    (b) A: Zooplanktons; B: Phytoplanktons; C: Small fish

(c) A: Zooplanktons; B: Small fish; C: Phytoplanktons

(d) A: Phytoplanktons; B: Small fish; C: Zooplanktons

Ans. (b) A: Phytoplanktons; B: Zooplanktons; C: Small fish

Explanation :

The correct sequence of the food chain is: Sunlight → Producers (phytoplanktons) → Herbivores (zooplanktons) → Carnivores (small fish) →Top Carnivores (Large Fish)

53. **Lakes and ponds do not require cleaning but an aquarium does because**
    (a) an aquarium is an artificial and an incomplete ecosystem
    (b) lakes and ponds are natural and incomplete ecosystems
    (c) an aquarium possesses a pool of decomposers
    (d) lakes do not possess any deomposers and thus BOD always remain low

Ans. (b) lakes and ponds are natural and incomplete ecosystems

Explanation :

Lakes and ponds do not require cleaning but an aquarium does because an aquarium is an artificial ecosystem. It is incomplete and lacks natural decomposers.

54. **If UNEP had not passed any regulation to control the CFC levels, then what could have been the possible consequences after a few years?**
    (a) Increase in CFC levels and thus increase in global warming.
    (b) Major amount of UV radiations reaching the earth, therefore, multifold increase in problems like cancer.
    (c) Increase in natural calamities like Tsunamis and cyclones.
    (d) Lowering of the temperature of the earth.

Ans. (b) Major amount of UV radiations reaching the earth, therefore, multifold increase in problems like cancer.

Explanation :

If UNEP has not controlled the CFC levels, then after 20 years there would have been major destruction of the ozone layer due to an increase in CFC levels in the environment.

55. **Which of the following sets represents the substances required for the formation of ozone?**
    (a) Oxygen andIR radiations
    (b) Oxygen and UV radiations
    (c) Oxygen and radiations of longer wavelengths
    (d) Carbon dioxide, water vapour and UV radiations

Ans. (b) Oxygen and UV radiations

Explanation :

Ozone is formed by the action of UV radiations on the oxygen atoms in the upper layers of the atmosphere.

56. **The most important trophic level in a terrestrial food chain is**
    (a) the one with the highest energy requirement per individual
    (b) the one withthe least energy requirement per individual
    (c) the one with moderate energy requirement per individual
    (d) not dependent on the energy requirement per individual, thus, all are equally important

Ans. (b) not dependent on the energy requirement per individual, thus, all are equally important

Explanation :

In any food chain, all the trophic levels are of equal importance.They maintain ecological balance.

57. **Which food chain is NOT a part of the given food web?**

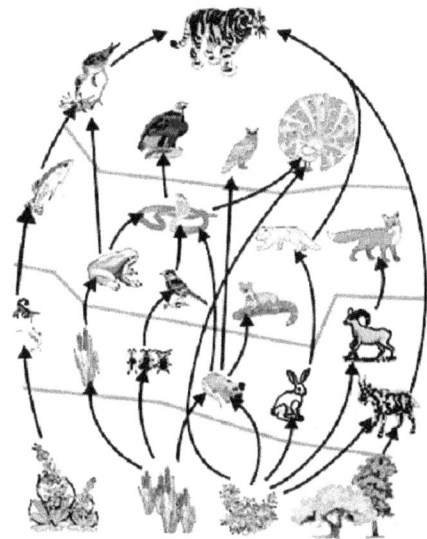

(a) Plants → Frog → Snake → Peacock
(b) Plants → Frog → Snake → Owl
(c) Hydrophytes → Crabs → Fish → Hawk → Tiger
(d) Both A and B

Ans. (b) Plants → Frog → Snake → Owl

Explanation :

The given image shows a food web in the ecosystem. A food web is formed when the different food chains are interconnected in the ecosystem. Food chain comprising Plants → Frog → Snake → Owl is not the part of this food we(b)

58. Which of the following options complete the statement given below?

Ozone is both harmful and beneficial because it is _____.
(a) not poisonous to the ecosystem
(b) poisonous but not for humans
(c) poisonous in very high amounts, and its concentration is very low in the atmosphere
(d) poisonous to humans but it also prevents UV rays from entering into the earth's atmosphere

Ans. (d) poisonous to humans but it also prevents UV rays from entering into the earth's atmosphere

Explanation :
Ozone acts as a blanket around the earth and prevents the UV rays from entering the earth's atmosphere. However, at the surface level, it acts as a pollutant.

59. The accumulation of the heavy metals in birds have caused a decline in their population. This is because
(a) the eggs produced by these birds have very thin and brittle shells
(b) heavy metals damage the eyesight of these birds
(c) heavy metals kill the fish that is the major diet of these birds
(d) heavy metals damage the feathers of these birds

Ans. (a) the eggs produced by these birds have very thin and brittle shells

Explanation :
The accumulation of the heavy metals causes a decline in the population of predatory birds because heavy metals interfere with bird reproduction by bringing about changes like thinning of the egg shells of the birds.

60. Which of the following statements is correct?
(a) All plants and bacteria are producers.
(b) All green plants and certain bacteria are producers.
(c) Only some species of green plants and all bacteria are producers.
(d) Only green plants are producers.

Ans. (b) All green plants and certain bacteria are producers.

Explanation :
All green plants and certain bacteria are producers in an ecosystem.

61. Ozone formation is possible in the upper layers of atmosphere because of the
(a) presence of active molecules of carbon
(b) presence of high energy UV rays
(c) presence of activated oxides of carbon
(d) presence of longer wavelength radiations

Ans. (b) presence of high energy UV rays

Explanation :
The high energy of UV rays help in the formation of ozone from oxygen.

62. Different types of enzymes are present in our body because:
(i) each enzyme has a specific function
(ii) each enzyme has a specific substrate
(iii) it makes the metabolic process faster
(iv) it makes the replacement of the defective enzymes easy
(a) (i) and (ii) (b) (iii) and (iv)
(c) (i) and (iv) (d) All of the above

Ans. (b) (i) and (ii)

Explanation :
Each enzyme has a specific substrate and has a specific function to perform. Each enzyme is a protein and each protein is made by a specific gene.

63. In _____ presence of _____, along with sunlight is required to make organic compounds.
(a) producers; chlorophyll
(b) decomposers; chlorophyll
(c) producers; carbon
(d) consumers; carbon

Ans. (a) producers; chlorophyll

Explanation :
In producers, the presence of chlorophyll, along with sunlight is required to produce glucose.

64. Which of the following statements holds true for the energy flow in an ecosystem?
(a) Energy can never be transferred bidirectionally between producers to consumers.
(b) Energy flows in a unidirectional manner in an ecosystem.
(c) Only 10% of the energy is transferred from one trophoc level to the next trophic level.
(d) All of the above

Ans. (d) All of the above

Explanation :
The flow of energy is always unidirectional. It flows from the sun to the producers and ultimately to the consumers. According to the 10% law, only 10% of the energy is transferred from one trophic level to the next.

65. The maximum number of levels in a food chain can be
(a) 7 – 8 (b) 5 – 6
(c) 3 – 4 (d) 1 – 3

Ans. (c) 3 – 4

Explanation :

At each trophic level, some amount of energy is lost; hence, food chains can have maximum 3-4 trophic levels. After four levels, there is no significant amount of energy left to pass on.

66. Fishes living in a crop field with standing water are the part of a/an _____ ecosystem.
    (a) natural   (b) artificial
    (c) indigenous   (d) None of these

Ans. (b) artificial

Explanation :

Crop fields are man-made ecosystems. If these have standing water as in the case of rice field, they can be used to culture fish. The fish in this water would be the part of an artificial ecosystem.

67. Which of the following would be affected by the decrease in the producer population?
    (a) All the organisms in the ecosystem.
    (b) The organisms in the next trophic level.
    (c) The organisms at the highest trophic level.
    (d) None of the organisms in the food chain will be affecte(d)

Ans. (a) All the organisms in the ecosystem.

Explanation :

A decrease in the population of producers would directly and indirectly affect all the organisms in that ecosystem.

68. Which activity would gradually reduce the occurrence of pests, thereby reducing damage to the crops year by year without affecting the environment?
    (a) Use of nitrogen based fertiliser
    (b) Crop rotation
    (c) Use of DDT
    (d) Use of manure

Ans. (b) Crop rotation

Explanation :

Crop rotation can gradually reduce the occurrence of pests, thereby reducing damage to crops year by year without affecting the environment

69. Fish diet can play significant role in biological magnification of pesticides like DDT because
    (a) harmful chemicals get washed into water bodies and enter the aquatic food chains
    (b) fishes can also produce these chemicals in their bodies
    (c) fishes increase in number rapidly
    (d) fishes have special enzymes in their body to digest these pesticides

Ans. (a) harmful chemicals get washed into water bodies and enter the aquatic food chains

Explanation :

Biological magnification occurs when the harmful chemicals used in the crop fields get washed into water bodies and enter the food chains.

70. Which of the following sets of substances can be used for vermicomposting?
    (a) Glass, sea shells, vegetable and fruit peels
    (b) Shells, vegetable peels, fruit peels and paper
    (c) Plastic cans, newspapers and cooked food
    (d) Styrofoam cups, disposable plates, cooked food and newspapers

Ans. (b) Shells, vegetable peels, fruit peels and paper

Explanation :

Only the degradable waste can be used for vermicomposting. Vermicomposting involves compost formation with the help of worms. Shells, vegetable and fruit peels and paper are some of the ideal substances that can be used in vermicomposting.

71. _____ are the smallest and the most important components of an ecosystem.
    (a) Decomposers   (b) Viruses
    (c) Algae   (d) Phytoplanktons

Ans. (a) Decomposers

Explanation :

Decomposers are the smallest and the important components of an ecosystem. They convert the complex organic molecules into the simpler ones. These simpler molecules then are available for reuse.

72. The direction of energy flow in an ecosystem is
    (a) unidirectional but in any direction
    (b) multidirectional
    (c) unidirectional but from lower trophic level towards the higher trophic level
    (d) bidirectional

Ans. (c) unidirectional but from lower trophic level towards the higher trophic level

Explanation :

Energy flows in a unidirectional manner in an ecosystem from the lower trophic level towards the higher trophic level.

73. Biological magnification is defined as
    (a) the accumulation of harmful chemicals at each trophic level of the food chain.
    (b) the accumulation of organic matter at the first trophic level of the food chain.
    (c) the reduction of energy at each trophic level of the food chain.
    (d) an increase in the population of a species at each trophic level of the food chain.

Ans. (a) the accumulation of harmful chemicals at each trophic level of the food chain.

Explanation :

The accumulation of harmful chemicals at each trophic level is called biological magnification.

74. **Which of the following is an eco-friendly activity?**
    (a) Use of fertilizers
    (b) Use of paper bags
    (c) Use of styrofoam cups
    (d) Use of insecticides and pesticides

Ans. (b) Use of paper bags

Explanation :

Using biodegradable substances instead of non-biodegradable substances is considered to be an eco-friendly activity.

75. **Classify the given activities under reuse and recycle.**
    (i) Using plastic bucket for growing plants
    (ii) Using old newspaper to make paper bags
    (iii) Using broken glass to melt and make a new glass
    (iv) Dissolving paper, bleaching and drying it to form a new paper.
    (a) (i) and (ii) are examples of reuse and (iii) and (iv) are the examples of recycle.
    (b) (ii) and (iii) are the examples of reuse and (i) and (iv) are the examples of recyle.
    (c) (i), (ii) and (iii) are the examples of reuse and (iv) is the example of recycle.
    (d) (i), (ii) and (iii) are the examples of recycle and (iv) is the example of reuse.

Ans. (a) (i) and (ii) are examples of reuse and (iii) and (iv) are the examples of recycle.

Explanation :

Reuse involves using again the same substance for some other purpose. Recycle involves forming a new substance from the old substance to be used for the same or different purpose.

76. **Which agricultural activites are affecting the environment?**
    (a) Overuse of fertlisers and pesticides
    (b) Using groundwater for irrigation
    (c) Extensive cropping in the same area of land
    (d) All of the above

Ans. (d) All of the above

Explanation :

Different agricultural activities are affecting the environment. Fertilisers and pesticides are non-biodegradable. They cause soil and water pollution. Soil loses fertlilty due to extensive cropping and water table is lowering due to the overuse of groundwater for irrigation.

77. **Which set of the organisms belong to the same trophic level?**
    (a) Plants; phytoplanktons
    (b) Rabbit; snake
    (c) Deer; tiger
    (d) Phytoplanktons; zooplanktons

Ans. (a) Plants; phytoplanktons

Explanation :

Plants and phytoplanktons belong to the same trophic level. Both are producers.

78. **Pesticide can disturb the balance within the ecosystem by**
    (a) indiscriminately killing pests and the predators of these pests
    (b) biomagnification
    (c) eutrophication
    (d) bioaccumulation

Ans. (a) indiscriminately killing pests and the predators of these pests

Explanation :

Pesticides can disturb the balance within the ecosystem by indiscriminately killing pests and the predators of these pests.

79. **If the energy at the third trophic level is 5J. What would be energy at the first trophic level?**
    (a) 5000 J   (b) 500J
    (c) 50J   (d) 5 J

Ans. (b) 500J

Explanation :

There is 10% transfer of energy at every trophic level. Therefore, the amount of energy at second trophic level must be 50 J and first trophic level must be 500 J.

80. **Which of the following is the best way for the disposable of kitchen waste?**
    (a) Landfill   (b) Composting
    (c) Incineration   (d) Reusing

Ans. (b) Composting

Explanation :

Kitchen waste contains all the organic waste that can be used in composting and manure formation.

81. **A large number of food chains are interconnected because the organisms at the higher trophic level can depend on different types of organisms at the lower trophic level. The existence of this phenomenon in nature is called**
    (a) food chain
    (b) ecological balance
    (c) ecological pyramid
    (d) food web

Ans. (d) food web

Explanation :

Different food chains interconnect to form food webs.

82. **The amount of energy absorbed by the plants in the form of solar energy is ___% and then ____% of this energy is transferred to the next level.**
    (a) 10%; 10% (b) 1%; 10%
    (c) 10%; 1%   (d) 1%; 1%

Ans. (b) 1%; 10%

Explanation :

Plants absorb only 1% of the solar energy and then 10 % of this 1 % is transferred to the next trophic levels.

83. **Which of the following is the set of greenhouse gases in the atmosphere?**
    (a) Ozone and CFC
    (b) Carbon monoxide and sulphur dioxide
    (c) Carbon dioxide and methane
    (d) Hydrogen sulphide and ozone

Ans. (c) Carbon dioxide and methane

Explanation :

Gases that maintain the temperature of the earth by trapping the solar energy in the earth's atmosphere are called greenhouse gases. Increase in the amount of greenhouse gases in the atmosphere can lead to global warming. Carbon dioxide and methane are the greenhouse gases.

84. **Which of the following occupies the top-most trophic level?**
    (a) Humans   (b) All producers
    (c) All carnivores (d) All omnivores

Ans. (a) Humans

Explanation :

Human beings are most intelligent of all the organisms. Hence, they occupy the top-most trophic level in the ecosyetm.

85. **Which of these is NOT a correct sequence of a food chain?**
    (a) Phytoplanktons → Zooplanktons → Fish
    (b) Seed grains → Rodents → Eagle
    (c) Grass → Insects → Frog → Snake
    (d) Seaweed → Zooplanktons →Phytoplanktons

Ans. (d) Seaweed → Zooplanktons →Phytoplanktons

Explanation :

Phytoplanktons are the primary producers. They should occupy the first trophic level in the aquatic food chain.

86. **The amount of a chemical used in a farmland was in nanograms. But its amount was found to be in milligrams in higher tropical levels. This happened because _____.**
    (a) of biological magnification
    (b) of the existence of the food web
    (c) organisms of lower trophic levels were consumed by the organisms of higher trophic levels
    (d) All of the above

Ans. (d) All of the above

Explanation :

Even if the usage is low, due to biological magnification, harmful chemicals get accumulated at the lower trophic level. These are then consumed by the organisms of higher trophic levels. As food chains are interconnected, the chemicals are also passed on from one organism to another easily. Gradually, the concentration of the chemicals increases at higher trophic levels.

87. **Four students gave 4 different statements about ecosystem. Who is incorrect?**
    Student A: "Energy can be recycled in an ecosystem."
    Student B: "Matter cannot be recycled in an ecosystem."
    Student C: "Energy cannot be recycled but matter can be recycled in an ecosystem."
    Student D: "Neither energy nor matter can be recycled in an ecosystem."
    (a) Both students A and B
    (b) Students A, B and D
    (c) Student C
    (d) Students A and C

Ans. (b) Students A, B and D

Explanation :

In an ecosystem, the sun is the only source of energy. The energy is not recycled, but the organic matter, which passes from one trophic level to the next, is recycled by the action of decomposers.

88. **Which of the following are environment friendly practices ?** [NCERT]
    (a) Carrying cloth bags to put purchases in while shopping.
    (b) Switching off unnecessary lights and fans.
    (c) Walking to school instead of getting your mother to drop you on her scooter.
    (d) All of the above

Ans. (d) All of the above

Explanation :

Being eco-friendly refers to a way of life that is better for the environment. It involves taking little measures towards ensuring that the Earth's environment is properly maintained for current and future generations. Carrying cloth bags to put purchases in while shopping, switching off unnecessary lights and fans, walking to school instead of getting your mother to drop you on her scooter are all examples of environment friendly practices.

89. **Several factories were pouring their wastes in rivers A and B. Water samples were collected from these two rivers. It was observed that sample collected from river A was acidic while that of river B was basic. The factories located near A and B are :***
    (a) Soaps and detergents factories near A and alcohol distillery near B.
    (b) Soaps and detergents factories near B and alcohol distillery near A.
    (c) Lead storage battery manufacturing factories near A and soaps and detergents factories near B.
    (d) Lead storage battery manufacturing factories near B and soaps and detergents factories near A.

Ans. (c) Lead storage battery manufacturing factories near A and soaps and detergents factories near B.

Explanation :

The lead storage batteries uses sulphuric acid which is acidic in nature while soaps and detergents are basic in nature.

90. **Disposable plastic plates should not be used because :** [NCERT Exemplar]
    (a) They are made of materials with light weight.
    (b) They are made of toxic materials.
    (c) They are made of biodegradable materials.
    (d) They are made of non-biodegradable materials.

Ans. (d) They are made of non-biodegradable materials.

Explanation :

There are some substances that cannot be acted upon by decomposers and hence, these item are called as non-biodegradable. Example- plastics, chemicals like DDT, etc. When items like disposable plastic plates are used they persist in the environment because they cannot be degraded and may cause hazardous effects on the other biotic components of the ecosystem. Therefore, usage of disposable plastic should be avoided as they have hazardous effects on the environment.

91. **Refrigerators have led to an environmental imbalance and destroyed ecosystems. How?**
    (a) Refrigerators emit CFCs that are harmful to only plant species.
    (b) Storing food in refrigerators makes them environmentally unhealthy.
    (c) Refrigerators use CFCs that are harmful to the ozone layer which forms a blanket around the earth.
    (d) Refrigerators emit greenhouse gases.

Ans. (c) Refrigerators use CFCs that are harmful to the ozone layer which forms a blanket around the earth.

Explanation :

CFCs are used in refrigerators. They are dangerous for the ozone layer that acts as a blanket around the earth and prevents UV rays from the sun to enter the atmosphere.

92. **Which of the following cannot be called a biodegradable substance?**
    (a) Dead leaves   (b) Cotton balls
    (c) Plastic coverings (d) Food wastes

Ans. (c) Plastic coverings

Explanation :

Plastics cannot be decomposed by the action of decomposers. Hence, the covering made up of plastic cannot be called a biodegradable substance.

93. **Some wastes stay in the environment for a longer duration because**
    (a) they are non-biodegradable materials and decomposers cannot decompose them
    (b) they are biodegradable materials but decomposers do not act on these materials
    (c) these play role in maintaining ecological balance
    (d) these are recyclable

Ans. (a) they are non-biodegradable materials and decomposers cannot decompose them

Explanation :

Some waste materials are non-biodegradable. Decomposers cannot break them into simpler forms. Therefore, these materials stay in the environment for a longer duration.

94. **The government of a country banned the use of plastic bags at various places. Is this step justified? Why?**
    (i) No; because it will not affect the environment in any manner.
    (ii) Yes; because it will reduce the amount of non-biodegradable waste (plastic) in the environment.
    (iii) Yes; because it will reduce the cost of waste management.
    (iv) Yes; because it would be replaced with paper bags which are more economical.
    (a) (i)   (b) (ii) and (iii)
    (c) (iii) and (iv)   (d) (ii), (iii), and (iv)

Ans. (b) (ii) and (iii)

Explanation :

Banning plastic will greatly reduce the amount of non-biodegradable waste in the environment. It will also decrease the amount spent in handling the non-biodegradable waste.

---
* are board exam questions from previous years

95. Which of the following sets contain only non-biodegradable materials?
    (a) Wood, detergent, leather
    (b) Polythene, detergent, paper
    (c) DDT, plastic, bakelite
    (d) Plastic, bakelite, kitchen waste

Ans. (c) DDT, plastic, bakelite

Explanation :

DDT, plastic and bakelite cannot be degraded by the action of decomposers. Hence, they are non-biodegradable.

96. Which of the following wastes is NOT broken down by decomposers?
    (a) Glass   (b) Dead leaves
    (c) Wood   (d) Carcass

Ans. (a) Glass

Explanation :

Decomposers breakdown biodegradable wastes. Hence, dead leaves, wood and carcass can be broken down by decomposers. However, glass and plastic form non-biodegradable waste. It cannot be broken down by the action of decomposers.

97. Which of the following statements is correct?
    (a) It is important to segregate biodegradable and non-biodegradable wastes.
    (b) Non-biodegradable substances cannot be buried in landfills.
    (c) We cannot dispose off non-biodegradable waste.
    (d) We can use the inorganic waste for vermi-composting.

Ans. (a) It is important to segregate biodegradable and non-biodegradable wastes.

Explanation :

It is important to segregate biodegradable and non-biodegradable wastes and treat them separately. Biodegradable waste can be used for composting and non-biodegradable waste can be reused or recycle(d) They can also be buried in landfills in extreme cases.

98. In the following groups of materials, which groups contain only non-biodegradable items ?
    [NCERT Exemplar]
    (i) Wood, paper, leather
    (ii) Polythene, detergent, PVC
    (iii) Plastic, detergent, grass
    (iv) Plastic, bakelite, DDT
    (a) (iii)   (b) (iv)
    (c) (i), (iii)   (d) (ii), (iv)

Ans. (d) (ii), (iv)

Explanation :

Those items which cannot be acted upon by detrivores or decomposers are called as non-biodegradable. As a result, such materials are unable to degrade or decompose. They are, in some ways, an inextricable part of the environment that cannot be removed. Polythene, thermosetting plastics such as Bakelite, insecticides such as DDT, detergent, and PVC are few examples of non-biodegradable items.

99. _____ is a biodegradable substance.
    (a) Polythene   (b) Paper
    (c) Plastic   (d) Glass

Ans. (b) Paper

Explanation :

Biodegradable substances are organic waste materials that can be decomposed biologically into compost or simple organic molecules. Examples are plant products such as wood, paper, food material.

100. _____ is a non-biodegradable substance.
     (a) Human/ animal waste
     (b) Newspaper
     (c) Aluminium
     (d) Plant products

Ans. (c) Aluminium

Explanation :

Non-biodegradable compounds are wastes that do not breakdown naturally in the environment, causing pollution and being detrimental to living things. Chemicals, paints, plastics, rubber, metals such as aluminium, and other materials are some examples.

Assertion and Reasoning Based Questions

101. **Assertion:** The flow of energy is unidirectional.

     Reason: Energy as it progresses through the various trophic levels is no longer available to the previous level.
     (a) If both assertion and reason are true and reason is the correct explanation of assertion.
     (b) If both assertion and reason are true, but reason is not the correct explanation of assertion.
     (c) If assertion is true, but reason is false.
     (d) If assertion is false, but reason is true.

Ans. (a) If both assertion and reason are true and reason is the correct explanation of assertion.

Explanation :

The flow of energy is unidirectional. The energy that is captured by the autotrophs does not revert to the solar input and the energy which passes to the herbivores does not come back to autotrophs. As it moves progressively through the various trophic levels it is no longer available to the previous level. Moreover, the energy available at each trophic level gets diminished progressively due to loss of energy at each level. Thus, both assertion and reason are true and reason is the correct explanation of the assertion.

102. **Assertion:** Energy available at each trophic level gets diminished progressively.

    Reason: Little usable energy remains after four trophic levels.

    (a) If both assertion and reason are true and reason is the correct explanation of assertion.
    (b) If both assertion and reason are true, but reason is not the correct explanation of assertion.
    (c) If assertion is true, but reason is false.
    (d) If assertion is false, but reason is true.

    Ans. (c) If assertion is true, but reason is false.

    Explanation:

    The energy available at each trophic level gets diminished progressively due to loss of energy at each level. The usable energy available at each trophic level gets diministed progressively due to loss of energy at each level.
    Thus, assertion is true but reason is false.

103. **Assertion:** Chemicals and toxins accumulate more and more as we move up the food chain.

    Reason: Anything that gets into biological tissue, that is not normally there, has the potential to accumulate and magnify.

    (a) If both assertion and reason are true and reason is the correct explanation of assertion.
    (b) If both assertion and reason are true, but reason is not the correct explanation of assertion.
    (c) If assertion is true, but reason is false.
    (d) If assertion is false, but reason is true.

    Ans. (a) If both assertion and reason are true and reason is the correct explanation of assertion.

    Explanation:

    Biomagnification is the increase in concentration of toxins up the food chain. Chemicals and toxins accumulate more and more as we move up the food chain, because they do not get broken down in the body. Anything that gets into biological tissue, that is not normally there, has the potential to accumulate and magnify as it moves up the food chain. Thus, both assertion and reason are true and reason is the correct explanation of the assertion.

104. **Assertion:** Green plants of the ecosystem are the transducers.

    Reason: Producers trap the radiant energy of the sun and change it into chemical energy.

    (a) If both assertion and reason are true and reason is the correct explanation of assertion.
    (b) If both assertion and reason are true, but reason is not the correct explanation of assertion.
    (c) If assertion is true, but reason is false.
    (d) If assertion is false, but reason is true.

    Ans. (a) If both assertion and reason are true and reason is the correct explanation of assertion.

    Explanation:

    Green plants of the ecosystem are the transducers because producers trap the radiant energy of the sun and change it into chemical energy. Thus both assertion (A) and the reason are correct and reason is the correct explanation of the assertion.

105. **Assertion:** Arctic's ozone depletion tends to be milder and short lived than the Antarctic's.

    Reason: CFCs, Frigid temperatures and sunlight are not present at the Arctic at the same time.

    (a) If both assertion and reason are true and reason is the correct explanation of assertion.
    (b) If both assertion and reason are true, but reason is not the correct explanation of assertion.
    (c) If assertion is true, but reason is false.
    (d) If assertion is false, but reason is true.

    Ans. (a) If both assertion and reason are true and reason is the correct explanation of assertion.

    Explanation:

    It is necessary to have all three at the same time for ozone layer to deplete. Thus, both assertion and reason are true and reason is the correct explanation of the assertion.

106. **Assertion:** Plastics are non-biodegradable.

    Reason: Enzymes cannot degrade plastics.

    (a) If both assertion and reason are true and reason is the correct explanation of assertion.
    (b) If both assertion and reason are true, but reason is not the correct explanation of assertion.
    (c) If assertion is true, but reason is false.
    (d) If assertion is false, but reason is true.

    Ans. (a) If both assertion and reason are true and reason is the correct explanation of assertion.

    Explanation:

    Substances which cannot be decomposed by the action of microorganisms are known as non-biodegradable substances. Mircroorganisms release enzymes which decompose the materials but these enzymes are specific in their action that is why enzymes cannot decompose all the materials. Thus, both assertion and reason are true and, reason is the correct explanation of the assertion.

Our Environment | 219

Case Based Questions

107. Refer the figure below carefully and answer the following questions.

Energy flow and trophic levels

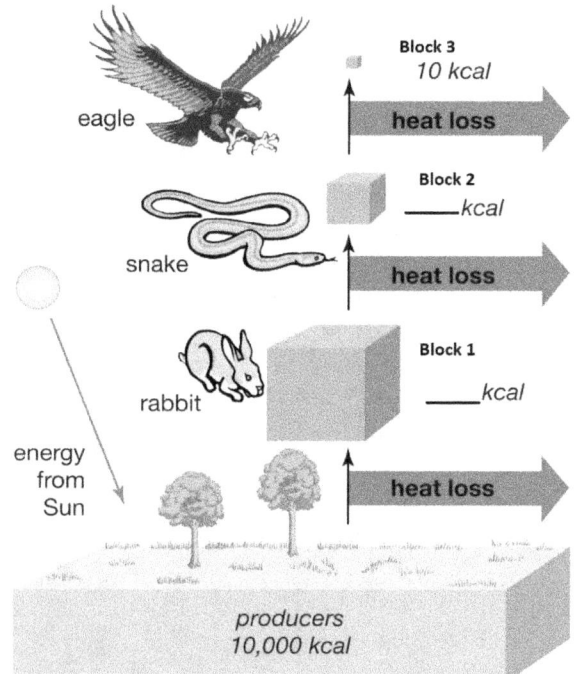

(i) How are the organisms on Block 1 level best described as:
  (a) primary consumers
  (b) secondary consumers
  (c) tertiary consumers
  (d) decomposers

(ii) In the figure given above what would be the amount of energy available at block 1 and block 2 levels if energy at producer level is 10,000 kcal?
  (a) 1000 kcal and 100 kcal
  (b) 100 kcal and 1000 kcal
  (c) 10,000 kcal and 100 kcal
  (d) 100 kcal and 10 kcal

(iii) What is represented by eagle at black 3?
  (a) decomposers
  (b) secondary consumers
  (c) tertiary consumers
  (d) predator

(iv) After solar energy enters our atmosphere, which statement does not hold good regarding subsequent the events?
  (a) Most of the radiation is absorbed by the Earth's surface and used to warm the surface.
  (b) Some of the solar radiation is reflected by Earth and atmosphere.
  (c) Some of the infra-red radiation is absorbed by the atmosphere and re-emitted in all directions by the green-house gases.
  (d) No infra-red radiation is emitted by Earth.

(v) Energy flow diagram definitely conveys all the points given below, except:
  (a) the flow of energy is multi-directional.
  (b) the energy captured by the autotrophs does not return to the solar input.
  (c) the energy that passes to the herbivores does not come back to the autotrophs.
  (d) the energy moves progressively through the various trophic levels and it is no longer available to the previous level.

Ans. (i) (a) primary consumers
(ii) (a) 1000 kcal and 100 kcal
(iii) (c) tertiary consumer
(iv) (d) No infra-red radiation is emitted by Earth
(v) (a) the flow of energy is multi-directional

108. Study the figure given below carefully and answer the following questions.

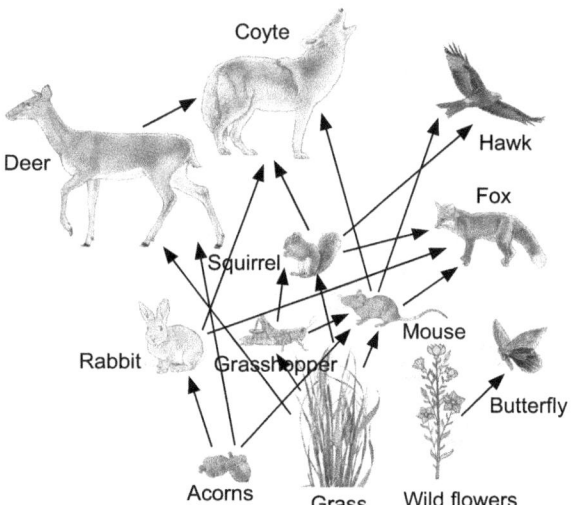

(i) What is the name of the interrelation shown in this figure?
  (a) Food chain
  (b) Food web
  (c) Trophic level
  (d) Energy conservation

(ii) The series of branching lines shown in above figure appears in nature because:
  (a) the length and complexity of food chains vary.
  (b) each organism is generally eaten by two or more other kinds of organisms.
  (c) straight line food chains are not practically possible.
  (d) all of the above

(iii) Which one of the following is true for a food web?
  (a) Food web does not help in stabilising the ecosystem.
  (b) secondary consumers cannot feed on other species in the event of decrease in population of prey.
  (c) A food web provides alternative pathways of food availability.
  (d) Food webs are straight.
(iv) The main source of energy flowing in any food web is the:
  (a) animals
  (b) consumer
  (c) primary producer
  (d) sun
(v) In the picture shown above concentration of a chemical absorbed from soil is likely to be highest in:
  (a) wildflowers   (b) grass
  (c) coyote   (d) rabbit

Ans. (i) (b) Food web
(ii) (d) all of the above
(iii) (c) A food web provides alternative pathways of food availability.
(iv) (d) sun
(v) (c) coyote

109. Read the following and answer the following questions.

The energy flow in the ecosystem is one of the major factors that support the survival of such a great number of organisms. For almost all organisms on earth, the primary source of energy is solar energy. It is amusing to find that we receive less than 50 per cent of the sun's effective radiation on earth. When we say effective radiation, we mean the radiation, which can be used by plants to carry out photosynthesis.

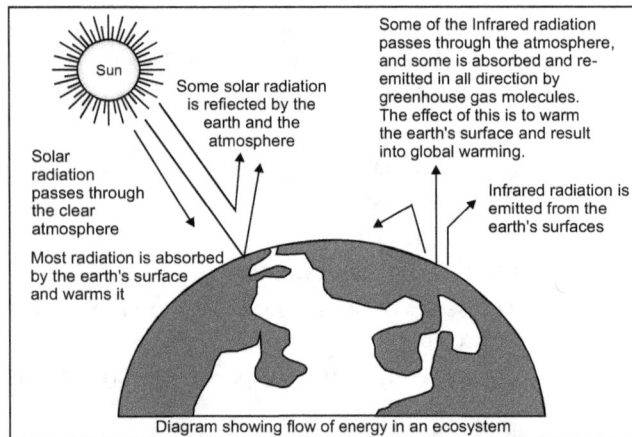
Diagram showing flow of energy in an ecosystem

(i) Every food chain in the ecosystem begins with _____. Which are the original?
  (a) saprophytes   (b) parasites
  (c) producers   (d) none of these

(ii) If 100 J energy is available at the producer level in a food chain then the energy available to the secondary consumer will be:
  (a) 10 J   (b) 0.1 J
  (c) 1 J   (d) 0.01 J
(iii) The constituents which do not form eco-system are:
  (a) Biotic constituents
  (b) Plastic bags
  (c) Abiotic constituents
  (d) All of the above
(iv) Which of the two sets belong to the same trophic level?
  (a) Frog : Lizard   (b) Rabbit : Tiger
  (c) Vulture : Crow   (d) Deer : Hawk
(v) A food chain comprising birds, green plants, fish and man. The concentration of harmful chemical entering the food chain will be maximum in:
  (a) plant   (b) man
  (c) birds   (d) fish

Ans. (i) (c) Producers
(ii) (c) 1 J
(iii) (b) Plastic bags
(iv) (a) frog : lizard
(v) (b) man

110. Read the following and answer the following questions. [CBSE Question Bank]

Frothing in Yamuna:

The primary reason behind the formation of the toxic foam is high phosphate content in the wastewater because of detergents used in dyeing industries, dhobi ghats and households.

Yamuna's pollution level is so bad that parts of it have been labelled 'dead' as there is no oxygen in it for aquatic life to survive.

(i) Predict the pH value of the water of river Yamuna if the reason for froth is high content of detergents dissolved in it.
  (a) 10-11   (b) 5-7
  (c) 2-5   (d) 7
(ii) Which of the following statements is correct for the water with detergents dissolved in it?

(a) Low concentration of hydroxide ion (OH⁻) and high concentration of hydronium ion (H_3O^+)

(b) High concentration of hydroxide ion (OH⁻) and low concentration of hydronium ion (H_3O^+)

(c) High concentration of hydroxide ion (OH⁻) as well as hydronium ion (H_3O^+)

(d) Equal concentration of both hydroxide ion (OH⁻) and hydronium ion (H_3O^+).

(iii) The table provides the pH value of four solutions P, Q, R and S:

P	2
Q	9
R	5
S	11

Which of the following correctly represents the solutions in increasing order of their hydronium ion concentration?

(a) P > Q > R > S (b) P > S > Q > R
(c) S < Q < R < P (d) S < P < Q < R

(iv) High content of phosphate ion in river Yamuna may leads to:

(a) decreased level of dissolved oxygen and increased growth of algae.

(b) decreased level of dissolved oxygen and no effect of growth of algae.

(c) increased level of dissolved oxygen and increased growth of algae.

(d) decreased level of dissolved oxygen and decreased growth of algae.

(v) If a sample of water containing detergents is provided to you, which of the following methods will you adopt to neutralise it?

(a) Treating the water with baking soda.
(b) Treating the water with vinegar.
(c) Treating the water with caustic soda.
(d) Treating the water with washing soda.

Ans. (i) (a) 10–11
(ii) (b) high concentration of hydroxide ion (OH⁻) and low concentration of hydronium ion (H_3O^+)
(iii) (c) S < Q < R < P
(iv) (a) decreased level of dissolved oxygen and increased growth of algae.
(v) (b) Treating the water with vinegar.

111. Read the following and answer the following questions. [CBSE Question Bank]

Biosphere is a global ecosystem composed of living organisms and abiotic factors from which they derive energy and nutrients. The ecosystem is defined as structural and functional unit of the biosphere comprising of living and non-living environment that interact by means of food chains and chemical cycles resulting in energy flow, biotic diversity and material cycling to form a stable, self-supporting system.

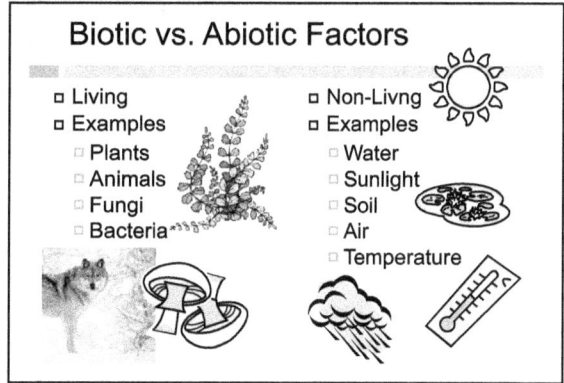

(i) Which trophic level is incorrectly defined?

(a) Carnivores–secondary or tertiary consumers.
(b) Decomposers–microbial heterotrophs
(c) Herbivores–primary consumers
(d) Omnivores–molds, yeast and mushrooms

(ii) The diagram below shows a food web from the sea shore.

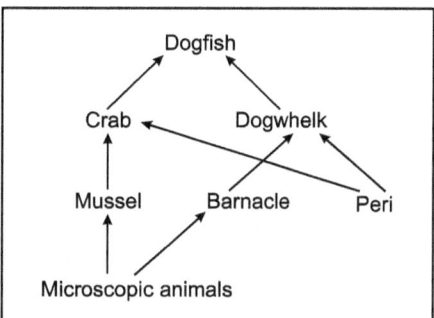

The mussel can be described as:
(a) Producer
(b) Primary consumers
(c) Secondary consumer
(d) Decomposer

(iii) The given figure best represents:

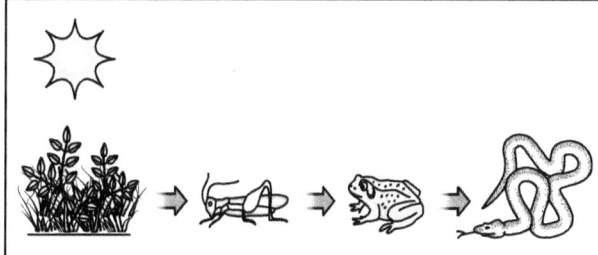

(a) Grassland food chain
(b) Parasitic food chain
(c) Forest food chain
(d) Aquatic food chain

(iv) Consider the following statements concerning food chains:

(i) Removal of 80% tigers from an area resulted in greatly increased growth of vegetation
(ii) Removal of most of the carnivores resulted in an increased population of herbivores.
(iii) The length of the food chains is generally limited to 3 – 4 trophic levels due to energy loss.
(iv) The length of the food chains may vary from 2 to 8 trophic levels.
Which two of the above statements are correct?
(a) (i), (iv) (b) (i), (ii)
(c) (ii), (iii) (d) (iii), (iv)
(v) Which of the following groups of organisms are not included in ecological food chain?
(a) Carnivores (b) Saprophytes
(c) Herbivores (d) Predators

Ans. (i) (d) Omnivores–molds, yeast and mushrooms
(ii) (c) Secondary consumers
(iii) (a) Grassland food chain
(iv) (c) (ii), (iii)
(v) (b) Saprophytes

112. Take a look at the picture carefully and answer the following questions.

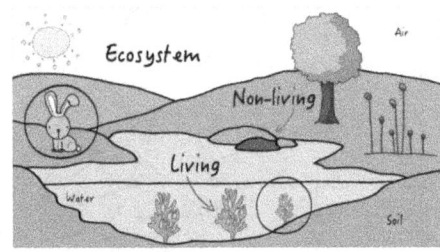

(i) While designing an aquarium what are the things you would like to include to make it a complete ecosystem?
(a) Fishes, aquatic plants, pleco fish (algae eating fish), aerator, pebbles, fish food.
(b) Fishes, grass, plants, pleco fish (algae eating fish), fish food.
(c) Fishes, plants, oxygen pump, food, stones.
(d) Animals, fishes, plants, oxygen pump, food.
(ii) Which one of the following is not a producer?
(a) Blue green algae (b) Cactus
(c) Fungi (d) Spinach
(iii) Herbivores, carnivores, omnivores, and parasites all come under:
(a) producers (b) consumers
(c) ecosystem (d) food web
(iv) Which one is not true about an ecosystem?
(a) Ecosystem consists of living and non-living things both.
(b) Living organisms interact with each other.
(c) Growth, reproduction, and other activities of living organisms are not affected by the abiotic components of ecosystem.
(d) A garden is considered an ecosystem.
(v) Ecosystems can be of how many types?
(a) Two types – man-made and natural
(b) Two types – terrestrial and aquatic
(c) Four types – forests, ponds, lakes, and garden
(d) All of the above imply as correct answer.

Ans. (i) (a) Fishes, aquatic plants, pleco fish (algae eating fish), aerator, pebbles, fish food
(ii) (c) Fungi
(iii) (b) consumers
(iv) (c) Growth, reproduction, and other activities of living organisms are not affected by the abiotic components of ecosystem
(v) (d) All of the above imply as correct answer.

113. Read the passage and answer the following questions.

Humans modify the environment around them through agriculture and urbanisation as the major activities. Human impact on the environment is so substantial that there is nothing left called pristine nature or ecosystems untouched by human intervention. The major impact of these interventions is ever increasing levels of all forms of pollution on our Earth. Waste disposal and depletion of ozone layer are two major concerns in this world.

(i) Which one of the following sentences is not true about ozone?
(a) Ozone is a deadly poison.
(b) Ozone protects us from harmful UV rays emitted by the sun.
(c) Ozone is formed from oxygen in presence of UV rays.
(d) Ozone causes skin cancer in humans.
(ii) Which one of the below given reason holds good for increase in the amount of waste generated by humans?
(a) Religious practices
(b) Change in packaging style and products
(c) Home cooking
(d) Use of plant-based products
(iii) An environment enthusiast would certainly not choose one of these for a tea party at her home.
(a) Paper cups (b) Thermocol cup
(c) Steel cup (d) Earthen cups
(iv) Which of the following groups contains a non-biodegradable item?
(a) Grass, flowers, lime-juice, and leather.
(b) Grass, wood, leather, and plastic.
(c) Cake, wood, flowers, and grass.
(d) Fruit-peels, cake, leather, and lime-juice.
(v) Which of the following waste management plan is likely to work the best?
(a) Integrated waste management plan
(b) Recycling waste management plan

(c) Reducing waste management plan
(d) Reusing waste management plan

Ans. (i) (d) Ozone causes skin cancer in humans.
(ii) (b) Change in packaging style and products
(iii) (b) Thermocol cup
(iv) (b) Grass, wood, leather, and plastic
(v) (a) Integrated waste management plan

114. Read the following and answer the following questions.

The amount of ozone in the atmosphere has begun to drop sharply from 1980s. This decrease has been linked to synthetic chemicals. In 1987, the United Nations Environment Programme (UNEP) succeeded in forging an agreement to freeze harmful chemicals production at 1986 levels.

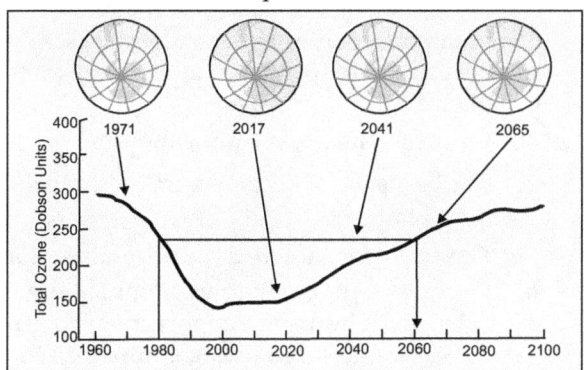

(i) At what level of atmosphere ozone layer is found?
(a) Troposphere (b) Stratosphere
(c) Biosphere (d) Ionosphere
(ii) At higher level of atmosphere radiations act upon oxygen molecule to form:
(a) oxygen
(b) ozone
(c) carbon monoxide
(d) all of the above
(iii) What is the major cause of ozone depletion?
(a) Chlorofluorocarbons
(b) Hydrochlorofluorocarbons
(c) Carbon tetrachloride and methyl chloroform
(d) All of the above
(iv) Which of the following sources is responsible for the depletion of ozone layer?

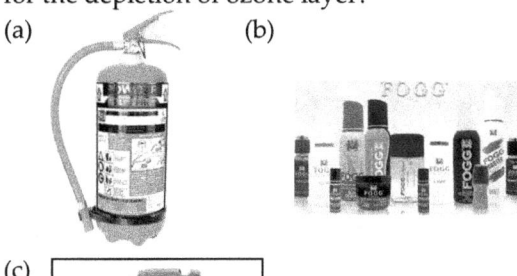

(d) All of the above

(v) In which of the following countries Ozone hole has appeared?
(a) Africa (b) North America
(c) Japan (d) Antarctica

Ans. (i) (b) Stratosphere
(ii) (b) Ozone
(iii) (d) All of the above
(iv) (d) All of the above
(v) (d) Antarctica

115. Read the passage carefully and answer the following questions from Q 115 (i) to 115 (v).

The waste generated by humans has been detrimental to our environment and is causing threat to our ecosystem. We are generating too much trash and failing to deal with it in a sustainable way. Every day we are disposing tons and tons of non-biodegradable and unrecyclable waste into our oceans and landfills. Plastic waste is an example. In 2017 the Environmental Protection Agency in the US calculated that the total generation of municipal solid waste in the United States in 2017 was 267.8 million tons; compared with 2015 levels, it was a 5.7 million increase.

(i) Non-biodegradable substances are:
(a) broken down by biological processes.
(b) not broken down by biological processes.
(c) prepared by biological processes.
(d) cannot be broken down by physical processes.
(ii) Which one of the following is not likely to happen in the case of solid waste disposal in landfills?
(a) Unpleasant odours
(b) Ground water pollution
(c) Fires and explosions
(d) Infrared radiation
(iii) Humans are not supposed to get any energy by eating coal, because:
(a) coal is harmful.
(b) coal is burnt.
(c) humans do not have enzymes to digest coal.
(d) coal is black.
(iv) Man-made plastics are not bio-degradable because:
(a) they are hard.
(b) bacteria and saprophytes do not contain enzymes to decompose plastics.
(c) plastics are made in industries.
(d) plastics do not absorb water.
(v) The depletion in the Ozone layer is caused by _____.
(a) nitrous oxide
(b) carbon dioxide

(c) chlorofluorocarbons
(d) methane

Ans. (i) (b) not broken down by biological processes.
(ii) (d) Infrared radiation.
(iii) (c) humans do not have enzymes to digest coal.
(iv) (b) bacteria and saprophytes do not contain enzymes to decompose plastics.
(v) (c) chlorofluorocarbons.

Reasoning Based Questions

116. Why do harmful chemicals concentrate as we go up in a food chain?

Ans. The process of increasing concentration of harmful chemicals at each trophic level of a food chain is called biomagnification. These substances are non-biodegradable so they persist in environment for a long time and are not easily degraded or excreted and when they move up in the food chain their concentration goes on increasing and gets accumulated in tissues or internal organs.

117. Why does vegetarian habit help us in getting more energy? In terms of energy who is at an advantageous position (vegetarian or a non-vegetarian) and Why?

Ans. Vegetarians obtain food directly from plants, while non-vegetarians get food from animals which feed upon plants. As a result animals which are herbivores get 10% of energy from plants suppose 100 J according to 10% rule. When non-vegetarians feed upon these animals they get only 10 J which is 10% of 100 J. But vegetarians which feed directly on plants get 100 J hence vegetarians are at an advantageous position and get more energy than non-vegetarians.

118. The first trophic level in a food chain is always a green plant. Why?

Ans. Green plants are the producers which prepare their own food by utilizing solar energy from inorganic sources and all other living organisms depends on them for food. Herbivores and carnivores depend upon green plants either directly or indirectly for food. Hence the first trophic level in a food chain is always a green plant.

119. Why is damage to the ozone layer a cause of concern? What steps are being taken to limit this damage? [NCERT]

Ans. Ozone layer is found in stratosphere which prevents the harmful UV rays of sun from entering earth's surface. Various ozone depleting substances like CFCs cause a great damage to ozone layer thus leading to its depletion. So harmful UV rays from sun can easily pass through this layer and cause various genetic disorders, mutations, cancer, eye diseases etc., in humans. UV rays also affect plants and animals.

In 1987, **UNEP [United Nations Environment Programme]** succeeded in forging an agreement called Montreal Protocol which states that to reduce the use of CFCs and replace CFCs with other alternatives.

120. Why is food chain having two trophic levels most advantageous in terms of energy?

Ans. A food chain having two trophic levels only would minimise the energy lost as heat which is an advantage in terms of energy.

121. Why is lake considered to be a natural ecosystem?*

Ans. A lake is considered as a natural ecosystem as it consists of both biotic and abiotic components and these components are interdependent on each other and do not require any human interference for their sustenance.

122. Give reason to justify the following:*
(i) The existence of decomposers is essential in a biosphere.
(ii) Flow of energy in a food chain is unidirectional.

Ans. (i) Decomposers breakdown complex organic substances into simple inorganic substance. These simple substances get mixed up in the soil and are used as nutrients by the producers. Thus, they replenish the soil naturally and help in degradation of biodegradable wastes. So, the existence of decomposers is essential in a biosphere as they maintain the balance in the ecosystem and provide space for new life in ecosystem.

(ii) In a food chain the energy moves progressively through the various trophic levels and it is no longer available to the previous trophic level. Energy captured by autotrophs cannot be reverted back to sun but it passes to herbivores then to carnivores following 10% Law. Thus flow of energy from sun to autotrophs then to heterotrophs to carnivores is unidirectional.

123. Why is it necessary to conserve the environment?

Ans. It is necessary to conserve the environment to prevent the damage to the environment and to protect the endangered species.

124. Why did United Nations act to control the production of CFCs used in refrigerators?

Ans. CFCs is an ozone layer depleting substance which is used in refrigerators, air-conditioners etc. So United Nations act to control the production of CFCs used in refrigerators.

125. Why is improper disposal of waste a curse to environment?

Ans. Improper disposal of waste would lead to environmental pollution, which causes harmful

---
* are board exam questions from previous years

effects on living organisms like plants, animals, human beings etc.

126. We do not clean ponds or lakes, but an aquarium needs to be cleaned. Why?

Ans. Ponds or lakes are natural, self-sustaining and complete ecosystem. They have decomposers like bacteria or fungi which break down the waste material and hence they remain clean. But an aquarium is a man-made, incomplete ecosystem and they do not have decomposers to clean the waste material. So an aquarium needs to be cleaned but we do not clean ponds or lakes.

127. Why non-biodegradable substances persist in environment for longer time?

Ans. Non-biodegradable substances cannot be degraded by microbes through biological process to simpler forms hence they persist in environment for longer time.

128. Why should biodegradable and non-biodegradable wastes be discarded in two separate dustbins?

Ans. Biodegradable wastes can be easily degraded by natural organisms like bacteria and fungi but non-biodegradable wastes cannot be degraded in a natural way by the action of microbes, they stay in environment as such. There are various techniques like recycling to degrade these non-biodegradable substances. Hence both biodegradable and non-biodegradable wastes should be discarded in two separate dustbins.

129. Why are some substances biodegradable and some non-biodegradable? [NCERT]

Ans. There are various types of waste substances released into our environment. Those substances which are degraded into simpler form naturally by the action of microbes like bacteria or fungi are called biodegradable substances. Examples–Vegetables and fruits peels, paper, agricultural wastes etc.

Those substances which cannot be degraded into simpler forms naturally by the action of microbes are called non-biodegradable substances. Examples–Aluminium foils, plastic bottles, glass apparatus etc.

Very Short Answer Type Questions

130. What is the role of decomposers in the ecosystem? [NCERT]

Ans. Decomposers act upon dead and decay organisms and convert them into simpler forms. These simple substances get mixed up in the soil and are used as nutrients by the producers. From producers it goes to consumers and so on. They maintain the balance in the ecosystem and provide space for new life in ecosystem.

131. What will happen if we kill all the organisms in one trophic level? [NCERT]

Ans. If we kill all the organisms of one trophic level, it will lead to an increase in the number of organisms at the lower trophic level and decrease in the number of organisms at the higher trophic level. This will result in disruption in the food web and hence the ecosystem.

132. In the following food chain, grass provides 4000 J of energy to the grasshopper.

Grass, grasshopper, frogs, snakes.

How much energy will be available to snakes and frogs?

Ans. If grass provides 4000 J energy, then according to 10 per cent law, it will give 10% of its energy to next trophic level.
Hence,
Grass ----> Grasshopper ------->
(4000 J)   (400 J)
Frogs ------> Snakes   (40 J)   (4 J)
So, for snakes and frogs, 4 J and 40 J energy will be available by 10 per cent law

133. Consider a food chain of the following:
Fish, crab, plankton, shark.

Arrange the above chain in proper order of trophic level. Assign trophic level to shark.

Ans. Plankton → Crab → Fish → Shark.
Shark occupies fourth tropic level (Tertiary consumer).

134. What limits the number of trophic levels in a food chain?

Ans. The flow of energy in each trophic level follows 10% law i.e., only 10% of the energy is available to the next higher trophic level hence the amount of energy goes on decreasing at each trophic level which limits the number of trophic levels in a food chain.

135. Write the full name of the group of compounds mainly responsible for the depletion of ozone layer?

Ans. CFCs (Chlorofluorocarbons) are mainly responsible for the depletion of ozone layer.

136. Mention one negative effect of our affluent lifestyle on the environment?

Ans. The affluent life style of few persons results in overuse of natural resources and in long term effects it can led to scarcity of resources. For example: usage of personal vehicles instead of public transport increases consumption of fuel, pollution, use of air conditioners, refrigerators etc., which contain CFCs when released into atmosphere leads to depletion of ozone layer.

137. In the following food chain, 100 J of energy is available to the lion. How much energy was available to the producer?*

Plant → Dear → Lion

Ans. There are three trophic levels the producer, the consumer and the secondary consumer according to 10 per cent law of energy transfer in trophic level, If the lion has 100 J of energy then, deer will have:
According to 10% law 100 J of energy is available to lion, so dear will get:

$$10\% \text{ of } x = 100 \text{ J}$$
$$x = 1000 \text{ J}$$

Plant is the producer, it will have:

$$10\% \text{ of } y = 1000$$
$$y = 10000 \text{ J}$$

138. In the following food chain plants provide 500 J of energy to rats. How much energy will be available to hawks from snakes?*

Plants → Rats → Snakes → Hawks

Ans. 500 J of energy is available to rats from plants is then according to 10 per cent law 50 J of energy will be available to snakes and only 5 J of energy will be available to hawks.

139. In a food chain of frog, grass, insect and snake assign trophic level to frog.*

Ans. Frog will be at third trophic level.

Grass → Insect → Frog → Snake

140. What will be the amount of energy available to the organisms of the second trophic level of a food chain, if the energy available at the first trophic level is 10,000 J?*

Ans. 1000 J amount of energy will be available to the organisms of the second trophic level of a food chain, if the energy available at the first trophic level is 10,000 J.

141. Why is biogas considered an excellent fuel?*

Ans. Biogas is considered as an excellent fuel because:
  (i) It causes no pollution, as it is environmental friendly.
  (ii) Biogas plant from which biogas is produced serves as an excellent way of waste disposal.
  (iii) It is economical and produces a large amount of heat per unit mass.

142. Write the name of the main constituent of biogas. Also state its percentage.*

Ans. Methane is the main constituent of biogas. Its formula is CH_4. Its percentage is approximately 50-75%.

143. If a harmful chemical enters a food chain comprising snakes, hawks, mice and plants which of these organisms is likely to have maximum concentration of the harmful chemicals in its body?

Ans. Hawks are likely to have maximum concentration of the harmful chemicals in their body as they are placed at top in this example of food chain.

144. Expand the term UNEP.

Ans. United Nations Environment Programme.

145. Write the common food chain of a pond ecosystem.

Ans. Phytoplanktons → Zooplanktons → Fish → Bird

146. What is an ecosystem?* [CBSE, 2017]

Ans. An ecosystem is a self-sustaining system where biotic and abiotic organisms of various communities interact with each other. Ponds, forests, grasslands etc., are the few examples of ecosystem.

147. Why is forest considered a natural ecosystem?

Ans. Forests are considered as natural ecosystem because they have species of plants and animals that grow without human intervention and they are naturally sustainable.

148. Name two natural ecosystems.*

Ans. River, pond, forest, ocean etc., are natural ecosystems.

149. Select the mis-matched pair and correct it:
  (a) Detritivores–Organisms which feed on detritus and degrade into simple substances.
  (b) Ecosystem–Abiotic and biotic components of environment.
  (c) Trophic level–It is made of interlinking of food chains
  (d) Producers–They synthesize their own food from inorganic substances

Ans. (c) Trophic levels are distinct sequential steps in the food chain where transfer of energy occurs.

150. What are the by-products of fertilizer industries? How do they affect the environment?

Ans. The by-products of fertilizer industries are oxides of nitrogen and sulphur which when released into atmosphere causes air pollution. They are mainly responsible for formation of acid rain. Acid rain damages marbles of monuments, statues etc. Acid rain also reduces the fertility of soil by decreasing the pH of soil thus growth of food crops is affected. They affect the microbes in soil and aquatic organisms in water bodies.

151. How can you help in reducing the problem of waste disposal? Give any two methods. [NCERT]

Ans. We can help in reducing the problem of waste disposal by the following two methods:
  (a) By separating biodegradable substances from non-biodegradable substances.
  (b) By putting the biodegradable organic waste into compost pits dug in the ground and preparing compost.

152. Why is improper disposal of waste a curse to environment?

Ans. Improper disposal of waste would lead to environmental pollution, which causes harmful effects on living organisms like plants, animals, human beings etc.

---
* are board exam questions from previous years

153. List two non-biodegradable wastes generated daily in kitchen which can be recycled?

Ans. Milk bags, tin cans are non-biodegradable wastes generated daily in kitchen which can be recycled.

Short Answer Type Questions

154. Define an ecosystem. Draw a block diagram to show the flow of energy in an ecosystem.*

Ans. Ecosystem refers to the interaction of all the biotic and abiotic components present in a particular area. Energy flows across the trophic levels following the 10% law. Only 10% of the energy, available to a trophic level is passed on to the next trophic level.

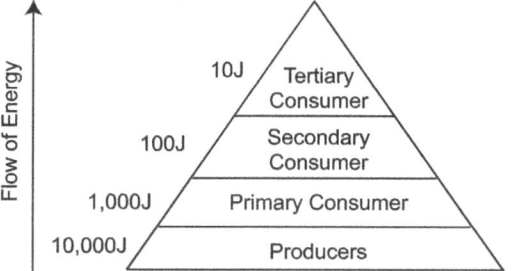

155. What are trophic levels? Give an example of food chain and state the different trophic levels in it? [NCERT]

Ans. The distinct sequential steps or levels in the food chain where transfer of energy occurs are referred to as trophic levels.

Example of a food chain is:

Grass → Grasshopper → Lizard → Snake → Hawk

Grass is producer, it belongs to first trophic level. Grasshopper is primary consumer, it belongs to second trophic level. Lizard is secondary consumer, it belongs to third trophic level. Snake is tertiary consumer and it belongs to fourth trophic level and hawk is quaternary consumer, it belongs to fifth trophic level.

156. Will the impact of removing all the organisms in a trophic level be different for different trophic levels? Can the organisms of any trophic level be removed without causing any damage to the ecosystem? [NCERT]

Ans. Yes, the impact of removing all the organisms in a trophic level will be different for different trophic levels. For example, If all producers will be removed then all herbivores will die of starvation. The various categories of carnivores which depend on herbivores for food will also be affected. Similarly if we will remove all organisms of higher trophic level the number of organisms in lower trophic level will increase thus creating imbalance in the ecosystem. So if organisms of any trophic level would be removed it will cause damage to the ecosystem.

157. What is biological magnification? Will the levels of this magnification be different at different levels of the ecosystem? [NCERT]

Ans. The increase in concentration of harmful toxic substances in the body of organisms at each trophic level of a food chain is called biological magnification. Yes, the levels of this magnification will be different at different levels of the ecosystem because the concentration of chemicals goes on increasing at different trophic levels. It is maximum at higher trophic levels and minimum at lower trophic levels. Suppose a food chain is Grass → Rabbit → Eagle, it will be the highest in eagle and minimum in grass.

158. What is a food web? Give few characteristics of a food web? Give an example of a food web?

Ans. Food web is a network of food chains which become interconnected at various trophic levels so as to form a number of feeding connections amongst different organisms of a biotic community.

Some characteristics of a food web are:

(a) Food web is an interlink of different food chains.

(b) It provides alternative pathways of food availability.

(c) Due to greater alternatives for food, it makes the ecosystem stable.

(d) It helps in development of an ecosystem.

Example of food web:

159. What are the characteristics of energy transfer in biosphere?

Ans. The characteristics of energy transfer in biosphere are:

(a) The ultimate source of energy is sun and is converted from one form to another.

(b) Energy gets continuously transferred through food chain and energy flow is unidirectional.

(c) There is loss of some energy during transfer from one trophic level to the next.

---
* are board exam questions from previous years

(d) Only 10% of energy is transferred from one trophic level to the next. The solar energy trapped by producers does not revert back to the sun.

(e) At each trophic level, some of the energy is utilized by organisms, rest is lost to environment and only 10% is available to the next trophic level.

160. What are decomposers? What will be the consequence of their absence in an ecosystem?

Ans. Decomposers are the microbes that feed on dead and decay organisms. Dead plants and animals will get accumulated in the ecosystem as there would be no decomposers to decompose them. The decomposers will act upon dead and decayed organisms into simpler forms and get mixed in the soil which is used by producers again. But in the absence of decomposers this whole process would not occur and the dead organisms will get accumulated in the ecosystem.

161. "The maximum concentration of harmful chemicals accumulates in human beings." State the phenomenon involved and justify this statement.

Ans. Human beings are always placed at the top of a food chain. The concentration of harmful chemicals [non-biodegradable substance] goes on increasing at every trophic level as a result as human beings are placed at the apex of every food chain so maximum concentration of harmful chemicals get accumulated in their body. This phenomenon is called biomagnification.

162. What is ozone and how does it affect any ecosystem? [NCERT]

Ans. Ozone is a triatomic molecule made of three oxygen atoms. It is present as a layer in stratosphere which prevents the harmful UV radiations of sun from entering the earth's surface, thus protecting us from skin cancers, genetic mutations, eye diseases like cataract etc. Ozone is a molecule made from three atoms of oxygen.

The harmful chemicals like CFCs which are used as coolants in refrigerators, air conditioners when released into atmosphere break down the ozone thus leading to depletion of ozone layer. Hence harmful UV rays can easily pass through ozone layer and cause various types of disorders in humans, plants and animals.

163. Show the reactions of formation of ozone from oxygen in the atmosphere? Name the pollutant and its role in depletion of ozone layer.

Ans. Ozone is formed by absorption of UV rays coming from sun.
$$O_2 \leftrightarrow O + O$$
$$O + O_2 \rightarrow O_3$$
UV radiations splits oxygen molecules to oxygen atoms and the oxygen atoms combine with oxygen molecule to form ozone.

CFCs are mainly responsible for ozone layer depletion. CFCs release chlorine atoms which break ozone to oxygen. More amounts of CFCs thus released will cause depletion of ozone layer.

164. You have been selected to talk on "Ozone layer and its protection" in the school assembly on Environment Day".*

(i) Why should ozone layer be protected to save the environment?

(ii) List any two ways that you would stress in your talk to bring in awareness among your fellow friends that would also help in protection of ozone layer as well as the environment.

Ans. (i) Ozone layer is present in stratosphere which prevents the ultra-violet rays from sun to penetrate the Earth's surface. But due to depletion of ozone layer ultra-violet rays enter into the surface of Earth and cause many health hazards like skin cancer, cataract in eyes etc. So, it is necessary to save the environment by protecting the ozone layer.

(ii) Some of the ways to protect the ozone layer are:
   (a) Banning the use of CFC's and other ozone depleting substances.
   (b) Reducing the use of fluorescent lights, limited use of supersonic planes, control over large scale nuclear explosions etc.

165. Write the essential function performed by ozone at the higher levels of the Earth's atmosphere? How is it produced? Name the synthetic chemicals mainly responsible for the drop of amount of ozone in the atmosphere. How can the use of these chemicals be reduced?*

Ans. Ozone layer absorbs most of the harmful ultraviolet radiations from the sun to the earth. It is formed high up in the atmosphere by the action of ultraviolet radiation on oxygen gas. Chlorofluorocarbons are the synthetic chemicals responsible for the drop of amount of ozone in the atmosphere.

The use of these chemicals can be reduced by:
(a) Replacement of chloroflurocarbons with hydrochlorofluorocarbons because it breaks down more quickly.
(b) Safe disposal of old appliances such as refrigerators and freezers.

166. Define a food chain. Design a terrestrial food chain of four trophic levels. If a pollutant enters at the producer level, the organisms of which trophic level will have the maximum concentration of the pollutant in their bodies? What is this phenomenon called?*

Ans. It is the sequence of arrangement of living organism in a community in which one organism consumes another organism to transfer food energy.

---
* are board exam questions from previous years

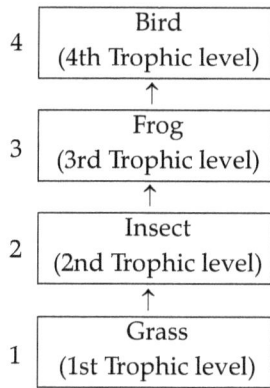

Grass ⟶ Insect ⟶ Frog ⟶ Bird

The organism at higer tropic level will have the maximum concentration of pollutants. This phenomenon is called biological magnification.

167. Give some characteristics of a food chain?

Ans. Some characteristics of food chain are:
(a) A food chain always progress in a straight chain.
(b) There is an unidirectional flow of energy from sun to producers to a series of consumers.
(c) There are 3-4 trophic levels or maximum upto 5 levels in a food chain.
(d) It helps in understanding the food relationships and interaction among various living organisms present in an ecosystem.

168. Give any two examples of each:
(i) Organisms occupying the first trophic level.
(ii) Carnivores.
(iii) Biodegradable wastes of humans.
(iv) Ecosystem.
(v) Abiotic factors of an ecosystem

Ans. (i) Grass, green plants
(ii) Tiger, Eagle
(iii) Kitchen waste like peels of vegetables, fruits, left over foods and old newspaper.
(iv) Natural ecosystem includes forest, pond and artificial ecosystem which include garden, parks, crop fields.
(v) Physical factors like temperature, sunlight and edaphic factors like soil.

169. The following organisms form a food chain.

Insects, hawk, grass, snake, frog.

Arrange them in proper sequence to form a food chain? Which of these will have the highest concentration of non-biodegradable chemicals? Name the phenomenon associated with it?

Ans. Grass, insects, frog, snake, hawk.
Hawk will have the highest concentration of non-biodegradable chemicals as it is placed at the top level of the food chain. This phenomenon is called Biomagnification.

170. Describe how decomposers facilitate recycling of matter in order to maintain balance in the ecosystem?

Ans. Decomposers act upon dead and decay organisms to convert them into simpler forms. These simple substances get mixed up in the soil and are used as nutrients by the producers. From producers it goes to consumers and so on. Thus there is recycling of matter which is done by decomposers that maintain the balance in the ecosystem.

171. Briefly describe different methods of wastes disposal?

Ans. The various methods of waste disposal are:
(a) **Land-fills:** In urban areas wastes are filled or deposited in low lying areas. These are also known as dumping grounds where wastes are buried.
(b) **Recycling of wastes:** Some wastes like papers, plastics, metals etc., which can be recycled are send to special recycling treatment plants so that new substances can be made from them.
(c) **Preparation of compost**: Biodegradable wastes like kitchen wastes, peels of fruits and vegetables etc., can be used to prepare compost which serves as a good manure to the plants.
(d) **Incineration:** Some wastes like medical wastes, chemical wastes are burnt at very high temperature in an incinerator and the ashes left behind are disposed by landfills.
(e) **Production of biogas:** Biodegradable wastes can be used in biogas plants to produce biogas which is used for several purposes like as a fuel.

172. What are the advantages of paper bags over plastic bags during shopping?

Ans. The advantages of paper bags are:
(a) They are made up of biodegradable material.
(b) They do not cause any environmental pollution.
(c) They can be recycled and reuse.
(d) They are capable of carrying more things and are washable.
(e) They are more strong and durable than plastic bags.

173. Suggest any four activities in daily life which are ecofriendly? [NCERT]

Ans. The four activities in daily life which are ecofriendly are:
(a) Carrying paper bags instead of polythene bags for shopping.
(b) Use of compost and biofertilisers, biopesticides instead of chemical fertilisers and pesticides.
(c) Segregating biodegradable and non-biodegradable substances and putting them in separate dustbins.
(d) Rain water harvesting.

174. Give any two ways in which biodegradable substances would affect the environment. [NCERT]

Ans. The two ways in which biodegradable substances would affect the environment are:
(a) Decomposition of biodegradable substances results in production of foul smell.
(b) The area where biodegradable wastes are accumulated serves as a good breeding place for mosquitoes, flies etc. which are the main carriers of germs for diseases like cholera, jaundice, typhoid etc.

175. What are the problems caused by the non-biodegradable wastes that we generate? [NCERT]

Ans. The problems caused by the non-biodegradable wastes are:
(i) As non-biodegrdable substances cannot be degraded naturally so they accumulate in the soil causing pollution and also reduces the fertility of the soil.
(ii) Some pesticides like DDT, mercury etc., which are non-biodegradable undergo biological magnification by entering into food chain.
(iii) If these substances do not undergo proper disposal techniques they will accumulate in soil thus reduces the fertility of soil.
(iv) Some harmful non-biodegradable substances may cause diseases in living organisms.

176. If all the waste we generate is biodegradable, will this have no impact on the environment? [NCERT]

Ans. If all the waste we generate is biodegradable then their decomposition at right time will not be possible as number of decomposers would be less as compared to the amount of biodegradable substances. It will get accumulated in the environment causing foul smell and will form a good breeding place for flies, mosquitoes etc., which will carry many disease causing germs. Thus various diseases like cholera, typhoid, jaundice, malaria, dengue etc., will be spread.

Long Answer Type Questions

177. What is an ecosystem? What are the components of an ecosystem? Also discuss the types of ecosystem? Draw a block diagram to show the flow of energy in an ecosystem?

Ans. An ecosystem is the structural and functional unit of biosphere where there is an interaction between living and non-living components to maintain balance between them.

The components of ecosystem are:
(a) **Biotic components:** They are the living organisms like plants, animals, human beings etc. Basing on the mode of obtaining food they are classified as producers, consumers and decomposers.
1. **Producers:** They are autotrophs which have the capacity to prepare their own food by trapping solar energy and converting them to chemical energy in the form of carbohydrates by the process of photosynthesis.
2. **Consumers:** They depend upon producers for food either directly or indirectly. They can be primary, secondary, tertiary or quaternary consumers.
3. **Decomposers:** They obtain food from dead and decayed organisms by breaking them down into simpler forms.
(b) **Abiotic components:** They are the non-living components i.e., the physical factors like temperature, light, wind, water, humidity and edaphic factors like soil, minerals etc.

The two types of ecosystem are:
1. **Natural ecosystem:** They are made by nature themselves without human interference. They can be terrestrial like forest, grassland and desert ecosystem and aquatic like freshwater and marine ecosystem.
2. **Artificial ecosystem:** They are made and maintained by human beings. Examples– Gardens, parks, croplands etc.

178. Explain energy relationships with trophic levels?

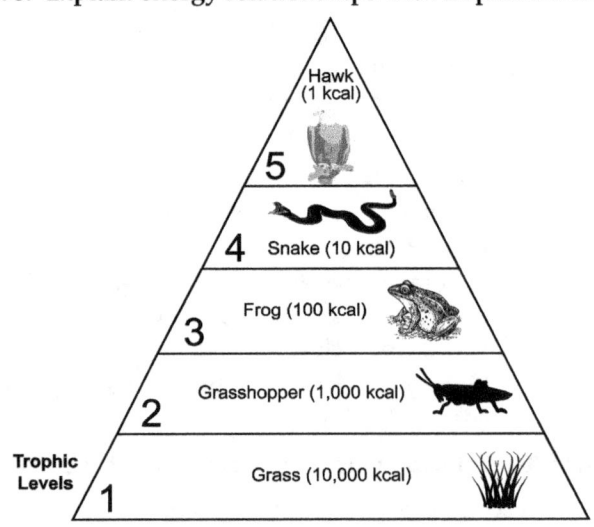

Ans. Each step or level of the food chain where transfer of food or energy takes place is referred to as a trophic level. The energy relationship within trophic levels is shown in a form of pyramid.

Consider a food chain Grass → Grasshopper → Frog → Snake → Hawk. This food chain can also be considered as energy chain. We can place these animals in different trophic levels, for example:

Grass: They are the producers so are placed in first trophic level. They utilize solar energy to prepare food. They transfer this energy to grasshopper, but only 10% of the energy is available to grasshopper according to Lindeman's 10% Law. If grass has 10,000 kcal of energy only 1000 kcal will be transferred to grasshopper. So energy at next trophic level is reduced.

Similarly grasshopper is placed at second trophic level; frog in third, snake in fourth and fifth trophic level is occupied by hawk. At each trophic level the energy goes on decreasing i.e., frog will receive 100 kcal of energy, snake 10 kcal and finally hawk only 1 kcal. Thus energy at each trophic level goes on decreasing and the animal placed at apex will receive lowest energy. Thus a food chain can be only up to maximum 5 trophic levels. In this way there exists a relationship between trophic levels and energy.

179. Answer the following questions:
(i) If Sita is consuming curd/yogurt for lunch, which trophic level in a food chain should she be considered as occupying?
(ii) Aquarium needs to be cleaned once in a while whereas ponds or lakes do not require any cleaning. Explain.
(iii) To protect the food plants from insects, an insecticide was sprayed in small amounts but it was detected in high concentration in human beings. How did it happen?

Ans. (i) In the predatory food chain, it consists of first, second, and third to fifth trophic levels where the first trophic level is occupied by producer's i.e, plants. The animals which consume plants are placed in the second trophic level. They are primary consumers. Herbivores are included in this trophic level. The organisms that depend on the organisms in the second trophic level are called secondary consumers; they are categorized under the third trophic level. Curd and yogurt are the products of cow or buffalo that belong to the second trophic level. So, Sita who is eating either curd or yogurt belongs to the third trophic level.

(ii) Aquariums are artificially built ecosystems which generally do not contain every aspect of a natural ecosystem. These artificial systems do not contain any form of natural decomposers and cleaners in the ecosystem as a result, food and waste generated by the organisms living in the aquarium accumulate and contaminate the water in the tank making it toxic. Hence, they have to be cleaned manually.

Ponds and lakes being natural ecosystems have natural decomposers and cleaners embedded as an integral part of the ecosystem, hence we do not have to clean them.

(iii) Insecticide are chemicals that are either washed down into the soil or into the water bodies. From the soil, these are absorbed by the plants along with water and minerals, and from the water bodies these are taken up by aquatic plants and animals. This is one of the ways in which they enter the food chain. As these chemicals are not degradable, these get accumulated progressively at each trophic level. As human beings occupy the top level in any food chain, the maximum concentration of these chemicals get accumulated in our bodies. This phenomenon is known as biological magnification. This is the reason why our food grains such as wheat and rice, vegetables and fruits, and even meat, contain varying amounts of pesticide residues. They cannot always be removed by washing or other means.

180. Study the given flow chart and answer the below given questions.

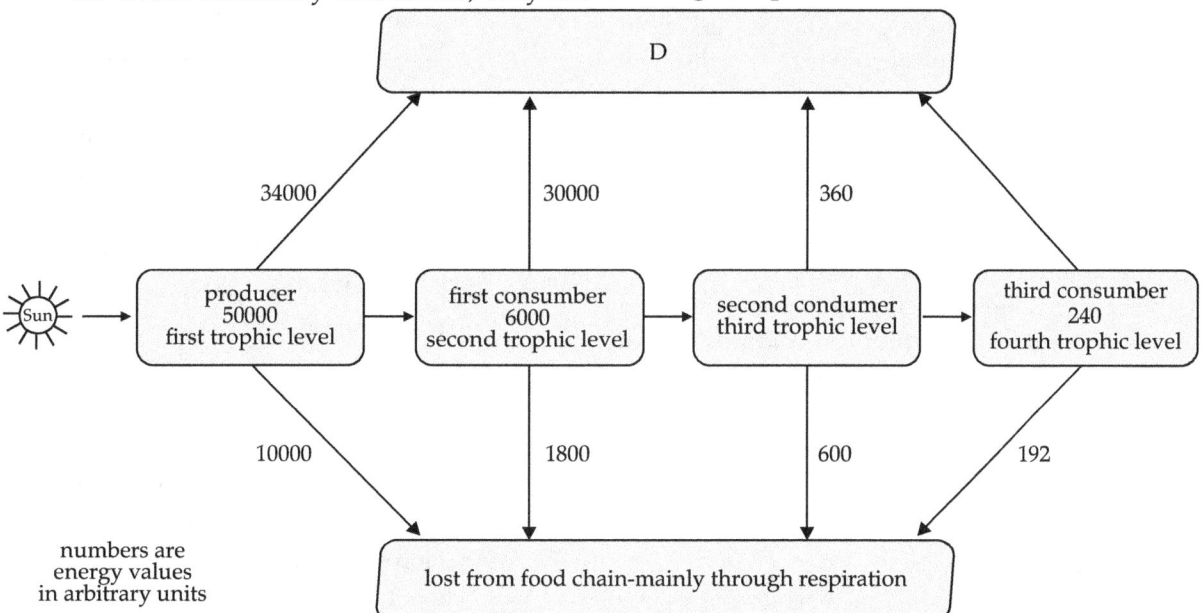

(i) Which form of the Sun's energy is trapped by the producer?
(ii) Into which energy form is the Sun's energy converted when it is trapped by the producer?
(iii) What does D refer to in the box?

Ans. (i) Sun's energy is trapped by the producer in the form of Light (or solar) energy.
(ii) Sun energy trapped by producer is converted into Chemical energy.
(iii) D refer to Decomposers like bacteria or fungi.

181. A team of Indian researchers went to Antarctica to study the ozone layer. They confirmed the presence of largest ozone hole over Antarctica and was just short of 27 million sq. km. After few days of their return, one of the scientists developed rashes, burning sensation and other skin problems which the doctors have confirmed as skin cancer.
    (i) What may be the cause of cancer just after return from Antarctica?
    (ii) What do we learn from this incident?

Ans. (i) The scientists were exposed to harmful UV-radiations of the sunlight as there was a big hole over Antarctica and this might be the cause of skin cancer. The ozone layer acts as an ozone shield and absorbs the harmful UV-radiations. The UV-radiations have extremely harmful effects on human beings, animals as well as plants.
(ii) We learn that the ozone layer is very important for the existence and survival of life on earth. Ozone layer absorbs high energy UV-radiations causing a rise in temperature of the stratosphere. The use of chemicals like CFCs has endangered the ozone layer. CFCs used as refrigerator coolants rise to the stratosphere where these molecules are broken down by UV-rays resulting in attack on the ozone molecules damaging the ozone umbrella of earth. Due to ozone layer depletion UV-rays reaching the earth cause skin cancer, cataracts, damage immune system, etc. UV-rays also decreases crop yield and certain fish larvae which are important constituents of aquatic food chains. It may also disturb global rainfall causing ecological disturbance. In this way all on the earth would be destroyed gradually.

182. Name the wastes which are generated in your house daily. What measures would you take for their disposal?

Ans. The wastes which are generated in our house daily are:
(a) Peels of vegetables and fruits.
(b) Old and used newspaper.
(c) Old plastics apparatus, broken glass apparatus.
(d) Plastic and polythene bags.
(e) Wastes from kitchen like left over foods, broken plates, cups etc.
(f) Old clothes, toys, utensils.

Measures that should be taken for their disposal are:
(a) Biodegradable and non-biodegradable substances should be separated and disposed separately.
(b) Kitchen wastes can be used to make compost.
(c) Old clothes, toys, utensils etc., can be reused by giving to poor and needy people.
(d) Plastic, polythene and glass apparatus can be recycled by using proper recycling techniques.
(e) Old and used newspaper can also be recycled.
(f) Safe disposal of plastic and polythene bags.

183. Answer the following:
    (i) What is meant by non-biodegradable waste? Identify non-biodegradable wastes from the following:
    Empty packet of chips, empty plastic bottle of mineral water, empty paper box of sweets, empty tin of cold drink.
    (ii) Pesticides added to the field are seen in increased amounts in the crop and in the birds that feed on them. What is this phenomenon called?
    (iii) Which gas shields the surface of the earth from the harmful UV radiations from the sun?
    (iv) Name the group of chemical compounds which adversely affects the ozone layer?

Ans. (i) The substances that cannot be degraded naturally by the action of microbes and persist in environment for longer period of time are called non-biodegradable substances.
The non-biodegradable wastes are empty packet of chips, empty plastic bottle of mineral water, empty tin of cold drink.
(ii) This phenomenon is called biological magnification.
(iii) Ozone gas shields the surface of the earth from the harmful UV radiations of the sun.
(iv) Chlorofluorocarbons [CFCs] are the group of chemical compounds which adversely affect the ozone layer.

Diagram Based Questions

184. Write the appropriate names of the trophic levels Z and X in the figure given below:

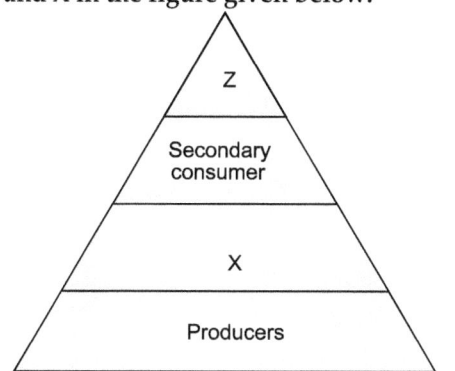

Ans. X – Primary consumers; Z – Tertiary consumers

185. Complete the below diagram by filling spaces marked as A, B, C and D:

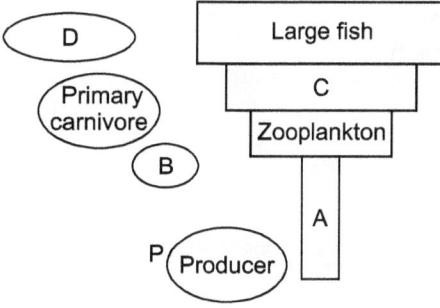

Ans. A – Phytoplankton; B – Herbivores
C – Small fish; D – Secondary carnivores

186. Which of the labelled arrows in the below diagram represents the smallest amount of energy transferred between organisms and the largest amount of energy lost to ecosystem?

Ans. The arrow which represents the smallest amount of energy transferred between organisms is Q and the largest amount of energy lost to ecosystem is R.

Differentiate Between

187. Distinguish between producers and consumers.

Ans.

Producers	Consumers
(a) They prepare their own food.	They depend on producers for their food.
(b) They prepare food from inorganic material by the process of photosynthesis.	They depend on readymade food.
(c) They always constitute the first trophic level.	They are placed at second or higher trophic levels.
(d) They possess chlorophyll which helps them in synthesising their own food.	They do not possess chlorophyll pigments.
(e) They have the capacity to trap solar energy and convert them to chemical energy in the form of carbohydrates. Examples – Green plants, algae etc.	They cannot trap solar energy and convert to chemical energy. They eat producers to get chemical energy. Examples – Humans, other animals like goat, rabbit, lion, tiger etc.

188. Differentiate between food chain and food web?

Ans.

Food chain	Food web
(a) The sequential interlinking of organisms where energy in the form of food is transferred from the producers through a series of consumers.	It is a network of food chains interlinking many organisms at different trophic levels which eat or being eaten and thus formed a number of feeding connections.
(b) A food chain shows one path how energy in form of food flows from producers to consumers.	A food web shows many paths i.e., it is a network of food chains where an organism eat several types of organisms or eaten by many different organisms.

189. Differentiate between biodegradable and non-biodegradable substances.

Ans.

Biodegradable Substances	Non-biodegradable Substances
(a) These substances are easily degradable in nature by the action of microbes like bacteria and fungi.	These substances are not degraded in nature by the action of microbes.
(b) These substances remain for a short period of time in environment. Examples – Peels of vegetables, fruits, paper etc.	They persist for longer period of time in the environment. Examples – Plastic, metals, glass objects etc.

Analysis and Evaluation Based Questions

190. Suggest one word for each of the following statements or definitions.
  (i) The physical and biological world where we live in.
  (ii) Each level of food chain where transfer of energy takes place.
  (iii) The physical factors like temperature, rainfall, wind and soil of an ecosystem.
  (iv) Organisms which depend on the producers either directly or indirectly for food.

Ans. (i) Environment
  (ii) Trophic level
  (iii) Abiotic factors
  (iv) Heterotrophs

191. Given below is a reaction which occurs in the stratosphere.
$$O_3 \leftrightarrow O_2 + [O]$$
  (i) Name the two reactions which are in equilibrium thereby maintaining steady concentration of ozone in the ozonosphere.
  (ii) What is being absorbed by the ozone for the occurrence of above two reactions?

Ans. (i) Photodissociation of ozone and generation of ozone are the two reactions which are in equilibrium thereby maintaining steady concentration of ozone in the ozonosphere.
  (ii) Ultraviolet radiations from sun are being absorbed by the ozone for the occurrence of above two reactions.

192. Why are crop fields known as artificial ecosystems?

Ans. Crop fields are made by man, most of the factors like sowing of seeds, watering etc., are done by man. Various types of crops are grown depending upon the type of soil and climatic conditions. Hence crop fields are known as artificial ecosystems.

193. Complete the following analogy.
  (i) Sewage : Biodegradable : : Mercury : _____
  (ii) Automobile exhaust : Gaseous waste : : Trash and rubbish : _____
  (iii) Paper and plastic : Recycling : : Hospital waste : _____
  (iv) Global warming : Troposphere : : Ozone depletion : _____
  (v) Household waste : Compost : : Incineration : _____

Ans. (i) Non-biodegradable
  (ii) Solid waste
  (iii) Incineration
  (iv) Stratosphere
  (v) Chemical waste

194. Why have been kulhads banned for serving tea on platforms? What types of cups are used in trains and platforms?

Ans. Kulhads are made from the top fertile layer of soil. Use of this soil to make kulhads on a large scale would lead to loss of fertile top soil. This fertile top soil is of great use for the growth of plants as it contains many useful nutrients. Hence kulhads have been banned for serving tea on platforms. Nowadays disposable paper cups are used in trains and platforms.

195. Given below is an energy flow diagram. Study it carefully and answer the following questions:

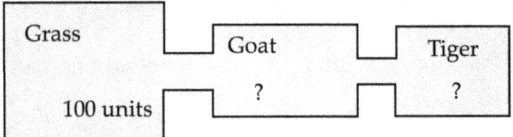

  (i) How much energy (in units) will pass from grass to goat?
  (ii) How much energy (in units) will pass from goat to tiger?
  (iii) Which law operates during the transfer of energy from grass to goat to tiger?

Ans. (i) 10 units of energy will pass from grass to goat.
  (ii) 1 unit of energy will pass from goat to tiger.
  (iii) Lindeman's Ten percent law operates during the transfer of energy from grass to goat to tiger.

196. What is energy pyramid? Why is it broader at base and narrower at the apex region?

Ans. An energy pyramid is a graphical representation of the flow of energy from the producers through the various consumers. It shows the amount of energy available and the loss of useful energy at each step of the food chain in an ecosystem. As the energy gets transferred from lower trophic level to the higher one, there is a loss of large amount of energy due to metabolism and as heat. As a result very little energy (i.e., 10%) gets transferred to the next level. So the trophic level at the base has maximum energy and that at the top has the least amount of energy. Hence energy pyramid is broader at the base and narrower at the top.

197. When plants are eaten by primary consumers a great deal of energy is lost as heat to the environment and some amount goes in carrying out various life processes. State the average percentage of energy lost in this manner.

Ans. The average percentage of energy lost when plants are eaten by primary consumers is 90%.

198. Write one word answer for the following statements or definitions?
  (i) Decline in the thickness of ozone layer over a restricted area.
  (ii) The substances which react with the ozone layer in the stratosphere and destroy it.
  (iii) The useless left over or discarded materials.

Ans. (i) Ozone hole
  (ii) Ozone depleting substances.
  (iii) Wastes

199. "Industrialization is one of the main cause of deterioration of environment." List any four reasons in favour of this statement.

Ans. (a) Industrialization leads to generation of harmful gases which when released to environment deteriorate the quality of air. It causes air pollution which affects life of plants, humans, animals etc.
  (b) The effluents generated from industries if comes in contact with water bodies like rivers, lakes etc., will cause water pollution.
  (c) Big machines used in industries produce a lot of noise causing noise pollution.
  (d) The harmful chemicals and toxic substances generated from industries if released into soil will contaminate the soil leading to loss of fertility of the soil thus causing soil pollution.

Application Based Questions

200. Your uncle has come from the village to renew the contract to supply frogs to the laboratories of the colleges of the town. While talking to you, he mentioned that cases of malaria have increased in his village. In addition population of grasshoppers has also increased that are damaging crops.
  (i) What could be the reasons for such problems faced by villagers?
  (ii) What suggestions will you give to your uncle?

Ans. (i) As uncle is supplying frogs from his village to laboratories so the number of frog population is decreasing. Frogs eat grasshoppers and mosquitoes. But as the number of frogs population is reduced so the population of grasshoppers and mosquitoes are increasing. So malaria is spreading in the village by mosquitoes and grasshoppers are causing damage to the crops.
  (ii) He must stop the supply of frogs to the laboratories as the reduced frog population is causing an imbalance in the food chain and proper ratio of frogs, grasshoppers and mosquitoes can not be maintained in the ecosystem.

201. Meera saw that her friend Reema was carrying polythene bags for shopping. She immediately stops her and told her not to carry polythene bags.
  (i) Why Meera stopped her friend Reema to carry polythene bags for shopping?
  (ii) What alternatives could be done to replace polythene bags?

Ans. (i) Polythene is made from a polymer which is a chemical and is non-biodegradable which needs proper disposal techniques. It can accumulate in soil causing loss of fertility or might block drains leading to water logging. If not disposed properly, animals like cow would eat them which might block their alimentary canal. So, Meera stopped her friend Reema to carry polythene bags for shopping.
  (ii) We can replace polythene bags with jute bags or paper bags for shopping.

202. Ayush went to a nearby park with his friends for a picnic. He saw that after picnic is over all his friends were throwing the leftover food, plates, cups, glasses here and there. He suggests them not to do like that and segregate the wastes and dispose them in red and green dustbins kept in park.
  (i) Why do you think Ayush told his friends to segregate wastes and throw in separate dustbins?
  (ii) How can we contribute in keeping parks, roads, sea beaches clean?

Ans. (i) Ayush told his friends to segregate wastes because there are two types of wastes- biodegradable wastes which include leftover foods, peels of vegetables, fruits, paper plates etc., and the other type of wastes is non-biodegradable which includes plastic cups, glasses etc. Both these wastes undergo separate techniques for their degradation hence they should kept in separate dustbin.
  (ii) We can help in keeping parks, roads, sea beaches clean by not littering, organise campaigns to create awareness among people about cleanliness, keeping dustbins in these places and throwing wastes only in dustbins, separating biodegradable and non-biodegradable wastes and proper disposal of these wastes.

203. A huge water body was being used for fishing, but after the set of industries near this water bodies when people consume fishes they start falling ill.
  (i) What might be the cause of their illness after setting up of industries?
  (ii) What steps must be taken by authorities to overcome this problem?
  (iii) Name the biological phenomenon involved in this case.

Ans. (i) The effluents of industries containing non-biodegradable wastes get mixed with water bodies. These non-biodegradable toxic wastes get accumulated in the body of the fishes and when people consumed these fishes they fall ill.
  (ii) Effluents should be properly treated before letting them into water bodies.
  (iii) This phenomenon is called biomagnification.

204. While going to school and coming back from school Tarun watches that in a slum area they burn plastics which produce lot of gases.
  (i) Is burning of plastic environmental friendly?
  (ii) Suggest two alternatives for proper disposal of plastics?

Ans. (i) No, burning of plastics is not environment friendly because it releases various harmful and toxic gases which may cause health hazards. Some of the gases are carcinogenic and they also cause respiratory problems.
  (ii) We should reuse plastics or we can recycle plastics in recycle plants.

Creating Based Questions

205. Why energy transfer is said to be unidirectional whereas biochemical transfer is said to be cyclic?

Ans. Energy transfer is said to be unidirectional because when the energy is absorbed by autotrophs from the sun, it is never reabsorbed by it. Similarly, when consumers eat up the producers directly or indirectly the energy transferred in this process can never be reversed in the food chain. In biogeochemical cycles chemical elements move from environment to organism and back to the environment.

206. Study the table and complete the missing terms.

S. No.	Nature of food chain	Producers	Consumers	Consumers	Consumers
1.	Forests	Trees, shrubs	Deer	……(a)……	Man
2.	Grasslands	……(b)……	Grasshopper/Frog	……(c)……	Vulture
3.	Pond	Decay plants	Worms	Fish	……(d)……

Ans. (a) Tiger
  (b) Grass
  (c) Snake
  (d) Shark

207. Rita wants to have an aquarium at home. What are the things that she needs to keep in mind in designing an aquarium?

Ans. The fish would need a free space for swimming, water, oxygen and food. Thus, she needs a good aquarium tank, oxygen can be provided through an oxygen pump (aerator) and fish food is available in the market.

Water parameters for nitrate, nitrite, ammonia and pH levels are to be maintained. To condition water properly, use a de-chlorinating and biological aquarium supplement. It is recommended to change 25 percent of the aquarium water at least once a month. This will help maintain a clean and healthy tank, plus it keeps nitrate concentrations at a safe level. Overcrowding can lead to low oxygen levels in the water. Another crisis of overcrowding includes excess waste, which clogs the filter and degrades the aquarium water.

208. Using the following information, form a pathway which shows the flow of energy at each trophic level. And also include information that is not mentioned below to complete it.

light energy, organic products, first trophic level, herbivores, second trophic level, energy.

Ans. Light energy green surfaces of plants ⟶ chemical energy stored in various ⟶ organic products in the plants first trophic level herbivores consume ⟶ plants as food second trophic level convert **chemical energy** into **kinetic energy** herbivores ⟶ are consumed by carnivores of the first order ⟶ **(secondary consumers)** third trophic level ⟶ **primary carnivores** are consumed by ⟶ **top carnivores** (last level) energy will be degraded.

209. Using the following information form a pathway showing the formation of ozone at higher levels. And also include information that is not mentioned below to complete it.

Ozone, UV, Molecular oxygen.

Ans. Ozone production ⟶ UV radiation acting on oxygen (O_2) molecule ⟶ the higher energy UV radiations split apart some molecular oxygen (O_2)
⟶ $O_2 \xrightarrow{UV} O + O$ ⟶ free oxygen (O) atoms then ⟶ combine with molecular oxygen ozone
$O + O_2 \longrightarrow \underset{\text{(Ozone)}}{O_3}$

210. Shyam was very upset after reading the news of a whale shark that was found dead in waters off the Tanjung Aru beach in Menumbok. Postmortem results showed the shark had died of starvation and indigestion as it had a huge plastic bag stuck in its stomach. Suggest some measures that can be taken to reduce plastic waste.

Ans. Cloth bags can be used instead of using plastic bags as they are washable, strong and more durable than plastic bags. They are made of biodegradable material and do not pollute the environment. They can be recycled and reused and are capable of carrying more things. These days, new types of plastics which are said to be biodegradable, are available.

Self-Assessment

211. What is the functional unit of the environment comprising of the living and non-living components called?

212. Name two natural ecosystems and two artificial ecosystems?

213. Which one term in the following includes the others?

    Air, flora, fauna, environment, water, sunlight, soil.

214. State a way to prevent accumulation of harmful chemicals in our bodies.

215. What is the difference between the food habits of organisms belonging to the first and third trophic levels? Give one example each of the organisms belonging to these two trophic levels.

216. What are planktons?

217. Give reasons:
    (i) Forest ecosystem is more stable than a cropland ecosystem.
    (ii) Available energy goes on decreasing at each trophic level in a food chain.

218. Give examples of the following:
    (i) Two step food chain in a forest ecosystem.
    (ii) Three step food chain in a forest ecosystem.
    (iii) Four step food chain in a pond ecosystem.

219. Name the following:
    (i) Organisms feeding on animal and plant food.
    (ii) Organisms breaking down wastes of living beings.
    (iii) The organisms occupying the first trophic level of any food chain.
    (iv) A complex network of many interconnected food chains and feeding relationships.
    (v) The cumulative increase in the concentrations of a persistent substance in successively higher levels of the food chain.

220. At which trophic level a person is feeding when he is eating:
    (i) Roasted chicken
    (ii) Bread
    (iii) Eggs
    (iv) Apple
    (v) Fish

221. A student went to study a local pond. In one part of the pond she noticed tadpoles scraping at some pond weed. In another part she saw a water beetle holding a tadpole in its jaws.
    (i) Construct a food chain for the pond ecosystem.
    (ii) How many trophic levels are there in this chain?

222. Explain why there are greater chances of accumulation of harmful chemicals in the body?

223. We often observe domestic waste decomposing in the by-lanes of residential colonies. Suggest ways to make people realize that improper disposal of waste is harmful to the environment.

224. What is Montreal Protocol? Why was it signed?

225. Very briefly explain the phenomenon of ozone layer depletion.

226. **Assertion:** Arctic's ozone depletion tends to be milder and short lived than the Antarctic's.

    Reason: CFCs, Frigid temperatures and sunlight are not present at the Arctic at the same time.

227. The amount of ozone in the atmosphere began to drop sharply in the 1980s. This decrease has been linked to synthetic chemicals like chlorofluorocarbons (CFCs) which are used as refrigerants and in fire extinguishers. In 1987, the United Nations Environment Programme (UNEP) succeeded in forging an agreement to freeze CFC production at 1986 levels. It is now mandatory for all the manufacturing companies to make CFC-free refrigerators throughout the world. Suggest an alternative coolant that can be used.

228. What kind of disposable cups being used on large scale in trains now a days and why?

Sustainable Management of Natural Resources

Chapter 16

Definitions

1. **Resources:** A resource is any means of supplying a material held in reserve which can be transformed into more valuable and useful item.
2. **Natural resources:** They are those substances or materials that exist in nature which are being exploited for supporting life and meeting the needs of human beings. These include air, water, forests, soil, minerals, fossil fuels etc.
3. **Pollution:** Any undesirable change in physical, chemical and biological characteristics of the soil, air or water which harmfully affects human lives or lives of other species.
4. **Ganga Action Plan:** It is a multi-crore project launched in 1985 which has been undertaken to clean the Ganga river.
5. **Namami Gange Programme:** It is an Integrated Conservation Mission, approved as "Flagship Programme" by the Union Government in June 2014 with budget outlay of ₹ 20,000 Crore to accomplish the twin objectives of effective abatement of pollution, conservation and rejuvenation of the National River Ganga.
6. **Biodiversity:** The existence of a wide variety of species of plants, animals, microbes in a natural habitat within a particular environment is called biodiversity.
7. **Fossil fuels:** The fuels that are obtained from dead remains of plants and animals which got buried beneath the earth millions of years ago are called fossil fuels.
8. **Sustainable development:** The development which can be maintained for a long time that meets the need of present generation without compromising the ability and needs for future generations without any damage to the environment.
9. **Conservation of natural resources:** The controlled utilisation of natural resources for the benefit of life so that it may yield sustainable benefit to the present as well as future generations is called conservation of natural resources.
10. **Watershed management:** Scientific conservation of soil and water to increase biomass production is called watershed management.
11. **Rain water harvesting:** The technique to capture and store rain water for future use by making special water harvesting structures is called rain water harvesting.

Multiple Choice Questions

12. **The major ill effect of monoculture practice in forests is on the:***
    (a) biodiversity which faces large destruction.
    (b) local people whose basic needs can no longer be met from such forests.
    (c) industries.
    (d) forest department.

    Ans. (a) biodiversity which faces large destruction.

    Explanation :

    Monoculture has a huge negative impact on forest biodiversity, which is rapidly diminishing. Growing a single type of flora or tree in the forest results in a loss of variety or variance among animal, plant, insect, and bird species.

13. **What is the name for the process of burning municipal solid waste in a properly designed furnace under suitable temperature and operating conditions ?**
    (a) Landfill   (b) Recycling
    (c) Vermi composting   (d) Incineration

    Ans. (d) Incineration

    Explanation :

    Incineration is the process of burning municipal solid waste in a properly built furnace at a temperature and operating pressure that is appropriate for the trash.

* are board exam questions from previous years

14. **Which of these statements are wrong?**
    (a) Fossil fuel is not a renewable source.
    (b) Natural gas is not a renewable source.
    (c) Sunlight is a renewable source.
    (d) Coal is a renewable resource.

    Ans. (d) Coal is a renewable resource.

    Explanation :

    Fossil fuels (petroleum, natural gas, coal) and nuclear power are examples of non-renewable resources of energy. Biomass energy and various kinds of inexhaustible energy, such as solar energy, hydropower, and wind power, are examples of renewable energy sources.

15. **Floods can be prevented by:**
    (a) Afforestation
    (b) Removing top soil
    (c) Deforestation
    (d) Agriculture

    Ans. (a) Afforestation

    Explanation :

    Afforestation also prevents mass wasting which reduces the amount of soil entering the river and keeps the rivers capacity high. When combined with floodplain zoning, afforestation can be very effective at reducing the risk of flooding. Planting trees help prevent erosion because the roots bind the soil.

16. **Which of the following is best method from environment point of view?**
    (a) Reduce
    (b) Recycle
    (c) Reuse
    (d) All of these

    Ans. (d) All of these

    Explanation :

    Reduce, reuse, and recycle are the three essential components of environmentally-responsible consumer behaviour. The 3 R's aims to educate individuals on how to avoid excessive and unneeded waste, as well as how to restrict non-renewable resource consumption.

17. **Select the eco-friendly activity among the following.** [NCERT Exemplar]
    (a) Using car for transportation.
    (b) Using poly bags for shopping.
    (c) Using dyes for colouring clothes.
    (d) Using windmills to generate power for irrigation.

    Ans. (d) Using windmills to generate power for irrigation.

    Explanation :

    Solar energy, wind energy, and geothermal energy are examples of non-polluting, non-exhaustible energy sources. These energy sources are not harmful to the environment. Wind energy, for example, can be harnessed using wind mills to irrigate crops and generate electricity.

18. **The most appropriate definition of a natural resource is that it is a substance or commodity that is :** [NCERT Exemplar]
    (a) Present only on land
    (b) A gift of nature which is very useful to mankind
    (c) A man-made substance placed in nature
    (d) Available only in the forest

    Ans. (b) A gift of nature which is very useful to mankind

    Explanation :

    Natural resources are substances that occur naturally and are valued in their unaltered (natural) state. The amount of material available and the demand for it determines the value of a natural resource.

19. **_____ is a not a greenhouse gas.**
    (a) Nitrous oxide
    (b) Methane
    (c) Carbon dioxide
    (d) Nitrogen

    Ans. (d) Nitrogen

    Explanation :

    Carbon dioxide, methane, chlorofluorocarbons, ozone, nitrous oxide, and water vapour are examples of greenhouse gases.

20. **Which of the following is not a natural resource?** [NCERT Exemplar]
    (a) Mango tree
    (b) Wooden house
    (c) Snake
    (d) Wind

    Ans. (b) Wooden house

    Explanation :

    Wooden houses are made by man. So, it is not a natural resource.

21. **How does organic material in the buried solid waste decompose ?**
    (a) By oxidation
    (b) By microorganisms
    (c) By flow of water
    (d) By soil particles

    Ans. (b) By microorganisms

    Explanation :

    Due to the action of microorganisms, the organic material will decay in the buried solid waste. The trash decomposes aerobically at first, until the aerobic bacteria consumes all of the oxygen in the freshly added fill.

22. **In our country vast tracts of forests are cleared and a single species of plant is cultivated. This practice promotes :** [NCERT Exemplar]
    (a) biodiversity in the area.
    (b) monoculture in the area.
    (c) growth of natural forest.
    (d) preserves the natural ecosystem in the area.

    Ans. (b) monoculture in the area.

Explanation :

The practice of removing enormous tracts of forest and planting a single variety of plant promotes monoculture in the area. As the number of species in the area decreases, this has a negative impact on biodiversity. It also has an adverse effect on the natural environment in the area. It slows down the growth of natural forests.

23. **The three R's that will help us to conserve natural resources for long term use are :**

    [NCERT Exemplar]
    (a) recycle, regenerate, reuse.
    (b) reduce, regenerate, reuse.
    (c) reduce, reuse, redistribute.
    (d) reduce, reuse, recycle.

Ans. (d) reduce, reuse, recycle.

Explanation :

The three R's – reduce, reuse, and recycle – all contribute to reducing the amount of garbage we generate. They save energy, natural resources, and landfill space.

24. **Which of the following is a greenhouse gas?**
    (a) Nitrogen dioxide (b) Sulphur dioxide
    (c) Carbon dioxide   (d) Carbon monoxide

Ans. (c) Carbon dioxide

Explanation :

Greenhouse gases generally trap the earth's radiations, resulting in an increase in the earth's temperature and are the primary cause of global warming. Water vapour, carbon dioxide, methane, nitrous oxide, and ozone are examples of greenhouse gases.

25. **The pH of water sample collected from a river was found to be acidic in the range of 3.5–4.5. On the banks of the river were several factories that were discharging effluents into the river. The effluents of which one of the following factories is the most likely cause for lowering the pH of river water ?**

    [NCERT Exemplar]
    (a) Soap and detergent factory.
    (b) Lead battery manufacturing factory.
    (c) Plastic cup manufacturing factory.
    (d) Alcohol distillery.

Ans. (b) Lead battery manufacturing factory

Explanation :

Lead battery production plants use acids in their batteries, which have a lower pH and are more likely to lower the pH of water when discharged into neighbouring bodies of water.

26. **Select the incorrect statement.**

    [NCERT Exemplar]

    (a) Economic development is linked to environmental conservation.
    (b) Sustainable development encourages development for current generation and conservation of resources for future generations.
    (c) Sustainable development does not consider the view points of stakeholders.
    (d) Sustainable development is a long planned and persistent development.

Ans. (c) Sustainable development does not consider the viewpoints of stakeholders

Explanation :

To prevent natural resource, development operations should be linked to environmental conservation efforts, all stakeholders, including local and indigenous people, should be considered partners in the development process, and development activities should be well planned.

27. **Coliforms are _____.**
    (a) bacteria present in the digestive tract of animals.
    (b) bacteria present in hot springs.
    (c) bacteria present in frigid cold environments.
    (d) All of the above.

Ans. (a) bacteria present in the digestive tract of animals.

Explanation :

Coliforms are bacteria that are always present in the digestive tracts of animals, including intestine of humans, and are found in their wastes. Their presence in water makes the water contaminated and unfit for use.

28. **The most rapidly dwindling resource in the world is _____.**
    (a) air   (b) water
    (c) sunlight (d) forests

Ans. (d) forests

Explanation :

Water, Wind, and Sunlight are natural resources that cannot be depleted, but forests are being cut down in vast quantities by humans for their own benefit, and as a result, they are rapidly depleting.

29. **Read the following sentences and select the correct option from those given below.**

    Statement: Sustainable development has an impact on socio-economic and environmental conditions.

    Reason: Environmental conditions helps in economic development.

    (a) Both the statement and reason are correct and the reason is the correct explanation of the statement.
    (b) Both the statement and reason are correct, but the reason is not the correct explanation of the statement.

(c) Both the statement and the reason are incorrect.
(d) The statement is incorrect.

Ans. (a) Both the statement and reason are correct and the reason is the correct explanation of the statement.

Explanation:

Sustainable development occurs by a change in all aspects of life. Change in the environmental conditions will affect the socio-economic conditions also.

30. **Kulhs is to Himachal Pradesh as bandharas is to _____.**
    (a) Rajasthan (c) Tamil Nadu
    (c) Kerala (d) Maharashtra

Ans. (d) Maharashtra

Explanation:

Kulhs and bandharas are the types of traditional rainwater harvesting systems in India.

31. **Savitri learnt about the different R's of waste management but she is confused about how can she can repurpose the old newspapers. Which of the following options solves her problem?**
    (i) Dissolving, bleaching and then drying
    (ii) Making paper bags
    (iii) Using newspaper to cover her notebooks.
    (a) (i) and (ii) (b) (ii) and (iii)
    (c) (i), (ii) and (iii) (d) (i) and (iii)

Ans. (b) (ii) and (iii)

Explanation:

Dissolving, bleaching and drying are the steps for recycling paper, whereas, making paper bags or using the newspaper to cover her notebooks are some ways of repurposing the old newspapers.

32. **Activities like cutting down trees not only reduce the forest cover but also adversely affect the**
    (a) government forest departments
    (b) industrialists
    (c) wildlife and nature enthusiasts
    (d) local people

Ans. (d) local people

Explanation:

Local people are mostly dependent on forests and forest products. They are the ones who are most adversely affected by the reduced forest cover.

33. **Which of the following sets has all the industries that depend on forests?**
    (a) Rubber, plastic and glass
    (b) Textile, ceramic and marble
    (c) Rubber, textile and glass
    (d) Paper, lac and sports equipment

Ans. (d) Paper, lac and sports equipment

Explanation:

Paper, lac and sports equipment industries are dependent on forest products. We get paper from wood pulp. Sports equipment are generally made from oak or maple wood that is obtained from the forests.

34. **Why do we need to manage our natural resources?**
    (a) To meet the demand of the increasing population
    (b) To save it for the future generations
    (c) Because natural resources are not unlimited
    (d) All of the above

Ans. (d) All of the above

Explanation:

We need to manage our natural resources because these are not unlimited. With the increasing population, the demand for natural resources is also increasing. If we will not manage it now, then they might get exhausted shortly and our future generations may suffer.

35. **What is the relationship between the utility of coal and petroleum and the efficiency of machines?**
    (a) More use of coal and petroleum increases the efficiency of machines.
    (b) More efficient machines use more coal and petroleum.
    (c) More efficient machines useless coal and petroleum.
    (d) More use of coal and petroleum decreases the efficiency of machines.

Ans. (c) More efficient machines useless coal and petroleum.

Explanation:

Machines with high efficiency use less fuel and give more work output.

36. **Which of the following sets contains all the resources that we need to manage sustainably?**
    (a) Forest, wildlife, water, coal and petroleum
    (b) Solar energy, water and coal
    (c) Tidal energy, coal and petroleum
    (d) Geothermal energy, coal and forests

Ans. (a) Forest, wildlife, water, coal and petroleum

Explanation:

Forests, wildlife, water, coal and petroleum are all exhaustible sources of energy. Therefore, we need to manage these resources sustainably.

37. **Which of the following stakeholders owns the land and controls the resources from forests?**
    (a) Tribal people
    (b) Forest department of the government
    (c) Nature enthusiasts
    (d) Industrialists

Ans. (b) Forest department of the government

Explanation :

The forest department of the government owns the land and controls the resources from the forests. Industrialists depend on the forests products. They do not own the land. Wildlife enthusiasts want to conserve nature. Tribal people were living in forests for centuaries. Britishers took over the control of the forests from these tribal people. In independent India, forest department finally took over the control of forests from britishers.

38. Which of the following statements is incorrect?
  (a) The five R's of resource management are for fossil fuels only.
  (b) Sustainable development also involves the safe disposal of wastes.
  (c) Equitable sharing is an important feature of sustainable development.
  (d) Earth has an unlimited supply of all-natural resources.

Ans. (a) The five R's of resource management are for fossil fuels only.

Explanation :

The five R's, that is Refuse, Reduce, Reuse, Recycle and Repurpose is the strategy used for the management of all the natural resources and not just the fossil fuels.

39. Which of the following sets contain all the materials that can be recycled as well as repurposed?
  (a) Wood, paper, water, coal
  (b) Plastic, glass and paper
  (c) Coal, plastic and paper
  (d) Natural gas, petroleum and paper

Ans. (b) Plastic, glass and paper

Explanation :

Plastic, glass and paper can be recycled and repurposed. For example, we can recycle paper or we can also use it for making paper bags.

40. Supriya listed some activities observed in the forest region. Which of the following given activities can be harmful to the region?
  (i) Cutting down trees for paper
  (ii) Collecting latex from the rubber trees
  (iii) People collecting the fallen berries and nuts
  (iv) Cattle grazing
  (a) (ii) and (iii)   (b) Only (i)
  (c) (i), (ii), (iii) and (iv)   (d) Only (iii)

Ans. (b) Only (i)

Explanation :

Collecting latex from rubber trees does not harm trees. Moreover, cattle grazing is part of the ecosystem activity. Such activities help maintain the ecological balance. So, these are not harmful activities. Cutting down trees for any purpose is a harmful activity.

41. Fossil fuels such as coal and petroleum are categorised as non-renewable sources of energy because
  (a) they are unlimited
  (b) they take millions of years to form
  (c) they are never renewed or reformed in nature
  (d) they cannot be formed by humans

Ans. (b) they take millions of years to form

Explanation :

Fossil fuels are considered non-renewable resources because they take millions of years to form.

42. The important message conveyed by the "Chipko Movement" is : [NCERT Exemplar]
  (a) to involve the community in forest conservation efforts
  (b) to ignore the community in forest conservation efforts
  (c) to cut down forest trees for developmental activities
  (d) government agencies have the unquestionable right to order destruction of trees in forests.

Ans. (a) to involve the community in forest conservation efforts

Explanation :

The 'Chipko Movement' sends a strong message to the public about the importance of community participation in forest conservation activities. People's involvement can aid in the expansion of forests as well as their conservation.

43. In our country there are attempts to increase the height of several existing dams like Tehri and Almati dams across Narmada. Choose the correct statements among the following that are a consequence of raising the height of dams.
[NCERT Exemplar]
  (i) Terrestrial flora and fauna of the area is destroyed completely.
  (ii) Dislocation of people and domestic animals living in the area.
  (iii) Valuable agricultural land may be permanently lost.
  (iv) It will generate permanent employment for people.
  (a) (i), (ii)   (b) (i), (ii), (iii)
  (c) (ii), (iv)   (d) (i), (iii), (iv)

Ans. (b) (i), (ii), (iii)

Explanation :

Raising dam heights will permanently submerge enormous tracts of land, displacing indigenous people and causing permanent loss of indigenous flora and fauna as well as agricultural land.

44. **Expand the abbreviation GAP.**
    [NCERT Exemplar]
    (a) Government Agency for Pollution control
    (b) Gross Assimilation by Photosynthesis
    (c) Ganga Action Plan
    (d) Governmental Agency for animal Protection

Ans. (c) Ganga action plan

Explanation :

Ganga Action Plan is abbreviated as GAP. As the quality of water in the Ganga was deteriorating owing to pollution, this multi-crore project was conceived in 1985.

45. **Narmada bachao andolan was to:**
    (a) clean Narmada   (b) expand Narmada
    (c) save Narmada   (d) none of these

Ans. (c) save Narmada

Explanation :

The Narmada Bachao Andolan (NBA) is an Indian social movement led by adivasis (indigenous people), farmers, environmentalists, and human rights activists who protested a series of huge dam projects on the Narmada River.

46. **Pick the right combination of terms which has no fossil fuel.** [NCERT Exemplar]
    (a) Wind, ocean and coal
    (b) Kerosene, wind and tide
    (c) Wind, wood, sun
    (d) Petroleum, wood, sun

Ans. (c) Wind, wood, sun

Explanation :

Fossil fuels are obtained from the decomposition of dead plants and animals. Wood is a source of energy as well, although it is not a fossil fuel. Unlike fossil fuels, which have a finite supply and so are exhaustible sources of energy, wind and sun are inexhaustible sources of energy.

47. **The practice of controlling the growth of trees and their quality to meet specific human needs is called _____.**
    (a) sericulture   (b) apiculture
    (c) silviculture   (d) agriculture

Ans. (c) silviculture

Explanation :

Silviculture is the activity of managing the growth, composition/structure, and quality of forests in order to accomplish certain goals and objectives, such as timber output.

48. **Which of the following statements refers to repurpose?**

(a) Using old plastic bottles for growing plants.
(b) Melting old plastic bottles to make new bottles.
(c) Replacing all plastic bottles with steel bottles.
(d) Cleaning the plastic bottle to use it again.

Ans. (a) Using old plastic bottles for growing plants.

Explanation :

Repurpose means using the product for some other purpose. Therefore, using old plastic bottles for growing plants is an example of repurposing.

49. **Which of the following is not a direct stakeholder of the conservation of forests?**
    (a) Industrialists like those having paper mills
    (b) Forest department
    (c) Nature enthusiasts
    (d) People living in urban areas

Ans. (d) People living in urban areas

Explanation :

People living in urban areas are not direct stakeholders in forest conservation. This is because they are not directly associated with the forests and their products.

50. **How does the uncontrolled exploitation of forests by industries affect the local people?**
    (a) Reduction of natural resources
    (b) Economic loss
    (c) Reduction in food for cattle
    (d) All of the above

Ans. (d) All of the above

Explanation :

The local people are highly affected in many different ways. Some of the effects include reduction of natural resources, economic loss and reduction in grazing area for cattle.

51. **Which of the following given sets has the sources of carbon that can also lead to global warming?**
    (a) Coal and petroleum
    (b) Methane and sulphur dioxide
    (c) Natural gas and oxides of nitrogen
    (d) Acid rain and petroleum

Ans. (a) Coal and petroleum

Explanation :

Fossil fuels, including coal and petroleum, are the sources of carbon. Their combustion releases carbon dioxide that increases the global temperature.

52. **Which of the following statements is true about fossil fuels?**
    (i) The burning of fossil fuels releases oxides of nitrogen.
    (ii) Fossil fuel is used for combustion in engines. It releases energy that is used for different purposes.

(iii) The burning of fossil fuels also releases carbon monoxide and carbon dioxide. Both these gases are taken up by the plants and hence are not harmful.
(a) (i) and (ii) (b) (ii) and (iii)
(c) Only (i) (d) Only (iii)

Ans. (a) (i) and (ii)

Explanation :

Fossil fuels are used for combustion in engines. On combustion, fossil fuels released different gases like nitrogen oxide, carbon dioxide and carbon monoxide, etc. All these gases are harmful.

53. **The Chipko Andolan movement first originated in**
(a) Reni in Garhwal (b) Rajasthan
(c) Madhya Pradesh (d) Punjab

Ans. (a) Reni in Garhwal

Explanation :

The Chipko Andolan first originated in Reni in Garhwal which is located high up in the Himalayas.

54. **Khejri trees in Khejrali village were saved by a group of**
(a) men (b) women
(c) children (d) old

Ans. (b) women

Explanation :

Amrita Devi Bishnoi in 1731 sacrificed her life along with 363 others while saving khejri trees in Khejrali village near Jodhpur in Rajasthan.

55. **It is important to make small check dams across the flooded gullies because they :**
[NCERT Exemplar]
(i) hold water for irrigation.
(ii) hold water and prevent soil erosion.
(iii) recharge ground water.
(iv) hold water permanently.
(a) (i), (iv) (b) (ii), (iii)
(c) (iii), (iv) (d) (ii), (iv)

Ans. (b) (ii), (iii)

Explanation :

Small check dams help recharge groundwater by retaining water and preventing soil erosion. Thus, it is important to construct small check dams cross flooded gullies.

56. **Why do the construction of dams, despite their benefits, face a lot of criticism?**
(a) Because it displaces a large number of tribals without adequate rehabilitation.
(b) Because it involves a huge amount of public money.
(c) Because it leads to loss of biological diversity.
(d) All of the above

Ans. (d) All of the above

* are board exam questions from previous years

Explanation :

Construction of dams despite their benefits face a lot of criticism because it displaces a large number of people in the nearby areas. It requires a lot of money and it also involves deforestation that may lead to the loss of biological diversity.

57. **A diagram of traditional water harvesting system is given below :***

The statement which defines the system and its parts is:
(a) This is an ideal setting of the Khadin system and A = Catchment area; B = Saline area and C = Shallow dugwell
(b) This is an ideal setting of the Shallow dugwell system and A = Catchment area; B = Saline area and C = Khadin
(c) This is an ideal setting of Catchment area and A = Khadin, B = Saline area and C = Shallow dugwell
(d) This is an ideal setting of Saline area and A = Catchment area; B = Khadin and C = Shallow dugwell

Ans. (a) This is an ideal setting of the Khadin system and A = Catchment area, B = Saline area and C= Shallow dugwell.

Explanation :

In India, the Khadin water collecting technique is a centuries-old concept that is mostly used in Rajasthan. The gathered water is primarily used in agriculture. It is divided into several sections: the catchment region, the Khadin or cropped area, the Khadin bund, the saline area, and the shallow dugwell.

58. **The pH range most conductive for life of fresh water plants and animals is :** [NCERT Exemplar]
(a) 6.5–7.5 (b) 2.0–3.5
(c) 3.5–5.0 (d) 9.0–10.5

Ans. (a) 6.5–7.5

Explanation :

In freshwater, a neutral pH is best for living things. This pH range, 6.5-7.5, is almost neutral.

59. **Water harvesting is a method which?**
(a) Increases ground water level.
(b) Not practiced in modern days.
(c) Has no relation with ground water.
(d) Decreases ground water level.

Ans. (a) Increase ground water level.

Explanation :

Rainwater harvesting is the process of collecting and storing rainwater rather than letting it flow off. By increasing the level of the water table, rainwater collecting recharges the groundwater supply.

60. **Khadins, Bundhis, Ahars and Kattas are ancient structures that are examples for :**

    [NCERT Exemplar]

    (a) Grain storage (b) Wood storage
    (c) Water harvesting (d) Soil conservation

Ans. (c) Water harvesting

Explanation :

Water harvesting is a centuries-old Indian notion that has been performed for many years. For water harvesting, Khadin structures are used in Rajasthan, Bundhis in Madhya Pradesh and Uttar Pradesh, Ahars in Bihar, and Kattas in Karnataka. Water harvesting is still done with these types of antique buildings.

61. **Which of the following was a local canal-based irrigation system and where was it found?**
    (a) *Kulhs*, Rajasthan
    (b) *Kulhs*, Himachal Pradesh
    (c) *Khadin*, Uttar Pradesh
    (d) *Kattas*, Karnataka

Ans. (b) *Kulhs*, Himachal Pradesh

Explanation :

Kulhs were the local canal-based irrigation system found four hundred years ago in Himachal Pradesh. The stream of water flowing down the hills was diverted into man-made canals.

62. **Groundwater is relatively purer than surface water. Which of the following best justifies the above statement?**
    I. Groundwater is collected after filtration through multiple layers of the soil.
    II. Mosquitoes do not breed in it.
    III. Human activities do not affect the groundwater.
    (a) Both II and III (b) Both I and III
    (c) I, II and III (d) Both I and II

Ans. (d) Both I and II

Explanation :

Groundwater is relatively purer than surface water because it is collected after filtration through multiple layers. Mosquitoes cannot breed in it. However, some human activities like overuse of the fertilisers can still pollute it.

63. **Near a residential area, sewage is directly dumped into the nearby river. Which of the following would best indicate the biological contamination level of the river?**

    (a) The total dissolved salts
    (b) The total coliform level
    (c) The total BOD
    (d) The total inorganic and organic matter

Ans. (b) The total coliform level

Explanation :

Contamination levels in a water body can be detected by determining the total coliform level in the water from that water body.

64. **Which of the following does NOT reduce the groundwater level?**
    (a) Irrigation activities
    (b) Diversion of water from water bodies for different purposes
    (c) Global warming
    (d) Acid rain

Ans. (d) Acid rain

Explanation :

Acid rain will not decrease the level of groundwater although, it may affect its quality.

65. **How does the collection of water underground, rather than on the surface, also help in the prevention of diseases?**
    (a) Groundwater is purer.
    (b) Groundwater does not allow the breeding of mosquitoes.
    (c) Groundwater has more dissolved minerals.
    (d) Groundwater boosts the immunity.

Ans. (b) Groundwater does not allow the breeding of mosquitoes.

Explanation :

Groundwater does not provide any breeding grounds to the disease-causing mosquitoes.

66. **Match the following traditional water harvesting with their respective region.**

Water harvesting system	Regions
1. *Khadins*	(a) Maharashtra
2. *Tals*	(b) Bihar
3. *Bundhis*	(c) Rajasthan
4. *Ahars*	(d) Madhya Pradesh

(a) 1. (a), 2. (c), 3. (d), 4. (b)
(b) 1. (c), 2. (a), 3. (d), 4. (b)
(c) 1. (d), 2. (a), 3. (b), 4. (c)
(d) 1. (c), 2. (b), 3. (a), 4. (b)

Ans. (b) 1. (c), 2. (a), 3. (d), 4. (b)

Explanation :

Khadins, tals, bundhis and ahars are different types of traditional water harvesting systems. They are named differently region wise. They may also differ in their structure and the method of use.

For example, khadin consists of a large earthen embankment that is build across the slopes to collect the surface-run off water.

Region wise classification of these systems is as given below.

Water harvesting system	Regions
1. *Khadins*	Rajasthan
2. *Tals*	Maharashtra
3. *Bundhis*	Madhya Pradesh
4. *Ahars*	**Bihar**

67. **The depletion of the groundwater can be prevented by**
    (a) increasing the number of wells and tubewells in an area
    (b) increasing the dependence on groundwater for irrigation purposes
    (c) preventing the deforestation
    (d) planting more trees in dry regions

Ans. (c) preventing the deforestation

Explanation :

Planting more trees in dry regions can further deplete the groundwater. Trees in the forests help bring about more precipitation. Preventing deforestation in nearby areas can also prevent the depletion of groundwater.

68. **In a largely levelled terrains, the water harvesting structures are mainly**
    (a) straight concrete check dams
    (b) crescent-shaped
    (c) star-shaped
    (d) Both A and B

Ans. (d) Both A and B

Explanation :

The water harvesting structures in a levelled terrain can be crescent-shaped earthen embankments or straight concrete check dams.

69. **The process of planting trees or sowing seeds in a barren patch of land to create a forest or a stand of trees is called:**
    (a) Agriculture (b) Aestivation
    (c) Vegetation (d) Afforestation

Ans. (d) Afforestation

Explanation :

Afforestation involves the planting of trees in a drainage basin to increase interception and storage while reducing surface runoff. This reduces a rivers discharge and so makes it less likely to flood.

70. **A successful forest conservation strategy should involve :** [NCERT Exemplar]
    (a) protection of animals at the highest trophic level
    (b) protection of only consumers
    (c) protection of only herbivores
    (d) comprehensive programme to protect all the physical and biological components

Ans. (d) comprehensive programme to protect all the physical and biological components

Explanation :

At one trophic level, a balance cannot be achieved. There is a need for a complete policy that protects both physical and biological components, rather than just animals, consumers, and herbivores.

Assertion and Reasoning Based Questions

71. **Assertion:** Reuse is better than recycling.
    Reason: Recycling uses some energy.
    (a) If both assertion and reason are true and reason is the correct explanation of assertion.
    (b) If both assertion and reason are true, but reason is not the correct explanation of assertion.
    (c) If assertion is true, but reason is false.
    (d) If assertion is false, but reason is true.

Ans. (a) If both assertion and reason are true and reason is the correct explanation of assertion.

Explanation :

Reuse refers to the use of the same material again and again. In the reuse of materials, no energy is consumed and the resources are saved. For instance, plastic bottles in which we boy various food items like jam and pickle can used for storing things in recycling certain used materials are converted into other useful materials in the kitchen. On the other hand, in recycling of materials, energy is consumed and the resources may be wasted. Thus, both assertion and reason are true and reason is the correct explanation of the assertion.

72. **Assertion:** There are abundant coliform bacteria in the river Ganga.
    Reason: Coliform bacteria are found in human intestines and in unburnt corpses.
    (a) If both assertion and reason are true and reason is the correct explanation of assertion.
    (b) If both assertion and reason are true, but reason is not the correct explanation of assertion.
    (c) If assertion is true, but reason is false.
    (d) If assertion is false, but reason is true.

Ans. (a) If both assertion and reason are true and reason is the correct explanation of assertion.

Explanation :

There are abundant coliform bacteria in the river Ganga and the presence of coliform bacteria indicates that the water is contaminated and unfit for use. These bacterias are found in the human intestine and therefore the immersion of the unburnt corpses are the reason behind the presence of abundance of coliform bacteria in the river Ganga. Thus, both assertion and reason are true and reason is the correction explanation of assertion.

73. **Assertion:** Sustainable development encourages development for present generation and conservation of resources for future generations.

    Reason: Sustainable development does not consider the viewpoints of stakeholders.
    (a) If both assertion and reason are true and reason is the correct explanation of assertion.
    (b) If both assertion and reason are true, but reason is not the correct explanation of assertion.
    (c) If assertion is true, but reason is false.
    (d) If assertion is false, but reason is true.

Ans. (c) If assertion is true, but reason is false.

Explanation :

Sustainable development takes into consideration both economic growth and ecological conservation simultaneously. Management of forest resources has to take into account the interests of various stakeholders. Thus, assertion is true but reason is false.

74. **Assertion:** Recycling of waste material can help in maintaining ecological balance.

    Reason: Non-biodegradable waste poses serious disposal problems.
    (a) If both assertion and reason are true and reason is the correct explanation of assertion.
    (b) If both assertion and reason are true, but reason is not the correct explanation of assertion.
    (c) If assertion is true, but reason is false.
    (d) If assertion is false, but reason is true.

Ans. (a) If both assertion and reason are true and reason is the correct explanation of assertion.

Explanation :

Certain Non-biodegradable waste like rubber and plastic pose serious disposal problems. Such substances can be recycled to manufacture usable articles, example: recycling of used polythene and aluminium foils. Thus, both assertion and reason are true and reason is the correct explanation of the assertion.

75. **Assertion:** Mining causes pollution.

    Reason: Large amount of slag is discarded for every tonne of metal extracted.
    (a) If both assertion and reason are true and reason is the correct explanation of assertion.
    (b) If both assertion and reason are true, but reason is not the correct explanation of assertion.
    (c) If assertion is true, but reason is false.
    (d) If assertion is false, but reason is true.

Ans. (a) If both assertion and reason are true and reason is the correct explanation of assertion.

Explanation :

Mining causes pollution because of the large amount of slag which is discarded for every tonne of metal extracted. Hence, sustainable natural resource management demands that we plan for the safe disposal of these wastes too. Thus, both assertion and reason are true and reason is the correct explanation of the assertion.

76. **Assertion:** One of the major objectives of conservation is to protect biodiversity.

    Reason: Conservation will help in making the resources available for our future generations.
    (a) If both assertion and reason are true and reason is the correct explanation of assertion.
    (b) If both assertion and reason are true, but reason is not the correct explanation of assertion.
    (c) If assertion is true, but reason is false.
    (d) If assertion is false, but reason is true.

Ans. (b) If both assertion and reason are true, but reason is not the correct explanation of assertion.

Explanation :

One of the major objectives of conservation is to protect the biodiversity because the loss in biodiversity can also lead to ecological imbalance. Thus both assertion and reason are true, but reason is not the correct explanation of assertion.

77. **Assertion:** Forests are 'biodiversity hotspots'.

    Reason: In forest we can find variety of species of both flora and fauna.
    (a) If both assertion and reason are true and reason is the correct explanation of assertion.
    (b) If both assertion and reason are true, but reason is not the correct explanation of assertion.
    (c) If assertion is true, but reason is false.
    (d) If assertion is false, but reason is true.

Ans. (a) If both assertion and reason are true and reason is the correct explanation of assertion.

Explanation :

Biodiversity hotspot means a place where large number of species are found. Forests satisfy this criteria. In forest we can find variety of species of both flora and fauna. The range of different life forms *i.e.,* bacteria, fungi, ferns, flowering plants, variety of animals likes insects, birds, reptiles, aves, mammals, etc., are all found in the forest. Thus, both assertion and reason are true and reason is the correct explanation of the assertion.

Case Based Questions

78. **Read the passage carefully and answer the following questions from Q 78 (i) to 78 (v).**

    Study the photograph of a forest given below carefully and then answer the questions.

    (i) Before Britishers came to our country, a lot of people lived in forests for centuries and still forests were alive. This is because:
    (a) they worshipped forests.
    (b) they did not use resources from forests.
    (c) they planted trees.
    (d) they developed sustainable practices to use the resources.

    (ii) Which one of the following industries is not based on forest produce?
    (a) sports equipment
    (b) lac
    (c) textile
    (d) paper

    (iii) Who are the important stakeholders those need to be considered when we discuss conservation of forests?
    (a) industrialists using forest produces
    (b) local people
    (c) conservation activists
    (d) all of the above

    (iv) We conserve forests so that:
    (a) we can preserve the biodiversity we have inherited.
    (b) we can preserve animal.
    (c) we can run forest-based industries.
    (d) we can use more plants.

    (v) Local people living in or around forests do not use forests for:
    (a) fishing and hunting.
    (b) getting firewood, timber and thatch.
    (c) getting fruits, nuts and medicines.
    (d) getting electricity.

Ans. (i) (d) they developed sustainable practices to use the resources
(ii) (c) textile
(iii) (d) All of the above
(iv) (a) we can preserve the biodiversity we have inherited.
(v) (d) getting electricity

79. **Read the passage carefully and answer the following questions from Q 79 (i) to 79 (v).**

    In present world, most of the energy sources comes from non-renewable energy sources such as petroleum, hydrocarbons (gases and liquids), natural gas, coal, and nuclear energy. All these sources of energy are called non-renewable because their supplies are limited to the amounts that we can mine or extract from the earth.

    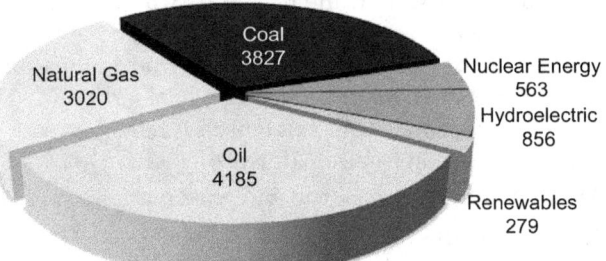

    World Energy Sources, nameplate capacity 2013 Million tonnes oil equivalent

    (i) When combustion takes place in insufficient air (oxygen), then _____ is formed instead of carbon dioxide.
    (a) carbonate
    (b) oxygen
    (c) carbon monoxide
    (d) carbon tetraoxide

    (ii) Coal and petroleum were formed from the _____ millions of years ago.
    (a) accumulations of metallic ores
    (b) decomposition of animals
    (c) burning of forests
    (d) degradation of biomass

    (iii) Along with carbon, coal is a source of:
    (a) chlorine, hydrogen, and nitrogen.
    (b) hydrogen, nitrogen, and sulphur.
    (c) oxygen, nitrogen, and sulphur.
    (d) hydrogen, nitrogen, and oxygen.

    (iv) Consumption of coal and oil can be reduced best by increasing the use of:
    (a) nuclear energy   (b) hydro-electricity
    (c) natural gas   (d) solar energy

    (v) Which of the following forms of non-renewable energy is not classified under a fossil fuel?
    (a) Nuclear   (b) Petroleum
    (c) Oil   (d) Natural gas

Ans. (i) (c) carbon monoxide
(ii) (d) degradation of biomass
(iii) (b) hydrogen, nitrogen, and sulphur.

(iv) (d) solar energy
(v) (a) Nuclear

80. **Read the passage carefully and answer the following questions from Q 80 (i) to 80 (v).**

India is one of the world's richest countries in terms of its vast array of biological diversity. For centuries, rural communities have relied on their local knowledge to conserve their environment. Through learning from experiences, imitating and observations, rural people have developed a body of knowledge on forest and wildlife conservation. The term conservation in this context refers to the processes of maintaining, protecting and managing forest and wildlife resources. Forests are indispensable for the provision of ecosystem goods and services, spiritual and cultural values, and nutrient cycles. The decline in biodiversity adversely affects rural livelihoods and threatens food, energy and health security of nearby communities.

(i) Endangered species are:
   (a) those that are in danger of extinction.
   (b) whose population has declined to levels from where it is likely to move into the endangered category.
   (c) species with small population may move into the endangered or vulnerable category.
   (d) none of the above

(ii) Amrita Devi Bishnoi National Award is given for:
   (a) Water harvesting
   (b) Wildlife conservation
   (c) Excellence in Science
   (d) Energy conservation

(iii) In which year Indian Wildlife Protection Act was implemented?
   (a) 1972   (b) 1983
   (c) 1999   (d) 2001

(iv) Which one of the following is a great achievement of the Chipko Movement?
   (a) More trees are planted.
   (b) Development in Himalayan region.
   (c) Successfully resisted deforestation.
   (d) Soil erosion gets declined.

(v) A local system of canal irrigation called kulhs is practised in which state?
   (a) Himachal Pradesh
   (b) Orissa
   (c) Uttar Pradesh
   (d) Madhya Pradesh

Ans. (i) (a) Those that are in danger of extinction.
(ii) (b) Wildlife conservation
(iii) (a) 1972
(iv) (c) Successfully resisted deforestation.
(v) (a) Himachal Pradesh

81. **Read the passage carefully and answer the following questions from Q 81 (i) to 81 (v).**

Natural resource management is the taking care of natural resources such as land, water, marine and biological systems, with a particular focus on how the management affects the quality of life for both present and future generations. It is about the long-term implications of thinking and actions about the future, and not just about present. Resource management is all about balancing of natural resources such as materials or substances occurring in nature, which can be exploited for economic gain such as mining, farming, utilising forest, fishing to name a few. Failed approaches to resource management are a big cause of pollution.

(i) Mining causes pollution because of the large amount of which is discarded for every tonne of metal extracted:
   (a) coal   (b) dust
   (c) slush   (d) slag

(ii) Despite nature's monsoon bounty, failure to sustain water availability underground has resulted largely due to:
   (a) loss of vegetation cover.
   (b) diversion for high water demanding crops.
   (c) pollution from industrial effluents and urban wastes.
   (d) All of the above

(iii) Which one of the following water resources ensures availability of water for irrigation, generating electricity and enough water for canal systems?
   (a) Ponds   (b) Dams
   (c) Lakes   (d) Rainwater harvesting

(iv) Which one of the given below is not an advantage of water stored in the ground:
   (a) Ground-water does not evaporate.
   (b) Ground-water spreads out to recharge wells.
   (c) Ground-water provides moisture for vegetation over a wide area.
   (d) Ground-water is not protected from contamination by human and animal waste.

(v) Best way to preserve forests is:
   (a) to enforce human non-intervention totally.
   (b) to stop building dams and roads.
   (c) to manage protected areas by keeping local people out.
   (d) to use the forest resources in a manner that is both environmentally and developmentally sound.

Ans. (i) (d) Slag
(ii) (d) All of the above
(iii) (b) Dams

(iv) (d) Ground-water is not protected from contamination by human and animal waste.

(v) (d) to use the forest resources in a manner that is both environmentally and developmentally sound.

82. **Read the passage carefully and answer the following questions from Q 82 (i) to 82 (v).**

Waste has become a big challenge for the environment and humans in modern times. Our water bodies, our grasslands, our fields, our public spaces; all of them are being affected by the waste we discard. The concept of 5R's is to decrease the amount of things we use and simultaneously also decrease the amount of things we throw away. Since we have limited space on earth to dispose all the waste, it is important to use the resources efficiently and create less waste. The 5Rs play an important role in solving the problems which can arise out of wrong waste management habits.

(i) Which of the following solid wastes describes the term 'Municipal Solid Waste'?
   (a) Toxic   (b) Hazardous
   (c) Non-toxic   (d) Non-hazardous

(ii) Why is it difficult to recycle plastics?
   (a) It is very hard.
   (b) It comes in different sizes.
   (c) It is adhesive.
   (d) It contains different types of polymer resins.

(iii) Which of the following is done on an individual level?
   (a) Burning   (b) Disposal
   (c) Recycling   (d) Source reduction

(iv) Why is recycled paper banned for use in food containers?
   (a) Because it creates a lot of spaces.
   (b) Because it creates contamination.
   (c) Because paper can be used only one time.
   (d) Because paper is very thick and can not cover the food containers.

(v) The burning of solid waste is not recommended because:
   (a) it is very costly.
   (b) it requires a lot of space.
   (c) it requires modern technologies.
   (d) it causes several environmental issues.

Ans. (i) (d) Non-hazardous
(ii) (d) It contains different types of polymer resins.
(iii) (d) Source reduction.
(iv) (b) Because it creates contamination.
(v) (d) it causes several environmental issues.

83. **Read the passage carefully and answer the following questions from Q 83 (i) to 83 (v).**

Observe the picture given below carefully before you answer the questions.

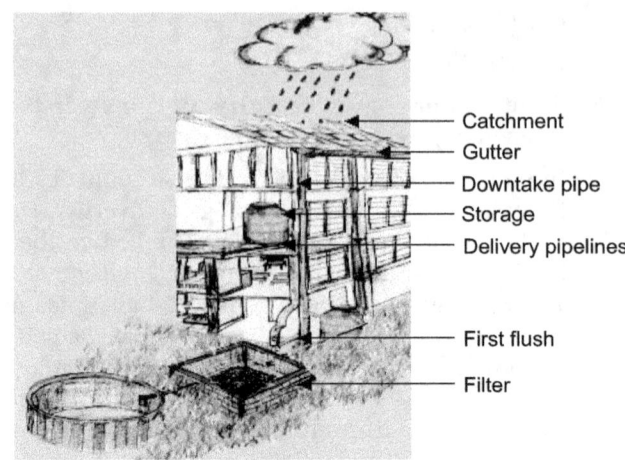

(i) Which process is described in the picture?
   (a) Rain water harvesting
   (b) Water cycle
   (c) Water purification
   (d) Desalting water

(ii) Bandhara, nadi, tals, bundhis, kattas are all names of:
   (a) water harvesting systems around the world
   (b) water harvesting systems in ancient India
   (c) weapons used in ancient India
   (d) forests around the world

(iii) Which of the following statements about water harvesting is not true?
   (a) Water harvesting techniques are highly locale specific and the benefits are also localised.
   (b) Water harvesting is an age-old concept in India.
   (c) Water harvesting processes mitigates droughts and floods.
   (d) Water harvesting cannot be considered as an alternative to the mega-projects like dams.

(iv) Watershed management cannot be used for which one of the following?
   (a) Scientific soil and water conservation.
   (b) Develop primary resources of land and water.
   (c) To run water transport.
   (d) To produce secondary resources of plants and animals.

(v) Various organisations are involved in digging small pits and lakes, building small earthen dams, constructing dykes, building sand and limestone reservoirs as a part of:
   (a) rooftop water collection.
   (b) watershed management.
   (c) community building project.
   (d) rearing fishes.

Ans. (i) (a) rain water harvesting.
(ii) (b) water harvesting systems in ancient India

(iii) (d) Water harvesting cannot be considered as an alternative to the mega-projects like dams.
(iv) (c) To run water transport.
(v) (b) watershed management.

84. Read the passage carefully and answer the following questions from Q 84 (i) to 84 (v).

Forest conservation is the practice of planting and maintaining forest areas for the benefit and sustainability of coming generations. The conservation of forest aims at a change in the composition of trees species and age distribution, and involves the upkeep of the natural resources within a forest that are beneficial to both humans and the environment. Forests are vital for human life because they provide a diverse range of resources; they act as carbon sink and produce oxygen which is vital for existence of life on the earth. Forests are rightly called as lungs of the earth. Not only this, forests help in regulating hydrological cycle, planetary climate, purify water, provide wildlife habitat (50% of the earth's biodiversity occurs in forests), reduce global warming, absorb toxic gases and noise, reduce pollution, conserve soil, and mitigate natural hazards such as floods and landslides.

(i) A dispute, between the local villagers and a logging contractor who had been allowed to fell trees in a forest close to the village, gave rise to a famous movement called:
 (a) Green Revolution
 (b) Sal Forest Movement
 (c) Chipko Andolan
 (d) Arabari Forest Movement

(ii) With increase in human population across the world, energy demand is increasing:
 (a) exponentially (b) linearly
 (c) quadratically (d) minimally

(iii) _____ are also called biodiversity hot spots.
 (a) Sea (b) Forests
 (c) National parks (d) Water reservoirs

(iv) Loss of forest diversity will definitely lead to loss of:
 (a) food and medicine options.
 (b) plants.
 (c) ecological stability.
 (d) resources.

(v) One of the easiest tests to check water quality is to check its:
 (a) pH
 (b) colour
 (c) particulate matter concentration
 (d) odour

Ans. (i) (c) Chipko Andolan
 (ii) (a) exponentially
 (iii) (b) Forests
 (iv) (c) ecological stability.
 (v) (a) pH

85. Read the passage carefully and answer the following questions from Q 85 (i) to 85 (v).

[Question Bank]

Waste management is essential in today's society. Due to an increase in population, the generation of waste is getting doubled day-by-day. Moreover, the increase in waste is affecting the lives of many people.

Waste management is the managing of waste by disposal and recycling of it. Moreover, waste management needs proper techniques keeping in mind the environmental situations. For instance, there are various methods and techniques by which the waste is disposed of. You must have come across 5 R's to save the environment: refuse, reduce, reuse, repurpose and recycle.

(i) Choose the waste management strategy that is matched with correct example.

(a)	Refuse	Choose products that use less packaging.
(b)	Reduce	Give unwanted toys and books to hospitals or schools.
(c)	Reuse	Not using single use plastic.
(d)	Repurpose	Making flower pot from used plastic bottle.

(ii) Recycling of paper is a good practice but recycled paper should not be used as food packaging because:
 (a) recycled papers may release color/dyes on food items.
 (b) recycled papers are not absorbent.
 (c) recycled papers can cause infection due to release of methane.
 (d) recycled papers are costly.

(iii) According to the 'Solid Waste Management Rule 2016', the waste should be segregated into three categories. Observe the table below and select the row that has correct information:

	Wet waste	Dry waste	Hazardous waste
(a)	Cooked food, vegetable peels	Used bulbs, fluorescent lamps	Plastic carry bags, bottles, newspaper, cardboard
(b)	Coffee and tea powder, garden waste	Plastic carry bags, bottles, newspaper, cardboard	Expired medicines, razors, paint cans

(c)	Leftover food, vegetable peels	Coffee and tea powder, garden waste	Insect repellents, cleaning solutions
(d)	Uncooked food, tea leaves	Old crockery, frying pans	Coffee and tea powder, garden waste

(iv) Effective segregation of wastes at the point of generation is very important. Select the appropriate statements giving the importance of waste segregation.
   (i) Less waste goes to the landfills.
   (ii) Better for public health and the environment.
   (iii) Help in reducing the waste.
   (iv) Resulting in deterioration of a waste picker's health.
   (a) Both (i) and (ii)   (b) Both (i) and (iii)
   (c) Both (ii) and (iii) (d) Both (i) and (iv)

(v) The given graph shows the amount of waste generated, dumped and treated in percentage. Identify the reason of low success rate of waste management process.

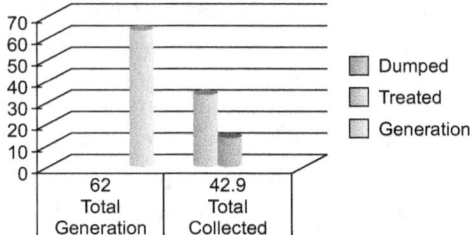

(a) Only 15% of urban India's waste is processed.
(b) Less than 60% of waste is collected from households.
(c) More than 60% of waste is collected from households.
(d) Both (a) and (b).

Ans. (i) (d) Repurpose — making flower pot from used plastic bottle
(ii) (c) Recycled papers can cause infection due to release of methane.
(iii) (b)

Coffee and tea powder, garden waste	Plastic carry bags, bottles, newspaper, cardboard	Expired medicines, razors, paint cans

(iv) (a) Both (i) and (ii)
(v) (d) Both (a) and (b)

Reasoning Based Questions

86. Why do you think that there should be equitable distribution of resources? What forces would be working against an equitable distribution of our resources?* **[NCERT]**

Ans. There should be equitable distribution of resources because everyone whether rich or poor has equal rights to use natural resources and get benefits from them. Geographical factors and economic factors are the forces working against an equitable distribution of our resources. The rich and powerful people take advantage and get more benefits by using resources as compared to poor people. Over exploitation and mismanagement of resources also work against equitable distribution of our resources.

87. Why do we need to manage our resources carefully? Why management of natural resources requires a long term perspective?*

Ans. We need to manage our resources carefully as resources are limited hence over-exploitation of resources would lead to its depletion and it may not be available for our future generations. Equitable distribution of resources is also important so that everyone can be benefitted equally without any discrimination between rich and poor. We should also see that it may not cause damage to our environment. Management of natural resources requires a long term perspective so that it helps in sustainable development and it should be available for our future generations also.

88. What are the two main objectives of sustainable development? Why is reuse considered better than recycling?*

Ans. The two main objectives of sustainable development are:
(a) The main objective is to provide economic well-being to the present as well as future generations as well as to maintain a healthy environment and life support system.
(b) Implement a massive ecological construction project to slow down ecological degradation.
Reuse is considered better than recycling as recycling consume some energy to generate new things which is not seen in case of reuse. Reuse prevents environment pollution by not creating any waste. Reuse also saves money as material is used again without any process.

89. Why is forest considered as natural ecosystem?*

Ans. Forests are considered as natural ecosystem as they have plants and animal species that grow without human intervention and these are naturally sustainable. All these species interact with each other and are interdependent.

90. Why should we conserve forests and wildlife? **[NCERT]**

* are board exam questions from previous years

Ans. Forests and wildlife are rich source of biodiversity. They maintain an ecological balance in nature. Forests provide us various valuable products like honey, medicines, lac, gums, resins, wood, prevent soil erosion and flood, brings rainfall, release oxygen to atmosphere which is a life supporter. Forests are habitat of variety of living organisms. Loss of biodiversity would lead to ecological imbalance so we need to conserve forests and wildlife.

91. **Although coal and petroleum are produced by the degradation of biomass even then we need to conserve them. Why?***

Ans. Coal and petroleum are formed from degradation of dead remains of plant and animals and it is a very slow process. It takes millions of years for the formation of coal and petroleum from the dead remains of plants and animals. But with increasing demand and consumption of these fossil fuels, they are depleting at a faster rate as compared to the rate of their replenishment. So, we need to conserve them.

92. **Why are the Arabari forests of Bengal known to be a good example of conserved forest?**

Ans. In 1972, West Bengal forest Department found that there is great degradation of Sal forests. So forest officer A.K. Banerjee involved the local villagers in protection of these forests. They were given employment in both silviculture and harvesting operations. By 1983, the sal forests of Arabari became thick and green. So, it is a good example of conserved forest.

Very Short Answer Type Questions

93. **How would these short term aims advantages differ from the advantages of using a long term perspective in managing our resources?*** [NCERT]

Ans. Exploiting resources for short term aim provides benefit to meet the needs of present generation only but exploiting resources for long term prospective to meet the needs of future generation also. The management of natural resources for future use is a sustainable practice. The judicious use of natural resources in present generation enables the future generation also to use them for their benefits.

94. **What is "repurpose"?**

Ans. Repurpose is the recovery of waste without any pre-processing. For example, waste oils that cannot be refined for reuse in vehicles can be burnt for energy recovery. Recovering the energy from waste oil reduces our dependence on coal and imported oil.

95. **Define sustainable development.**

Ans. Sustainable development refers to the process of economic development where resources are used judiciously to satisfy needs of not only present generation but also to conserve them for the use of future generations.

96. **Write two advantages associated with water harvesting at the community level.***

Ans. (a) Exploitation of water resources will be reduced.
(b) It helps to recharge natural wells.

97. **If you could use any source of energy for heating your food which one would you prefer? State one reason for your choice.***

Ans. I would prefer a solar cooker for heating food because solar cooker is environmental friendly and causes does not any pollution.

98. **Name few industries based on forest produce.**

Ans. Rubber, paper, timber, sports goods manufacturing industries are based on forest produce.

99. **Which fossil fuel is conserved:**
(i) When we save on electricity.
(ii) When we use bicycle for covering short distances instead of a motor bike.

Ans. (i) Coal is conserved when we save on electricity.
(ii) Petroleum is conserved when we use bicycle for covering short distances instead of a motor bike.

100. **Name two industries based on forest produce.***

Ans. Timber industries and paper manufacturing industries are based on forest produce.

101. **What is major cause of Ganga river pollution?**

Ans. The main cause of water pollution in the Ganga river are the increase in the population density, various human activities such as bathing, washing clothes, the bathing of animals, and dumping of various harmful industrial waste into the rivers.

102. **How does increasing demand for energy adversely affect the environment?**

Ans. To meet the increasing demand for energy we are exploiting the natural resources and mainly using fossil fuels like coal and petroleum which also emits pollutants that cause air pollution and this in turn adversely affects the environment.

103. **Find out the traditional systems of water harvesting or management in your region?** [NCERT]

Ans. Ponds, pits, lakes etc., are the traditional systems of water harvesting or management in the regions where rain water is stored.

104. **Find out the source of water in your region or locality. Is water from this source available to all people living in that area?**

Ans. The source of water in our region is through borewell and municipal water supply. Municipal water is obtained from dams or rivers and it is

are board exam questions from previous years

available to all people living in the area. Some people in some areas have their own borewell.

105. List two advantages associated with water harvesting at the community level?*

Ans. The two advantages are:
(a) Recharging of wells increases the level of ground water.
(b) The water can be stored in rainy season and we can use it when there are no rain or when there is water scarcity.

106. Write the energy conversion that takes place in a hydropower plant.*

Ans. In a hydropower plant, the turbine converts the kinetic energy of falling water into mechanical energy and after that generator converts mechanical energy into electrical energy.

107. Find out the traditional systems of water harvesting or management in your region ? [NCERT]

Ans. Ponds, pits, lakes etc., are the traditional systems of water harvesting or management in the regions where rain water is stored.

108. Name two factors which can be used to find whether river water has been contaminated.

Ans. The presence of coliform bacteria in water and BOD value can be used to find whether river water has been contaminated.

109. Name the group of bacteria that confirms the contamination of water ?

Ans. Coliform group of bacteria confirms the contamination of water.

110. Which canal has brought greenery to considerable areas of Rajasthan ?

Ans. Indira Gandhi canal has brought greenery to considerable areas of Rajasthan.

111. Name the dam on the river Narmada whose height government want to raise.

Ans. Government want to raise the height of Sardar Sarovar dam on Narmada river.

112. Write the energy conversion that takes place in a hydropower plant.

Ans. In a hydropower plant, the turbine converts the kinetic energy of falling water into mechanical energy and after that generator converts mechanical energy into electrical energy.

113. What would be the advantage of exploiting resources with short term aims? [NCERT]

Ans. The advantage of exploiting resources with short term aims is to provide benefits to meet the requirements of present generations.

114. What are the main uses of coal and petroleum products?

Ans. Coal is used as fuel in homes and in thermal power plants to generate electricity. Petroleum products like petrol, diesel etc., are used as fuel in transports like buses, cars, trucks, scooters etc.

Short Answer Type Questions

115. We saw in chapter (Management of natural resources) that there are four main stake-holders when it comes to forests and wildlife. Which among these should have the authority to decide the management of forest produce? Why do you think so? [NCERT]

Ans. The local people who live in or around Forest and Forest Department of Government should have the authority to decide the management of forest produce because local people know the practices to use these resources in a sustainable manner without causing any harm or damage to environment. Since we have seen in our past how local people protect the Sal forests of Arabari and tribal women of Tehri-Garhwal district of UP protest against the felling of trees by hugging them. There should also be a governing body which should take steps and create awareness among people for conserving and managing forests and wildlife resources.*

116. In the context of conservation of natural resources, explain the terms reduce, reuse, recycle, refuse and repurpose? From among the materials we use in daily life, identify two materials for each category?

Ans. Reduce means less use of commodities or natural resources. Examples–Electricity, water.

Reuse means use of things again and again instead of throwing it away. Examples– Plastic bags, bottles, paper, envelopes etc.

Recycle means by using specific recycling technique new things can be produced from old ones. Examples – Metals, glass apparatus, plastic materials, papers etc.

Refuse to buy products that can harm you and the environment. Examples - Refuse single use plastics, like disposable coffee cups, utensils, and straws. These materials are often made of plastic and thrown away after one use.

Repurpose means converting waste into resources. Examples - Waste plastic bottle can be used to make boat, waste oils that cannot be refined for reuse in vehicles can be burnt for energy recovery.

117. On the basis of the issue raised in this chapter, (Management of natural resources) what changes would you incorporate in your life style in a move towards a sustainable use of our resources? [NCERT]

Ans. Changes that I would incorporate in my life for sustainable use of our resources are:

---
* are board exam questions from previous years

(a) Use of energy efficient bulbs instead of conventional bulbs.
(b) Planting more trees.
(c) Switching off lights, fans, TV, computer when not in use.
(d) Closing off water taps while shaving, brushing.
(e) Repairing leaky taps and pipes on time.
(f) Separating biodegradable and non-biodegradable wastes before disposing them in dustbins.
(g) Walking to nearby places and using of public transport to conserve fuels.
(h) Use of renewable sources of energy like solar energy.

118. Write the negative effect on the environment of affluent life style of few persons of a society.*

Ans. Use of air-conditioners, personal transport etc., releases very harmful gases like CFCs, oxides of sulphur, nitrogen into our environment. This may be responsible for ozone layer depletion and acid rain. Excessive use of non-biodegradable material may cause hazardous problem and excessive exploitation of resources may cause depletion of the environment.

119. What changes can you make in your habits to become more environment friendly? [NCERT]

Ans. We can make the following changes in our habits:
(a) We can segregate biodegradable and non-biodegradable wastes and dispose them in separate dustbins.
(b) We can collect paper, plastics, metals, glass apparatus and recycle them to make new products.
(c) By closing the water taps and repairing leaky pipes and taps on time to save water.
(d) By switching off lights, fans, computer, television etc., when not in use.
(e) By using solar energy for cooking, heating water etc., instead of using fossil fuels.
(f) By planting more trees.
(g) By reusing things instead of throwing away. Example – old clothes, toys etc., can be given to needy people, plastic bottles of jam, pickles can be used to store other things etc.

120. What changes would you suggest in your home in order to be environment friendly?* [NCERT]

Ans. The following measures can be taken in our home in order to be environment friendly:
(a) We can segregate biodegradable and non-biodegradable wastes and dispose them in separate dustbins.
(b) By closing the water taps and repairing leaky pipes and taps to save water.
(c) By switching off lights, fans, computer, television etc., when not needed.
(d) By using solar energy for cooking, heating water etc., instead of using fossil fuels.
(e) By reusing things instead of throwing away. Example – old clothes, toys etc., can be given to needy people, plastic bottles of jam, pickles can be used to store other things etc.
(f) Use of energy saver lights like CFLs bulbs.

121. Three advantages of exploiting resources with short term aims:*
(i) Immediate benefit to few people.
(ii) Progress in science and technology for development in a country.
(iii) Urbanisation and Industrialisation of an area.

Ans. Three advantages of using a long time perspective:
(i) Resources will be made available for sustainable development.
(ii) Provides valuable contribution to the socio-economic development.
(iii) Quality of environment will be conserved.

122. What can you as an individual do to reduce your consumption of the various natural resources? [NCERT]

Ans. I would follow 5 R's techniques *i.e.*, Reduce, Reuse, Refuse, Repurpose and Recycle.
(a) Use of lights, fans, televisions, music players etc., when required.
(b) Using CFLs bulbs, fluorescent tubes which consume less energy instead of conventional bulbs or tubes.
(c) Repairing of pipes and taps that cause leakage of water.
(d) Using solar energy for cooking and solar heater to heat water during winters.
(e) We can use waste water that is produced from water purifier in watering plants, moping floor, cleaning vehicles etc.
(f) We can write on both sides of a paper, we can give our unused and old things to needy and poor people, bottles of jams, jellies, pickles when finished can be used to store other things etc.
(g) We can recycle things like paper, plastics, metals, glass etc.

123. Explain 5 R's in the conservation of environment.

Ans. Refuse: The word 'refuse' refers to ' to deny or to say no'. Refusing will help to eliminate a lot of waste from the very beginning. It is simply about saying no to the things that you do not need and looking into reusable alternatives. It includes the activities:
(a) To say no to buy products that can harm you and the environment.
(b) Looking into reusable alternatives.
(c) Refuse single use plastics, like disposable coffee cups, utensils and straws. These materials are often made of plastic and thrown away after one use.

---
* are board exam questions from previous years

Reduce: The word 'reduce' refers to ' use less'. It includes the activities:
(a) Do not waste food.
(b) Save electricity by switching off electrical appliances when not required.
(c) Saving the fuel such as petrol, diesel etc. by walking or cycling to go for shorter distances.
(d) Repairing the leaking taps.

Recycle: The word 'recycle' refers to 'processing of waste articles to form new products'. A number of materials such as tins, cans, glass, plastics, polythenes etc. The following articles can be recycled are:
(a) Broken glass to form new glass.
(b) Waste polythene sheet to form a new sheet.
(c) Plastic articles can be recycled to produce inferior quality of plastics.

Reuse: The word 'reuse' refers to ' using of articles till it gets broken'. It is more advantageous than recycling as it does not require energy. It includes the activities:
(a) Writing on both sides of paper.
(b) Using cloth carrying bags.
(c) Use of metals, ceramics, glass containers.

Repurpose: The word 'repurpose refers 'to recover'. Repurpose means converting waste into resources. This requires a bit of thinking and craftiness, but does not have to be beautiful. It includes the activities:
(a) Waste plastic bottle can be used to make boat.
(b) Waste oils that cannot be refined for reuse in vehicles can be burnt for energy recovery.
(c) Recovering the energy from waste oil reduces our dependence on coal and imported oil.

124. Why should there be equitable distribution of resources? List three forces that would be working against an equitable distribution of our resources.*

Ans. There should be equitable distribution of the resources so that all the people irrespective of being rich and poor have access and makes use of the resources. Equitable resource distribution also leads to sustainable development.

Three factors that work against equitable distribution of resources are:
(a) Over exploitation of resources by industrialists for short-term gains.
(b) Improper management which has led to access of natural raw material to certain group of people which are either influential.
(c) Wastage by the people who have indifferent attitude towards environment, use the resources with short-term aim hence leading to depletion of resources.

125. List three advantages each of:*
(i) Exploiting resources with short-term aims.

---
* are board exam questions from previous years

(ii) Using a long-term perspective in managing our natural resources.

Ans. (i) (a) Short-term exploitation will meet the demand of present generation.
(b) There will be no shortage of resources.
(c) Larger aspect regarding the details of a reserve can be studied also.

(ii) (a) Long-term management of natural resources would meet the demand of present and future generation.
(b) No harmful impact on the environment.
(c) Equitable distribution of resources amongst the rich and poor.

126. Major rivers in India have high bacterial contamination, Yamuna and Ganga top the list of most polluted rivers.

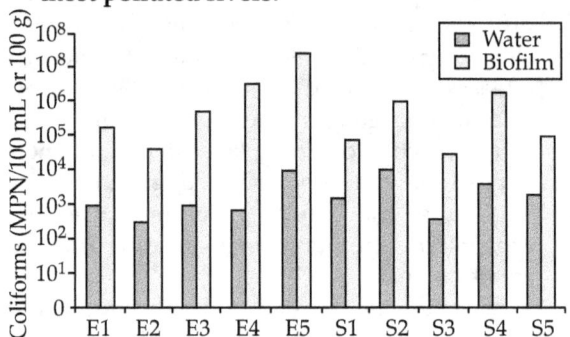

The graph above shows the Distribution of total coliform bacteria in river water and biofilms. E1 to E5.
(i) Which among the following is the most polluted?
(ii) State the reason for bacterial contamination in water body.

Ans. (i) E5 is most polluted river body.
(ii) Bacterial contamination in water is indicated by the presence of coliform bacteria. Bacterial contamination in water is mostly through untreated sewage and cause waterborne diseases.

127. Advancement of the technology has resulted in improvement of our lifestyle and has also changed our attitude. When the human population was low and technology was in its infancy, the various kinds of solid wastes generated due to human activities were easily degraded by decomposers present in nature and it did not create any Significant harmful effect on the environment. In the recent times, however human population has increased tremendously and the technology has become greatly advanced. These two factors have contributed Significantly in the deterioration of our environment due to addition of number of wastes.

(i) Samaira took three different types of solid wastes P,Q, R and buried them under the soil in a pot, as she wanted to study their rate of decomposition. Her findings are shown in the given graph

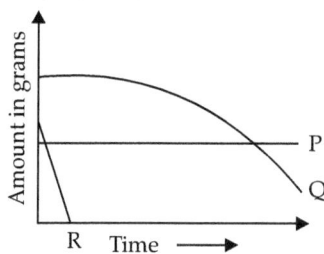

Select the option that correctly identifies P, Q and R

	P	Q	R
(a)	Polythene bag	Leather bag	Fruit peel
(b)	Used syringes	Broken glass	Leather purse
(c)	Cardboard	Cow dung	Rubber mat
(d)	Human excreta	Paper cup	Cow dung

(ii) Which of the following statements regarding solid wastes is correct?

(a) Change in the packaging technology has resulted in generation of lot of solid wastes.

(b) Dumping of solid wastes could reduce the fertility of the soil leading to reduction in crop yield.

(c) Accumulation of solid waste could cause increased incidents of disease in a locality.

(d) All of these

Ans. (i) (a) According to the given graph, P is a waste that is not decomposed with the time. Hence, it can be a non-biodegradable waste such as glass and plastic wastes, synthetic polymers, pesticides, etc. Q took sometime for decomposing; hence it can be a waste made up of biodegradable material such as leather bag. As R starts decomposing in a very short span of time, this means it is a biodegradable waste such as fruit peel, cow dung, human excreta, etc.

(ii) (d) Increased use of plastic material in packaging has resulted in generation of lot of solid wastes. Dumping industrial chemical waste affects the soil fertility and subsequently reduces crop yield. Solid waste can block drains creating pools of water which can become breeding ground for mosquitoes and therefore, could increase the incidents of disease in the locality.

128. (i) How industry is affecting the forest?*

(ii) State the main aim of the management of forests and wild life.

Ans. (i) Industries depend on forests as a resource provider and exploit all the resources to the maximum without any scope of conservation. The various industries which are based on forest produce are; timber industry, paper manufacturing industry, 'lac' industry and sports equipment industry. Forests are also treated as hunting and fishing sites and a source of raw materials for many industries. The deforestation caused due to the development projects and industrialisation is a serious issue.

(ii) The main aim of the management of forests and wild life is to conserve the biodiversity which we have inherited.

129. State the significance of Chipko movement.

Ans. The Chipko movement awakened people to the importance of maintaining trees as it allows a nation's ecosystem to function properly and also helps people live healthily and have a prosperous lifestyle. The Chipko movement quickly spread across communities and media, and forced the government, to whom the forest belongs, to rethink their priorities in the name of forest produce. Due to the participation of local people, it led to the efficient management of forests.

One of the movement's major successes was that the Uttar Pradesh government ensured zero tolerance for commercial forest felling and saved thousands of trees from being felled, which resulted in the conservation of abundant forest resources for local benefits.

The Chipko movement was a movement in India to protect forests. Thus, individuals took up this campaign and organised a number of demonstrations to raise people's consciousness. They protested against logging operations for trade. And deforestation has finally been stopped.

130. Water is an elixir of life, a very important natural resource. Your science teacher wants you to prepare a plan for a formative assessment activity– "How to save water, the vital natural resource."

(i) Write any two ways that you will suggest to bring awareness in your neighborhood on how to save water.

(ii) Name and explain any one way by which the underground water table does not go down further.*

Ans. (i) Water is a very precious natural resource which can be saved by the following ways:

(a) Turning off taps while brushing, shaving.

(b) Use of buckets instead of shower while bathing.

(c) The waste water from purifier can be used for moping, watering plants, etc.

(ii) Underground water can be recharged by rain water harvesting. The technique to capture

and store rain water for future use by making special water harvesting structures is called rain water harvesting. There are two ways of rain water harvesting:
- (a) Surface run off where rain water that flows away from the surface can be collected and used.
- (b) Rooftop rain water harvesting is the technique where rain water from roof tops of the buildings is collected through canals and drains the water to ground reservoir. This stored water can be used in future.

131. How did Chipko Movement ultimately benefits the local people? Explain briefly.*

Ans. Chipko movement was originated from a small village Reni in 1974 where a group of women under the leadership of *Gaura Devi* protested against indiscriminate felling of trees by hugging them. The Chipko movement spread slowly to other parts under the leadership of *Shri Sunderlal Bahuguna* of Silyara in Tehri region. Chipko movement is the movement where people form a circle around the tree and hug them to prevent falling of trees. The local people of Tehri-Garhwal district of Uttarakhand, then a part of UP realise the importance of forests and protest against felling of trees as well as giving forest products to other regions.

This prevention of cutting down of trees help in conservation of soil, bringing rainfall, maintenance of ecological balance in nature. The local people can use the products of forests for their benefits.

132. Suggest some approaches towards the conservation of forests? [NCERT]

Ans. Some approaches towards the conservation of forests are:
- (a) Large scale afforestation programmes.
- (b) Avoid cutting of trees (deforestation).
- (c) To educate people about the importance of forests by organising programs and campaigns.
- (e) Forest fires should be checked.
- (d) By implementing law for severe punishment to anyone who is involved in illegal cutting down of trees.
- (f) Local people should be included in conservation of forests and they should be given proper employment.

133. How can you as an individual contribute or make a difference to the management of: [NCERT]
- (i) Forests and wildlife
- (ii) Water resources
- (iii) Coal and petroleum

Ans. (i) Forests and wild life:
- (a) Large scale afforestation programmes.
- (b) Avoid cutting down of trees.
- (c) To educate people about the importance of forests by organising events, programs and campaigns.

(ii) Water resources:
- (a) By closing the water taps and repairing leaky pipes and taps to save water.
- (b) Harvesting and conserving water.
- (c) Avoid polluting water and create awareness among people to save water.

(iii) Coal and petroleum:
- (a) Minimum utilisation of fossil fuels and using more alternative sources of energy like solar energy.
- (b) We can use public transport instead of our personal vehicles.
- (c) We can walk to nearby places instead of using vehicles.
- (d) Proper maintenance of vehicles and use of efficient internal combustion engines.
- (e) Use of CNG instead of petrol or diesel.

134. State two advantages of conserving:*
- (i) Forests
- (ii) Wildlife

Ans. (i) Advantages of conserving forests:
- (a) It supports life and purifies air by releasing oxygen by photosynthesis process.
- (b) It holds the soil and prevents soil erosion.

(ii) Advantages of conserving wildlife:
- (a) It balances ecology and biodiversity.
- (b) It provides important things to sustain life like life saving drugs, ivory, musk, leather etc.

135. List three environmental consequences of using fossil fuels. Suggest three steps to minimise the pollution caused by various energy sources.*

Ans. The combustion of fossil fuels releases different harmful products. Three environmental consequences of using fossil fuels are:
- (a) It release CO_2 which is a greenhouse gas which traps the solar energy falling on earth and it leads to global warming.
- (b) Carbon monoxide is poisonous gas which when enters in the blood stream stops the functioning of red blood cells to carry oxygen from lungs to other parts of the body. It also causes death.
- (c) Sulphur dioxide released during the burning of fossil fuels is harmful for lungs and causes bronchitis and other diseases.

Steps to minimise the pollution caused by various energy sources are:
- (a) Solar cookers should be used to cook food wherever possible.
- (b) Use of biogas as domestic fuel should be encouraged in rural areas.
- (c) Five R's strategy—Refuse, Reduce, Reuse, Repurpose and Recycle should be practiced.

136. Compare the traditional system with the probable systems in hilly or mountainous areas or plains or plateau regions. [NCERT]

Ans. Water harvesting system in hilly or mountainous areas is different from plains or plateau regions because in hilly regions like in Himachal Pradesh local systems of canal irrigation which are man-made channels through which water flows from streams and were carried to various villages. These were called Kulhs. This method was practiced nearly 400 years ago. But in plains or plateaus water is stored in dams, tanks etc.

137. What is water harvesting? List two main advantages associated with water harvesting at the community level. Write two causes for the failure of sustained availability of groundwater.*

Ans. Water harvesting means capturing rain where it falls or capturing the run off in village or town. It can be done by capturing run off from rooftops and local catchments.

Advantages:

(a) Harvesting water allows capturing better utilisation of an energy resource or when there is an immediate need.
(b) This water is suitable for irrigation.

Causes for failure of sustained ground water availability are:

(a) Increase in agricultural activities leads to depletion of ground water.
(b) Increase in population and industries are also responsible for the same.

138. Discuss the advantages of storing water in ground.

Ans. The advantages of water stored in the ground are:

(a) It does not evaporate, but spreads out to recharge wells and provides moisture for vegetation over a wide area.
(b) It does not provide breeding grounds for mosquitoes like stagnant water collected in ponds or artificial lakes.
(c) The ground-water is also protected from contamination by human and animal waste.

Long Answer Type Questions

139. What do you understand by sustainable development? Explain.

Ans. Sustainable development, is a kind of development that takes into account the needs of the economy, and the environment without compromising either of the aspects. If the economic development is sustainable then the present use of natural resources will not limit us from their use in the future. Thus, sustainable development tells us that development must be of a kind which can take care of our needs as well as the needs of future generations. In other words, "sustainable development refers to the process of economic development where resources are used judiciously to satisfy needs of not only present generation but also to conserve them for the use of future generations". Sustainable development takes places without depleting the present natural resources.

140. Discuss the objectives of Namami Gange Programme.

Ans. The Ganga is the most important river of India both from the point of view of its basin and cultural significance. But water in the Ganga river is polluting day-by-day due to increase in the population density, various human activities such as bathing, washing clothes, the bathing of animals, and dumping of various harmful industrial waste into the rivers.

Much of the effort to clean the Ganga over the last 30 years has been centred around creating sewage treatment capacities in major urban centres along the river. 'Namami Gange Programme', is an Integrated Conservation Mission, approved as "Flagship Programme" by the Union Government in June 2014 with budget outlay of Rs.20,000 Crore to accomplish the twin objectives of effective abatement of pollution, conservation and rejuvenation of the National River Ganga. Namami Gange is being implemented by the National Mission for Clean Ganga (NMCG), and its state counterparts—State Programme Management Groups. NMCG would establish field offices wherever necessary. The National Mission for Clean Ganga is the implementation wing set up in October, 2016.

Main pillars of the Namami Gange Programme are:

(a) Sewerage Treatment Infrastructure
(b) River-Front Development
(c) River-Surface Cleaning
(d) Bio-Diversity
(e) Afforestation
(f) Public Awareness
(g) Industrial Effluent Monitoring
(h) Ganga Gram

The government's Namami Gange programme seeks to tackle the problem at several levels at the same time. "Rejuvenation" of the Ganga includes reviving 'Aviral Dhara', or continuous flow in stretches that have gone dry due to natural or man-made reasons, regenerating the river ecology, making the river an important inland waterway, reviving it as a habitat for dolphins and gharials, and spreading awareness about the need to keep the Ganga clean.

---
* are board exam questions from previous years

141. What is the importance of forest as a resource? What are the causes of deforestation?

Ans. Forests are an important natural resource due to following reasons:
(a) Forests provide us wood, dry fruits, spices, gums, resins, dyes, tannins and various products like honey, camphour, rubber etc.
(b) The roots of trees hold the soil firmly preventing soil erosion.
(c) It absorbs carbon dioxide from atmosphere and release oxygen which is life supporter.
(d) It absorbs carbon dioxide which is a greenhouse gas thus plays an important role in reducing global warming.
(e) It increases frequency of rainfall and regulates water cycle.
(f) It serves as a shelter for wildlife.

Causes of deforestation are:
(a) Large scale deforestation for demand of wood, timber as raw materials for industries, domestic purposes etc.
(b) Construction of dams, reservoirs, roads, railways.
(c) Setting up of factories and industries.
(d) Construction of big apartments to provide space to the growing population.
(e) Shifting cultivation for agriculture.
(f) Overgrazing by livestock.

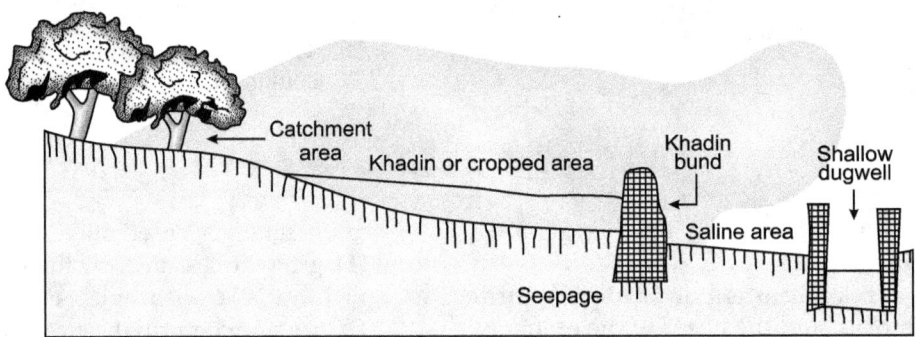

Fig. Traditional water harvesting system an ideal setting of the Khadin System

142. Answer the following questions:
(i) What are fossil fuels and why are they called so?
(ii) How are they important for us?
(iii) Name two fossil fuels?
(iv) Give some methods to conserve fossil fuels?

Ans. (i) Fossil fuels are obtained by degradation of dead remains of plants and animals which are buried under the surface of earth over a million years ago. They are called so as they are produced by degradation of biomass over a million years ago.
(ii) They are an important source of fuels. Petroleum products like petrol, diesel etc., are used as fuel in automobiles. Coal is used in thermal power plants to generate electricity and also used as a fuel for domestic purposes. Natural gas is also used as a fuel in automobiles in the form of Compressed Natural Gas (CNG).
(iii) The two fossil fuels are coal and petroleum.
(iv) Methods of conserving fossil fuels are:
  (a) Use of CNG in place of petrol and diesel as a fuel in automobiles.
  (b) Switching to renewable sources of energy like solar energy, wind energy, hydroelectric energy instead of using non-renewable energy sources like fossil fuels.
  (c) Wastage during extraction and transportation of fossil fuels should be minimised.
  (d) Protecting them from accidental fires.
  (e) Over consumption and wastage of petrol or diesel should be checked in automobiles by proper servicing and efficient internal combustion engines.

143. What are dams? Give some examples of major dams in our country? State some benefits of constructing dams?

Ans. Dams are large water storage bodies built by government agencies to regulate the flow of water and utilise it for benefit of human beings. There are many dams constructed across major rivers in different parts of our country. For examples:
(a) Bhakra dam across river Sutlej in Punjab.
(b) Tehri dam on river Ganga in Uttaranchal.
(c) Mettur dam on river Cauvery in Tamil Nadu.
(d) Sardar Sarovar dam on river Narmada in Gujarat.
(e) Hirakud dam on river Mahanadi in Odisha.

Some benefits of constructing dams are:
(a) It stores adequate amount of water which can be used for irrigation.
(b) Water can be supplied to villages and towns when there is shortage of water through pipelines.

(c) It can be used to generate hydroelectricity.
(d) It can be used for flood control.

144. Answer the following questions:
(i) What is meant by rain water harvesting? Name some of the ancient structures used for rain water harvesting by the rural people.
(i) What are the various advantages of water stored in ground?

Ans. (i) Rain water harvesting is a process of collecting and storing rain water by using special techniques for future use when there is shortage of water or during non-rainy days. There were various traditional methods by the rural people for rain water harvesting. These include Khadins, Nadis, Bandharas, Kulhs, Kattas, Tals etc.

(ii) The various advantages of water stored in ground are:
(a) Water is not polluted.
(b) Water does not get evaporated but it spreads out to recharge wells.
(c) It does not serve as breeding places for mosquitoes, flies.
(d) It does not get contaminated due to human activities.
(e) It provides moisture for vegetation.
(f) Mitigates flood and droughts.

145. What do you mean by watershed management? What is its main aim? What are the advantages of watershed management?

Ans. Watershed management is concerned with scientific soil and water conservation to increase the production of biomass.

Its main aim is to:
(a) To develop land and water resources, to produce secondary resources of plants and animals without causing any ecological imbalance.
(b) To implant the sustainable management of natural resources to improve the quality of living.
(c) Improvement of quality of soil for better productivity.
(d) Supplying clean and safe drinking water to all.

Advantages of watershed management are:
(a) It enhances the life of downstream dam and reservoirs.
(b) It minimises the risk of droughts, landslides and floods.
(c) It increases ground water level.
(d) It increases crop production.
(e) Various developmental activities like hydroelectric power generation, supply water for irrigation and other domestic uses.

146. Explain Khadin system of water harvesting with diagram?

Ans. Khadins are a traditional way of harvesting rain water and it is mainly followed by people of Rajasthan. These are very long earthen embankments which are built across the lower edge of the sloping farmlands which are called bund. Rain water flows down the slopes and fills the bunds to form a reservoir. Pathways are made from bund to nearby well which are mainly dug behind the bund where water seeps and fills the wells.

Differentiate Between

147. Differentiate between watershed management and Water Harvesting.

Ans.

Wastershed Management	Water Harvesting
Watershed management means to conserve soil and water in a watershed so as to increase the bio-mass production.	Water Harvesting means storing rain water and reusing it, rather than allowing it to run off.
Watershed management includes both the land and water area that runs off to a common point.	In Water Harvesting, we store the water and use them for irrigation, drinking and other purposes.
Watershed management system are natural systems.	Water Harvesting Systems are artificial.

Analysis and Evaluation Based Questions

148. The environmentalists are insisting upon "sustainable natural resource management". State its advantages?

Ans. The advantages of sustainable natural resource management are:
(a) It provides resources for the benefit of both present and future generations.
(b) It would reduce pollution and helps in conservation of natural resources.
(c) It enables equal distribution of resources to everyone whether rich or poor.
(d) It provides steady economic growth and misuse of natural resources.

149. If you find coliform bacteria in a sample of potable water, what does it mean? Explain.

Ans. The presence of coliform bacteria in water indicates that water is contaminated by sewage as sewage contains human excreta. Human excreta contains a lot of disease causing microbes and when this sewage is dumped into rivers or lakes or ponds they get contaminated as coliforms from sewage will come into water.

150. Give four characteristics of a good fuel?

Ans. Four characteristics of a good fuel are:
(a) It causes little to no pollution.
(b) It should have high calorific value.
(c) It should be economical, easily available and easily transported.
(d) It should have moderate ignition temperature.

151. Suggest ways to strike a balance between environment and development?

Ans. (a) Use of renewable sources of energy instead of non-renewable sources.
(b) Large scale afforestation programmes should be carried out and use of forest resources effectively.
(c) Segregation of biodegradable and non-biodegradable wastes and use of recycling technology for efficient use of resources.

152. List few problems that may arise by planting trees of single variety over vast tracts of forest?

Ans. The problems which arise by planting trees of single variety over vast tracts of forest are:
(a) Loss of biodiversity.
(b) Various needs of the local people cannot be met by monoculture.
(c) If a disease occurs to that particular plant it would affect large areas.
(d) Different organisms require different types of food from different plants but if one variety of plants is planted many organisms will not get food.

153. What is the slogan of Chipko Movement?

Ans. Slogan of Chipko Movement is *"five Fs"* – Food, Fuel, Fibre, Fodder, Fertilizer.

154. Answer the following:
(i) Locate and name the water reservoirs in figure A and B.
(ii) Which has an advantage over the other and why?

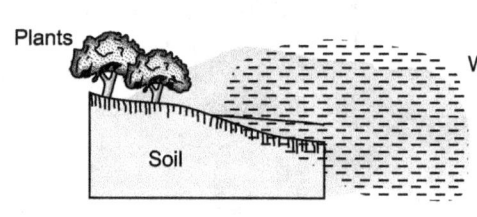
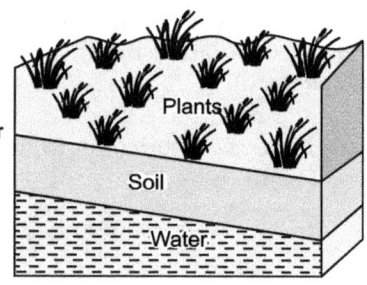

Figure (A)   **Figure (B)**

Ans. (i) A is pond and B is underground water body.
(ii) Underground water body has an advantage over pond as:
  (a) Water is lost by evaporation.
  (b) Water does not get contaminated due to human activities.
  (c) It does not serve as a breeding place for mosquitoes, flies which are carriers of several diseases.
  (d) It provides moisture for vegetation over a large area.
  (e) It spreads out to recharge wells.

155. Which of the two is better option:
(i) To collect rain water in ponds or artificial lakes
(ii) To let it recharge ground water by water harvesting.

List two causes for the failure of sustained availability of ground water.

Ans. To let it recharge ground water by water harvesting is better option than to collect rain water in ponds or artificial lakes because there is no loss of water by evaporation, water does not get contaminated due to human activities, it does not provide a breeding place for mosquitoes, flies etc.

The causes for the failure of sustained availability of ground water are :
(a) Rising population demands more water which leads to depletion of ground water level.
(b) Growing industries and dumping of effluents and wastes from them causes pollution of ground water.

Application Based Questions

156. **Chipko movement was stared in 1970s in a small village of Garhwal high up in Himalayas. Villagers stood against greedy contractors.**
Women folk hugged the trees. The Chipko – movement spread slowly to all nearby areas under the leadership of Shri Sunder Lal Bahuguna.
 (i) Do you feel inspired by this movement which prevented felling of trees?
 (ii) Who do you think are real stakeholders?
 (iii) Which old belief has been challenged by Chipko movement?

Ans. (i) Yes, we feel inspired by this movement which prevented felling of trees because it is one of the suitable methods to conserve the forests and protect the environment from getting damaged.
 (ii) Local people are real stakeholders.
 (iii) Chipko movement has challenged the old belief that forests only give us timber but they help in sustaining our lives, they serve as a rich source of biodiversity, they are a habitat of wildlife. They give us oxygen which is life supporter. So, we should conserve our forests.

157. **In a village in Karnataka, people started cultivating crops all around a lake which was always filled with water. They add fertilizers to their field in order to enhance their yield. Soon they discovered that the water body was completely covered with green floating plants and fishes start dying in large numbers. Analyse the situation and give reasons for excessive growth of plants and death of fishes in the lake?**

Ans. The fertilizers that were added by farmers washed away to the lakes by rain water. Fertilizers contain many chemicals like nitrates and phosphates which provide nutrients for excessive growth of algal blooms and the entire water body gets covered by them. This process is called eutrophication. Since the entire water body gets covered by these green algal blooms sunlight and air cannot enter to the lake. So fishes found in lakes due to insufficient availability of dissolved oxygen died.

158. **Water finds a very important role in our day to day life but a large portion of our population has no access to pure drinking water. Many of them are also suffering from waterborne diseases.**
 (i) What makes water unsafe for drinking?
 (ii) What steps should an individual take to prevent pollution of water?

Ans. (i) Release of untreated effluents of industries to water bodies, dumping of garbage in water, throwing domestic waste, sewage etc., into the water bodies make the water unfit for drinking. These wastes contain heavy metals, coliform bacteria, various disease causing microbes, salts etc. The high TDS and BOD value also makes the water unfit for drinking.
 (ii) Following measures should be taken to prevent water pollution:
  (a) We should treat waste water in treatment plants before letting them into water bodies.
  (b) We should not dump garbage, domestic waste in water bodies.
  (c) We should test the water for BOD, TDS value and coliform count from time to time.

Creating Based Questions

159. **Ramesh is concerned about the quality of water in the river flowing in his village. On the banks of the river several factories were discharging effluents into the river. There were soap and detergent factory, lead battery manufacturing unit, plastic cup manufacturing unit and alcohol distillery in the nearby area.**
He collected the water samples and sent them for testing in a laboratory, the pH of water sample collected from a river was found to be acidic in the range of 3·5-4·5. The effluents of which one of the following factories is the most likely cause for lowering the pH of river water? Suggest what should Ramesh do?

Ans. Acid spillage from lead battery manufacturing factory can lower down the pH. Ramesh should talk to management authorities of lead battery manufacturing unit to make alternative arrangements for disposal of their effluents.

160. **In our country, there are attempts to increase the height of several existing dams like Tehri and Almati, dams across Narmada. People living in nearby area are afraid of the consequence of raising the height of dams. Can you suggest some such consequences that might affect these people.**

Ans. People might face social problems because such projects displace large number of peasants and tribals without adequate compensation or rehabilitation, economic problems because these projects swallow up huge amounts of public money without the generation of proportionate benefits, environmental problems because they contribute enormously to deforestation and the loss of biological diversity.

The people who have been displaced by various development projects are largely poor tribal who do not get any benefits from these projects and are alienated from their lands and forests without adequate compensation. The oustees of the Tawa Dam built in the 1970s are still fighting for the benefits they were promised.

161. Using the following information form a pathway showing the meaning of three R's with example. And also include information that is not mentioned below to complete it. Reduce, Recycle, Reuse, save electricity, plastic, use again.

Ans. Reduce → use less → example → save electricity by switching off unnecessary lights and fans.

Recycle → recycle materials to make required things → example → recycle the products like plastic, paper, glass and metal.

Reuse → use things again and again → example → Like the plastic bottles in which you buy various food-items like jam or pickle can be used for storing things in the kitchen.

Self-Assessment

162. Give two examples of wastes that can be recycled and reused.

163. Everyone of us can do something to reduce our personal consumption of various natural resources. List four such activities based on 5-R approach.

164. How does refusing helps to eliminate waste?

165. What is meant by 5-R's strategy?

166. Name the raw material used in the formation of coal and petroleum.

167. What are non-renewable resources? Give examples.

168. Explain the term sustainable development.

169. What is the objective of 'Namami Gange Programme'?

170. List four stakeholders which may be helpful in the conservation of forests.

171. Name the tree for which Amrita Devi Bishnoi and others sacrificed their lives.

172. Mention the role of forests in conserving the environment. How do the forests get depleted?

173. There is a garbage bin installed near your school gate where children and other staff of the school throw waste food, tetra pack, plastic, waste paper, empty mineral water bottle etc. The bin is cleared by municipality everyday which they dump in a landfill area.

(i) Can you suggest any improvement in this waste disposal system of your school?

(ii) What action will you take in your school to conserve energy?

(iii) Give an idea which can discourage travelling of students by personal car.

174. How local people can be used for successful forest management ?

175. List the products of combustion of fossil fuels and what are their adverse effects on environment?

176. Write in detail about coal and petroleum conservation?

❏❏

www.ingramcontent.com/pod-product-compliance
Lightning Source LLC
LaVergne TN
LVHW061932070526
838199LV00060B/3828